D1562082

German Immigrants

Lists of Passengers Bound from Bremen to New York, 1855–1862

GERMAN IMMIGRANTS

Lists of Passengers Bound from Bremen to New York, 1855–1862

With Places of Origin

Compiled by
Gary J. Zimmerman &
Marion Wolfert

Baltimore
GENEALOGICAL PUBLISHING CO., INC.
1993

Copyright © 1986 by
Genealogical Publishing Co., Inc.
Baltimore, Maryland
All Rights Reserved
Second printing, 1993
Library of Congress Catalogue Card Number 86-80830
International Standard Book Number 0-8063-1160-6
Made in the United States of America

To Guenther ❧
for your understanding.

❧ Marion

Explanation of the Text

The destruction of the Bremen passenger lists has been a great hindrance to the historical and demographic study of German immigration to America. In many cases the Bremen lists were the sole source of information concerning the place of origin of an immigrant family. The importance of Bremen as a port of departure makes this loss even more lamentable. In the period 1855–1862, the period which this volume covers, only 160,000 people sailed from Hamburg, while 225,000 emigrants left via Bremen.

As far as can be ascertained by German archivists, lists of emigrants sailing from Bremen were kept beginning in 1832. These lists were used to compile statistical reports for the government and port authorities. Owing to a lack of space, the lists from 1832 to 1872 were destroyed in 1874. Thereafter the lists were shredded every two years. From 1907 the original lists were again kept on a permanent basis, but with the destruction of the Statistical Land Office on October 6, 1944, all remaining lists perished. Transcripts of some twentieth-century lists (1907, 1908, 1913, 1914) were recently discovered at the German State Archives in Koblenz—the product of a college study—but no nineteenth-century transcripts have as yet been uncovered.

This partial reconstruction of Bremen passenger lists, 1855–1862, is based on American sources, specifically, *Passenger Lists of Vessels Arriving at New York* (National Archives Microfilm Publication M237), and is a continuation of an earlier volume covering the period 1847–1854. Not all Bremen passengers of the 1855–1862 period are included in this work, however; only those for whom a specific place of origin in Germany is given. Of the total number of passenger arrival records, roughly 21% provide such information; the other 79% give only "Germany" as the place of origin. The benefit of having these 35,000 passenger arrivals indexed is that it provides immediate access to place of origin information, which the voluminous nature of the New York arrival lists heretofore prevented. Future volumes in this series will cover later years of arrival, and eventually Bremen arrivals at other major U.S. ports.

Imperfections and peculiarities in the original lists, as well as difficulties encountered in the computerization process, make it imperative that all entries found herein be compared against the original manifests. It is apparent from the lists themselves that the information had been supplied verbally by the passengers, since obvious name and place-name misspellings occur frequently. Therefore, all possible spelling variations must be searched for. A good example is the surname MEYER, which is found in the lists under eight different spellings: Meyer, Meier, Mayer, Meir, Mayr, Myar, Myer and even Mjar. The majority of spellings may vary only slightly, but because of the alphabetical arrangement of this work these variants are often separated.

In the original lists many given names and surnames were partially or completely anglicized. More often than not given names were carried over into their English equivalents; and on rare occasions a surname was translated. The name SCHMIDT, for example, might be listed as SMITH; BRAUN as BROWN, etc. When this occurs, as with other questionable spellings, an entry is added under what is assumed to be the original German spelling, to facilitate the researcher.

Misspelled place names have been corrected on a limited basis. Place names with spellings grossly in error were examined, and an accurate spelling sought. Sometimes a correct spelling could not be established, and the spelling as found in the original was retained. The corrected spellings sometimes represent the compilers' opinion of the way the original should read; but since there is the risk that an incorrect judgment was made, all entries should be compared with the original.

Some names may be difficult to locate because of peculiarities in the German language. German surnames that carry an "umlaut," i.e. a modified vowel (Ä, Ö, Ü), have been changed to their English equivalents; thus Ä = AE, Ö = OE, Ü = UE, and are so indexed. Some surnames that should have had modified vowels were left unmodified in the originals. The name MÜLLER is found as both MUELLER and MULLER in the text, as well as the anglicized form MILLER. Surnames composed of two or more distinct words have been alphabetized under the final word. Thus von WEGNER is found as WEGNER, v.; de GREVE as GREVE, de; and AUF DEM KAMP as KAMP, auf dem. French names like D'ARTENAY are not separated.

The majority of the records contain abbreviations that vary from list to list. Many are standard German abbreviations, but some given-name abbreviations are odd, and are therefore difficult to recognize. A table of the most frequently used abbreviations is included in this work. Names that have been abbreviated often make it difficult to tell the sex of the passenger. In many cases, therefore, the sex of the passenger is noted in parenthesis. Several lists were composed entirely of initials, and several others employed the use of German nicknames, which may be unfamiliar to researchers. Some of the more commonly used nicknames and their equivalents are listed below:

Bernhard = Bernd	Johann = Hans
Catharina = Trina	Magdalena = Lena
Elisabeth = Beta, Louise, Elise	Margaretha = Greta
Friedrich = Fritz	Matthias = Theiss
Friederike = Rika	Valentin = Veit
Georg = Joerg	Wilhelmine = Minna
Helena = Lena	

German regional dialects account for a great deal of inconsistency in surname and place name spellings. Certain consonants can be pronounced alike, allowing for a variety of spelling possibilities. The following table of equivalent consonants will assist in determining alternative spellings:

B = P	as Ebstein = Epstein	TZ = Z	as Dietz = Diez = Tietz
F = V	as Focke = Vocke	C = K = G	as Cunkel = Kunkel
D = T	as Dentel = Tendel		= Gungel
S = Z	as Seidler = Zeidler	I = J = Y	as Ide = Jede = Yde

German dipthongs also allow for a great deal of variety in spelling. Some combinations of vowels produce exactly the same sound, which make them interchangeable. Some examples of these are:

AE = E = EE as Faendrich = Fendrich = Feendrich
AI = AY = EI = EY as Kaiser = Kayser = Keiser = Keyser
OI = EU = AU = AEU as Broihahn = Breuhahn = Bräuhahn
= Braeuhahn
I = IE = IH as Bilke = Bielke = Bihlke = Biehlke
E = EE = EH as Frese = Freese = Frehse
Also sometimes I = UE as Gingerich = Guengerich = Juengerich

Use of the German unasperated "H" occurs frequently in these manifests. Not having a sound, this letter can be placed in several locations without affecting the pronunciation. The process of alphabetization will make such spellings widely separate, however, such as WOLLEBEN = WOHLLEBEN, WALTER = WALTHER, OELSNER = OEHLSNER. The doubling of letters is also frequently found, as in the names HERMANN = HERRMANN and ULMANN = ULLMANN. All possibilities should be sought, although duplicate entries have been added under the more common spellings of some surnames.

The computerization process has necessitated the abbreviating of place names. Most of these are suffixes and prefixes, and have been abbreviated as follows:

Unt.	= Unter	---fd.	= ---feld
Ob.	= Ober	--hsn.	= --hausen
Gr.	= Gross	--bch.	= ---bach
Kl.	= Klein	---bg.	= ---berg or ---burg
Ndr.	= Nieder	---df.	= ---dorf

Increasing numbers of Poles and Czechs appear in the manifests, many of whose names are grossly misspelled. The ships' captains who made these lists often transposed these names into German phonetic spellings, such as KUTSCHERA for KUČERA, NÜRSCHAN for NÝŘANY, etc. Additional problems were encountered in trying to read the captains' handwriting. Easily mistaken were the letters "u" for "n", "o" for "a", "t" for "f" and "l". A good example of this is the name HAUSCHILDT, which was several times mistaken for HANSCHILDT. With the more common names these problems were corrected, but undoubtedly some errors are still to be found. With any questionable spelling, great care has been taken to preserve the manifest's original version.

When more than one person of a particular surname travelled together (as in a family), they have been grouped under the name of the first family member appearing on the list. Thus the wife and children of a passenger will follow on the line just below that of the head of household. The integrity of the family was in this way retained, but it is necessary to scan all entries of a particular surname in case the individual sought is listed under another family member.

The reference numbers are composed of two parts. The first part is the year of arrival, the second the number of the passenger list for that year. Within each year all the lists are numbered. The table of references included in this volume provides the name of the arriving vessel, the date of its arrival in New York, and the call number of the National Archives' microfilm (series 237). A typical entry follows:

BEIERLEIB, Johann 60 Lustberg 61-1640

This entry states that the 60-year-old Johann Beierleib arrived in New York in 1861 (61 = 1861) and appears on list 1640 for that year. The table of references, under 61-1640, gives

Norma 10 Nov 1861 107

This indicates that Johann Beierleib was on the ship *Norma* which arrived in New York on November 10, 1861. The original list can be found on microfilm roll 107.

Questions regarding the transcription of the names and places which appear in this volume can be directed to the German Immigration Archive, P.O. Box 11391, Salt Lake City, Utah 84147. This archive retains the original transcriptions and can attempt to identify places for which correct spellings were not available.

We would like to thank Richard C. Hansen for his assistance in compiling this book.

Gary J. Zimmerman
Marion Wolfert

TABLE OF ABBREVIATIONS

Places

A., Aus.	Austria
B., Ba.	Baden, Bavaria
Bad., Bd.	Baden
Bav., Bv.	Bavaria
Br.	Braunschweig
C.H., Curh.	Kurhessen
H.	Hessen, Hannover
Ha., Hann.	Hannover
He., Hess.	Hessen
KH., KHe., Kurh.	Kurhessen
Na., Nass.	Nassau
N.Y.	New York
O., Old.	Oldenburg
Oest.	Austria
P., Pr., Prss.	Prussia
S., Sa., Sachs., Sax.	Saxony
W.	Wuerttemberg, Waldeck
Wa., Wald.	Waldeck
Wu., Wue., Wuert., Wrt.	Wuerttemberg

Ages (infants)

bob	born on board ship
by	baby
d	days old
m	months old
w	weeks old

Given Names

A.	Anna
Ad.	Adam, Adolph, Adalbert
Alb.	Albert, Albin, Albrecht
Andr.	Andreas

Ant.	Anton
Aug.	August, Augusta
Balt.	Balthasar
Bar., Barb.	Barbara
Bern., Bernh.	Bernhard
Carol., Carole.	Caroline
Cas., Casp.	Caspar
Cat., Cath.	Catharine
Charl.	Charles, Charlotte
Chr., Christ.	Christian, Christoph
Chr'tne	Christine, Christiane
Clem.	Clement, Clementine
Con., Conr.	Conrad
Dan.	Daniel
Diedr.	Diedrich
Dom.	Dominicus
Dor.	Dorothea, Dorette, Doris
Eberh.	Eberhard
Ed., Edw.	Eduard
El., Els.	Elisabeth
Em.	Emil, Emanuel, Emma, Emilie
Eman.	Emanuel
Eng.	Engel
Ern.	Ernst, Ernestine
Ferd.	Ferdinand
Fr.	Friedrich, Franz
Fr'd, Friedr.	Friedrich
Fr'ke	Friederike
Fr'z	Franz
Geo.	Georg
Gert.	Gertrude
Gottfr.	Gottfried
Gotth.	Gotthard
Gottl.	Gottlieb
Gust.	Gustav
Heinr., Hr., Hch.	Heinrich
Hen., Henr., Hen'tte	Henriette
Her., Herm.	Hermann, Hermine
Ign.	Ignatz
J.	Johann
Jac.	Jacob
Jas.	James
Joh., Johs.	Johannes
Jos.	Joseph
Jul., Juls.	Julius, Julie
Kath.	Katharine

Lor., Lor'z	Lorenz
Lud., Ludw.	Ludwig, Ludolph
M., Mar.	Maria
Magd.	Magdalena
Marg.	Margaretha
Mart.	Martin
Matth.	Matthias, Mathilde
Max.	Maximilian
Mic., Mich.	Michael
Nic., Nicol.	Nicolaus
Pet.	Peter
Ph., Phil.	Philipp
Reg.	Regina
Rob.	Robert
Ros.	Rosine, Rosalie
Rud.	Rudolph
Sal., Sol.	Salomon
Seb.	Sebastian
Sim.	Simon
Soph.	Sophia
Th.	Theodor, Thomas, Theophilus
Theo., Theod.	Theodor, Theophilus
Ther.	Therese
Traug.	Traugott
Val., Valen.	Valentine
Vic., Vict.	Victor, Victoria
Vin., Vinc.	Vincent
Wilh., Wm.	Wilhelm, Wilhelmine
Wilh'mne	Wilhelmine
Wolfg.	Wolfgang

TABLE OF REFERENCES

YR–LIST	SHIP	DATE OF ARRIVAL			FILM #
55-413	Republic	29	May	1855	152
55-538	Mimi	22	Jun	1855	153
55-544	Anna Delius	23	Jun	1855	153
55-628	E.M. Arndt	10	Jul	1855	154
55-630	Aeolus	10	Jul	1855	154
55-634	E. Delius	10	Jul	1855	154
55-698	Therese	26	Jul	1855	155
55-757	Johanna	7	Aug	1855	155
55-812	Pres. Smidt	24	Aug	1855	156
55-845	Geo. Williams	1	Sep	1855	156
55-932	Republic	25	Sep	1855	157
55-1048	Hudson	23	Oct	1855	157
55-1082	Julia	5	Nov	1855	158
55-1238	New York	24	Dec	1855	159
55-1240	Anna Lange	24	Dec	1855	159
56-279	Eberhard	6	May	1856	161
56-354	Joh. Wilhelmine	21	May	1856	162
56-411	Wursata	2	Jun	1856	162
56-413	Emigrant	2	Jun	1856	162
56-512	Dorette	19	Jun	1856	163
56-527	Alfred	23	Jun	1856	163
56-550	North Star	24	Jun	1856	163
56-589	New York	3	Jul	1856	164
56-629	Republic	10	Jul	1856	164
56-632	Teresa	11	Jul	1856	164
56-692	Amaranth	22	Jul	1856	164
56-723	R. Jacobs	30	Jul	1856	165
56-819	Shakespeare	20	Aug	1856	165
56-847	Therese	25	Aug	1856	166
56-951	Ohio	18	Sep	1856	166
56-1011	Wursata	30	Sep	1856	167

YR–LIST	SHIP	DATE OF ARRIVAL			FILM #
56-1044	Johann Lange	8	Oct	1856	167
56-1117A	Louis Henry	25	Oct	1856	168
56-1204	Herder	17	Nov	1856	168
56-1260	Amalie	2	Dec	1856	169
57-21	Union	8	Jan	1857	170
57-80	Hermine	2	Feb	1857	170
57-365	Republic	21	Apr	1857	172
57-422	Hansa	2	May	1857	173
57-436	Albert	5	May	1857	173
57-447	Jubilaum	6	May	1857	173
57-509	Agen & Heinrich	22	May	1857	174
57-555	Concordia	26	May	1857	174
57-578	Ariel	30	May	1857	174
57-606	New Orleans	2	Jun	1857	174
57-654	Arago	12	Jun	1857	175
57-704	Trls	20	Jun	1857	175
57-754	Rastede	1	Jul	1857	175
57-776	H. von Gagern	3	Jul	1857	176
57-847	Hermine	16	Jul	1857	176
57-850	Lina	17	Jul	1857	176
57-918	Ariel	29	Jul	1857	177
57-924	Magdalene	31	Jul	1857	177
57-961	Argo	8	Aug	1857	177
57-1026	Pres. Smidt	28	Aug	1857	178
57-1067	Aequator	5	Sep	1857	178
57-1113	Meridian	16	Sep	1857	178
57-1122	Jubilaum	17	Sep	1857	179
57-1148	Indiana	23	Sep	1857	179
57-1150	Ariel	24	Sep	1857	179
57-1192	Argo	6	Oct	1857	179
57-1280	Dorette	2	Nov	1857	180
57-1407	Juno	8	Dec	1857	181
57-1416	Aristedes	12	Dec	1857	181
58-261	Dorette	17	Apr	1858	183
58-306	Ariel	5	May	1858	183
58-399	Albert	24	May	1858	184
58-545	Aristedes	24	Jun	1858	185
58-563	Republic	28	Jun	1858	185
58-576	Juno	1	Jul	1858	185
58-604	Bremen	6	Jul	1858	185

YR–LIST	SHIP	DATE OF ARRIVAL			FILM #
58-815	New York	28	Aug	1858	187
58-881	Union	15	Sep	1858	187
58-885	Bremen	15	Sep	1858	187
58-925	Hudson	27	Sep	1858	187
59-47	Herzog Brabant	26	Jan	1859	190
59-48	New York	26	Jan	1859	190
59-214	New York	5	Apr	1859	190
59-372	Neptune	13	May	1859	191
59-384	Weser	16	May	1859	192
59-412	Ernst M. Arndt	20	May	1859	192
59-477	New York	30	May	1859	192
59-535	Therese	13	Jun	1859	192
59-613	Bremen	27	Jun	1859	193
59-951	New York	22	Sep	1859	195
59-990	Herzog Brabant	3	Oct	1859	196
59-1017	Jubilaum	14	Oct	1859	196
59-1036	Bremen	18	Oct	1859	196
59-1216	Bremen	16	Dec	1859	197
60-52	Helene	26	Jan	1860	198
60-334	New York	2	May	1860	200
60-371	Johann	11	May	1860	200
60-398	Gerhard	31	May	1860	201
60-411	Leontine	2	Jun	1860	201
60-429	Elizabeth	6	Jun	1860	201
60-521	New York	26	Jun	1860	202
60-533	Herzog Brabant	28	Jun	1860	202
60-622	Helene	15	Jul	1860	202
60-785	New York	21	Aug	1860	204
60-998	New York	17	Oct	1860	205
60-1032	Anna	26	Oct	1860	206
60-1053	Herzog Brabant	30	Oct	1860	206
60-1117	Lina	20	Nov	1860	206
60-1141	Geestemunde	27	Nov	1860	207
60-1161	Jubilaum	1	Dec	1860	207
60-1196	New York	14	Dec	1860	207
61-47	Elena	19	Jan	1861	208
61-107	New York	14	Feb	1861	208
61-167	Bremen	15	Mar	1861	209
61-478	Hermann	27	May	1861	211

YR–LIST	SHIP	DATE OF ARRIVAL			FILM #
61-482	New York	28	May	1861	211
61-520	Geestemunde	7	Jun	1861	212
61-669	Shakespeare	15	Jul	1861	213
61-682	Republic	16	Jul	1861	213
61-716	New York	25	Jul	1861	213
61-770	Thusnelda	10	Aug	1861	213
61-779	Herzog Brabant	12	Aug	1861	214
61-804	Bremen	20	Aug	1861	214
61-897	New York	18	Sep	1861	214
61-930	Hermann	28	Sep	1861	215
61-1054	Fanny Kirchner	11	Nov	1861	215
61-1132	Hansa	13	Dec	1861	216
62-1	Europa	2	Jan	1862	216
62-100	Aristedes	1	Feb	1862	217
62-111	Hansa	6	Feb	1862	217
62-166	Bremen	5	Mar	1862	217
62-232	Hansa	25	Mar	1862	217
62-306	Emilie	17	Apr	1862	218
62-342	Anton Gunther	25	Apr	1862	218
62-349	John Kepler	28	Apr	1862	218
62-401	Hansa	12	May	1862	219
62-467	New York	27	May	1862	219
62-608	E.F. Gabain	25	Jun	1862	220
62-712	Goshen	19	Jul	1862	221
62-730	City of New York	22	Jul	1862	221
62-758	Orpheus	29	Jul	1862	221
62-836A	Hansa	18	Aug	1862	222
62-879	Herzog Brabant	30	Aug	1862	222
62-938	New York	15	Sep	1862	223
62-983	Fortuna	1	Oct	1862	223
62-993	Bernhard	2	Oct	1862	223
62-1042	Hansa	15	Oct	1862	223
62-1112	New York	13	Nov	1862	224
62-1169	Hansa	10	Dec	1862	224

German Immigrants

Lists of Passengers Bound from Bremen to New York, 1855–1862

NAME	AGE	RESIDENCE	YR-LIST
ABBY, A.L.	24	Suelza	59-1036
ABE, Elisabeth	27	Sdt.Lengsfeld	60-0429
Anna 4			
ABECK, G.	29	Neuendorf	59-0990
ABEGG, George	19	Bremen	57-0080
ABEKEN, M.(f)	30	Hannover	55-0544
Fritz 7, Fanny 2			
ABEL, Anton	28	Winterberg	62-0879
ABEL, C.	45	Westchreisen	56-0527
Dorothea 16			
ABEL, Ch.	14	Deischheim	59-1036
ABEL, Ferd. Heinr.	25	Dorummerdeich	55-1082
Dorothea 25			
ABEL, G.N.	26	New York	62-0938
ABEL, Johann	34	Cassel	57-1280
ABELE, Christ.	25	Philadelphia	56-1216
Carol. 4			
ABELER, Scholastic	18	Reichau	56-0512
ABELS, Meta	18	Sievern	61-0897
ABOT, (m)	26	France	58-0306
ABOTT, J.L.	17	Paris	62-0938
ABRAHAM, Adolph	26	Kempen	61-0682
ABRAHAM, Dorchen	20	Niederuf	57-0850
ABRAHAM, Isaac	40	New Orleans	56-1216
ABRAHAM, M.(m)	30	Golluh	62-0730
ABRAHAM, Salomon	19	Bapparch	59-0951
ABT, Theo.	20	Schwalenberg	62-1112
ACCARIAS, Joseph	30	France	57-1192
ACH, Cunigunde	29	Heldburg	59-0214
ACHERBACH, Jacob	22	Nieder Dieten	60-0371
ACHILIS, Th.	55	New York	62-1112
Julie 41, Marie 17, Anna 15, Johann 11			
Julie 9			
ACHINE, Leopold	48	Guben	56-0550
ACHMANN, Elise	8	Boitzen	62-0879
ACHSTE, Caroline	18	Hagen	61-0478
ACHTERBERG, Wilh.	23	Teschendorf	60-0371
ACHZIGER, Barbara	22	Hammenader	61-0770
ACKELMEYER, August	25	Heiden	55-0812
ACKER, Joh.Fr.	30	Schnelldorf	57-1113
ACKER, Wilhelm	34	Sachs.-Weimar	57-0606
ACKERMANN, A.Marta	41	Hersfeld	60-1053
Adam 12, Margaretha 14, Elise by			
ACKERMANN, Augusta	59	Breslau	61-0897
ACKERMANN, C.G.	27	New York	62-0467
Henriette 25, CHarles Fr. 11m			
ACKERMANN, J.H.	18	Goermer	62-0938
ACKERMANN, Joh.Fr.	49	Utenberg	59-0214
ACKERMANN, Johanna	23	Remptendorf	59-0613
ACKERMANN, Marie	21	Bavaria	60-1161
Anna 18			
ACKERMANN, Theod.	35	Germany	57-0578
ACKERT, Marie	28	Hofgeismar	56-1044
ADAM, Aug.Heinr.	35	Langenheim/He	62-0608
ADAM, Christine	30	Meissen	62-0938
ADAM, Minna	23	Rechallau	62-1112
ADAMI, Christ.	20	Hausen	59-0384
ADAMS, Aug.	25	Milburn	58-0306
(wife) 20			
ADAMS, Nicolaus	29	Hirten/Pruss.	55-1238
ADDIKS, Dora	17	Midlum	62-0879
ADDISON, William	27	Southampton	59-0384
ADE, Friederike	18	Wuerttemberg	61-0682
ADELBERG, J.	35	New York	62-0836
Josephine 30, Fr.(f) 5, Alma 4			
ADELER, L.(m)	40	Baltimore	62-0730
ADELMANN, J.P.	45	Heilbronn	60-0785
ADEN, J.F.		Driftsethe	57-1192
ADERHALT, Elisab.	40	Kernern	59-0412
Friedrich 10			
ADERHOLD, Carl	17	Nordhausen	56-0629
ADEROLD, Georg	24	Koerna	57-1280
ADLER, Abraham	20	Ernsbach	57-0961
ADLER, Anna	53	Neustadt	58-0815
ADLER, Aron	19	Hintersteinau	60-0785
ADLER, Bertha	16	Meiningen/Sax	55-0538
ADLER, Caroline	24	Obersemen	62-0836
ADLER, Friedrich	27	Neustadt	58-0815
Barbara 18			
ADLER, Lazarus	38	Csenzy	62-1112
Carl 19, Rudolph 9, Heinrich 8			
Maximilian 6, Ludwig 3, Eugenia 6m			
ADLER, Marianne	17	Urspruengen	60-0521
ADLER, Moritz	24	Gudensberg	60-0411
ADLER, Salomon	19	Laupheim	59-0477
ADOLPH, Louis	35	Posen	60-0785
Johanna 37, Joseph 5, Charles 4			
Augusta 2, Hermann 11m			
ADOLPH, Wilhelmine	29	Oberstadt/SW.	60-0429
ADRIAN, A.	28	Milford	60-0334
AESCHMANN, F.	24	London	62-1042
AFFELDER, Jacob	15	Furth	58-0306
AGNITSCH, Johann	23	Swicknick	56-1260
AGRICOLA, H.	31	Heiligenstein	56-0512
Friedericke 30, Hulda 2, Dorothea 3m			
AHL, Nicolaus	35	Schlesingen	57-0847
AHLBORN, Aug.Fr'dr	26	Langensalza	58-0545
AHLDERS, Heinr.	34	Aschendorf	59-0214
AHLERS, Cord	30	Wilstedt	58-0885
AHLERS, Elisab.	31	Moorsum	61-0482
Anna 4			
AHLERS, Lueder	20	Holzkamp	58-0925
AHLERS, Marie	16	Meinburg	61-0482
AHNERT, Joh.Christ	46	Daumitsch	56-0819
AHRENBERG, Andreas	54	Twieflingen/B	55-0628
Charlotte 55, Henriette 19			
AHREND, Burckhard	36	Elspe	57-0422
AHREND, H.H.(m)	19	Drangstedt/Ha	60-0622
AHRENDT, Heinrich	18	Cassel	59-0951
Nicolaus 20			
AHRENS, Anna	18	Wallhoefen	56-1204
AHRENS, Anna	20	Bredbeck	59-1036
AHRENS, Augusta	23	New York	56-1216
(son) 11m			
AHRENS, Charlotte	9	Bovenden	62-1169
AHRENS, Gertrude	27	Neuenkirchen	57-0606
AHRENS, Heinr.	28	Wallhoefe	62-1112
AHRENS, Herm.	24	Bonames	57-1150
AHRENS, J.C.(m)	16	Liswareshold	60-0521
AHRENS, Justine	43	Echt	58-0881
F.A.W. 18, August 12, Wilhelm 9			
AHRENS, L.(m)	25	Germany	62-0166
AHRENS, Mich.	22	Koehlen	56-1117
AHRENS, Sophie	28	Bremen	62-0879
Gesine 5			
AHRENS, Wilhelm	17	Oese	59-0535
AHRING, Joh. Fr.	27	Rabber	56-0951
AICHLER, Franz	41		61-0770
AIGELTINGER, Anna	48	Jever	62-0836
Leopold 15			
AIGNER, Franz	34	Baiern	59-0535
AINSCHULD, Wmne.	30	Carlsruhe	58-0925
AKKEN, Gesche	59	Campen	57-0422
AKMANN, Fr.	19	Altenhagen	61-0804
ALAHNKEN, D.H.	12	Worpswede	59-0535
ALBACH, Elisabeth	24	Hattenbach	59-0047
ALBACH, Joh.J.P.	31	Lick	58-0815
Wilhelmine 29, Georg 21			
ALBACH, P.	29	Darmstadt	62-0993
ALBERG, Christian	43	Anger	56-1044
Dorothea 39, Dorothea 17, August 14			
Wilhelm 8, Wilhelmine 8, Heinrich 6			
Carl 3			
ALBERHARDT, Ludwig	14	Diepholz	59-0214
Lina 16			
ALBERS, Diedrich	18	Suling	59-0412
Caroline 55, Sophie 27, Maria 14			
ALBERS, F.E.	20	Mittelhausen	62-0993
ALBERS, Hendrike	18	Lahr/Hannover	56-0692
Marie 16			
ALBERS, Joh.Heinr.	60	Goldswarten	58-0563
Anna Marg. 57, Anna Elisa 27, Heinrich 17			
Friederike 15			
ALBERS, Joseph	36	New York	62-1169
Francisca 39			
ALBERS, Marie	16	Brockhausen	56-0951

NAME	AGE	RESIDENCE	YR-LIST
ALBERS, Ulfert	55	Wrisse	57-0422
Ontje 44, William 22, Luebbe 20			
ALBERSDOERFFER, J.	24	Biedenkopf	57-1067
Therese 23, Caroline 34, Ulka 7			
Friedrich 5			
ALBERT, Adolph	28	Besse	59-0214
ALBERT, Barbara	37	Siegelsgrund	61-0779
ALBERT, Christ.	38	Louin	60-0521
Elisabeth 36, Christ.(m) 9, Peter 7			
Christ.(m) 5, Elisabeth 3, Agnes 11m			
ALBERT, Geo.	27	Braach	62-0232
ALBERTE, Hermann	47	Kruspis	55-1082
Louise 24			
ALBERTS, Mike(f)	65	Wremen	60-0521
ALBERTSON, Carl	37	Pommern	58-0399
Augusta 34, Wilhelm 11, Carl 9, Ernst 5			
Augusta 3, Hermann 2			
ALBES, Wilhelm	23	Apelern	56-1260
ALBES, Wilhelmine	23	Goettingen	55-0634
Elise 18			
ALBINGER, Ludw.	33	Newark	57-0918
Antonia 36			
ALBITZ, Augustin	45	Lochmatt	60-0622
Martha 38, Fridolin 19, Adelheid 15			
Augustina 13, Rosalia 8, Ottmar 5			
ALBORN, Marie	27	New York	60-0334
Ida 3, August 11m			
ALBORN, Milus(f)	20	Wahmbeck	60-0334
ALBRECH, Christian	18	Mooring	57-1122
ALBRECHT, Adolph	22	Meppen	55-0845
ALBRECHT, Adolph	56	Brackel	59-1036
ALBRECHT, Anna	20	Brakel	60-0521
ALBRECHT, F.A.	18	Muehlhausen	62-0938
ALBRECHT, Francis	41	Gr.Hirschau	56-1011
Antonia 32, Francis 6			
ALBRECHT, Friedr.	15	Coburg	57-0447
ALBRECHT, Gertrude	18	Roda	60-1141
ALBRECHT, Gust.	16	Friedland	60-0998
ALBRECHT, Heinrich	33	Bremervoerde	57-0447
Justine 42, Friedrich 2			
ALBRECHT, Heinrich	28	Rhoden	61-0520
Louis 28			
ALBRECHT, Marie	41	Liegnitz	60-0411
Agnes 18, Emilie 16, Louis 9, Gustav 7			
ALBRECHT, Thalia	17	Cassel/Hesse	60-0622
Louise 14			
ALBRECHT, William	26	Brunswick	57-0422
ALBRECHT, Wm.	30	Havana	59-1036
ALERS, (Dr.)	38	San Francisco	62-0836
ALEXANDER, Prinzch	18	Wolfshagen	62-0712
ALFTER, Armand	37	Bonn	57-0654
ALHEIT, Johannes	17	Hadamar	57-0754
ALJEST, Juergen	46	Vosberg	62-0758
ALLBRECHT, Adolph	19	Zweibruecken	57-1067
ALLEN, John	33	US.	62-0938
ALLENDOERFFER, Fdr	26	Cassel	57-1192
ALLENSEN, E.(f)	15	Heidelbach	57-0555
ALLENSEN, H.(m)	47	Wohnfeldt	57-0555
ALLENSTEIN, Christ	58	Draupchen	61-0107
Annerle 55, Ferdinand 9			
ALLENSTEIN, Georg	40	Koenigsberg	61-0107
ALLES, Catharine	21	Niederstoll	57-0654
ALLES, Conrad	30	Weaver	57-1113
ALLES, Maria	17	Wallenrode	61-0682
ALLGAUER, Andr.	39	Ebingen	59-0951
ALLINE, A.	19	Switz.	62-0467
ALLOIS, Ph.(m)	21	Germany	62-0467
ALLSTADT, Georg Fr	29	Burgheim/Hess	62-0608
ALMANDINGER, Magd.	42	Degerloch	62-1112
Carl 14, Gette 12			
ALMENDINGER, Joh.	17	Unterboringen	62-0879
ALMERS, Friedrich	22	Nortwede	57-1122
ALMSTEDT, Wm.	22	Hildesheim	60-0521
ALOTH, Geo.	33	Bessel	56-0512
M. 30, Heinrich 3, John 9m			
ALPERS, Gepse	17	Fahnendorf	60-0334
ALPERS, Joh.August	14	Scharmbeck	57-0754
ALPI, Giovanni	31	Italy	61-0167

NAME	AGE	RESIDENCE	YR-LIST
ALS, Caspar	32	Rain	59-0384
ALSGUTH, Heinr.Chr	29	Wellen	56-0629
ALSGUTH, Ludwig	19	Beverstadt	59-0412
ALSTER, Ferd.		Cassel	59-1036
Emilie			
ALSWEDEL, Joh.Chr.	56	Eimbeck	56-0589
ALT, Caspar	32	Rain	59-0384
ALT, Georg	22	Graefenberg	59-0535
ALT, v. Catharina	17	Eichenrod/CH.	60-0622
Margarethe 14			
ALTEN, Ernest	16	Hannover	57-1192
ALTENBERN, Wm.	29	Leopoldstein	60-0998
Conrad 23			
ALTENBURG, Minna	16	Stadthagen	58-0881
ALTERMANN, Friedr.	24	Leipzig	61-0682
ALTERS, Henry	22	Louisendorf	57-0422
ALTHAUS, Carl	19	Rinteln	56-1260
ALTHAUS, Heinrich	20	Gross Fehden	61-0779
ALTHAUS, Jacob	27	Perleburg/Pr.	60-0371
Philippine 28, Christian 1			
ALTHAUS, Johannes	26	Kurhessen	61-0779
ALTHAUSER, Georg	26	Opfingen	60-1117
ALTHEIM, Casp.	54	Hochelheim	55-0413
Louise 24			
ALTHEN, Anton	23	Hochhelheim	56-0527
ALTHOF, Fr.(m)	19	Detmold	61-0482
ALTMANN, Aug.Carl	28	Haltensleben	59-0372
Elisabeth 24			
ALTMANN, Catharine	53	Oldenburg	58-0399
ALTMANN, Franz	24	Friedland	57-0654
ALTMANN, M.	24	Poppendorf	59-0613
ALTMANN, Robert	38	Breslau	56-0411
ALTMICKS, Servat.	30	Warendorf	58-0885
AMAND, Carl	19	Wahrer	60-0998
AMAND, Friedrich	18	Erfurt	58-0399
AMANN, Adele	51	Oldenburg	57-0961
AMANN, Catharine	41	Durlach	62-0879
AMANN, Jac.	29	Regensburg	59-1036
AMBACH, Emilie	39	Kreitz	55-1048
Julius 24, La. 16, Franz 14, Gustav 9			
Carl 8, Hermine 6			
AMBACH, H.F.(m)	52	Greiz	62-0111
AMBACHER, Caroline	32	Willhermsdorf	59-0951
AMBERG, Phil.	35	Arnsberg	57-1148
AMBERG, Philip	35	Arnsberg	57-1148
AMBRON, Valent.	58	Niederwoellst	59-1036
Marie 58			
AMELING, Heinrich	34	Koenigsberg	58-0399
AMEN, Heinr.	21	Hohenems	60-1196
AMEND, Georg	29	Kleinheubach	59-0412
AMENDE, Fr.(m)	36	Geilshausen	61-0669
Christine 34, Pauline 5			
AMENDE, Minna	21	Belera	56-1044
Eduard 18			
AMEREIN, Catharina	23	Speckswinkel	57-0754
AMHEIM, Rosalie	23	Rodenburg	61-0682
August 4			
AMMANN, Minna	23	New York	62-0938
AMMER, Louis	18	Gruenberg	55-0630
AMMERMANN, Gesine	22	Elsferth	59-0613
AMMERMANN, Rosette	37	Dransfeld	57-1192
AMRAM, Moses	27	Leipzig	58-0604
AMRAU, David	59	Echte	59-0951
Minna 54			
AMRHEIN, Heinrich	32	Hessen	62-0758
Dorothea 56			
AMSCHULD, Wilh'mne	30	Carlsruhe	58-0925
ANACKER, William	20	Herrenbreit	60-0411
ANDAP, Sovier	40	Rouen	62-0836
ANDERSON, F.	30	New York	60-0785
ANDERSON, Hanson	32	France	62-0938
ANDING, Magdalena	21	Burgpreppach	60-0533
ANDREAS, Joh.Ph.	36	Leipzig	57-0961
ANDREAS, Wm.	23	Engelsbach	60-0785
ANDREE, Will.	31	St.Louis	57-1148
ANDRES, Christine	17	Koenigswald	60-1032
ANDRES, George	44	Geinsheim	60-1141
Mary 47, Jacob 15, Barbara 13			

NAME	AGE	RESIDENCE	YR-LIST
ANDRESS, Andrew	27	Wrisse	57-0422
Gretje 24			
ANDRESSEN, Math.	30	Neukirch	62-0938
ANDREUS, Chr.	25	Cassel	56-0411
ANDREW, Fortuna(m)	12	California	60-0785
(f) 26			
ANDREWS, Ed.	34	Southampton	59-0384
ANGEL, Wilhelm	39	Kieslegg	59-1036
ANGELRODT, Antonia	58	St.Louis	58-0885
ANGELROTH, v. (m)	19	St.Louis	60-0334
ANGER, Ernst	25	Writzen	56-0819
ANGER, Julius	18	Creuznach	59-0477
ANGERER, Anton	16	Fuerth	59-0477
ANGERER, Mich.	58	Hartmannsteut	55-0932
Marie 44, Jacob 14			
ANGERMUELLER, Fr.	17	Coburg	50-1017
ANHALT, Joh. Fr.	24	Bollstedt	56-0589
Joseph 27			
ANHALT, Johanne	26	Ziegenheim	60-0785
Hirsch 14			
ANKEL, Friederike	25	Fulda/Hess.	55-1238
ANKELE, Joh. Georg	20	Gormaringen	62-0001
ANKEN, v.Heinrich	17	Zeven	61-0682
ANNACKER, Georg	34	Langenfeld	60-1161
Catharina 32, Catharina 55, Catharina 26			
Barbara 3, Louis 6m			
ANSBACHER, Julchen	19	Achim	60-1196
Georgine 17			
ANSCHITZ, Cathrina	22	Hempfeshausen	57-0447
ANSCHUETZ, Joh.G.	33	Wisconsin	59-0214
ANSCHUETZ, Pet.Jac	23	Asslar	59-0214
Johannette 24			
ANSCHUETZ, Philip	23	Muenster/Darm	62-0342
ANSORG, Friedrich	54	Meiningen	62-0758
Ottilie 44, Friedrich 25, Sophie 17			
ANTENRIETH, Cath.	29	Bretten	59-1036
ANTERAR, Christine	22	Hasselbach	60-0334
ANTHER, Philipp	23	Engelsbach	60-0785
APEL, Anna	16	Nentershausen	56-1216
APEL, Carl	18	Heinersdorf	56-0629
APEL, Charlotte	18	Culmbach	59-0951
APEL, Friedrich	30	Liebstedt	56-0589
APEL, Friedrich	23	Liebstedt	56-0723
APEL, Friedrich	34	Nordhausen	57-1026
APEL, Heinr.	22	Hersfeld	55-1082
Louise 24			
APEL, Johanna	21	Sudwasi	55-1048
Wilhelmine 17			
APEL, Jos.	29	Brueck	61-0669
APELT, Joh.	26	Trogau	57-1026
Eva 20			
APFELBECK, Martin	55	Landau/Bav.	55-0628
Eva 45, Anna Maria 16, Victoria 15			
Joseph 13, Therese 10, Crescens 9			
Franziska 6, Anna 4, Martin 3			
APIARIUS, F.	49	New York	62-1042
APOHR, Augusta	21	Kassel	55-1048
APOHR, Friedrich	44	US.	55-1048
APOHR, Gustav	14	Hannover	55-1048
APPEL, Adolph	22	Allheim	59-0048
APPEL, Conrad	18	Hesse-Darm.	62-0712
APPEL, Elisabeth	22	Nordhausen	55-0845
APPEL, Fanny	16	Borken	62-0938
APPEL, Fritz	34	Luethorst	57-1407
Caroline 18			
APPEL, Heinrich	30	Oberlais	62-0712
APPEL, Johann	31	Tiefenklein	60-0429
APPEL, Johann	28	Olmbach	57-1407
APPEL, Johann	22	Allheim	59-0048
Martin 17			
APPEL, Johannes	19	Kappeln	57-1067
APPEL, Kunigunde	16	Redwitz/Bav.	60-0429
APPEL, S.	29	Herchenhain	62-0993
E. 16, D. 61			
APPEL, Sebastian	21	Maishofs	55-0932
APPELHOFF, Joh.Fr.	37	Vilsen	60-0398
Henriette 37, Charlotte 6, Augusta 3			
APPELL, Johannes	18	Muenchen	62-0232

NAME	AGE	RESIDENCE	YR-LIST
APPELMANN, Ernstne	17	Langenheim/He	62-0608
APPELMANN, Susanne	28	Heubach	59-0477
APPELT, Mart.	30	Duesseldorf	62-1112
APPENZELLER, Peter	60	Ween	58-0306
(wife) 54, Heinrich 34, Jacob 23			
Peter 21, Georg 18, Caroline 15			
Catharine 6			
ARAN, (f)	38	France	57-1150
ARANDIZ, Abrh.	29	Havre	62-0938
ARB, Cath.	21	Soell	57-0578
Georg 40, Georg 19, Johann 13, Peter 13			
Alwine 9, Marie 8, Barbara 6			
ARENBECK, A. Elis.	29	Warendorf	59-0384
ARENBECK, Georg	59	Warendorf	62-0836
Minna 21			
AREND, Catharina	18	Koerle	57-0754
AREND, Catharina	26	Lutternsberg	57-0606
AREND, Ernst	16	Moederath	58-0885
ARENDS, J.K.(m)	25	Pichelwarf	62-0232
ARENS, Eberhard		Nuenkirchen	56-0550
ARENS, Gottlieb	33	Bisperode	56-0629
Marie 33			
ARENS, H.(m)	41	New York	62-0836
E.(f) 27, Betty 6, Adelheid 4			
ARENS, H.J.	17	Wedel	59-0477
ARENS, Hagen D.	58	Campen	55-1082
D. Dirks 26			
ARENS, Helene	23	Hasberge	56-1117
ARENS, Henriette	23	Muenden	57-1192
ARENS, Herm.	31	Cincinnati	61-0897
Rebecca 24, Anna Louise 3, J.Heinr. 9m			
ARENS, Jacob	41	Bremen	62-0342
Wilhelmine 41, Jacob 14, Heinrich 9			
Clemens 8, Meta 6, Wilhelmine 5			
Hermann 2, Eduard 3m			
ARHOLD, Johann	34	Salz	56-0847
ARINGTON, Georg	30	Boston	59-1036
ARLT, Carl	30	Frankenstein	60-0622
ARMANN, Louis	25	Baltimore	56-1216
ARMBRECHT, Heinr.	14	Seesen	57-1148
ARMBRUESTER, Jacob	24	Tuebingen	60-0411
ARMBRUESTER, P.J.	25	Solling	58-0576
Caroline 30, Carl 5			
ARMBRUST, Anna	46	Perouse/Wuert	56-0819
ARMHEIM, Joh.	40	New York	59-1036
ARMSBERG, Doris	31	Schiffdorf	62-0306
Maria 4, Johanna 2, Rebecc(died) 6m			
ARNADY, Georg	26	Oppeln	61-0107
ARNBRON, Ernst	14	Ndr.Wollstadt	58-0563
ARNDS, J.	27	Aschendorf	62-0993
M. 25			
ARNDT, Friedrich	17	Budzyn	56-1117
ARNDT, Julius	32	Schoenau/Sil.	60-0622
ARNDT, Wilhelm	34	Selters	58-0576
ARNDT, William	27	Leopoldshagen	57-0654
Friederike 30			
ARNECKE, Wilh'mine	29	Honterlagen	61-0897
ARNNEBERG, Raphael	25	Arnsberg	57-1148
ARNOLD, A.	28	Wittersleben	56-0512
Amalie 25			
ARNOLD, A.(m)	15	Oberstross	62-0730
ARNOLD, Barbara	19	Meiningen	61-0478
ARNOLD, Bramby	31	London	57-1148
ARNOLD, Carl	20	Esslingen/Wrt	60-0371
ARNOLD, Friedricke	32	Weissenfeld	56-0589
Mary 40			
ARNOLD, G.H.(m)	33	Thalheim	62-0401
ARNOLD, Herrmann	16	Birkenbrinkha	55-0628
ARNOLD, Louis	47	New York	62-1112
ARNOLD, M.(f)	28	New York	62-0836
Emma 9, Martha 8, Arthur 7, Louise 5			
Milton 3, Clara 1			
ARNOLD, Marg.	23	New York	59-0613
ARNOLD, Sophie	19	Meiningen	56-0723
ARNRAM, Moses	27	Leipzig	58-0604
ARNSBERG, v. Georg	36	Hildesheim	58-0925
ARNSTEIN, Cathrina	54	Triemen	56-1117
A. (f) 24			

NAME	AGE	RESIDENCE	YR-LIST
ARNSTEIN, Martin	56	Triemen	56-1117
ARNTZ, Ges.	29	Germany	62-1112
ARNZEMANN, Maria	19	Bremen	56-1117
AROLD, Maria	26	Frankenberg	60-1053
ARON, Jeanette	25	Graetz	61-0482
ARONSTEIN, Fanny	18	Ansbach	56-0723
ARRAS, Peter	22	Oberkleigumpe	59-0477
ARTHMANN, Eduard	48	Osnabrueck	62-0342
ARTMANN, Friedrich	40	Cathrinhagen	57-0847
ARTMANN, Hermann	25	Greven	59-0214
ARTMEYER, Joh.	27	Chemnitz	59-0384
ARVES, Elisabeth	27	Ndr.Willstedt	57-1280
ARZBERGER, Marg.	23	Doerfglas	56-0527
ARZT, August	16	Baden	60-1196
Christ. 23			
ARZT, Catharina	21	Regenberg	56-0632
ASBACHER, Wilhelm	30	Ludwigsburg	59-0048
ASCH, Adelheid	14	Posen	61-0716
ASCHBRENNER, Fr'dr	45	Hasfelde	56-0819
Wilhelmine 39, Gustav 18, Friedrich 16			
Adolph 14, Hermann 10, Mathilde 8			
Wilhelmine 9m			
ASCHEBERG, A.H.	26	Emdessen	61-0107
Herm. 27			
ASCHEMOOR, Cathar.	22	Lauiston	58-0815
ASCHEN, Amalie	18	Kaldorf	57-0606
Sophie 21			
ASCHENBACH, August	33	Chedorff	60-0334
ASCHENBACH, Peter	18	Schleid	60-1161
ASCHENBRAND, Wolf	25	Sontra	60-0533
ASCHENMOOR, Georg	16	Wagenfeld	60-0334
ASCHENPRENTER, Jac	30	Curhessen	55-0634
Elise 27, Christine			
ASCHER, Rosalie	21	Piesslitz	59-1036
ASCHERMANN, J.H.	48	Eberschuetz	57-0578
Caroline 26			
ASCHHEIM, Jos.	27	Posen	57-1148
ASCHUETZ, A.Rosina	54	Sachsenmeinin	59-0412
Georg Ernst 15, Eleonore 22			
Eva Elisab. 18			
ASMANN, Conrad	23	Eisenach	60-1196
Ludwig 20			
ASMUS, Anton	38	Frauenbreitin	61-0770
ASMUS, G.(m)	35		62-0401
ASMUS, Heinrich	21	Norden	59-0412
ASMUS, Wilhelm	34	Goettingen	55-0634
Johannette 34, Dorette by			
ASPELMEIER, Heinr.	17	Hille	56-0411
ASPELMEIER, Wm.	15	Minden	58-0399
Friedrich 19			
ASSAUER, Chr.	45	Elmira	62-0938
ASSER, Meyer	18	Cassel	60-0411
ASSMANN, Friedrike	23	Nordhausen	62-0758
ASSMUSS, Carl	29	Zitzenrode	58-0576
Sophie 24			
AST, August	27	Stemmen	56-1260
Louise 16, Conrad 49, Friedricke 22			
ASTE, Dominicus	24	Italy	62-1042
ASTHOLZ, Adolf	17	Gronau	58-0563
ATTENBORN, Ed.	18	Hamburg	60-0998
ATTHANS, Carl	19	Rinteln	56-1260
AU, Jos.	59	Allmannshofen	62-0730
AUBEL, Christian	58	Albshausen	57-0754
AUBEL, Juliane	21	Grefenhausen	62-0111
AUCH, C.	51	New Orleans	62-1169
AUE, H.Aug.	27	New York	62-0467
AUERBACH, Elise	59	Eberstadt	61-0669
AUERBACH, Geo. Fr.	42	Freyburg	56-0413
Henriette 20			
AUERBACH, Mor.	25	Bockenheim	57-0654
AUFFERHART, Mary	19	Genselohe	59-1036
AUFHAEUSER, Pippi	24	Hainsfahrt	60-0521
AUFNARDE, Joh.W.	28	Dwergse	59-0214
AUGUSTA, Jacques	34	France	62-0467
AUGUSTIN, Antoine	18	France	62-0111
Marie 20			
AUGUSTIN, Wilhelm	19	Osnabrueck	57-1407
AUKAMP, Wilhelm	15	Wagenfeld	60-0334

NAME	AGE	RESIDENCE	YR-LIST
AUL, Elis.	48	Aufenau	59-0990
AUMANN, C.	34	Braunschweig	59-1036
AUMANN, Friedrich	20	Petershagen	60-0533
Heinrich 26			
AUMANN, Louise	34	Braunschweig	59-1036
AUMUELLER, Mary	14	Villmar	59-1036
AUMUELLER, Michael	29	Dankenfeld/Bv	61-0770
AURACHER, Marie	19	Holzkirchen	60-1032
Ursula 24, Johann 3			
AUSCHUETZ, Aug.	19	Prussia	60-1161
AUSKA, Jos.	28	Bohemia	60-1161
Asbert 28, Joseph 6, Isede(m) 2			
AUSSING, Louise	21	Osnabrueck	60-1032
AUSTERHOFF, Herrm.	23	Wadersloh	59-1036
AUTH, Alonisa	25	Magdlose	60-1141
Victoria 22			
AUTH, Victoria	22	Stark	60-1141
AUWAERTTER, Johann	39	Schlichten	57-0422
AWES, Elisabeth	27	Ndr.Willstedt	57-1280
AX, Chr.	40	Baltimore	62-1169
Nanny 28, Marie 7, Carl 5			
AXELL, Franz	40	New York	62-0730
AXT, Ernst	31	Weimar	62-0758
AXT, Heinr.	34	Koenigstein	55-0413
AXT, Hermann	32	Germany	57-0578
Agnes 28			
BAAKE, Friedr.	18	Breslau	56-0527
Fr. 45			
BAARS, August	31	Oldenburg	61-0520
BABBIN, Friedrich	12	Seesen	56-0527
BABENAU, Louise	26	Altenbusek	59-0951
Cath. 25			
BABRACH, Israel	24	Koestrich	62-0879
BACH, Carl	38	Muenchstadt	62-0758
BACH, Elisabeth	20	Eisenach	59-0372
BACH, Eva Marg.	26	Zinbrand	55-0812
BACH, Jacob	16	Morsheim	59-1036
BACH, Joh.Christ.	16	Voga	57-1416
BACH, Louis	48	US.	59-0951
(wife) 36, Carl 8			
BACH, Math.	33	Lenau	60-0334
Barbara 29			
BACH, Wm.	51	Richrath	62-0111
BACHA, Wenzel	40	Budicowitz	59-0477
Maria 39, Math. 9, Joseph 11m			
BACHARACH, Wolf	18	Nentershausen	62-0712
BACHFELD, Jacob	20	Cassel	60-0334
BACHHOFEN, T.	49	Weinheim	56-0512
BACHMANN, Adam	19	Altenburg	56-0527
Catharine 18			
BACHMANN, Anna M.	23	Obersuhl	56-0723
BACHMANN, Barb.	59	Dottingen	61-0482
BACHMANN, Bernhard	22	Salzungen	57-1067
BACHMANN, Dar.	9	Augsburg	57-0918
BACHMANN, Elisab.	22	Kuenig	61-0482
BACHMANN, Eliza	27	Ziegenheim	57-0654
BACHMANN, Ester	30	Zirden	56-0951
BACHMANN, Jacob	24	Hadamar	57-0754
Anna Elisab. 29			
BACHMANN, Johannes	30	Kerstenhausen	55-0812
BACHMANN, Michael	30	Louisville	62-0467
Barbara 28, Catharine 20			
BACHMANN, Robert	25	Zwickau	59-0477
BACHMANN, Wmne.	26	Neuenhoff	59-0412
BACHT, Wilhelm	29	Roemersberg	55-0932
Anna 24, Heinrich 5			
BACHUS, Heinr.	42	Madison	59-0214
BACK, Augusta	25	Coppenbruegge	62-0938
BACK, Dorothea	21	Burghausen	61-0482
BACKE, Louise	24	Ortendorf	60-0334
BACKEMEIER, Heinr.	35	Lerbeck	57-1067
Marie 26, Heinrich 2			
BACKER, Friedr.	24	Bremen	60-0785
Franz 28			
BACKER, John	45	Pittsburg	59-0477
Catharine 44, Wilhelm 9m			
BACKER, Justus	23	Altenhausen	57-0847
Maria 29, Justus 3			

NAME	AGE	RESIDENCE	YR-LIST
BACKER, Marg.	24	Arheilgen	60-0785
Cath. 25			
BACKHAUS, A.	28	Lintorf	56-0951
Johann 23			
BACKHAUS, Carl	44	Amsterdam	56-0951
Heinrich 3			
BACKHAUS, Carl Aug	21	Muehlhausen	57-1148
BACKHAUS, Friedr.	27	Muehlhausen	59-1036
BACKHAUS, Godfrey	27	Uder	57-0422
Francis 25			
BACKHAUS, Heinrich	20	Rennbach	57-1280
BACKOETTER, Theres	24	Greven	59-0214
BACKOFEN, T.	49	Weinheim	56-0512
BACKSEITZ, Anna	18	Miess	59-0613
BACKSMEYER, Friedr	18	Rahden	59-0412
BAD, Carl	36	England	60-0785
Marie 26, Paul 7, Marie 6, Ernestine 5			
Blanch 3, Sabina 1			
BADDIKER, Franz	19	Bergheim	59-0214
BADE, August	33	Neu Lewin/Pr.	60-0622
BADE, Augusta	41	Rothenitz	61-0804
Anna 10m			
BADE, Friedrich	19	Bierde	55-0812
BADE, Gottfried	25	Prellwitz	56-0819
BADEN, Joh.Heinr.	36	New York	58-0885
BADEN, John	24	Bremerhafen	59-1036
BADER, Gertrude	53	Muenster	60-0521
Therese 21, Gertrude 17, Engelbert 9			
BADER, Johanna	39	Reichenberg	59-0951
Anton 9, Carl 7, Johanna 5, Eduard 3			
BADER, Joseph	26	Bavaria	60-1161
Marianna 20			
BADER, Peter	22	Darmstadt	57-0606
BADERSCHNEIDER, J.	39	Christesgruen	61-0478
Joh. Rosine 33, Joh. Fritz 8m			
BADESTOCK, C.A.	48	Carsdorf	61-0482
Johanna 42, Friedr. 19			
BADEWITZ, C.W.L.	32	Magdeburg	62-0993
E.M. 25			
BADO, Giov.	50	Genna	61-1132
BADUENZ, Albertine	24	Ritzig	56-0629
BADUM, Friedrich	35	Hemhoffen	59-0412
Maria 31, Caroline 9, Margaretha 6			
BAECHMER, Ernst	30	Haselbeck	61-0520
BAECHT, Andreas	33	Zennern	60-0334
BAECKER, Dennis	46	Schonau	57-0422
BAEFEIN, Crescenza	29	Biesendorf	58-0604
BAEGER, Wm.	26	Drackenburg	60-0521
BAEGLER, Gregor	30	Neuwege	62-0879
BAEHMER, Carl	30	Gertzig	55-0411
BAEHR, Johanna	18	Herford	59-0384
BAEHR, Leop.	27	Chemnitz	59-0535
BAER, Anna	20	Mistelgau	58-0563
Kunigunde 16			
BAER, Anna	42	Fluchshof	61-0478
Magdalena 16, Leonhard 10, Maria 9			
Susana(died) 7, Elisabeth 5			
Joh. Bernh. 18			
BAER, Carl Friedr.	21	Ramptendorf	61-0716
BAER, Conrad	34	Cruz	56-1117
BAER, Friedrich	27	Mistelgau	61-0520
Margaretha 24, Margaretha 3, Johann 2m			
BAER, Jacob	26	Eberstadt	61-0047
BAER, William	23	Hoelst	60-1141
BAER, de Johanna	35	Nemor	55-0812
BAESELER, Eduard	33	Altenburg	62-0758
BAETJER, Diedrich	16	Arsten	57-1148
BAETJER, Henry	20	Habenhausen	57-0422
BAEY, de John	35	Louisendorf	57-0422
BAFF, Louise	32	Holzhausen	56-0512
Charles 5			
BAFFERT, Pierre	22	France	62-0467
BAGE, Philipp	34	Herford	56-1260
BAGEMUHL, Mich.Gtf	27	Tanto	57-0704
Carlne.Luise 21			
BAGGELER, Marie	32	Moederath	59-1036
BAGGER, H.B.	47	Neermoor	55-0413
Louise 24			

NAME	AGE	RESIDENCE	YR-LIST
BAHA, Barbara	20	Bischoff	57-1280
Anna 18			
BAHDE, Heinrich	32	Klanhorst	57-1067
BAHDE, Louise	34	Giessen	57-1067
Friedrich 1			
BAHE, Ernst	33	Rohrsen/Hann.	57-0847
Sophie 21, Wilhelm 3			
BAHLEN, Catharine	60	Wetruck	59-0047
Augusta 8			
BAHLERT, Christian	17	Lohe	57-1122
BAHLSEN, Em.(f)	21	Hannover	61-0669
BAHN, Valentin	22	Friedrichsrod	56-0279
Catharine 2			
BAHR, A.(m)	47	Noerenberg	61-0897
C.(m) 20			
BAHR, Conrad	15	Obernerich	57-1067
BAHR, Mrs.	28	Bremen	59-0477
BAHTKE, August	32	Ritzig	56-0629
Wilhelmine 27, (baby) bob			
BAIER, Carl	28	Kaichen	58-0881
BAIER, Joh.Andreas	24	Kunstenhaus	59-0372
BAIER, Johann	23	Weismein	57-0606
BAIERL, Anton	20	Wien	61-0047
BAILLEU, Joh.	21	Ziethen	61-0478
August 50			
BAISON, Francois	26	France	56-1216
BAIST, Elisab.	26	Philadelphia	61-0804
Marie 6, Wm. 2			
BAIST, Nicolaus	26	Seidenrodt	60-1141
BALD, Wilhelm	33	Berleburg	56-0847
BALDEWEIN, Anna E.	32	Bierschied	56-1117
BALKE, Henry	45	Vlotho	59-0384
Johanna 43, Johanna 16, Anna 9, Emma 13			
Johannes 3			
BALKE, Henry	42	Loirs	57-0654
Augusta Engl 23, Wilhelm 15			
BALKE, Marg.	21	Lerau	59-0613
BALKE, Robert	18	Polzberg	60-1161
BALL, Caroline	18	Ederheim	62-0836
Wilhelmine 22			
BALL, Gottlieb	40	Berlin	56-0819
BALLAUF, Carl Luis	57	Muenden	57-1192
BALLAUFF, Charles	43	Minden	57-0961
BALLES, Anton	38	Burgstadt	60-0533
BALLIN, Henriette	16	Hebenhausen	61-0167
BALLIN, J.M.(m)	15	Oldenburg	62-0401
BALLMANN, Chr.	48	Veckenstedt	57-0654
Friederike 50, Friederike 7, Chr. 20			
BALLMANN, Ida	48	Leipzig	61-0930
Elise 18, Max 20			
BALLUFF, Minna	42	New York	60-0521
Marie 6, Ida 4, Louis 6m			
BALLZER, Ad.(m)	19	Germany	62-0467
BALSEN, Jos.	24	Soell	57-0578
BALSER, Johanna	14	Frankfurt	59-0951
Herrmann 7			
BALTE, Jos. Ant.	27	Warendorf	60-1196
BALTEN, C.	40	US.	57-1192
Mary 30			
BALTHASAR, F.	16	Elsfleth	62-0993
BALTZER, Ludw.	21	Muenster	62-0836
BALTZER, Ludwig	29	Pohlgoens	59-1036
Elise 21, Cath. 24			
BALUNINGER, Wilh.	40	Trabelsdorf	59-0047
Caroline 22, Friederike 7m			
BALZ, Barb.	22	Breitenstein	60-0521
BALZ, Casp.	53	St.Louis	56-1216
BALZ, Philip	17	Tramersheim	59-0477
BALZKE, F.A.(m)	19	Rosendorf	61-0930
BAMANN, Ernst	21	Lesester	62-0467
BAMBEI, Georg	22	Kirchheim/KHe	62-0342
BAMBERG, Bierkchen	19	Lengerich	59-0951
BAMBERGER, Herm.	16	Burgkundstadt	62-0730
BAMBERGER, Lina	17	Mittwitz	62-0730
Therese 18			
BAMBERGER, S.	15	Eberstadt	62-0938
Simon 16			
BAMBERGER, S.(m)	19	Fuerth	62-0401

NAME	AGE	RESIDENCE	YR-LIST
BAMIG, Carl Friedr	19	Friedorf	56-0629
BANDES, Anna Cath.	21	Weiler/Pruss.	55-1238
BANDES, Elisabeth	15	Hirten/Prus.	55-1238
BANDMANN, Daniel	24	Cassel	61-1054
BANDMANN, F.(m)	27	Boston	62-0166
BANF, Casp.	34	Philadelphia	61-0897
BANGE, F.L.(m)	30	New York	62-0232
BANGER, Therese	25	Wuerzburg	59-1036
Barbara 29			
BANGERT, Jacob	21	Darmstadt	57-0606
Christian 18			
BANKAEMPER, J.Hch.	32	Muenster	58-0881
Diena 21			
BANNAMANN, Cathar.	20	Stambach	56-1117
BANNASCH, Fr.	24	Berlin	57-1148
BANTEL, Joseph	14	Metzingen	59-0613
BANTJEN, Bernh.	44		58-0815
BANTZ, E.	15	Hildburghause	62-0993
BANZE, Ekhardt	33	Besse	56-0527
Rudolph 9			
BAPP, Joh.Chr.	28	Indianopolis	59-0214
BAPPERT, Franz	52	Creuznach	62-0001
BARANDON, Augusta	19	Verden	62-0166
BARBER, Ch.	18	England	60-0521
Anne 22			
BARBER, J.	55	England	60-0521
BARBERI, Joseph	55	Italy	61-0716
BARBRACK, Fr.(m)	25	Holtrum	61-0669
BARDET, Elisabeth	27	US.	61-0167
(child) 9m			
BARDILOWSKY, W.	40	Boehmen	62-0467
Marie 48, Marie 9m			
BARDORFF, Georg	24	Nordheim	56-0847
Franziska 30			
BARELMANN, Gerh.H.	56	Wartenburg	57-1113
BARFEIND, Heinrich	24	Oldendorf/Han	60-0429
Joh. Heinr. 21			
BARGEMANN, (m)	29	Norden	57-0578
G.J.(f) 22, Johann 8m			
BARGEN, v.Heinrich	27	Zeven/Hann.	60-0622
Maria 23			
BARGMANN, Ludwig	22	Varel	62-0879
BARING, Carl Jul.	22	Hannover	55-0634
BARK, Georg	42	Duerkheim	62-1169
BARK, Peter	34	Borhoff	57-1122
BARK, Phil.	29	Riederhausen	59-1036
BARKHOLZ, John M.	29	Abtswind	62-0467
BARLAGE, G.	33	Quakenbrueck	57-1150
BARMUELLER, Reinh.	26	Suhl	56-1117
BARNASS, Helene	39	Fordon	57-1150
Doris 30, Jette 9, David 7, Hanna 6			
Julius 4, Louise 3			
BARNICK, Friedrich	44	Brallina	56-1117
BARNOWSKY, William	28	Husenberg	57-0422
Francis 19			
BARNSCHIER, Cath.	19	Weissenhausen	57-1026
BARNSTORFF, H.	45	New York	62-1112
Augusta 31			
BARRE, de la Emily	19	Strassburg	57-0961
BARRELMANN, D.G.	26	Warfenburg	56-0723
BARTALDERS, Marie	14	Borgentreich	60-1196
BARTASCH, Jos.	54	Boehmen	62-0938
Rosalie 53, Rosalie 20, Therese 18			
Joseph 26, Johanna 25, Jos. 10m			
BARTEL, Gertrude	24	Oberzwehren	56-0527
BARTEL, Leonh.Casp	50	Untersambach	57-1026
Martha M.Chr 20, Joh. Friedr. 7			
BARTEL, M.M.(m)	29	Cloppenburg	61-0897
BARTELMAE, Marie	22	Altorf	61-0520
BARTELS, (m)	40	Paderborn	58-0306
BARTELS, (widow)	50	Paderborn	58-0306
Marie 30, Augusta 28			
BARTELS, Anna	23	New York	62-0938
Louise 2			
BARTELS, Diedrich	29	Bremen	60-0052
BARTELS, Dorothea	24	Reher	61-0520
Johann 27			
BARTELS, E.(m)	20	Braunschweig	62-0232

NAME	AGE	RESIDENCE	YR-LIST
BARTELS, Elisabeth	22	Hoya	57-0924
BARTELS, Friedrich	27	Hannover	56-0279
BARTELS, Heinrich	30	Harburg	57-0924
BARTELS, Johann	21	Frankfurt/Ma.	55-1238
BARTELS, Johann	18	Hannover	62-0467
BARTELS, Trine	21	Beckedorf	56-0589
BARTENSTEIN, Heinr	21	Westhausen	62-0712
Margaretha 52			
BARTESCH, Joseph	23	Boehmen	56-1044
BARTH, Amalie	27	Frankenhausen	56-0512
BARTH, August	46	Luckenwalde	60-0533
BARTH, Caroline	49	Stuttgart	58-0576
BARTH, Christian	36	Luckenwalde/P	60-0371
Charlotte 42, Paul 9, Oscar 8, Ida 7			
BARTH, Christian	25	Poppenburg	57-1407
Dorothea 23, Anna by			
BARTH, Elisabeth	19	Boehmen	61-0897
BARTH, Elisabeth	32	Ebingen	62-0938
BARTH, F.	62	Hausen	62-0993
BARTH, Mathilde	32	St.Louis	58-0885
Elise 9, Friedrich 7, Felix 6, Robert 1			
BARTH, Tobias	42	Baltimore	62-0938
BARTHELD, v. H.(m)	16	Sielen	62-0467
BARTHELEMES, M.(m)	25	Laibach	61-0478
BARTHING, Wilh.	18	Halle	56-1216
BARTHLING, Chr.	19	Hille	55-0411
BARTHNAGEL, Hartw.	42	Tuemmelsee	57-1148
Augusta 43, Louis 16, Carolina 14			
Augusta 11, Charles 8			
BARTHOLD, August	27	Leese	57-0422
BARTHOLD, Wilhelm	16	Nordheim	57-1067
BARTHOLMAES, P.H.	30	Gypersleben	61-0482
Dorette 25, H.Franz 2, (boy) 6m			
BARTHOLOMAE, Aug.	30	Effien	56-1044
BARTHOLOMAEUS, Edw	23	Deutschthal	57-1192
BARTHOLOME, Johann	25	Prussia	56-1044
BARTLING, Friedr.	33	Roehr	59-0372
Ludwig 18			
BARTLINGS, An Mary	19	Wittlage	56-0589
BARTMANN, Anton	49	Burgsteinfurt	58-0885
BARTOLOMAI, Heinr.	40	Magdeburg	56-0847
BARTRUFF, Joh.(f)	58	Spatzenhof	57-0555
BARTSCH, Daniel	49	Hammer	61-0779
Anna Rosine 40, Anna Rosine 23, Carl 17			
Christian 15, Ernst 12, Helene 8			
Caroline 5, Wilhelm 2, Anna Susanna 30			
Carl Gustav 8			
BARUCH, Bar.	16	Landau	58-0563
BARUCH, Joseph	17	Schrode	57-0654
BARY, de Julie	34	New York	62-1042
Eugenia 3			
BARZHORN, Helene	20	Burhave	56-0723
BASCH, Amalie	30	Bovenden	59-0477
BASCHER, Julie	23	Niederassbach	55-0845
BASEL, Jacob	63	Thierenbach	59-0477
Maria 53, Michael 26, Margaretha 28			
Marge 21, Marianne 5			
BASSE, Dorothea	52	Wissenbrick/P	57-0847
BASSE, Franz	20	Braunschweig	62-0342
BASSELER, Georg	47	Tyrol	55-0812
BASSON, Aug.Rud.	22	Hannover	60-1032
BAST, Peter	21	Bavaria	59-0214
BASTIANE, Maria	53	Waldernbach/N	60-0371
Catharina 30, Clara 25, Elisabeth 23			
Georg 19, Joseph 16, Daniel 9			
BATCHING, J.(m)	30	Schebingen	62-0111
BATEFELD, Elisa	20	Frankenberg	56-0692
BATH, Peter	38	Pittsburg	59-0951
BATH, Ph.(m)	31	Philadelphia	61-0804
BATHMANN, Christof	25	Glaskowo	57-0704
BATHMANN, Maria L.	16	Bremen	61-0482
BATJAMANN, Martin	27	Bockeln	55-1082
BATMER, Friedr.	24	Kalbe	62-0306
BATT, Fridolin	25	Witterau	59-0477
BATTENFELD, Jean	36	France	62-0938
Anna 32			
BATTER, Elisabeth	24	Cloppenburg/O	60-0371
BATTERMANN, Heinr.	19	Haste/Hessen	55-0628

NAME	AGE	RESIDENCE	YR-LIST
BATTERMANN, Joh.	24	Cincinnati	62-1169
Fritz 20			
BATZ, Leonhard	32	Arnsberg	58-0885
BATZLER, John	34	Baltimore	60-0785
Babette 9			
BAU, Georg	28	Neustadtl	55-1082
BAUCHMANN, Hermann	25	Baltimore	59-0214
BAUDLER, (f)	22	Koburg	57-0555
BAUER, Adam	30	Nitzkau	56-0847
BAUER, Andreas	29	Kleinpardorf	60-0521
Margaretha 9, Friedrich 6			
BAUER, Andreas	4	Reuth	57-1026
BAUER, Anna D.	22	Walmannshofer	60-0622
BAUER, Carl	27	Gaisberg	59-0214
BAUER, Caroline	20	Mohrenbach	60-0521
BAUER, Casp. Fred.	40	Hildburghsn.	55-0812
Johanna 48			
BAUER, Casper	29	Ugenhopen	57-1416
BAUER, Cath.	23	Alsfeld	61-0669
BAUER, Catharina	20	Weissenhard	56-1260
BAUER, Cathrina	21	Eltershoffen	60-1141
BAUER, Conrad	32	Schwabach	56-0589
BAUER, Conrad	29	Baiern	58-0399
Cath. 30, Elisabeth 3, Kunigunde 3m			
BAUER, Elisabeth	27	Geisnidda	56-0723
BAUER, Elise	52	Schesslitz	57-1148
John 20, Mary 20, Anna 16			
BAUER, Ferd.	55	Geisselhardt	59-1036
Cath. 47, Gottfr. 9, Joh. 8, Jacob 7			
BAUER, Friedrich	24	Fuerstenberg	59-0613
Minna 16, Johann 8			
BAUER, Genofeva	34	Wendelsheim	62-0938
BAUER, Gottfried	38	Scherndorf	59-0412
BAUER, Joh.Andr.	34	Scherndorf	59-0412
Therese 29, Emilie 5, Louis 2			
Friedrich 10m			
BAUER, Joh.Leonh.	28	Deckingen	57-0754
BAUER, Johann	25	Walkersbrun	60-0429
BAUER, Johann	37	Hummendorf	62-0001
BAUER, Johannes	58	Alsfeld	55-0634
Elisabeth 40, Joh. Cathr. 7, Emma 6			
BAUER, Joseph	44	Schmierreuth	57-0850
BAUER, Joseph	40	Hill	57-0850
Anna 28, Katharina 6, Johann 4			
BAUER, Magdalena	25	Weydingsfeld	55-1238
Louise 24			
BAUER, Michael	23	Wassbuhl	62-0001
BAUER, Nicolaus	32	Reinerscheidt	58-0399
BAUER, Robert H.	37	Altengesee	57-1067
BAUER, Sebastian	42	Neubronn	56-0413
Maria 6			
BAUER, Stephan	40	New York	61-0682
Magdalena 40, Johann 14, Susanna 11			
Maria 10, Joseph 8			
BAUER, Susanne	24	Wuerzburg	60-1032
BAUER, Sussmann	26	Lehe	56-1260
BAUER, V.(m)	21	Naila	62-0730
BAUER, W.	30	Krupp	56-0512
Christine 21, Catharine 4			
BAUERLE, Gottfr.L.	27	Mondelsheim	57-0606
BAUERMANN, Heinr.	19	Hannover	57-0847
BAUERMANN, Julie	32	Pronenberg	59-0951
Hulda 1, Martha 5m			
BAUERNMEISTER, Fr.	40	Bessendorf	57-0847
Anna Doroth. 36, Augusta 15, Otto 10			
BAUERREISS, J.	27	Voggendorf	56-1044
BAUERSCHMIDT, Adam	28	Oberginsbach	60-0334
BAUG, Wilhelm	18	Darmstadt	55-0634
BAUM, Elisabeth	21	Laichingen	56-0951
BAUM, Gustav	26	Breslau	60-1117
BAUM, Leopold	22	Oldenburg	61-0897
BAUM, Moses	14	Merzhausen	59-0372
BAUM, Peter	36	Wetzlar	61-0482
BAUMANN, Andreas	32	Krumbach	57-0422
BAUMANN, Balthasar	33	Giessen	55-0634
Catharina 26, Johannes 18, Heinrich 12			
BAUMANN, Baruch	19	Curhessen	55-0634
BAUMANN, C.G.	44	Waldfischbach	62-1042

NAME	AGE	RESIDENCE	YR-LIST
BAUMANN, Carl	15	Lauffen	62-0166
Cath. 17			
BAUMANN, Catharine	16	Menderferbach	62-0730
BAUMANN, Charles	36	New York	62-0730
Christine 48, Johann 9, Jacob 8			
BAUMANN, Conrad	30	Deissel	56-0723
Christine 34			
BAUMANN, Heinrich	21	Erligheim	61-0107
BAUMANN, Joh.	39	Richmond	57-1150
BAUMANN, Joh.	33	Kirchaick	59-0990
BAUMANN, Louise	48	New York	59-0384
BAUMANN, Louise	17	Muehlhausen	62-1169
BAUMANN, Otto	16	Mayenberg/Han	60-0622
BAUMANN, Rosine	20	Wittenberg	62-0758
BAUMANN, Sophie G.	18	Hilsedorf/Han	60-0622
BAUMANN, W.(m)	25	Traxelmoor	62-0730
Anna 21, Therese 1, Franziska 20			
Mathies 20			
BAUMEISTER, A.(m)	22	Selgau	61-0804
BAUMEISTER, Henry	26	Hemmersen	57-0961
BAUMEISTER, Max	21	San Francisco	61-0804
BAUMER, Joh.	34	Doerfles	57-0447
BAUMER, Mathias	70	Weimersheim	57-0754
Anna Maria 35, Maria Barb. 23			
Carolina 11, Barbara 6			
BAUMGAERTEL, S.W.	20	Asch	57-1067
BAUMGARDT, A.Cath.	20	Oberstoppel	60-1053
Maria 16			
BAUMGARDT, Sara	22	Werssels	60-0521
BAUMGART, Andreas	23	Kieselbach	57-1026
BAUMGART, Elisab.	17	Kieselbach	57-1026
BAUMGART, Heinr.	18	Wensheim	56-1216
BAUMGARTEN, Ch.(m)	24	Kirchzandern	60-0785
BAUMGARTEN, Ernst	20	Lemfoerde	59-0214
BAUMGARTEN, Fanny	17	Erfurt	55-1082
BAUMGARTEN, Georg	19	Stolzenau	57-1148
BAUMGARTEN, Georg	32	Schoenau	57-1280
Anna 27			
BAUMGARTNER, Marg.	17	Muenster a/Na	59-0214
BAUMSHORST, Herm.	21	Freiburg	60-0785
BAUNSMANN, Jos.	24	Greven	59-0214
BAURMEISTER, Chr.	20	Hillen	55-0932
BAURMEISTER, Diedr	18	Anderstein	56-1117
BAURMEISTER, Juls.	20	Carlshafen	55-0634
BAURSACHS, Wilhelm	17	Schweina	55-0932
BAUSCH, Carl	20	Leipzig	59-0951
Louis 30			
BAUSCH, H.E.(m)	31	Philadelphia	62-0111
BAUSCHEL, Friedr.	27	Duesseldorf	57-1067
BAUSEWEIN, Chr.	58	Versbach	60-0521
Doroth. 56			
BAUSEWEIN, Emil	17	Wuerzburg	60-1196
BAUSIL, Francis	34	Tegowous	56-1011
Barbara 24			
BAUSS, Caroline	17	Lasphe	62-0938
BAUSTIAN, Johann	40	Wucharir	62-0401
Sophie 36, Louise 8, August 6, Ernst 9m			
BAUTZ, Maria	18	Wutburg	57-1026
BAUZE, Andreas	25	Steigra	60-0398
BAX, Heinrich	20	Gontershausen	56-0847
BAX, Heinrich	19	Lippe Detmold	57-1280
BAXMANN, Edward	23	Hanover	57-0654
BAY, C.(f)	16	Wuertemberg	57-0555
W.(f) 23			
BAYER, Barbara	30	Schrieheim	56-1011
BAYER, Eva Marg.	25	Germany	61-0167
BAYER, Gottlieb	20	Aichelbach/Pr	60-0622
Adam 17			
BAYER, Johann	27	Reisach	60-0533
BAYER, Peter	24	Bremen	56-1117
BAYERL, Andreas	28	Waldau	55-0630
BAYERLEIN, Marg.B.	18	Ipsheim/Bav.	60-0429
BAYERLEIN, Martha	28	Johannisthal	55-0932
BEAR, William	23	Hoelst	60-1141
BEAU, Georg Wm.	39	Strut	62-0306
Margaretha 25, Franz 5, Margaretha 3			
Elisabeth 9m			
BEAUHIN, v. Ad.(m)	22	Goettingen	61-1132

NAME	AGE	RESIDENCE	YR-LIST
BEAURARD, (f)	60	Bordeaux	62-0401
BECHER, A.Marie	29	Mergesheim	57-1067
Johann 7, Michel 9m			
BECHER, Conrad	58	Baiern	58-0399
BECHER, Elis.	23	Rosenbeck	61-0897
BECHER, Elisabeth	28	Schotten	59-0477
BECHER, Joh.Michel	30	Unt.Schwaning	57-1067
BECHERER, Lina	21	Malberg	61-0107
BECHERER, Ludwig	22	Saarlouis	59-0214
BECHT, Anna Cath.	58	Oberleis	57-1067
Maria 5			
BECHTEL, Albert	20	Stuttgarth	50-1017
BECHTEL, Geo.Jonas	19	New York	60-1196
BECHTHOLD, Cath.	20	Ndr.Wollstadt	58-0563
BECHTLUFFT, Carl	28	Burgsteinfurt	58-0885
Fritz 20			
BECHTOLD, Amand	28	Magdeburg	61-0716
BECHTOLD, Carl	28	Lissberg/Hess	62-0608
BECHTOLD, Conr.	19	Schmikartshsn	55-0932
Elisabetha 50			
BECHTOLD, Conrad	56	Schotten	57-0924
Margarethe 44, Heinrich 18, Carl 16			
Elisa 14, Johannes 12, Wilhelm 7			
BECHTOLD, Jacobine	30	Buechenau	61-0107
Gallers 8, Friedr. 2			
BECHTOLD, John	27	Oberbergen	57-0654
BECK, Anna M.	22	Gniebel	60-0411
BECK, August	32	Chicago	62-1112
Louise 28, Willy 5, Carl 1, Franziska 1m			
BECK, Balth.	45	Pittsburg	57-1192
BECK, Balthasar	45	US.	57-1192
BECK, Carl	26	Orp	58-0563
BECK, Christian	28	Burghofen	57-0850
A.Marie 33, Heinrich 5, Anton 3, Anna 10m			
Anna Cathr. 24, Martha 5m			
BECK, Eduard	32	Indianapolis	57-1192
BECK, Eva	25	Rilsen	60-1117
BECK, Eva	20	Coburg	62-0712
BECK, Friedrich	40	Ohrdrup	61-0897
BECK, Georg	31	Schwann	59-0613
BECK, Gottfried	37	Almenhausen	56-0819
Christ.Elis. 35, Joh.Friedr. 9			
Anna Doroth. 8, Wilhelm Carl 6			
Joh. Robert 2			
BECK, Heinr.	19	Waldkappel	57-1416
Dorothee 43, Johannes 17, Margaretha 22			
BECK, Heinrich	18	Prague/Bohm.	56-0819
BECK, Heinrich	21	Leipzig	57-0918
BECK, J.F.	21	Freudenthal	59-1036
BECK, Joh. Adam	42	Kirchenlamitz	56-0723
Louise 30			
BECK, Johann	52	Bleichenbach	60-1053
Caroline 46, Dorothea 9, Heinrich 8			
BECK, Lorchin	21	Bleichenbach	58-0576
BECK, Louise	40	Backnang	59-1036
BECK, S.M. (m)	20	Leidingen	55-0413
BECK, Sarah	23	New York	62-1042
BECK, Simon	59	Oberlauringen	57-0422
Jane 37, Mary 6, John 9			
BECK, Victoria	62	Augsburg	58-0399
Marie 7			
BECK, Wm.	43	Hochelheim	62-0836
Marg. 42, Marie 18, Heinrich 12			
BECKE, Christopher	28	Gross Furra	56-1011
John 31, Augusta 6, Charlotte 2			
Ferdinand 3m			
BECKE, Godfrey	57	Gross Furra	56-1011
Maria 57, Ferdinand 27, Christian 24			
BECKEN, Albert	18	Bassum	61-0107
BECKENSTROETER, J.	33	Honeburg	56-0847
Maria 44			
BECKER, A.(m)	22	Merlau	57-0555
BECKER, Adam	38	Ronshausen	55-0413
Louise 24			
BECKER, Anna	23	Bremen	59-0477
BECKER, Anna	11	Worpswede	59-1036
BECKER, Anna	31	Worpswede	59-1036
Henry 5			

NAME	AGE	RESIDENCE	YR-LIST
BECKER, Anton	28	Wildbach	62-0836
BECKER, Aug.	26	Prussia	57-0555
BECKER, August	17	Coesfeld	56-0951
BECKER, August	22	Dipenau	59-0412
BECKER, Ba.	38	Schoenwalden	58-0881
Rudolph 9			
BECKER, Barbara	17	Giessen	57-0606
BECKER, Bernhard	26	Doessel	56-1044
BECKER, C. Arnold	29	Oberluebbe	60-0533
BECKER, Carl	16	Sulbach	61-0482
BECKER, Carl	30	Chicago	61-0482
BECKER, Carl	23	Grefenhausen	62-0111
BECKER, Caroline	50	Kalkhorst	57-0654
BECKER, Carsten	21	Sueste	57-1148
BECKER, Caspar	65	Leitmar	57-1067
Elisabeth 55, Joseph 16			
BECKER, Catharina	66	Weinheim	60-0533
Gerhard 18			
BECKER, Catharine	27	Wehrdorf	57-0704
BECKER, Catharine	29	Gr.Buseck	62-0467
Marie 21, Heinrich 8			
BECKER, Charles Jo	26	Lorck	57-0654
Mary 34			
BECKER, Cilly	26	Schrimm	60-0521
BECKER, Conr.	22	Muenster	62-1042
Elise 20			
BECKER, Conrad	17	Gr.Rohrheim	56-0847
BECKER, D.Wm.	16	Beverstedt	57-0654
BECKER, Dorothea	33	Magdeburg	62-0730
BECKER, Elise	23	Bleiwaesche	56-0723
Barbara 46			
BECKER, Elise	31	Kirchforo	62-0467
BECKER, Fr.	21	Melle	57-0606
BECKER, Fr.Wm.	34	Mahlwinkel	62-0166
BECKER, Friedrich	23	Muenden	57-1192
BECKER, G.(m)	27	Dubuque	62-0836
Fanny 29, Anton 4, Joseph 11m			
BECKER, Georg	21	Nassau	55-0630
BECKER, Georg	30	Schotten	58-0563
BECKER, Gottfried	55	Wickersdorf	57-1407
Margaretha 45, Fritz 21, Martin 34			
Johanna 29, Marie by			
BECKER, Gust.	24	Pyrmont	62-1112
BECKER, Gustav	34	Gozlow	61-0770
BECKER, H.B.(m)	29	Lohne	62-0401
J.(f) 54			
BECKER, Heinrich	22	Speel	56-0819
BECKER, Heinrich	59	Bohra/Hessen	62-0608
Ludwig 8			
BECKER, Henriette	41	Berlin	56-0819
Franz 13, Emma 11, Ernst 6, Oscar 4			
BECKER, Hermann	23	Goettingen/Ha	55-0628
BECKER, J.C.W. (m)	24	Belm	61-0482
H.L. (m) 22			
BECKER, J.G.	56	Dasdorf	55-0932
Elisabeth 47, Reinhold 16, Carl 11			
BECKER, J.H.C.	32	Aldenahausen	57-0447
Catharine 24, Conradine 7m			
BECKER, Joh.	29	Maehren	61-0478
Elise 50, Catharine 15, Anton 11			
BECKER, Joh.	26	New York	56-1216
BECKER, Joh. C. G.	51	Saalfeld	56-0951
Henriette 46			
BECKER, Joh.Friedr	29	Essnerberg	55-0812
M. Ilsebein 29, Cath. Engel 2			
Cath.Ilsbein 4w			
BECKER, Johann	37	Unt.Schwaning	58-0604
BECKER, Johannes	34	Wellingerode	56-1044
Anna Elisab. 30, Elise 6, Joh.Aug. 1			
BECKER, Johannes	20	Neustadt	61-0478
BECKER, John	35	Penna.	61-0897
BECKER, John C.	42	America	62-1112
BECKER, Joseph	38	Kluk	57-1026
Anna 39, Elisabeth 16, Anna 9			
Catharina 7, Stephan 5, Friedrich 6m			
BECKER, Jost	15	Hochweisel	59-0384
BECKER, Kilian	60	Godensberg	60-1161
Cathr. 22, Kilian 24			

NAME	AGE	RESIDENCE	YR-LIST
BECKER, Louis	30	Polle	59-0477
Minna 26			
BECKER, Ludwig	19	Osnabrueck	56-0589
BECKER, Ludwig	14	Redgen	61-0047
Caspar 8			
BECKER, Ludwig	68	Herbershausen	62-0608
Dorette 58, August 20, Ludwig 11			
BECKER, Ludwig	22	Baden	59-0477
BECKER, Maria	24	Sondorf	56-0629
BECKER, Mary	54	Driftsethe	59-1036
BECKER, Math.(m)	20	Muenster	62-0111
BECKER, Max	46	Ulsfeld	57-0776
Elisabeth 27			
BECKER, Peter	27	Birstadt	55-1048
Caroline 23, Dorette 9m			
BECKER, Peter	22	Ndr.Ofleiden	62-0712
BECKER, Rupert	17	Niederweimar	62-0730
BECKER, Sophie	19	Herbertshsn.	56-1044
BECKER, Theodor	28	Ochtrup	60-0411
BECKER, Wilhelm	35	Battenberg/He	62-0342
BECKER, Wm.	27	Ruilsch	62-0467
BECKERMANN, Joh.	46	New York	59-0951
BECKERR, Carl	29	Darmstadt	59-0613
BECKERT, Caroline	3	Catharinenbrg	59-0951
Anton 9, Julie 4			
BECKERT, Clemens	20	Dresden	56-0632
BECKERT, Herm.	44	Luenten	60-0334
Adelheit 44, Marie 14, Wilhelm 6			
BECKERT, Joseph	38	Catharinenbrg	59-0384
BECKMANN, E.H.	50	Hesepe	55-0932
Cornelia 19			
BECKMANN, Fr'drika	30	Cassel	57-1148
BECKMANN, Fr.(m)	27	St.Louis	62-0730
BECKMANN, G.H.	23	Westercappeln	55-0932
BECKMANN, Johann	22	Zeven	59-0535
BECKMANN, Meta	30	New York	57-1192
Emily 9m			
BECKMANN, Minna	17	Suderup	60-1032
BECKMANN, Rebecca	15	Prehlsdorferm	61-0478
BECKMANN, Robert	32	Oberneuland	57-1148
BECKSTEDE, T.	32	Rehda	62-0993
BEDIKOWSKY, Bernh.	17	Flatow	57-0704
BEEKER, Elisabeth	15	Lora/Hess.	61-0770
BEEMSTRUN, Jan Eym	42	Persene	56-0629
Albertje 42, Berentje 18			
BEENDERS, Claus Ev	24	Suederneuland	57-0422
BEENES, Franz	28	Hadamer	60-0334
BEENING, A.	32	Leer	57-0578
BEER, Franz	24	Prag	56-1044
BEER, Jacob	18	Illsitz	56-0632
BEERING, Caroline	17	Rahden	57-1280
Henriette 17			
BEERMANN, August	25	Plane	57-1407
BEESE, Christian	27	Wirode	57-0776
BEGEMANN, Ad.	15	Hiddessen	57-0422
BEGEMANN, Fritz	20	Hildesin	56-0629
August 22			
BEGREISS, Christof	44	Bischoffsrode	60-0398
Maria 44, Johannes 22, Georg 14			
Catharina 9, Christoph 6, Michael 1			
BEHACKER, Margreta	19	Hagenbuecher	61-0478
BEHLE, Ch.	22	Vasbeck	60-0998
BEHLERS, Amand	21	Dorum	62-0879
BEHLERT, Gottlieb	24	Helba	57-1067
Marie 26, Rosina 18, Gustav 5			
BEHLING, Heinrich	29	Polle	56-0819
Friederike 30			
BEHM, Anna	36	Hochstall/Bav	62-0608
BEHM, Ernestine	26	Molsdorf	57-0961
BEHM, Joh.L.	56	Neu Wuhrow	57-1113
Charlotte 55, Wilhelm 30, Siegfried 24			
BEHM, Louise	20	Bergholz	57-0654
BEHMANN, Marie	32		59-0477
BEHME, Pauline	26	Cracau	55-0812
BEHMER, Fz.	22	Bonn	62-0938
BEHNKEN, Friedrich	56	Neufeld/Capln	57-0961
BEHNKEN, Meta	16	Langwedel	59-1036
BEHR, Cathinka	20	Rothenburg	59-0613

NAME	AGE	RESIDENCE	YR-LIST
BEHR, Elisa	30	Duisburg/Pr.	55-1238
BEHR, Emilie	22	Graben	62-0730
BEHR, Friedrich	58	Landau	58-0576
BEHR, Georg	55	Burgprepach	57-0754
Anna Maria 35			
BEHR, Joh.	29	Euskirchen	61-0716
BEHR, Ludwig	39	Mt.Vernon	62-0232
BEHR, Samuel	25	Lima	60-0785
BEHREND, Seibern	41	Wittmund	60-1032
BEHRENDS, Hch.Eden		Nebraska	58-0925
BEHRENDSEN, Gerhd.	19	Gr. Starau	58-0815
Angel.Marg. 60			
BEHRENDSEN, Hm.Hch	60	Flatterlothsn	58-0815
BEHRENS, Christian	43	Klein Ilsede	61-0779
BEHRENS, Claus	6	Weihe	60-0533
BEHRENS, Engelke	21	Freisenbuttel	62-0608
BEHRENS, H.C.	28	Aurich	62-0879
BEHRENS, Henry H.	16	Strackholt	57-0422
BEHRENS, Herm.	15	Geestdorf	61-0478
BEHRENS, Wilhelm	28	Silbeck	57-0850
Charlotte 28			
BEHRING, Peter	56	Proebsten/Han	57-0847
Maria 47, Heinrich 18, Foecke 16			
Christopher 14, Minna 12, Heinrich 10			
Lotte 7			
BEHRMANN, Engel	24	Westerharre	58-0881
BEHRMANN, H.(m)	21	New York	62-0730
BEHRMANN, Henry	35	Walsrode	57-0422
Wilhelmine 34, Augustus 9, Emily 7, Ida 3			
William 6m			
BEHUKE, Wilhelm	37	Posen	57-0776
Anna 40, August 9, Christiana 7, Anna 4			
Caroline 9m			
BEIER, Carl	24	Hameln	60-0521
BEIER, E.M.(m)	23	Corlitz	61-0482
BEIERLEIN, Johann	31	Breitenlesau	57-1280
Barbara 24, Frantz 3			
BEIERSDOERFER, C.	29	Marbach	61-0520
BEIERSDORF, Ernst	53	Neubronn	56-0413
Christiane 35			
BEIFUSS, Hermann	19	Giesen	59-0372
BEIKIRCH, Joseph	40	Hausen	57-0924
Florentine 24			
BEIKIRCH, Sebast.	28	Steinbach/Han	60-0622
BEIL, Adam	15	Maden/Curhess	60-0622
BEIL, Christ.	14	Besigheim	60-0334
BEIL, Simon	23	Proelsdorf	59-0990
BEILE, Marianus	38	Warendorf	58-0885
BEILER, Catharina	34	Wehe	57-0704
Carolina 18			
BEILING, Rosalie	17	Butterwiesen	62-0938
BEIMBORN, August	28	Hessen	62-0758
BEINHAUER, Johann	22	Cassel/Hessen	60-0052
BEINHORN, Charlott	25	Grohndel	56-0632
BEINKAMPE, Ed.	24	Dissen	56-1044
BEINKEN, Dorothea	20	Bremen	56-0723
BEINZ, Anna M.	41	New York	62-0730
BEISCHEL, Victor	25	Beteford	58-0885
BEISENKOTTER, Joh.	37	Drensteinfurt	60-1196
BEISS, Margaretha	55	Hellingen/Pr.	60-0622
BEITZ, Christiana	25	Vegesack	57-1407
Carl by			
BEITZ, Valent.	22	Wenjes	55-0413
Louise 24			
BEJEE, Elise	18	Havre	62-0836
BEKEL, Cath.	50	Glashuetten	55-0932
BEKETT, Marie	30	US.	62-0938
Marie 17			
BEKS, Charlotte	28	Wittringhause	56-0589
BELINA, Wenzel	45	Boehmen	62-1042
Johanna 35, Franz 15, Anton 13, Wenzel 6			
Johann 4, Joseph 9m			
BELING, Fr.(m)	38	New Orleans	62-0836
BELISIER, H.(m)	16	Bruchsal	62-0730
BELL, Bachelder	22	Maine	60-0785
BELLA, Joh.	53	Adelsdorf	55-0845
Anna 52			
BELLENKAMP, Gerhd.	39	New York	57-1192

NAME	AGE	RESIDENCE	YR-LIST
BELLINGER, Heinr.	34	Quickborn	62-1169
BELLKNAP, Clayton	21	London	62-1042
BELLOF, Maria	20	Giessen	57-0606
BELONE, H.H.	27	Honolulu	59-0613
BELSNER, Barb.	24	Entringen	55-0932
BELZ, Daniel	38	Schwandau/Pr.	62-0608
Caroline 40, Carl 14, Justine 12			
August 9, Heinrich 5, Johann 8m			
BEMBENECK, Michael	33	Matezko/Polen	56-1260
Josephine 29, August 4, Herrmann 2			
Michael 6m			
BENDA, Conrad	20	Hackborn	60-0334
BENDA, Martin	28	Borek	61-0779
Barbara 30, Matthias by			
BENDA, Paul	30	Schapfurth	61-0107
BENDEL, August	52	Schodtheim	60-0533
Henriette 26, Emil 2			
BENDEL, Jacob	45	Guentersdorf	57-1148
Clara 41, Clara 16, Jacob 14, Anna 7			
Johannes 2			
BENDELE, Moritz	24	Wien	60-0521
BENDER, Andreas	18	Niederhorfeld	56-0847
BENDER, Anton	29	Alsfeld/KH.	60-0622
BENDER, Cath.	16	Grueningen	62-0111
BENDER, Dorothea	22	Marburg	58-0885
BENDER, John J.	20	Caldern	62-0467
BENDER, Joseph	17	Carlsruhe	58-0881
BENDER, Laurence	16	Berge	57-0422
BENDER, Marie	18	Heidelberg	59-0990
BENDER, Max	19	Duesseldorf	56-1216
BENDER, Philip	17	Eltwyl/Nassau	57-0924
BENDICKTER, Louis	22	Baiern	57-0776
BENDIX, Rosa	25	Muenster	59-1036
BENDT, Georg	19	Bremen	57-1148
BENEDICT, Amalie	20	Lichtenstadt	59-0477
BENEDICT, C.Gottl.	21	Lichtenberg	57-0654
BENEDICT, Ferd.	19	Lichtenstadt	61-0482
BENEDICT, Joseph	32	Peine	58-0399
BENEDICT, Magdalen	20	Wilhelmsdorf	62-0712
BENGARD, Wilhelm	24	Weikersheim	56-1260
BENGER, August	33	Breslau	59-0477
BENGER, Ferd.	28	Camford	61-0482
BENICKE, F.Wilhelm	49	Schoeneberg	60-0533
Caroline 50, Augusta 24, Caroline 18			
Fr. Wilhelm 10			
BENJAMIN, Elias	22	Borgentreich	60-0533
BENJE, Julia	28	New York	62-0836
BENKER, Cathar.	32	Leutendorf	56-0527
BENKER, Christian	31	Wordorf	56-0589
BENKER, Johann	36	Texas	56-0589
Amalie 37			
BENKER, Marie	22	Leipzig	58-0306
BENKERT, J.	26	Philadelphia	62-1042
BENKERT, John Jac.	19	Bretten	57-1192
BENKERT, Ph.S.	32	Philadelphia	62-1042
BENKUS, Rudolph	28	Cloppenburg/O	60-0371
BENNDORF, F.(m)	19	Teuchern	62-0730
BENNECKE, Alma	22	Holtdorf	57-0654
BENNER, Ed.	31	Muekhausen	62-0166
BENNINGHAUS, B.	35	Ohio	57-1148
BENNINGHAUS, Wm.	35	New York	57-1148
BENNOT, Gottlieb	22	Thumlingen/Wt	61-0770
BENOIT, Fermo	29	US.	61-0716
BENSE, Helena	15	Braunschweig	62-0730
Wilhelm 14			
BENSE, Louise	35	Toledo	59-1036
Aug. 6, John 3			
BENSELER, Wilhelm	29	Minden	57-0924
Friederike 45, Wilhelm 3			
BENSEMANN, Dorothe	56	Westenholz	58-0563
Carsten Hch. 21, Sophie 19, Marie 15			
BENSEN, Friedrich	29	New York	58-0885
Friedrich 4			
BENSY, de (f)	16	France	62-1112
BENTE, Marie	20	Aschaffenburg	60-1032
BENTTCHER, Santa	34	Prussia	57-0961
BENZ, A.E.(m)	37	New York	62-0730
BENZ, Lorenz	18	Voelkersheim	59-0477

NAME	AGE	RESIDENCE	YR-LIST
BENZING, Jac.	25	Thomingen	62-0467
BENZINGER, Bernh.	27	Kaferthal	62-0166
Mary 19			
BEOUBAY, B.	34	France	62-1112
BER, Maria	34	Kl. Rindefeld	61-0478
Barbara 14			
BERBENICH, Wilhelm	21	Bissigheim/Bd	60-0622
BERBERICH, Juliane	31	Auerbach	61-0482
BERBIG, C.	21	Gr.Kromsdorf	62-0993
M. 18			
BERCKBACH, Robert	18	Hornburg	57-1026
BERCUETTE, Jean	45	Paris	62-1112
BERDEN, Ferdinand	33	Alsfeld/Hess.	62-0608
BERENDS, Evert	38	Westermarsen	57-0654
Ulfert 43			
BERENDS, Georg H.	69	Iheringsfehn	58-0815
Fritze 64			
BERENDS, Joachim	28	Mannschlacht	55-0812
Metje 24, Eduard 5, Catharine 3			
Friedrich 1, Wilke 11w			
BERENDS, Joh.Wm.	22	Bilshausen	57-0924
BERENS, Louise	26	New York	62-0836
BERENTZ, Dietrich	18	Stuttgart	57-0365
BERESHEIM, Marie	48	Kleinensee	57-1067
Johann 21, Elizabeth 13, Catharine 25			
BERG, Anna Cath.	46	Kurhessen	56-1044
BERG, Catharine	20	Hannover	61-0682
BERG, J.B.(m)	30	Boston	60-0521
BERG, Lucie	21	Giessen	59-1036
BERG, Marie	48	Ratzik	56-0723
Marie 26			
BERGEMANN, Th.	36	New York	57-0422
BERGEN, Margaretha	52	Goettingen	57-1122
BERGER, Carl	21	Rechenburg	59-0477
Rosine 52			
BERGER, Caroline	10	Detmold	59-1036
BERGER, Eduard	21	Lugnitz	57-1026
BERGER, Gottfried	27	Bayern	57-0850
BERGER, Gottlieb	28	Reutgen	56-0819
BERGER, Henriette	35	Liegnitz	60-0533
Otto 16, Agnes 14			
BERGER, Johann	25	Heidenheim	60-1032
BERGER, John	42	Prag	57-0654
BERGER, Meta	19	Nortwede	57-1122
BERGER, Mich.	24	Wuertemberg	57-0606
BERGER, Therese	21	Unt.Breitenba	60-0334
Sebast 11m			
BERGER, Wilhelm	28	Badegast	60-0429
BERGES, Pierre	27	Rouen	62-0836
BERGFELD, Anna	25	Schuttorf	57-1192
BERGHOEFER, Philip	25	Doeringhausen	56-0413
BERGHOEVER, Adam	23	Raussenberg	57-1280
BERGHOF, Joseph	21	Behre	56-0632
BERGHOFF, Marie	19	Meiningen	61-0478
BERGHOLZ, J.(m)	37	Cleveland	61-0897
Johanna 28			
BERGHORN, Heinrich	16	Stolzenau/Han	55-0628
Sophia 32, Minna 22			
BERGK, Louis	18	Kohden	59-0214
Conrad 21			
BERGLOCHER, Marg.	24	Neudorf	58-0399
BERGMAN, Christoph	59	Eisenhain	57-1122
Margaretha 55, Anna 19, Elisabeth 16			
Johann 9			
BERGMANN, A. (m)	49	Cincinnati	62-0836
BERGMANN, Aug.	21	Schlettau	59-0951
BERGMANN, August	22	Oelze	60-1161
BERGMANN, Charles	22	Chodzisen	57-1148
BERGMANN, Conrad	27	Proebsten	57-0847
BERGMANN, Doris	18	Pommern	61-1132
BERGMANN, Ed.	28	Kahle	61-0669
BERGMANN, Ferdin'd	25	Kluetzkon	56-0629
Caroline 26, Friedrich 9m			
BERGMANN, Frantz	57	Lichtingen	57-1407
Heinrich 25			
BERGMANN, Friedr.	16	Zels/Pr.	55-0538
BERGMANN, Friedr.	20	Loh	57-1067
Heinrich 17			

NAME	AGE	RESIDENCE	YR-LIST
BERGMANN, Heinrich	51	Rumeln	61-0482
Gertrude 42, Elise 13, Cath. 11, Mary 5			
Diedr. 3, Jacob 3m, Gerhard 3m			
BERGMANN, Joseph	22	Lohne	59-0613
Josephine 20			
BERGMANN, Margaret	27	Kitzingen	56-1117
BERGMANN, Moritz	24	Kobylin	56-0951
Evelina 20			
BERGMANN, Sophie	26	Celle	61-0482
BERGMANN, Wm.	24	Uchte	62-0111
Chr. 26, Elise 21, Sophie 19			
BERGMAYER, Gottl.	50	Sudersfeld	60-0785
Marie 43, Gottlieb 19, Sophie 9, Engel 4			
Marie 7, (f) 11m			
BERGREIS, Ernst	15	Uderfleben	60-1032
BERGSTEDE, E.(f)	50	Lemfoerde	62-0467
Marie 28			
BERING, Eva Maria	19	Freiburg	57-0509
Maria E. 27			
BERK, Georg	29	Mannsbach	57-1407
Elise 34			
BERKA, Math.	45	Boehmen	62-0938
Maria 48, Cathar. 9, Alois 7, Maria 19			
Franz 13, Johann 15			
BERKA, Wenzel	32	Boehmen	62-0938
BERKEFELD, Adolph	27	Hannover	60-1161
BERKEFELD, Sophie	19	Hessen	57-0850
BERKEMEYER, Ant.	29	Delbrueck	61-0482
BERKING, Charles	29	US.	59-0613
BERKLAGE, Joh.	22	Otting	59-0535
BERKNER, Carl Wilh	22	Bruck	58-0563
BERKNER, Gottfried	45	Carzig	57-0776
Anna 52, Carl 19, Friedrich 17, Emilie 11			
BERLINER, Seligm.	16	Vestheim	58-0815
BERLS, Fr. Georg	20	Noda	60-0411
BERMANN, Anna	15	Achim	60-0334
BERMANN, Gustav	20	Pyrmont	60-0429
BERMQUIER, Leop.	40	Berlin	62-0938
BERNARD, Louise	27	Merseburg	55-0411
Gesine 21			
BERNARDI, M.	38	Havre	62-0401
(wife) 30			
BERNASCHEK, Franz	26	Gruenhoff	61-0779
Marie 37, Bartholomeus 14, Joseph 7			
Anna 17			
BERNBERGER, Paul	28	Steinbach	59-0384
BERND, J.B.(m)	29	Leipzig	61-0682
BERNDORFF, C.W.(m)	30	Bremen	62-0111
BERNDT, E.	48	Covington	57-0918
BERNDT, Gottfried	54	Blumfeld	57-0924
Wilhelmine 56, Charlotte 19, Albert 17			
BERNECKE, Carl	25	Hassenhausen	61-0482
BERNECKER, Eduard	27	Weimar	60-1032
BERNEKING, Carolne	25	Holzhausen	58-0399
BERNER, Eduard	47	Endschuetz/Sx	61-0770
Rosine 49, Hermann 8			
BERNER, G.	38	Burglehn	58-0885
BERNER, Pauline	25	Stuttgart	57-0924
BERNER, Sebald	25	Protbach	57-1280
Barbara 33, Kunigunde 4, Johann 2			
BERNETT, Marie	35	Grindelwald	62-1169
Franz 8, Caroline 7, Maria 7, Johann 3			
Jacob 60			
BERNHARD, D.L.	43	New York	59-0214
(son) 13, Peter 31			
BERNHARD, Ed.	20	Lebau	56-1216
BERNHARD, Elisab.	54	Wenkbach	59-0047
Helene 22			
BERNHARD, Franz	24	Austria	60-0411
BERNHARD, Jul.(m)	19	Luxemburg	60-1196
BERNHARD, Louis	28	Bremen	57-1067
BERNHARD, Mar.Chr.	27	Hirschberg	56-0354
BERNHARD, Marie	20	Gr. Almerode	60-1032
BERNHARD, Melchior	44	Southpen	62-0306
BERNHARD, Sophie	24	Ritterhude	57-1067
Anna 9m			
BERNHARDT, Amalie	56	Minden	56-0279
BERNHARDT, Carl	40	Dresden	56-0279
Josephine 50			
BERNHARDT, Gertrud	18	Wenighoesbach	60-0429
BERNHARDT, Selke	40	Herdenheim	61-0482
BERNHARDT, Wilhme.	20	Darmstadt	58-0885
BERNHEIMER, Joseph	39	Ems	59-0477
BERNIGER, Fr.A.	18	Duhlhausen	57-0654
BERNING, Conrad	26	Lesen	56-0819
BERNING, J.H.	30	Elbergen	62-0993
BERNINGER, Cathar.	31	Burgstadt	60-0533
Anna 3			
BERNIUS, Georg L.	18	Biebera	58-0885
BERNKHOF, Herman	19	Sudingen	61-0047
BERNRATH, Fr.	25	Altrath	56-1216
BERNRATH, Heinr.	25	Allrath	60-1196
BERNS, Carl	36	Swinemuende	61-0897
Emilie 36			
BERNSDORF, Rebecca	19	Lilienthal	57-1122
BERNSTEIN, Louis	24	Rawitz	56-0951
BERONIS, Stephano	35	Italy	61-0107
BERR, Wilhelmine	19	Pitzerie	56-0632
BERROTH, Christina	21	Nordhausen	60-1141
BERSTECHER, Joh.	16	Gaeltlingen	60-0334
BERTH, Amalie	27	Frankenhausen	56-0512
BERTHALOTH, Sophie	22	Erda	59-0214
BERTHOLD, Maria	30	Leipzig	60-0785
BERTHOLT, Hermann	38	Altenburg	62-0758
Augusta 38, Ernst 12, Augusta 10, Clara 9			
Gustav 8, Sophie 4			
BERTLE, Theresia	54	Herrenstetten	60-0398
BERTRAM, Agnes	13	Conreith	60-0785
BERTRAM, Carl	18	Mariensee	62-0712
BERTRAND, (m)	22	Troyes	62-0401
BERTRAND, Hermann		Egeln	56-0629
BERTRUM, Josephine	45	Braunschweig	60-1141
Alwina 16, Otto 14			
BERTSCH, Albert	30	Heilbronn	57-1192
BERTSCH, Jacob	17	Cappisshacurz	57-0847
BERTSCH, John F.	33	New York	62-0232
Pauline 20			
BERTSCHLINGER, Ar.	24	Quincy/IL	59-1036
BESCHKE, Friedrike	44	Calbe/Saale	57-0021
BESECK, Franz	39	Bohemia	60-1161
Therese 38, Caspar 61, Therese 16			
Maria 14, Cathar. 10, Anna 6			
BESEL, Friedr.	44	New York	59-1036
BESSER, William	31	Stadthagen	57-0422
BESSERT, Friedrich	26	Colberg	56-0723
BESSLER, Lorenz	24	Germany	61-0167
Eva 21			
BESSOLD, Georg	30	Cincinnati	57-0422
BETHGE, C.	19	Arnsee	62-0993
BETHHAEUSER, Babet	18	Querbach	60-0521
BETS, Mathias	59	Strunpfede	57-1122
Magdalene 54, Pauline 17			
BETSCHE, Christ.	22	Baden	60-1196
BETTFUEHR, Theodor	32	Stettin	61-0682
BETTICH, Anton	26	Voelkersheim	59-0477
BETTIGHEIMER, C.	46	New York	61-0897
Caroline 18			
BETTINGER, Maria B	47	Herbstein	60-0998
BETZ, Gottlieb	23	Altenfeld	58-0399
BETZ, Joh.	35	New York	62-0938
BETZ, Theresia	21	Urspringen	60-1053
BETZELL, Friedrich	26	Walheim	60-0334
BEUME, Joseph	13	Heid/Austria	59-0047
Wentzel 9			
BEUNOTTE, W.	44	Neuhof	59-0990
(f) 38, (m) 6, (baby) by			
BEURMANN, C.H.(m)	55	Pittsburgh	61-0482
BEUSE, Heinrich	18	Holzhausen	61-0482
BEUSS, Lina	31	Schluechtern	60-0521
BEUSS, Moritz	18	Schluechtern	60-0521
BEUSSEL, Carl Wilh	52	Hoya	60-0398
Emilie 21			
BEUST, Ludwig v.	36	Rudeburg	59-0214
Augusta 36, Helene 3, Hulda 2			
BEUTEL, Joachim	57	Mecklenburg	57-0776
Johanna 24, August 19			

NAME	AGE	RESIDENCE	YR-LIST
BEUTLER, Albert	16	Vaihingen	62-0879
Gottlieb 14			
BEUTLER, Mich.	44	Runau	56-0527
Johann H. 39			
BEUTLER, Wilhelm	29	Muehlhausen	62-0879
BEVERFOERDE, Jul.	25	Bramsche	61-0669
BEVERING, Carl	19	Altendorf	59-1036
BEYER, Agneta	26	Malchow	57-0961
BEYER, Anna Cath.	20	Minchhosbach	55-1238
BEYER, Catharina	18	Goldmuehl	58-0563
BEYER, Friederike	76	Greiz	58-0604
BEYER, Heinrich	26	Bremen	59-0990
BEYER, Johannes	45	Frankenberg	57-0924
Christina 27, Fr.Conrad 12, Susanna M. 10			
A. Catharina 2			
BEYER, Louis	29	Mainshaim	59-0477
BEYER, Rosa	19	New York	59-0951
Johann 11m			
BEYER, Theodor	24	Loueznik	56-0589
BEYER, William	21	Wulften	59-0384
Augusta 24			
BEYERER, Theresia	17	Zwiesel	59-0384
BEYERS, Joh.(died)	42	Philadelphia	60-0785
BEYNA, Barb.	25	USA.	56-0527
Sophia 47			
BEYNE, Friederike	24	Doessel	56-1044
BIBOL, Marie	25	Oestrich	59-1036
Jos. 16			
BICK, Elise	51	Cincinnati	59-0951
BICK, Fr.W.	14	Osterkappeln	61-1132
BICK, Georg H.	40	Osterappeln	56-0411
Marie 20			
BICKEL, Carl	38	Donaueschinge	62-0608
Heinrich 14			
BICKENFELD, August	19	Billerbeck	59-0477
Franzisca 20			
BICKER, Cath.	26	Wahlen	62-0232
Elis. 9m			
BICKER, Genoveva	24	Alnzefahr	62-0467
BICKER, Veronica	20	Neustadt	61-0482
BICKHUS, Bernhard	24	Legden	56-0819
Elisabeth 25			
BICKNASE, Caroline	20	Landsbergen	60-1053
BICKNASE, William	24	Winzlar	56-1011
BIDOLL, Catharina	25	Rheinland	60-0371
BIEBER, Friedrich	26	Okarben/Hess	62-0608
BIEBER, Peter	27	Erdhausen	60-0533
Anna 28, Peterine 4, Wilhelm 6m			
BIEDEBACH, Franz A	33	Volkmarsen	60-1053
Caroline 29, August 5			
BIEDEKOPF, Johann	22	Wuchersheim	58-0604
BIEDENKOPF, Peter	55	Oberlais	62-0712
Caroline 19, Ernst 16, Gustav 14, Adam 10			
BIEDERMANN, J.(f)	15	Reutlingen	60-0521
BIEDERMANN, Marg.	40	Culmbach	58-0881
Julie Cath. 13, Bartholomaus 11			
Margarethe 9, Conrad 5			
BIEHL, Ludw.	24	Katzenellenbo	59-0990
BIEK, Gerh.Heinr.	43	New York	59-0372
BIEL, Dorothea	20	Gandersheim	57-0606
BIELITZ, Fr. Gust.	24	Naumburg	55-0845
BIENEMANN, Rosalie	15	Annroechte	57-0924
Benjamin 14			
BIENEN, Johanna	19	Cassel/Hessen	55-0628
BIERBAUM, Maria	22	Ledenburg	59-1036
Cath. 20, Eberhard 16			
BIERBAUM, Sophie	22	Lienen	60-0334
BIERBERG, Louise	24	Markoldendorf	57-0924
BIERER, Johann	43	Schonau	55-1048
Susanna 42			
BIERGANS, Fr.	36	Ottendonn	57-0961
BIERHACKE, Reinh.	34	Detmold	56-1044
BIERHOFF, Samuel	14	Borgentreich	60-0533
BIERL, Michael	20	Kritzenorst	58-0885
BIERLE, August	56	Ulm	55-0932
BIERMANN, August	37	Gutenmuehlen	57-1067
BIERMANN, E.W.(m)	30	Kurhessen	57-0555
BIERMANN, Georg	17	Sieke	57-0447
BIERMANN, Georgine	36	Osterode	57-1067
BIERMANN, Heinrich	33	Nienburg	57-0850
BIERMANN, Heinrich	17	Boitzen	62-0879
BIERMANN, Johann	47	Halberstadt	55-0812
Friedrich 43, Auguste 6			
BIERSCHWALD, Carl	38	New Orleans	62-0712
BIERWIRTH, Conrad	24	Kurhessen	56-1044
BIESEMEYER, Friedr	30	Struecken	57-0509
BIESER, Maria	23	Niederweinhei	59-0613
BIESSE, Ferdinand	30	Minden	57-1026
BIESTERFELD, Gottl	22	Ottensen/Curh	60-0429
BIETSCH, Friedrich	24	Waldburg	59-0613
Evelina 20, Sidonia 17			
BIEWALD, Paul	32	Oppeln	62-1042
BIGOLTI, A.	39	Switz.	62-0467
BIHL, Friedrich	45	Iserlohn	57-1150
BIHLER, Juditte	17	Reutlingen	60-0521
BILDERMANN, J.(f)	15	Reutlingen	60-0521
BILFINGER, Ammian	34	New York	57-1192
BILLEMANN, Elise	30	Sudkirchen	62-0467
BILLER, Bernhard	14	Lehe	57-1026
BILLHARDT, Adolph	25	New York	58-0399
BILLINGER, Joh.	50	Unterleinach	61-0669
Barb. 17			
BILLMANN, Friedr.	26	Cassel	56-0411
BILZ, Anna	9	Reichenberg	57-0606
Therese 7			
BILZING, Friedrich	45	Schlotheim	58-0881
Minna 25, Oscar 1, Hermann 9m			
BINDENBERGER, Ludw	20	Ohausen	57-1407
BINDER, Carl	36	Ostheim	61-0669
BINDER, Carl	35	St.Louis	59-0040
BINDER, Heinrich	31	Noertingen	59-0214
Friederike 27			
BINDER, Jacob	43	Schlegelhof	62-0836
Christine 41, Cath. 18, Marie 17			
Fr.(m) 9, Wm. 8, Sam. 5, Chr. 2			
BINDER, Louise	42	Meiningen	60-0334
Bertha 11, Clara 9, Emil 8			
BINDER, M. Pauline	19	Wuertenberg	56-0411
BINDER, Math.(f)	44	Acham	62-0730
Rosine 47			
BINDER, Wilhelm	20	Oberdorf/Pr.	55-1238
BINDHAMMER, Carl	20	Laubach	59-0477
BING, Henry	24	Frischborn	58-0545
BINGEL, Johannes	69	Ilsehhausen	60-0622
Heinrich 38, Catharina 22, Dorothea 22			
Carl 9m			
BINGER, Carl	32	Bettmer	57-1407
Caroline 28, Johanna 6, Carl 4, Marie by			
BINGER, H.C.	22	Nindorf	59-0535
BINNER, Adolph	25	Langbielau	57-1067
BINZER, Conrad	17	Pohlgoens	55-0413
BIRCHER, Rudolph	50	St.Louis	59-0951
BIRCKBACH, Robert	18	Hornbvrg	57-1026
BIRGE, v.Heinr.Fr.	30	Westenholz	57-0847
Maria 21			
BIRK, Marr.	38	Trollingen	62-0730
BIRKEL, John	58	Bavaria	55-1082
Louise 24			
BIRKENBUSCH, Conr.	24	Battenberg/He	62-0342
BIRKENHAUER, John	56	Geismar	60-0533
Elise 57, Marie 15			
BIRKNER, Catharine	34	Froschenreuth	60-0533
BIRNBAUM, Sigmund	19	Krakau	59-0613
BIRTNER, Louis	26	New York	62-0467
BIS, Fr.	28	Nemschuetz	62-0993
M. 34, A. 4, R. 60			
BISAGNE, Giralino	28	Italy	61-0107
BISCHER, Jac.	56	Rottingen	59-0951
Pauline 52			
BISCHOFF, B.(m)	59	Achim	62-0730
BISCHOFF, Bernhard	30	Hucherieden	60-0334
BISCHOFF, Franz'ka	39	Philadelphia	61-0804
BISCHOFF, Franz'ke	18	Bremen	58-0399
BISCHOFF, Georg J.	28	Kruckenau	55-1082
BISCHOFF, H.(m)	15	Ottersberg	56-1117
BISCHOFF, Heinrich	9	US.	55-0845

NAME	AGE	RESIDENCE	YR-LIST
BISCHOFF, Herm.	39	Javerden	61-0482
Marg. 38, Marg. 7, Diedr. 4, Heinrich 2			
Anna M. 59			
BISCHOFF, Johann	30	Lehe	60-0521
BISCHOFF, Johann	27	Hofstaedten	57-0509
Dorethe 30, Georg 1			
BISCHOFF, John F.	27	Wittorf	57-0847
BISCHOFF, Rob.	39	Posen	62-0166
BISCHOFF, Sylvest.	28	Bueckenau	61-0520
BISCHOFF, Wilh'mne	55	Desdel	60-0521
Wilhelmine 22			
BISCHOFF, Wilhelm	59	Muenchen	57-1148
Charlotte 23			
BISMANN, Margareta	23	Tedinghausen	55-1048
BITTANI, Wm.	35	Switz.	62-0467
BITTER, Andreas	60	Bavaria	59-0214
BITTER, August	22	Oldenburg	61-0107
BITTER, Conrad	25	Hiddingsen	60-1141
BITTER, Jos.	28	Illinois	62-1042
BITTER, Justine	22	Weiler	59-0951
BITTNER, Franz Ant	45	Hromitz/Boehm	57-0924
Catharine 42, Catharine 16, Jacob 12			
Franz 6, Anton by, Agnes by			
BITTNER, Johann	37	New York	60-0785
BITTON, Johann	19	Bamberg	62-0001
BITZER, Ludw.	27	Burgfelden	59-0384
BLACH, Johann	40	Samotschin	57-0704
Chrlt.Emilie 30, Ernst.Emilie 3			
Ernst Ludwig 10m			
BLAESEL, Fritz	32	Alendorf/Pr.	55-0538
BLAESER, M.	24	Kleinern	57-1192
BLAEUER, Friedr.	51	Grindelwald	62-1169
Anna 48, Friedrich 26, Elisabeth 16			
Margaretha 18, Marianna 9, Susanna 8			
Rosine 6, Catharine 4			
BLAEUER, Samuel	35	Aarau	59-0951
Elisabeth 30, Adolph 7, Elisabeth 6			
Wilhelm 4, Amia 2, Carl 3m			
BLAHR, Franz	39	Czernheit	61-0779
Anna 22			
BLAICH, Wilh.	10	Calen	59-0951
BLAIICH, Carl	20	Neuenburg	59-1036
BLAJENS, Erdmann	26	Prussia	62-0758
Louise 33, Henriette 3, Justine by			
BLANCK, E.(f)	24	Bischhausen	57-0555
BLANDE, de C.S.	25	France	60-1196
BLANK, Ferdinand	43	Repzin	61-0478
Wilhelmine 39, Albert 11, Emilie 8			
August 4, Hermann 1, Wilhelmine 19			
BLANK, Franz Herm.	21	Vollmersdorf	61-0167
BLANK, J.	18	Aschaffenburg	62-1112
BLANK, Joh. Caspar	23	Hannover	55-0634
BLANK, Johann	47	Thann/Bav.	55-0628
Margarethe 55, Leonhard 23, Catharine 18			
BLANK, Ph.(m)	27	New York	61-0482
BLANKE, G.F.	46	Hannover	59-0214
Dorothea 47			
BLANKEN, Lina	24	Diepholz	59-0214
BLANKENSTEIN, Bert	21	Hagen	56-0847
BLANKMUELLER, Gotl	25	Veckenstedt	57-0654
BLASCHECK, Caspar	37	Obermensching	62-1112
BLASCHECK, Franz	37	Ratchendorf	59-0384
Franz 12			
BLASCHEN, Rosine	44	Kraschen	56-0847
Johanna 43			
BLASE, Louise	21	Ippenberg	56-0951
Heinrich 3			
BLASS, Philipp	39	Ob.Hilbertshm	56-1216
Cath. 37			
BLASSHERK, Johann	36	Reitschendorf	59-0951
Ernst 9, Robert 6, Heinrich 4, Amalie 2			
BLASZ, Carl	40	Kruhningsfeld	56-0847
BLATTAU, Joseph	50	Mistich/Aust.	56-0819
Franz 30			
BLAUFUSS, F. Wilh.	18	Huelselrieth	60-0533
BLAUM, Jacob	23	Nentershausen	59-0951
Anna 21			
BLAUROCK, Heinr.	37	Soenna	57-1113

NAME	AGE	RESIDENCE	YR-LIST
BLEARIUS, Joseph	28	Reith	61-0482
BLECHER, Sophie	17	Bremen	61-0930
BLECK, Heinrich	31	Nail	58-0881
BLECKMANN, Mary	58	Vluym	57-0422
BLECKMANN, Robert	21	Barmen	57-1067
BLEESLANE, H.(Dr.)	29	Berlin	60-0998
BLEICHRODT, E.P.	25	Ziegelrode	62-0993
BLEIER, Catharine	22	Halewitz	57-1067
BLEIGART, Carl	21	Westerburg	61-0482
Blondine 9			
BLELL, Charles	25	Brandenburg	57-0961
BLENDERMANN, Marg.	24	Lilienthal	58-0925
BLESSIN, Gust.	30	Aussond	57-0961
BLEY, Anna	19	Warmstedt	62-0938
BLEY, Bernh.	21	Bosel	60-0785
BLEY, Friedrich	19	Pulvermuehle	57-0422
BLEY, Friedricke	47	Trepto	57-1026
Carl 12			
BLEY, Joh.	24	Schaar	60-0521
BLEYER, Ad.	34	Fallingborste	56-0527
BLIEDUNG, Charlott	51	Clettenburg	62-1169
BLIEN, Salomon	20	Worms	57-0918
BLIND, Lisette	20	Grumstadt	57-0606
Caroline 28			
BLOCH, Ferdinand	25	Hessen	60-0371
BLOCH, Hanna	20	Floss	57-0654
BLOCH, Moritz	44	Vreeland	60-0998
Therese 22, Ernestine 20, Moritz 9			
Victor 8, Philipp 7, Regine 6			
BLOCK, Anna			59-1036
(f) 15, (f) 8, (f) 6, (f) 4, (f) 2			
BLOCK, Bernhard	43	Volkmarsen/He	62-0608
Margaretha 45, Mathilde 17, Lorenz 15			
Philipp 8, Wendelin 6, Juliane 4			
Florenz 9m			
BLOCK, Conrad	31	Uesen	57-1148
Sophie 31, Hinrich 5, Dietrich 3			
BLOCK, Emil	34	Germany	59-0951
BLOCK, J.	48	Bremen	57-1148
BLOCK, John	28	New York	62-0730
BLOCK, Theo.	29	Berlin	61-0804
BLOCKS, Caroline	23	Griebau	62-0758
BLODES, Theodor	24	Haynau	57-1067
BLOEMER, Bertha	28	New York	62-0938
BLOEMER, Steffan H	36	Westercappeln	57-1192
Cath. Marie 30			
BLOESER, Catharine	29	Neukirchen	62-0879
BLOHM, Carol.	18	Goettingen	56-0512
BLOHM, Friedrich	22	Hamburg	55-0634
BLOHM, John	30	Darmstadt	57-0654
BLOMER, Anna	26	Stenste	59-1036
BLOMER, Clemens	28	Kalum	59-0951
BLONDE, Julius	18	Bleschen/Prus	61-0770
BLONER, George	18	Eplingen	56-1011
BLOOTH, A.	45	New York	62-0938
Anna 36, Albert 9, Johann 7, Heinr. 11m			
BLOSSFELD, Eva Mag	58	Preussen	57-0606
BLOTZER, Wilh'mine	24	Berlin	61-0897
BLUCH, Moritz	44	Vreeland	60-0998
Therese 22, Ernestine 20, Moritz 9			
Victor 8, Philip 7, Regine 6			
BLUEMEL, Carl	38	Suessenbach	57-0754
Johanna 36, Ernestine 6, Gottl. Ernst 28			
BLUEMEL, Friedrich	54	Kraschen	56-0847
BLUEMKE, Stanislas	18	Czarnikau	60-0411
BLUHM, Anna	18	Hessen	60-1161
BLUM, Anna	15	Gorma	59-0477
BLUM, Carl F.	16	Thal	61-0520
BLUM, Catharine	16	Guntersblum	62-0879
BLUM, Conrad	27	Auhagen	61-0520
BLUM, Edw.	21	Eihausen	60-0334
Justine 15			
BLUM, Elise	18	Basertt	60-0521
BLUM, Elise	20	Engelsdorf	58-0576
BLUM, Heinrich	22	Timmerland	57-1280
BLUM, Ignatz	18	Enentack	56-1216
BLUM, John	37	Ohio	62-1042
BLUM, Joseph	17	Friedendorf	56-0629

NAME	AGE	RESIDENCE	YR-LIST
BLUM, Louise	21	Eichelsachsen	59-0214
BLUM, Louvisa	18	Suedfelde	57-1122
BLUM, Malchen	23	Koestrich	62-0879
BLUMANN, M.(m)	20	Brugstemmen	59-0951
Betty 18			
BLUMBERG, Carl Fr.	38	Bremen	57-1192
BLUME, Aug.	38	New York	62-1042
Christiane 36			
BLUME, Dorothea	20	Waltringhsn.	59-0384
BLUME, Elisabeth	24	Braunschweig	56-1044
BLUME, Sophie	20	Anhagen	60-0533
BLUME, Wilhelm	27	Erfurt	55-0634
BLUMENHOFF, Friedr	29	Suthorf	62-0712
BLUMENKAMP, Jacoba	20	Aachen	62-0111
BLUMENSTEIN, Heinr	42	Wattenbach	57-0924
Cath.Elisab. 42, Georg 14, Friedrich 10			
August 3			
BLUMENTHAL, Guido	18	Springe	58-0399
BLUMENTHAL, Hulda	21	Obornik/Pr.	62-0608
BLUMENTHAL, Joseph	12	Linke	57-0924
BLUN, Salomon	20	Worms	57-0918
BLUT, Heinrich	23	Schneeberg	57-1026
BLYDEN, M.(m)	25	France	62-0467
BOAM, Jacob	50	Bavaria	59-0214
BOAT, Ferdinand	21	Luebbecke	56-1044
BOBEL, Anna	47	Maden	59-0412
Catharine 8, Elisa 5			
BOCHLOWITZ, Frana.	24	Burchlowitz	50-1017
BOCHTLUFT, Albt.	18	Borghorst	60-0521
BOCK, (f)	40	New York	57-1150
Emilie 20			
BOCK, Albert	26	Vitzig	57-0704
BOCK, Anna M.	19	Laudershausen	57-0847
Anna C. 27			
BOCK, Caroline	28	Bremen	59-1036
Bernhardine 4			
BOCK, Charles	27	Muenden	57-0422
BOCK, Chr.Fr.	40	Muehlberg	61-0482
Johanna Ma. 37			
BOCK, Engel	20	Gressendorf	59-0535
BOCK, F.	29	Amboeck	57-0961
BOCK, Fr.	22	Herbsen	57-0578
Wilhelmine 26			
BOCK, Georg	20	Hilmes	57-0924
BOCK, Heinrich	26	Prussia	61-0770
BOCK, Hermann	26	New York	56-1011
BOCK, Jacob Friedr	30	Zezenow	57-0704
Wmne.Henr'te 29			
BOCK, Johannes	31	Echzell	61-0779
BOCK, Marg.	32	Windheim	61-0669
BOCK, Maria	55	Beilstein	55-0630
Friederike 23			
BOCK, Mary	18	Huenfeld	60-0411
BOCK, Rosa	24	Niederraunen	61-0770
Caecilie 19			
BOCK, Rosamunde	21	Eichfir	61-0478
BOCK, S.M. (m)	24	Ulm	61-0804
F.C. 9			
BOCKEL, Heinrich	18	Finna	56-1044
BOCKERT, Alex	24	Iburg/Hann.	61-0770
BOCKLET, Albert	15	Dankenfeld	57-0754
BOCKLET, Anna	22	Dankenfeld	57-0754
BOCKLINGER, Lucia	58	Mollis	62-0401
BOCKMEYER, Heinr.	20	Apelern	56-1260
BOCKOCH, Carl	28	Vlettindorf	60-0785
Eleonore 29, Friedr. 1			
BOCKSBERGER, Wilh.	30	Meiningen	62-0758
Rosina 38, Carl 7			
BOCKSTEDE, Cathar.	33	Osnabrueck	56-0847
Anna 23			
BODANGEL, v.Fritz	24	Muehlhausen	59-1036
BODBECK, Arnold	28	Hettingen	58-0815
BODE, Christiana	20	Oelfen	57-1407
BODE, Friedrich	18	Olxhain	57-1407
Ludwig 22			
BODE, Heinrich	35	Hortheim	57-0578
BODE, Heinrich	22	Brinkum	59-0047
Meta 19			

NAME	AGE	RESIDENCE	YR-LIST
BODE, Johann	33	Cassel/Hess.	61-0770
BODE, Nicolaus	20	Obergeis	56-0819
Cath. Elise 18			
BODE, Wilhelm	23	Bisberode	60-0521
BODECKER, Louis	21	Todenhausen	60-0785
BODEMANN, Caroline	20	Friedingsen	59-1036
BODEN, F.W.	64	Brooklyn	57-1148
Louise 60			
BODENBERG, Friedr.	21	Anderstein	56-1117
Dorothea 17			
BODENBERGER, Erstn	24	Schweidnitz	56-0512
BODENHOPP, (m)	32	Prussia	60-0785
BODENSTEIN, Dor.	29	Nesselrode	59-1036
Cath. 10, Joh. 9, Heinr. 7, Joh. 5			
BODENSTEIN, E.(m)	20	Halle	62-0166
BODENSTEINER, Joh.	27	Bernreidh	59-0613
BODENSTEINER, Ther	14	Bernreuth	60-0334
BODERBENDER, Joh.	20	Wittelsburg	60-0334
BODERMUND, Carolne	40	New York	62-0166
BODMANN, Christina	59	Seburg	57-0422
Jesbena 26			
BODO, Magd.	23	Bodensee	60-1161
BODRIAN, Thomas	28	Volksheim	57-1416
BODSTEDT, Friedr.	41	Marburg	57-0704
Louise 36, Margaretha 7, Elisabeth 5			
BOEBEL, Wilhelm	18	Hessen	57-0847
BOECHER, Adam	28	Oberlais	62-0712
Maria 29, Carl 3			
BOECK, Chr.(m)	16	Prussia	57-0555
BOECK, Georg	26	Doellnitz	60-0521
BOECKE, Clemens		Buke	58-0881
BOECKEL, Marie	21	Donaueschingn	60-0521
BOECKER, Bernh.	20	Muenster	60-0521
BOECKER, Henry	19	Polle	59-0477
BOECKER, Michel	36	Carzig	57-0776
Augusta 30, Emilie 9, Louise 5			
BOECKMANN, H.	17	Bremervoerde	59-0990
BOECKNER, Johannes	23	Niederofladen	57-0776
BOEDEKER, Heinr.W.	18	Rieste	62-0879
BOEDIGER, Joh.Mich	58	Nordhausen	59-0214
Christiane 48			
BOEGE, Doris	19	Syek	59-0613
BOEGEL, C.L.	18	Zeven	59-0535
Heinrich 22			
BOEGEL, Christ	42	Silberg	61-0107
BOEGER, Anna	34	Karlburg/Bav.	60-0429
BOEGER, Friedr.	56	Bruchhausen	55-0411
BOEHLIG, Gustav	26	Meiningen	62-0758
Anna 23			
BOEHLKEN, Johanna	21	Wulfsdorf	59-0214
BOEHM, Catharina	21	Ebensfeld	55-0630
BOEHM, Cathr.	28	Vollmerz/Curh	60-0622
BOEHM, Elisabeth	23	Strut	62-0306
BOEHM, Ely	24	New York	62-1169
BOEHM, Gustav	30	Schloppe	61-0930
Augusta 30, Emil 4, Franziska 1			
BOEHM, Joh. Ernst	18	Guegleben	57-1026
BOEHM, Joh.Pet.	27	Eberbach	56-1117
BOEHM, Johann	58	Mies	58-0881
Josepha 38, Hermann 27, Johann 24			
Marie 21			
BOEHM, John	31	Kreuznach	61-0107
Peter 28, Peter 24, Peter 24			
BOEHM, John Jacob	20	Ndr.Vorschutz	57-0754
Anna Cath. 22			
BOEHM, Joseph	18	Tetschen	56-0951
BOEHM, Lilli	14	Eibenschitz	62-0730
BOEHM, Magdal.	24	Burgsolms	60-1053
BOEHM, Magdalena	25	Hollenbach	60-1053
Barbara 20, Conrad by			
BOEHM, Martha Elis	35	Weissenborn	56-1117
BOEHME, August	32	Schmiedeberg	55-1238
BOEHME, Carl	26	Prussia	57-0555
BOEHME, Carl Aug.	21	Auerswalde	56-0723
BOEHME, Christ.Wm.	18	Celle	57-0754
Louis Georg 15			
BOEHME, Fr. Aug.	25	Auerswalde	56-0723
BOEHMER, Friedr.	27	Elinghausen	56-0411

NAME	AGE	RESIDENCE	YR-LIST
Sophie 24, Adolph 9m			
BOEHMER, Joh.H.	18	Lahe	57-1113
Ilsabein 58, Cathar. 28			
BOEHMER, Joseph	27	Borntosten	57-1067
BOEHMER, Louise	20	Goettingen	59-0372
BOEHR, Julie	19	Bremen	58-0885
BOEHRINGER, Elis.	20	Grosshebach	61-0520
BOEKE, Heinr.	26	Erder	58-0306
Charlotte 24			
BOELKE, Friedrich	29	Two Rivers	57-0961
Bertha 28, Ida 2			
BOELKER, Maria	17	Osnabrueck	62-1042
BOELTER, Michael	25	Gr.Woelwitz	56-1260
BOEMCKE, Johann	33	Bremen	58-0576
BOEMER, August	18	Raalkirchen	62-1169
BOEMERS, Mary Soph	25	Helsinghausen	56-0589
BOEN, Stephan	25	Pyritz	56-0632
Catharina 40			
BOENIG, Dan.	26	Neustadt	62-1042
BOENING, Dietrich	47	Warflieth	57-0578
BOENRING, J.B.	29	Schoeppingen	58-0604
Antonia 22			
BOER, H.	30	Vlotho	56-0512
Susan 28, Wilhelmina 3m			
BOERCHERT, Friedr.	31	Langenstein	56-0629
BOERLIN, Christ.	24	Basel	59-0951
BOERMANN, Eva	22	Sulzbach	57-1148
Lena 22			
BOERMANN, Sophie	38	Uslar	56-0819
Louise 9, Heinr. Wilh. 11m			
BOERNER, Anna	35	Hatten	60-0521
BOERNER, Cath.	39	Baltimore	61-0482
Valt. 4, Caroline 6m			
BOERNER, Doris	52	Herfa	59-1036
BOERNER, Elias	18	Seeba	58-0563
BOERRIG, Andreas	30	Germany	57-0578
BOESCHE, Andreas	17	Sieke	58-0399
Johann 15			
BOESCHEN, Diedrich	61	Hassendorf	60-0521
BOESCHEN, Diedrich	18	Kustett	59-0535
BOESCHEN, Joh.Hch.	16	Altenbruck	57-0436
BOESCHLING, Friedr	26	Braunschweig	57-0422
BOESE, Caroline	26	Peine	59-1036
Dorothea 21			
BOESE, Fr.	26	New York	62-0938
BOESE, Heinrich	25	New York	62-0879
BOESE, Henry	32	New York	62-0730
BOESE, Julius	29	Braunschweig	62-0758
BOESE, Magdalene	25	Hoppenhof	56-0819
BOESE, Marie	22	Bremen	60-1032
BOESE, Wilhelm	22	Peine	55-0932
BOESE, Wilhelmine	16	Windheim	58-0545
BOESSER, Johanna	18	Neunkirchen	62-1169
BOESSMANN, Maria	19	Bolsten	56-1011
BOETE, Wilhelm	24	Lauingen	60-0334
BOETTCHER, August	27	Kl.Ruchter/Th	60-0429
BOETTCHER, Dr.	16	Leeste	62-0938
BOETTCHER, Ernst	18	Crimmitschau	55-1238
BOETTCHER, Gottl.	50	Indianapolis	59-1036
BOETTCHER, H.	49	Barmen	62-0938
Wm. 33			
BOETTCHER, Johanna	32	Klein Rieden	62-0879
Wilhelm 2			
BOETTGER, Johann	20	Ostendorf	56-0847
BOETTICHER, Alb.	50	Liegnitz	59-0384
Anna 14, Alfred 5			
BOETTICHER, Fr'dke	26	Ndr.Stolzingn	60-0521
Marianne 18			
BOETTINGER, Adalb.	19	Herbstein/Hes	62-0342
BOETTINGER, J.Zach	23	Lauterbach	57-0606
BOETTINGER, Lud.F.	18	Darmstadt	59-0384
BOETTJER, Meta	24	Hannover	58-0545
Elise 22			
BOETTNER, Caroline	21	Wuertemberg	57-1192
BOEVING, Hermann	41	New York	58-0885
Adelheid 25, Hermann 3, E. 3			
BOGE, August	30	Cloppenburg/O	55-1238
Elisabeth 28			

NAME	AGE	RESIDENCE	YR-LIST
BOGEN, Henry	22	Berlin	60-1141
BOGENA, Carl Wm.	20	Sophienhof	58-0306
BOGENA, Trintje	26	Norden	61-0520
Gesine 24			
BOGER, Jacob	27	Schwaigern	56-1044
BOGGS, W.L.(m)	28	New York	61-0716
BOGNER, Wendelin	21	Loehringen	60-0533
BOHE, Augusta	20	Oberneulande	57-1122
BOHL, Anna	15	Coburg	62-0712
BOHLANDER, Philipp	39	Guetersdorf	57-0704
Mary Elisab. 23, Johannes 3m			
BOHLE, Heinrich	18	Hannover	62-0758
BOHLEN, Henry	33	New Orleans	59-1036
BOHLENDER, Conr.	19	Unterstoppel	59-0990
BOHLENDER, G.	17	Breitenbach	59-0990
BOHLENS, Eduard	22	Bremen	56-0413
BOHLER, Emilie	19	Borna	60-0785
BOHLING, Otto	32	Petershagen	57-1122
Margarethe 27, Charlotte 11m			
BOHLMANN, Herm.	18	Emtinghausen	59-0384
BOHMAUER, Saphir	27	Baiern	57-1280
BOHMS, Sophia	22	Bassum	57-0961
BOHN, A.(m)	25	Noerenberg	61-0897
BOHN, Engel	56	Roennebeck	59-0372
BOHN, Peter	27	Hettdorf	62-0467
BOHNE, Anna	17	Hessen	57-0776
BOHNE, Ernst	22	Louisville	61-1132
BOHNEMANN, Marie	28	Rodinghausen	57-1113
BOHNENBERG, Carol.	18	Mindnerheide	56-0411
BOHNER, M.Engel	24	Borringhausen	59-0477
BOHNLEIN, Johann	25	Steinach	60-0785
BOHREN, Johann	55	Grindelwald	62-1169
Anna 52, Johann 30, Margaretha 20			
Catharine 13			
BOHRINGER, Marg.	30	Weitheim	61-0482
Sophie 23			
BOHRMANN, H.(m)	26	Moorsum	61-0804
BOIKER, R.J.	36	New York	62-1112
Chris. 23			
BOISSELIER, T.H.	30	Bremen	61-1132
BOKEL, J.A.(m)	41	Springfield	62-0836
BOKELMANN, C.	35	New York	62-0836
Louise 25			
BOLENDER, Adam	50	Mengshausen	58-0576
Anna 42, Anna 8			
BOLENDER, Conr.	20	Mengshausen	56-1117
BOLENDER, Henry	36	Columbus	57-1192
BOLENDER, Philipp	20	Hessen	57-0776
BOLITZKY, E.	38	Liegnitz	59-0990
BOLLAGE, Anton	32	Ludbrach	57-1416
BOLLE, Charles	56	Spanbeck	56-1011
Charlotte 58, Christina 35, Louisa 30			
Charlotte 24, Wilhelmina 14			
BOLLENDER, Elisab.	47	Schletzenroth	55-0630
Jacob 14, Wilhelm 8, Anna 12			
BOLLIER, Caroline	25	Markgroeninge	59-0477
BOLLMANN, Chr.	48	Veckenstedt	57-0654
Friederike 50, Friederike 7, Chr. 20			
BOLLMANN, Diedr.	19	Glitten	59-0535
BOLLMANN, Friedr.	29	Hallage	57-0654
BOLSTER, Johann	23	Neustadt	57-1407
BOLTE, Caroline	22	Verden	62-0836
Heinrich 9			
BOLTE, Diedr.Heinr	31	Beusen	60-0398
Henriette 25			
BOLTE, Emilie	21	Hoexter	56-0723
BOLTE, Ferdinand	30	Hoexter	57-0021
BOLTE, Friedrich	38	New York	57-1407
Johanna 26, Fred. 4			
BOLTE, Georg	23	Hofgeismar	57-1026
BOLTE, H.	46	Bremen	62-0938
(wife) 32, Anni 1			
BOLTE, Louise	28	Hextor	57-1407
Johanna 4, Mimi 3, Bertha by			
BOLTZE, Christian	33	Madison	57-1148
Friederike 26			
BOMANN, Heinrich	26	Celle	57-1150
BOMBATZ, Johann	35	Heinrichsstad	55-0845

NAME	AGE	RESIDENCE	YR-LIST
BON, Mathilde	25	San Francisco	62-0232
BONACKER, Mich. H.	24	Dreislar/Pr.	60-0622
BONE, Heinrich	20	Damme	59-0214
BONETTI, G.	22	Switz.	62-0467
BONITZ, Carl R.	28	Koettensdorf	56-0723
BONNET, Marie	25	Fortwaerne	59-0613
BONNHAG, Johann	16	Muehlhausen	60-0533
BONTJEN, (m)	35	Norden	57-0578
J.G. 30			
BOOM, Jos.	41	New York	61-0482
Minna 39, Josephine 9, Pauline 8			
Moritz 5			
BOOMGARDEN, P.	35	Campen	57-0422
Mentje 27, Eltje 27, Jantje 23			
BOORMANN, Robert	26	England	56-1216
BOORMANN, Robert	48	America	56-1216
Edw.H. 37			
BOOS, Eduard	46	Schwerin	60-0785
BOOS, Heinrich	34	Petershagen	57-1122
Christiana 35, Wilhelm 20, Heinrich 14			
Herman 11, Wilhelm 10, Christian 5			
Friedrich 3, August 11m			
BOPP, Antony	31	Rusk	60-1141
BOPP, Philipp L.	27	Damm/Bav.	60-0622
BOPPART, Julius	23	Rheineck	58-0815
BORADT, Heinrich	21	Bremervoerde	60-0533
BORCHERDT, A.	51	Wolfenbuettel	62-0993
E. 51, R. 17			
BORCHERLING, L.(m)	45	Newark	62-0467
BORCHERS, Anna	29	Hedeminden	58-0399
BORCHERS, Ernst	23	Melle	55-0634
BORCHERS, Friedr.	15	Hofgeismar	60-1032
Sophie 19, Dorette 30			
BORCHERS, H.	34	Diedesdorf	58-0306
BORCHERS, Juergen	30	New York	59-0048
BORCHERS, Wilhelm	18	Sudingworth	62-0001
BORCHERT, Wilhelm	29	Gladebach	57-0924
Friedericke 36, August 4, Caroline by			
BORCKELMANN, Joh.H	18	Bramsche	56-1117
Dorothea 20			
BORDMANN, G.	66	Wardenburg	62-1112
BORGER, Jacob	24	Weinheim	62-0879
BORGERDING, Louise	35	Damme	57-1148
BORGERDING, Wmne.	16	Stroehen	59-0412
BORGHOLS, Heinrich	37	Voerden	56-0629
Theresa 36, Alexander 7			
BORGMANN, Fr.(m)	41	Osterlumme	59-0951
BORGMANN, Heinrich	25	Minden	60-1053
BORGSTEDE, Hch.Wm.	30	Gerde	56-0413
BORINGER, Fr.	24	Berka	60-0398
BORITZKY, Johann	48	Schondorf	57-1026
Anna 50, Catharina 22, Anna 17, Johann 13			
Maria 9, Elisabeth 6			
BORK, Eduard	34	Muenster	61-0779
BORKICY, Jos.	49	Muchingen	59-1036
BORKOWSKY, Mor.	30	Schrimm	57-0961
BORMANN, Wilh.	30	Adenstedt	55-1082
Heinr. 28			
BORN, Catharine C.	23	Schoenbach	62-0467
BORN, Georg Heinr.	28	Wingerhausen	58-0563
Carl P. 16			
BORN, Heinrich	21	Wultersbach	57-1407
BORN, Ludwig	28	Damstedt	57-0776
BORN, W.	16	Berghausen	59-0990
BORNBRUCH, Lucie	27	New York	62-0938
BORNEISER, Elisab.	24	Randenhausen	57-1113
Hinrich 30			
BORNEMANN, Ernst	27	Poetzen	56-0589
BORNEMANN, H.	23	New York	58-0399
BORNEMANN, Ludwig	41	Wenzen	61-0682
Hanchen 35, Heinrich 18, Wilhelmine 14			
August 11, Hermann 9, Wilhelm 6m			
BORNEMANN, Magdal.	22	Hohenwart	62-0879
BORNER, Jul.	22	Obergrafenhm.	55-0932
BORNHARDT, Johanna	31	Haltum	60-0521
(daughter) 6m			
BORNHOFF, Elene	24	Liebnau	57-1122
BORNSCHEIN, Franz	34	Grosshelmdorf	57-1067
Friederike 30, Albert 11, Pauline 8			
Wilhelm 6, Wilhelmine 3			
BORNSCHEUER, Anna	20	Dainrode	55-0630
BORNSCHIER, Cath.	19	Weissenhausen	57-1026
BORNTRAEGER, Ludw.	50	Eichelsachsen	62-0712
BORO, Benedette	22	Italy	56-1216
BORO, Georgia	32	America	56-1216
BORRIE, G. (m)	29	Friedrichstal	62-0730
H. (m) 31			
BORST, Georg	19	Galingen	57-1122
BORTH, Caroline	20	Griebau	62-0758
BORTH, Heinrich	37	Grieben	56-0723
Christiane 48			
BORTH, Wilhelm	25	Grieben	56-0723
BOSALIA, Augusta	37	Wolfersdorf	57-1122
Franz 13, Joseph 10, Eduard 8, Marie 4			
Aderf. 11m			
BOSCH, Marie Anne	30	Kl. Ordlangen	56-0632
Elisabeth 19			
BOSE, Christ.	23	Kuhrstedt	58-0306
BOSE, Friedr.	15	Dedesdorf	57-0654
Charles 19			
BOSECKER, Christ.	28	Voilsdorf	61-0478
Ottilie 23, Victor 5, Wilhelm 3			
BOSER, Lambert	19	Steinberg	59-0477
BOSKEN, Marie	21	Gehrde	60-0521
BOSS, Anna	30	Bannheim	60-0785
BOSS, L.M. (m)	36	Osternuland	62-0306
Gesina 32, H.L.(m) 10, Marta 9			
Hendricus 7, Johanna 9m			
BOSS, S.W.(m)	29	Unthuisen	62-0306
Cornelia 27, Willem 2, Harm 3m			
BOSSE, Augusta	35	Kl.Michelstn.	61-0482
BOSSE, Augusta	23	Schoeppensted	62-0730
BOSSE, Engel	20	Preuss.Minden	60-0371
BOSSE, Gottfried	32	Schlanzsched	57-0447
BOSSHARDT, Anna	28	Woelflingen	62-0712
BOTE, Friedrich	16	Hagenburg	58-0885
Diedrich 17			
BOTH, Georg	24	Chicago	58-0604
BOTH, Louise	45	Molsdorf	56-0589
Jette 18			
BOTING, Heinrich	21	Sottrum/Hann.	60-0622
BOTL, Anna	15	Coburg	62-0712
BOTSCH, Geo. Andr.	35	Rothenburg/Bv	55-0628
BOTT, Anton	24	Bernharz/Hess	62-0608
BOTT, August	19	Steinbach/CH.	60-0622
BOTT, Maria	27	Cassel	59-1036
BOTTCHER, Wilhelm	17	Wulstorf	56-0512
BOTTEMIS, P.(m)	59	Muehlheim	61-0897
Amalie 59			
BOTTO, Cecilia	23	Italy	56-1216
BOTTO, Dominione	30	America	56-1216
BOUCSING, Alex.	33	Pittsburg	57-0754
BOURBON, de Nicl.	28	Spain	61-0482
(f) 58			
BOUREARD, Jacques	54	New York	62-1042
BOUSESET, Isa	20	Prag	57-0654
BOWHERS, Anna	30	New York	59-0951
Wilhelm 9, Friedr. 6, Marg. 3			
BOWMAN, James	22	England	60-0334
BOX, Ad. Aug.	24	Wurgassen	57-1148
BOY, Carl A.W.	33	Celle	58-0881
Johanne 6			
BOY, Leopold	49	Lindenberg	61-0779
Anna 51, Emil 17			
BOYCARD, M.(m)	30	France	61-0167
L.(f) 25			
BOYER, Heinrich	20	Gudesberg/Hes	57-0847
BOYSEN, Thomas H.	28	England	59-0613
BRAADT, Elise	30	Fahrenholz	59-0535
BRAASCH, August	28	Zimdorf	58-0881
Caroline 23, Wilhelm 2, Bertha 6m			
BRAASCH, Charlotte	29	Glamsee	57-0704
Caroline 23			
BRAASCH, Friedrich	34	Hagnow	58-0881
Caroline 34, Marie 4, August 1			
BRAASCH, Peter	62	Glanse	58-0881

NAME	AGE	RESIDENCE	YR-LIST
Dorothea 55, Ferdinand 18, Gottlieb 15			
Maria 12			
BRABAND, Christine	19	Luedingworth	56-0413
BRABETZ, Simon	60	Kestran/Boehm	57-1067
Wenzel 30, Anna 24, Catharina 22			
Rosalie 18, Joseph 36, Josepha 21			
BRACHT, Victor	29	Effien	56-1044
BRADMANN, Caroline	20	Ottenau	60-0521
BRAENNLICH, Chr'ne	21	Badbergen	62-0467
BRAENNLICH, G.(m)	57	Rudelswalde	62-0467
Christine C. 52			
BRAEUCHLE, C.	20	Aurich	59-0990
BRAEUNIG, Elisab.	17	Flensungen	62-0467
BRAEUNING, Conr.	47	Ahorn	56-0629
Conr. 39			
BRAEUNING, Valent.	24	Maroldsweisac	56-1011
BRAEUNINGER, Wilh.	23	Wuerttemberg	61-0682
BRAEUNLICH, Chr'ne	21	Badbergen	62-0467
BRAEUNLICH, G.(m)	57	Rudelswalde	62-0467
Christine C. 52			
BRAEUTIGAM, Amalie	22	Veilsdorf	55-0413
BRAEUTIGAM, Carl	21	Landau	60-0334
BRAEUTIGAM, Melch.	17	Hadamar	57-0754
BRAHM, Josephine	22	Millenberg	59-0477
BRAND, Eliza	30	Berlin	57-0961
Hedwig 6			
BRAND, Gottfried	26	Schueren	56-0411
Joseph 24			
BRAND, Henriette	23	Frankenhausen	60-1032
Sophie 16, Louise 57			
BRAND, Herm.Heinr.	22	Dreeke	59-0412
BRAND, Johann	18	Ettenhausen	60-0334
Conrad 20			
BRAND, Lisette	18	Freienohl	56-0411
BRAND, Louise	36	Richenau	60-0785
BRAND, Maria	18	Esrod	56-1011
BRAND, Minna	26	Vlotho	59-0384
BRANDAU, Heinr.	19	Solz	57-0850
BRANDEIS, Gerhard	21	Prag	59-0477
BRANDEIS, Jonas	20	Prag	56-1260
BRANDER, Emil	34	Stamheim	62-0712
BRANDES, Andrew	26	Pulvermuehle	57-0422
BRANDES, Heinrich	32	Winzlar	59-0613
Amalie 26			
BRANDES, Marie	26	Bernstrupp	60-0334
Sophie 15			
BRANDES, Wilhelm	19	Hashausen	55-1082
Augusta 17			
BRANDES, v. H.	27	Hannover	62-0938
BRANDFUSS, August	19	Heisebeck	57-0924
BRANDHORST, Cathr.	34	Gehrden	57-1113
BRANDMEYER, Charl.	21	Verden	57-1148
BRANDMUELLER, Ros.	52	Horlachen	56-0819
BRANDMULLER, Anna	16	Greislbach	57-0847
BRANDNER, Franz	45	Washington	62-1112
Therese 6			
BRANDS, William	58	Louisendorf	57-0422
Mathilda 56, Theodora 36, Minna 18			
Peter 16			
BRANDT, Carl	26	Vlotho	56-0512
BRANDT, Christ.	45	New York	59-0951
BRANDT, Christ.(m)	14	New York	61-0804
BRANDT, Christian	32	Bernhausen	55-0630
BRANDT, Georg	24	Philadelphia	60-0334
BRANDT, Heinrich	24	Weimar	56-0951
BRANDT, Heinrich	27	Uchte	57-0447
BRANDT, Joh. Carl	19	Rotenburg	61-0520
BRANDT, Johannes	45	Dietzhausen	55-0630
Anna 42, Catharina 19, Ludwig 15			
Louise 13			
BRANDT, Meta	21	Vegesack	58-0576
BRANDT, Ph.Casp.	20	Bischofsheim	59-0477
BRANDT, Sophie	27	Hafern	62-0938
BRANDT, Wilhelmine	33	Preuss.Minden	56-1044
BRANDUS, Ida	20	Magdeburg	57-0961
Sidonie 17			
BRANDY, Bernhard	17	Damme	57-0961
BRANEL, Anton	42	Muenich	59-0951

NAME	AGE	RESIDENCE	YR-LIST
Marie 42, Anton 9, Eugen 6, Marie 1			
BRANN, Thilo	24	Halle	55-1082
BRASCH, Anna M.	24	Arp/Bavaria	59-0047
Catharine 1, Philipp 16			
BRASCH, Rachel	27	Lobsens	57-1148
Hanne 9			
BRASS, C.W.	40	Bremen	59-0613
Anna 30, William 20m, Emil 5m			
BRASSE, Heinr.	16	Minden	58-0399
BRAUCLAIR, de Wm.	19	Homberg	57-1113
BRAUDAN, An Margr.		Obergeis	56-0819
BRAUE, Meta	63	Vegesack	61-0682
BRAUER, Anton	20	Freienburg	61-0107
BRAUER, Carl	16	Hille	56-0411
BRAUER, Carl	25	Bremen	60-0334
BRAUER, Christine	41	Richmond	60-0785
Johann 19, Elisabeth 9, Marg. 7			
BRAUER, Dor.	25	Marburg	62-1112
BRAUER, Friedr.	18	Hille	56-0411
BRAUER, Gustav	22	Bremen	59-1036
BRAUMONT, Joseph	26	Berlin	59-0951
BRAUN, August	18	Gypersleben	61-0482
BRAUN, Bertha	18	Lemgo	61-0930
BRAUN, Carl	20	Allendorf	56-0589
BRAUN, Carl Aug.	18	Bischleben	58-0306
BRAUN, Conrad	54	Niederthalhsn	55-0630
Anna 49, Martin 26, Barbara 13, Conrad 9m			
BRAUN, Conrad	24	Bavaria	60-0371
BRAUN, Ed.(m)	24	Rawitz	62-0166
BRAUN, Elise	20	Oberschmitten	58-0576
BRAUN, Elise	14	Reinswoode	59-0384
BRAUN, Elise	21	Hildeshausen	60-0398
BRAUN, F.L.A.(m)	25	Michelstadt	60-1196
BRAUN, Fed. August	32	Barmen	60-1141
BRAUN, G.A.	17	Michelstadt	59-0477
BRAUN, Gustav	25	Baltimore	62-0938
BRAUN, H.	24	Mariensee	57-1192
BRAUN, H.J.H.	38	Bremen	59-0477
Wilhelmine 27			
BRAUN, Heinrich	23	Gleba	57-0704
BRAUN, Hermann	19	Stuttgarth	50-1017
BRAUN, Joh.Mich.	62	Adrian	59-0214
BRAUN, Johann	25	Lauterbach	62-0879
BRAUN, M.	29	Boston	62-0993
J. 5, W. 8			
BRAUN, Maria	17	Oberlindenbac	59-0214
BRAUN, Nicolaus	56	Sternbach	62-0712
BRAUN, Seb.	58	Noerdlingen	57-1148
BRAUN, Theodor	26	Wien	56-1260
BRAUN, Wilhelm	33	Spiescappeln	55-0812
Anna Elisab. 33, Adam 2			
BRAUN, v. F.C. (m)	23	Uffenheim	61-1132
BRAUNE, Bertha	17	Altenburg	57-0606
BRAUNE, J.H.(m)	20	Dresden	61-0478
BRAUNROCK, Christ.	30	Solz	57-1113
Barbara 29, Luise 1			
BRAUNSCHWEIGER, Ch	21	Braunschweig	57-1148
BRAUNSCHWEIGER, He	20	Braunschweig	59-0477
Albert 16			
BRAUNSDORF, Gottl.	40	Wittenberg	62-0758
Wilhelmine 40, Emilie 10, Amalie 7			
Wilhelmine 3			
BRAUT, Louis	31	Ronneburg/Alt	55-0538
BRAUTWEIN, Dorothe	19	Bernhausen	60-1053
BRAUWEILER, Friedr	36	Germany	56-1216
BRAUWEILER, M.F.	38	Dueren	61-0482
Marie 8, Mathilde 7, Fritz 5			
BRAWARD, Jacob	60	Grindelwald	62-1169
BRECHELEIN, Sebast	31	Bavaria	62-0758
Margaretha 33			
BRECHN, Hinrich	24	Wittstedt/Han	56-0819
BRECHT, Augusta	20	Uslar	57-0578
BRECHT, F.A.(m)	20	Lauffen	62-0111
BRECHT, Fd.	15	Rettmar	57-1148
BRECHTEL, Casp.	44	Niederreith	55-0413
Louise 24			
BRECHTEL, Georg	48	Bavaria	62-0938
BRECHTEZENDE, J.B.	28	Wener	57-1067

NAME	AGE	RESIDENCE	YR-LIST
BREDE, August	21	Besse	59-0214
BREDE, Georg	20	Altendorf	57-0754
BREDEN, Anna	22	Sandstadt	56-0819
BREDEN, Wilhelm	17	Pennigbuechel	60-0334
BREEK, Friedrich	53	Minden	57-0776
Carl 14			
BREHM, Carl	59	Molzdorf/Goth	55-0538
Catharine 58, Henrietta 28, Therese 19			
Louis 17			
BREHM, F.	33	Heiligenfelde	62-0993
E. 34, F.A. 4, C.O. 1			
BREHM, G.	26	Hennyhausen	56-0512
BREHM, Magnus	30	Harberstein	55-0538
BREHME, Ad.	31	Neustadt	57-0578
BREHME, Therese	27	Umpferstadt	56-0589
BREIDENBACH, C.(m)	33	Beienheim	62-0166
BREIER, Charles	36	St.Louis	62-0730
BREIN, Hirsch	29	Suwacken	62-0938
BREIS, Joh.	24	Wittelsburg	60-0334
BREIT, A.(m)	29	Hohenfeld	62-0836
BREITBARTH, Julius	24	Schlesien	59-0412
BREITENMEYER, J.	46	Philadelphia	62-0938
BREITHAUPT, Math.	17	Duerrenmettst	60-0334
BREITHAUPT, Minna	19	Fuerstenau	60-0411
BREITKRIENTZ, L.	30	Wucharir	62-0401
BREIVOGEL, Joh.	22	New York	59-0384
Elise 21			
BREM, Elisabeth	34	Niederlande	58-0563
BREMEHR, H.(m)	24	Wiedenbrueck	62-0232
BREMEL, Johannes	34	Ebinger	59-0613
BREMENCAM, Heinr.	31	Brockenfeld	61-0770
BREMER, Carl	23	Diepholz	58-0563
Antonia 21			
BREMER, Gottfried	18	Braunschweig	58-0881
BREMER, Heinrich	27	Beckedorf	56-0589
BREMER, Hermine	23	Bremen	61-0804
BREMER, Joh Chr.	29	New York	57-1192
Dorette 32, Marg. 33			
BREMER, Johann	36	Colberg	56-0723
BREMER, Peter	33	Bermoel	57-1122
BREMER, Ph.	26	Michelbach	62-1112
BREMERMANN, Veron.	38	Bremen	62-0349
Elisabeth 13, Veronica 9			
BREMJES, H.	28	U.S.	55-1082
BRENDEL, Carl	30	Schmiedehause	56-0819
BRENDLER, Fr.Chr.	50	Seitendorf	57-0654
Christine 40			
BRENKE, Diedr.	26	Uchte	62-0111
BRENNECKE, John	15	Brostedt	57-1148
BRENNEKE, August	24	Bassum	60-1141
Ferd. 26			
BRENNEKE, Bernhard	30	Hildesheim	57-0447
BRENNER, Jacob	18	Ellweiler	59-0384
BRENNING, Adam	31	Gettenbach	57-0447
Anna 37			
BRENNSFLECK, C.(m)	26	Grosseibstadt	62-0730
BRENZ, Jac.	25	Bestenscheid	60-0334
BRESE, Carl	27	Queensstadt/P	55-0538
BRESLAUER, Ida	27	Berlin	60-0998
BRESTEL, Charles	34	Wien	57-1148
BRESTIL, Charles	34	Wien	57-1148
BRETENBECK, Wilh.	23	Mussnershutte	57-1192
BRETH, (f)	20	Cologne	59-0384
BRETTMANN, Wilhelm	32	Uenzen	58-0881
Margaretha 29, Heinrich 16			
BRETTSCHNEIDER, J.	31	Schlesingen	57-1280
BREUDENBAUER, F.	25	Salgedorf	56-0512
BREUER, Marie	18	Altwistedt	59-0990
BREUKMANN, Louis	28	Westfahlen	59-0412
BREUL, Alwin Richd	14	Saalfeld	61-0478
BREUNIG, Ludwina	25	Mechenhart/Bv	60-0429
BREUNING, Catarine	27	Hessen	59-0412
BREUNING, Jacob	25	Baden	60-0429
BREUNING, Rosine H	18	Wangen	59-0047
BREUNS, Julius	36	Helmstadt	59-0214
BREUT, Carl	24	Pava	57-0365
Elise 22			
BREYER, Heinrich	46	Suhlingen	62-0712

NAME	AGE	RESIDENCE	YR-LIST
Sophie 47, Marie 15, Dorothea 64			
BREYMEYER, Charlot	19	England	60-0785
Robert 1			
BRICE, J. (m)	44	S.Carolina	60-0785
BRICKLIN, Chrstne.	20	Carlsruhe	58-0925
BRICKWEAIL, Margar	31	Lehe	59-0477
Matthias 5			
BRICKWEDE, Joh.	57	Osnabrueck	59-1036
BRICKWEDEL, (f)	48	England	62-1112
BRICKWEDEL, Franz	15	Drangstedt	57-1150
Arend 20, Gerhard 31			
BRICKWEDEL, John A	30	Lehe	58-0604
BRICKWEDEL, Mart.H	34	New York	58-0925
BRIEBACH, Andreas	22	Fulda	61-0107
BRIEDE, Joh. Peter	30	Kurhessen	56-0632
BRIEKWEDDE, Heinr.	31	Ankunf	57-1280
Mina 20			
BRIEL, El.	22	Marburg	59-0990
BRIGGENMEYER, Elis	23	Cappeln	61-0804
BRILAWSKY, Mariane	40	Krotoschin	57-1148
Hannch. 14, Eisig 9, Aaron 5			
BRILL, Joh. Fr.	24	Lauterbach	60-1053
BRIMLER, Anna	46	Boehmen	56-1044
Christine 9			
BRINCKWEDEL, H.(m)	50	New York	61-0897
Gesina 44, Marie 18, Heinr. 16, Gesina 8			
Ida 7, Diedrich 5			
BRINDEL, Caspar	42	Koenigswarth	56-0629
Agathe 29, Franz 6m			
BRINGELMANN, Heinr	70	Bath	58-0815
BRINGMANN, Diedr.	50	New York	59-0951
(son) (died) 6			
BRINGMANN, J.Henry	22	Rinteln	57-0422
BRINIKE, Christine	55	Halchte	60-0398
Augusta 18			
BRINKER, Fr.(m)	24	Arensberg	61-0482
BRINKER, Heinrich	55	Ahausen	59-0535
Bernhard 14			
BRINKHOFF, Fr.	26	Muenster	62-1042
BRINKHOFF, Johann	20	Werder	58-0563
BRINKHOFF, Sophie	28	Bavaria	57-0847
BRINKM, Elise Wilh	21	Bremerhafen	55-0634
BRINKMANN, Anna C.	26	Darup	62-0232
BRINKMANN, Arend	17	Oese	59-0535
BRINKMANN, August	36	Hardorf	61-0682
Sophie 32, Wilhelmine 4, Georgine 9m			
BRINKMANN, Carolne	38	Luebbecke	62-0836
Charlotte 20			
BRINKMANN, Charlot	22	Hartum	56-0951
Wilhelmine 58			
BRINKMANN, Chr'ne	25	Loh	55-0812
BRINKS, Johann B.	26	Grafsfeld	59-0047
BRINKWEDEL, Beta	20	Hannover	55-0634
BRINNING, C.(m)	29	Oysterbreiten	61-0804
BRISTER, Joh.	56	Steinfeld	59-0951
BRITLOH, Caroline	56	Werder	57-0654
Ulricka 19, Emily 14			
BRITT, Louis	36	Boston	62-0467
BRIX, Sophie	56	Hannover	58-0604
BRIZOLAVA, Maria	24	Italy	56-1216
BROCK, Emilie	22	Witzhaus	62-0467
BROCK, Joseph	24	Darop/Pr.	62-0342
BROCKELMANN, (f)	49	Bramsche	61-0804
BROCKHAGEN, Heinr.	24	Calbeck	57-1067
Carl 10m			
BROCKHAGEN, Jos.	17	Garbeck	60-0521
Elise 20			
BROCKHAUSEN, C.(m)	27	Muenster	61-0107
BROCKHAUSEN, Edw.	21	Muenster	56-0819
BROCKHUS, Eduard	24	Wisconsin	61-0047
BROCKMANN, Elisab.	27	Blaisee	57-1192
BROCKMANN, Elise	20	Lengwich	62-0730
BROCKMANN, Johann	18	Lueneburg	56-1260
BROCKMEIER, Hch.Wm	29	Lengerich	57-0422
BROCKMEIER, Lisett	26	Doehren	62-0111
Christ. 22			
BROD, Cathrina	22	Nilbel	61-0047
BRODA, Maria	25	Nickenich	57-1416

NAME	AGE	RESIDENCE	YR-LIST
BRODBECK, Friedr.	9	Mundingen	61-0482
BRODKORB, Johann	28	Wetteich	58-0815
BRODKORB, W.	30	Weimar	59-0535
BRODMANN, An.	21	Heuthen	61-0669
BROECKER, Johann	32	Papenhofen	61-0779
BROELL, Adam	24	Steinau/Curh.	60-0429
BROEMER, Alex.	14	Aufenau	62-0730
BROERMANN, Theod.	25	New York	60-0521
Angelica 24			
BROESCHER, Henriet	24	Romannshof	57-0704
BROESMANN, A.M.	56	Klost. Oesede	57-0422
BROESSLER, Adam	59	Heinrichsthal	60-1141
Cathrina 58			
BROHHUHN, Charles	23	Weissenborn	57-1192
BROHN, Bertha	20	St.Louis	57-1192
BROKENHAGEN, Ludw.	33	Pannovo	57-0776
Anna 33, Bernhard 4, Amalie 9			
BROKTEN, zu C.F.J.	18	Brokten	61-0482
BROKUSCH, Franz	15	Mertesdorf	57-0654
BROME, Johanna	30	New York	56-1216
BROMIGA, Heinrich	32	Schanebeck	60-0052
BRONING, Wilhelm	15	Ricking	60-1032
BRONNER, Heinrich	25	Boubach	59-0372
BROSANG, Marie	19	Hannover	62-1042
BROSCH, Franz	34	Boehmen	62-0467
Elisabeth 25, Franz 3			
BROSKE, Ernst	32	Borken	59-1036
BROSON, John	44	America	62-1112
BROTT, Marie	27	Luenighausen	62-0836
BROTT, Marie	27	Luenighausen	62-0836
BROVING, Richard	25	Suedlohn	62-1112
BROWN, G.Ross	49	San Francisco	62-1169
BROWN, John	37	Pittsburg	59-0214
BROWN, Robert	25	Southampton	59-0384
BROWNSEN, H.F.	23	New York	60-1196
BROZIZEK, Joseph	29	Boehmen	56-1044
BRUCH, Therese	24	Sellbach	61-0107
BRUCHEL, Wilhelm	23	Wetzlar	59-0384
BRUCHHOFF, Elise	22	Butzbach	62-1042
BRUCHSAL, Adam	25	Altengeseke	59-0412
BRUCKER, Christian	32	Tado	60-0533
BRUCKER, Jacob	17	Denkendorf	62-0879
BRUCKHOF, Amalie	20	Butzbach	61-0482
BRUCKNER, Andreas	26	Wasserlos	56-0819
BRUDER, Margarethe	24	Langenzenn	61-0167
BRUDER, Mariane	25	Hesse-Darmst.	60-0371
BRUEBACH, Elisab.	23	Holstein	60-1053
BRUECHER, Franz J.	15	Klingenberg	60-0429
Barbara 50, Justina 17, Valentin 12			
Wilhelm 10			
BRUECHWEH, August	24	Darmstadt	59-0613
BRUECK, Margaretha	19	Prussia	60-0371
Angela 51			
BRUECKMANN, Heinr.	29	Solingen	61-0716
BRUECKNER, Carl	29	Ndr. Striegis	59-0951
Charlotte 27			
BRUECKNER, Johanna	18	Coburg	61-0804
BRUECKNER, Leopold	33	Dresden	59-0951
BRUECKNER, Max	17	Wellhausen	56-1216
BRUEGGEMANN, Bernh	23	Ostercappeln	62-0983
Louise 18			
BRUEGGEMANN, Dd.Wm	21	Bremen	57-0924
BRUEGGEMANN, Fr'dr	26	Osnabrueck	58-0576
Charlotte 25			
BRUEGGEMANN, Grebk	32	Tergast	58-0563
BRUEGGEMANN, H.(m)	28	Osterlumme	59-0951
BRUEL, Edward	29	Giessen	59-0477
BRUEL, Th.(m)	27	Albersloh	57-0654
BRUELL, Julius	28	Glogau	56-0279
BRUEMLEINE, Bernh.	41	Louisville	60-0785
Wm. 12			
BRUENER, Dorette	20	Holtensen	57-0924
BRUENING, Bernhard	46	Osnabrueck	57-1192
BRUENING, Caroline	33	Bodenwerder	60-1141
BRUENING, Chrstine	23	Leinen	57-1407
BRUENING, Derrick	20	Loestedt	57-0422
BRUENING, Elise	30	Wessum	59-0951
BRUENING, Fr.	20	Bolenborg	57-0850
BRUENING, Heinrich	25	Bremen	57-0447
BRUENING, Louise	16	Sievern	57-1148
BRUENING, Mary	41	New York	62-0938
Herm. 9, Johanna 10m			
BRUENING, Sophie	30	New York	62-1112
Chr. 9m			
BRUENJE, Joh.Math.	18	Schiffdorf	56-1117
BRUENJES, N.(m)	17	Hambergen	62-0730
BRUENJES, Trina	17	Hambergen	56-1117
BRUENN, Eva	27	Sand	57-0754
BRUENNER, Kunig.	35	Windischnlaib	60-0521
BRUENNER, Valentin	58	Zimmern	59-0477
BRUENNING, Cath.	15	Sievern	60-0785
BRUENNOW, Dr.	36	Annaber	57-1150
Rebecca 21			
BRUENO, (m)	22	France	58-0306
BRUENS, H.C.(m)	18	Langen/Han.	60-0052
BRUENSTEDT, Bernh.	18	Emsteck	59-0951
BRUENYES, P.O.	25	Germany	62-0166
BRUESSEL, Johannes	35	Kederasphe	61-0682
Anna 32, Peter 8, Marie 5, Anna 3			
Catharina 6m			
BRUETING, John H.	32	Treppendorf	57-0961
BRUETT, Amalie	18	Zeren	58-0815
Carl 15			
BRUETT, Theodor	22	Gr. Flettbeck	57-0961
BRUGER, Wm.	34	New York	62-0232
BRUGGEWARTH, Marie	31	Herzfeld	58-0399
BRUMER, Martin	23	Haltenbrunn	56-0951
BRUMMELHAUS, Joh.	29	Luenten	60-0334
BRUMMER, Claus	26	New York	58-0815
BRUMMER, Johann	15	Koehten	58-0815
BRUMSLICK, Moses	36	Witznike	55-0845
BRUMSTERMANN, Carl	28	Stadthagen	57-1122
BRUNDEN, Anna	29	France	57-0847
George 18			
BRUNE, Carl	16	Hilberthausen	55-0845
BRUNE, Catharina	25	Melle	56-0819
BRUNE, E.A.	32	Neuhaus	62-0993
Elise 60			
BRUNE, Friedrich	28	Brinkhausen	56-0413
M.M. 32			
BRUNE, Louis	18	Lingen	60-0533
BRUNING, Joh.	34	Sievern	56-1117
BRUNINGEN, Christ.	27	Wiedern	57-1122
BRUNJES, Anna	17	Beverstedt	60-0521
BRUNJES, H.(m)	27	Schoenebeck	60-0521
BRUNK, Christ.	22	Hohe	59-1036
BRUNKE, Wilhelm	26	Jerze	60-1032
BRUNKE, Wilhelm	16	Radehorst	57-1067
BRUNKHORST, Friedr	17	Gihum	57-0961
BRUNKHORST, Heinr.	32	Schweringen	56-0723
Heinrich 3			
BRUNNER, Carl	18	Herzenheim	59-0951
BRUNNER, Georg	30	Asch	57-0924
BRUNNS, H.(m)	23	Bueckeburg	57-0555
BRUNOTTE, Wm.	27	Hameln	60-0785
BRUNS, (m)	36	Cincinnati	58-0306
(wife) 31, (baby) 4m			
BRUNS, Carl	57	Bemen Kreis	59-0384
BRUNS, Chr.(m)	43	Algermissen	61-1132
BRUNS, Christian	52	Bierde	55-0812
Wilhelmine 19			
BRUNS, Christian	29	Neustadt	57-0961
BRUNS, Christian	21	Pohle	59-0384
William 19			
BRUNS, Christine	24	Scharmbeck	55-0634
BRUNS, Elise	25	Neuenkirchen	57-0704
BRUNS, Fr.	30	New York	61-0804
Claus 28			
BRUNS, H.	18	Horsteln	59-1036
BRUNS, Hanne	20	Schmarje	59-0384
BRUNS, Heinrich	26	Sievern	56-0413
BRUNS, Hermann	28	Minden	56-0413
Anna 11m			
BRUNS, J.	34	Brooklyn	59-0951
BRUNS, Joh.Chr.	43	Goettingen	57-0606
BRUNS, Johann	26	Koehlen	56-1117

NAME	AGE	RESIDENCE	YR-LIST
BRUNS, Johann	25	Emsen	58-0925
BRUNS, Johann	17	Boesel	62-0467
BRUNS, Joseph	17	Osterloh	59-0951
BRUNS, M.	6m	Brooklyn	59-0951
BRUNS, Marie	18	Bremen	57-0606
BRUNS, Peter	25	Dettum	57-1026
BRUNS, Ph.(m)	15	Nordholz	57-0555
BRUNS, Reb.	58	Scharmbeck	59-0990
BRUNS, Rudolph	41	Lehnen	59-1036
BRUNSCHOFF, Joh.H.	34	Fallingbostel	57-0847
Margaretha 30, Heinrich 7, Friedrich 4m			
BRUNZLICH, Ferdin.	32	Miess	59-0613
BRUSEMA, Henr. E.	46	Osternuland	62-0306
BRUSSOK, Carl	30	Kl. Ujeschutz	61-0779
BRUST, Caroline	18	Wennigs	57-1407
BRUST, Wilhelmine	17	Hessen	60-1161
BRUT, Franz	46	Reichenberg	55-0845
BRUTSCHER, Elise	23	Baiern	57-0606
BUBE, Heinrich	14	Gelnhausen	56-1216
BUBLITZ, Peter	65	Griebau	62-0758
Friedricke 29, Caroline 10			
BUBSER, Christoph	51	Ipplingen	62-0879
Caroline Fr. 27, Carl 25, Jacob Friedr 21			
Anna 17, Johann Jacob 15, Caroline 3			
BUCH, A. Augusta	29	Dresden	56-0629
BUCH, Agnes	24	Dobberschuetz	60-0521
BUCH, Bernh.	35	Weitheim	60-0334
Marie 35, Louis 12, Cath. 33			
BUCH, Caroline	19	Soldin	60-0533
BUCHBACH, Barb.E.	23	Petersberg	62-0467
BUCHBINDER, Bruno	14	Leipzig	56-0629
BUCHBINDER, Maria	21	Krisch/Boehm.	57-0924
BUCHENAU, Georg	16	Storndorf	55-0413
BUCHENBACHER, Ad.	16	Nienburg	57-1192
BUCHER, Georg	23	Ruedenheim	60-0334
BUCHHEIM, Johann	20	Liebensee	57-0961
BUCHHEISER, Chstne	51	Palitzsile	61-0047
BUCHHOLTZ, H.D.	18	Buehren	59-0535
BUCHHOLZ, August	36	Schoenewald	56-0632
Friederike 18			
BUCHHOLZ, Eduard	16	Budziszewo	56-0819
Christine 16			
BUCHHOLZ, Ferd.	22	Neu Schonewld	57-0704
BUCHHOLZ, Fr.(m)	27	Schweringen	56-0723
Louise 9			
BUCHHOLZ, Georg	36	Cincinati	59-0384
Charlotte 23			
BUCHHOLZ, Heinrich	30	Schlange	61-0520
BUCHHOLZ, William	30	Bulinghausen	57-0422
BUCHNER, Margar.	24	Grossgarnstad	56-0512
BUCHOLT, Johanna	56	Laasen	60-1032
BUCHSPIESS, Friedr	56	Dristedt	59-0477
Martha 53, Friedr. 33, Hy. 25, Auguste 21			
Theodor 9			
BUCHTERKIRCH, Mary	40	Mahner	56-0527
Bertha 8			
BUCHTOLD, John	27	Oberbergen	57-0654
BUCHWALD, Carl Aug	24	Schoenau	62-0712
BUCK, Albert H.	17	New York	60-0521
BUCK, Catharine	17	Buechel	60-0334
BUCK, Charles	17	Giessen	57-0654
BUCK, Dorothea	22	Wuertt.	55-0634
BUCK, Johanna	21	Oldenburg	58-0399
BUCK, L.(m)	19	Oppendorf	59-0951
BUCKE, Ernst	34	Appelfeld	56-0512
BUCKEL, Catharina	30	Treysa	55-0812
BUCKSPIESS, Carl F	19	Olbersleben	56-0951
BUDDE, Cath.E.	17	Oberhalsten	59-1036
BUDDE, Jos.	40	Waarendorf	62-1042
Marie 37, Gertrud 9m			
BUDDE, Wilhelm	30	Rhoden/Wald.	60-0622
BUDDENBORN, Wmne.	28	Suling	59-0412
BUDDENDICK, Heinr.	27	Dissen	56-1044
Charlotte 36, Heinrich 29, Catharine 35			
Minna 9, Charlotte 7			
BUDELMANN, Meta E.	29	Drifsethe	62-0467
BUDENS, Ludwig	23	Rasdorf	56-0819
BUDESHEIM, Elis.	18	Konshausen	55-0413
BUECH, Gottlieb	41	Selchow	56-0819
Beata Louise 40, Adolph 9			
BUECHEL, Carl	26	Passen	60-0398
BUECHEL, Franz Aq.	29	Wuerzburg	61-0167
BUECHEL, Friedrich	17	Dillstedt	55-0630
Christiane 13			
BUECHEL, Johann	29	Grossentorsdo	56-0589
Helena 44			
BUECHER, Rosine	26	Innsbruck	56-0632
Heinrich 3			
BUECHHARDT, Heinr.	18	Beckum	58-0399
Dora 30			
BUECHNER, Carl	36	Trebra	62-0712
BUECK, Heinrich	58	Queckborn	58-0576
BUECKERT, Justine	24	Holsheim	56-1216
BUECKING, Gertrud	22	Homberg/Hesse	57-0924
BUECKING, Wilhelm	34	Alsfeld	56-1216
BUECKMANN, Gretche	19	Assendorf	59-0613
BUEDNER, Carl Fr.	20	Altenbeuschen	61-0779
BUEGLER, John	52	Prossekel	56-1011
Justine 38			
BUEHER, Caroline	21	Wierborn	59-0613
BUEHLER, G.	24	Nellingsheim	62-0938
BUEHLER, Mary	36	Berka	57-0422
Bertha 16, Minna 13			
BUEHLING, Anna	13	Neumarschen	56-0411
BUEHMANN, Heinrich	24	Steinhude	56-0411
BUEHNER, G.(m)	20	Marburg	62-0467
Minna 22			
BUEHSE, Amalie	24	Jever	62-0938
BUELOW, Gottfried	48	Poplob	56-1260
Carl 10, Wilhelmine 12, Heinrich 22			
Augusta 25, Albertine 3, Bertha 1			
Amalie(died) 5d			
BUELTE, Augusta	24	Stemmen	56-1260
BUELTEL, Bern.	25	Spelle	57-1148
BUELTEL, J.H.	40	Listrup	62-0993
E. 16			
BUELTER, Wilhelm	38	Posen	58-0399
Wilhelmine 34, Carl 8, Henriette 4			
August 11m			
BUEMANN, Fr.(m)	40	New York	62-0467
BUENKER, Ferd.	16	Cincinnati	61-0804
BUENNING, Johann	25	Bassum	61-0107
BUENNING, Sophie	23	Schierenhop	61-0107
BUENTE, Carl	27	Magdeburg	60-0521
BUENTIND, Tede	24	Wrisse	57-0422
BUERGER, A.	27	Berge	62-0993
BUERGER, Ana Elis.	21	Beuren	57-0754
BUERGER, Carl	23	Detmold	56-1044
BUERGER, Conrad	24	Kalmberg/Hann	61-0770
BUERGER, Heinrich	30	Massaville	58-0815
BUERGER, J.G. (m)	57	Niederlommatz	55-0630
Johanna 55			
BUERGER, Joh.Fr.	28	Baiern	59-0412
BUERGER, Johann	33	Oberbreisnig	57-0578
BUERGER, Justine	27	Eversberg	60-0334
BUERGER, W.A.	37	Hameln	56-0951
BUERGER, Wilh'mine	23	Niederlommatz	55-0630
Amalie 18, Pauline 16, Franz 14			
BUERGERMEISTER, El	27	St.Johann	59-0613
Christina 7			
BUERO, Ger.	25	Paris	59-0214
BUERSCHAPER, Doret	32	Hannover	61-0167
BUERSCHEN, J.H.	35	Reidlage	57-1148
Anna 28			
BUESCHER, A.C.	29	Cincinnati	62-1042
Lina 25, Gerhard 11m			
BUESCHER, Wilh.	42	Marbke	59-0951
Mary 41, Cath. 16, Elisabeth 15			
Wilhelm 14, Marie 12, Franz 11			
Margaretha 9, Caspar 8, Anton 3			
Friedrich 1, Heinrich 11m			
BUESCHERS, Marie	20	Wittlage	56-0589
BUESCHING, Dr.	30	Hafen	62-0938
Louise 22			
BUESING, Bernhard	22	Rechtenfleth	57-1407
BUESINGA, M.T. (m)	23	Schwarzenwald	55-0413

NAME	AGE	RESIDENCE	YR-LIST
BUETTER, Heinrich		Oberzwehren	56-0527
BUETTNER, Georg	29	Bavaria	60-0371
BUETTNER, Heinrich	24	Altenburg	62-0758
Therese 24			
BUETTNER, Heinrich	22	Fulda	62-1042
BUETTNER, Joachim	30	Meiningen	58-0815
Joh.Mart. 34			
BUETTNER, John	31	Arnsbach	59-0477
BUETTNER, Marg.	24	Cincinnati	62-0938
Martin 19			
BUETTNER, Margaret	28	Stadelhofen	62-0608
BUETTNER, Marie	32	Marburg	57-0850
BUETZ, Ferdinand	24	Briesen/Prus.	55-1238
Henriette 30, Julius 1			
BUFF, Louis	31	Giessen	59-0951
BUHLAU, Anna	28	Zeven	61-0682
BUHLERT, Julius	17	Zelle/Hann.	59-0047
BUHNKEN, Adelheid	17	Bockeln	55-1082
BUHR, Joseph	26	Weiler/Pr.	55-1238
BUHR, de Gerd Popp	28	Ostfriesland	57-0606
Simon Eden			
BUHRMANN, Cathrina	50	Messlingen	57-1122
Elisabeth 17, Marie 14			
BUISCHENKE, Doroty	58	Meiningen	57-0654
Fr.William 19, Mary M. 14			
BUISCHKER, Engel	32	Rohrichum	58-0563
BUKELSHAUSEN, E.	17	Appenrod	57-0555
BUKH, Joh.	26	Waldenbruch	60-0785
BUKOWSKY, Franz	66	Raudnitz/Aus.	62-0342
Catharine 63, Johann 23			
BULAU, Carl	20	Berga	59-0613
BULLIG, Matthias	57	Boston	62-1169
BULLMANN, Julie	28	Grossostheim	60-0334
BULLWINKEL, Anna	20	Heissenbuttel	59-0990
BULTMANN, Heinrich	19	Hille	55-0411
BULTMANN, Heinrich	16	Behling	56-0723
BULWER, Wilhelmine	53	Solingen	60-1141
BULWINKEL, Sophie	18	Osterholz	56-1117
BULZ, W.	25	Remscheid	62-1169
BUMANN, Conrad	52	Wallingh.	59-0214
BUMANN, Louise	58	Brueggen	59-0214
BUMILLER, Theod.		Cincinnati	62-0111
BUMMERSCHEIN, H.	23	Bettenhausen	57-0422
BUNCK, Friedrich	24	Boerschken	56-0819
BUNDSCHEN, Mary Th	18	Glashaven	61-0167
BUNDSCHUH, Carl	28	Alsace	60-0371
BUNG, Mrs.	25	Paris	59-0214
BUNKER, Johann	24	Arenswalde	58-0885
BUNNER, Casper	39	Tauberettersh	58-0925
BUNTE, Carl	19	Farrenholz	50-1017
BUNTE, Georg	19	Preuss.Minden	58-0563
BUNTKE, Carl	28	Bresco	56-0629
BUNZ, David	17	Wain	60-0334
BUNZ, Margaretha	17	Unterbalzheim	60-0334
BUNZEL, Christiane	30	Suessenbach	57-0754
BUOSCH, A.	20	St.Antarien	59-0477
BURBACH, Ludwig	59	Leun	57-0704
Louise 50, Louise 31, Elisabeth 22			
Wilhelmine 19, Christian 14, Friedrich 4			
Caroline 24, Jacobin G. 16			
BURCHARD, A.	23	Neise	56-0512
BURCHARD, Carl	25	Goerlitz	58-0881
BURCHARD, Maria	24	Feuchtwangen	55-0628
Margarethe 18			
BURCHARDT, Antonia	28	Bremen	58-0885
BURCHARDT, Catrina	24	Wernswig	55-0845
BURCHARDT, Friedr.	11m	Cincinnati	59-0951
BURCHHARDT, Casper	30	Zelhausen	60-1117
BURCK, Wilhelmine	59	Bessel	56-0512
Anna 20, Wilhelmine 22			
BURDENSICK, Heinr.	26	Bremervoerde	55-1082
BURDORF, Cath.	26	Bremen	59-0951
BUREZ, Georg	45	Boehmen	61-0897
Elisabeth 49, Wenzel 22, Georg 20			
Johann 17, Franz 14, Mathias 8			
Casparine 6, Friedrich 10m			
BURFEIND, Heinrich	24	Oldendorf/Han	60-0429
Joh.Heinrich 21			

NAME	AGE	RESIDENCE	YR-LIST
BURFEIND, Sophia	19	Bremervoerde	60-0622
BURG, Paul	16	Ludwigsburg	59-0047
BURGERT, Anton	31	Nottungen/Pr.	62-0342
Elisabeth 29			
BURGHARDT, Carolne	19	Engelbrand	59-0951
Magdalene 32, Lina 2			
BURGHAUSER, Heinr.	16	Bingen	61-0779
BURGHEIM, R.	20	Minden	62-1042
BURGKARD, L.	29	Knittlingen	62-1042
Henriette 22			
BURGMANN, Gustav	14	Gr. Rodnitz	59-0613
Marie 37			
BURGUIN, Samuel	52	France	61-0107
Joseph 12, J.G.Luoys 55, (dau.) 19			
BURHMANN, Cathrina	50	Messlingen	57-1122
Elisabeth 17, Marie 14			
BURIZ, Joseph	38	Boehmen	61-0930
Maria 30, Wenzel 9, Johann 4, Victorina 2			
BURKART, Louise	18	Tucherfeld	59-0951
BURKE, J.H.(m)	37	Baltimore	62-0111
BURKERT, J.C.H.(m)	14	Doerzbach	62-0730
BURKHARDT, Franz	26	Voilsdorf	61-0478
BURLAGE, Joh.Heinr	30	Talge	60-1032
BURMANN, Maria	23	Bassel/Old.	60-0371
BURMEISTER, Carl	18	Hille	55-0411
BURMEISTER, Carl	17	Hille	56-0411
BURMEISTER, Claus	22	New York	62-0467
BURMEISTER, Heinr.	22	Hannover	56-0847
BURMEISTER, J.(m)	40	New York	62-0232
BURMEISTER, J.Hch.	24	New Orleans	62-1169
(wife) 20			
BURMEISTER, Louise	22	Minden	57-0776
BUROGEL, Doris	24	Bremen	60-0411
BURRI, Peter	42	Basel	59-0048
BURRICHTER, Heinr.	25	Diepholz	59-0214
BURWIRTH, Heinrich	20	Spiescappeln	55-0812
BUSCH, Aide	23	Dorum	56-1044
BUSCH, Anna	18	Ruttel	57-1148
BUSCH, Antonia	21	Roerebeck	62-1042
Johanna 20			
BUSCH, Armand	24	Ruttel	57-1148
BUSCH, Daniel	51	Solingen	60-1141
Anna Cathar. 52			
BUSCH, David	15	Westhofen	59-0048
BUSCH, Helene	27	Badbergen	60-0521
BUSCH, Joh.	30	Huemme	61-0804
Caroline 31, Fr.(m) 9, W.(m) 6, Ed.(m) 9m			
BUSCH, Johann	18	Obersheisen	61-0482
BUSCH, Johann	25	Grosskarber	59-0047
BUSCH, Lina	3	New York	62-0166
Josephine 2			
BUSCH, Ludwig	40	Waldsleben	56-1117
Hermann 16, Louise 28, Henriette 18			
Fr.Wilhelm 9, Emil 4			
BUSCH, Martin	10	Hagen	57-0654
BUSCH, Rebecca	18	Mulsum	62-1042
BUSCH, Wilhelm	17	Oldenburg	57-1150
BUSCHE, Charles	42	Leckwegen	57-0654
Caroline 52, Julia 22, Friedrich 20			
Henry 18, William 16, Gottl. 14			
Charles 12, Christine 9			
BUSCHEK, Johann	32	Hohenflies	56-0723
Anna 42			
BUSCHHAUPT, Henrit	28	Prussia	56-1044
BUSCHMANN, Friedr.	49	Bremen	59-0951
Louise 49, Heinrich 20			
BUSCHMANN, Furchtg	26	Eibenstock	56-1011
BUSCHMANN, Gottl.	44	Muehlhausen	59-1036
BUSCHMANN, Hermann	25	Baltimore	59-0214
BUSCHMANN, Mariana	9	Damme	57-0961
BUSCHMANN, W.C.	48	Mittelhausen	61-0482
Louise 54			
BUSCHMANN, William	54	Winzlar	56-1011
Katharina 56, Friederica 21, Caroline 14			
William 9			
BUSCHNER, Ernstine	31	Roschuetz	57-1026
BUSE, Sophie	24	Ellville	55-1082
BUSE, William	18	Dedendorf	57-0961

NAME	AGE	RESIDENCE	YR-LIST
Friedrich 9			
BUSHING, Christine	24	Eldaxen	57-1122
BUSIAHN, Carl	25	Grunau	57-0924
BUSING, (m)	23	Bremen	58-0306
BUSS, J.A. (m)	24	Simonswolde	55-0413
BUSS, Joh.	34	Aurich	59-0990
BUSSE, Friedrich	22	Halberstadt	57-0422
BUSSE, Friedricke	40	Schwartje	61-0520
Friedrich 15, Louise 11			
BUSSE, Wilhelm	23	Hannover	56-1044
BUSSENIUS, Adam	22	Duingel	61-0047
BUSSERT, John Fr.	30	Puttbus	57-0654
BUSSET, Jean	30	France	60-1196
BUST, Conrad	25	Wimmar	57-1122
BUSWINGER, Gerold	17	Friegelhof	60-0411
BUTALA, Michael	20	Grifsch	56-0589
BUTHAN, Fr.(m)	45	Ft.Madison	62-0232
BUTHE, Franz	19	Paderborn	59-1036
BUTLLOH, Caroline	56	Werder	57-0654
Ulrika 19, Emily 14			
BUTTE, August	26	Sandewalde	56-0819
BUTTE, Hermann	25	Braunschweig	59-0384
BUTTE, Sophie	17	Dichberg	57-0847
Wilhelmine 16			
BUTTERS, G.W.(m)	23	Steingruen	62-0730
BUTTMANN, Heinrich	16	Behling	56-0723
BUTTMANN, J.B.	33	Aumundorf	62-0467
BUTTNER, Anton	27	Coburg	61-0047
BUTTSTEDT, Joh.Gus	24	Sachsen	59-0412
BUXBAUM, A.	20	Marburg	62-1112
BYRNE, F.P.O.(m)	32	London	60-0785
Brink, Alexander t	24	Vilbel	59-0613
CABANIS, Albert	34	New York	62-0306
CACH, Fr.Wilhelm	26	Taucha	57-0654
Rosina 20			
CADIX, Euguene	13	France	62-1112
CAEN, Marie	28	San Francisco	61-0804
Diedr. 3			
CAESAR, August	20	Hilenburg	59-0951
CAESAR, Carl	16	Varel	62-0836
CAHEN, Rosalie	52	Oldendorf	59-0951
Emma 19, Salomon 14, Jacob 13, Caroline 9			
CAHN, Lina	16	Altenstadt	57-0918
CAHN, Peter	26	Rehnbach	56-0411
CALESSE, August	34	Breslau	57-0776
Eleonora 29			
CALLENBACHER, Andr	21	Schwan	60-0398
Louise 26			
CAMMANN, Johana C.	27	Himbeck/Hann.	60-0622
CAMMANN, Marie	17	US.	59-0951
CAMMERA, Wilhelm	17	Stuttgart	62-0938
CAMPADOMICE, Jean	25	Italy	60-0334
CAMPE, J.H.(m)	17	Wersage	60-0521
Anna 16			
CAMPE, John	22	Sansteth	56-1011
CAMPEN, Claus	17	Abbenseth	60-0334
CANDES, F.H.	21	Bothel	59-0535
CANUS, Doris	63	Wardsfelde	57-1122
Sophie 19, Doris 13			
CAPE, Oliver	25	Philadelphia	59-1017
CAPLE, Edmund	24	England	59-0613
CAPP, Franz	59	Guellstein	62-0879
CAPPEL, Joh.	25	France	62-0467
CAPPELER, Joh.	32	Elbingenalp	55-0413
CAPPIA, Francis	37	Switzerland	61-0482
CAPULLO, Angela	24	Genna	61-1132
CARCERA, (m)	16	Rangoon	62-0401
CARFAZNO, Achille	25	Napoli	62-1042
CARILLA, Jean	30	Corsica	62-1042
CARL, Augusta	21	Celle	55-0845
Elisabeth 17			
CARL, C.Fr.(m)	42	Borsleben	61-0897
Friedricka 42, Edw. 15, Adelheid 3			
Caroline 5, Adele bob			
CARL, Friedrich	48	Darmstadt	59-0613
CARL, L.	22	Schoenhagen	59-0990
CARL, Paulus	70	Bayern	56-1044
Catharina 17			

NAME	AGE	RESIDENCE	YR-LIST
CARLSHEIM, Eduard	34	Dortmund	59-0047
CARO, Simon	19	Berlin	57-0704
CARRA, Joh.Bapt.	19	Waltershofen	59-0613
CARRE, Louis	38	Rouen	62-0836
CARRER, Johannes	25	Menningerberg	62-0983
CARRY, Clementine	34	France	57-1192
CARRY, Const.	24	Hechingen	57-1192
CARSTANZEN, Hugo	21	Coeln	60-1196
CARSTEN, Henry	19	Ruttel	57-1148
CARSTEN, Janken	49	Jever	56-1044
Heinrich 6			
CARSTEN, Sophie	23	Muenster	57-0436
CARSTENS, Cathar.	32	New York	62-0938
Catharina 11m			
CARSTENS, Margaret	14	Dedendorf	57-0961
CARSTLES, Wenzel	47	Boehmen	62-0306
Anna 48, Peter 20, Anton 16			
CARTNER, J.	24	Leipzig	56-0550
CASANOVA, A.M.		Obersaxen	59-0477
CASPAR, G.	26	Bremke	62-0938
CASSEBART, Marg.	17	Horn	61-0520
CASSEGNE, Chr.	45	France	62-0938
CASSIUS, Franz	27	Minden	57-0847
Louise 21			
CASTAGNETO, Giacom	23	Italy	61-0716
CASTEDE, Bertha	41	France	62-0938
CASTELHUN, Elise	18	Guntersblum	59-0477
CASTENDYCK, Carl	30	New York	59-1036
CASTENS, Friedrich	22	Wardenburg	57-1113
CATLIN, Marg.	28	England	62-0938
CAVALLS, Jean	27	Wolpiano	59-0535
CAVIEZEL, Christ.	18	Rheinwald	59-0477
CAZIER, Charles	29	France	59-0384
CECHOTA, Matthias	37	Bianza	56-1011
Barbara 24, Petrolina 10, John 7			
Barbara 6, Maria 5, Katharina 3, Maria 29			
CEHYLI, Marie	25	Porischitz	55-0845
Franz 7, Joseph 4, Marie 2, Anna by			
CEOPEDES, de C.M.	22	Manzanilla	62-1042
CERGE, Gertrude	29	Muenster	58-0399
Elisabeth 2			
CERIZAC, (m)	38	France	62-0730
CERVENZ, Wentz	49	Schwalitz	60-1141
Mary 50, Wentz 19, Anna 14, Cathrina 11			
John 13			
CESNY, Anna	27	Cittow	57-0850
CESSLER, Johanna	18	Bengershausen	55-0812
CHABRUL, Ad.(m)	22	Prussia	62-0401
CHADE, Eliza	16	Germany	57-0578
CHALUPSKY, Wenzel	34	Boehmen	61-0716
Rosalie 29, Clara 5, Wenzel 3, Marie 8m			
CHANCE, Georg	29	London	59-0214
CHASTMER, F.W. (m)	20	Offenbach	60-0998
CHERST, Adam	45	Hessen	56-1044
Cath.Elisab. 34			
CHEVALIER, (f)	24	New York	62-0836
CHEVREUX, Alfred	31	France	62-0467
CHEVROLET, (m)	50	Troyes	62-0401
CHIAPPINO, Aug.	24	Illinois	60-0785
CHIAPPINO, Heinr.	25	US.	55-0845
CHIOT, Albert	7	England	61-0482
CHLADECK, Anton	58	Mediz	59-0951
Therese 44, Johanna 17, Florentine 13			
Clementine 9, Joseph 15, Zenka 8			
CHRASTEL, Johann	27	Welwaren	59-0384
CHRIST, Georg	48	Baltimore	60-1032
CHRIST, Louise	28	Frankenhausen	60-0533
Adolph 8, Emma 3			
CHRISTIANI, Th.Hch	30	Fulda	62-0879
CHRISTIANS, Lewis	37	Berlin	60-1141
CHRISTIANSEN, (m)	29	Foehr	61-0478
CHRISTINE, (f)	19	New York	62-0467
CHRISTMANN, Ferd.	26	Kraehfeld	57-0436
Elisabeth 24, Caroline bob			
CHRISTMANN, Jacob	10	Arheilgen	55-0413
CHRISTOFELSMEIER,C	37	Hensdorf	61-0478
CHRISTOPH, J.(m)	42	Herrnhut	57-0080
Albertine 36, Marie 9m			

NAME	AGE	RESIDENCE	YR-LIST
CHRISTOPHERS, Anna	16	Meinburg	61-0482
CHUDOWA, J.F.	33	Bremen	62-0879
CHUEBEL, Carl Fr.A	18	Heitersbach	57-0704
CHYNOWETH, James		Canada	56-1216
CIALDEA, Augusta	51	Wien	59-0477
CICHACK, Adalbert	35	Boehmen	62-0712
Barbara 27, Joseph 5, Anna 10m			
CIHA, Wenzel	32	Butschek	61-0779
Ludwika 21, Wenzel by, Catharina 19			
CIZECH, Wenzel	45	Wostrow	56-0411
Anna 40, Marie 3, Johann 20, Franz 9			
CLAASEN, P.J.	30	New York	61-0482
CLAASSEN, Frientje	23	Ochtelbur	55-0413
CLAPROTH, Caroline	31	Poehlde	58-0885
CLARIUS, Catharine	19	Heldenberg	60-0533
Marie 17			
CLARODE, Jos.	28	Bavaria	62-1169
CLASNER, Heinrich	32	Muenchberg	55-0630
CLAUDE, Seroph.	25	France	62-1112
CLAUS, Christian	28	Steindorf	56-0847
Theresia 19			
CLAUS, Heinz	22	Bielefeld	60-1161
CLAUS, J. (m)	26	Berlin	59-0951
CLAUS, Joh. Christ	19	Philippsthal	60-0622
CLAUS, Justus	26	Hessen	57-0606
CLAUS, Sophia	22	Marburg/Gotha	60-0622
CLAUSEN, Anna	26	Achim	60-0785
CLAUSEN, Friedrich	30	Schweringen	60-0533
CLAUSER, J.A.	20	Freudenstadt	59-0990
CLAUSS, Marie C.	16	Kleinkoff	62-0836
CLAUSSEN, Armand	25	New York	57-0961
CLAUSSEN, August	20	Augusta	58-0885
CLAUSSEN, Caspar	33	Bausendorf	59-0214
John 5			
CLAUSSEN, Diedr.	18	Ottersberg	55-0413
CLAUSSEN, Hermann		Blender	58-0885
CLEMENS, Christian	34	Salzung	57-1122
CLEMENS, Sophie	17	Hannover	57-1192
CLEMENT, Catharina	24	Mies	58-0881
CLEMENT, Jacques	30	Havre	62-0836
CLOEM, Eliza	19	Rottendorf	60-1141
CLOSE, Rob.	24	Schweidniz	57-1113
CLOSS, August	26	Polle	56-0819
CLOUDT, Jost Wm.	34	Uchte	57-0924
CLUEVER, Heinr.	25	Blumenthal	59-0048
Catharine 25			
CMEJLA, Joseph	23	Hrachotusk	57-1067
Barbara 25, Franz 1, Elisabeth 3m			
COBERG, Heinrich	25	Lokum	62-0712
COHEN, J.M.(m)	23	Rotenberg/Hes	55-0544
COHEN, Max	17	Germany	59-0613
COHEN, Solomon	19	Germany	61-0167
COHN, (f)	19	Koenigsberg	62-0836
COHN, Abraham	18	Staukenburg	57-1148
COHN, Ad.	26	Gehaus	57-0961
COHN, Alex.	15	Dobschau	62-0467
COHN, Ambros Anton	17	Colditz	57-0924
COHN, Anna	19	Gnesen	58-0399
COHN, Assan	33	Welmanrod	62-0306
COHN, Barbara	19	Ruegenwalde	57-1148
COHN, Caroline	43	Amonegruen	60-0785
COHN, Diana	22	Breslau	56-0847
COHN, Friedrich	18	Zirken	57-1192
Johann 20, Bertha 31, Paul 19, Hirsch 5			
Philipp 3, Heinrich 11m			
COHN, Henry	27	California	62-0467
COHN, Hirsch	59	Lobsens	57-1148
COHN, Hulda	18	Posen	58-0604
COHN, Joseph	18	Fordon/Posen	57-0422
COHN, Jul.(m)	25	Bremen	62-0401
COHN, Marichen	31	Krotoschin	62-0467
COHN, Meyer	22	Zeppelburg	56-0411
COHRS, Claus	16	Hoenau	60-0334
COHRS, Claus	19	Barcheln	56-1117
COHRS, Mart.	27	St.Louis	60-0334
COLANDER, Martin	30	Ilanz	59-0477
Charles 56, Agnes 55, Barbara 19			
COLAREUS, Elias	56	Alsfeld	57-1122

NAME	AGE	RESIDENCE	YR-LIST
Anna 58			
COLBMANN, Clara	19	Schneibach	59-0372
COLDEWEG, August	25	Bremerhafen	60-0622
COLGATE, R.	54	US.	62-1042
S.A. 20, G. 18			
COLLMANN, Claus	27	Neermoor	55-0413
Louise 24			
COLMAN, Maier	17	Geroda	60-0521
Nisam 13			
COLOHNE, Wilh'mine	25	Grodmada	56-0411
COLZHAUSEN, v.Magd	48	Cologne	56-0354
Margaretha 28			
CONRAD, Carl	43	Bochum	60-1196
CONRAD, Friedrich	49	Halberstadt/P	55-1238
CONRAD, Gottfried	48	Neusaltz	59-0412
Louis 44, Adolph 18, Heinrich 15			
Emilie 17, Emma 10, Hulda 5			
CONRAD, Henriette	38	Worlitz	61-0779
CONRAD, Hugo	30	Konigsberg	60-0411
CONRAD, Jacob	39	Climbach	55-0630
CONRAD, Jacob	17	Clumbach/Han.	60-0622
CONRAD, Lorenz	32	Neuenkirchen	61-0897
Johanna 25			
CONRAD, P.(m)	32	Schertendorf	57-0555
CONRAD, Wilhelm	21	Langensalza	57-0924
CONRADI, Charlotte	18	Windheim	60-0533
CONRADI, Georg	19	Rudolsdorf	57-1113
CONRADY, Georg	57	Hessen	59-0412
Georg 20, Maria 54, Augustina			
CONRIOL, Friedrich	49	Halberstadt/P	55-1238
CONSERVE, C.C.	40	England	59-0384
(wife) 36			
CONSTEDT, Berthold	28	Lissa	59-0477
CONWAY, Th.G.	22	Philadelphia	62-1042
CONZELMANN, Gottl.	50	St.Louis	59-0951
Georgine 37, Emilie 9, Wilhelm 3			
Theophilus 1			
COOK, Emilie	18	England	62-1112
COOK, John	20	England	60-0334
(wife) 20			
COORS, J.William	21	Bremen	60-0533
CORBACH, Lina	25	Baltimore	61-0167
CORBY, Henry	32	London	59-0477
CORDEL, Anna Elis.	16	Guxhagen	57-0754
CORDES, Albert	28	Hannover	62-0758
Orfka 28, Anna by			
CORDES, Antoinette	30	New York	61-0716
CORDES, Fr.	18	Bremervoerde	62-1042
CORDES, Fr.(m)	40	New York	61-0804
CORDES, Fr.D.	32	Hannover	61-0482
CORDES, Gesche	15	Asterbroch	57-0654
CORDES, Heinrich	18	Hastedt	62-0879
CORDES, Jac.	19	Bremervoerde	59-0990
CORDES, Joh.	18	Verden	62-0836
CORDES, Jurg.	15	Neuenbilstedt	62-0938
Gesche 20			
CORDES, Maria	22	Dedersdrf/Old	60-0622
CORDES, Mary	18	Stemmen	57-1148
CORDESMEYER, W.(m)	27	Lieme	57-0422
CORDS, Hinrich	44	Leer	59-0412
Hinricka 42, Lea 13, Johannes 11			
Catarina 9, Jacob 6, Luebbert 3, Berend 1			
CORDUAN, Wilhelm	38	Koeln	56-1117
CORFES, L.	29	New York	62-1169
CORND, Heinrich	31	Bederkesa	57-0847
Carolina 27, Henriette 5, Hinrich 4			
CORNELIUS, August	17	Imshausen	57-0924
CORNELSEN, Ch.	28	Wilmington	59-1036
Agnes 18			
CORNELY, Leopold	27	Duelken/Pr.	62-0608
CORNETH, Nicholas	34	Dorum	57-0422
Anna 34, Henry 4			
CORS, Elisabeth	20	Bieren	57-1148
CORSEN, Adolph	20	Bremen	55-0812
CORSS, Jos.	17	Albjen	59-0951
CORVES, Louis	24	Polle	55-0932
Johanna 18			
CORYN, M.	27	England	59-0613

NAME	AGE	RESIDENCE	YR-LIST
COSINSKY, August	21	San Francisco	59-0048
COURT, Anna	20	Rheinland	62-0758
COWARZICK, Louise	27	Cassel	59-1017
Emilia 3, Maria 10m			
CRAEBER, Georg	25	Hannover	62-0730
CRAMER, Cath.	28	Steinfeld	61-0669
CRAMER, Dora	59	Eschwege	59-0477
Adolf 21			
CRAMER, Friedrich	18	Herrnhof	56-1117
CRAMER, H.P.	28	Norden	57-0918
CRAMER, Th.	18	Hemmelte	58-0306
CRANK, Joseph	27	Hungary	57-0847
Anna 24, Maria 3, Theresa 10m			
CREICK, Geo.W.	20	Louisville	62-1169
CRESNER, Anna	21	Baiern	58-0399
CRESS, Elis.	21	Elm	62-1042
CRIEHL, John	15	Illienworth	59-1036
CRISSEY, (m)	36	London	62-0401
(f) 27			
CROBBODH, Carl	55	Ladowitz	57-1416
CROHN, Otto	22	Luedingworth	58-0563
CROLL, M.	51	Cassel	62-0993
Th.W. 19, G.H.T. 11			
CRON, Henry	26	Opperhausen	56-1011
Anna 46, John 24, Anna Maria 21, Georg 18			
Charles 15, Caroline 9			
CRON, Hermann	16	Neundorf	59-1017
CRONE, Wilhelm	46	Paderborn	58-0576
Antonia 40, Marie 19, Antonia 6, Anton 4			
Gertrud 3			
CRONEBERG, Emilie	21	Solingen	60-1141
Edward 17			
CROON, Marie	18	Bremen	60-0785
CROOT, Samuel	50	England	59-0384
CROWN, John	42	Adamaweiler	61-0107
Christ 21, Barbara 20			
CRUEGER, Hugo	35	Schweidnitz	58-0399
CRUSIUS, Ludwig	29	New York	58-0576
CUBITZKY, Anton	28	Munster	62-0758
Anna 26, Leonidas by			
CULVERWERE, J.	30	New York	62-1042
CURDTS, Carl	18	Buemmelse	60-1053
CURITZ, Paul	28	Magdeburg	62-1169
CUSTER, Jean	34	St.Gallen	62-1112
CYNADR, Joh.	36	Boehmen	61-0482
Rosina 30, Agnes 3			
CYRIACI, Heinr.	41	Gerstungen	60-0398
CZAPIWKSY, Lorenz	30	Danzig	62-0758
Antonia 24, Augustina by			
CZERIONSKY, Anton	19	Posen	57-0776
D'AGOSTINO, Luc.	30	Napoli	62-1042
DACHS, Hedwig	15	Ulm/Wuertt.	55-0628
DAECHE, Dorothea	48	Rotenburg	61-0779
Elisabeth 23			
DAEHLKE, Henry	26	Schoenhof	57-1148
Magn. 25			
DAENEMARK, Lina	17	Stotel	59-0535
DAENGES, Jacob	16	Munchhausen	61-0520
Philipp 20			
DAESER, Rosalie	46	Reichenberg	59-1036
Rosalie 16, Anna 14, Marie 8, Augusta 6			
Helene 9m			
DAEUFEL, Susanna	23	Baiern	59-0412
Kunigunde 17			
DAHL, Peter	42	Barmen	60-1141
DAHLEN, Johanna	18	Bruecken	58-0399
DAHLEN, v. H.	14	Frischlembach	59-0951
DAHLKE, Ferdinand	45	Griebnitz	58-0576
Therese 35, Caroline 13, Hulda 7			
Louis by			
DAHLMANN, Meta	29	New York	62-0467
DAHMANN, Gerhard	19	Gaste	56-1117
DAHMS, Heinrich	26	Hannover	57-0847
DAHN, George F.	28	New York	61-0520
DAHNBUSTEL, Jacob	29	Hannover	57-0847
DAHNKAMP, H.(m)	25	New York	61-0482
DAHNKEN, Metta	17	Hannover	62-0758
DAIKER, E.	20	Poll	62-0993
DAIMINGER, Joseph	35	Limbach	57-1407
Catharina 29			
DAIS, Elisabeth	20	Gruessen	57-0924
DALHOFF, Conrad	25	Borchhorst	59-0412
DALKEMEIER, Carl		Dubuque	61-0770
DALMEYER, Georg	39	Schlangesdorf	61-0478
DAMANN, H.(m)	17	Badbergen	62-0467
DAMBKE, Carl	17	Polichus	61-0897
DAMM, Heinrich	24	Obermaehler	57-0509
DAMMANN, Catharine	16	Westenholz	58-0563
DAMMANN, Friedrich	25	Westenholz	57-0847
Marie 19			
DAMMANN, H.	34	Bavaria	57-0847
DAMMENGIL, Victria	48	Worms	61-0897
DAMMEYER, H.(m)	32	Essern	62-0836
DAMMVAL, Henry	25	Osterode	57-0422
DANCKER, Diedr.	29	Bremen	59-0951
DANELIUS, Johanna	23	Stolp	60-0521
DANEMANN, Diedrich	23	Beverstadt	59-0412
DANGEL, Christine	15	Neckartheidin	60-0411
DANHOF, Johann	34	Unthuisen	62-0306
Lambert 30			
DANICKER, Theresia	22	Immendingen	60-1196
Jacob 2			
DANIEL, W.	55	Salzgitter	56-0527
Marg. 58			
DANIEL, William	20	US.	57-1148
DANIELE, Cavalhi	23	Italy	61-0167
DANK, Heinr. Chr.	35	Nordlida	59-0047
DANK, Peter	24	Effien	56-1044
DANKEN, Joseph	18	Hinfeld	57-0704
DANKERS, Jacob	25	Molsum	58-0563
Johann 23			
DANKERT, Babette	18	Bavaria	55-0628
DANKMEYER, Theodor	34	Baltimore	58-0925
DANNEBROCK, Marg.E	20	Wersen	62-0836
DANNENBERG, Elise	16	Hille	56-0411
DANNENBERG, Fanny	20	Trendelburg	62-1169
DANNENBERG, Joseph	19	Trendelberg	59-0477
DANNENFELD, Ferd.	39	New York	56-0723
Amalia 35			
DANNHARDT, Joh.A.	28	Hochstall/Bav	62-0608
DANNHAUER, Lucie	21	Bremen	58-0881
DANNHEIM, Heinrich	41	Bochel	56-0411
Dorothea 38, Dorothea 13, Henriette 10			
Wilhelm 5			
DANSING, Minna	16	Wansdorf	62-0730
DANT, Leonhard	24	Erleswind	59-0214
DANTER, P.S.	24	New York	56-1216
Clara 19			
DANTZE, Carl	35	US.	59-0951
DANZ, Georg	28	Neidershausen	58-0545
Christiane 56, A.Catharine 21			
Elizabeth 12, Gottfried 3m			
DANZEBLOCK, Anna	17	Wabern	62-0712
DANZIGER, Ad.(m)	17	Posen	60-0521
DANZIGER, J.(m)	35	New Orleans	62-0836
DAPPEN, Edward	26	Crab	57-1192
DAPRICH, Theodor	24	Niederassbach	55-0845
DARFOSS, Leonh.	25	Rosenbach	60-0785
Cath. 20, Johanna 3			
DARHAMMER, Gottlb.		Elbingen	59-0613
Anna 28			
DARINSKY, Daniel	37	Cincinati	61-1132
DARKELSCHERS, Anna	19	Greven	60-0785
DARTSCH, Wladislaw	17	Gnesen	61-0779
DASCHER, Bernh.	23	New York	58-0815
DASKE, H.L.A.(m)		Schonfeldbaum	56-0723
DASS, Conrad	16	Hesse-Cassel	56-0512
DATZEL, Maria Aug.	26	Furth	55-0812
DAUB, Caspar	48	Darmstadt	57-0654
Eliza 46, Anna 18, Johannes 13, Henry 11			
A.Eliza 9, (son) 1			
DAUB, Valentin	30	Treisa	57-0422
DAUBERMERKL, Ther.	22	Waltershof	61-0482
DAUBERT, Caroline	56	Dassel/Hann.	62-0608
DAUGHTY, K.(m)	19	England	60-0521
C.(m) 17			

NAME	AGE	RESIDENCE	YR-LIST
DAUKE, Dorette	16	San Francisco	59-0951
DAUME, Augusta	18	Salzdetfurth	56-1260
DAUN, Cath.	46	Weiss	60-0334
DAUPEL, Jos.	34	Thonhausen	61-0669
DAUPHIN, Dor.Chrlt	34	Wetzlar	57-0704
Wm.(Willing) 7			
DAUSCHEL, G.	17	Waltroth	62-1042
DAUZ, Marg.	19	Ramsthal	61-0669
DAVID, (f)	40	Cincinati	62-0836
DAVID, Paulina	30	Berlin	57-0961
DAVIDS, Christian	38	Hohenbostel	55-0630
DAVIDSMEYR, Hch.Ch	17	Osnabrueck	57-1148
DAVIDSOHN, D.(m)	30	Rotenberg/Hes	55-0544
DAVIDSOHN, John E.	60	Bremen	59-0477
Edgar 24			
DAWSON, J.J.	37	Southampton	59-0384
DAY, Theresia	29	St.Louis	59-1036
Laura 6			
DEBENKER, G.	26	France	62-0938
DEBUS, Elisabeth	16	Maibach	62-0401
DEBUS, Eliza	16	Bergholz	60-1141
DEBUS, Valentin	23	Borgholz/Hess	62-0608
Elisabeth 20, Elisabeth 19			
DECHANT, Leonhard	27	Bayern	56-1044
DECHER, Georg	32	Lehrbach	61-0779
DECK, Rudolph		Welzheim	59-0613
DECKER, Heinr. Wm.	30	Epe	56-1117
DECKER, Heinrich	12	Wallersheim	61-0779
DECKER, John T.	25	U.S.	55-1082
DECKERT, Friedrich	17	Bensheim	56-1216
DECORTIN, Stephen	23	Bavaria	59-1017
DECTER, William	45	Dresden	57-1148
Emily 25			
DEDE, Claus	21	Bremervoerde	56-1260
DEEHNE, Joh.	24	Elelsen	59-1036
DEESEN, v. G. (m)	26	New York	62-0467
Heinrich 16			
DEETJEN, (m)	33	Germany	62-0166
DEFELDER, Geo.Fr.	22	Grossburga	57-0924
DEGEN, Ludwig	25	Wengershausen	62-0879
DEGENER, Gotlieb	36	Bromberg	55-1082
DEGENFELDER, John	20	Wideberg	56-1011
Christine 16			
DEGENHARD, Christn	19	Holzhausen	59-0214
DEGENHARDT, J.(m)	53	St.Louis	61-0804
Franziska 53, Emma 13, Henriette 25			
DEGENHARDT, S.(f)	32	Leega	62-0730
DEGENHARDT, W.	33	Drensteinfurt	59-0990
(f) 33			
DEGENKOLBEN, J.Fr.	30	Nichtsheim	58-0563
DEGLEINSBACH, Cath	36	Schweina	56-0819
DEGNER, Claus	20	Lammstedt	56-1260
DEHLA, Kunigunda	56	Baiern	58-0399
DEHN, Andreas	28	Zaisenhausen	59-0412
Christiane 29, Caroline 5, Friedricke 1			
DEHN, Carl Friedr.	15	Zaisenhausen	59-0412
DEHN, Joh. Wilh.	20	Westerbeck/Ha	62-0608
DEHNE, Joh.	30	Osnabrueck	59-1036
DEHNE, Joh.Friedr.	40	Ankum	57-0924
Marie 50			
DEHNERT, Heinrich	15	Rittenau/Hess	55-0628
DEIBEL, Catharina	30	Lola/Hesse-D.	60-0371
DEIBEL, Elise	33	St.Louis	62-0836
Elise 11m			
DEICHER, Carl	19	Mannheim	59-0048
DEICHMULLER, Chrlt	21	Philippsthal	60-1032
DEICKE, August	28	Mehle	58-0399
DEICKE, Fr.	21	Bremervoerde	59-0990
DEICKE, Heinrich	17	Dexendorf	56-0723
DEIGMANN, Martha	41	Hebenhausen	56-1117
Elise 14, Wilhelm 7, Marie 4			
DEILEN, v.Heinrich	17	Tisselhode	59-0535
DEILER, Joseph	25	Memmingen	60-0334
DEIM, Johann	27	Coburg	57-0509
DEININGER, Robert	29	Hof	62-0879
DEISCH, Marie C.	59	Dobel	62-0836
DEISS, Elisabeth	56	Kreuzberg	56-0819
DEISS, Georg	20	Rohe	57-1026
DEISSE, H.	27	Ruppertsburg	59-1036
DEISTE, Carl	26	Spangenberg	55-1082
DEISTER, Wilh.	40	Horner/Hesse	62-0712
DEITSCH, Babette	31	New York	59-0048
Maria 29			
DEITZKE, Carl	32	Lauburg	57-0704
Augusta 27			
DEIVERMANN, Joh.	28	Louisville	56-1216
DELAIN, Georg	26	Chalan	59-0047
DELAIN, Lina	22	Muenzheim	59-0047
DELBRUEGGE, F.	20	Halle	56-0951
DELIUS, Charles	19	Bielefeld	60-0411
DELIUS, Emilie	26	New York	62-0836
DELKESKAMP, J.H.	28	Heithoefen	59-0384
DELLERE, Julius	18	Durmstedt	59-0951
DELLMANN, Catharin	30	Muenden	50-1017
DELLMER, Christine	17	Melsum	57-1122
DELVENDAHL, Josefa	27	Buchholz	59-0951
DELWER, Heinr.Died	23	Nesse	56-0819
DEMANDT, Joh.	26	Boehmen	61-0897
Marie 21, Johann 10m			
DEMAREZ, Fr. (m)	18	Friedrichstal	62-0730
DEMARIA, Bern.	45	Genna	61-1132
DEMARTEAU, Michel	26	Coeln	61-0167
DEMIAN, Wilhelm	52	Neuwied/Pr.	55-0628
DEMIAN, Wilhelm	54	Neuwied	57-1150
DEMME, Christian	20	Muehlhausen	57-1192
DEMMELMEYR, Sophie	29	Thalmessing	60-1196
DEMMERT, Carl Frdr	33	Sudeck	57-1026
DEMMERT, Christ.	28	Meyn	57-1026
DEMSEY, Anna	20	US.	62-0938
DEMUTH, Mathilde	17	Eulenberg	57-1407
DEMUTH, Moses	17	Rimbach	61-0804
DEMUTH, Nicolas	28	Luxemburg	61-0482
Clara 20			
DENGLER, Cath.Marg	28	Wuertemberg	57-0606
DENGLER, Franz	53	Konigswart	59-0613
Barbara 44, Joseph 21, Johannes 9			
Elisabeth 7			
DENGLER, G.F.(m)	22	Sulzdorf	61-0482
DENGLER, Joh.	29	Loebenstein	59-0384
DENGLER, Joh.Georg	20	Waldorf/Wuert	62-0342
DENGLER, Wm.	17	Erbach	62-0836
DENKER, Heinrich	20	Strichelt	59-0613
DENKER, M.	24	Herxwarden	62-0938
DENNER, Christian	35	Wiesbach/Wuer	55-0628
DENNER, Eva	24	Muennerstadt	58-0881
DENNER, Franz	29	Than/Bav.	61-0770
DENNINGER, Heinr.	21	Jagsthausen	59-1036
DENSTETTEN, Sophie	35	Maue	56-0589
DENTZ, Richard	12	Coeln	58-0885
DENZELMANN, Henry	31	St.Louis	62-0730
DEPKE, Gottfried	55	Wohlau	55-0812
DEPP, Marie	22	Ahlsfeld	61-0478
DEPPE, Anne M.	24	Beckum	61-0482
DEPPE, Heinrich	19	Grossberkel	56-0819
DEPPERMANN, Marie	21	Doehren	59-1036
DERBERG, Carl Fr.	17	Wiedersheim	57-0422
DERFUSS, Georg	35	Rosenbach	57-1113
DERHARD, Johann	18	Schluechtern	60-0521
DERKHEIM, Agnes	35	Germany	59-0951
DERN, Anton	23	Langgoens	55-0413
DERN, P.A.	59	Hausen	61-0804
Marie 52, Elisabeth 19, Christiane 16			
Heinrich 9, Georg 8			
DERRER, Heinrich	23	Hofheim	57-0606
DERRER, Joh.	13	Burgweisach	59-1036
DERSCH, Conrad		Halsdorf	56-0723
DERSCH, Ernst	30	Amonau	62-0879
Margaretha 35			
DERSCH, Joh. Georg	24	Gunzenhausen	55-0812
DERTER, Caspar	23	Bavaria	57-0847
DESENBERG, Mayer	26	Kalamazoo	62-1169
DESENDIE, H.(m)	29	France	61-0482
DESENIS, Joh.Phil.	17	Hohenhorst/CH	60-0429
Engel Marie 17			
DESSAUER, Friedr.	23	Aschaffenburg	59-0384
DESSELBERG, Wm.	16	Schwarzennach	57-1122

NAME	AGE	RESIDENCE	YR-LIST
DESSENER, Jan	18	Aschaffenburg	59-1036
DETERMANN, Adolph	23	Lengerich/Pr.	55-1238
DETERMANN, Anton	27	Neuenhaus	57-0961
Anna 2, (f) 9m			
DETERMANN, Carolin	24	Neuenkirchen	59-0214
DETERS, Elisabeth	40	Damme	57-0961
Charles 4, Mary 11m			
DETRICHE, Andree	31	Ampsen	59-0613
DETTMANN, Ferdin.	22	Dorlar	58-0545
DETTMAR, Heinrich	33	San Francisco	59-1036
DETTMAR, Pauline	20	Hextor	57-1407
DETTMER, Emilie	20	Hoexter	56-0723
DETTMER, Johann	24	Wulmsdorf	59-0047
DEUBNER, Christoph	56	Bischoffsrode	60-0398
DEUS, Franz	21	Rierenbach	62-0836
DEUSEN, C.W.	26	Wien	62-1112
Elisabeth 23, Anna 2			
DEUTZ, Anton	41	Lampertshause	59-0477
DEUTZ, Richard	12	Coeln	58-0885
DEVERMANN, Hermann	33	Grothe	62-0879
Johann H. 39			
DEYST, Barbara	31	Bonshausen	62-1042
Adam 3, Wm. 9m			
DHIEL, Adam	16	Curhessen	60-0371
DIBEL, J.	47	Herdelsbach	56-0512
Christina 19			
DICK, Adolph	15	Ulm	60-1141
DICKEL, Heinrich P	25	Romrod/Hessen	62-0608
DICKERT, Marg.	18	Sandlofs	57-0654
Cath. 16			
DICKHAUT, Marie	32	New York	62-0730
Johann 7, Marie 6m			
DICKMANN, Hinrich	40	Rehren/Hann.	57-0847
Hinrich 15			
DIDIER, Nicol.	34	Havre	62-0836
DIEBOLD, Ann Marie	38	Baden	61-0167
Ludwig 13, Emma 12, Franz 9, Eduard 7			
Carl 4			
DIEBOLD, Ursula	24	Hechingen	57-1192
DIECK, Marie	17	Stondorf	61-0669
DIECKHOEMER, Heinr	18	Bielefeld	57-0447
DIECKMANN, Carolne	20	Versmold	56-1044
DIECKMANN, Heinr.	28	Spahden/Hann.	62-0608
DIECKMANN, Ilsabe	23	Holsen	56-0723
DIECKMANN, Sophie	59	Menslage	57-1026
Anna 24			
DIECKMANN, Wm.	59	Westendorf	60-0334
Wilhelmine 51, Christ. 16, Ernestine 9			
Heinr. 7			
DIEDEL, Herm.	22	Greiz	59-0384
DIEDEL, Louis	15	Kreutz	59-1017
DIEDEL, Marie	24	Cassel	62-0938
DIEDOLPH, Susanne	31	Lindheim	58-0576
Charlotte 7, Marie 3, Wilhelm by			
DIEDRICH, Adam	26	Koenig	62-0836
DIEDRICH, Barbara	39	Gemuend	59-0214
Benedikt 5			
DIEDRICH, Daniel	21	Homberg	56-1204
DIEDRICH, Friedr.	30	Hannover/Han.	55-1238
DIEDRICH, Georg	19	Genzungen	58-0576
DIEDRICH, Joh.Conr	59	Lichtenau	58-0925
Anna M. 56			
DIEGMANN, Carl Jos	30	Heuthen	57-0606
DIEHL, Adam	16	Curhessen	60-0371
DIEHL, Conrad	32	Muenster	62-0111
Marg. 30, (daughter) 9m			
DIEHL, Helene	22	Alsfeld	59-0412
DIEKAMP, Heinr.	27	Albertloh	59-0951
DIEKER, Georg	20	Wehr	62-0232
DIEKERT, Barth.	20	Almus	59-0047
DIEKERT, Cornelius	35	Grosstaibach	59-0047
DIEKKRUGER, Sophie	26	Wohe	57-0776
DIEKMANN, H.J.	19	Westendorf	59-0384
DIEKMANN, Joh. Fr.	16	Lehe	56-0629
DIEKOP, Catharina	18	Neuwied/Pr.	55-0628
DIEL, Christiane	23	Bavaria	62-0758
DIEL, Sophie	24	Villingen	59-0214
DIEMAC, v. Aug.	51	Philadelphia	59-1036

NAME	AGE	RESIDENCE	YR-LIST
Marie 17, Emilie 13, Wm. 11			
DIEMAR, Francis	36	Rasdorf	57-0961
Johanna 37			
DIEMER, Joh.	18	Bieringen	61-0482
DIEMER, Johann	24	Hohenstein	58-0815
DIENSTBACH, Heinr.	14	Alsfeld	56-0951
DIENZELNAR, Heinr.	26	New York	58-0815
DIEPHAL, Friedrich	25	Messlingen	57-1122
DIEPHOLZ, Wilh'mne	10	Sulingen	56-0819
DIERHOFF, Augusta	26	Messfeld	57-0509
Eva M. 35			
DIERING, H.J.	59	Baltimore	59-0477
H.J.Ludw. 15			
DIERK, Herm.	33	San Francisco	58-0815
DIERKS, Gertrud	64	Ibbenbuehren	60-0521
DIERKS, Gretchen	28	Emden	60-1196
DIERKS, Saake	20	Wisers	58-0815
DIERS, Harm	69	Ruttel	57-1148
Henry 41, Anna 41, Armand 12, Friedrich 9			
Anna 4			
DIERS, Herm.Heinr.	16	Wartenburg	57-1113
DIERSING, Heinrich	23	Damme	59-0214
DIESSEL, Caroline	20	Nichtsheim	58-0563
DIESTLER, Conrad	39	Fuerth	60-1032
DIETERICH, Johann	44	Unt.Stuerming	61-0478
Barbara 37			
DIETERLE, Gottlieb	28	Ludwigsburg	62-0342
Maria Cath. 30			
DIETMANN, Friedr.	13	Dehlen	59-0535
DIETRICH, Christne	20	Havel/Bav.	55-0628
DIETRICH, Friedr.	19	Cassel/Hess.	55-0628
DIETRICH, Friedr.	58	Rothenburg	60-0521
DIETRICH, Henry	25	New York	59-1036
DIETRICH, J. Claus	56	Hitzerode	56-0723
Wilhelmine 41			
DIETRICHS, H.(m)	29	Wattenhausen	56-0723
Heinrich 3			
DIETSCH, Joh. Wmne		Netschka	62-0983
DIETSCH, P.W.(m)	41	Chicago	61-0897
DIETZ, August	24	Eichsen	56-0512
DIETZ, C.	57	Siegenhausen	62-0993
Car. 22			
DIETZ, Conrad	23	Steinheim	56-0589
E. 16			
DIETZ, Emma	18	New York	62-1042
Rosalie 17			
DIETZ, Ernst	19	Jagsthausen	62-0879
Charlotte 20			
DIETZ, Ferdinand	52	Wilhelmsdorf	61-0478
DIETZ, Franz	34	Kleinerstadt	61-0482
DIETZ, Friedr.	37	Vochawind/Bav	60-0429
Elisabeth 38, Sophia 12, Philip 10			
Johann 3, Friedrich 9m			
DIETZ, Georg	13	Wilhelmsdorf	61-0478
DIETZ, Georg	28	Liech	61-0669
DIETZ, Johann	31	Hirschfeld	55-0845
Catharine 34			
DIETZ, Johann	17	Gleimesheim	55-0845
Friedr. 17			
DIETZ, Johann	33	Ostheim	60-1141
Augusta 18, Hansford 9			
DIETZ, Nicolaus	20	Neukirchen	60-0533
DIETZ, Wilh.Dan.	24	Eberbach	56-1117
DIETZE, Carl Oswld	28	Dresden	56-0819
DIETZE, Friedrich	30	Rehsen	56-1117
DIETZEL, Andreas	27	Reppendorf	56-0847
DIETZEL, Margareta	26	Wengershausen	58-0563
DIETZEL, Valentin	59	Strut	62-0306
Elisabeth 58, Franz 32, Catharina 4			
Eva 28, Joseph 9m			
DIETZOLD, F.R.	19	Teich-Wolfram	62-0993
DIEZEL, Catharine	20	Eringshausen	61-0478
DIFFANE, Friedr.	20	Stuttgart	60-1196
DIHL, Catharina	34	Wilsdorf	55-0812
DIHLER, Jost	31	Beilstein	55-0630
DILCHERT, Daniel	18	Gudensberg	55-0932
DILCHERT, Elisab.	24	Hadamar	57-0754
DILGER, Anna	24	Illerrieden	61-0804

NAME	AGE	RESIDENCE	YR-LIST
DILGER, Robert	27	Illrieden	60-0521
DILL, Anna	23	Eckersdorf	61-0520
DILL, Joh.Georg	34	Eichenheim	59-0372
DILLEMUTH, Jacob	23	Hainchen	56-0723
DILLMANN, Agatha	18	Wiesenthaid	59-0214
Babette 22			
DIMAND, Alois	22	Buchau	60-0334
DINER, Maria	16	Suntheim/Wuer	55-1238
DINGFELDER, Sara	16	Uhlfeld	60-0521
DINKEL, Margaretha	36	Untermerzbach	60-1053
DINKELDAY, Heinr.	40	Konitz	61-0482
DINKENBILLER, Joh.	34	Aufsess	61-0669
DINOECKE, Joh.	61	Brackel	56-0512
Eliza 60, Wilhelm 16, Anna 18, Adolph			
DINTRUP, John	36	Werne	57-0422
DIPEL, Adam	25	Niederbeishm.	55-0630
Elisabeth 19			
DIPFEL, Jacob	28	Milwaukee	62-1042
DIPPEL, Anna	44	Schiffelbach	59-0535
Daniel 20, Catharine 16, Elisabeth 7			
DIPPEL, Eduard	18	Bremen	55-0634
DIPPEL, Jost	54	Lensel	56-0847
DIPPOLD, Kunigunde	18	Lochow	60-0521
DIPPOLD, Margareta	18	Zeckendorf/Bv	60-0429
DIRKS, Ant.Fr.Gun.	23	Hucksiel	57-1148
DIRKS, Johann	20	Osterode	56-0819
DIRKS, Johann	19	Borgholz/Pr.	60-0622
DIRKS, Jules	24	Bevergen	60-0411
DIRKS, Valentin	24	Elberberg	60-0411
DIRKSEN, Herm.	34	Aschendorf	59-0214
DISCHINGER, Cath.	53	Rielinghausen	59-0477
Anna M. 18, Jacob Friedr 15, Jos.Gottl. 9			
DISCHNER, Geo.Alb.	24	Obermassing	57-0754
DISDORE, Delphine	37	France	62-0166
DISSEL, Franz	47	Hoechst	58-0885
DISTELMANN, Emilie	20	Berlin	56-1216
DISTLER, Lorenz	15	Westheim	61-0520
DITE, Ferdinand	16	Boehmen	62-0001
Maximilian 14			
DITERS, Anna M.	28	Oberhaugstedt	56-0951
DITTERICH, Gg.Fr.	24	Forchheim	57-1192
DITTMANN, Agatha	18	Wiesenthaid	59-0214
Babette 22			
DITTMANN, Caspar	30	Zeilitzheim	57-1067
DITTMANN, Heinrich	24	Weilburg/Nass	62-0608
DITTMANN, Henry	25	Hannover	56-1011
DITTMANN, Marie	35	Eibelstadt	59-0477
DITTMAR, A.(m)	24	Blankenheim	62-0232
DITTMAR, Christine	24	Oldisleben	55-0630
DITTMAR, Elisabeth	19	Holzhausen	59-0214
DITTMAR, Hannchen	24	Rottenburg	60-0429
DITTMAR, Henriette	21	Naila	62-0730
DITTMAR, Philipina	29	New York	62-1112
Catharine 9			
DITTMER, Christian	40	Stettin	55-0812
Caroline 38, Caroline 28, August 13			
Emilie 10, Heinrich 7, Franz 6, Emilie 6			
Emil 4, Albert 2			
DITTMER, Johann	1	Rieda	62-0730
DITTMER, Louise	34	Oberstetten	62-0730
Marie 38, Sophie 30, Friedrich 9			
DITTMERS, Friedr.	26	Frillsdorf	56-1117
DIZINGER, Joh.	40	Wittenberg	62-0758
Magdalena 50			
DLAG, Joh.	32	Bensheim	62-0232
Sophie 27, Heinr. 27			
DOBBERT, Wilhelm	26	Carzig	57-0776
Sophie 23			
DOBLOG, Carl	18	Gr.Schmoele	56-1117
Sophie 15, Dorothea 12			
DOBRENTEI, Marie	28	Tyrnau	59-0477
Adelbert 7, Edward 3			
DOCKENBACH, Elise	23	Geden	61-0897
DODGE, Robert	28	London	62-0938
DOEBEL, Hartmann	45	Berka	60-0398
Elisabeth 17, Adam 9, Magdalena 6			
DOEBEL, Joh.	54	Berka	60-0398
Catharine 49, Hartmann 24			
DOEBLER, Simon	32	Katzenberg	57-1192
Magdalena 29, Jacob 8			
DOEGELMAN, Leopold	39	Burgstal	56-0847
Friedericke 33			
DOEHLEN, Anna M.	20	Dorum	56-1044
DOEHLER, Albert	25	Schleusingen	62-0401
DOEHLER, Carl	29	Clausthal	56-1216
DOEHNER, Wm.	33	Cronenburg	59-0951
DOELEN, v. F. (m)	28	Spickerneufld	62-0836
DOELER, Elisa	19	Rossdorf/Pr.	60-0622
DOELL, Cath.	24	Marburg	60-0334
DOELL, Elise	50	Altenberg	60-0334
Johanna 22			
DOELL, Johannes		Villingen	57-1067
DOELLE, John Georg	46	Schwarzburg	60-0411
Henriette 47, Fr. Charles 16			
Ch. Edward 5, Charles 15			
DOELLER, Barbara	59	Iphofen	60-1141
Christina 30, Mary 3			
DOELTZ, Ernst	32	Goslar	57-0436
DOENELT, Julius	23	Reinbach	57-0654
DOENJES, Chr.	17	Frankenau	56-0723
DOEPP, August	18	Rodenburg	60-0533
DOEPPEL, Joh.Nic.	27	Culmbach	56-1044
DOERBAUM, J.F.	40	Bremen	62-0938
DOERFLER, Johannes	40	Hirschfeld	57-0704
Margaretha 31			
DOERIES, Henry C.	44	Oehrsen	56-1117
Caroline 44, Anna 16, Wilhelm 10			
Christ. 7, Lina 4			
DOERING, A.	20	Elberfeld	59-0613
DOERING, Carl	26	Illinois	62-0342
Louise 21			
DOERING, Heinr.	19	Altendorf	56-0629
DOERING, Johannes	49	Altendorf	57-0754
Anna 48, Sophie 23, Marie 18, Wilhelm 15			
Johannes 10			
DOERNAU, J.Wm.	24	Beverstedt	59-0477
Sophie 20			
DOERNER, Joh.	21	Hildesheim	56-1216
DOERNTE, Ernst	30	Bartshausen	62-0608
DOERR, Elisabeth	17	Dorfgill	62-0111
DOERR, Heinr.	51	Rueddinghause	59-0951
Marie 52			
DOERRINKEL, Friedr	36	New York	59-0048
DOERSCH, Anna Gert	30	Halsdorf	57-0606
Catharina 6			
DOERSTOW, Max	27	Roldisleben	61-0779
DOESCHER, Carsten	16	Ringstedt	59-1036
DOESCHER, Fr'drke.	24	Dorum	58-0306
DOESCHER, Friedr.	25	New York	57-1150
DOESCHER, Hch.Fr'd	14	Nesse	61-0520
DOESCHER, Heinrich	16	Ringstedt	59-0613
DOESCHER, Mary	45	New York	62-1169
Anna 7			
DOESE, Ernst	46	Neu Wuhrow	56-1260
Wilhelmine 34, Wilhelm 11, Albert 6			
Henriette 4, Rudolph 3m			
DOESEKER, Gerhard	21	Koehlen	56-1117
DOFT, J.H.(m)	19	Kederasphe	61-0682
DOHE, Joh. Bernh.	34	Schale	56-0819
Georg 7			
DOHM, Emilie	31	New York	59-0384
Sophie 40, Caroline 1			
DOHMEYER, Heinrich	45	Langenholz	59-0535
DOHMSTREICH, F.(m)	59	Alsmouth	61-1132
DOHRMANN, Diedr.	22	Buchel	59-0535
DOHRMANN, Fr'drke.	18	Bremen	61-0779
DOHRMANN, Georg	20	Bremen	56-1216
DOHRMANN, Gerhard	30	Rumeln	61-0482
Marg. 30, Marg. 4, Anna 9m, Wilhelm 72			
DOHRMANN, J.H.	32	Narten	57-1192
DOHRMANN, Philp'ne	21	Reichenberg	56-0847
DOKTOR, Thomas	33	Budweis/Boehm	62-0608
Anna 35, Anna 4			
DOLD, Maria Eva	52	Freyburg	58-0604
Gustav Adolf 18, Josephine 15			
DOLEISCH, Joseph	30	Boehmen	61-0930

NAME	AGE	RESIDENCE	YR-LIST
Anna 30, Franz 9m			
DOLES, Johann	37	Haibach	60-1053
Sara 37, Nicolaus 8, Barbara 5, Joseph 4			
Margaretha by			
DOLEZAL, Rud.	16	Boehmen	62-1112
DOLGEMAR, C.(m)	25	Warendorf	62-0836
DOLGER, Peter	36	Niedenberg/Bv	60-0429
DOLL, George	40	Philadelphia	60-0785
DOLLER, John Mich.	24	New York	59-0372
DOLLINGER, Heinr.	24	Wisconsin	59-0613
DOLPHINE, Elise	27	Halle	56-0354
DOLZZN, Johann	60	Prussia	62-0758
Marianne 52, Joseph 22, Carl 19			
Victoria 16, Pauline 12			
DOMIANNS, Carsten	49	Fallingen	57-1148
Mary 40, Engel 9, Emily 3			
DOMINIQUE, Ch.	26	Wolpiano	59-0535
DOMKE, August	28	Moabit	60-0533
Julie 26, Alexander 1			
DOMKE, Martin	39	Posen	57-0776
Christine 38, Julie 5, August 3			
DOMMES, Fr.	29	Dorste	62-0993
DOMS, Christoph	23	Jankendorf	56-0819
DOMSCH, Gotth.Hch.	46	Bautzen	57-0924
DOMSCHKE, Louis	23	Klitten/Pr.	55-0628
DONATH, Gottf.	33	Forisville	61-0107
DONECKE, William	30	Weimar	57-0654
Friedricke 25, Rosalie 4			
DONGES, Heinrich	25	Bleichenbach	57-0924
DONHAUSER, Kunig.	44	Unterimmendrf	61-0770
Elisabeth 21			
DONNER, Christ.A.	26	Brockenauland	60-1053
DONNER, Elisabeth	23	Guenthers	61-0482
DONNER, Louis	32	Greiz	56-1216
Adrienne 28, Henry 11m			
DOPHEIDE, A.	34	Halle	56-0354
DOPPELMEYER, Mayer	48	New York	59-1017
DORA, Elisabeth	62	Graefenberg	55-1238
Louise 24			
DOREY, K.(m)	24	England	60-0521
DORMANN, Ernst	18	Vahlsen	60-1032
DORMANN, Heinrich	16	Kamschaide	62-1169
DORN, Conrad	28	Brugenau	62-0306
DORN, Maria	19	Oberzell	60-0429
DORN, Martin	19	Hattersheim	56-1204
DORN, Meier	15	Tachau	58-0885
DORNBERGER, Fr'dke	35	Berka	57-0422
DORNBUSCH, E.J.	31	Bastede	59-0214
DORNBUSCH, H.	38	Huelshagen	61-0804
Anna 34, Engel 2, Anna 8, Dorothea 7			
Catharina 5, Wilhelm 3, Heinrich 11m			
DORNBUSCH, H.(m)	25	Huelshagen	61-0804
DORNENBUSCH, Marie	22	Wessum	59-0951
DORRIES, Wilhelmne	52	Dankelsheim	62-0938
Amalia 19, Heinrich 15			
DORSCH, August	29	Hessen	60-1053
Amalie 21			
DORSCHKY, Christne	28	Bayern	56-1044
DORSCHNER, Wilhmne	42	Friedland	56-0819
Wilhelmine 22, Bertha 21, Therese 20			
Friederike 18, Carl 16			
DORSSEN, Maria	23	Leeste	62-0938
DORSTEWITZ, Max	33	Jaegersdorf	61-0930
DORTMANN, Ernstine	30	New York	60-0521
Henny 4			
DOSEDEL, Wenzel	53	Boehmen	61-0482
Anna 26, Johann 14			
DOSS, Carl Friedr.	16	Zeulenroda	62-0879
DOTERS, Joh.	38	Oldenburg	57-1150
DOTTER, Johann	29	Wambach	60-1196
DOTZERT, Cath.	18	Lauterbach	59-0990
DOUBROWSKI, Sophie	19	Boehmen	62-1042
DOUTHEIL, John	30	Neukirchen	57-0422
DRACH, v. Wilhelm	24	Ellershausen	57-0754
DRACK, Simon	59	Wertheim	60-0334
Barbara 66			
DRACKE, Adolph	34	Valbruch	57-0021
Sophie 24, Christian 37			

NAME	AGE	RESIDENCE	YR-LIST
DRALLE, Charles	23	Bergkirchen	56-1011
DRALLE, Sophie	26	Neuenbrueck	62-0836
DRANDORF, Albert	21	Altenburg	60-0533
DRANGENSTEIN, Gert	22	Schlierbach	58-0563
DRATHMANN, W.F.	31	Bremen	62-1042
DRAVE, August	48	Dittenburg	62-0938
Marg. 47			
DRDA, Franz	29	Boehmen	62-1112
Anna 35, Franz 5, Joseph 11m			
DRECHLER, Julius	27	Braunsdorf	60-0533
DRECHOTER, An.Mary	22	Moosbach	58-0563
DRECHSEL, C.W.	46	Thalheim	61-0716
Wihlelmine 40, Christiane 9			
Heinrich W. 3			
DRECHSLER, Christ.	22	Cassel	55-0634
Conrad 18			
DRECKMEYER, Marie	29	Linne	56-0589
DRECKSCHMIDT, Fr'z	52	Enniglohe	56-0723
Bruno 11			
DREGE, Heinrich	36	Bomte	59-0613
DREHER, Fr.(m)	27	Stuttgart	62-0111
DREIFUSS, Caecilie	21	Buttenhausen	60-0521
DRENGBERG, Marie	38	Eimbeck	62-1169
DRESCHE, Barbara	26	Gestungshausn	56-0512
DRESCHER, Ad.	25	Rimba	61-0669
DRESCHER, Gabriel	25	Muenchberg	61-0682
Margaretha 26, Margaretha 6m			
DRESCHER, Ph.	36	Louisville	62-0467
Barbara 23, Valentin 9			
DRESSEL, C.	34	Eishausen	62-0993
DRESSEL, Heinrich	32	Grossmannsrod	61-0478
DRESSEL, M.	35	Voilsdorf	61-0478
Christiane 34, Laura 10, Carl 7, Rosa 8m			
DRESSEL, M.M.E.	14	RoemhilD	57-0606
DREUS, Christian	36	Neu Luboza	56-0629
Wilhelmine 34, Carl 9, Regine 7			
Augusta 5, Wilhelm 6m			
DREVES, Anton	29	Oenhausen	59-0214
DREVES, Irenaus	37	Warendorf	58-0885
DREWES, Anna	19	Bremen	59-1036
DREWES, Heinrich	42	Bremervoerde	56-0632
Caroline 26			
DREWES, Maria	33	Bremervoerde	56-0632
DREWES, Rosine	33	Baiern	59-0412
Catharina 3			
DREYER, Carl	36	Petershagen	62-0836
DREYER, Chr.Fr.	30	St.Louis	62-0166
DREYER, Christian	43	Halvesdorf	62-0983
DREYER, Ernestine	21	Lickwegen	61-0482
DREYER, Fr.(m)	34	Erichshagen	60-1161
DREYER, Fr.(m)	26	Brake	62-0111
DREYER, Heinr.Conr	27	Sarstedt	56-0629
DREYER, Heinrich	49	Ostenholz	58-0563
Christine 50, Heinrich 25, Dorothea 23			
Dorothea 3, Heinrich 1			
DREYER, Maria Elis	58	Vitzerode	57-1026
DREYER, Paul	28	Prenzlau	57-1026
DREYER, Rosa	22	Koenigsheim	60-1141
DREYER, Therese	41	Wetzel	62-0983
DREYER, William	10	Wetzel	62-0983
Mary 6, Franz 2			
DRIESLER, Cathar.	36	Drehle	57-0654
DRINCKE, Francis	24	Forstentrup	57-0422
DRISCH, Joh.Christ	29	Urbach	62-0879
Carl 38, Marie Elisab 43, Friedr.Andr. 12			
Anna Fr'drke 11, Doro.Fr'drke 8			
Carl Conrad 5, Emma Augusta 3			
DRIUCKE, Francis	24	Forstentrup	57-0422
DROBRUECK, Joseph	26	Kollin	57-1113
Catharina 24			
DROEGE, Carl	30	Ottenstein	57-0606
DROEGE, Henriette	36	Bomte	59-0613
Louise 9, Heinrich 7, Engel 5, Marie 3			
Elise 9m			
DROEGE, Louise	19	Hille	56-0411
DROELLER, Johann	30	Endorf/Pruss.	56-0632
DROST, Fried.	21	Bremen	59-0214
DROST, Joh. Nicol	43	Coburg	55-0634

NAME	AGE	RESIDENCE	YR-LIST
DROST, Wm.	26	Bremen	62-1042
DROSTE, Herm.	24	Voiden	61-0167
DROSTE, July	20	Rinteln	57-1026
DRUCKGRAF, Ferd.	25	Schuppinnen	61-0107
DRUECK, Siegm.	30	Kurz	56-0723
DRUMMER, J.	28	Leutenbach	59-0477
DRUSEL, Daniel	56	Perlberg	58-0563
DRUSSEL, Margareta	53	Schwarzburg	58-0399
DRZEIVOZNIAK, Jos.	28	Posen	58-0399
Josephine 22, Johann 32, Wilhelmine 25			
DUBBER, Joh.H.	40	Haren	57-1067
DUBBERS, H.(m)	18	Brooklyn	62-0467
DUBISAR, N.	42	Nemschuetz	62-0993
C. 42, J. 16, M. 11			
DUBOEG, M.	34	England	62-1169
DUCHINE, Alexander	23	France	60-0334
DUCKWITZ, Arnold F	22	New York	62-1112
DUDENHAUS, Friedr.	48	Wottingerode	60-0785
Wm. 38, Helena 16, Wm. 13, Wilhelmine 8			
DUECKER, Peter	15	Flogeln	58-0563
DUEDER, Nicolaus	23	Asmushausen	57-1280
DUEFFNER, Sabine	44	Schonoch/Bav.	60-0622
Antonia 13			
DUEHL, Louise	15	Braunschweig	59-0384
DUEHLMEYER, H.W.	19	Niedernholz	56-0589
DUELFER, Henry	28	Spiescappel	60-0411
Anna Cath. 25			
DUELFER, L.(m)	25	Holzminden	61-0804
DUELL, Wm.	21	Frankfurt	59-0477
DUEMKE, Heinrich	29	Berlin	61-0930
DUENBOSTEL, Fr.	26	Grindau	62-0938
DUENEL, Conrad	58	Heinum	56-0629
Hanne 48, Hanne 17, Carl 14, August 11			
DUENK, John	39	Milwaukee	59-1036
DUENKLAU, Margrete	50	Heringhausen	60-1032
Friederike 17, Elisabeth 14, Heinrich 9			
Casper 7			
DUENNINGER, Georg	26	Lumbach/Bav.	57-0754
DUENSING, Louis	23	Mariensee	57-1192
W. 16, Henriette 16			
DUERING, Cath.	19	Hosfeld	60-0334
DUERING, Fr.	27	Bremen	62-1042
Elisabeth 21, Friedricke 9m			
DUERKER, Heinrich	15	New York	59-0951
DUERKER, Peter	20	Herborn	55-0630
(female) 18			
DUERR, Cath.	48	Lochingen	61-0669
DUERR, Catharina	21	Marburg/K-Hes	62-0342
DUERR, Friedrich	17	Madorf/K-Hess	62-0342
DUESTERHOEFT, Chr.	37	Posen	58-0399
Wilhelmine 27, Augusta 4, Wilhelmine 9m			
DUETHORN, Michael	35	Zeckendorf/Bv	60-0429
DUETTMANN, Heinr.	27	Osnabrueck	59-0372
DUEVEL, Mina	35	Peine	57-1280
Caroline 11, Fritz 10, Marie 8			
Catharina 70			
DUFOUR, Sebastian	45	France	62-0938
Josephine 37, Marie 7, Luciel 3			
DUFT, Ernst	30	Erfurt	62-1169
DUGMANN, Martha	41	Hebenhausen	56-1117
Elise 14, Wilhelm 7, Marie 4			
DUHNE, Trina	16	Achim	55-0634
DUHNKE, Wilhelm	26	Danzig	56-0951
DUHR, Lon.	30	Selchow	57-1148
DUIS, Friedrich	56	Oldendorf	57-0422
Trientje 50, Himpe 16, Volkert 14			
Vocke 12, Gesche 6			
DUISBURG, E.(m)	28	New York	59-0214
DULION, Leon	17	Italy	62-0166
DULKES, Bernhard H	29	Legden/Pr.	60-0622
DULLINGER, Xaver	28	Sheboygan	57-0961
DUMCKE, Peter	34	Langenbergen	56-0723
DUMOULIN, Adeline	23	France	62-0166
DUMPROFF, Andr.	36	Steinfeld/Bav	60-0429
Bar.(Wunner) 31			
DUMSTORF, Anton	24	Cloppenburg	58-0306
DUNDES, M.	72	England	62-0938
DUNHEIM, Christine	19	Kolleda	57-0447

NAME	AGE	RESIDENCE	YR-LIST
DUNKEL, Marie	8	Tiedelsen	61-0478
DUNKELBERG, Edward	23	Baden	60-1053
DUNKER, L. Ad. (m)	16	Selsingen	61-0897
DUNKER, Minna	29	Nienburg	55-1082
DUNKRAK, Sophia	18	Dedendorf	57-0961
DUNREG, Otto Louis	21	Laar	59-0951
Huldine 27			
DUPATZ, Jos.	35	St.Louis	59-0477
Anna 28, Elsbeth 7, K. 6, Anna 9			
DUPPER, Peter	32	Kistany	57-1416
Margarethe 26, Peter 3, Max. 2			
DUQUEMARE, Alfr.	24	France	62-0467
DURAND, Dorothee	28	Hannover	57-1148
Dora 4			
DURENBERGER, Cath.	18	Frankenthal	59-0951
DURHOFF, Bernhard	25	Oelde	58-0306
DURKINGHAUS, Crlne	18	Boston	58-0815
DURR, Julius Wm.	26	Tunnshewalde	57-1416
DUSENBERG, (f)	19	Eimbeck	62-1042
DUSK, Joh.	42	Bohemia	60-1161
Anna 43, Marie 14, Mathias 12			
Anastasia 3, Franz 1			
DUTE, Anna Maria	22	Rockensuess	60-0533
DUTHORN, Marg.	16	Steinfeld	57-1113
Johannes 37, Marg. 24, Marg. 2			
DUTINE, Catharine	22	Stockstadt	60-0398
DUX, Elisabeth	26	Volkmarsen/He	62-0608
DVORAK, Wenzel	32	Pento Zahosie	56-1011
Rosalia 40, John 6, Antonia 4			
DWERSTEG, Victor	23	Borghorst	59-0951
EAFRINGEN, L.	24	Bavaria	59-0214
EBBING, Gustav	33	Borken	59-0477
EBE, Petrus	25	Griermingen	60-0521
EBEL, Dorothea	25	Bremen	55-1082
EBEL, Gustav	20	Curhessen	60-0371
EBELICH, Carl	37	Rolfshagen	59-0372
Sophia 33, Sophia 9, Caroline 5			
Wilhelmine 2			
EBELING, August	25	Lauenfoerde	59-0214
EBELING, Georg	20	Oldenburg	58-0576
EBENHOCK, Marie	31	Wuerzburg	58-0604
Carl 6, Franz 5			
EBENSTEIN, Loeb	39	Poland	62-0712
EBER, Wilhbert	13	Merbach	62-0306
EBERBACH, Jacob	22	Laufen/Wuertt	60-0429
EBERDING, Otto	29	Luedersfeld	56-0589
EBERHACK, Ulrich	21	Rangen/Bav.	60-0429
EBERHARD, Ernst	24	Wensdorff	56-1216
EBERHARD, Wm.	55	Altensielbach	55-0413
Louise 24			
EBERHARDT, Henriet	39	Langenhausen	57-0654
Lina 20, Udo 16, Hulda 13, Doska 9			
Arnold 6			
EBERHARDT, Regina	25	Detmold	57-0422
EBERHARDT, Wilhelm	15	Marburg	60-0334
EBERLE, Caecilie	32	Wuerttemberg	60-0411
EBERLEIN, Wilhelm	20	Wirtenberg	57-0776
Susanne 50, Sophie 27, Caroline 17			
Ernst 5			
EBERLING, Carl	16	Nidda	60-1141
EBERLING, Valentin	35	Eich/Hessen	60-0622
EBERS, August	17	Hannover	57-1192
EBERS, Tamme	28	Odendorf	57-0422
EBERT, Christ. W.	22	Goldhausen	56-1117
EBERT, Dorothea	16	Vochawind/Bav	60-0429
EBERT, Heinr.	39	Eisenach	61-0107
Franz 20			
EBERT, Heinrich	17	Greiz	57-0509
EBERT, Joh.	16	Betziersdorf	59-1036
EBERT, Ludwig	38	Langenburg	57-0422
EBERT, Mich.	28	Walkershausen	61-0482
EBERT, Sebald	22	Eisenach	60-1032
EBERWEIN, Balthas.	22	Ilstein	56-1216
EBERWEIN, Wilhelm	17	Ulm/Wuertt.	60-0622
EBINGER, Adam	22	Backnang	57-0422
EBSTEIN, Bertha	23	Fulda	60-0785
Israel 14			
EBSTEIN, Marie	24	Untersigginge	61-0716

NAME	AGE	RESIDENCE	YR-LIST
Louise 32, Therese 29			
EBSTEIN, Rosi	22	Kasalup	61-0716
ECHER, Louisa	17	Goettingen	56-0512
ECHLER, Elisabeth	19	Hessen	60-0371
ECHTERLING, Freidr	32	WInsebeck	59-0214
Marie 26, Anton 6, Fritz 5, Therese 3			
ECK, Conrad	22	Hinjerath	61-0682
ECK, Conrad	25	Bischoffsthro	59-0214
ECK, Friedrich	24	Steinfeld	60-1053
ECK, Margaretha	51	Thalmessing	60-1196
Anna 24, Leonhard 15, Maria 14, Sophie 12			
Carl 11, Walburga 5, Catharina 4			
ECK, Peter	28	Erfurt	59-0477
ECK, Sophia	26	Culmbach	57-0422
ECK, Wm.	20	Struth	62-0401
ECKARD, Henriette	59	Philadelphia	58-0881
ECKARDT, Caroline	19	Wahmbeck	60-0334
ECKARDT, Conr.	17	Kurhessen	57-0555
ECKARDT, Conrad	37	Kurhessen	56-1044
Martha 27, Johannes 9, Anna Cathar. 7			
Joh.Heinrich 3, Peter 3m			
ECKARDT, John	30	Naida	60-0411
ECKARDT, Therese	32	Philadelphia	62-0730
ECKART, Chr.	19	Metze	56-0411
ECKBERT, J. Bernh.	28	Leer	62-0712
ECKE, Friedrich	25	Ziegelrode/Pr	61-0770
ECKE, Maria	59	Ballenstedt	62-0712
ECKEL, Conrad	50	US.	59-0047
ECKEL, Otto	23	Buedingen	58-0563
ECKELMANN, G.H.	25	Vehrte	57-0654
ECKELMEYER, Cath.L	19	Westercappeln	57-1192
ECKELS, J.F.	22	Stennebergen	58-0399
ECKENBRECHER, Elis	20	Roemhild	57-0606
ECKENBURGER, Emma	20	Roemhild/Sax.	61-0770
ECKERT, Andreas	24	Bruchsal	62-0712
Martin 23			
ECKERT, Andreas	22	Bruchsal	62-0879
ECKERT, Carl	26	Schlesien	56-1044
Heinrich 20, Adolph 18			
ECKERT, W.(m)	40	Bavaria	57-0555
ECKERTZ, Wilhelm	21	Neuwied/Pruss	55-0628
Elisabeth 46, Wilhelmine 19			
ECKHARD, Catarina	19	Hetzerode	57-0776
ECKHARDT, Anne	19	Heubisch	56-1011
ECKHARDT, Jacob	21	Nausis	56-0819
ECKHARDT, Joh.H.	20	Kurhessen	56-1044
ECKHARDT, Johanne	22	Muenden	56-1117
Emilie 16			
ECKHARDT, Johannes	31	Niederaulau	57-0704
Anna Elisab. 28, Anna Margar. 2			
ECKHARDT, Ludwig	27	Lohme	57-0754
ECKHART, August	19	Heinersdorf	56-0629
ECKMEIER, Barbara	19	Baiern	58-0399
ECKRIS, Adam	14	New York	57-0654
ECKSTEIN, Anna	28	Gnadsberg	57-0654
ECKSTEIN, Babette	13	Nuernberg	55-1082
ECKSTEIN, Christne	27	Schwarzenbach	59-0384
ECKSTEIN, David	30	Pilsen	59-0477
ECKSTEIN, G.(m)	27	Kissingen	61-0804
ECKSTEIN, J.(m)	21	Neustadt	61-0804
ECKSTEIN, Michel	35	Storndorf	56-0527
Henriette 47			
EDELER, Lenore	21	New York	57-1148
EDELMANN, Clara	22	Kriegshaber	57-1148
EDELMANN, Elisab.	27	Schonau	60-1161
EDELMANN, Ursula	48	Hohenlinden	61-0478
EDELSTEIN, S.(m)	21	Nienburg	62-0836
EDEN, Ede	21	Marx	58-0925
C.Elisabeth 19			
EDEN, Herman Wm.	24	Minsen	60-1141
Theda 25, Anna Mary 2			
EDEN, Meta	22	Horsten	57-0850
EDER, Charlotte	21	Schwabing	58-0306
EDER, Joh. B.	16	Breitenbach	58-0885
EDINGER, G.	32	Mannheim	59-0990
EDLER, Sophie	21	Langenholzhsn	57-0606
EDLER, Wilhelm	33	Goettingen	57-1280
Regine 36, Elise 4, Christian 3			

NAME	AGE	RESIDENCE	YR-LIST
EDLICH, Theodor	20	Sachsen	59-1017
EGAN, Marg.	46	Ireland	61-0804
EGBERGER, Carl	55	Dinkelsbuehl	60-0334
Josephine 27, Caroline 10			
EGBERT, Gerh.	36	Gehrden	57-1113
Louise 30			
EGELING, C.A.(m)	37	Richmond	60-0785
EGER, Friederike	22	Gr.Breitenbch	58-0881
EGER, Mich.	16	Seligenstadt	60-0521
EGERD, Joh. H.	57	Padingbuttel	60-0622
Dorothea 57, Johanna 30, Hermann 17			
Julius 12			
EGERSDORF, Theo.FC	22	Hannover	60-1032
EGERT, Elisabeth	26	New York	62-1112
EGERT, Joh. Georg	22	Weichersbach	61-0520
EGG, an den M.		St.Gallen	62-0111
EGGER, Margaretha	21	Dunsfeld	59-1017
EGGERING, Cathrina	24	Neuenlande	58-0563
EGGERMANN, Gerhard	17	Bevsten	59-1036
EGGERS, Albert	17	Leeste	62-0938
EGGERS, Anton	40	Davenport/IA	59-0951
EGGERS, Aug.	42	Cincinnati	62-1042
EGGERS, Carsten	17	Westenholz	57-0847
EGGERS, Ernst	25	Philadelphia	62-1042
EGGERS, Friedr.	17	Lasse	61-0482
EGGERS, Friedrich	38	Schweringen	56-0723
Antoinette 23			
EGGERS, Friedrich	21	Fallingbostel	57-0422
EGGERS, Hedwig	20	Nesse	61-0482
EGGERS, Henry	25	New York	62-0938
EGGERS, Lueder		New York	57-0365
EGIDY, Wolff	25	Dresden	62-0401
EGLOFFSTEIN, (m)	25	Eisenach	61-0716
EHALT, Peter	29	Seligenstadt	60-0334
Anna 22			
EHERT, J.G.(m)	30	Neuendorf	61-0804
EHESCHEID, Jacob	31	Vohburg	57-0961
EHLE, Bernhard	27	Eisfeld	59-0951
Marie 25, Friedrich 8			
EHLE, Louise	19	Meisselbach	59-0951
EHLERMANN, Diedr.	19	Visselhoevede	60-0622
EHLERS, D.H.	25		62-0938
EHLERS, Dorothea	22	Asendorf	56-0723
EHLERS, Dorothea	19	Affstaedt	57-0850
EHLERS, Friedr.Wm.		Bremerlehe	57-0924
Betty 2, Wilhelmine by			
EHLERS, Joh.Heinr.	48	Ostenholz	58-0563
Anna Christ. 40, Heinrich Fr. 13			
Wilhelmine 11, Christine 7, Charlotte 4			
EHLERS, Julia	26	New York	62-0938
Anna 4, Louise 9m			
EHLERS, M.(m)	21	New York	61-1132
EHLERT, Johann	27	Hollen	56-0723
EHLERT, Johanna	30	New York	62-0836
Kathi 6, Augusta 8			
EHLICHS, Fr.(f)	23	Aachen	62-0111
EHLING, Georg	44	Huettenhof	60-1032
EHMANN, Johann	28	Niederbach	57-1122
EHMANN, Philipp	16	Merchingen	59-0477
EHMER, Andreas	23	Tiefenort	57-1026
EHMER, Therese	30	Herzheim	61-0804
Mich. 17			
EHNTHOLT, A.L.	20	Bremen	59-0535
EHRENBECK, Wilhelm	19	Bremen	59-0477
EHRENBERGER, Sara	41	Gunzendorf	61-0482
EHRENREICH, Sara	23	Langenschweiz	61-0770
EHRHARDT, Gottfr.	30	Doebris	58-0925
Liberta 24, Robert 6			
EHRHARDT, Heinr.	59	Ramptendorf	61-0716
Marie 57, Caroline 18, Christian 21			
EHRHARDT, Johanna	21	Remptendorf	59-0613
EHRLEN, Jacob	22	Oldendorf	61-0520
EHRLICH, Jos.	20	New York	62-0938
EHRLICH, Julie	31	Leobschuetz	61-0930
EHRLICH, Robert	21	Langenhausen	59-0951
EHRLICH, Wm.	29	Hartenstein	62-0836
EHRMANN, J.(m)	26	Koenigshofen	62-0836
EHRMANN, Sara	23	Homburg	60-0785

NAME	AGE	RESIDENCE	YR-LIST
EIBS, Henning	46	Dorum	56-0819
EICH, Johann	31	Jacobsthal	61-0520
EICHBAUM, Joh.	22	Gunzenhausen	59-1036
EICHBERG, Char.(f)	23	Spatzenhof	57-0555
EICHBERG, Emilie	26	Stuttgart	62-0836
EICHBERG, Pauline	20	Stuttgart	59-0477
EICHBERG, W.(f)	36	Neuenburg	57-0555
EICHBORN, Lehne	20	Wertheim	60-0334
EICHE, Heinrich	20	Minden	55-0845
EICHELBAUM, G.(m)	59	Interbogk	62-0836
Dor. 58			
EICHELMANN, Bernh.	22	Wittenburg	56-0819
Caroline 25			
EICHENBERG, Andr.	38	Cassel	60-0411
Christine 40			
EICHENBERG, Heinr.	30	Oberleden	56-0411
Catharina 50, Martha 9, Nicolaus 8			
EICHENBERG, Levy	24	Beringhausen	56-0632
EICHENGRUEN, Emily	18	Gehrde	60-0533
EICHENHAUER, Conr.	24	Bann	60-1053
EICHENHAUER, Minna	20	Brutenbach	56-0632
EICHENHOF, Friedka	23	Noertingen	59-0214
EICHERER, Christ.	21	France	61-0107
EICHHOLTZ, Betty	22	Ndr.Elsungen	60-1141
EICHHOLZ, Friedr.	26	Hoelten	57-0021
EICHHOLZ, Otto	17	Potsdam	56-0512
EICHHORN, Eleanore	28	Leipzig	61-0897
EICHHORN, Eva	16	Burggruss	56-0512
Margaret 22			
EICHHORN, Gottfr.	16	Walduern	60-1053
EICHLER, Christine	48	Hersfeld	55-1082
EICHLER, E.R. (f)	58	Muegel/Sax.	55-0538
W.A. (f) 18			
EICHLER, Fred	32	Dansa	56-0512
Rosine 26, Hermann 5			
EICHLER, Heinr.	17	Herspenhausen	55-1082
EICHLER, Heinrich	24	Herfa	62-0983
EICHLER, Wm.	45	Washington	62-0938
EICHMANN, Carl	16	Windhausen	56-0527
EICHMANN, Friedr.	34	Lothe	56-1216
EICHMANN, Johannes	18	Kloten	55-0630
EICHMEIER, Herm.	25	Lippe-Detmold	58-0399
EICHMEYER, Hermann	56	Kaldorf	57-0606
Wilhelmine 58, Hermann 18			
EICHMUELLER, Fr'dr	22	Spiess	57-1113
EICHMUELLER, Georg	44	Spies	57-1113
Catharina 13, Leonhard 9			
EICHNER, Marie	17	Selters	58-0576
EICHNER, Simon	27	Osterhofen/Bv	55-0628
EICHORN, Conrad	55	Brooklyn	60-0398
Albertina 53			
EICK, Elisabeth	22	Thalmessing	59-0384
EICK, Friedrich	55	Recklinghause	58-0576
Minna 54, Minna 17, August 14, Eduard 10			
Ferdinand 13			
EICK, John Adam	22	Billfingen/Bd	57-0847
EICKHOFF, Albert	26	Celle/Hann.	60-0622
EICKHOFF, Cathrine	40	Oettingen/Han	57-0847
Carsten 42, Heinrich 3			
EICKHOFF, Franz	14	Bonninghausen	60-0334
EICKHOLTZ, Fr.(m)	23	Rheda	62-0836
EICKHOLTZ, Fr.(m)	23	Rheda	62-0836
EICKHORN, Carl	25	New York	62-0730
EICKHORST, Michael	28	Posen	58-0399
A.C. 26, Augusta 9m			
EICKMANN, Margar.	25	Sottrum/Hann.	60-0622
EICKMEYER, Aug.	24	Wetzlar	59-0951
EICKMEYER, C.(m)	18	Melbergen	62-0836
Marie 20			
EICKMEYER, Fred.	56	Vlotho	56-0512
Sophia 58, Gottlieb 26, Wilhelmine 24			
Louisa 19			
EIDAM, Catharina	21	Cappeln	60-0334
EIDMANN, Georg	23	Baltimore	62-0342
EIF, Johann II	50	Leihgestern	57-0924
EIFERT, Adam	33	Staden/Hessen	60-0622
EIFERT, Nicl.	11	Burkhard	60-1161
EIFFERT, Carl	16	Ortenberg	62-0712

NAME	AGE	RESIDENCE	YR-LIST
EIFLER, Bernhard	36	Steinau	56-0589
Anna 42			
EIKELBERG, Ernst	27	Goettingen	57-0776
Dorothea 34, August 7			
EIL, Wulfgang	30	Filsfich	57-1280
EILERS, Elisabeth	48	Mensfelden	59-0384
Friedrich 20, Emma 12			
EILERS, Helene	36	New York	60-0785
EILEXMANN, Hermann	28	Westphalia	60-0371
EIMESS, Georg Fr.	20	Roemhild	57-0606
EINFELDT, Ernst	28	Kl.Barkau	61-0482
EINSTEIN, Alex.	19	Laupheim	59-0477
EINTANZ, Elisabeth	22	Herbethausen	57-0776
EIPP, Anna Maria	32	Gimbsheim/Bad	60-0429
EIRING, Heinrich	36	Frieberg/Darm	62-0342
EIRING, Marie	20	Philippsthal	60-1032
EIRLER, H.(m)	37	Unter Sorg	61-0669
Carl 2, Henr.(f) 28			
EISBERG, Ernst L.	18	Minden	57-0654
EISCHHORN, Eva	16	Burggruss	56-0512
Margaret 22			
EISEL, Barbara	40	Doringstadt	57-0847
Joh.Friedr. 10, Georg 8			
EISEL, Georg H.	39	Quarthaven	57-0847
EISELE, Anton	34	Emmerfeld	60-0334
EISELE, Jacob	26	Herbolzheim	60-0398
EISELE, Joseph	17	Vogt	59-0613
EISELE, Louise	18	Laufen	57-1280
EISELE, Otto	23	Dettlingen	60-1196
Caroline 20			
EISELL, A.	19	Waiblingen	59-1036
EISENBACH, G.H.	26	Eberstadt	57-1148
Georg 20			
EISENBRENDER, Her.	18	Weiblingen	59-0477
EISENDRAUT, J.Geo.	16	Konigsberg/Sx	60-0622
EISENER, Mathilde	28	Giessen	57-0606
EISENFELDER, John	29	Hundelshausen	60-0411
Joseph 22, Barbara 23			
EISENHARD, Louise	22	Zimmersrode	56-0847
EISENHARDT, Christ	17	Muehlhausen	59-1036
EISENHAUER, Elisab	24	Hessen	60-1161
EISENHUT, Cathrina	22	Hungen	57-1122
EISENMANN, Junette	21	Masbach	61-0482
EISFELD, Theod.	40	New York	57-1150
EISFELDER, Wilhelm	56	Zellerfeld	55-0932
EISING, Arend	21	Germany	62-1112
EISKAMP, Herrmann	17	Hoya/Hannover	55-0628
EISSLER, Jos.M.	21	Thachum	62-0730
EISTERHOLM, Johann	30	Brake	59-0477
EITEL, Joseph	51	Staffelstein	61-0478
Franz 15, Carl 13			
EITELSJOERGEN, Joh	57	Rothleben	59-1036
Friedr. 19, Aug. 17			
EITERMANN, Friedr.	22	Ankum	57-0924
EITMEYER, Daniel	32	Elvershausen	56-0847
EITS, Johannes	15	Wittmund	59-1036
EITZMANN, H.	32	Oettingen	57-0847
Catharina 24, Heinrich 3m			
EITZMANN, Wilhelm	33	Dueshorn/Hann	57-0847
Hermann 35, Marie 38, Heinrich 8			
Hermann 6			
EKARDT, Hieronymus	21	Bieber	60-1053
EKEL, Johannes	59	Bringhausen	58-0925
ELASSER, Moritz	17	Tuchterfeld	57-1148
ELBEL, Eduard	32	Saalfeld	60-0398
ELDUME, Anna	28	Mustolde	58-0399
ELERS, Marie	54	Fischback	55-1082
G. Friedr. 14, Henriette 10			
ELFERS, Heinr.	35	New York	60-0334
Friedericke 34, Heinr. 7, Emmy 2			
ELFERS, J.D.	31	Ihligenworth	57-0961
Hannchen 26			
ELFLEIN, A.(m)	40	Hochheim	61-0482
Wilhelmine 41, Amand 7, Ricke 9			
ELFRICH, Carl W.	24	Breddin	57-1113
ELFRICH, Christ.W.	23	Koppenbrueck	57-1113
ELGER, Marie	33	Reichenberg	59-0951
ELHARDT, H.(m)	26	Muehlhausen/P	55-0544

NAME	AGE	RESIDENCE	YR-LIST
M. (m) 19			
ELIAS, Carl	13	Dedesdorf	58-0885
ELIAS, Heinrich	28	Obermeiser	56-0723
ELINGEN, Wilhelm	29	Messlingen	57-1122
ELITZER, Marg.	18	Kleinseebach	60-0334
ELLENBERG, Elisab.	18	Dorl	56-0819
ELLENBERGER, Carl	18	Rielingen	57-1067
ELLENBERGER, Crlne	25	Biedenkopf	57-1067
ELLENHARDT, Heinr.	32	Charleston	59-1036
ELLENHORST, D.Wm.	35	New York	59-1036
ELLERBACH, H.Ratje	28	Vilsen	60-0398
ELLERBROOK, Ludw.	28	Vegesack	55-1082
ELLERICH, Heinr.	49	Curhessen	55-0634
Elisabeth 46, Johannes 20, Catharina 13			
Joh. Heinr. 6			
ELLERMANN, Gott.	25	Runau	56-0527
ELLIGEN, Therese	20	Frankenhausen	57-0776
ELLING, Fried.	39	Renzen	59-0535
Elisabeth 37, Heinrich 9, Wilhelm 4			
ELLING, Heinrich	48	Cordingsmuhle	57-0847
Anna 43, Heinrich 19, Catharina 16			
Friedrich 15, H. Friedrich 8, Heinrich 7			
Wilhelm 6, Anna 10m			
ELLING, Hinrich	37	Hannover	57-0847
Cath. Ilse 30, Charlotte 7, Hinrich 5			
Maria 3, Dorothea 9			
ELLING, Joh. Herm.	23	Brokel	60-1141
ELLINGER, Georg	27	Riethnordhsn.	57-0850
ELLINGER, H.F.	56	Mittelhausen	61-0482
Sophie 44, Wm. 22, Heinrich 13			
ELLINGER, Moniz	26	New York	59-0477
ELLINGHAUSEN, John	30	Brinkum	57-1148
Lisette 28, Meta 11m			
ELLWERMANN, J.	29	Lembeck	59-0477
ELMEIRICK, Gustav	43	Perleberg	61-0107
ELMEN, v. Doris	33	Dorum	61-0047
ELMSMANN, Henry	22	Nuernberg	57-0654
ELPING, Lambert	42	Schale	56-0819
Sophia 13			
ELSAESSER, Magd.	21	Edelbach	56-1117
ELSASS, Jacob	18	Frankfurt a/M	61-0482
ELSASSER, August	46	Neustadt	59-0047
ELSASSER, J.(m)	30	New York	61-0897
Gottlieba 24			
ELSBACHER, Johanna	19	Muenchen/Bav.	55-1238
ELSEN, Elisabeth	29	Varelbruch	57-0961
ELSENBERG, John	32	Gensbach	57-0654
ELSENBROCK, Anna	20	Bremen	59-1036
ELSINGER, Sigism.	24	Cleveland	57-0654
ELSNER, Carl	27	Naumburg	61-0047
ELSNER, Reinh.	34	Glaz	60-1196
EMANUEL, Jos.	33	New York	62-0836
EMDE, Marie	20	Corbach	58-0881
EMDE, van d. Louis	51	Mengringhsn.	61-0520
Ludwiga 51, Ludwig 13, Christian 9			
EMERZ, Joh.	28	Boos	57-0578
Caecilie 27, Jacob 10m			
EMICH, Georg	23	Oberamstadt	56-0527
EMMEL, August H.	15	Langensalza	59-0535
EMMEL, Babette	28	Ruedesheim	62-0730
EMMEL, Johanna	28	Ruedesheim	60-1196
EMMERICH, Gust.	16	Oberlais	62-0712
EMMERICH, Mansche	18	Horstein	59-0613
Emilie 17			
EMMERICH, Rieke	25	Sandbeck	56-0512
EMMERT, Conrad	37	Helsen	57-0447
EMMINGER, Heinrich	30	Laprairie	58-0815
EMMRICH, Joh. Wm.	32	Villingen/Hes	62-0342
EMWERKAMP, Christa	24	Lembeck	59-0477
ENCE, Emil		England	61-1132
ENCINGER, Anna	52	Neumark/Bav.	55-0628
Anna 17			
ENDELE, Jacob	33	Geisingen/Wrt	55-1238
Louise 24			
ENDER, August	16	Wichthausen	55-0630
ENDERS, Anna	24	Hausen	61-0520
ENDERS, Conrad	52	Steinheim	56-0413
Maria 6			

NAME	AGE	RESIDENCE	YR-LIST
ENDERS, Elise	23	Alsfeld	62-0730
Catharine 14			
ENDERS, Joh.	26	Alsfeld	60-0334
ENDERS, Johann	35	Baiern	58-0399
ENDERS, Margaretha	46	Hockenheim	56-0819
Catharina 20, Elisabeth 18, Theresa 3			
ENDNES, August	23	Stuttgart	62-1112
ENDRES, Cathrina	23	Niederahr	60-1141
ENDRES, Fr.	35	Malsdorf	55-0932
Maria 30, Friedr. 9, Doroth. 2, Anna 2m			
ENDRES, Kunigunde	25	Horlachen	56-0819
ENGEL, Carl	26	Neutrebbin/Pr	62-0342
ENGEL, Christine	26	Cappeln	57-1122
ENGEL, Daniel	53	Pitzerie	56-0632
Christiane 45, Johann 22, Apolonia 20			
Ernestine 16, Henriette 10, Augusta 8			
Ottilie 6, Anna 60			
ENGEL, Elis.	19	Gruenberg	60-0785
ENGEL, Georg	31	Hausen	57-0606
ENGEL, Johannes	22	Roeddenau	57-0754
ENGEL, Johannes	58	Frankenberg	57-0578
Wilhelmine 56			
ENGEL, Johannes	18	Enzberg	62-0879
ENGEL, Jurgen	33	Cappeln	57-1122
Cathrine 29, Charlotte 10, Wilhelm 9			
Heinrich 3, Friedrich 10m			
ENGEL, Margarethe	27	Reimerod	57-1113
ENGEL, Ulrich	27	Germany	59-0613
ENGEL, Wm.	26	Neutrebin	62-0111
ENGELAGE, Friedr.	19	Oppendorf	60-0521
ENGELBART, Charles	20	Lutter	58-0925
ENGELBERT, H.A.	49	Barmen	56-0589
ENGELBRECHT, C.L.	38	Unterluebbe	60-0533
Caroline 32, Ernst 9, Friedrich 7			
Sophie 58			
ENGELBRECHT, Joh.	36	Doberschuetz	60-0521
Anna 30, Susanne 4			
ENGELBRECHT, Wm.	30	New York	59-1036
ENGELBREIT, Marg.	23	Ruedenheim	59-0990
Dorothee 22			
ENGELHARD, Barbara	22	Gestungshause	56-0512
ENGELHARD, Casper		Villersbrun	57-1026
ENGELHARD, Conrad	30	Bayern	61-0930
ENGELHARD, Elisab.	23	Kalchreuth	57-0447
ENGELHARD, Franz	30	Eichis	56-0629
ENGELHARD, L.	23	Wilmershausen	56-0512
ENGELHARDT, August	43	Gradebeck/Han	62-0342
ENGELHARDT, Carl	24	Reichenberg	59-0384
ENGELHARDT, Charlt	21	Schwartitz	61-0482
ENGELHARDT, Fr'zka	27	Idensburg	60-0785
ENGELHARDT, Kunig.	15	Burgpreppach	60-0533
ENGELHARDT, Margar	30	Rechenburg	59-0477
ENGELHARDT, Minna	28	Kirchhain	62-0401
ENGELHAUSEN, Heinr	27	Osterbruch	59-0951
ENGELKE, Aug.	28	Suettorf	62-1042
ENGELKE, Wilhelm	26	Hannover	59-0214
Wilhelm 24			
ENGELKING, Ludwig	28	Kirchhorsten	57-1150
ENGELKING, Sophie	20	Beckedorf	56-0589
ENGELKINK, Hans	52	Hohnhorst	55-0630
Sophie 46, Conrad 12, Engel 15, Maria 15			
Wilhelm 9, Trina 7			
ENGELKRAUT, Conrad	32	Hof	62-0100
ENGELMANN, Alio(f)	25	Eisenbergen	55-1082
ENGELMANN, Carolne	33	Einigsdorf	56-0951
ENGELMANN, Chr.	30	Kuhne	57-0654
ENGELMANN, Louis	9	Saalfeld	56-0951
Engel Doroth 16			
ENGELMANN, Otto	26	Wuertt.	55-0634
ENGELS, C.E.	22	Hueckelswagen	56-0354
ENGELS, Rick (m)	20	Chicago	60-0521
Emilie 41, Bertha 2			
ENGELSKIND, H.(m)	49	Petershagen	61-0482
Lore 50, Louise 21			
ENGELSKIND, Heinr.	49	Petershagen	60-0371
Wilhelm 17			
ENGELSTAEDTER, Fr.	14	Coburg	61-0478
ENGERT, Gottlieb	21	Neudorg	55-0932

NAME	AGE	RESIDENCE	YR-LIST
Christine 18			
ENGLER, A.	32	Hermsdorf	56-0589
ENGLERT, William	45	Charleston	58-0815
ENHUS, Hermann	15	Bremerhaven	57-0436
ENKE, Johanna	29	Cassel	55-0634
ENNECKER, Aug.	18	Damme	59-0951
ENSTE, Mina	20	Warstein	57-1148
ENTNER, Eleonore	33	Muenchen	61-0716
Lina 12, Agnes 7, Franz 9, Theodor 8			
ENZELEIN, Fr.(m)	25	Insterburg	62-0836
ENZINGER, Anna	52	Neumark/Bav.	55-0628
Anna 17			
ENZLIN, Theodor	27	Breslau	57-1122
EPLER, Elizabeth	29	Hardthausen	58-0545
EPP, Magnus	31	Kempton/Bav.	55-0538
EPPE, Christ.	18	Wuertemberg	57-0555
EPPELEIN, Joseph	30	Illstadt/Bav.	61-0779
EPPINGER, Caroline	22	Nitzingen/Wrt	62-0608
EPPINGER, Caroline	20	New York	62-0938
EPSTEIN, Hermann	31	Poppelau	55-0812
EPSTEIN, Moses	46	Kirchheim	60-0785
Henriette 56			
EPSTEIN, Seligman	20	Trilou	57-1416
EPTING, And.	26	Quakertown	62-0467
ERATH, Heinrich	18	Metze	56-0411
ERB, C.	21	Weidenau	62-0993
ERB, Carl	19	Wuertemberg	59-0990
ERB, J.F.(m)	22	Hagsfelden	62-0730
ERB, Louis	15	Landershaugen	59-0477
ERBACH, Charles	32	Eisenach	59-1036
Carl 9			
ERBBROCKHAUSEN, B.	16	Detmold	61-0482
ERBE, Julius	18	Stuttgart	60-0398
ERBELE, (m)	14	Heidelsheim	56-0527
ERD, Georg	66	Bils/Tyrol	61-0770
Marie 35			
ERDERS, Savine	19	Berka/Weimar	55-0538
ERDINGER, Maria	23	Faltenthal	57-0754
ERDLEN, Christian	23	Noerdlingen	56-1260
ERDMANN, Adolph	26	Prussia	57-0961
ERDMANN, Albert	18	Mollenhausen	57-0447
ERDMANN, Andreas	31	Mittelsdorf	58-0563
Margaretha 28			
ERDMANN, August	22	Osterowke	56-0819
ERDMANN, Carl	33	Zempelburg	56-1260
Augusta 29, Carl 3, Augusta 9m			
ERDMANN, Daniel	46	Colberg	56-0723
Wilhelmine 40			
ERDMANN, Emilie	17	Griebau	62-0758
ERDMANN, Johanne	58	Leipzig	56-0847
ERDMANN, Otto	22	Isernhagen	57-0961
ERDMANN, Wilh'mine	36	Isernhagen	57-0961
Carolina 1			
ERDWIENS, Henry	34	Schuerum	57-0422
Anna 30, Henry 4, Anna 11m			
ERFURT, S.	25	Danzig	62-0993
ERFURT, S.	25	Straussberg	62-0993
ERHARD, Ferdinand	35	Selchow	56-0819
Friederike 38, Pauline 19, August 17			
Emilie 12, Augusta 9, Hermann 7, Albert 5			
Marie 3, Robert 10m			
ERHARDT, Johannes	36	Black River	60-0429
ERHARDT, Joseph	30	Etzingen	59-0384
ERICH, C.N.	31	Memphis	62-1042
ERICHS, L.	38	New York	59-1036
Meta 27, Johanna 1, (baby) 8m			
ERICHSON, Caroline	19	Dorum	60-0411
ERKE, Dorothea	21	Quedlinburg	59-0384
ERKEL, Georg	42	Ruettershause	55-0812
Dorothea 42, Heinrich 14, Catharina 9			
Gretje 3			
ERKMANN, Barbara	23	Baden	60-1196
Cathrina 22			
ERLENBACH, M.	29	Nuernberg	62-0938
ERLLE, Carl	26	Hatsfeld	61-0478
Anna Maria 23			
ERMEDING, Anna	17	Lobenstein	62-0467
ERMER, Johann	32	Hochdorf	56-1117
ERMETTE, Daniel	21	Naumburg	56-0819
ERMISCH, Rosalie	28	Magdeburg	61-0482
ERNAU, Louise	19	Germany	56-1216
ERNESTI, Wilhelm	33	New York	61-0779
ERNST, Catharina	18	Rottendorf	60-1141
ERNST, Catharine	20	Rohrbach	62-0730
ERNST, Christine	21	Stoeckheim	56-0951
ERNST, Christine	59	Jena	59-0535
Renolde 18			
ERNST, E.(m)	30	New York	62-0401
ERNST, Elisabeth	24	Baiern	58-0399
ERNST, Hermann	25	Nordsungen/Pr	60-0371
ERNST, Jacob	19	Curhessen	58-0399
ERNST, Joh.	28	Ebenhausen	60-0398
Carl 30			
ERNST, Margaretha	16	Bodisgruen	55-0413
ERNST, Marie	24	Schweitz	62-0836
ERNSTE, Gust. Chr.	28	Soemmerda	55-1082
Louise 24			
ERSSE, Cath. Elis.	38	Hersfeld	55-0634
Christoph 26			
ERTE, George	27	Altenstadt	59-0384
ERZBERGER, J.H.(m)	47	Doerfles	62-0730
Johann 45, Catharine 38, Margaretha 59			
Chr. 15, Margaretha 14			
ESAU, Wilhelmine	18	Elleringshsn.	59-0951
Christine 16			
ESCH, Robert	26	New York	57-0961
ESCHBACH, Jos.	48	Ottenbrueck	60-0334
ESCHEN, (m)	24	Savannah	57-0578
ESCHENBURG, J.	27	Chicago	60-0334
Bertha 25			
ESCHER, Fanny	18	Sonnenberg	62-0730
ESCHER, Minna	23	Sonneberg	62-1112
ESCHERBACH, G.J.	24	Alsleben	60-1196
ESCHERING, Margret	17	Grafenberg	56-0847
ESCHMANN, Joh.H.	24	Diethers	56-1117
ESER, Sebastian	15	Wuerttemberg	56-0512
ESFELD, F.(m)	40	California	62-0467
ESFELD, Franz	36	Achim	58-0925
Elise 30			
ESMERK, Ferd.	36	New York	62-1169
Mrs. 32, William 7			
ESSELMANN, J.B.(m)	36	Muenster	62-0166
ESSEN, Erich	17	Osnabrueck	55-0634
ESSENWEIN, C.Barb.	18	Battmannsweil	56-1117
ESSENWEIN, Jane	26	Neustadt	57-0654
ESSING, Georg	30	Hemstedt	61-0478
ESSLEBEN, Friedr.	23	Alsleben	58-0563
ESSMAN, Albert	6	Mannheim	60-0334
ESSMANN, August	18	Frankenhausen	60-0533
ESSMANN, Ernst	23	Schaumb.-Lipp	55-0634
ESSMANN, William	24	Bavaria	59-0214
ESTE, Chr.	25	Cincinnati	62-0467
ETSCHEL, Georg	32	Wald	55-0812
ETTE, Charles	32	Berlin	62-0730
Edw. 23, Dorothea 59			
ETTLING, H.A.	31	Alsfeld	62-0836
ETTLING, H.Cath.	36	Alsfeld	57-0654
ETTLING, J.(m)	33	New York	62-0730
ETZEL, Carl	37	Appelhachs	59-1036
ETZEL, Catharina	29	Ortzelbach	60-0398
Amandus 16			
ETZEL, Friedrich	54	Gerstungen	58-0563
Christine 25, Gottfried 16, Johannes 11m			
ETZEL, Philipp	29	Schleidt	59-0047
Caroline 22, Wilhelmine 4m			
ETZMANN, Heinrich	21	Lebenstedt	56-0723
ETZNER, Elise	22	Hoya	59-1017
EUCHMANN, Johann	19	Soell	57-0578
EUKE, Friedrich	25	Deutschthal	57-1192
EULEI, Theodor	28	Mengeringhsn.	62-0306
EULER, Jean	20	Frankfurt	59-0048
EULER, Marie	22	Beuren	57-1067
EULER, Marie	26	Hailer	59-0990
EULER, Martin	33	New York	57-1192
EULITZ, Carl Gotl.	28	Chemnitz	59-0613
EURICH, Marie	19	Kirchheim	60-0533

NAME	AGE	RESIDENCE	YR-LIST
EUSENROTH, Peter	32	Herborn	62-0401
Caroline 30, Louis 4, Lina 2, Lisette 6m			
EUTHOEFER, Edw.	26	Muenster	62-1112
EVERBECK, Johannes	30	Lemgo	62-1169
EVERDING, Augusta	25	Bueckeburg	61-0897
EVEREN, Charles	36	New York	59-0613
EVERS, J.H.	26	Elbergen	62-0993
M. 27, A. 64			
EVERSMEYER, Hen'te	24	Lengerich	62-0836
EWALD, Anton	26	Senden	56-0723
A.M. 43			
EWALD, Elise	20	Uttershausen	57-1067
Nicolaus 16, (baby) bob			
EWALD, Marie	24	Hessen	60-0398
EWE, Caroline	32	Blankenburg	57-0422
Gustav 8, Alwine 3			
EWE, Otto	23	Walthersleben	57-0422
EWIGMANN, B.(m)	27	Schoppeln	62-0730
Gerhardine 28			
EYBERGER, Joseph	27	Knittelsbach	61-0779
Theresia 33, Joseph by			
EYCK, v. Peter	42	Louisendorf	57-0422
EYCK, van Wilhelm	50	Ospern	58-0306
(wife) 55, Margaretha 21, Elisabeth 17			
Johanna 13			
EYE, v. Arnold Fr.	25	Fuerstenau	57-1026
FAASS, Chr. Friedr	22	Iptingen	56-0411
FABER, D.F.(m)	20	Fuerth	61-0804
FABER, Elise	28	Meiningen	62-1042
FABER, Johann	51	Dambach	57-1280
FABER, Mary	58	Gestungshause	56-0512
Barbara 23, Elisabeth 15			
FABER, Robert	22	Neckarweihing	61-0770
FABERI, Simon	39	Evansville	62-0232
Francisca 43, Caroline 9, Barbara 8			
Eugen 6			
FACKENER, Anna E.	19	Oberholzhsn.	60-0533
FAEC, Minna	29	Prussia	62-0758
FAEHNDRICH, Julius	40	Breslau	59-0372
FAENZLER, Herrmann	23	Corbusen	59-0613
Pauline 24, Meta 2, Emilie 18			
FAESENFELDT, Diedr	57	New York	57-1148
FAEZBURGER, Jacob	14	Schweitag	57-1026
FAHL, John	23	Bremen	59-0951
FAHLBURCH, Sophie	20	Neuenbruck	62-0836
FAHLBUSCH, Andreas	33	Gillersheim	56-0819
FAHLBUSCH, Aug.F.	29	Lindau	59-1036
FAHLEN, Johanna	25	Baltimore	62-0938
FAHRBACH, Sophia	20	Meichingen	59-1036
FAHRENHOLZ, Claus	48	New York	59-0951
FAHRION, Magd.	48	Deizisau	61-0669
FAIGLE, Johann	27	Rintingen	62-0836
FAIST, Andreas	23	Baiersbronn	58-0563
FAIST, John	25	Baden	60-1196
FALG, Augusta	27	Gawshorst	59-0951
FALK, Georg	28	Brausbach	57-0422
FALK, Josepha	21	Wallkofen	62-0111
FALKE, Marie	20	Bethen	59-0951
FALKE, Sophie	5	Bremen	62-1169
FALKEN, Anna	22	Sudwalde	62-1112
FALKENBERG, W.(m)	42	France	61-1132
FALKENS, Pauline	23	Hannover	58-0925
FALLBROCK, Heinr.	28	Stadthagen	57-1122
Elisabeth 28, Friedrich 10m			
FALSER, Jacob	18	Neuhausen	59-0951
FALSING, Cath.	45	Herbstein	60-0998
FALTEMEYER, Theres	22	Karthaus Prul	62-0467
FALTENSTEIN, (f)	52	New York	62-1169
(f) 19, Henry 14			
FALTER, Joh. Geo.	14	Hohenstadt	56-0951
E.M. 25			
FANGEMANN, Christ.	47	Hasbergen	62-0712
Johann 9, Anna 7, Gesine 6, Adeline 3			
FANGMANN, Franz	33	Strihen	60-0334
FAREISS, Margareth	33	Doelnitz	60-1053
FARGEL, M.	12	Weimar	62-0993
FARICKI, Marc.	17	Posen	57-0654
FARMBACHER, Joh.Gg	24	Bernbach	58-0881

NAME	AGE	RESIDENCE	YR-LIST
FARR, Heinrich	38	Leisenwalde	58-0563
Katharina 26, Wilhelmine 1			
FARTHMANN, Charlot	19	Bieren	56-1011
FASS, Moses	24	Obornik/Posen	62-0342
FASSBINDER, Hen'te	26	Detmold	56-1117
Gustav 8			
FASSE, Gottlieb	18	Aplern	61-0520
FATTHAUER, Friedr.	19	Osterkappeln	61-0167
FATUM, Johann	23	Niederofladen	57-0776
FAUE, Catharina	23	St.Johann	59-0613
FAULBAUM, Aug.	19	Bueckeburg	57-1148
FAULHABER, Oscar	20	Chicago	62-0938
FAULSTICH, Fr.(m)	41	Allendorf	61-0669
H.(m) 15			
FAULSTICH, Valent.	15	Fulda/Prussia	57-0847
FAULSTICK, Elise	27	Herfa	57-1067
FAULWETTER, Joh.	22	Roda	61-0669
FAURE, Barbe	30	France	56-1216
(f) 6, (m) 2			
FAUSER, Wilhelm	26	Iserlohn	57-0924
Carol. Luise 25, Gust. Robert by			
FAUST, Andreas	31	Kirchberg/Prs	61-0770
Anna Maria 33, Heinrich 4, Christine 1			
FAUST, Christ. M.	19	Lohlbach	60-1053
FAUST, Franz	30	Gerstedt	56-1260
FAUST, Johannes	15	Elsrode/Hess.	57-0924
FECHHEIMER, Mary	23	Mitwitz	57-1148
FECHTEMEIER, Henrt	22	Tevennau	61-0478
FECHTIG, Franz	17	Moeskirch	60-0521
FECHTNER, Friedr.	34	Pyritz	56-0632
Henriette 24			
FECKE, Carl	19	Osnabrueck	56-0411
FECKEN, Gertje	26	Rysum	58-0563
FEDDEN, Betha	28	Driftsethe	57-1148
FEDDERWITZ, Diedr.	18	Wallhoefen/Ha	60-0622
FEDERLOHNER, J.Hch	30	Untersambach	57-1026
FEDITZ, Christiane	15	Atter	57-1148
FEES, Friedrich	53	Dinkelsbuehl	55-0630
Catharina 40			
FEESS, Johannes	25	Loechau	59-0613
Jacob 9, Joh.Jac. 18, Wilhelm 15			
FEGE, Catharine	20	Amthagen	57-1280
FEGH, Philippine	26	Gehdern	58-0576
FEHD, Andreas	29	Walgermar	57-0924
FEHL, Dorothea	51	Wintersheim	62-0100
FEHL, Maria	15	Wintersheim	61-0520
FEHLHABER, Carl	53	Prosekel	56-0819
Ernstn.Carl. 48, Emilie 20, Hermann 17			
Wilhelm 15, Carl 11, Augusta 8			
FEHR, Casper	30	Bergheim	60-1141
FEHR, Maria	20	Huettweiler	61-0167
FEHR, Martha Elis.	20	Guxhagen	57-0754
FEHRENKAMP, Chr(m)	17	Holzberge	56-0723
Maria Elise 46			
FEHRING, Conrad	48	Bonenberg	56-0632
Heinrich 3			
FEHRING, Johann	27	Neuhaus	60-1032
FEHRING, Ludwig	44	Bonenberg	56-0632
FEHRING, M.	25	Listrup	62-0993
FEHRMANN, Heinrich	52	Minden	58-0399
Caroline 50, Louise 16, Friedrich 7			
Marie 4			
FEHRMANN, J.	19	Bremen	59-0990
FEHRMANN, Joh.	58	Seifhennerdrf	56-0847
Louise 18			
FEICKENHEIMER, F.	17	Meiningen	62-0467
FEICKERT, Antonia	30	Deutz	62-0401
FEIGE, Friederike	19	Bitterfeld	62-0983
FEIGE, Juls. Franz	24	Calbe/Saale	62-0983
FEIGEL, Jos.	59	Saaz	57-1148
Th. 58, Anth. 24			
FEIGERWALD, Joh. P		Sommershausen	58-0815
FEIL, Carl	24	Baden	58-0925
FEIL, Ernst	29	Waldheim	56-1260
FEIL, Gottlieb	30	New York	62-0401
FEIL, Therese	28	Schleissheim	59-0613
FEILER, Bernh.	18	Duesseldorf	60-0785
Herm. 15			

NAME	AGE	RESIDENCE	YR-LIST
FEIN, Catharine	22	Kleebrunn	57-1280
FEINAENGELE, Fanny	27	Philadelphia	57-1192
FEINE, Henry	29	Weinsdorf	57-0654
FEISEL, Martha	20	Rottendorf	60-1141
FEISS, Fr.(f)	19	Herzheim	62-0836
FEIST, Nanny	26	Heusenstamm	58-0563
FEISTKORN, C.(m)	19	Eckartsberga	61-0482
FELDER, Louis	29	Noettingen	60-0785
FELDHUSEN, Wm.	30	Ritzebuettel	57-1150
FELDKAMP, Joseph	19	Alfhausen	56-1117
FELDMANN, Anna	26	Riemsen	60-0521
FELDMANN, C.(m)	19	Herzebrock	60-0334
FELDMANN, Caroline	22	Wartjenstedt	62-0879
FELDMANN, Friedr.	25	Barnstorf	60-0533
FELDMANN, Heinr.	32	Neuenkirchl	59-0951
FELDMANN, Jettie	20	Blowitz	57-1067
FELDMANN, L.(f)	27	San Francisco	61-0804
Emma 10m			
FELDMANN, R.	28	New York	62-0836
(wife) 22			
FELDSTEIN, Hedwig	23	Vegesack	62-1169
FELLDER, Heinrich	4	Daubringen	57-0924
FELLER, Maria	24	Haackenburg	59-0372
FELLER, Michael	36	Nassau	62-1042
FELLERMANN, J.Hch.	50	Uenzen	58-0881
Dorothea 50, John Henry 17			
FELS, Carl	20	Hessen	57-0606
FEND, Johannes	16	Ronshausen	60-0429
FENDRICH, Julius	40	Breslau	59-0372
FENKER, F.Xaver	34	Erlangen	61-0482
FENNA, August	28	Posen	57-0776
Beate 20			
FENNEBERG, Julius	35	Kirchhain	56-0723
FENNEL, John	42	Berlin	59-0951
FENNEL, Maria	19	Waldeck	57-0776
FENNER, J.F.(m)	29	Neumark	57-0555
W.(f) 26			
FENSEL, Conrad	23	Frauenaurach	60-0533
FENSKE, Franz	24	Marienfeld/WP	57-0924
Caroline 24, Carl by			
FERBER, Carl	22	Gera/Reuss	60-0371
FERMANN, Marie	50	Hille	56-0411
FERNANDER, R.	22	New York	62-1042
FERNAU, Catharine	16	Breitenbach	60-0052
FERNBACH, Heinr.	45	Lutterscheid	56-1216
FERNDER, Gottlieb	68	Neu Schonewld	57-0704
Christine 60, Friedrich 23			
FERNE, Elisabeth	15	Hebel	57-1067
FERNEDING, Elise	21	Ihorst	59-0951
Marie 9			
FERNEDING, Joseph	56	Damme	57-0961
FERNHOLZ, Johann	58	Attendorn	57-0606
Elisabeth 28, Wilhelm 26, Marianne 22			
Theodor 18			
FERNKUSS, Adam	30	Hochstein	57-0447
FERRIER, Henr'tte	40	Hildburghsn.	59-0951
Georgine 8			
FERSTEGGE, J.	35	New York	62-0836
Antonia 32, Elise 9			
FERTSCH, Carl	17	Kaichen	59-0990
FESENFELD, Anna	28	Uesen	57-1148
FESENFELDT, Dr.(m)	59	New York	61-0482
FESSEL, Heinrich	45	Landwehrhaven	55-0538
Sophie 45, August 16, Louise 14			
Heinrich 8			
FESTNER, Bernhard	27	Halle	59-1017
FETTER, Ed.	25	Berne	60-0998
Francisca 47, Josephine 17, Friederika 13			
FETZERT, Friedrike	19	Gr.Breitenbch	58-0881
FETZERT, Johanna	46	Gr.Breitenbch	58-0881
Johanna 21			
FEUERSTEIN, Marg.	45	Stangenrod	56-0951
Caroline 23			
FEULNER, Joh. A.	22	Unterlangenst	60-1053
Barbara 15			
FEY, Heinrich	58	Mitterode	56-0279
Catharina 45			
FEY, John	30	Schwarzenhaus	56-1011
Catharine 23, (baby) bob			
FEY, Joseph	24	Zell	61-0779
Victor 27			
FEY, Martha	35	Weissenhard	56-1260
Caroline 28			
FEZECK, Wenzel	32	Boehmen	61-0930
Theresia 33, Franz 9, Maria 10, Joseph 7			
FIALA, Franz	54	Boehmen	62-0306
Maria 58, Maria 14, Anna 29, Agnes 23			
Rudolph 9m			
FICHTERMEIR, Joh'a	30	Bevern	56-0723
FICHTNER, Friedr.	34	Pyritz	56-0632
Anna 48			
FICK, Ch.Friedr.	27	Ludwigsthal	57-1026
Wilhelmine 20			
FICKE, Amalie	23	Duermentingen	60-0521
FICKE, Bernhard	16	Eggestedt	57-1026
FICKE, Fritz	46	Salzkotten	58-0545
FICKE, J.C.(m)	25	Limstedt/Han.	60-0622
FICKEN, S.	21	Ohlenstedt	56-0512
FICKENSCHER, Jos.	23	Wuerzburg	60-0371
FICKER, John	19	Denekamp	57-1148
FIDDELLEKE, Joh.	17	Margelse	55-0413
FIDEKE, Wilhelm	17	Laskowo	62-0100
FIEBICH, Clara	19	Hildrighausen	62-0836
FIEDEL, Elise Marg	20	Starnbach	56-0819
FIEDLER, Adam	27	Uhlmannsdorf	61-0482
Ernestine 21, Herm. 23			
FIEDLER, August	38	Guntersdorf	62-0608
FIEDLER, August	34	Sammerien	59-0951
FIEDLER, Georg	19	Burgkundstadt	62-0938
FIEDLER, Ludwig	14	Beverstedt	56-1117
FIEDTKE, Aug.	32	Marienwerder	61-0804
Juliane 24, Bertha 11m			
FIEGLER, Marie	20	Emsteck	59-0951
FIEREDAG, Johann	50	New York	59-1036
Anna 50, Henry 9			
FIGGE, Carl	18	Niederense	56-0629
FIGGE, Pauline	24	Peckelsham	61-0804
Dina 9m			
FIHLER, Georg	32	Graperthofen	57-1026
Mihna 34, Friederich 1			
FILBRICHT, Carl	27	Minden	60-0785
FILIPPO, Galians	54	Italy	61-0167
FILLE, Antoina	27	Wolpiano	59-0535
FILLER, Hermann	24	Schmalkalden	62-0758
FINCK, A.M.(f)	58	Prussia	57-0555
FINCK, Arend	16	Rinstedt	58-0563
FINCK, Caspar	50	Obersuhl	55-0413
Louise 24			
FINCK, Charles	15	Obernsuhl	56-1011
FINDEISEN, Hugo	26	Chala	60-0521
FINGER, Eleanore	20	Tuschka	57-1067
FINGER, Emanuel	20	Rottendorf	60-1141
Eliza 22			
FINGER, Martin	24	Bleiwaesche	56-0723
FINGERHUT, Carolne	20	Neukirchen	62-0879
FINGERLE, Joh.	32	Esslingen	59-0990
(f) 24, (m) 2, (baby) by			
FINIS, Gebharda	26	Ehrsten/KH	60-0622
FINK, Anna	55	Wollingst	56-0512
Wilhelm 14, Mathilde 12			
FINK, Anna Cathar.	24	Ottrau/Hess.	55-0628
FINK, Caroline	17	Salzhausen	55-0413
Louise 24			
FINK, Dorette	19	Halsel	59-1036
FINK, Eleanore	20	Rendel	58-0881
FINK, Heinrich	15	Hosel	59-1036
FINK, Jacob	17	Schlitz	60-0521
FINK, Jacob	39	Bremen	59-0477
Johann 9			
FINK, Joh.	15	Kaichen	59-0990
FINK, Johann	27	Bresbach	57-1122
FINK, Justus	30	Immichenhain	58-0925
FINK, Magnus	26	Weitnau	57-0918
FINK, Wilhelm	27	Cassel	56-1044
FINKE, Eide	35	New York	59-1036
FINKE, Elisa.	20	Vilsen	57-1192

NAME	AGE	RESIDENCE	YR-LIST
FINKE, Friedrich	44	Wehden	56-0413
Cintra 28			
FINKE, Marie	21	Suedhemmen	60-0533
FINKE, Meta	21	Bottlersiel	60-0334
FINKE, Sophia	21	Preuss.Minden	60-0371
FINKE, Wm.	18	Pyrmont	57-1150
FINKELDEY, Cath.	40	Frankenberg	59-0990
(son) 9			
FINKELENBURG, Wm.	30	Bonn	58-0815
FINKENSTAEDT, Mary	20	Germany	56-1216
FINKERS, Dorothea	18	Rahden	59-0412
Marie 16			
FINNENSTEDT, Ernst	15	Lamstadt	59-1036
FINSEE, Anna	24	Heidelberg	57-0447
FINSTERER, Therese	17	Fuerth/Bav.	55-0628
FINSTERL, W.(m)	30	Wien	61-1132
FINSTERWALD, Meyer		Yacha	57-0961
FIRME, Rosette	25	Nordhausen	57-0924
FIRME, Wilh.	18	Wiehe	56-0527
FIRMETEU, Joh.	23	Hitzerode	61-0669
Heinr. 14			
FISCH, Chr.	29	Wennholshause	56-0411
FISCHBECK, Meta	22	Gestendorf	60-0411
FISCHEL, Sophie	18	Koenigswarth	59-0613
FISCHER, Adam	20	Kaltensundhei	56-0527
FISCHER, Andreas	20	Eger	56-1216
FISCHER, Anna	25	Aulfingen	60-0521
FISCHER, Anton	37	Moenchmotchel	57-1280
Elisabeth 30, Carl 7, Oskar 4			
FISCHER, Barb.	18	Schopfloch	60-1161
FISCHER, Barb.	25	Coburg	57-0422
FISCHER, Carl	26	Unterkessach	59-0214
(wife) 26, (dau.) 2, (dau.) 3m			
FISCHER, Carl	20	St.Worbis	59-1036
FISCHER, Carl Aug.	23	Brunswick	57-0555
FISCHER, Cathar.	24	Bischwind/Bav	60-0622
FISCHER, Catharina	20	Motten/Bav.	55-0628
FISCHER, Catharina	33	Oberried	61-0478
FISCHER, Catharine	25	Hutzdorf	56-1117
FISCHER, Chr.	32	New York	59-0951
FISCHER, Christ.	43	Lenn	58-0604
Margarethe 34, Margarethe 4, Christine 4			
(dau.) 6m			
FISCHER, Christian	23	Erligheim/Wrt	60-0429
FISCHER, Clemens	20	Stade	62-1112
FISCHER, Conrad	28	Cassel	56-1117
FISCHER, Dittmar	14	Elbern	57-0754
FISCHER, Emma Fr.	15	Unterkesfach	59-0214
FISCHER, Friedrich	31	Kieselbach	57-1026
Anna Cath. 38, Georg 9, Anna Barbara 8			
Anna Marg. 6			
FISCHER, Friedrich	45	Kieselbach	57-1026
Cath. Elis. 38, Friedrich 17, Heinrich 9			
Georg 7, Cath. Elis. 2			
FISCHER, Friedrich	23	Wiederau	59-0535
FISCHER, Friedrich	26	Backnang	59-1036
FISCHER, Friedrike	30	Bevern	56-0723
FISCHER, Georg	35	Borch	60-1032
FISCHER, Georg	33	Vicksburg	57-0704
FISCHER, Georg	48	Kieselbach	57-1026
Annette Dor. 35, Cath. Elis. 18			
Anna Marg. 6, Maria Elis. 2			
FISCHER, Georg	21	Wernshausen	58-0576
FISCHER, Georg	32	Ettenhausen	61-0669
FISCHER, Godfrey	32	Tremnitz	56-1011
Maria 44			
FISCHER, Gottlieb	20	Heskem	55-0845
FISCHER, Gottlieb	24	Streetz/Bav.	56-0819
Babette 25			
FISCHER, H.	35	Berghausen	59-0990
(f) 37, (f) 58, (f) 9, (f) 7, (f) 5			
(m) 3, (baby) by			
FISCHER, Heinrich	28	Horb/Bav.	60-0429
FISCHER, Heinrich	27	Hesken	56-1117
FISCHER, Henriette	41	Oschersleben	60-0521
Minna 19, Marie 17			
FISCHER, Henry	16	Cassel	59-0384
FISCHER, Henry	54	Texas	59-1036

NAME	AGE	RESIDENCE	YR-LIST
Marcy 42, Caroline 13, Mary 9, Molly 7			
Henry 3			
FISCHER, J.E.(m)	28	Willingen	62-0467
FISCHER, J.W.	27	Elbergen	62-0993
FISCHER, Jacob	49	Thalau	56-0819
FISCHER, Joh.	22	Oberohmen	61-0897
FISCHER, Joh. Aug.	30	Stressenhsn.	57-1026
Elisabeth 22			
FISCHER, Joh. G.	25	Unterlauter	55-0932
FISCHER, Joh.Georg	34	Lenn	58-0604
Jacobine 34, Georg 8, Catharine 4			
(dau.) 6m			
FISCHER, Johann	23	Hachborn	55-0630
Anna 22			
FISCHER, Johann	18	Cannstadt	56-0512
FISCHER, Johann	29	Storndorf	56-0527
FISCHER, Johann	22	Eichstadt	60-1141
FISCHER, Johann	73	Lenn	58-0604
Sophie 46, Elisabeth 25			
FISCHER, Johanna	34	Goettingen	59-0613
FISCHER, Josepha	24	Mittelfeld	62-1042
FISCHER, Julius	35	Mettingen	62-1042
FISCHER, Kunigunde	50	Maroldsweisac	60-0429
Catharine 20			
FISCHER, Ludmilla	39	Zarletzlitz	58-0925
FISCHER, Ludwig	38	Brechthausen	62-1112
Christine 36, Ludwig 13, Helene 6			
Fried. 3			
FISCHER, Magdalena	22	Maroldsweisac	56-1011
FISCHER, Magdalena	19	Heldburg	57-0654
FISCHER, Margareta	25	Hoechst	60-0521
FISCHER, Margarete	18	Offenbach	59-0613
FISCHER, Marie	59	Amoeneburg	62-0836
FISCHER, Meta	30	New York	59-0951
Dietrich 8			
FISCHER, Nathalie	25	Saalfeld	55-1082
FISCHER, Oswald	23	Podelwitz	58-0885
FISCHER, Peter	25	Damme	59-0214
FISCHER, Richard	30	New York	62-0836
(wife) 28			
FISCHER, Simon	19	Boehmen	55-0634
FISCHER, Sophie	16	Carlsruhe	56-0819
FISCHER, Valentin	20	Netzhausen	55-1082
Louise 24			
FISCHER, Valentin	27	Brettlar	56-0413
Maria 6			
FISCHER, Valentin	23	Hartershausen	57-0654
Barbara 22			
FISCHER, Victorina	55	Ichstedt	61-0897
Elisabeth 24, Caroline 20, Otto F. 14			
John C. 3, Marie 3m			
FISCHER, Wilh'mine	28	New York	62-0401
Albert 11m			
FISCHER, Wilh'mine	21	Baltimore	62-1112
FISCHER, Wilhelmne	23	Ilfeld	57-0422
FISCHLER, Franz	25	Baiern	57-0776
FISENER, Catharine	24	Germany	61-0167
FISKER, Gerhd.	32	Woquard/Ostfr	62-0712
Edo Behrend 22			
FISSMER, Gustav	19	Minden	62-0879
FISTER, Helena	27	Hannover	57-0847
FITMEYER, Heinrich	26	Hohnhausen	56-0411
Sophie 56, Augusta 6			
FITSCH, John	23	Hartford	59-0214
FITTING, Friedrich	37	Schoneberg	56-0819
Charlotte 25			
FITTLER, Barb.	51	Selten	55-0932
FIX, M.(m)	32	Brussel	62-0232
FLACH, Joseph	27	Schwaldorf/Wu	60-0429
Dorothea 28, Elisabetha 10m, Marianna 10m			
FLAGGE, Augusta	21	Markoldendorf	56-0951
FLAMERSCHMIDT, Wmn	40	Neu Schmidt	57-1416
Martin 7			
FLAMM, Johann	50	Neuhausen	56-0847
Anna Cath. 38			
FLAMMER, John D.	37	New York	62-0730
Conrad 14, John 8			
FLATAU, Louis	15	Zduny	57-1148

NAME	AGE	RESIDENCE	YR-LIST
FLATO, Emil	22	Breslau	56-1117
FLATO, Louise	27	Cassel	57-1148
Mary 17, Georg 15			
FLECK, Caroline	17	Altendorf	57-0754
FLECKE, Catharina	10	Herrnhausen	57-1407
FLECKE, Marie	25	Heimarshausen	62-0938
FLECKE, Wm.	26	Heimarshausen	62-0938
Theodea 23			
FLECKENSTEIN, An.C	18	Hoesbach/Bav.	60-0429
FLECKENSTEIN, Con.	21	Wildflecken	55-1082
Louise 24			
FLECKENSTEIN, Geo.	54	Hoerstein	61-0779
Margaretha 55, Rosine 26, Elisabeth 22			
FLECKENSTEIN, J.	22	Hoerstein	62-0836
FLECKENSTEIN, John	31	Aschaffenburg	60-0411
FLEEK, Chr.	28	Italy	62-1042
FLEGEL, Adelheid	16	Schweidnitz	57-1113
FLEGEL, Eduard	19	Schweidniz	57-1113
FLEGENHEIMER, Wilk	20	Thairnbach	61-0107
FLEINER, Ernst	18	Emden	55-0845
FLEISCHER, Anton	59	Einbeck	57-1113
Louise 30, Carl 28			
FLEISCHER, Carl	31	Erfurt	56-0629
FLEISCHER, Heinr.	23	Gerstungen	58-0576
Anna 47, Gertrude 14			
FLEISCHMANN, Gust.	35	US.	59-0951
FLEISCHMANN, J.	22	Ruhla	62-0938
FLEISCHMANN, M.	57	New Orleans	56-1216
Elise 42, Daniel 18			
FLEISCHMANN, Marg.	18	Hallerhuette	58-0563
FLEISCHMANN, Mich.	29	Baiern	57-1280
Elisabeth 26			
FLEISCHMANN, Oscar	23	Erlangen	57-0447
FLEISSNER, Fr'zka.	18	Ragenwies/Bav	60-0622
FLENTY, Georg	25	Hildesheim	59-0477
FLESSA, Mich.	23	Haila	61-0669
FLETTER, Joh.	15	Balzheim	60-0334
FLEUCHAUS, Franz	26	Galochstein	58-0815
FLIEDNER, Heinrich	20	Storkhausen	57-1067
FLIEGER, Jacob	20	Shellbach	57-0447
FLINK, Karien	28	Oldersum	58-0563
FLINK, Nicol.	28	Achtern	56-1216
FLINTJE, L.(m)	40	New York	60-0785
FLINZ, Hermann	25	Wachtum	60-0533
FLOCH, Eva	60	Ernsthausen	57-0754
FLOHR, Arnold	33	St.Louis	57-1192
Sophie 24			
FLOHR, Heinr.	22	Haudorf	62-1112
Wilhelm 18, Caroline 23, Dorette 45			
FLOHR, Peter	40	Bendorf	59-0047
Marie 36, Ida 5, Hugo 4, Rosa 3			
FLORA, Gustav	31	Wulfingerode	57-1416
Friedricka 33, Friedr. 7			
FLOTTMANN, August	19	Bueckeburg	59-0613
FLOXTER, Hirsch	20	Grossenglis	57-1416
FLUCK, Georg	36	Hannover	57-1416
Louise 30, Antonia 9, Rosine 3m			
FLUEGEL, Charlotte	16	Amenau/Curh.	60-0622
FLUEGEL, Eduard	21	Amenau/Curhes	60-0371
FLUEGEL, Ludwig	48	Neuenburg	57-0555
Cath.(f) 18			
FLUEGEL, Simon	24	Obernfuhl/Pr.	55-1238
FLUEGEL, Wilhelm	24	Prussia	57-0555
Johanna 24			
FLUEGGE, Fr.	15	Seesen	57-1148
FLURER, Georg	15	Doelsberg	58-0604
FOCKEN, Wilhelm	24	Weener	61-0682
Susanne 22			
FOECKEL, Elis.	33	Liebloss	60-0785
FOEGE, Marg.	18	Steinau	62-1042
FOEHRING, Ed.	30	Golcanda	58-0306
FOELKER, Chr.	28	Lech	58-0563
Christina 24, Heinrich 6m			
FOELL, Wilhelm	16	Giegelbach	56-0847
FOELSING, Conrad	26	Alten Schlirf	62-0879
FOERSTE, Joh.Edw.	16	Schleberoda	56-0411
FOERSTER, Andrew	54	Wien	57-0422
Josephine 44			
FOERSTER, Anna	24	Elberberg	60-0411
FOERSTER, Christne	60	Walzleben	57-0436
Louise 35			
FOERSTER, Cunig.	24	Glotzdorf	55-0932
FOERSTER, Eva	19	Lugenheim	60-0334
Babette 17			
FOERSTER, Harry	25	Dornbern	57-0654
Mary 25			
FOERSTER, Joh.	29	Blasbach	60-0521
FOERSTER, John	34	Philadelphia	62-1042
FOERSTER, Louise	24	Hoexter	59-0214
FOERSTER, Margaret	16	Windecken/CH.	60-0622
FOERSTER, Michael	15	Hoholz	61-0478
FOERSTER, Paul	52	Hoholz	61-0478
Barbara 50, Barbara 10, Michael 15			
FOERSTERLING, Wm.	27	Hannover	57-0422
FOERSTNER, M.	27	New York	62-1112
FOLEDO, de A.M.(m)	36	Arolsen	62-0306
FOLKERTS, A.H.B.	21	Fachinggerode	61-1132
FOLKMANN, Johanna	38	Copenhagen	62-0467
FOLKWEIN, Jacob	27	Westhoyel	58-0604
FOLLE, H.	15	Goettingen	59-0613
FOLLER, Joseph	41	Schoenach	60-1141
FOLMERDING, Marie	24	Bremen	60-0334
FOLTO, Fritz	24	Nebelsdorf	57-1416
FONTAINE, Hubert	28	Belgium	61-0107
FORDEMANN, (m)	30	Sachsen	62-0938
FORDUERER, E.	16	Frankenhausen	56-0512
FORKEL, Julius	18	Coburg	55-0634
FORMANN, Jacob	55	Boehmen	62-0712
Louise 30			
FORNDRAN, Elise	26	Sachs.-Mein.	57-0606
FORSCH, Wilhelm	14	Luedenstaedt	61-0482
FORST, Bertha	19	Barmen	61-0682
Joseph 14, Heinrich 12			
FORSTER, Carl Gotl	31	Erdmansdorf	57-1416
Elise 36, Robert 7			
FORSTER, Jacob	20	Edungen	60-0411
FORSTER, Josepha	18	Leuchtenberg	60-0429
FORT, Anna	25	Mainz	59-0951
Franz 8m			
FOSSEN, Elise	58	Lehe	60-0785
FRAAS, A.M.	19	Stammbuch	58-0399
FRAAS, Johann	29	Baiern	58-0399
Catha. 26, Catha. 11m			
FRABERT, H. (m)	25	Bischoffroda	62-0836
Anna C. 32, Georgine 8			
FRABERT, Maria Eva	54	Fraiersbach	62-0306
FRACHER, Heinrich	28	Steinbach	57-0447
Elisa 22			
FRACKMANN, Wilhelm	26	Hamm/Pr.	55-0628
FRAEDRICH, Wm.Frdr	49	Ziegenhagen	59-0477
Maria Elisab 59, Ernestine 18			
FRAENKEL, Caroline	19	Fuerth	59-0613
FRAENKEL, Jacob	37	Formbach	59-0613
FRAENKEL, Therese	39	Louisville	59-0951
Henry 9			
FRAENTZEL, Barbara	31	Appeln	60-0521
FRAGGE, Elisabeth	19	Eit	59-0412
Anna 16			
FRANCK, Heinrich	31	Feuchte	58-0563
FRANCK, Simon	36	Unterkassach	59-0477
FRANDZ, Zackarias	28	Herbstein	60-0998
Francisca 29, Constantina 4, Marzell 2			
Jos. 55			
FRANGEN, A.(m)	47	Sinzig	62-0730
FRANK, Abraham	16	Meinelsdorf	62-0730
FRANK, Babette	18	Berkasch	59-0048
FRANK, Bernhard	17	Iphofen	56-0847
FRANK, C.A.C.	20	Bremen	62-1112
FRANK, Caroline	29	Dresden	56-0629
FRANK, Catharine	48	Marburg	60-0334
Ottilie 15			
FRANK, Ch.	29	Duesseldorf	59-1036
FRANK, Fanny	17	Coppenbruegge	57-0422
FRANK, Fanny	23	Burgkundstadt	61-0482
FRANK, Fanny	24	Aumenau	62-0730
FRANK, Georg	60	Bretten	59-1036

NAME	AGE	RESIDENCE	YR-LIST
FRANK, H.	40	Norwich	62-0467
Johanna 40, Carl 14, Theodor 9			
FRANK, Heinrich	37	Philippsthal	60-0622
Elisabeth 38, Elisabeth 6, Louise 3			
FRANK, Heinrich	59	Fritzlar	60-0521
Fulda 57, Johanna 22, Minna 20, Moritz 17			
FRANK, Helene	22	Bruck	60-0785
FRANK, Jacob	55	Berlin	61-0804
FRANK, Joh.Georg	22	Bayern	56-1044
FRANK, Johanna	26	Besigheim/Wrt	61-0770
FRANK, Jos.	25	Hammelberg	62-0401
FRANK, Lehna	20	Heidingsfeld	61-0897
FRANK, Leopold	16	Bibra	59-0048
FRANK, Meyer	33	Weimar	50-1017
FRANK, Moritz	17	Duesselsheim	59-0477
FRANK, Moritz	17	Ruesselsheim	59-0477
FRANK, Rosa	59	Weidnitz	62-0730
FRANK, Rosalia	24	Duesseldorf	59-1036
Sibilla 22, Julia 20			
FRANK, Salomon	41	Willmen	57-1067
FRANK, Simon	40	Unterkesbach	62-0836
FRANK, Thomas	22	Hoepfingen	59-0047
FRANKE, Adam Fr.	25	Seidenroda	55-0932
FRANKE, Carl	44	Geepisdorf/Pr	55-0538
Anna 42, Anna 18, Carl 16, Caroline 9			
Johann 7, Gottlieb 4			
FRANKE, Elise	38	Bilbergen	60-0521
FRANKE, Fr.	27	Stadthagen	57-0654
FRANKE, Georg	41	Herstelle	62-0730
Augusta 24			
FRANKE, Gust	30	Kamenz	60-0334
FRANKE, Henriette	18	Neuenbrook	62-0712
FRANKE, J.W.	29	Saalfeld	56-1044
Friedrike 22, Carl 11m			
FRANKE, Joh.	36	New York	56-1216
FRANKE, John	25	New York	59-0214
FRANKE, Louise	20	Louisville	60-0785
FRANKE, Philipp	20	Fritzlar	59-0214
FRANKE, Reinh.Ferd	34	Guben	56-0819
FRANKE, Theodor	35	Ravicz	58-0925
FRANKE, Wm.	23	Rondorf	57-1416
FRANKE, Wm.	48	Columbus	62-0401
Gertrude 19			
FRANKEL, Solomon	20	Wien	61-0107
FRANKENBERG, T.	27	Charley	62-0938
FRANKENBERGER, Ph.	15	Vestheim	58-0815
FRANKENBURG, C.(m)	26	Hanau	60-0521
Anna 23			
FRANKENBURG, Joh.	27	Wilstedt	60-0334
FRANKENHEIM, Nann.	27	Nordhausen	56-0629
FRANKENHOFF, Anton	23	Suedlohn	62-0983
FRANKFORT, Christ.	20	Heyna	60-0411
FRANKL, Gottl.	18	Wien	61-0804
FRANKLIN, (Capt.)	42	Luhdun	59-0048
FRANSCH, Math.	37	Skau	59-0477
FRANTZ, Catharine	15	Bohra/Hessen	62-0608
FRANZ, Agnes	37	Mussen	57-1280
Wilhelm 20, August 18, Carl 14, Gustav 12			
Heinrich 7, Emilie 6			
FRANZ, Anton	32	Stockstadt	59-0214
FRANZ, Conrad	33	Prussia	57-0847
FRANZ, Emanuel	28	Westphalen	61-0897
FRANZ, Friedrich	30	Tromnau	56-0411
FRANZ, Heinrich	23	Groenfeld	60-0398
FRANZ, Jacob	26	Meiningen	58-0815
FRANZ, Johann	24	Hochhelheim	56-0527
Regine 36			
FRANZ, Johanna	29	Ummerstadt	60-0398
FRANZ, Joseph	27	Tuschkau	58-0881
Theresia 31, Margaretha 4			
FRANZ, M.(f)	18	Hagen	59-0477
FRANZ, Magdalene	18	Waldau	56-1117
FRANZ, Philippine	19	Germany	61-0167
FRANZEN, Mathias	33	Kester	59-0214
FRANZES, Fritz	24	Schueren	56-0411
FRATZ, Anna	63	Cerlin/W.Prus	57-0924
FRATZKE, Ferdinand	45	Selchow	56-0819
Joh.Louise 44, Carl Hermann 22, Julius 18			
Wilhelm 14, Carl 9, Gustav 7			
Marie Elise 3			
FRATZKE, Marie	59	Prosekel	56-0819
August 34, Wilhelmine 26, Hermann 8			
August 6, Albertine 4, Bertha 6m			
FRATZSHER, G. Chr.	26	Neustadt	56-0629
FRAUCKE, Ad.Gottfd	17	Muehlhausen	57-1192
FRAUENHOF, Julius	25	Haan	60-0411
Henr. Cath. 22, Emilie 11m			
FRAUSCHOLD, Friedr	28	Coburg	55-0845
FRECH, Conrad	20	Koenigsheim	60-1141
Antony 22			
FRECH, Johannes	38	Wetzlar	62-0467
FRECK, Louis	29	Stuttgart	62-0467
FRECKMANN, Andrew	21	Seburg	57-0422
FREDDERSDORF, Elis	24	Eichfir	61-0478
FREDE, Philip		Braunschweig	57-1026
FREDEMANN, Joh.Hch	28	Bueckeburg	57-1026
FREERKS, Henry	25	Wolpedorf	57-0654
FREES, Cath.	20	Ostheim	62-0401
FREESE, Ant.Friedr	25	Wayens	57-0422
FREESE, Hermann	22	Bennigen	56-1117
FREESE, Joh.Lud.	22	Bremen	62-0401
FREHLICH, Heinr.	16	Wahlen	61-0478
Jost 16			
FREIBARD, Carl Wm.	18	Marbach	62-0001
FREIBER, Christian	16	Wildbach	56-0589
FREIBERG, Betty	58	Grossneder	58-0815
Friedrich 28			
FREIBERG, Joh.Ferd	16	Cassel	57-0754
FREIBIG, J.Friedr.	29	Meiningen	61-0478
FREIDENFEHT, (f)	33	New York	57-1150
FREIGANG, Johanna	59	Ronneburg/Alt	55-0538
FREIHAMMER, Franz	58	Uhrfahr	59-0535
Marie 48, Franz 11, Allois 8			
FREIHOEFER, Elisab	18	Ordenhausen	61-0682
FREILING, Caspar	27	Holzhausen	57-1067
FREILING, William	24	Greven	57-1192
FREIMUTH, Friedr.	22	Rothuffeln	59-0384
Maria 33			
FREISE, Ludwig	20	Wirgassen	59-0990
FREISE, Ulrich	44	Hemmendorf	57-0422
Rosina 38, Lewis 14, Charsine 9, Minna 7			
FREISLEBEN, Lazar	25	Portchoir	59-1036
FREITAG, Anna	18	Dainrode	55-0630
FREITAG, August	34	Luerdissen	60-0334
Louise 21, Gustav 50, Hermandine 45			
Caroline 17, Henriette 14, Wilhelmine 11m			
FREITAG, Augusta	31	New York	57-1148
George 8, Anna 11m, Friederike 23			
Henriette 15			
FREITAG, Carl	45	Repzin	61-0478
Henriette 46, August 21, Albert 17			
Hermann 15, Friedrich 11			
FREITAG, Christian	22	Kuenzelsau	61-0478
FREITAG, Conrad	36	Wienhagen	55-0812
Anna Marie 39, Johanna 16, Simon 13			
Louise 10, Charlotte 7, Heinrich 5			
Amalia 3			
FREITAG, Daniel	36	Ziegelein	56-1011
Albertine 36, Maria 6, Gustavus 4			
Emily 3m			
FREITAG, Friedrich	42	Eisenach	62-0712
Therese 46			
FREITAG, Gottlob	50	Cembschen/Pr.	62-0608
Eleonore 25, Wilhelmine 22, Amalie 12			
Friederike 8			
FREITAG, Henry	28	Rentorf	57-0422
S. 18			
FREITAG, Michael	34	Halsbach/Bav.	55-0538
FREITAG, Theresa	37	Hohenstettin	62-0712
FREITEL, Henry	20	Hannover	57-0422
FREITZ, Jac.	34	Gonnesweiler	59-0384
FREMDLING, Carl	22	Bremervoerde	60-0622
FRENEDING, Cathar.	40	Damme	57-0961
Mary 24, Mina 14			
FRENKAMP, Heinrich	26	Lohne	62-0401
FRENTZER, Carl	36	Muenster	59-0047

NAME	AGE	RESIDENCE	YR-LIST
FRENZEL, Catharine	22	Culmbach	60-1032
FRENZEL, Lothar	19	Melborn	56-0354
FRERMANN, Engelbr.	28	Epe	56-0819
FRERS, Heinrich	14	Buttel	55-0544
FRESE, Carl	23	Schmillinghsn	57-1113
FRESENBURG, Aug.	27	Essen	56-0527
FRETHOLD, Friedr.	15	Osnabrueck	59-0951
FRETZ, Wenzel	32	Bemen	57-1280
FRETZKE, Ferdinand	45	Selchow	56-0819
Joh. Louise 44, Carl Herm. 22, Julius 18			
Wilhelm 14, Carl 9, Gustav 7			
Marie Elise 3			
FRETZKE, Marie	59	Prosekel	56-0819
August 34, Wilhelmine 26, Hermann 8			
August 6, Albertina 4, Bertha 6m			
FREUDENBERG, Fr'dr	30	Pulvermuehle	57-0422
FREUDENBERG, Wilh.	24	Lemke	56-0413
FREUDENSTEIN, Joh.	23	Philadelphia	59-0214
FREUDENSTEIN, Joh.	23	Holzhausen	59-0214
FREUDENTHAL, Fr'dr	28	Walsrode	57-0422
FREUND, Augusta	19	Kirchen	62-0467
FREUND, Conr.	31	Damm	61-0669
Franz 22			
FREUND, Elise	24	Hessen	57-0776
FREUND, Maria	23	Luxen/Prus.	55-1238
FREUNDT, Joseph	24	Schlesien	59-0372
FREY, Adam	17	Hamm/Pr.	62-0608
FREY, Clara	16	Darmstadt	57-1148
FREY, Jacob	30	New York	62-0111
FREY, Joseph	35	Stockstadt	59-0214
Maria Anna 36, Georgius 9, Franz Joseph 5			
Elisabeth 2			
FREYBE, Ferdinand	39	New York	62-0401
FREYBERG, Leopold	20	Durlach	57-1148
FREYTAG, Heloise	27	Bremen	56-0512
Henry 21			
FRIBIS, Isaac	23	Sachs.-Mein.	60-0371
FRICK, August	25	New York	62-0938
FRICKE, Andreas	52	Goslar	57-0606
Henriette 45			
FRICKE, Johann F.	14	Weihe	60-0533
FRICKE, Louis	20	Bremervoerde	59-0990
FRICKE, Marie E.	21	Hordinghausen	56-0951
FRICKE, Wilhelm	26	Witzenhausen	56-0279
FRICKEN, v. Anton	21	Vechta/Old.	60-0371
FRIDERICI, Louise	19	Han. Muenden	60-1032
FRIDERICI, Theodor		Gehaus	57-0961
FRIDRICI, Friedr.	33	Gehaus	60-0785
FRIEBEL, Charles	27	Posen	57-0961
FRIEBERTSHEUSER, J	29	Hasbach	60-0521
FRIEDBERGER, Leop.	15	Laupheim	59-0477
FRIEDE, Catharina	18	Auerbach	58-0815
FRIEDEMANN, Johann	43	Preussen	58-0399
Caroline 40, Wilhelmine 17, Louise 13			
August 9, Marie 3			
FRIEDERICHS, H.L.A	19	Hannover	62-0467
FRIEDERICI, Franz	39	Baiern	55-0634
Elisabeth 38, Friedr. 11, Catharina 9			
Maria 7, Elisabeth by			
FRIEDHEIM, Arnold	21	Muender	58-0399
FRIEDLAENDER, C.F.	23	Berlin	62-0836
FRIEDLAENDER, S.	23	Thoren	59-0477
FRIEDLANDER, Wilh.	20	Berlin	58-0604
FRIEDMANN, David	18	Heinrichs	56-0847
FRIEDMANN, Eva	24	Lengsfeld	62-0730
FRIEDMANN, Hirsch	57	Koebylin	56-0629
FRIEDMANN, Jette	26	Auerbach	56-0413
FRIEDMANN, Margart	20	Redwitz/Bav.	60-0429
FRIEDMANN, Samuel	20	Hochheim	58-0815
FRIEDNER, D.	34	Emmershausen	55-0845
Caroline 34, Clara 4, Louise 3, Joseph 2			
Hermann by			
FRIEDRICH, Conr.	28	Nimbodden	55-1082
FRIEDRICH, F.H.	26	Grebenstein	62-0993
FRIEDRICH, G.(m)	20	Karlsruhe	62-0730
FRIEDRICH, G.(m)	49	Detroit	62-0730
Johanna 29, Wilhelm 2, Julius 11m			
FRIEDRICH, Gottfr.	29	Erlangen	56-0819
FRIEDRICH, Hermann	29	Mainz	57-0924
FRIEDRICH, Joh.	35	Ernsthausen	60-0334
Margaretha 38, Helena 14, Conrad 8			
Wilhelm 2			
FRIEDRICH, Joh.Hch	28	Buffalo/NY	58-0815
FRIEDRICH, Johann	36	Ermreuth	60-0533
FRIEDRICH, Richard	22	Berlin	57-1122
FRIEDRICHS, Anna	28	Suefershausen	57-1407
August 28, Carolina 26, Johanna 15			
Carolina 7, Elise 5			
FRIEDRICHS, Ed.	33	Brakel	61-0669
FRIEDRICHS, Elise	18	Hitzerode	61-0669
FRIEDRICHS, G.W.	21	Gliessen	56-1117
FRIEDRICHS, J.Adlf	26	Bachband/Hann	62-0342
FRIEKE, Sophie	18	Steinbring	59-0412
FRIEMANN, Herm.	25	Nordhorn	57-1192
FRIES, Joh.Martin	50	Laufach	60-1053
Catharina 45, Sophia 17, Theodor 14			
Lina 12, Jacob 9, Magdalena 6, Anna 4			
FRIES, Philippine	34	Buettenhausen	56-1216
FRIESE, Chr.	58	Silkrode	62-0938
Sophie 57			
FRIESE, Ernst Lud.	56	Dachwig	55-1082
Louise 24			
FRIESE, Florentine	30	Lugde	62-1112
FRIESELMANN, Fr.	56	Linsburg	59-0535
Christine 55, Marie 23, Friedricke 19			
Caroline 16, Rosette 14, Louise 14			
FRIESER, John W.	23	Wildenreuth	57-1192
FRILLS, Theodor	25	Eppe	59-0951
FRINKNER, Elias	65	Erlingheim	59-0613
FRISCH, Cath.	17	Koethen	59-1036
FRISCH, Heinrich	24	Kaschau	58-0881
FRISCHEMEIER, Ludw	16	Westphalia	60-0371
FRISCHIN, E.Friedr	19	Bremen	60-0533
FRISIUS, Anton	21	Delmenhorst	56-1216
FRISIUS, Cath.Soph	55	Oldenburg	59-0412
FRIT, Jacob	29	Wallerstein	59-0951
FRITJES, Nicolaus	39	Goetzen	62-0712
FRITSCH, Amalia	20	Saalfeld	55-1082
FRITSCH, Joh.Chr.	30	Urbach	58-0563
FRITSCHE, Fr. Bern	27	Creuzburg	55-0812
FRITSCHE, Hermann	33	Waldenburg	59-0384
FRITSCHE, William	24	Prussia	55-1240
FRITZ, Augusta	18	Lehnberg	60-0334
Adolph 16			
FRITZ, Jacob	44	Cammstadt	62-0758
FRITZ, Joh. Geo.	21	Weilheim	60-1196
FRITZ, Joh.Gottl.	22	Kaiserbach	56-1117
FRITZ, Michael	29	New York	59-0613
FRITZ, Wilhelmine	18	Wanningheim/W	55-1238
FRITZE, Carl	45	Bremen	61-1132
Adelaide			
FRITZE, Rosalie	36	Berlin	59-1017
Ida 2			
FRITZE, Wilhelm	19	Schwarza	57-0847
FRITZENMEIER, Aug.	29	Kaldorf	57-0606
Carl 25			
FRITZSCHE, Carolne	47	Grossenstein	60-1053
Friedr. Wm. 17, Elise 10, Felix 8, Max 7			
FROBA, Johann	23	New York	59-0214
FROEBE, W.	14	Berghausen	59-0990
FROECHLE, L.(m)	29	New York	62-0467
FROEHER, Georg	42	Schwanfeld	55-0413
FROEHLICH, Conrad	14	Arnsheim	56-0413
FROEHLICH, Franz	37	Ronneberg	60-0533
FROEHLICH, H.(m)	33	Nesselrode	62-0730
FROEHLICH, Johann	22	Wornswig	57-1067
FROEHLICH, Johanna	20	Zittau	61-0804
FROEHLICH, Matth.	56	Pirk	59-0535
Barbara 56, Catharine 20, Johanna 11			
FROEHLIG, Joseph	58	Maulbach	61-0047
FROELD, John	25	Gross Waraula	56-1011
Henrietta 20			
FROELICH, Wilhelm	33	Wichmannshsn.	57-0847
FROELING, Heinrich	18	Western	56-0413
FROHBACH, Adolph	19	Leipzig	59-0613
FROHBACH, Hermann	21	Eilenburg	59-0613

NAME	AGE	RESIDENCE	YR-LIST
FROHBACH, William	50	Benrath	59-0613
FROHBERG, Elisab.	58	Eswangen	60-0785
FROHM, Fritz	24	Luebeck	57-1122
FROHMANN, Andreas	32	Erfurt	59-0613
Christiane 48, Anna 14, Maria 11			
August 9, Carl 7			
FROHN, Anna Maria	58	Baden	62-0712
FROHNFHOFER, Cath.	52	Mkt.Einershm.	61-0779
FROHSINN, L. (m)	40	Bruchhausen	55-0845
FROLICH, Mary	22	Tiefenort	57-0654
FROM, Valentin	54	Frankenthal	60-0622
FROMENT, Josephine	26	Bordeaux	62-0401
FROMEYER, Georg	19	Voxtrup	62-0983
FROMHOLZ, Gustavus	22	Berlin	56-1011
FROMME, Bernhard	31	Greven	57-1192
FRONING, Philipp	28	Moesfeld/Pr.	55-1238
FROSCH, Catharina	21	Muthmannsreut	61-0520
Catharine 18			
FROSCH, Margaretha	21	Bavaria	60-0371
Friedrich 17			
FROST, Barbara	27	Kleinberghsn.	55-0628
FROST, Franz	20	Brucks	55-0812
FROST, Joh.	37	Oberbrechen	59-1036
Magdalena 26			
FROST, Joh.	27	Oberbrechen	59-1036
Joh. 26			
FRUEHINSFELD, Marg	21	Nuernberg	56-0847
FRUEHLING, Susanna	21	Vlettindorf	60-0785
FRUEST, Jacob	27	Simonswolde	55-0413
FRUISON, Mich.	27	Rochester	62-0232
FRUK, Anna	21	Kurhessen	56-0512
FRUNK, H.	33	Berlin	62-1042
FRUST, Johannes	22	Kalkofen	56-0512
FRUTH, Georg	33	Kemnatheroed	61-0770
FRUTSCHEL, Julius	22	Leidewitz	59-0048
FRUTZSCHNER, J.F.	35	Holzhausen	56-1117
FUCHS, Ann Christ.	22	Ehringen	56-0632
Marie 37			
FUCHS, C.J.G.A.	25	Grafenberg	61-0482
Anna 25, Cath. 2			
FUCHS, Cath.	22	Aalen	60-0334
FUCHS, Cath.	42	Burkhaus	60-0334
Marie 9, Johannes 4			
FUCHS, Catharine	25	Schenksalz	57-0924
FUCHS, Emil	19	Coburg	62-0467
FUCHS, Emily	29	Berlin	57-1148
FUCHS, Emma	24	Saalfeld	62-0467
Hulda 11m			
FUCHS, Eugen	24	Meiningen	61-0478
FUCHS, Friedrich	17	Worbswede	61-0682
FUCHS, G.Michael	34	Illmenau/Sax.	62-0342
FUCHS, H.	18	Aschaffenburg	62-1112
FUCHS, Jac.	25	Sietzingen	59-0384
FUCHS, Jacob	40	Honolulu	60-0785
Anna 22, Jacob 9, Anna 9m			
FUCHS, Joh.Georg	39	Oberstreu	57-1416
FUCHS, Joseph	30	Ellwangen	60-0334
Anna 32, Anna 10m			
FUCHS, Marg.	28	Mannheim	60-0334
FUCHS, Mathias	36	Skomelns	57-1026
Rosalia 32, Maria 9, Joseph 3			
FUCHS, Michael	29	Rippeshausen	56-0819
FUCHS, Michel	34	Ewin	61-0520
FUCHS, Wilh.	19	Bremen	58-0399
FUCHSHUBER, Conrad	30	Rickingen	58-0576
FUCKE, Carl	49	Spiegelberg	57-1416
Carl 14			
FUEGLEIN, Joseph	31	Hofham	56-0847
FUEHRER, Margareta	37	Hohensolms	61-0682
Minna 11, Caroline 9, Catharine 7			
Sophia 5, Elise 4			
FUEHRER, Valentin	18	Schwarzenborn	57-0754
FUEHRING, Johann	29	Wartdorf	57-1407
FUELLBRANDT, Aug.	28	Rowno	61-0779
Caroline 27, Augusta 3, Emilie 2			
Bertha by			
FUELLER, Joseph	28	Ilvesheim/Bad	60-0429
FUELLING, Wilh'mne	25	Wehrendorf	56-0951
FUERGANG, Ed.	23	Aalen	62-0166
FUERLH, Julie	26	Tueschau	60-0521
FUERST, David	45	Althuettendor	61-0482
Wilhelmine 38, Caroline 13, Storustine 12			
Augusta 9, Ernestine 7, Louise 5, Emma 3			
August 15, Wilhelm 11m			
FUERST, Isaac	19	Rothenkirchen	59-0214
FUERST, Johann	31	Boxbrunn	61-0520
FUERST, Julie	26	Tueschau	60-0521
FUERST, Leontine	17	Berlin	57-0422
FUERST, Louis	32	Walsdorf	57-1148
FUERST, Louise	16	Huettendorf	60-0521
FUERSTENAU, Louise	22	Spenge	57-1113
FUERSTER, Cath.	20	Nellighoff	62-1042
FUERSTER, Rich.	21	Wangen	60-0334
FUERTH, Jacob	25	Tereschow	60-0521
FUERTHER, Otto	20	Pappenheim	59-1036
FUESSLER, Marg.	13	Semd	61-0669
FUESZLER, Fr. (m)	27	Friedrichstal	62-0730
FUG, J.G.	24	Elpersheim	59-0990
FUHRHAUSE, Hermann	19		59-0477
FUHRKEN, Heinrich	18	Stollham	56-1044
FUHRMANN, Johann	31	Ungedanken	57-0754
Elisabeth 37, Crescentia 11m			
FUHRMANN, O.(f)	17	Schertendorf	57-0555
FUHRMANN, Thomas	20	Borstadt	56-0819
Franziska 22			
FUHS, Friedrich	17	Worbswede	61-0682
FULLRIDE, Heinrich	24	Libenau	57-0447
FULLWALD, Herrmann	25	Stimmen/Lippe	55-1238
FUND, Johann	24	Marienkulm	56-0847
FUNK, Herm.	32	Koenigsberg	59-0951
FUNK, Martha	25	Weissenborn	60-0533
FUNK, Valentin	24	Hitzerode	56-0723
Christiane 29			
FUNK, Wilhelmina	31	Strassburg	57-0961
Emmy 5, Louis 5m			
FUNKE, C.(m)	25	Hagen	61-0482
FUNKE, Elisabeth	52	Volkmarsen	58-0925
FUNKE, Emma	23	Rochlitz	58-0815
Anna 22, Metta 15, Maria 14			
FUNKE, Franciska	39	Arnsberg	59-0412
Johann 8, Franziska 6, Gertrude 3			
Maria 9m			
FUNKE, G.	38	Wolmirstedt	62-0730
Caroline 38, Carl 3			
FUNKE, Joh.Bernh.	46	Wesecke	62-0983
FUNKE, Joh.Wilhelm	26	Holte	56-0951
FUNKE, Ph.(m)	25	Bodensee	62-0836
FURCH, Georg	33	Thueringen	57-0606
FURCH, Julius	25	Ludwigsruhe	60-0429
FUREDINK, Joseph	53	Janken	55-0845
Magdalena 53			
FUSCHS, Augusta	23	Gr.Oschersleb	59-0412
FUSS, J.Fr.	17	Ebingen	62-0938
FUSS, Joh. Th.	36	Buchenberg/Bd	60-0622
FUSS, Johannes	25	Loechau	59-0613
Jacob 9, Joh.Jac. 18, Wilhelm 15			
GAAB, Jac.	18	Speyer	61-0897
GABEL, Fr.	27	Waldeck	56-0512
GABEL, Joseph	28	Krehlau	59-1017
GABLER, Wilhelmine	30	Dinkelsbuehl	60-0334
GABRIEL, August	24	Homberg	62-0401
GABRIEL, Carl	21	Fogenau	59-1017
GABRIEL, Magdal.	17	Boehmen	60-0411
GACH, Margaretha	31	Koeppern	59-0613
GADE, Peter	42	Himmelpforten	60-1141
GADE, William	48	New York	58-0885
Friedricke 30, Anna 17, William 10			
Henry 8, Catharine 5, Friedricke 3			
GAEBE, Dora	19	Aplern	61-0482
GAEBEL, Cath.	17	Pfordt	59-0214
GAEBEL, Jac.	19	Langerdiebuch	59-0951
GAEBELEIN, Carl	38	Schips/Sax.	61-0770
Christian 38, Johann 38, Heinrich 6			
GAEDE, A.	32	Bahrendorf	62-0993
L. 9			
GAEHMANN, Wilhelm	22	Eschershausen	59-0412

NAME	AGE	RESIDENCE	YR-LIST
GAENSEHALS, Franz	39	Ringleben	56-0692
GAERSSELMEIER, M.	19	Walkring	62-0467
GAERTNER, F.	16	Oschrode	62-0993
GAERTNER, Michael	40	Altungl	58-0925
Eva 24, Oswald 4			
GAESAR, Carl	33	New York	62-0730
GAETJEN, Chr.	28	New York	57-1148
Catharina 28, Johann 3, Meta 6m			
GAETJEN, Diedrich	31	St.Magnus	60-1161
Adelheid 25, Elise 2, Berend 6m			
GAETZEN, Heinrich	16	Dedesdorf	59-0477
GAGS, (m)	27	Boston	60-0334
GAHN, Carl	27	Alsheim	62-0836
Minna 22			
GAHN, Johann	24	Philadelphia	61-0897
GAIBEL, A.	43	Neuenhain	62-0993
L. 40, M. 13, A. 7, Johann 4, M. 2			
Eberhard 3m			
GAILING, Friedrich	45	Abstadt	57-0924
Caroline 34			
GAILLE, Bapt.	30	France	59-1036
GAJER, Trina	30	Achim	59-1036
Herrmann 9m			
GALL, Johann	29	Guentersdorf	58-0881
GALL, Martin	25	Eppelsheim	61-0716
GALLEN, Theodor	41	Chicago	59-0477
GALLMEYER, Friedr.	25	Windheim	58-0545
GALMEYER, Louis	25	Rehburg	57-0578
GALSTER, Margarete	30	Weingratz	56-0632
GALSTERER, Babette	25	Schwabach	58-0563
GAMAGE, G.C.W.	38	New York	61-0804
GAMMERT, Daniel	38	Breslau/Pr.	55-0628
Anna Rosine 31, Friedr. Wm. 9			
GANEWITZ, Frid.	31	Lennep	59-0477
GANGENAGEL, C.	48	Krumstadt	62-0993
GANNSEN, Joh.	59	Thiernau	59-1036
Antje 54, Anke 23			
GANS, Christine	54	Lembach/Hess.	55-0538
GANS, Emanuel	18	Neustadt	61-0804
GANS, Leiser	19	Doensburg	60-0411
GANS, Mayer	17	Langenschwarz	56-0629
GANSKE, Ernestine	26	Selchow	56-0819
GANTER, E.	24	England	62-1112
GANZBERG, Robert	26	Berlin	62-0730
GANZWEIL, Cathrina	38	New York	56-1117
GARBARINO, Joh.	32	Genoa	62-0232
Joseph 25			
GARBRICHT, D.	23	Eisenach	55-0845
GARCIA, Alexander	24	Nizio	60-0785
GARDAU, (Capt.)	33	Luhdun	59-0048
GARDON, Johann	42	Burgstadt	56-1216
Marg. 42, Friedr. 9, Louise 5, Marie 4			
Carl 2, Louise 11m			
GAREIS, Joseph	19	Deutsch Boehm	57-1280
GARLICH, Fritz	27	Lestedt	56-0819
GARMS, Caroline	34	New York	62-1042
Sarah 9, Emilie 8			
GARMS, Peter	38	New York	62-0836
Anna 42, Marg. 8, Sophie 7, Peter 5			
GARNJOOT, Joh.	19	Detmold	59-1036
GARREL, Christ.	61	Essen	59-1036
GARREL, Honore	23	France	59-0613
GARRIGUS, Augusta	25	Dresden	62-0608
GARTE, Heinrich	20	Rittenau/Hess	55-0628
GARTELMANN, Johann	24	Wollings	56-1117
GARTEN, Auf Dem L.	15	Wehden	62-1042
GARTEN, auf d. Aug	17	Roedinghausen	60-0334
John 15			
GARTENBACH, Elisab	20	Niederheim	62-0938
GARTHE, Elisabetha	20	Geismar	60-1053
GARTHER, Bernhard	23	Burgsteinfurt	57-0509
GARTNER, Friedrich	18	Friedland	57-0654
GARTNER, J.	24	Leipzig	56-0550
GARTZKA, Friedrich	27	Prussia	62-0758
GASMANN, Louise	20	Uhlenberg	60-0521
GASS, Johannes	21	Schoenbach/He	62-0608
GASS, John	31	Cincinnati	57-0422
GASS, Martin	28	Oberzell/Bav.	60-0429

NAME	AGE	RESIDENCE	YR-LIST
GASSDORF, Christ.	25	Heuthen	56-1216
GASSERT, Joseph	21	Bruchsal	62-0879
GAST, Stephan	20	Soell	57-0578
Gertrude 23			
GASTORF, Carl Jos.	20	Heuthen	57-0606
GASTORF, Johannes	24	Heuthen	57-0606
GATESLEBEN, H.	36	Wisconsin	59-0951
GATMANN, Andreas	29	Deitstadt	57-0776
GATTERMANN, Wilh.	21	Grewe	58-0576
GATTUNG, August	20	Braunschweig	57-1280
GAUE, Joh.	28	Rollhammer	55-1082
GAUER, Heinrich	27	Seeligfeld	56-0629
Henriette 22			
GAUL, Georg	29	Tlacht	60-0785
GAULCKE, Carl	44	Nessin	56-0723
Katharina 40			
GAUME, Proper	62	France	61-0482
Philomele 25, Anastasia 24, Charles 34			
Caecilie 25, Marie 6, Leonia 4			
Martha 11m			
GAUNSEN, Joh.	59	Thiernau	59-1036
Antje 54, Anke 23			
GAUSE, Cathrine	25	Cappeln	57-1122
Elisabeth 19			
GAUSSEN, Joh.	21	Bremervoerde	60-0622
GAUTIER, Pauline	40	Paris	62-0938
GAUTIER, Reinhart	18	Rauschenberg	61-0682
Helene 20			
GEBAUER, A.Elisab.	48	Hersfeld	60-1053
GEBAUER, Martha	23	Hersfeld	62-1042
GEBCKE, Hinrich	33	Falster	57-0847
Christine 23, Conradine 2m			
GEBELER, Sophie	59	Grosshelmdorf	57-1067
GEBEN, Heinr.Aug.	19	Altenbruch	58-0563
Johanna Marg 22			
GEBER, August	28	Lippe	58-0545
GEBERT, Catharine	22	Volkshausen	59-0477
GEBHARD, Georg	29	Strahlenfels	57-1113
Alma 26, Georg 4m			
GEBHARDS, Bernh.	24	Repsholt	59-0535
GEBHARDT, August	33	Elvershausen	56-0847
Catharina 13			
GEBHARDT, Ernst	35	Unterwirrbach	60-0429
GEBHARDT, Friedr.	22	Neustadt	56-1117
GEBHARDT, Johann	25	Bepsfeld	57-1280
Hilke 28			
GEBHARDT, Julie	26	Neustadt	60-0411
Oscar (died) 9m			
GEBHARDT, Ulrich	32	Stadelhofen	62-0608
GEBNER, Wilhelm	20	St.Louis	59-1036
GEDDGE, Rebecca Ma	23	Exin	59-0214
GEEHN, Hinr. v.	34	Wallingh.	59-0214
GEERKE, Aug.F.	29	Berlin	59-1017
GEERKEN, Georg Nig	18	Brunshausen	57-0654
GEERKEN, Heinr.	20	Worpswede	56-0723
GEERKEN, J.(m)	30	New York	62-0836
GEERKEN, Lina	24	Hopswede	62-0836
Gesche 9			
GEESEN, Joh.H.	19	Bremerhaven	62-0401
GEFFKEN, Cath.	35	New York	59-0951
Joh. 9, Heinrich 3, Diedrich 9m			
GEFFKEN, Elise	18	Westewede	56-0723
GEGNER, Joh.	26	Untertanbach	60-0334
GEHBAUER, Ernst.	44	Oberhusdorf	57-1113
Johann 29, Friedrich 1			
GEHEL, Michael	24	Hermannsfeld	56-0413
Barbara 30			
GEHLE, Carl	24	Windheim	58-0545
GEHLERT, Eduard	26	Schlettau/S.	60-0429
Christ.Frdka 31, Marie Aug'ta 7			
GEHLING, Bernhard	56	Wessum	59-0951
GEHLING, Elisabeth	50	Wessum	59-0951
Herrmann 7			
GEHNER, Franz	45	St.Louis	59-1036
Charlotte 42			
GEHR, Barbara	28	Eckenhaid	57-1113
Anna 4			
GEHR, J.G.(m)	19	Pliezhausen	60-0411

NAME	AGE	RESIDENCE	YR-LIST
GEHRING, Charles	49	Naumburg	57-0961
Bertha 19			
GEHRING, Elisabeth	20	Coburg	56-0847
GEHRING, Gertrud	21	Osnabrueck	56-1216
GEHRING, Wilhelm	6	Prellwitz	56-0819
Christ 42, Friederike 32, Wilhelmine 14			
August 31, Emilie 23, Bertha 10m			
Friedrich 59			
GEHRS, Johann	25	Ostereistedt	58-0563
GEIBEL, Adam	21	Boehmen	58-0399
Julius 18			
GEIDEHUS, J.Fr.Chr	21	Bremervoerde	58-0563
GEIDER, F.(m)	22	Mannheim	62-0836
GEIER, Gottfried	18	Konigsberg/Sx	60-0622
GEIGEL, Ludwig	26	Wuerzburg	58-0604
GEIGER, Christiane	20	Zell	56-1260
GEIGER, Friedricke	16	Fuerstenberg	57-1407
GEIGER, Johannes	13	Waldstetten	60-0371
Franziska 44, Franz 9			
GEIKOFF, Joh.	30	Burgsteinfort	56-0512
Marie 30			
GEILHARDT, Ernstne	27	Freidelberg	58-0563
GEILHORN, Joseph	48	Hildesheim	56-1260
GEINZER, Catharina	27	Erlangen	57-0447
GEINZER, Georg	27	Weissendorf	57-0447
GEIRTH, Carl	25	Breslau	59-0412
GEIS, Barbara	45	Ob.Altenbusch	61-0779
Josepha 8			
GEISEL, Anna	14	Langenhain	59-1036
GEISENBERGER, Lea	23	Biebergau	60-0521
GEISENDOERFER, Dor	19	Weigersheim	60-0334
GEISENHOEFER, Elis	34	New York	62-0712
GEISLER, Amalie	20	Sackwitz	60-1196
GEISLER, Augusta	27	Prausewitz	57-0754
GEISLER, J.Georg	56	Pennsylvania	59-1036
GEISLER, Joh.Gotfr	36	Annaberg	56-0819
GEISLER, Robert	13	New York	58-0604
GEISLER, Rosine	23	Tutlingen	59-1036
GEISLER, Wilhelm	28	Lignitz	56-0847
Theresia 33			
GEISS, Andreas	58	Neudorf	60-1053
Caroline 21			
GEISS, Bar.	20	Rhina	58-0576
GEISSDORFER, Wm.	14	Weikersheim	57-0924
GEIST, J.G.	70	Grossforst	61-0669
Ros. 23			
GEIST, Wilhelm	28	Osterode	57-1407
GEIWITZ, Barbara	53	Guplingen	62-0879
GEIZ, Peter	20	Buttenstadt	59-1036
GELCKE, Hinrich	33	Falster	57-0847
Christine 23, Conradine 2m			
GELFIUS, Martin	18	Darmstadt	57-1407
GELLENBERG, Maria	22	Gutenthal	61-0682
GELLERMANN, Joh.H.	18	Wiesedermer	58-0925
GELLERT, Carl	21	Niederlosnitz	55-0538
GELLERT, Elisabeth	17	Koenigsberg	57-1067
Christina 20			
GELLINGS, Th.	36	Keppeln	58-0306
GELZHAUSEN, Carl	15	Bauerbach	62-0467
GEMEINER, Johann	35	Tirschenreuth	57-0754
GEMEINHARD, Eduard	24	Rehau	62-0306
GEMEINHARDT, Anna	29	Berg	56-0723
GEMLING, Adelheid	26	Schale	56-0819
GEMPP, Wm.	23	St.Louis	60-0785
GENEROTH, Adam	20	Hainershausen	57-1407
GENF, Louise	21	Homburg	62-0730
GENNERT, Cordelia	30	New York	59-1036
GENNERT, Gottl.	33	New York	59-1036
GENSLER, Pauline	29	Posen	57-0654
GENTZ, August	34	Zerben	56-0411
GENTZEL, E.	22	Brick	56-0512
GENTZEN, L. (m)	27	Prussia	57-0555
P.(m) 10			
GENTZOCH, Moritz	28	Liebenwerda	56-0279
GENZBERGER, Louis	36	Alexandria/VA	58-0815
GENZLER, Franz	39	Oberfeld	61-0779
Verena 30, Gotthardt 2, August by			
Heinrich 19, Ludwig 22, Johann 24			

NAME	AGE	RESIDENCE	YR-LIST
GEORG, Marie	18	Loesheim	60-0521
GEORGE, Peter	25	Esterode	58-0563
GEORGI, Fr'dr.Bern	21	Laubegast	60-0429
GEOVANNY, Gellania	41	New York	59-0951
GEPHARDT, Elise	24	Dortmund	58-0576
GERALD, Baronin v.	52	Bremen	59-0613
Carlotta 20, Dorothea 16, Bertha 15			
GERAND, Ant.	37	France	62-1112
GERARD, D.F.	35	Louisville	62-1042
Elise 27, Julie 3m			
GERBACH, Joh.	34	Oberreichenba	56-0411
GERBEDING, Berndne	32	Berklen	59-0951
Sophie 9			
GERBEDING, C.O.	42	San Francisco	56-1216
GERBER, Elisabeth	22	Hostann	58-0925
Caroline 16			
GERBER, Fr.(m)	24	Heidelberg	62-0836
GERBER, Franz	18	Lissa	60-0785
GERBER, Marg.	33	Waldthann	62-0836
GERBER, Veronica	60	Bern	59-0951
GERBER, Wilhelm	19	Wolfenbuettel	57-1280
GERBERS, Christian	30	Reimern	57-0847
GERBIG, Georg	23	Lauterbach	58-0545
GERBIG, Louise	18	Alsfeld	55-0630
GERBRAST, Elisab.	21	Hessen	56-1044
GERCK, Anna Adelhd	48	Uenzen	58-0881
Johann 16			
GERDERS, Reinke	28	Horsten	56-0629
GERDES, Dirk	41	California	60-0052
Anna 31, Gilke 8			
GERDES, M.D.	20	Rustersiel	59-0613
GERDES, Marie	45	Apen	60-0533
GERDTS, Carst.	16	Alt Lueneburg	56-1117
GEREK, Carl	20	Barsinghausen	57-0436
GERETH, Fried.Ph.	50	Washington	59-0477
GERHARD, Augusta	16	Roemershag	60-0533
GERHARD, Elise	23	Feldar	57-0776
GERHARD, Emilie	20	Barknau	56-1044
Elisabeth 20			
GERHARD, Ferdinand	26	Neustadt/Sax.	55-0538
GERHARD, Gotth.	35	Wiederau	59-0535
Augusta 32, Augusta 9, Therese 7			
Emilie 4, Amalie 1			
GERHARD, Otto	23	Danzig	56-1011
Katharine 34			
GERHARDT, Carl	23	Jena	57-0918
GERHARDTS, C.	25	Remscheid	62-1169
GERICKE, G.	39		59-0990
(f) 32, (f) 7			
GERICKE, Theodor	33	Joachimsthal	57-0578
GERIDES, Heere	27	Repsholt	59-0535
Anna 17			
GERIDES, Marie		Repsholt	59-0535
Hilke			
GERKE, Carl	60	Padile	57-0847
Christine 64			
GERKE, Catharine	19	Nienburg	57-0606
GERKE, Hermann	28	Hannover	57-0847
GERKE, Zacharias	27	Stockheim	56-0951
Catharina 24			
GERKEN, Anna	20	Hagen	58-0925
GERKEN, Bertha	9	New York	62-0467
GERKEN, Catarina	19	Bremervoerde	57-0776
Ernst 16			
GERKEN, Claus	47	Cassebruch	56-0589
Elisabeth 41			
GERKEN, Claus	25	Heise	59-0047
GERKEN, G.	29	US.	59-0951
Catharine 29			
GERKEN, Hinrich	23	Westendorf/Ha	57-0847
GERKEN, Lueder	20	Loxstedt	61-0520
GERKER, Joh.Heinr.	42	Badbergen	57-0704
Cath.M.Adel. 51, Cath.Marie 17			
GERKHARDT, Emma	22	Weisheim	62-0401
GERLACH, Chr.	25	Minsleben	57-0654
GERLACH, Elise	18	Gedern	60-0334
GERLACH, Ernestine	54	Mussleben	61-0482
GERLACH, Isabella	19	Frankfurt	62-1112

NAME	AGE	RESIDENCE	YR-LIST
GERLACH, Joh.	25	Constanz	60-1161
GERLACH, John H.Ch	26	Bayern	57-0654
GERLACH, Lucas	20	Warnitz	60-0533
GERLACH, Margar.	24	Frauensee	56-0512
GERLACH, Philipp	16	Frieberg/Darm	60-0371
GERLING, Friedr.	33	Hille	56-0411
Louise 29, Friedrich 6m			
GERLING, Friedrich	47	Hille	55-0411
Elisabetha 35, Carolina 5, Heinrich 4			
Marie 34			
GERLING, W.L.	35	Minden	58-0399
GERMANN, Helene	36	Darmstadt	59-0951
GERMANN, Wilhelmne	16	Weisensee	59-0412
GERMANNS, Geo.Hch.	27	Hochstedt	57-1067
GERMER, H.(m)	52	Baltimore	61-1132
Hch.(f) 26			
GERMEROTH, Cathar.	37	Heimershausen	57-1280
Johann 15, Maria 9, Heinrich 7			
GERNAND, Louise	32	Hermannstein	59-0214
Catharine 8			
GERNENDT, J.Geo.L.	29	Wuerttemberg	59-0372
GERNER, Cath.	16	Hofheim	57-0606
GERNGROSS, Minna	22	Thalmassing	56-0819
GERNREICH, Marcus	38	Liverpool	56-1117
GEROET, Anna	22	Alt Lueneburg	60-0785
GEROLD, Emma	22	Gera	58-0881
GEROT, Marie	24	Germany	61-0167
GERSON, Dina	20	Erbecn	59-0951
GERSON, Gottlieb	25	Landorf	59-0951
GERST, Bernh.	16	Vechta	59-0951
GERSTENSCHLAEGER,J	14	Hessen	60-1161
GERSTNER, Moser	16	Listberg	57-1067
GERSTNER, Therese	64	Bavaria	60-1161
GERTH, Christian	26	Bantorf	57-0021
GERTH, W.(m)	21	Breslau	61-0804
GERTZEN, A.(m)	37	Philadelphia	61-0804
GESCHWITZ, Herm.	25	Dresden	50-1017
GESSLER, Adolph	32	Heichlatte	59-0951
Pauline 32			
GESTATTENER, Math.	50	Soell	57-0578
GESTENBERGER, F.	27	Schweinsdorf	56-0512
GEUMANN, Albert	17	Heuthen	57-0606
GEUTER, Anna	60	Gestungshause	56-0512
Johanna 23, Anna 21			
GEUTNER, Franz	25	Burgpreppach	61-0520
GEUZEL, Augustus	22	Gr.Weschungen	56-1011
GEWEHR, Johannes	19	Obernfuhl/Pr.	55-1238
Anna Maria 21			
GEYER, Carl	26	Steppach	56-0819
GEYER, Friedrich	17	Gotha	56-0819
GEYER, Mathias	30	Linden	62-0712
Marianna 24			
GIANONE, V.	27	Italy	61-0107
Augusto 26, Antonio 57			
GIARETTY, Giovanny	29	Italy	60-1161
GICK, Hermann	20	Osnabrueck	57-1407
GIEBEL, Johanna	25	Meiningen	61-0478
GIEBELHAUS, Sophia	15	Frankenberg	57-0924
GIEGERITH, Barbara	27	Raetz	56-0589
Eugenia 50			
GIENEN, Johannes	24	Olsbruecken	62-0401
GIERECKE, H.C.	17	Loxstedt	62-0836
GIERL, J.B. (m)	28	Iowa City	61-0804
GIES, Anna	26	Niedergoss	56-1260
GIES, George	40	Ronshausen	56-0279
Heinrich 3			
GIES, Margar.	26	Steinbach	56-0512
GIESCH, Joseph	34	Minten	56-0411
Amalia 24			
GIESCHEL, Carl	20	Hohenwart	62-0879
GIESE, Augusta	20	Carlshafen	60-0398
GIESE, Conrad	16	Cassel	56-0512
GIESE, Ferdinand	14	Cassel	57-0754
GIESE, Gustaf	26	Posen	59-0412
Wilhelmine 22, Gustav 11m			
GIESE, Julius	36	Mohrin	56-0819
Wilhelmine 36, Gustav 3, Emilie 3m			
GIESECKE, Augusta	28	St.Louis	58-0604

NAME	AGE	RESIDENCE	YR-LIST
GIESECKE, Conrad	26	Schmarje	59-0384
GIESELBACH, Christ	38	Rodebach	59-0613
Martha 23, Cath. 4			
GIESS, Eduard	20	Neustadt	59-0535
GIESSELMANN, Moriz	20	Volmerdingsen	57-0021
GIESSENHAUS, Fr'dr	25	Bridenei	57-1280
GIESSING, Dan.	23	Nuernberg	60-0334
GIESSLER, Anna	21	Guxhagen	57-0754
Elisabeth 33			
GIFHORN, August	24	Lippe/Detmold	57-1280
(child) 1			
GILBERT, Christina	30	Bavaria	60-0371
Theodora 6m			
GILDEMEISTER, A.	40	New York	62-1042
Mrs. 36, Cath. 11, Mary 10			
GILDERMANN, Fr.H.	30	Oldendorf	56-1204
GILEG, Louise	32	Nesselgrund	57-0847
Wilhelm 10m			
GIMBEL, Heinr.	24	Welfterode	55-1082
GIMBER, Georg	24	Lobenfeld	57-0847
GIMPEL, Marg.	35	Cassel	57-1192
Elisabeth 56, Margaretha 27			
GIMSCH, Emilie	21	Wallendorf	61-0520
GINDIA, Anna	19	Cologne	56-0512
Bertha 12, Otto 8			
GINDRICH, Matthias	25	Hodina	61-0779
Anna 51			
GINGERICH, Barbara	27	Raetz	56-0589
Anton Bernh. 9m			
GINGERICH, Dan.	26	Braunfeld	62-0467
GINOCCHIO, Pietro	35	Italy	61-0107
GIOBBEE, Emilie	21	Bordeaux	62-0401
GIOVANNETTI, A.	19	Switz.	62-0467
GIPPRICH, Joseph	39	Michigan	59-0477
Dina 41, Marie 5, Elisabeth 3			
GIRAND, Eduard	32	America	56-1216
GIROU, Jean	30	France	62-0938
GISSEL, H.	17	Marburg	59-0990
GISTEL, Johann	69	Weissenburg	62-0100
Louise 6			
GLACKEMEYER, Carl	10	Oldendorf	60-1032
Charlotte 13			
GLADEN, v. Anna	19	Wollings	56-1117
GLAESER, Caspar	19	Curhessen	60-0371
GLAESER, Fr.	27	Baltimore	61-0167
Wm. 29			
GLAESER, Johann	36	Baltimore	59-0951
Marg. 37, Georg 11m			
GLAESSNER, Henr'tt	29	Clausthal	55-0413
GLAHN, J.H.	28	New York	62-0938
GLAHN, Lena	28	Beverstedt	60-0785
GLAHN, Nie.	22	Fressdorf	59-0535
GLAHN, v. Claus	22	Bremerhafen	59-1036
GLAHN, v. Fr.	18	Habichhorst	56-1117
GLAHN, v. Gesche	21	Lehe	60-1161
GLAHN, v. John	30	New York	62-0467
GLAISNER, Chr.Fr.	59	Goslar	57-0606
Marie 49, Louis 7, Chr.Fr. 31			
GLANDER, Wilh'mine	17	Oldenburg	62-0758
GLANZ, Julius	20	Markgroningen	57-0422
GLANZEL, Aug.Jul.	38	Dresden	58-0885
GLAS, Adam	27	New York	59-0535
GLASER, Ad.	15	Tereschau	62-0730
GLASER, Adolph	31	Weimar	61-0682
Ernestine 25, Carl 2, August 3m			
GLASER, August	32	Janau	60-1161
Johanna 31, Edward 4, August 1			
GLASER, August	41	Leindorf	62-0712
Charlotte 40, Herrmann 12, Anna Augusta 9			
Carl 6, Heinrich 4, Anna 11m			
GLASER, Barbara	21	Doberschuetz	60-0521
GLASER, Ernst	35	Leindorf	62-0712
Wilhelmine 34, Bertha 5, Herrmann 3			
GLASER, Franz	14	Cronach/Bav.	60-0429
GLASER, G.F.(m)	21	St.Louis	62-0111
GLASER, Louis	14	Tereschau	59-0477
GLASS, Carl	22	Baltimore	59-0951
GLASS, Friedr.	47	Rittwitz	55-1048

NAME	AGE	RESIDENCE	YR-LIST
Wilhelmine 41, Babetta 17, Siegfried 15			
Johanna 13, Carl 11, Caroline 7			
Augusta 5, Heinrich 2			
GLASS, Sophie	60	Darmstadt	60-1161
GLASSICK, F.	31	Memphis	62-1042
GLAUBER, Anna	21	Melzting	55-0932
GLAUBIT, J.(m)	28	Prussia	57-0555
GLAUBITZ, August	31	Wuestenroth	60-1053
GLAUBITZ, Charlott	51	Lauburg	57-0704
Caroline 16, Emilie 14			
GLAWATZ, Gustav	30	Liebenau	62-0938
GLEBE, Joh.Ernst	21	Niedergoss	56-1044
GLEICHMANN, Carl	17	Schleusingen	57-0924
GLEICHMANN, Dan.	38	Themar	57-0578
Barbara 41, Rosamunde 9, Johann 8			
Marie 6, Georg 48			
GLEICHMANN, Louis	21	Berlin	62-0730
GLEIM, Friedrich	50	Homberg	61-0520
Elisabeth 54, Heinrich 19			
GLEIM, Johann	18	Homburg	58-0545
GLEISSENBERG, Rosa	32	Berlin	57-0961
GLENAU, Louis	40	US.	61-0167
GLESER, Georg	34	Schweinshaupt	60-0622
Margaretha 33, Margaretha 14			
GLEYER, Heinrich	10	Oehrbeck	57-1407
Carl 8			
GLIES, Conrad	18	Erdmannrode	57-1067
GLIEWER, Ignatz	31	Nordheim	61-0478
GLINKE, Wilhelm	37	Marienwerder	57-0704
Wilhelmine 34, Johanna 7, Caroline 5			
Hermann 3, Theodor 2			
GLISS, Heinrich	36	Schlitz	56-0629
Barbara 39, Johannes 8, Catharina 23			
GLOCK, Elise	18	Hessen	60-1161
GLOCKMEYER, S.A.	27	Dramfeld	59-0477
GLOECKLER, Joh.	60	Unterbalzheim	60-0334
Marg. 57, Marg. 24, Anna 18, Barbara 16			
Georg 13			
GLOECKNER, Bernhar	20	Lich	59-0214
Marie 22, Marie 9m			
GLOECKNER, Friedr.	24	New York	59-0214
GLOGACOSKA, Anna	26	Neustadt	60-0521
GLUCKER, Barbara	27	Neidingen	60-0398
GLUECK, A.	35	Windheim	62-0993
E. 28			
GLUECK, Dietr.H.	32	Mattfeld	57-0850
Margaretha 33, Anna 6, Adelheid 11m			
GLUECK, Ph.K.	23	Dettingen	62-0166
GLUECK, Philipp	20	Dettingen	59-0951
GLUECKAUF, Gottfr.	24	Ratnitz	57-0924
Lotte 21			
GLUECKAUF, Jacob	22	Raudnitz	61-0779
GLUESNER, Chr.Fr.	59	Goslar	57-0606
Marie 49, Louis 7, Chr.Fr. 31			
GLUSER, Friedrike	21	Grosbach/Wrt.	60-0052
GLUTH, Christoph	51	Grunau/Pruss.	57-0924
Henriette 37, Friedrich 21, Johann 14			
Ludwig 11, Stephan 9, August 7			
Wilhelmine 4, Daniel 1			
GNEISIG, Chr.	42	Merseburg	59-1036
GNIRSZ, Karl	64	Emmingen/Egg	57-0080
Katharine 62			
GOBEL, Jacob	25	Arheilgen	60-0785
GOBEL, Johannes	27	Allendorf	55-0630
GOBRECHT, Christ.	24	Wilhelmshsn.	57-0578
Georg 16			
GOCK, John Friedr.	23	Bergen	57-0654
GOCKE, Edwin	18	Blomberg/Lipp	57-0847
GODA, Therese	22	Eber	60-0785
GODDAR, Caroline	29	Duesseldorf	61-0897
GODDE, Carl	16	Sottinghausen	58-0925
GODE, Christoph	27	Wobbe	57-0847
GODKNECHT, Hartwig	26	Kaickhorst	57-0654
GOEBEL, Albert	20	Almenhausen	57-1067
GOEBEL, Anna Elis.	30	Niederurf	57-0754
GOEBEL, Caroline	44	Hersfeld	60-0521
Adam 14			
GOEBEL, Caroline	37	Reinhardshsn.	61-0478

NAME	AGE	RESIDENCE	YR-LIST
GOEBEL, Gustav	26	New York	56-1216
GOEBEL, Heinrich	18	Holzhausen	57-0924
GOEBEL, Johann	27	Nassau	55-0630
Peter 19			
GOEBEL, Johann	27	Gausschasch	61-0779
Catharina 24			
GOEBEL, Salamene	25	Wittenberg	57-1067
Albert 8			
GOEBET, Otto	24	Glaudenbach	56-0629
GOECKE, Georg	17	Pyrmont	57-0509
GOECKEMEYER, Engel	20	Halden	56-0951
GOEDECKE, August	24	Halle	56-0723
GOEDECKE, Hermann	18	Hastede	60-0429
GOEDHALS, W.	59	Moorlage	62-0993
GOEGELEIN, Fr.	28	Wuertemberg	57-0606
GOEHMANN, Ludw.	29	Allendorf	56-0723
GOEHRING, Rosalie	19	Buessleben	56-0589
GOEHRING, W.R.F.	25	Ronneburg	58-0576
GOELFERT, Lorenz	30	Meiningen	55-0634
GOELKEL, Georg	35	New York	56-1216
Antonie 25			
GOELLNER, Math.	27	Graag	59-0477
GOENNEL, Franz	18	Reichenbach	58-0576
Ernestine 16			
GOENNER, Friedrich	36	Assendorf	61-0478
Wilhelmine 32			
GOENNERMANN, Carl	18	Luederbach	60-1141
GOEPPEL, Heinr.	34	Baltimore	62-0401
GOEPPERT, Christ.	22	Milwaukee	57-0654
GOERING, Joh.	51	Hoerner	60-1161
Dorothea 39, Henriette 19, Caroline 12			
August 9, Herman 3			
GOERKEN, Beta	27	Schlat	56-1117
GOERTZ, Rudolph	40	Saalfeld	60-1053
GOERZIG, Sophie	20	Rotenburg/Hes	55-0628
GOESKER, Friedrike	40	Esten	56-1044
GOESSMANN, C.(m)	40	Goettingen	57-0578
GOETHEL, Fr.(m)	24	Bitterfeld	56-0723
GOETTEN, Marie	18	Giershagen	56-0951
GOETTING, Herrmann	31	Philadelphia	57-0365
Lisette 26			
GOETYEN, August	18	Dorum	60-1141
GOETZ, Barbara	17	Schwirbitz	56-1044
GOETZ, Elias	16	Hargasthausen	60-0521
GOETZ, Elisabeth	21	Coburg	57-1067
GOETZ, Friedrich	30	Rohdach	59-1017
GOETZ, Hermann	32	Neuenburg	57-0776
Dorothea 32, Martha 4, Maria 2			
GOETZ, Joh. Georg	46	Haueneberstn.	60-0622
GOETZ, M.(m)	41	Vilseck	62-0730
GOETZ, Michael	35	Jettelhofen	57-0754
GOETZ, Moses	19	Fuerth	60-0785
GOETZ, Pauline	17	Coburg	57-1067
GOETZ, Romann	51	Oberroth	55-0845
Elisabeth 47, Daniel 25, Ferdinand 18			
Antoni 16, Emilie 10, Anna 6			
GOETZE, Abraham	30	Flemmingen	61-0482
GOETZE, Christine	22	Alack	58-0604
GOETZE, Doris	32	New York	61-0897
GOETZE, Ernst	26	Koehlen	56-1117
GOETZE, Friedrich	27	Sachsenhausen	61-0682
GOETZE, Heinrich	34	Gottsburen	58-0563
Amalia 35, Wilhelm 2			
GOETZE, Louis	29	New York	60-1196
Emmy 22, Helene 3			
GOETZE, Wilhelm	52	Obermehler	57-0924
Joh.Dorothea 13			
GOETZE, X.(m)	26	Chemnitz	62-0836
GOEY, Marie A. de (f)	28	Baltimore	59-0613
GOGARYA, F.	46	Panama	59-1036
GOLDBACH, Mar.Elis	26	Dietershausen	56-0819
GOLDFUSS, Barbara	23	Haselbrunn	62-0467
GOLDHAHN, Johanna	23	Dresden	59-1036
GOLDKAMP, Friedr.	29	Belm	60-0521
GOLDKAMP, Louise	36	Hurg	62-0467
GOLDMANN, Gretel	31	Bavaria	55-0628
GOLDMANN, Sophie	18	Zirden	56-0951

NAME	AGE	RESIDENCE	YR-LIST
GOLDMEIER, R.(m)	17	Lotte	62-0836
GOLDNER, Therese	45	Senna/Pr.	60-0371
GOLDNER, Wilhelm		Aschaffenburg	57-0578
GOLDSCHMIDT, Bernh	26	Nordwalde	59-0951
GOLDSCHMIDT, Carln	28	Geisa	61-0107
GOLDSCHMIDT, Greta	18	Voerden	56-0629
GOLDSCHMIDT, H.(m)	22	Berlin	62-0836
GOLDSCHMIDT, Janas	38	Hammelburg	58-0815
Sara 24			
GOLDSCHMIDT, Janet	17	Wehrda	60-1161
GOLDSCHMIDT, M.Ann	20	Furth	57-1148
GOLDSCHMIDT, Mark	20	Zuellicken	59-1036
GOLDSCHMIDT, Ph.	45	New York	61-0804
GOLDSCHMIDT, Rika	21	Lutzbuerg/Bv.	55-0538
Julie 18			
GOLDSCHMIDT, S.(m)	24	Breitzbach	61-0482
GOLDSTEIN, Ad.	38	New York	62-0467
Louise 33, Henry 6, Anna 2, August 11m			
GOLDSTEIN, Bertha	17	Zduny	57-1148
GOLJENBOOM, Jan E.	21	Upleward	57-0422
GOLKE, Mar.Justin	40	Kossel	57-1416
GOLL, Anna Marie	38	Dannberg	56-1117
GOLL, Joseph	42	Dannberg	56-1117
GOLLER, Maria	17	Wuestenselbit	55-0628
GOMBERG, Henry	17	Gomberg	58-0545
GOMBERT, Johanna	20	Ruderichshsn.	57-0447
GOMMER, Zacharias	55	New York	60-0334
GOMPF, Georg	52	Niederofleide	62-0712
Margaretha 53, Margaretha 22, Johannes 18			
Wilhelm 16			
GONNER, Christian	41	Marienhagen	61-0930
GONNERMANN, Adam	24	Luderbusch	55-0932
Anna 24, Jacob 9m			
GONZALES, L.(m)	25	Campeche	62-0836
GOODMAN, N.	25	LaGrange	56-0550
GOPPERT, Sophie	28	Coburg	60-1161
GORATH, Heinrich	28	Oldenburg	57-0754
Anna Maria 30, Anna Cathar. 11m			
GORDNER, Peter	23	Bricken	59-0384
GORDOERFER, Emily	17	Furth	57-1148
GORENFLO, L.	22	Friedrichstal	62-0938
Gottfr. 24, Gustav 19, Wilhelm 32			
Catharina 33, Caroline 4, Wilhelm 2			
Louise 6m			
GORGE, Anna	21	Ellenberg	59-0214
GORGES, Margaretha	50	Wellmich/Nas.	55-1238
GORGES, Philipp	28	Frankfurt/M.	55-1238
GORIG, Peter	17	Wallenrode	61-0804
Carl 14			
GORR, Ph.(m)	27	Heuchelheim	62-0467
GOSBECHER, Ludwig	23	Curhessen	58-0399
GOSLAR, C.H.	29	Bueckeburg	56-0629
GOSS, Joh.	22	Ruppertsburg	59-1036
GOSSERT, Christian	31	Nierstein	59-0048
GOSSLER, Elise	22	Ronshausen	56-0279
GOSSMANN, Salomon	39	Breslau	57-1122
Fegele 37			
GOSTERMANN, Carl	17	Singen	57-1122
GOTKE, Joh.	54	Essen	59-0613
GOTSBECK, Gottfr.	28	Hutzdorf	56-1216
GOTSCHILLING, Gotl	34	Schoenwalden	57-0754
GOTSCHING, Otto	30	Waterburg	62-0836
GOTTAS, Johann	34	Blattnitz	58-0881
Barbara 29, Anna 1			
GOTTBEHOERDE, Fz.	20	Demme	57-1192
GOTTBRECHT, Sebast	24	Edling	56-1117
Franciska 25			
GOTTE, Helen	16	Osnabrueck	57-0654
GOTTENDIECK, Elise	19	Oldendorf	60-0521
GOTTER, Florentine	23	Essen/Pr.	62-0608
GOTTFRIED, Haths	36	Hornau	57-0654
GOTTHELF, Henriett	21	Hofgeismar	62-0712
GOTTHOLD, Margaret	26	Meisenheim	60-0785
GOTTING, Christian	50	Krackau	57-1026
Friederike 31, Franziska 3			
GOTTLIEB, Ignatz	20	Koenigsberg	56-1216
GOTTO, Levy	25	Alsace	61-0716
GOTTSACKER, Jac.	16	Maisschofs	55-0932

NAME	AGE	RESIDENCE	YR-LIST
Marie 25, Sabaste 3			
GOTTSCHALG, J.Gotl	27	Lennewitz	57-0422
Louisa 28, Anna 11m			
GOTTSCHALK, Heinr.	23	Speckwinkel	57-0754
Johannes 16			
GOTTSCHALK, Ma.(f)	30	New York	60-0334
GOTTWALD, Franz'ka	26	Glatz	57-0754
GOTTWERTH, Christ.	25	Kirtorf	55-0630
Maria 22			
GOYTIZOLA, de D.A.	57	Cienfuegos	62-1042
GRAAF, Peter	63	Louisendorf	58-0306
(wife) 47, Anna Christ. 25, Maria Eva 22			
Heinr. Peter 20, Maria Elis. 14			
Christine 7, Anna 6, Wilhelm 4, Jacob 17			
GRAAT, Julia	32	New York	62-1169
GRAB, Louis	23	Achenen	59-0951
GRABAU, Armand	20	Adolphsdorff	57-0654
GRABAU, Henry	19	Nordsohl	57-0422
GRABE, J.C.	24	Charleston	59-0951
GRABEN, v. Wilh.	35	USA.	55-1082
Adolph 6			
GRABENKRUEGER, Fr.	28	Indiana	62-0342
GRABENSCHROEDER, W	19	Herzfeld/Pr.	62-0608
Elisabeth 23			
GRABENSTEIN, Henry	23	Lauterbach	60-1053
GRABNER, Adam	40	Gogl	55-0932
Cath. 36, Franziska 12, Elisabeth 3			
Joseph 9, Matthias 7, Adam 4			
GRADMANN, Thomas	33	New York	57-0961
Madlen 22, Lina 2m			
GRAEBE, Wilhelm	22	Rodenberg	56-0589
GRAEBER, Carl	36	Schlesien	62-0758
GRAEBER, D.F.(m)	19	Wahlheim	62-0111
GRAEBER, Jacob	48	Marbach	60-1161
Marie 35, Marie 1			
GRAEBER, Joh.	42	Ahsweiler	56-1216
GRAEBER, Minna	22	Gulz	60-0521
GRAEBER, Saphier	18	Buchau	59-0384
GRAEBNER, Joh.Geo.	57	Schellert	60-1053
Margaretha 18			
GRAEBNER, Mart.	19	Fuerth	60-0334
GRAEF, Baldin	55	Breitenbach/S	55-1238
Louise 24			
GRAEF, Cunigunda	20	Wrisse	57-0422
GRAEF, Pauline	26	Meiningen	62-0758
GRAEFER, Heinrich	21	Charleston,SC	60-0622
GRAEFFRATH, Daniel	51	Solingen	60-1141
Amalie 42, Julius 11, August 6, Carl 2			
Amalie 8			
GRAEHLING, Margar.	26	Hanau	61-0779
GRAENZER, Minna	17	Thueringen	57-0606
GRAESER, Johanna	42	New York	62-1112
GRAESER, Magdalene	42	Brooklyn	62-0232
Louise 18			
GRAESS, Ludwig	17	Andernach	57-1416
GRAESSLE, Max	26	Laupheim	59-0477
GRAETZ, Catharine	24	Brukenau/Bav.	55-0628
GRAETZER, J.(m)	32	Brieg	62-0111
GRAEVE, J.Ch.W.	17	Bremen	59-0477
GRAEVE, Maria	27	Ahlden	58-0399
GRAF, Christine	15	Muenster	57-0924
GRAF, Eduard	20	Gestendorf	61-0167
GRAF, Johann	27	Hoessbach/Bav	60-0429
GRAF, Peter	52	Baiern	57-0606
GRAFF, Caroline Wm	44	Cassel	57-1026
Anna Elisab. 15			
GRAFF, Ernst	20	Halle	59-0048
GRAFFT, Carl	31	Gera	58-0881
GRAFT, Traugott	40	New York	62-0836
GRAHE, Elisabeth	18	Weimelsheim	57-0436
GRAHEL, W.	29	St.Louis	57-1192
GRAHN, Valentin	17	Darmstadt	58-0563
GRAMANN, Carl	32	Siegelbach	56-0589
GRAMANN, Gottliebe	17	Meiningen	62-0758
GRAMBOW, Wilh'mine	23	Laerkerick	62-0401
GRAME, Friedr.	19	Bremen	59-1036
GRAMSTEDT, Frnz'ka	19	Minden	60-1161
GRAMT, Wilhelmine	22	Aschenfort	56-0819

NAME	AGE	RESIDENCE	YR-LIST
GRANATE, Franz	55	Settchau	55-0845
Maria 22, Maria 5, Franz 3, Joseph 1			
GRAND, Susan	24	England	56-0550
Johann 32			
GRANDJOT, Lisette	20	Schoeneburg	55-0932
Joseph 27			
GRANDKEY, Nicholas	31	France	62-0111
Augustin 28			
GRANZ, Christian	21	Korbach/Pruss	61-0770
GRAP, C.Fr.(m)	36	Neuenburg	57-0555
GRAPE, Sophie	6	Teggendorf	59-0384
GRASHOF, Catharine	60	Bremen	62-0938
GRASKE, August	33	Neu Wuhrow	56-1260
GRASMAEDER, Conrad	20	Gleichen	57-0754
GRASMUCK, Anton	24	Coburg	56-0847
GRASS, Salomon	23	Posen	58-0604
GRASSBERGER, Josep	26	Kreutz	59-0214
GRASSEL, Boniface	33	Mittelharkhsn	59-1036
GRASSEL, Seraphine	29	Gengweiss	59-1036
GRASSMANN, Geo. M.	26	Graefenholz	60-1053
GRASSMANN, Marie	25	Bernroth	60-0521
GRASTROFF, Carl	37	Krichlitz	57-1280
Christiane 35			
GRATE, Gust.	36	Haune	60-0998
GRATZ, Barbara	23	Tiefenort	57-1026
GRAU, Daivd	28	Hohengeren	60-0398
Barbara 19			
GRAU, Gottfried	32	Gaildorf/Wrt.	60-0411
John 18			
GRAU, Marie	23	Brom	58-0815
Franciska 17			
GRAUE, Herman	21	Bremen	56-0819
GRAUE, Joh. Gerh.	29	Elberfeld	55-0634
GRAUER, Jacob	21	Kusterdingen	61-0482
GRAUER, Louise	22	Cassel	62-0938
GRAUERHOLZ, Herm.	26	Dorferden	57-1113
GRAUERT, Eduard	22	Mannheim	56-0847
GRAULICH, Anna	55	Darmstadt	60-0371
GRAULICH, Margaret	20	Mahlbach	61-0478
GRAUN, Gertrude	26	Fulda	58-0399
GRAUN, Jacob	15	Ostheim	61-0482
GRAUPNER, Guenther	45	Sonderhausen	57-0555
GRAVERMANN, Gertr.	18	Aschberg	57-0422
Francis 32, Anna 26			
GRAWE, Hermann	21	Brunswick	57-0555
GREB, H.	23	Wallersdorf	62-0993
GREBB, Johann	16	Alten Schlirf	62-0879
GREBE, Anna Martha	21	Wattenbach	57-0924
GREBE, Elisabeth	22	Kl.Kladenbach	60-0371
GREBE, Jost	25	Breidenbach	60-0371
GREEB, Cath.	20	Metzlos	59-0990
GREEN, Marga.	50	England	56-0550
GREF, Maria	17	Worms	61-0897
GREFEN, Anne	18	Bolsten	56-1011
GREGORI, Christina	20	Romelshausen	57-0776
GREGORI, Heinrich	35	Camberg	57-0365
GREGORIE, Marcus	35	Havre	57-0578
GREGORIUS, Jac.	23	Breitscheid	59-0477
Catharine 18			
GREGORIUS, Rose	34	Erfurt	58-0399
Rudolph 13, Ernst 11, Richard 9, Julius 5			
Hedwig 4			
GREGORVIZ, Martin	33	Amtmannsdorf	56-1260
GREHLING, J.Heinr.	18	Schwarzenfels	60-0429
GREIF, Margaretha	30	Schwiltz	61-0478
GREIF, Mathias	35	Austria	55-1048
Theresia 24, Franz 9m			
GREIFELD, Julius	15	Suhl	57-1280
GREIFENSTEIN, Joh.	36	Sommerstadt	56-0847
Julius 24			
GREIFF, de A.(m)	30	Prussia	62-0836
GREIFZU, Caspar	40	Reichenhausen	57-1280
Sophia 36, Ernestine 9, Rebecca 7			
Therese 5, Margarethe 59			
GREIM, Marie	34	Erlangen	60-1032
GREIN, C.(f)	22	Heidelbach	57-0555
GREIN, Julie	34	Cassel	58-0815
GREIN, K.(f)	24	Heidelbach	57-0555

NAME	AGE	RESIDENCE	YR-LIST
GREINBAUER, Joh.	29	Nenndorf	59-1036
GREINER, Balsher	16	Stangenbach	60-1053
GREINER, Fr.(m)	20	Holheim	57-0654
GREINER, J.B.(m)	16	Wuertemberg	57-0555
GREISLEBEN, Minna	19	Burschau	56-0951
GREISS, Johann	43	Eisenach	57-0509
Anna Elis. 34, Mathilda 14, Johanna 9			
Adam 6, Johanna 3m			
GREIWE, M.(m)	30	Washington	62-0836
GREIWE, M.(m)	30	Washington	62-0836
GREIZ, Catharine	46	Neustadt	59-0047
GRELL, Friedr.	17	Suess	61-0520
GRELLER, Johann	42	Morschreuth	60-0533
Margaretha 38, Georg 16, Barbara 4			
Johann G. 8, Kunigunda 5, Johann 2			
Margaretha 3m			
GRELLJOHANN, Diedr	20	Walhofen/Hann	62-0608
GREMCKE, Heinrich	33	Bremervoerde	59-0477
GRENAU, (f)	24	London	62-0836
GRENLICH, H.O.	25	Oelo	57-1067
GRESE, Gottl.	29	Bremerhaven	61-0482
GRESMANN, H.	40	New York	60-0785
Marie 30, Marie 5, Oscar 3m			
GRESS, Margaretha	16	Gissigheim/Bd	60-0622
GRESSER, Theresia	35	Fulda	62-0401
GRESZLE, Carl	44	Grossgota	56-0847
GREUL, Carl	38	Colberg	62-0758
Friederike 39, Gustav 6, Emil by			
GREULICH, Johannes	24	Freiensteinau	62-0879
GREVE, Franz	30	Paderborn	57-0606
GREVE, Friedrich	26	Hildesheim	56-1260
GREVE, Gg.Pet.Nic.	19	Franzenburg	60-0429
GREVE, Maria	17	Boitzen	62-0879
GREVE, Marie Anna	30	Hapsen	57-1416
GREVE, Peter Niels	14	Luedingworth	56-0413
GREVENHORN, Caspar	48	Tiefenort	60-0398
GREVES, Joh.G.	24	Bremerhaven	62-0401
GRIEBER, Franz	24	Gotha	57-0447
GRIEN, Hede.	20	Tarmstedt	57-1148
GRIES, Ed.	26	Volmerhausen	61-0107
GRIES, Heinrich	12	Dens	56-1204
Cathrine 20			
GRIES, Martin	16	Metze	56-0411
GRIESE, Carl Henry	35	Luetjenburg	57-0422
Dav. Fr. 59, Caroline 58, Mary 29			
GRIESE, Charl.	59	Riepen	59-0384
GRIESE, Friedrich	40	Schneidemuehl	57-0924
A.Rosina 25, Joh.Gottlob 2			
GRIESEL, Adam	16	Holzhausen	56-0527
GRIESEL, Mary	28	Gilsa	60-0411
Elisa 21			
GRIESEMANN, Conrad	40	Soell	57-0578
Anna 38, Conrad 12, Joseph 9, Johann 8			
Anton 6, Mathias 3, Aloys 1			
GRIESEMANN, Friedr	20	Bavaria	62-0758
GRIESER, (m)	33	Germany	59-1036
(female) 19			
GRIESINGER, Adolph	28	Eutendorf	62-0100
GRIESMANN, Marie	19	Philipsthal	57-1026
GRIESSE, Christian	21	Hemmendorf	57-0422
GRIESSE, Franz	56	Volkmarsen/He	62-0608
Magdalena 52, Theodor 26, Augusta 20			
Adelbert 14, Bernhard 9, Dorothea 6			
GRIESSLER, Wilh.	59	Calen	59-0951
GRILL, Johann	32	Wiederzug	56-1260
GRIMM, Anton	39	Wisconsin	60-0334
GRIMM, Caroline	26	Schopfloch	60-0334
GRIMM, Johanna	18	Freesau	56-0847
Aloisia 34			
GRISEKE, Wilhelm	23	Braunschweig	55-0845
GRISZ, Rudolph	26	Salz	56-0847
GROBEN, Veronica	27	Karsee	59-0613
GROBER, Friedr.Aug	26	Merseburg	59-0412
GROEBEN, v.d. A.	31	Koensgebrueck	62-1112
GROEBER, Engel M.	16	Dielingen	59-1036
GROEFFEL, Mary	16	Rettmar	57-1148
GROEGER, August	36	Schmiedelberg	57-1026
Aug.Henriett 34, Gustav 8			

NAME	AGE	RESIDENCE	YR-LIST
GROEGER, Fanny	16	Bekackon	60-0785
GROENINGER, Elisb.	8	Manheim	60-0521
GROENNER, Friedr.	40	Galena	56-1044
Dorothea 35			
GROEPPER, Heinrich	25	Aplern	61-0520
GROESCHEL, Joh.W.	22	Lippendorf	57-0578
GROESSE, Elisabeth	21	Schreufa/Hess	57-0924
GROETSCH, Simon	36	Heimaden	58-0563
Margaretha 24, Katharina 3			
Anna Kathar. 1			
GROETZINGER, C.(m)	21	Ulm	61-0897
GROEVER, Peter	23	Neunkirchen	61-0682
Elisabeth 24			
GROH, Johanna	29	Duesseldorf	61-0897
Emilie 3, Gustav 9m			
GROH, Ph.	26	Weidensass	57-1148
GROH, Wm.	33	Chligs	62-0467
GROHE, Elise	15	Godensberg	60-1161
GROHNHAGEN, Heinr.	29	Westenholz	57-0847
Marie 27, Dorothea 10			
GROLACH, Alb.	25	Colberg	61-0897
GROLL, Elisabeth	18	Curhessen	58-0399
GROLL, Franz	20	Neustadt	59-0535
GROLL, Jos.	25	Eschenbach	61-0716
GROLL, Mary	19	Wittershausen	56-0512
GROLLMANN, J.Luisa	26	Tempelburg	56-0629
Amalie Chrst 24			
GROM, Teresa	21	Wollbach	56-0629
GROMBERG, William	18	Dedendorf	57-0961
GRONEMANN, Louis	30	Avadessen	56-0411
Heinrich 25			
GRONEMEIER, Heinr.	31	Guetersloh/Pr	55-0628
Sophie 28			
GRONEWEG, C.A.	34	Lemfoerde	56-1117
Augusta 30, Louis 8, Rudolph 6, Wilhelm 4			
Maria 1			
GRONEWEG, Wilhelm	21	Lemfoerde	59-0613
GRONHAGEN, Hch.	27	Hannover	57-0847
H.Friedr. 21			
GRONHOLZ, Josefina	17	Westen	60-0411
GRONING, Hermann	20	Hoya	55-0634
GRONLOH, Marie	48	Badbergen	60-1032
GROOS, (m)	26	Bocholt	62-0111
(f) 21			
GROOS, Eduard	23	Homberg	55-0630
GROP, Ph.(m)	21	Gueldesheim	60-0334
GROPP, J.M.(m)	23	Doerfles	62-0730
GROPP, Johanne	20	Doerfglas	56-0527
GROPP, Zacharias	55	Sheboygan	58-0604
GROS, Ida	28	Labes/Pruss.	55-1238
GROSCH, Barbara	16	Heubach	59-0477
GROSCH, Caroline	23	Dalherda	60-0533
GROSCH, Clara	14	Neustadt a/O	59-0477
GROSERIKY, Paul	17	Constadt	55-0812
GROSS, Adam	17	Moellerich	57-1148
GROSS, Barbara	59	Marburg	61-0482
GROSS, Carl	18	Marianowo/Pr.	60-0622
GROSS, E.	40	Salzungen	56-0512
GROSS, Elisabeth	25	Langenstein	57-0754
GROSS, Eva Elisab.	25	Mayertsdorf	57-0776
GROSS, Geo. Philip	24	Bremen	59-0535
GROSS, H.	41	Bonnstedt	62-1169
Mrs. 38, Barbara 16, Robert 12, Emil 1			
GROSS, Henry	24	Langenaubach	59-0477
GROSS, J.	29	Saxe-Coburg	56-0512
GROSS, Johann	28	Berliswagen	62-0836
GROSS, Leonhard	34	Rodh	59-0412
GROSS, Ottilie	23	Wichtshausen	62-0608
GROSSBRECHBERGER,S	50	Ebersberg	61-0478
GROSSE LEFERT, Aug	21	Hollich	60-0398
Heinr.Lefert 17			
GROSSE, Juliane	25	Marschluchham	61-0779
GROSSER, Kunigunde	32	Weingarst	56-0632
GROSSHAEUSER, Chr.	27	Erlangen	57-0447
GROSSHAUSER, Georg	24	Bachhausen	59-0384
GROSSHEIM, Fr.(m)	28	Hannover	57-0555
M.(f) 30			
GROSSHEIM, Hch.Aug	23	Altena	61-0779
GROSSKOPF, Heinr.	59	Gittilde	62-0306
GROSSKURT, Louise	30	Drausfeld	56-0629
GROSSMANN, Maria	32	Elbeschrot/Bv	55-0628
GROSSMANN, Ottilie	18	New York	59-0951
GROSSMUCK, John	45	Baltimore	60-0785
GROTE, G. (m)	25	Braunschweig	56-0512
GROTE, H.	26	Cloppenburg	57-0578
GROTE, Herm.	40	New York	61-0804
GROTENHAUS, Bernh.	29	Ochtrup	60-0411
GROTH, Therese	19	Bolshausen	56-1044
GROTHE, Juliane	26	Linkwegen	61-0482
GROTHEER, Heinrich	19	Osterode	56-0819
GROTHER, Johann	22	Culm	60-0785
GROTIAN, Louis	20	Braunschweig	57-1148
GROTRIAN, L.W.	22	New York	61-0167
GROTTER, Anna	20	Achim	60-0785
GROVE, Fr. Anton	44	Sandt	57-0961
GROVINGER, Anna	17	Duerrenmettst	60-0334
GROVS, Georg	28	Niedernepfen	55-0812
GRUBE, Friedrich	54	Wolbrechtshsn	57-0422
Carolina 52, Friedrich 24, Augustus 19			
Henry 14, Caroline 21, Dorothy 17			
GRUBE, Gesine	25	Buechel	60-0334
GRUBE, W.(m)	43	Bremen	61-1132
GRUBE, Wilhelm	40	Rheder	59-0214
GRUBE, Wm.Heinr.	22	Wolfenbuettel	57-1026
Heinrich 20			
GRUBER, Arnold	18	Pest	62-0836
GRUBER, Jacob	20	Nassbach	56-0847
GRUBER, Moritz	32	Jugetz	57-1067
GRUBER, Soph.	22	Ladenburg	59-1036
GRUBER, Sophie	19	Muenchen	62-0001
GRUBER, Veit	62	Bischoff	57-1280
Eva 53			
GRUBER, Wolfgang	25	Loewenherz/Bv	57-0924
GRUBERE, Louis	20	Muenchen	62-0232
GRUBNER, Christine	27	Steinzell	57-1280
GRUEM, Diedrich	59	Beierberg	57-1280
GRUEN, Christian	21	Erfurt	55-1082
GRUEN, Margaretha	35		57-1192
John 59, Elisabeth 17			
GRUEN, Wilh.	29	Diepholz	59-0951
GRUENBAUM, Dina	20	Geisa	59-0477
Regina 26			
GRUENBAUM, M.(m)	24	Aschenhausen	56-1044
Mathilde 58			
GRUENDLER, August	19	Gr.Oschersleb	59-0477
GRUENE, Alexander	38	Braunschweig	56-1117
GRUENEBAUM, Regina	21	Grambach	62-1042
GRUENEBERG, Edel.		Grossmedor	56-0819
GRUENEBERG, Raph.	25	Arnsberg	57-1148
GRUENER, Anne	22	Voccawind	56-1011
GRUENER, Margareta	28	Marolsweisach	61-0520
GRUENER, Therese	18	Wilder	60-0785
GRUENER, Wolfgang	30	Auerbach	61-0520
Anna 34, Wolfgang Seb 3, Carl 6m			
GRUENEWALD, Elis.	15	Elberfeld	55-0634
GRUENEWALD, M.(m)	58	Wurschborn	62-0836
GRUENEWALD, Marg.	22	Philadelphia	62-0111
Ludw. 2			
GRUENHUT, Joseph	17	Raudnitz	56-0629
Anna 21			
GRUENING, Wilhelm	20	Bromberg	55-1082
GRUENINGER, Heinr.	28	Neussen/Wuert	60-0622
GRUENSTEIN, Rebec.	25	Meisenheim	62-0730
GRUENTHALER, Cath.	19	Sulzbach	55-1082
GRUENWALD, Moritz	21	Seippendorf	60-0334
GRUESS, Ludwig	17	Andernach	57-1416
GRUETTER, Georgine	38	Walsrode	62-0836
Gustav 9			
GRUIN, (m)	21	France	58-0306
GRUIS, Charles	27	Kentucky	57-1192
GRUMBACH, Elisab.	23	Richtenbach	55-1082
GRUMBRECHT, Ernst	29	Goettingen	55-0413
Louise 24			
GRUMSYK, Conrad	26	Lippe-Detmold	58-0399
GRUNDBERG, Conrad	23	Alsfeld	57-1122
GRUNDEI, Rosalia	35	Langdorf	58-0399

NAME	AGE	RESIDENCE	YR-LIST
GRUNDMEYER, Johann	51	Wiersen	57-0578
Caroline 52, Sophie 19, Caroline 17			
GRUNDRUM, Mary	18	Hornau	57-0654
GRUNDTMANN, Johann	52	Kalefeld	56-0512
August 18			
GRUNE, Anna	19	Brackel	56-0512
GRUNENHAGEN, Fz.	59	Koenigsberg	60-0521
GRUNER, Fr.	46	Cienfuegos	62-1042
GRUNER, H.H.	45	St.Thomas/VI	62-1042
Mrs. 40, Cora 13, Fr. 10, Pamela 7			
Guil 3, Mary 20, Malo 25			
GRUNER, Mathias	30	Ohmenhausen	61-0482
GRUNSTEWITZ, Mart.	30	Posen	58-0399
Anna 27, Johann 2, Marianne 6m			
GRUNTZMANN, J.Fr'd	26	Potsdam	56-0589
GRUNWALD, O.	21	Sorau	62-0993
GRUNWALD, Raphael	9	Posen	57-0654
Jul. 17			
GRUPE, Christina	16	Westphalia	60-0371
GRUPE, William	37	Antendorf	59-0384
Wilhelmine 40, Wilhelmine 18			
GRUPE, Wm.	51	Washington	62-1042
Doris 51			
GRZYL, Casimir	29	Smiesczkowo	61-0779
GUBLER, Jacob	25	Basel	50-1017
GUBMANN, Elisabeth	36	Gr.Deckendorf	61-0897
GUCKENBERGER, Sim.	23	Cincinnati	60-0334
GUCKENHEIM, Samuel	29	Baden	55-0634
GUCKSTATTER, Barb.	23	Zuckenheim	56-0632
GUDE, Augusta	22	Henderson	62-0879
GUDEMUSH, Casp.	30	Schuchtern	57-0654
GUDERA, M.	17	Annaberg	62-0938
GUEHL, Chr.	37	Schmieden	62-0730
Catharine 34, Friedrich 9, Louise 5			
Catharine 3, Roeschen 10m			
GUELKEN, Ernst	28	Heithoefen	57-0754
GUEMMLING, Elisab.	50	Michelsbach	60-0398
GUENDEL, Philipine	26	Hesse-Darmst.	60-0371
GUENGERICH, Dan.	26	Braunfeld	62-0467
GUENGERICH, Wm.	22	Bogel	57-0555
Cath. 32			
GUENNE, Joseph	28	Leder	56-0847
GUENTER, Anton	27	Schwerstedt	56-0819
GUENTHER, Alex'ine	29	Cassel	55-0634
GUENTHER, Arm.Hch.	37	Boston	57-1192
GUENTHER, August	25	Gotha	55-0634
Marie 24, Ida by			
GUENTHER, Carl	38	Greiz	62-0712
Johanna 38, Heinrich 6, Caroline 10m			
GUENTHER, Carl	26	Chemnitz	62-0938
Friedr. 24			
GUENTHER, Clara	23	Berlin	57-0961
GUENTHER, Conrad	28	Detmold	56-1044
Henriette 29			
GUENTHER, Daniel	24	Scharmbeck/Ha	62-0608
GUENTHER, Elise	19	Walburg	60-1032
GUENTHER, Ernst	46	Atenburg	62-0730
GUENTHER, Friedr.	22	Landolfshsn.	57-0924
Caroline 20			
GUENTHER, Gottlieb	17	Greiz	62-0712
Herrmann 14, Christiane 53			
GUENTHER, H.	31	Kriegsreuth	62-0993
M.M. 32, M. 3			
GUENTHER, Heinrich	24	Grossensee	61-0779
GUENTHER, Hermann	36	Weimar	56-1260
GUENTHER, Maria	34	Diedorf	57-1280
GUENTHER, Wilh'mne	20	Verden	57-1148
GUENTNER, Anna	20	Machtlos	55-0413
Louise 24			
GUENZEL, C.G.	30	Veilsdorf	55-0413
Louise 24			
GUENZEL, Joach.	35	Niederreith	55-0413
GUENZEL, Mich.	25	Masbach	61-0482
Marie 30, Marie 9m, Johann 3, Cath. 3			
GUERTLER, Joh.	54	Gintershof	55-1082
Mar. Marg. 53			
GUETL, Gregor	24	Oberisling	62-0467
GUETZ, Ernst	44	Rumian/Aus.	56-1260

NAME	AGE	RESIDENCE	YR-LIST
Caroline 33, Fritz 9, Carl 7, Albert 6			
Johann 2, Ludwig 6m			
GUGEL, Christina	21	Esslingen/Wrt	60-0429
GUGEL, Joh. An.	29	Bavaria	61-0482
GUICHELOT, J.(m)	54	Paris	62-0111
GUILLOUF, Samson	39	France	61-0167
GULDE, Adalb.	25	Bleicherode	59-1036
GULDE, Jacob	30	Aldingen	62-0467
GULDENBERG, Jette	16	Kestrich	59-0951
GULDNER, Adam	15	Willofs	55-1082
GUMANN, John	28	Cincinnati	61-0716
GUMMERT, Peter	56	Halberstadt	58-0399
Friedr. 19, Justine 13, Wilhelm 9			
August 7			
GUMPPER, Barbara	36	Oberleningen	62-0001
GUNDACKER, An.Dor.	19	Linden/Bav.	60-0429
GUNDELFINGER, Dan.	22	New York	59-0214
GUNDER, Eta	25	Aurich	60-0785
GUNDERMANN, Georg	15	Rodenbach	57-1067
GUNDERMANN, Heinr.	37	Rodenbach	57-1067
GUNDERT, Hermann	23	Stuttgart	62-0608
GUNDERT, Peter	23	Koblenz/Main	56-0632
GUNDLACH, C.M. (f)	22	Grossalmerode	55-0538
J.J. (m) 4			
GUNDLACH, Conrad	42	Graevenhagen	55-0845
Anna 46, Barbara 9, Johannes 34			
Martha 25, Barbara by			
GUNDLACH, Louis	18	Preuss.Minden	60-0622
GUNDRUM, H.(m)	20	Alsfeld	62-0730
Ferd. 15			
GUNKEL, Anna	20	Kruckenau	55-1082
GUNKEL, Anton	24	Bergrothenfel	61-0779
GUNKEL, August	20	Schwarzenberg	57-1280
GUNKEL, Peter	16	Passau	57-1407
GUNKEL, Wilhelm	13	Wuerzburg/Bav	60-0371
Genoveva 18			
GUNTERMANN, Elis.	23	Kirchwald	57-0776
GUNTHER, Fr.Erholt	20	Heitersbach	57-0704
GUNTHER, Friedr.Wm	26	Gerlitz	62-0306
GUNTLA, Heinrich	23	Breitenbach	57-0704
Anna Martha 22, Gorg 2			
GUNZ, Catharina	19	Allheim	59-0048
GUNZELMANN, Cath.	19	Bamberg	62-0712
GUNZENHAUSEN, Sal.	16	Wunderthausen	60-0533
GURRE, Heinr.	16	Damme	59-0951
GUSBERLET, Eva	22	Whershausen	59-0613
GUSMANN, Marie	17	Overdingen	62-0730
GUSSFELDE, Julie	18	Fuerth	56-1044
GUT, Max	20	Moehringen	60-0398
GUTEMANN, Robert	21	Frankfurt	56-0692
GUTERMANN, Philpne	21	Burgkundstadt	61-0482
GUTFREUND, Ignatz	23	Glosau	57-1067
Anna 22			
GUTH, Chr.	30	Philadelphia	57-0422
Susannah 26, Mary 3, Fredrika 6m			
GUTH, Eliza	30	Darmstadt	57-0422
GUTHARD, Lorenz	17	Borken	57-1280
GUTHEIL, Johann	57	Leichertshsn.	61-0770
Christiane 42, Georg 13, Anna 10			
Wilhelm 7			
GUTHEIL, Reinhold	26	Detmold	58-0545
Charlotte 28, Louise 3, Anna 9m			
GUTHMANN, Gabriel	16	Flatow	57-0704
GUTIKE, P.	20	Berlin	62-0993
GUTKNECHT, Carl	24	St.Gallen	60-0533
Barbara 22, Lena 11m			
GUTKNECHT, HArtwig	26	Kaickhorst	57-0654
GUTMANN, Carl	29	San Francisco	59-0214
GUTMANN, Caroline	24	Egenhausen	62-0879
GUTMANN, Isaac	21	Bohenheim	62-0232
GUTMANN, Maria	28	Baiern	62-1112
GUTMANN, Philippin	27	Boehmen	61-0478
Richard 18			
GUTMANN, Rosa	23	Thalmessing	60-1196
GUTMANN, Rosalia	17	Cronheim	56-0819
GUTMANN, Zelline	20	Fuerth	59-0477
GUTSTADT, Jacob	27	Rothenburg	57-1148
GUTTHARD, M.E.	23	Sachsen	58-0399

NAME	AGE	RESIDENCE	YR-LIST
HAACK, Johann	15	Zeven	62-0879
Catharine 18			
HAAG, Fritz	30	Landau	56-0847
Catharina 30			
HAAG, Joseph	22	Lauda	57-0021
Johann 24			
HAAK, Conrad	31	Luebena	57-1280
HAAK, Wm.	45	Washington	61-0107
HAAKE, Diedrich Wm	31	Beckedorf	56-0589
Pauline 18			
HAAKE, Dorothea	27	Bremen	59-0951
HAAKE, Wilhelmine	24	Minden	58-0399
HAAR, v.d. Fritz		Fuerstenau	59-1036
HAARS, Marie	28	Alzenau	60-1032
HAARSTRICH, Christ	22	Farmensen	56-0629
HAAS, Anna	21	Hessia	56-0847
HAAS, Anna	15	Linzheim	56-1011
HAAS, Casper	15	Oberissigheim	60-1141
HAAS, Chr.	31	Spahl	59-0951
HAAS, Elisabeth	24	Herchenhain	56-0723
HAAS, Georg	25	Mertesdorf	57-0654
Elisabeth 24, Mary 4, Catharine 2			
(dau.) by			
HAAS, Heinrich	18	Dankmarshausn	56-0279
HAAS, Ida	21	Nordhausen	59-1036
HAAS, Jacob	27	Engelbach	60-0785
Elise 30, Georg 11m			
HAAS, Johannes	15	Sachs.-Weimar	55-0634
HAAS, Joseph	20	Winterbach	62-0712
HAAS, Josephine	53	Wiesbaden	61-0482
HAAS, Rosine	9	Widden	60-0521
HAASCHE, H.H.	20	Brettorf	62-0879
HAASE, Diedrich	18	Emsen	58-0925
HAASE, Friedrich	18	Dissen	56-1044
HAASE, Margaretha	24	Hessen	60-0371
HAASE, Wilhelm	47	Greussen	56-0723
Henriette 56			
HABBE, Johann	31	Gutsdorf	56-1044
HABBERT, Caroline	18	Lewera	57-0422
HABBIG, Anna	44	Offenbach/H-D	60-0622
HABER, Carl	59	Achen	62-0836
Josephine 56, Mathilde 22			
HABERKORN, Cathar.	17	Balkhausen	59-0477
HABERLAND, J.C.L.	44	Bremen	62-0342
Henriette 40, Diana 20, Franziska 1			
HABERLAND, Johann	17	Magdeburg	62-0712
HABERMANN, Andreas	29	Falkenau	56-0847
Maria 4			
HABERMANN, Eduard	18	Pilzdorf	61-0478
HABERMANN, J.(m)	30	Kurhessen	57-0555
HABERMANN, Joh.	19	Hanau	57-0606
HABERMANN, Ludwig	40	Coburg	61-0478
Pauline 39, Martin 16, Mathilda 14			
Marcus 12, Gottfried 9, Wilh. (died) 9m			
HABERMANN, Maria	15	Wallenrode	61-0682
HABERMANN, Peter	46	Elsa	62-0166
HABERMANN, Robert	23	Neuenburg	57-0776
HABERMAYER, Jacob	28	Bavaria	55-0538
Therese , Marie 36			
HABERMEHL, Elisab.	17	Weisskirchen	62-0712
HABERMEHL, Heinr.	18	Allenrod	55-1082
HABERMEHL, Johann	47	Storndorf	56-0847
Julie 18			
HABERS, J.D.	52	Uphusen	55-0413
Louise 24			
HABERSTOCK, Cath.	31	Southofen	57-0918
HABERSTROH, Matias	26	Boston	59-0384
HABIG, Rosine	27	Webelsburg/Pr	55-0628
HABLIEN, Cath.	26	Wuertemberg	57-0606
HABSCH, Gottfr.	40	Berlin	56-0629
Mathilde 34			
HACH, Adalbert	34	Strigowitz	57-1113
Anna 24, Adalbert 6, Johann 4, Wenzel 1			
HACHE, Margarethe	19	Strihen	60-0334
HACHMANN, J.H.	28	New York	59-0477
HACHTING, J.B.	24	Madison	59-0384
HACK, Carl	23	Darmstadt	60-1141
HACKE, Sophie	18	Rade	59-0412

NAME	AGE	RESIDENCE	YR-LIST
HACKE, Wilhelmine	20	Suling	59-0412
HACKENBERG, Herm.	24	Neisse	58-0399
HACKENBROCK, Marg.	26	Coblenz	60-1032
HACKENFURT, M.Cath	31	Ahaus	61-0482
HACKER, Carl	22	Dinkelsbuehl	57-1026
Elise 27			
HACKER, Georg	31	Lichtenfelde	60-0429
Dorothea 40, Elisabeth 13, Dorothea 9			
Carl 6			
HACKER, Joh.Conrad	38	Bavaria	60-0371
Margaretha 31			
HACKER, Michael	30	Christand	62-0712
HACKEWESSEL, Reinh	30	Hartford	57-0365
Augusta 26, Carl 5, Reinhold 2			
HACKMANN, Joh.Fr.	25	Hasbergen	57-0924
Wilhelmine 28			
HACKMANN, Max	18	Wierup	59-0951
HACKMANN, N.H.(m)	45	Cincinnati	60-0785
HADELER, Gesche M.	46	Sudbruch	59-0990
(m) 10			
HADELER, H.	19	Strange	59-0990
C. 18, G. 16			
HADGE, (m)	40	France	58-0306
HADLER, Wm.	25	Scheinfuerden	61-0482
HAECKSTOCK, Michel	54	Kurbach/Aus.	55-0538
Elisabeth 38, Franz 20, Anna 11			
HAEFEL, Wilhelmine	59	Beverungen	57-1280
Anna Rosine 14			
HAEFENER, G.P.(m)	23	Zuerich	61-0482
HAEFFNER, Anna	57	Anlishagen	61-0669
Marie 24, Joh. 18			
HAEFFNER, Cathrina	25	Widdern/Wurtt	60-0429
HAEFFNER, Jacob	28	Berk	57-0850
HAEFKER, H.J.	24	Thedinghausen	59-0477
HAEFNER, Cathar.	24	Lichtenstn/Bv	60-0622
HAEFNER, Johann	43	Jankersdorf	60-0334
Marie 35, Johann 7			
HAEFNER, Polikarp	26	Schweinberg	57-0924
HAEGEL, Johann G.	29	Bayern	56-1044
HAEGELE, Catharina	16	Geschwend	56-1117
Rosine 20			
HAEGERICH, Heinr.	19	Niederstein	57-0924
Maria 17			
HAEMEL, Conrad	33	Oberleis	57-1067
HAENDEL, Hch. Got.	57	Lobenstein	55-0932
HAENDLER, Anton		Austria	55-0538
Theresia , Johann 7, Anton 3, Theresia 2			
HAENER, Ferd.	24	Sandhausen	59-0214
HAENSEL, Augusta	27	Spieledorf	56-1044
HAENSEL, Louis	19	Reinboltshaus	56-1117
HAENSEL, Maria	20	Altenschlirf	60-0334
HAENSER, Bernh.	21	Niederweissel	59-0384
HAENTROCHEL, Carl	30	Plauen	60-1117
HAEPER, Friedrich	15	Bremen	59-0048
HAERDER, Bett.	54	Neuhaus	58-0604
Carol. 24			
HAERENZ, Fr.(m)	17	Eckartsberga	61-0482
HAERING, Benedict	59	Marburg	60-0334
HAERING, Daniel	52	Frankenhag	61-0520
Wolfgang 15			
HAERRING, August	29	Elberfeld	55-0634
Louise 24, Maria 6, Lydia 2			
HAERRING, Friedr.	40	Elberfeld	55-0634
Amalie 38, Friedr. 12, Maria 7			
Hannchen 6, Johannes 5, Paul 3			
Christine by			
HAERRY, Caroline	29	Otmarsingen	59-0951
Oscar 4			
HAERTEL, Friedrich	30	Lengfeld	57-0704
HAERTNER, Carl	20	Laufen/Wuertt	60-0429
HAERTNER, Rudolph	20	Laufen/Wuertt	60-0429
Heinrich 17			
HAESELER, August	24	Hannover	55-0413
HAESEMEYER, Diedr.	53	Wenden	59-0535
Marie 53, Wilhelmine 20, Fritz 9			
Wilhelm 8			
HAESEMEYER, Wlhmne	16	Holtdorf	61-0930
HAESSLER, Augusta	7	Walperndorf	61-0482

NAME	AGE	RESIDENCE	YR-LIST
HAEST, Gerhard	36	Wengsel	57-1148
HAETTMANN, Joh.	26	Reinsecke	59-1036
HAETZLEIN, Johann	30	Ob.Schrambach	57-1026
Barbara 23			
HAEUM, Adolph	24	Weissenfels	56-0723
HAEUSER, Chr.	59	Eicherhausen	60-0521
Marie 18			
HAEUSER, Lisette	16	Langenhain	59-1036
HAEUSER, Marie C.	17	Watzenborn/He	62-0608
Catharine 15			
HAEUSERMANN, Fr.	21	Affalterbach	60-1161
HAEUSSNER, Carolne	21	Stuttgart	60-0429
HAEVEN, van John	22	Aurich	61-0520
HAFEMANN, Heinr.	26	Greven	59-0214
HAFEMEYER, Henry	31	New Orleans	58-0815
HAFENER, Waldburga	30	Turnhausen	57-0754
HAFTEN, v. Alex.	14	Dresden	55-0630
HAGA, Adalbert	25	Alkum	61-0716
HAGDORN, Julius	27	Giershausen	60-0398
HAGE, (m)	29	France	58-0306
HAGE, August	18	Elze	59-0214
HAGE, August	37	Gadderbaum	59-0951
Augusta 2			
HAGE, Franz	18	Alsfeld	60-0334
HAGE, Heinrich	25	Buttlau	57-1067
HAGE, Susanne	24	Heingoldshsn.	57-1067
HAGEDORN, Heinrich	25	Bremen	59-0951
HAGEL, Johann	32	Birkbach	57-1407
Permel 30			
HAGEMANN, Adolph	27	Stemmen	56-1260
Henriette 20			
HAGEMEIER, Friedr.	21	Neuhausen	55-0932
HAGEMEIER, Lorenz	21	Neuhausen	57-1067
HAGEMEISTER, Cath.	55	Solms	56-1117
Christine 16			
HAGEMEISTER, Fr'dr	34	Detmold	55-1048
Maria 31			
HAGEMEYER, Louise	24	Werffen	60-0334
HAGEN, Gust. Ad.	36	Berlin	58-0885
HAGEN, Gutje	28	Campen	55-1082
HAGEN, Joh.Christ.	46	Putzenmuehle	58-0604
Sophie 46			
HAGEN, Joh.H.	24	Dwergse	59-0214
HAGEN, Lusette	39	Boston	60-0521
HAGEN, Marie	29	New York	60-0411
HAGEN, Nestor	21	Berlin	57-0654
HAGEN, Otto R.	22	Minsen	57-0422
HAGEN, Th. (m)	36	Suspension Br	60-0785
Moritz 3			
HAGEN, v. H.	45	Bremen	62-1112
HAGENAU, Herm.Geo.	36	Hagen	58-0563
HAGENBUCHER, Joh.	29	Greitz	58-0399
Elisabeth 27, Elisabeth 3, Kunigunde 11m			
HAGENS, Carolina	32	Bremen	57-0654
HAGENS, Henry	19	Bremen	57-0961
HAGENSIEK, C.W.	35	Garnaville	59-0613
HAGER, Caroline	23	Rahfeld	60-0334
Simon 21			
HAGER, Marg.	16	Schwarzenbach	59-0384
HAGET, Bernhard	37	Hecke	59-0412
Gertrude 26			
HAGIS, (f)	49	England	60-0334
HAGMANN, Adam	39	Chicago	59-0613
Therese 29			
HAGREFE, Louis	24	Wallrode	59-1036
HAGSEN, Charlotte	44	Vogesack	59-0214
Augusta 36			
HAHL, Clementine	18	Baiern	58-0399
HAHN, Adam	18	Hessen	57-0606
HAHN, Armand	35	Bremen	57-1148
HAHN, Barbara	22	Germany	61-0167
HAHN, C.F.(m)	40	Indiana	61-0804
HAHN, Caroline	21	Petzkowetz	57-1026
HAHN, Catharine	21	Niederamstadt	56-0847
Helene 3			
HAHN, Eliese	28	Metze	56-0411
Anna 24			
HAHN, Elisabeth	23	Arheilgen	62-0938

NAME	AGE	RESIDENCE	YR-LIST
HAHN, Friedr.	25	Groeplitz	59-0535
HAHN, Friedr. G.	21	Hedelfingen	60-1053
HAHN, Gottfr.	23	Wuertemberg	57-0606
HAHN, H.	26	USA.	56-0550
HAHN, Isaac	33	Runkel	57-1026
HAHN, J.A.(m)	32	Sachsen	61-0682
HAHN, Jacob	25	Wuertemberg	57-0606
HAHN, Joh. Ch.	24	Neidenstein	60-1053
HAHN, Joh. Heinr.	42	Tiefenbach/Pr	55-0628
Anna Marg. 35, Catharina 13, Fritz 10			
Philipp 7, Johannette 5, Georg 2			
HAHN, John Georg	18	Penach	57-0422
HAHN, Ludwig	24	Alsfeld	57-0606
Heinrich 16			
HAHN, Margarethe	40	Ofte	57-1122
Conrad 12, Cathrine 11, Wilhelm 14			
HAHN, Maria	64	Bordorf	61-0047
HAHN, Maria	26	Langensalza	58-0545
HAHN, Michael	15	Gundlitz/Bav.	60-0429
HAHN, Otto	17	Hannover	58-0399
HAHN, Wilhelm	17	Wienesdorf	59-0372
HAHNE, C.	24	Frankenhausen	56-0512
HAHNE, Emilie	20	Hannover	62-1042
HAHNER, Dorothy	27	Ziegenheim	57-0654
HAHSE, Dorothea	21	Juliusberg	57-0754
Augusta 13, Ernst 7			
HAIL, Lisette	23	Memmingen	55-0630
HAILER, Franziska	26	Neuler/Wuertt	55-0538
HAILER, Thomas	45	Schorndorf	60-0334
HAIMANN, Anna	55	Munssen	57-0654
Ant. 17			
HAISCHER, Emma	18	Neukirch	62-1112
Victor 16, Anton 12			
HAISS, Theodora	27	Daitzingen	62-0467
HAJCH, Wenzel	40	Boehmen	62-0467
Marie 44, Antonia 11m			
HAJECK, Johann	65	Bohemia	60-1161
Marie 64			
HAKE, Carl	30	Charleston	60-0334
Minna 24			
HALBACH, Gustav	22	Barmen	59-0048
HALBERS, H. (m)	18	Uphusen	55-0413
HALBERSTADT, Chr.	40	Misburg	57-1192
HALBERSTADT, Conr.	40	Misburg	57-1192
Sophie 32, Caroline 8, John 50			
HALBERSTADT, Joh H	43	Nolhfelden	60-0411
Anna Mary 46, Margaretha 16, Catharina 13			
HALBERSTADT, Wilh.	21	Bremen	60-1032
HALBFLEISCH, C.H.	29	Neukirchen	59-0477
HALDA, Joseph	46	Radwanow	56-1011
Katharine 45, John 10, Maria 7, Antonia 3			
HALDENEGGER, Conr.	56	Louisville	61-0482
Josephine 34, Wilhelmine 6, Pauline 9m			
HALDRIG, Wilhelm	33	Wispacheldelh	56-0819
HALECK, Mary Anna	24	Luedinghausen	60-1141
HALHORN, H.W.Georg	24	Bruchhausen	59-0372
HALL, Jane	23	England	57-1148
HALL, Maria	40	France	60-1196
Leopold 11, Master 9			
HALLE, August	59	Foerste	62-0938
Heinrich 33, Louise 34, Louise 7			
HALLE, Carol.	57	Herford	59-0384
HALLEN, Henry	36	Chicago	57-0654
HALLER, Friedrich	29	Roessing	57-1067
HALLER, Rudolph	20	Koenigsheim	60-1141
HALLET, Ella	9	New York	59-0613
Megie 8, Lesly 7, Irene 9m			
HALLSTEIN, Lina	37	Koenig	62-0730
HALSMANN, Christ.	24	Stockam	59-1036
HALTENSTEDT, B.	35	New York	62-0836
(wife) 35			
HALTMANNSHIN, A.M.	36	Alsingen	57-0704
HAMAN, Friedrich	25	Saarweiler	60-1053
HAMANN, Carl H.	43	Weniger Jena	61-0716
Henriette 27, Rosine 59, Ernst 3			
HAMANN, Ludwig	30	Goslar	57-0606
Conradine 27			
HAMANN, Marie C.	16	Bachheim/Hess	62-0608

NAME	AGE	RESIDENCE	YR-LIST
HAMANN, Minna	22	Hemmendorf	57-0422
Dorothy 18			
HAMBERG, Gerhard	32	Damme	59-0214
HAMBURGER, Clara	19	Fuerth/Bav.	55-0628
HAMBURGER, Lob.	34	Kissingen	57-1148
HAMEL, Conrad	30	Erxdorf	59-0613
HAMEL, H.	19	Buergel	62-0993
HAMELE, Vinc.	30	Michelsdorf	55-0932
Johanne 30, Ludwig 9m, Emilie 5			
Emdwig 9m, Emilie 5			
HAMERDING, Franz	21	Munster	57-1416
HAMM, Casp.	42	Hall	59-1036
HAMMANN, Carl	22	Frankenthal	59-0951
HAMME, Louise	20	Bremen	59-0951
HAMMEL, Caroline	28	Grossgota	56-0847
HAMMEL, Eulilie	20	Leusel	55-1082
HAMMER, Anna Eva	23	Frielingen	57-0704
HAMMER, Friedr.	17	Schwarzburg	60-0411
HAMMERMUELLER, J.G	54	Colditz	57-0924
An Christine 54, Aug. Moritz 27			
Hanna Veron. 27			
HAMMERS, Charlotte	50	Kalisch	58-0815
Olga 9			
HAMMERSCHIDT, Wmne	40	Neu Schmidt	57-1416
Martin 7			
HAMMERSCHLAG, A(m)	17	Bingen	60-1053
HAMMERSCHLAG, S.	21	Schlusselburg	58-0881
Moritz 25			
HAMMERSCHLAG, Sim.	27	Trent	60-0785
HAMMERSCHLAG, Sim.	18	Bederkesa	60-0521
HAMMERSCHMIDT, Joh	25	Westheim	60-1161
HAMPKE, D.H.	29	Hannover	58-0399
M.C. 30, Mathias 2, C.M. 19			
HANAK, Dorothea	24	Boehmen	62-0730
Wenzel 19			
HANASPEL, Ph.(m)	32	Neuendorf	56-0723
Marie 28			
HANAUER, Caroline	21	Burgkundstadt	61-0482
HANDER, Mathias	28	Haldenwang	60-0533
HANDS, Cannel	26	Pennsylvania	59-0214
HANEFELDT, H.D.	17	Dorfhagen	62-1169
HANEKAMP, Elisab.	31	Osterloh	59-0951
HANENKLAU, Johann	34	Hotteln	60-0334
HANF, Georg C.	18	Niederbach	57-1113
HANF, Pauline	22	Ellwangen	62-0938
HANFT, Bernh.	28	New York	61-0804
HANFT, G.(m)	25	New York	61-0804
HANG, ANton	30	Pfortzheim	59-0477
HANG, Anton	31	Berchtenroth	56-0589
Heinrich 3			
HANG, Christine	30	Strunpfede	57-1122
Hermann 3			
HANGES, Anna	19	Blaisee	57-1192
HANGK, Jos.	49	Munster	60-0998
HANITSCH, Gertrud	28	Bieden/Hessen	62-0608
HANK, Elisabeth	36	Opittwitz	55-0845
HANK, Michael	40	Baden	60-0371
HANKAMMER, Dan.	51	Heringen	61-0482
Wilhelm 25, Christ 18, Carl 14, Herm. 7			
Christine 23, Wilhelmine 20, Catharine 9			
HANKE, Constantin	30	Woipelsdorf	61-0779
HANKE, Franz	18	Falkendorf	56-0692
HANKEN, Gerhartrud	23	Amthagen	57-1280
HANNA, Johann	24	Schneiderhof	57-0578
HANNE, Fritz	23	Schlessinghsn	59-0535
HANNEL, Michel	25	Gramsdorf	56-0819
HANNER, Justine	23	New York	59-1036
Wm. 9m			
HANNES, Adalbert	52	Boehmen	61-0930
Maria 46, Theresia 17, Joseph 15			
Albert 13, Rumann 11, Marie 9, Barbara 1			
HANSAM, Jacob	17	Oberbalzheim	60-0334
HANSEN, Carl	20	Plockingen	58-0885
HANSEN, Johann	15	Frellstorf	62-0938
HANSEN, Thomas	24	Flensburg	58-0576
HANSING, Louis	27	Steinhuden	57-0606
HANSTEIN, Barbara	19	Langendorfles	62-0712
HANTF, Christ.	29	Marktbreit	56-1216

NAME	AGE	RESIDENCE	YR-LIST
HANZOW, Ludwig	30	Selchow	56-0819
HAPP, Friedrich	51	Messingen/Wrt	55-1238
HAPPEL, Conrad	47	Wolfenrod/CH.	60-0429
Elisabeth 47, Elisabeth 13, Helena 11			
Anna Cath. 9, Wilhelm 7, Marie 6			
Eva(Ketting) 58			
HAPPINGA, Anna Ma.	24	Furth	55-0812
HAPPMANN, Christ.	18	Hille	56-0411
HARBACH, Reinhd.	32	Grossenbuseck	61-0482
Elisabeth 32, Margareth 5, Louise 3			
Anna 26			
HARBAUER, Joseph	33	Lanz	50-1017
Ottilie 28, Carl 9m, Carl 9m			
HARBECK, Elisabeth	21	Trebes/Bav.	60-0622
HARBORTH, H.	40	Gehrden	62-0993
HARCHON, Celestin	22	Nancy	62-0608
HARCHROTH, Franz	29	Gumbuennen/A.	56-1260
HARDEKOPF, Heinr.	16	Lindhorst/Lip	55-0628
HARDELL, Martin	52	Salm	56-0819
Maria Elise 46, Wilhelm 25, Wilhelmine 23			
Hermann 20, Augusta 18, Julius 15			
Julie 9			
HARDER, Fritz	21	Diepholz	58-0563
HARDER, Nicolaus	30	Bremen	56-1117
HARDOERFER, Helene	30	Puschendorf	61-0520
HARDRATH, Friedr.	43	Carzig	57-0776
Anna 52, Louise 14, Maria 12, Gottfried 8			
Sophie 6, Augusta 5			
HARDT, Elise	21	Pirstling/Bav	61-0770
HARDTE, Cath.	40	Griedelbach	55-1082
HARDWIG, Anne	30	Muenchen	61-0482
HARF, Maria	31	Hannover	56-0413
HARFE, Philip	50	Effolderbach	59-0047
HARFING, Cath.	41	New York	57-1150
HARHAN, G.	18	Redwitz	58-0604
HARJES, Dr. (m)	26	Ndr.Blockland	61-0804
HARKEN, A.(m)	21	Jever/Old.	55-0544
HARKER, Sophie	40	Paddingmittel	58-0306
HARLIECK, Ths.(m)	20	Boehmen	62-0730
HARLING, Joh.B.	20	Wallen	57-0578
HARM, Friedrich	31	Adelebsen	57-1026
Betty 51			
HARMANN, J.L.		New York	59-0613
(f) , (f) , (f) , (f)			
HARMMING, Johann	48	Wolpinghausen	55-1238
HARMS, Anna	20	Ochtmannien	60-0785
Cord 15, Herm. 5			
HARMS, August	24	Stollheim	55-1082
HARMS, August	17	Falster	57-1280
HARMS, Betty	19	Land Hadeln	57-0924
HARMS, Diedr.	55	Teatzville	60-0785
HARMS, Friedr.	26	New York	59-1036
HARMS, H.	32	Grasberg	62-1112
Anna 25			
HARMS, Hans H.	32	Harten	57-0847
HARMS, Henry	19	Sievern	57-1122
HARMS, Juergen Fr.	24	Hannover	57-0606
HARMS, Kasten	34	Horsten	58-0563
Marie 20			
HARMS, Louise	20	Lafayette	61-0804
HARMS, P.(m)	19	Hipstedt	57-0555
HARMS, Sophie	37	Hannover	57-0847
HARN, John	20	Frankfurt/M	60-1141
HARN, Mary	30	Damme	57-0961
HARNACH, Alois	36	Wien	62-1112
HARNEMANN, Wilhmne	33	Peine	59-0214
HARNISCH, Johanna	58	Bertsdorf	55-0932
August 18			
HARNISCHFEGER, Aug	53	Soden	60-0398
HARNSTEDT, Charles	25	Steinbruecken	57-0961
HARNUNG, Minna	20	Cassel	57-0365
HAROLD, v. A. (m)	25	Frostberg	62-0467
HARON, Pierre	32	Buffalo	62-0467
Angelique 70			
HARPAMPER, Wilhelm	16	Rheda	57-1026
HARPE, Wilhelm	21	Schmillinghsn	57-1113
HARPICH, Christian	37	Dainthal	61-0478
Elisabeth 38			

NAME	AGE	RESIDENCE	YR-LIST
HARRER, Lorenz	57	Forst	57-0654
HARROCK, John	30	England	59-0613
HARTEL, Adam	28	Oberfranken	58-0399
HARTEN, Agnes	20	Badbergen	62-0879
HARTEN, Albert von	16	Altenwistedt	59-0412
HARTEN, Burkardina	20	Blumenthal	59-0048
HARTEN, Joh.Ed.	22	Jever	57-1148
HARTENHORST, v.(m)	17		57-0447
HARTH, Hirsch	20	Gemuenden	60-0411
HARTIG, Elis.	25	Niederroden	56-1117
Marg. 21			
HARTIG, W.	27	Heinsdorf	59-0990
HARTING, Engel	24	Bueckeburg	57-0555
HARTING, Jacob	27	Inchenhofen	57-1192
HARTING, Ph.(m)	35	Bueckeburg	57-0555
HARTJE, Heinrich	16	Klauen	56-1117
HARTKE, Christian	42	Glarnsee	57-0704
Maria 36, Maria 7, Wilhelmine 4			
Augusta 6m			
HARTL, Marie	26	Waltershof	61-0482
HARTMANN, A.M.	23	Geisa	59-0477
HARTMANN, Albert	53	Arolsen	62-0306
Wilhelmina 54, Robert 21, Moritz 17			
Hermine 14, Hermann 9			
HARTMANN, Aloys	26	Fellen/Bav.	62-0608
HARTMANN, Anton	16	Wernigerode/P	60-0622
HARTMANN, Anton	25	Cammer	57-1067
Christine 23			
HARTMANN, Aug.	28	Erfurt	55-1082
Anna Cath. 50			
HARTMANN, August	22	Hannover	57-0447
HARTMANN, Bernhard	22	Hammel	60-0334
Marie 30			
HARTMANN, Carl	15	Steinberg	60-1141
HARTMANN, Cath.	53	Dornapenstein	60-0785
HARTMANN, Cathar.	26	Rudersdorf	56-0951
HARTMANN, Chr.	19	Bremen	56-1117
HARTMANN, Chr.Frdr	31	Cammer	57-1067
Anton 22			
HARTMANN, Christne	31	Baden-Baden	62-0758
HARTMANN, Conrad	21	Leichenbach	60-0052
HARTMANN, Conrad	20	Homburg	57-1067
HARTMANN, Conrad	20	Horsten	59-0384
HARTMANN, Eva	21	Elters	58-0563
HARTMANN, Friedr W	21	Isnitz	56-0411
HARTMANN, Friedr.	28	Meiningen	56-0847
HARTMANN, Georg	57	Oberbellbach	55-1082
Louise 24			
HARTMANN, Georg	21	Hessen	60-0371
HARTMANN, Gertrude	22	Hamberg	57-1067
HARTMANN, H.	23	Haenigsen	62-0993
HARTMANN, Heinrich	14	Hasebicke	55-0845
HARTMANN, Heinrich	58	Darmstadt	58-0885
Susanna 52, Peter 28			
HARTMANN, Heinrich	40	Uffhofen	59-0047
HARTMANN, Henry	21	Windheim	58-0545
HARTMANN, J.P.(m)	20	Winterkasten	61-0716
HARTMANN, Jacob	28	Aarau/Switz.	60-0371
Anna 23			
HARTMANN, Joh.Val.	53	Heidelberg	60-1161
Johanna 52, Elisab. 26, Johanna 17			
HARTMANN, Johann	38	Altenburg	58-0399
Hinrich 48			
HARTMANN, Jos.	28	Warburg/Pr.	62-0608
HARTMANN, Louisa	20	Isernhagen	57-0961
HARTMANN, M.(m)	28	Lindau	62-0467
HARTMANN, Margaret	19	Neidenstein	60-1053
HARTMANN, Margaret	21	Bamberg	57-0436
HARTMANN, Marie	17	Heynau	60-0411
HARTMANN, Philipp	62	Darmstadt	60-0785
HARTMANN, R.	19	Arolsen	59-0535
HARTMANN, Sophie	17	Babenhausen	62-0836
HARTMANN, Theresia	24	Ankum	59-0214
HARTMANN, Ursula	27	Baiern	58-0399
HARTMANN, Wilh.	18	Gudensberg	55-0932
HARTMANN, Wilhelm	16	Coburg	57-1113
HARTMANN, Wilhelm	33	Beelen/Pr.	62-0608
Elisabeth 24			
HARTNER, Eva	57	Tuebingen	60-1032
HARTNER, Susanne	22	Kitzingen/Bav	61-0770
Magdalene 28			
HARTNOTH, Fr.	34	Cleveland	59-1036
HARTUNG, Andreas	44	Dietenborn	57-0924
Christine 52			
HARTUNG, Barbara	33	Fliegenhockst	60-0429
HARTUNG, Carl G.	23	Balstedt	62-0306
Christina 21			
HARTUNG, Franz	21	Baiern	58-0399
HARTUNG, Friedr.	28	Bretten	59-1036
HARTUNG, Friedrich	58	Hedemuende	59-0951
Louise 48, Carl 16, Augusta 11, Ernst 8			
HARTUNG, Friedrike	22	Ostheim	61-0482
HARTUNG, Geo.Heinr	38	Woellmarshsn.	57-0021
HARTUNG, Georg	27	Eisenach	56-0723
Anna 21			
HARTUNG, Georg	36	Berka/Weimar	60-0622
Christine 39, Magdalena 11, Maria 10			
Andreas 7, Valentin 6, Anna 3, Johann 9m			
HARTUNG, Gustav	20	Goslar	59-1036
Dorothea 18			
HARTUNG, Heinrich	37	Haran	56-0847
Bernhardine 4			
HARTUNG, Heinrich	19	Wennigstedt	57-0447
Christian 17			
HARTUNG, Jacob	49	Steinbach	56-0819
HARTUNG, John	34	Herford	59-0477
HARTUNG, Robert	20	Gr.Weschungen	56-1011
HARTUNG, Wilhelm	34	Nordhausen	57-0924
Augusta 33, Henriette 6, Carl 2			
Heinrich by			
HARTWIG, Anne	30	Muenchen	61-0482
HARTWIG, Aug.F.	30	Berlin	56-0951
HARTWIG, Elise	17	Besse	59-0214
HARVEY, Georg	34	Montreal	62-1112
HARYE, Catharine	26	Gertdorf/Han	60-0622
HARZ, de Henry	39	Winzlar	56-1011
Dorothy 32, Henry 10, Caroline 8			
Friedrich 3			
HASANECK, Johann	44	Willegwi	57-1067
Marie 33, Marie 7, Franz 4, Johann 2			
HASCHEL, C. Gottl.	26	Dresden	56-0629
HASE, Gesina	17	Kirchhatten	61-0897
HASE, J.C.(m)	29	Neuenburg	57-0555
Justine 27, Wilhelm 3, Emilie 1			
HASE, Metz	59	Huchting	62-1042
Gesine 24			
HASE, Richard	23	Altenburg	55-0812
HASE, Wilhelm	57	Neuenburg	57-0555
M. 53			
HASE, Wilhelm	17	Braunschweig	56-1216
Julius 16			
HASEBIRCK, John	32	Quendorf	57-1148
HASEBROCK, Armand	39	Quendorf	57-1148
William 31			
HASELMANN, Marg.	22	Redwitz	55-0630
HASEMANN, Christ.	16	Lindhorst	59-0214
HASEMANN, Heinrich	16	Hagen	57-0776
HASEMANN, Joh.Otto	47	Schottlingen	61-0520
Maria 40, Joh.Heinrich 15, Engel Maria 12			
Engel Doroth 7, Engel Sophia 7			
Caroline 4, Engel Sophia 9m			
HASEMEYER, Casp.C.	17	Fritzlar	62-0879
HASENAUER, An.	18	Eichschiss	55-0845
HASENFLUG, Elisab.	29	Wasendorf	57-0021
HASENKAMP, Jenne	20	Vechta	62-0730
HASHAGEN, Elise	18	Blumenthal	59-1036
H.G. 27, Anna 19			
HASRREN, Franziska	58	New York	60-0533
HASS, Chr.	15	Hersfeld	59-1036
HASS, Heinrich	19	Ordendorf	57-1280
HASS, Johann	28	Oldenburg	58-0399
HASS, Marie	16	Kirchheim/Wrt	62-0608
HASS, Peter	56	Luedingworth	56-0413
Carl 9			
HASSALD, Fr.(m)	31	Philadelphia	61-0897
HASSBERG, Mag.	19	Zeven	57-1026

NAME	AGE	RESIDENCE	YR-LIST
HASSE, Dorothea	20	Sabbenhausen	59-0214
HASSELBACH, Helfr.	20	Frankenberg	56-0847
HASSELBACH, Wlhmne	19	Sansteth	56-1011
HASSELBACHER, Jete	22	Desterbergenr	60-0521
HASSELBAUER, Barb.	23	Lauz	50-1017
HASSELMEYER, Justn	44	Irendorf	60-0411
HASSELN, v.A.D.(m)	17	Neukirchen/Ha	60-0622
HASSENFLUG, Anna	17	Lehrbach	55-0630
HASSERT, Eduard	24	Naumburg	59-0613
HASSFELD, Georg	51	Weiterode	55-1082
Cath. Elise 53, Anna Marg. 14, Conrad 16			
HASSIG, Anton	30	Nafenau	60-0334
HASSLER, Anna	37	Unterbalzheim	60-0334
HASSMANN, Ulrich	36	Gerich	57-1122
HASTEDT, Gesine	18	Hemelingen	57-1192
Lise 18			
HASTEDT, Marie	25	Hannover	55-0634
HASTING, J.T.	29	Hanover	57-0654
HASTORF, Louise	20	Hamburg	55-1048
HATH, Johann	19	Solz	57-0850
HATTEMEYER, John	45	Kl.Kitzighofe	61-0482
Felicita 21, Aloisia 20			
HATTENDORF, Aug'ta	18	Quetzen	61-0897
HATTENDORF, Conrad	26	Kohlenfeld	61-0520
HATTENDORF, H.(m)	25	Bueckeburg	61-0897
HATTENDORF, Maria	22	Rothenburg	59-0412
HATTFELD, Henry	36	New York	57-1192
Anna 32			
HATTUNG, Christina	26	Solze	59-0535
HAUB, Wilh.	21	Pforzheim	59-0214
HAUBER, Magdalena	26	Willburgstett	57-1026
HAUBERT, Joseph	65	Saarbruecken	57-0509
Anna 52, Peter 18, Helene 7			
HAUBOLD, Ernst Fr.	35	Rischberg/Sax	60-0622
HAUBRICHS, An Mary	22	Hesweiler	57-0924
HAUCH, Anna M.	18	Tuebingen	60-0411
HAUCK, Barbara	51	Lohr/Bav.	60-0622
HAUCK, Dorothea	31	Leutzendorf	60-0622
HAUCK, Marg.	21	Grefenhausen	62-0111
HAUCKE, Julius	29	Bischoffswald	60-0622
HAUEISEN, Marg.	29	Poppengruen	55-0413
HAUENSTEIN, Joh.C.	46	Mistelbach	56-0951
HAUENSTEIN, Marg.	23	Mistelgau	61-0520
HAUENSTEIN, Oscar	13	Sonnenberg	62-0730
HAUER, G.(m)	21	Blankenbach	62-0730
HAUF, Herm.	24	Schwerin	61-0897
HAUG, Adam	26	Gaildorf	60-0411
Gottfried 13			
HAUG, C.F. (m)	27	Magdeburg/Pr.	55-0538
HAUG, Fer.	24	Calen	59-0951
HAUG, Mary	19	Friegelhofe	60-0411
HAUGK, Jos.	49	Munster	60-0998
HAUKE, Adolph	32	Detmold	59-1036
HAUKE, Cathrina	40	America	59-1036
Wm. 6m			
HAUKERN, Johann	37	Gerkswalde/Au	55-1238
Magdalene 36, Johann 6, Maria 5			
Joseph 6m			
HAUMACHER, Johann	57	Markgroningen	62-0836
Wilhelmine 58			
HAUN, Ant.Jos.	21	Oberbalbach	57-0961
HAUNS, Ida	32	Hermesdorf	59-1036
Gustav 9, Paul 4, Johanna 8			
HAUPT, Henriette	38	Berlin	56-0819
HAUPTFUEHRER, Dan.	18	Geismar/Hess.	55-0628
HAUPTFUEHRER, J.H.	22	Ernsthausen	57-0924
HAUPTMANN, Peter	23	St.Louis	62-0467
HAUPTMEYER, August	42	Aerzen	57-0447
Johanne 41, Friedrike 9, Wilhelmine 10m			
HAUPTNER, Barb. C.	23	Roggenstein	57-0924
HAUPTVOEGEL, Albt.	30	Leipzig	59-0047
Louise 19			
HAURY, Rud.	15	Basel	62-0730
Albert 19			
HAUSCHILD, Agnese	19	Lilienthal	57-0606
HAUSCHILD, Fr.Wm.L	34	New York	59-0372
Wilhelmine 28			
HAUSCHILD, J.D.	28	Lilienthal	62-0730

NAME	AGE	RESIDENCE	YR-LIST
HAUSCHILD, Johann	20	Nortwede	57-1122
HAUSCHILDT, Elis.W	18	Verden	61-0482
HAUSELMANN, Johann	19	Zwerenberg	56-0951
Caroline 32			
HAUSEMER, Lilly	17	Moenschroth	62-0836
HAUSEN, Jos.W.	59	Marotterode	61-0482
HAUSENER, Joseph	24	Goekelsbug/Bv	55-0628
HAUSER, Aldrich	48	Havre	57-0578
Gottfried 38, Sophie 16, Schlatter 30			
HAUSER, Catharina	22	Baden	60-1196
(child) 1			
HAUSER, Louis	38	Philadelphia	62-0730
HAUSER, Minna	21	Oberndorf	62-0836
HAUSER, P.(m)	29	New York	61-0804
HAUSER, Victoria	52	Landau/Bav.	55-0628
HAUSFELD, Joh.	40	Voiden	61-0167
Cath. M. 60			
HAUSINN, Ed. C.G.	16	Varel	58-0604
HAUSLEUTNER, Ernst	24	Breslau	60-0334
Seraphine 18			
HAUSMANN, August	19	Fridolinghaus	59-0477
HAUSMANN, Friedr.	28	Breslau	56-1044
HAUSMANN, Sophie	18	Bovenden	56-0279
HAUSMANN, Wm. Fr.	28	Kirchhain	56-0723
HAUSTEIN, Esther	20	Langendorf	59-1017
HAVENBERG, Conrad	21	Broistedt	56-0723
HAVERKAMP, Heinr.	36	Haldorf	59-0951
HAVERMANN, Eduard	38	Spandau	59-0047
HAVICKHORST, Heinr	43	Baltimore	60-1196
HAWEL, Adelbert	58	Stupno	57-1026
Anna 57			
HAWLISECK, Johann	36	Piesack	57-1113
Maria 3			
HAY, Engelbert	18	Oeflingen	58-0881
HAYEN, E.	21	Oldenburg	59-0990
HAYENGA, Lina	30	Andreasberg	62-1169
Marie 8, Agnes 6, Hermann 4			
HAYES, Rebecca	59	Bramstadt	59-0477
HAYMORIES, Ludw.	23	Lamas	59-0477
HAYNS, (m)	30	New York	62-1169
HAYWARD, Giles	34	Minnesota	59-0477
Margaretha 23			
HEANNY, Jean	22	France	62-1112
Gottl. 15, Marie 12			
HEARD, Robert	36	England	62-0938
HEARNE, David	38	Southampton	59-0384
HEBBEL, Johanne	22	Ottenberg	57-0704
HEBEISEN, Helene	19	Diebeisen	58-0885
HEBELER, Elisabeth	36	New York	59-0214
HEBELZAND, Martha	24	Kurhessen	56-1044
HEBENER, Conrad	54	Daubringen	57-0924
Margarethe 50, Catharine 26, Heinrich 4			
HEBER, Heinr. Alf.	19	Dresden	56-0819
HEBERLEIN, Hugo	17	Wiesbaden	57-1148
HECHER, Adam	35	Meckershausen	62-1112
HECHLER, C.	30	Horningen	62-1112
HECHLER, Wilhelm	28	New York	62-1112
HECHT, B.	27	New York	62-0938
HECHT, B.(m)	40	Griesbach	62-0401
HECHT, Dorothea	24	Horsten	59-0384
HECHT, Esther	15	Oberzella/Hes	62-0608
HECHT, G.	33	Wollmirstedt	62-0993
HECHT, Geo. Martin	24	Hatzelsdorf	56-1044
HECHT, Georg	27	Bremen	59-1017
HECHT, Isaac	19	Gellenhausen	60-0398
HECHT, Isaac	19	Gelnhausen	60-0398
HECHT, Jette	20	Weimarschmied	62-0730
HECHT, Joh.Gottlob	40	Jueterborg	59-0412
HECHT, Joseph	30	Darmstadt	57-1407
Marie 26			
HECHT, Regina	16	Ruttenheim	57-1148
HECHT, Regina	22	Buttenheim	61-0482
HECHT, Sophie	24	Lichtenberg	59-1017
HECHT, Wilhelm	24	Lichtenberg	59-1017
HECK, Catharine	44	Bodehausen	57-0447
HECK, Elisab.	57	Schuetzingen	59-1036
HECK, Heinrich	18	Sandheim	56-0411
HECKEL, Peter	31	Hillpoldstein	58-0576

NAME	AGE	RESIDENCE	YR-LIST
Margarethe 23, Catharine by			
HECKEL, Sebastian	49	Henfstedt	61-0478
Joh.Marie 45, Marianne 24, Johannes 22			
Ernst 19, Friedrich 8			
HECKELBERG, F.	20	Lingen	58-0399
HECKELL, Mart.	17	Leidingen	55-0413
HECKER, Bertha	22	Oldendorf	59-0951
HECKER, Carl	32	Berlin	59-0951
HECKER, J.F.	29	Weimar	57-0606
HECKERT, Elisabeth	36	Rauschenberg	57-0754
Maria 14			
HECKETHIER, Susana	57	Branderode	55-0812
HECKMANN, Bernhard	26	Werne	59-0214
HECKMANN, Jane	33	Schuettorf	57-0422
HECKMANN, Minna	48	Uslar	57-0578
HECKMANN, Wilhelm	50	Burghoven	57-0776
Elisabeth 41, Heinrich 9m			
HECKNOTH, Conrad	18	Treysa	60-0533
HEDDAEUS, Christ.	22	Koenig	57-1192
Sophie 20			
HEDEMANN, Wilhelm	18	Raden	59-0412
HEDER, Adam	20	Bebra	59-0047
HEDKE, Eduard	24	Boin	56-0819
HEDTKE, Gottlieb	39	Alt Paleschke	61-0779
Wilhelmine 39, Adam 13, Pauline 9			
Henriette 7, Juliane 6, Mathilde by			
HEDTKE, Gottlieb	50	Alt Paleschke	61-0779
Caroline 45, Susann 17, August 10			
Henriette 5			
HEDTKE, Jacob	35	Lienczewo	61-0779
Caroline 33			
HEDTKE, Johann	49	Alt Paleschke	61-0779
Florentine 31, August 13, Theodor 10			
Friedrich 8, Adolph 5, Alvine 3			
HEDTKE, Martin	31	Lienczewo	61-0779
Caroline 38, Henriette 17, Carl 14			
Julius 9, Caroline 7, Theodor 3			
Wilhelm 2, Rudolph by			
HEEB, Johann	28	Ruggell	60-0533
HEELEIN, Johanna	22	New York	57-1280
Helene 1			
HEER, H.W.W.	21	New York	62-1042
HEEREN, Ed.(m)	39	Bremen	56-0847
HEEREN, H.	60	Hesel	55-0932
Margareth 58, G.M. 38, Enkel 28, Hasin 23			
Johanna 19, Johanna 2			
HEERING, H.(m)	26	Muehlberg	61-0482
HEERMANN, Felix	20	Boehmen	61-0897
HEERZ, Caroline	18	Gruenholz	61-0804
HEESE, Rosalie	26	Schneith	57-0776
HEFEN, Charles	20	Suelbeck	57-0654
HEGEL, Armand	21	Neustadt	57-0654
HEGELER, H.	28	Oldenburg	62-1042
HEGENBART, Stephan	38	Franzberg	57-1148
Marianne 35			
HEGER, Geo.	30	Gusthol	60-0521
HEGMANN, Tabitha	29	Unt.Altenbush	61-0779
HEHE, Christoph	24	Heithoefen	57-0754
HEHL, Marg.	21	Stuttgart	62-0730
HEHN, J.P.	23	Margoldsheim	58-0576
HEHN, Pierre	28	America	56-1216
HEHRIEGEL, Jul.	33	Moebisburg	59-0990
(m) 15, (m) 14, (baby) 9m			
HEICHEL, Ernst	32	Oberelen	55-0630
HEICHKE, Carl	46	Auma	57-1280
Wilhelmine 41, Carl Hein. 14, Franz 12			
August 9, Eduard 6, Minna 5			
HEID, Carl	25	Darmstadt	60-1161
HEID, Friedrich	29	Wimmer	56-0589
HEID, Joh.Valentin	26	Baden	61-0779
HEID, Theodor	30	Laibach	56-0951
HEIDBRING, John	31	Strackholt	57-0422
HEIDBRINK, Anna	23	Harpenfeld	56-0589
HEIDE, Bernh.	49	St.Paul	60-0334
Augusta 30, Johann 16, Raphael 17, Paul 2			
HEIDE, Friedrich	56	Ratzik	56-0723
Ida 3			
HEIDE, auf d.Engel	18	Voiden	61-0167

NAME	AGE	RESIDENCE	YR-LIST
HEIDE, v.d. C.	31	Muender	60-0334
Dorothea 28, Dorothea 6m			
HEIDE, v.der Mag.	34	Lamstedt	59-0477
Margaretha 8, Catharina 4			
HEIDEL, Carl	36	Schneeberg	57-1122
Caroline 30, Emma 10, Ida 9, Bertha 7			
Ferdinand 3, Adolph 8m			
HEIDELBACH, Anna C	53	Leusel	56-0951
August 15			
HEIDELOFF, Marie	23	Gutenburg	58-0545
HEIDEMANN, Cath.	50	Pungehn	61-0779
HEIDEMANN, Wilhelm	24	Steinhude	56-0411
HEIDENBLUTH, Carl	30	Eisenach	57-1113
HEIDENREICH, Jos.	34	Bottendorf/Bv	55-0538
HEIDENREICH, W.(m)	26	Steppach	61-0478
HEIDER, Charlotte	33	Dittersdorf	60-0429
HEIDER, Friedr.	22	Schluesselbg.	62-0111
HEIDGADT, Wilhelm	13	Mintzlage	60-0334
HEIDGERDT, Hermann	25	Haten	59-1036
HEIDGERT, Diedrich	13	Menslage	57-1026
HEIDIG, Peter	35	Blankenfeld	57-1407
HEIDINGSFELDER, J.	28	Rappenau	58-0576
Marie 34			
HEIDKAMP, Bernhard	43	Reischendorf	57-1148
Anna Maria 33, Maria Eng. 55, Fr. 7			
Bernhardine 5, Elisabeth 3, Bernhard 6m			
HEIDMANN, Margaret	34	Bremen	60-0334
Conradine 1			
HEIDMANN, Wilhelm	19	Bremen	57-0850
H. 25			
HEIFER, Johannes	59	Alsfeld	55-0634
Anna Elisab. 58			
HEIGEROTH, Casper	31	Newrode	57-0776
HEIGMANN, Anna	16	Duerrenmettst	60-0334
HEIKER, Carl	26	Windheim	58-0545
HEIL, Johann	14	Meiningen	56-0527
HEIL, Rudolph	34	Brueckenau	62-1169
HEILAND, Hugo	36	Hofstaetten	60-1053
HEILAND, Therese	24	Hungen	57-1416
HEILBOM, Marie	25	Schluechtern	58-0604
HEILBORN, Marie	25	Schluechtern	58-0604
HEILBRONN, Abraham	25	Oberaula	60-0533
HEILER, Mathilde	18	Albertriet	56-0847
HEILIG, J.	33	Rosenberg	62-0993
HEILING, Reno	23	Nuernberg	57-1067
HEILING, Wilhelm	16	Bersan	57-1192
HEILMANN, F.J.	56	Borgloch	57-0654
HEILMANN, Joh.G.	27	Wuerm	62-1169
Cath. 24			
HEIM, Heinrich	22	Attendorn	57-0606
HEIM, Henry	27	Coburg	57-1192
HEIM, Johann	19	Faurndau	59-0613
HEIM, Marger.	20	Bavaria	57-0606
HEIM, Sophie	13	Heiningen	59-0535
HEIMANN, Aug.	24	Runau	56-0527
HEIMANN, Carl	30	Emsteck	59-0951
Alex. 30			
HEIMANN, Johann	24	Ruhden/Pr.	62-0608
Caroline 24			
HEIMANN, Julius	20	Oldenburg	59-1036
HEIMANN, Louis	17	Sonneberg	56-0629
HEIMBACH, Johan J.	49	Reimerod	57-1113
Maria 29, Johannes 9, Heinrich 6, Marie 1			
HEIMBACH, Rosalie	31	Hafenlohe	61-0482
Adam 3			
HEIMBERG, L.(m)	23	Prussia	57-0555
HEIMBOCHEL, Sophia	20	Linde/Hann.	60-0622
HEIMBURG, v. Emil	19	Jever	57-0924
HEIMBURG, v.Carol.	24	Worpswede	59-0951
Jenny 18			
HEIMEL, Jacob	49	Farrenbach	58-0576
Elise 31, Georg 19, Catharine 8			
HEIMERDINGER, Chr.	69	Goppingen	60-0334
HEIMERDINGER, Frdr	27	Boekingen	60-1053
HEIMES, Joseph	22	Febecke	62-0879
HEIMROTH, Ana Cath	16	Kruspis	55-1082
HEIMSFURTHER, Clar	21	Bechhofen	56-0723
HEIN, Anna	20	Bremen	60-0052

NAME	AGE	RESIDENCE	YR-LIST
HEIN, Armand	20	Bremervoerde	57-0654
HEIN, Elisabeth	6	Rothenburg	57-0436
HEIN, J.D.	30	New York	62-0730
Anna 24			
HEIN, Johann	46	Wittelsberg	60-0334
Elisabetha 43, Johannes 8, Johann 6			
Catherina 7			
HEIN, Marie	16	Badbergen	62-0467
HEIN, Marie	24	Wilangheim	59-0613
Eva 22			
HEIN, Sally	23	Fischerhude	58-0885
HEIN, Wilhelmine	19	Altona	57-0704
HEINA, Catharine	35	Illinois	60-0052
Alfred 3, Oskar 6, Edmund 1			
HEINBACHER, Elisab	24	Billertshsn.	62-0608
HEINBURG, Dorothea	18	Neuhaus	56-0629
HEINDEL, Georg Fr.	27	Daubersbach	57-0578
HEINE, (f)	23	France	57-1150
HEINE, Emilie	28	Strelitz	57-1067
HEINE, Engel Marie	22	Hohnhorst	55-0630
Engel Doroth 16			
HEINE, Eugen	27	Wasungen	57-1416
HEINE, Gottlob	21	Pollhagen	61-0478
Franz 50			
HEINE, Heinrich	45	Jever	61-0520
Caroline 45, Carl 6, Bernhard 3			
HEINE, Hinrich	32	Rosenthal/Hes	57-0847
HEINE, Joh.Gottfr.	28	Erfurt	57-1067
HEINECKE, Doris	22	New York	62-0730
HEINEKEN, Averick	51	Bremen	61-0482
Adele 19, Mary 11			
HEINEKEN, Fr.P.	21	Bremen	62-0938
HEINEMANN, Armand	24	Hildesheim	59-0214
HEINEMANN, August	17	Volkmarsen/He	62-0608
HEINEMANN, C.C.	24	Alabama	57-1192
HEINEMANN, Dietr.	14	Landsbergen	60-1053
HEINEMANN, Heinr.	26	Wellingerode	56-1044
HEINEMANN, Johann	32	Sand	55-0812
HEINEMANN, Math.	19	Osnabrueck	56-0512
HEINEMANN, Regine	20	Schluchtern	58-0604
HEINEMANN, W.(m)	27	Hannover	61-0107
HEINEN, Heinrich	26	Rumeln	61-0482
Sophie 20			
HEINER, Georg	18	Walldorf	59-0477
HEINER, Johann	32	Hirten/Pr.	55-1238
Louise 24			
HEINER, Joseph	32	Passau	55-0845
HEINERL, Anton	25	Darchau	55-0932
HEINKE, Ernest	22	Sohland	56-0632
HEINLEIN, A.Barb.	30	Freidenbach	59-0412
HEINLEIN, Cathrina	21	Dandorf	57-0754
HEINMUELLER, Johs.	22	Curhessen	55-0634
HEINOTH, C.(m)	52	New York	61-0897
HEINRICH, Carl	28	Bilitz	56-0847
HEINRICH, Elisab.	22	Bavaria	62-0758
HEINRICH, Maria	22	Wuestenroth	60-1053
Caroline 15			
HEINRICH, Wilhelm	36	New York	57-1280
Mathilde 30, August 9, Wilhelm 1			
HEINRICHS, Pet. J.	22	Illmen/Pruss.	55-1238
HEINS, Chr.	26	Westen	61-1132
Wm. 26			
HEINS, H.	30	New York	62-1169
HEINS, Heinrich	22	Milkendorf	61-0520
HEINS, Johanna	26	Gera	60-1141
HEINS, Meta	20	Otterstein	57-0654
HEINS, Sophie Marg	16	Drangstedt	58-0563
HEINSCHEN, Anna M.	18	Wersabe	57-0847
HEINSKE, William	27	Wronke	57-0422
HEINSON, Anna	20	Bremen	61-0897
HEINTZ, Heinrich	21	Kaiserslauter	59-0613
HEINTZE, Melanie	28	Elmslohe	62-1112
HEINZ, Christine	46	Hochhelheim	56-0527
Johanna 22			
HEINZ, Fritz	33	Pohlgoens	55-0413
HEINZE, Otto	30	New York	62-1042
Lyda 24			
HEINZERLING, Heinr	23	Sontra	61-0520
HEINZIG, Bernh.W.	29	Leipzig	62-0608
HEIPEL, Johann	20	Breitenbach	56-1260
HEIRMANN, Johann	17	Donaueschingn	60-0521
HEIROCK, Martha	17	Curhessen	57-0847
Barbara 15			
HEISE, Christ.	36	Iber	57-1113
Henriette 26, Wilhelm 9, Johanne 5			
Georgine 2, CHristian 1			
HEISE, Eduard	30	Sulza	55-1082
HEISE, J.C.	26	Prussia	57-0555
Henriette 28			
HEISE, Johann	40	Salza	55-1082
HEISE, Wilhelm	22	Braunschweig	55-0932
HEISECK, Heinrich	19	Schlesien	58-0399
HEISENER, W. (m)	17	Halden	56-0951
HEISER, Catharine	48	Arnsheim	56-0819
Anna Margar. 15, Carl 10, Elisabeth 8			
Caspar 6, Anna Maria 4			
HEISER, Johann	28	Zernin	57-0776
HEISNER, Catharina	23	Rockenfuess	57-0924
HEISSINGER, Gertr.	23	Neustadt a/R.	57-1067
HEISSNER, Clara	20	Zwickau	59-0951
HEISTER, Heinrich	28	Heingruenden	59-0048
HEISTERHAGEN, Mina	24	Deckbergen	58-0881
HEITERKESS, Anton	18	Coelln	56-0819
HEITKAMP, Maria A.	30	Reischendorf	57-1148
Friedrich 34, Henry 1			
HEITMANN, Henry	25	Bextehoevede	60-1141
HEITMANN, J.D.	28	Otterndorf	57-0961
Mary 28			
HEITMANN, Joh.	47	Krepen	60-0521
Meta 47			
HEITMANN, M.(f)	32	Sand	57-0555
W.(m) 9, E.(f) 7			
HEITMANN, Sophie	22	Ricklingen	56-1044
HEITZ, John	32	Rouen	62-0836
HEITZMANN, Lorenz	23	Urach	59-0477
HEIXEL, Johann	54	Wien	56-0723
A.(f) 16			
HEIZMANN, Cathrina	22	Thumlingen	58-0563
Margaretha 18			
HELBERG, Christian	38	Rethem/Hann.	57-0924
HELBIG, Georg	26	Kleinmehlsa	62-0166
HELD, David		Wrunbach	60-1196
HELD, Fr.	38	Kaldorf	57-0606
Amalie 43, Friedrich 7, Amalie 5			
August 1			
HELD, Jacob	31	Balzheim	60-0334
Maria 29, Marg. 4, Christian 22			
HELD, Joh. Georg	25	Ephausen/Wurt	62-0608
HELD, Martin	28	Mosbach/Bav.	60-0429
HELDENBERG, Ludwig	24	Muenchen	61-0930
HELDERLIN, Andreas	22	St.Gallen	57-1407
HELEMEYER, Louise	18	Blomberg	56-0512
HELFEN, B.(f)	21	Kleinlangheim	59-0951
HELFRICH, An Elis.	23	Altendorf	57-0754
Heinrich 19			
HELFRICH, Joseph	18	Nuesig	56-1260
HELGENBERG, Theod.	15	St.Louis	59-1036
HELKES, J.	31	Kirchweichede	59-1036
Peter 3, Elisab. 1			
HELL, Franz	18	Seligenstadt	60-0334
Sophie 16			
HELLBERG, Gustav	45	Westenholz	58-0563
Marie 48, Dorothea 18, Sophie 10			
HELLE, J.G.	48	Wiersen	59-0384
Caroline 38			
HELLENBERG, Bernh.	22	Schmalkalden	57-0924
HELLER, Adolf	15	Koenigswarth	50-1017
HELLER, Adolph	24	Weissungen/Sx	62-0342
HELLER, B.	20	Darmstadt	59-0613
HELLER, C.(m)	35	New York	60-0521
HELLER, Friedrich	45	Dissen	56-1044
Johanne 27			
HELLER, Isaac	29	Pennsylvania	62-0730
HELLER, Joh.	22	Loewenstein	61-0669
HELLER, Matthaeus	46	Schmalkalden	58-0576
Catharine 41, Caroline 17, Susanne 15			

NAME	AGE	RESIDENCE	YR-LIST
August 13, Margaretha 11, Elise 8			
Marie 4			
HELLER, Moritz	16	Koenigswart	58-0885
HELLER, Rosine	50	Schwarzenbach	60-0521
HELLER, Salomon	43	Raunitz	56-0411
HELLGOTH, A.Marie	36	Nordhalben	56-1117
HELLING, Carl	54	Elderich	56-0629
HELLING, J.H.(m)	16	Dillingen	56-0951
HELLINGEN, Stephen	32	Backe	62-0306
Franz Wh. 23			
HELLMANN, Heinrich	18	Hottorp	57-0850
HELLMANN, Johannes	48	Fischbach	57-1067
HELLMANN, Wilh'mne	26	Hottorp	57-0850
Dorothea 23			
HELLMER, Franz	21	Huelskotten	57-0021
HELLMUTH, Andr.	58	Zirden	56-0951
Wilhelmine 38			
HELLMUTH, Henry	29	Wildungen	57-0961
(wife) 23, Anna 22			
HELLMUTH, Herm.	35	Grossenritte	56-0527
Anna 2			
HELLMUTH, Johann	29	Wettringen	59-0412
HELLMUTH, Rosine	23	Altenstein	57-0509
HELLRICH, Johann	41	Schwarzennach	57-1122
HELLRIEGEL, Theres	65	Rothenfels	58-0881
HELLWIG, Adam	58	Hadamar	57-0754
Catharina 51, Anna Elisab. 22			
Cath.Elisab. 13			
HELLWIG, Carl	29	Waechtersbach	62-1169
Lisette 39			
HELLWIG, Conrad	16	Hadamer	57-0754
HELLWIG, Elise	19	Roth	56-0589
HELLWIG, Jacob	16	Busserode	55-1082
HELLWIG, Maria	23	Dorbe/Curhess	60-0429
HELM, Ernst Louis	22	Gera	58-0881
HELM, Hermann	25	Homberg	61-0520
HELMBOLD, Joh.G.	24	Oberwaid	59-0535
HELMENTAG, Louise	18	Buhlen	62-0111
HELMHOLZ, Heinrich	38	Gronau	58-0563
Marie 36, Josephine 9, Elise 8, Fritz 6			
Wilhelmine 4, August 2			
HELMHOLZ, Mathilde	26	Braunschweig	55-0628
Otto 4			
HELMKAMPF, W.	19	Goettingen	59-0613
HELMKE, Marie	26	Bederkesa	58-0563
Wilhelm 16			
HELMKE, Martin Hch	21	Nesse	61-0520
HELMKEN, Johann	23	Scharmbeck	59-0477
HELMRICH, Geo. Hch	59	Celle	56-1117
Marie 7			
HELMS, Ch.	34	Milwaukee	59-0951
Elise 8m			
HELMS, Charles	27	Brinkum	62-0232
Anna 25			
HELMS, Friedrich	28	Siedenburg	58-0925
HELMS, Justine	44	Gronau	58-0563
Augusta 16, Wilhelmine 12, Louise 10			
Christian 4			
HELMS, Marie	30	Assendorf	59-0613
HELMSEN, Franz	58	Hildesheim	59-0951
Therese 52			
HELMUTH, Michael	59	Meiningen	62-0758
Elisabeth 50, Anna 36, Friederike 26			
Andreas 18, Wilhelm 10			
HELSCHER, An Fr'ka	35	Potsdam	56-0589
HELVIG, Cath.	24	Hundshausen	55-0413
HELWEG, Georg	27	Reichensachse	55-0628
Elisabeth 27, Carl 2			
HELWICH, Gertrude	20	Oberfuhl/Pr.	55-1238
HELX, Anna	19	Oberbalzheim	60-0334
HEMETER, Mathilde	27	Baltimore	62-0467
Robert 2			
HEMMANN, Wilhelm	39	Weimar	61-0682
Caroline 29, Pauline 12, Franz 9, Ida 5			
Carl 9m			
HEMMER, Matthaeus	26	Ehrl	59-0214
Anna Maria 23			
HEMMERICH, Magd.	22	Tessendorf	61-0897

NAME	AGE	RESIDENCE	YR-LIST
HEMPEL, Carl	42	Greiz	60-0785
HEMPEL, Conrad	40	Gellhausen	58-0563
Elisabetha 29, Conrad 3, Eleonore 11m			
HEMPEL, Franz	24	Marpersdrf/Wm	60-0622
Amalie 33			
HEMSING, Anna	19	Osterwik	62-0232
HENBACH, Alfred	30	New York	59-0613
(f) 25, (f) 19			
HENBIG, Jeronimus	24	Brueckenau/Bv	55-1238
HENCKE, Carl	40	Romannshof	58-0576
Louise 55, Ernestine 32, Johann 8			
Emilie 6, Hermann 4, August by			
HENCKE, Friedrich	42	Romannshof	58-0576
Johanne 42, Emilie 16, Pauline 14			
Ernestine 10, Friedrich 6, Mathilde by			
HENCKE, J.D.	20	Nettenauberge	59-0384
HENCKE, Lotte	16	Britefeld	60-0334
HENCKEL, Catharine	18	Alsfeld	57-0606
Christine 16, Friedrich 21			
HENCKEL, Friedrike	26	Spahl	58-0545
HENDEL, Jac.	23	Posen	57-0654
HENDELBERGER, Isak	11	Furth	58-0306
HENDERICKS, Fr.	28	France	61-0897
HENDING, Barbara	55	Gockelheim	61-0520
Celestin 14			
HENES, Johann	59	Mainsheim	59-0477
Johann 26, Catharina 20, Rosine 17			
Christian 13			
HENFTLING, Georg	35	Mainbernheim	61-0779
HENGESBACH, Casper	33	Velmede	58-0925
HENGESBACH, Heinr.	23	Callenharz	56-1260
HENGGE, Joh.B.	34	Baiorn	57 0606
HENKE, August	30	Colberg	56-0723
Johanna 36			
HENKE, Heinr.	30	Collhorst	57-0447
HENKE, Hermann	18	Ebersbach	55-0932
HENKEL, Eva	19	Rauschenbach	57-0754
HENKEL, Heinrich	19	Burgholz	59-0384
HENKEL, Marie	23	Cassel	56-0589
HENKEL, Marie Anna	22	Wiekers	61-0478
HENKEL, Valentin	17	Wichthausen	55-0630
HENKELMANN, Heinr.	45	Uiha	60-0785
Sophie 40, Bernhard 16, Ludwig 14			
Regina 10, Amalia 9, Sophie 6, Wm. 5			
HENKELMANN, Herman	30	Spenge	58-0881
HENKELMANN, Wilmne	21	Eicha	60-0334
HENKEN, Anna	27	Achim	57-1192
HENKEN, Ernst	17	Dorum	61-0478
HENKEN, Hanke	14	Debstedt	57-0578
HENKEN, John	38	New York	61-0716
HENKEN, Lisette	36	New York	62-1042
Georg 9, Alex 7			
HENKEN, Trina	31	Zeven	61-0682
HENLE, Mary	30	Billenhausen	57-1148
Felicita 28			
HENLE, Ottilie	22	Billenhausen	56-0847
HENNE, Johannes	42	Vernewakshaus	56-0723
Johanne 27			
HENNE, Xaver	17	Oningen	61-0167
HENNECK, Johann		Kamnade	58-0881
HENNECKE, Agnes	52	Steinfeld	57-0961
Elisabeth 18, Metta 23, Louis 27			
Franz 17			
HENNECKE, Aug.	13	Sickershausen	62-0730
HENNECKE, August	32	Hannover	57-1192
Charlotte 24, Johanne 4, Caroline 5			
Minna 9m			
HENNECKE, Henry	34	Hannover	57-1192
HENNECKE, Ignatz	20	Steinfeld	57-0961
HENNEICK, Ernst	30	Bremen	62-0879
HENNEMANN, Cunig.	34	Ebensfeld	58-0925
HENNIES, Chr.Adolf	33	Verden	58-0815
HENNIGER, Johann	37	Schoelen	57-1280
HENNING, Cath.	17	Unterstoppel	59-0990
HENNING, Heinrich	28	Mihla	60-0398
HENNING, Johann	27	Zeven/Han.	55-1238
HENNING, Louise	24	Hohenhausen	55-0932
HENNING, Philipp	38	Oberstoppel	59-0990

NAME	AGE	RESIDENCE	YR-LIST
(f) 22			
HENNINGER, Johann	39	Mayville	58-0881
HENNINGS, E.M. (m)	32	Weener	55-0413
HENRI, A.		New York	59-0613
(f)			
HENRICH, Johannes	58	Schwanheim	56-0723
HENRICHS, Christne	21	Wuerttemberg	60-0411
Anna B. 20			
HENRICHS, Frd.	16	Peterhof	57-1192
HENRICI, H.A.(m)	27	Lehe	61-0482
HENRICI, H.H.	30	Lehe	59-0613
HENRICKES, Hermann	36	Wessum	59-0951
HENSCHEL, Rosine	48	Scheidelwitz	61-0804
Louise 17			
HENSCHEL, Theresia	28	Hainsbach	59-0384
Maria 3			
HENSEL, Carl	35	Neisse	56-1260
Franzisca 32			
HENSEL, Johann	45	Fauerbach	59-0384
Elisabeth 42, Elisabeth 19, Balthazar 17			
Anna 15, (baby) 10m			
HENSELER, Hinrich	52	Bielefeld	57-0447
Friedrike 57, Georg 26, Cecilie 24			
Friederike 18, Franz 15, Antoinette 19			
HENSLER, M.A.	25	Leustetten	59-0990
HENSSEN, J.D.(m)	29	Stuckhausen	60-0998
HENTSCHEL, Emanuel	21	Kratzbasch	56-1204
HENTZE, William	23	Ottbergen	60-0411
HENZE, Anna	23	Luethorst	57-1407
HENZE, August	29	Liegnitz	57-1407
Christian 18, Wilhelmine 26, Elise 54			
Johanna 3, Marie by			
HENZE, Carl	30	Pyrmont	58-0881
(wife) 25			
HENZE, Christ.	66	Nienburg/Hann	62-0712
Louise 18			
HENZE, Wilhelm	32	Nordheim/Hann	62-0608
HENZEL, Salome W.	21	Lich	59-0214
HEPP, Georg	33	Emmertshausen	57-0754
HEPPER, Carl	35	Chicago	61-0482
Henriette 22			
HEPPERLE, Walburga	27	Schelking	59-1036
HEPPLER, A.(m)	38	Illinois	61-1132
HEPPLER, Catharine	20	Oefingen	62-0938
HERAS, Gustav	23	Wulfsbach/Hes	62-0608
Catharine 33, Barbara 7			
HERB, Engelbert	30	Oberhausen	56-0847
HERBERT, Georg	18	Prussia	60-1161
HERBERT, Joh.	29	Hofbieber	59-0951
HERBST, Benedict	28	Bavaria	60-0371
HERBST, Franz J.	40	Preussen	60-0785
Clementine 24			
HERBST, Marcus	22	Krotoschin	57-0578
HERBST, Pankratz	29	Altendorf	61-0047
HERBSTLEB, Martha	23	Herbstleben	58-0545
HERCHE, Peter	17	Ranstadt	59-0990
HERDNER, Christ.	20	Roeningheim	59-0613
HERDRICH, Johann	25	Ansbach	56-0723
Franciska 32			
HERGENROETHER, J.	28	Wuerzburg	62-0836
HERGERT, Ferd.	26	New York	59-0951
HERGESELL, Charles	26	Tamowitz	57-1192
HERHOLT, Christ.	36	New York	61-0804
HERING, Conrad	35	Berka/Weimar	60-0622
Christ(died) 34, Dorothea 7, Heinrich 6			
Georg 5, Elisabeth 2			
HERING, Maria	30	Goettingen	59-1036
HERKING, Johann	31	Freden	59-0951
Johanna 58			
HERKING, Wilh.	41	Eppe	59-0951
HERKLOTZ, Ed.	41	Dresden	62-0166
HERLAU, Friedricke	18	Friedrichstal	62-0938
HERLAU, Johann	22	Friedrichstal	62-0730
HERLING, Sophia	23	Pyrmont	55-1048
HERMAN, W.(m)	35	Hamilton	61-0804
HERMANN, August	31	Carzig	57-0776
HERMANN, C.	32	Hof	62-1112
Cath. 26, Carl 6, Caroline 4, Babette 2			

NAME	AGE	RESIDENCE	YR-LIST
Cath. 10m			
HERMANN, Casper	39	Baiern	62-0306
HERMANN, Catharina	25	Hessen	60-0371
Magnus 4			
HERMANN, Catharina	27	Schellenwald	57-0847
HERMANN, Catharina		Hamitbor	59-0613
William			
HERMANN, Christine	19	Althattendorf	60-0622
HERMANN, Fr.	20	Hamberg	57-1067
HERMANN, H.	19	Niederommer	59-0990
HERMANN, Helene	36	Darmstadt	59-0951
HERMANN, Henry	20	Gitzen	57-1148
HERMANN, J.	43	New York	62-0730
Helene 40			
HERMANN, Ludwig	19	Feuchtwangen	56-0847
HERMANN, Ludwig	23	Hopfstadt/Bav	60-0371
HERMANN, Luwdig	48	Siegen	62-0758
HERMANN, Marten	32	Paschenberg	57-0422
HERMANN, Math.	23	Dinkelsbuehl	60-0334
HERMANN, Valentin	32	Germa	56-0589
HERMANN, Winfried	27	Wesel	58-0306
HERMANNS, Carl	35	Chicago	62-0401
HERMELING, Joh.Fr.	30	Westercappeln	57-1067
HERMERS, Marie	18	Reihne	56-0847
HERMES, Eduard	18	Crefeld	60-0785
HERMFREISE, Franz	20	Westerwehe	56-1216
HERMING, Christian	34	Niengraben	60-0533
Sophie 19, Sophie 9m			
HERMS, Andreas	27	Anger	56-1044
HERMS, Charles	21	Wehdem	57-1192
HERMS, Heinrich	18	Widlar	58-0399
HERN, Anna Elis.	55	Cassel	57-0654
HERNATZ, Peter	23	Pittsburg	60-0785
Marg. 19			
HERNING, F.A.	18	Dresden	62-0938
HERNRING, Chr.	33	Huettendorf	60-0521
Augusta 24, Chr. 9m			
HEROLD, Anna	30	San Francisco	59-0048
Rudolph 3, Oscar 1			
HEROLD, Armand	21	Teutleben	57-0422
HEROLD, Charles	29	New York	57-0961
HEROLD, Friedr.	35	Wolfenbuettel	57-1113
HEROLD, Georg	30	Birkach/Bav.	60-0429
HEROLD, Lorenz	34	Kilzberg	61-0478
HEROLDT, E.(m)	16	Connifeld	61-0804
HERPICH, Elisabeth	22	Dreisigacker	56-0819
HERR, Elise	24	Lohr	60-0785
HERR, Georg	29	Pfarrweisach	60-1053
HERR, Johann	38	Pfarrweisach	60-0622
Dorothea 21			
HERR, Juliane	24	Steinbach/Bav	60-0371
HERR, Valentin	25	Bavaria	60-1161
HERREILERS, Marie	27	Wardenburg	57-1113
HERRENREDER, C.	30	Offenbach	59-0951
HERRING, Carl	27	Varel	62-0879
HERRING, Johann	26	Pittlow	57-0776
HERRLICH, Adam	15	Hessen	57-0776
HERRMANN, Adam	26	Grossachsen	62-1169
HERRMANN, Caroline	22	Wien	57-0961
Mary 4, Gustav 9m			
HERRMANN, Cathrina	24	Steinfeld	61-0520
HERRMANN, Emma	19	Hainsfurth	59-1036
HERRMANN, Ezechiel	19	Friedingen	60-0411
Lydia 21			
HERRMANN, Fr'drke.	22	Obernkirchen	59-0951
HERRMANN, Friedr.	27	Sachsen	55-0634
HERRMANN, G.	46	Neukirchen	59-0951
Richard 9			
HERRMANN, Lorenz	25	Schopbug	61-0047
HERRMANN, Marianne	16	Cronach	59-0951
HERRMANN, Martin	15	Glaesdorf	57-1148
HERRMANN, Michel	25	Poos/Pruss.	55-1238
HERRMANN, Robert	34	New York	58-0885
HERRNSTADT, Aug.	22	Militsch	59-0477
Amalie 18			
HERSCHEL, C.	23	Bonn	62-0993
HERSCHENHAND, Mor.	39	Mannsfeld	56-0413
Ferdinand 10			

NAME	AGE	RESIDENCE	YR-LIST
HERSCHENVOETHE, J.	16	Schnellenbach	57-1122
HERSCHLER, Magdal.	24	Volkhoz	57-1122
Elisa 9m, Louisa 9m			
HERSLEB, J.(m)	34	Grottstedt	61-0669
HERSRIECK, Johann	28	Hessen	57-0776
HERTEL, Elisa	17	Oberweslau	56-0589
HERTEL, Johann	22	Rehau	62-0306
HERTER, Ezech	22	Marbach	60-1161
HERTHHEIMER, Herm.	16	Loberstein	59-1017
HERTING, Ad.	29	Muehlhausen	59-1036
HERTING, J.A.(m)	31	Cincinnati	62-0467
HERTLEIN, Joh. G.	31	Muehlhausen	60-0533
Anna 23			
HERTNER, Rudolph	20	Laufen/Wuertt	60-0429
Heinrich 17			
HERTWIG, Elisabeth	8	Leipzig	58-0885
HERTWIG, Ludwig	18	Roda	57-1067
HERTWIG, Wilhelm	27	Waldenburg/Pr	57-0924
HERTZ, August	32	Heiligenstadt	57-0447
HERTZOG, Anton	56	Damme	58-0925
(wife) 53			
HERUNG, Albrecht	37	Lovant	59-1017
HERWIG, Helene	20	Trendelburg	55-0932
HERWIG, Sophie	28	Allendorf	61-0520
HERYES, Heinrich	31	Brooklyn	62-0166
HERZ, Alexander	16	Ottersberg	56-1117
HERZ, August	35	New York	62-0730
HERZ, Barb.	23	Feuchtwangen	61-0669
HERZ, Isaak	22	Hanau	56-1216
Herm. 15			
HERZ, J.J.	39	Steeg	59-0477
HERZ, Jacob	30	Nahbollenbach	61-0930
Louise 50			
HERZ, Johannette	28	Guntersblume	59-0613
HERZ, Wilhelmine	28	Cincinati	61-1132
HERZBERG, Christ.	22	Prussia	62-0758
HERZBERG, Herm.	22	Lamen	59-1036
HERZBERG, Hermann	27	Colberg	56-0723
Catharina 28			
HERZBERG, Isaac	14	Camen	59-0477
HERZBERG, Meyer	59	Camen	59-0477
Henriette 50, Herz 27, Elise 14			
Abraham 9, Regina 8, Moses 7			
HERZBERG, Wilhelm	17	Zeven/Hann.	60-0429
HERZER, Carl	30	Weimar	59-1036
HERZING, Johann	26	Pittlow	57-0776
HERZINGER, Elise	20	Elschwege	56-0632
HERZLER, Franz	31	Nuernberg	56-0632
HERZOG, Anna	21	Bremen	57-0924
HERZOG, Elis.	18	Reselage	59-0951
HERZOG, Elisabeth	26	Obersteinbach	60-0371
HERZOG, Heinrich	24	Damme	58-0306
HERZOG, Joh.	22	Struth	62-0401
HERZOG, Johann	28	Sperndorf	59-0535
HERZOG, Louise	20	New York	62-0730
HERZOG, Sebastian	28	Sohlar/Bav.	55-0628
HERZOG, Ursula	14	Weissmein	58-0399
HERZSTEIN, Goldine	23	Willebadessen	60-0521
HESEN, Charles	20	Suelbeck	57-0654
HESER, Ludwig Ph.	49	Dittahausen	57-0704
Anna Cath. 47, Joh. Ludwig 19, Conrad 13			
Cath. Doroth			
HESLING, H.J.	30	Neuenkirchen	62-0467
HESPE, D.H. (m)	20	Bremen	55-0413
HESPE, Daniel H.	20	New York	59-0048
HESPEL, Wilhelm	19	Unterkessach	59-0214
Carl 16			
HESPP, Nicolaus	17	Wahheim	57-1416
HESS, (m)	30	Ballenstadt	55-1048
Bertha 21			
HESS, Casper	18	Philippsthal	60-0622
HESS, Casper	34	Neustadt	61-0779
Ernestine 27, Carl 2, Therese by			
HESS, Catharina	15	Homberg	57-0776
HESS, Elise	14	Maibach	59-1036
HESS, Joh.	25	Rohrbach	56-0512
HESS, John	25	Havre	57-0578
HESS, Margaretha E	24	Schenkbergsfe	57-0847

NAME	AGE	RESIDENCE	YR-LIST
Eva Elisab. 22			
HESS, Solomon	17	Geroda	60-0521
HESS, Thomas	26	Scheinfeld	56-1011
Joseph 21			
HESS, Valentin	32	Bodes	56-0629
Elise 32, Christina 9, Heinrich 9m			
HESSE, Anna	25	Tocherode	56-0819
HESSE, Anna Cath.	30	Frankenau	56-0723
HESSE, B.D.	40		62-0836
(wife) 32			
HESSE, Carl	20	Wanfried	60-0411
HESSE, Caspar	36	Hessen	62-0758
Louise 33, Georg Friedr 11, Marie 10			
Christoph 5			
HESSE, Dietrich		New Jersey	55-1240
HESSE, Friedrich	26	Wermsdorf	55-0630
HESSE, Georg Dan	38	Borkin	61-0167
HESSE, Heinrich	20	Immenrode	62-0712
HESSE, Henriette	31	Iserlohn	57-0924
HESSE, Johann	17	Bothen	58-0399
HESSEL, Georg	38	Bischoff	57-1280
Catharina 25, Maria 9, Georg 7, Martin 1			
HESSEN, Augusta	17	Ringklew	57-0776
HESSEN, Joh.H.	31	Brickwede	57-0578
HESSENBERGER, Fr'z	39	Austria	55-1048
HESSLER, Barb.	35	Echzell	59-0990
(f) 9			
HESSLER, Jos.	24	Usingen	59-0384
HETHUCHER, Magdal.	26	Hafenloar	59-0372
HETLEIN, Georg	21	Baiern	58-0399
HETT, Magdalene	21	Culmbach	60-1032
HETTJE, Catharine	25	Aachenstein	61-0478
HETTLACHER, Carl	41	Neustadt	57-0654
HETZEL, Wilhelm	38	Herzhausen	56-0512
HEUBACH, E.	31	New York	59-0613
HEUBELEIN, Gustav	27	Sanneberg	57-0447
Wilhelmine 22			
HEUBER, Bernhard	20	Eisenach	56-0723
HEUBERT, Mathias	32	Wulsburg	61-0682
HEUBLEIN, Caroline	30	Weimar	59-0535
HEUER, Adeline	20	Bremen	56-1117
HEUER, Heinr.	34	Oldendorf/Han	55-1238
HEUER, Johann	31	Oerbke	57-0847
Sophie 32			
HEUER, W.	44	Bremen	59-0990
HEUER, Wilhelm	26	Wunstorf	59-0535
HEUERMANN, Anna	26	Oldenburg	60-0521
HEUERMANN, Cathar.	30	Westenholz	57-0847
HEUM, Clara	42	Obertiefenbch	57-0422
Margaret 20, Anna Mary 18, Elisa 16			
HEUMANN, Elis.	24	Weida	56-0723
HEUMANN, Juliane	26	Suelbeck	60-0622
HEUMANN, Rud.	23	Gaste	56-1117
HEUMANN, Wilh'mine	18	Wiedensahl	59-0535
HEUNE, Friedr.Bern	22	Olbersleben	62-0983
HEUNEWIG, Dominic	51	Warendorf	58-0885
HEUPKE, August	13	Holtensen	57-0924
HEUSEL, Peter	42	Penna.	61-0897
HEUSELER, Th.	28	Blockwinkel	61-0167
HEUSER, H.(m)	26	Herbstein	62-0232
HEUSING, Maria	26	Hann.Muenden	58-0399
HEUSS, Martha	20	Bornheim	61-0897
HEUSSNER, Aug.	28	Ronnebeck	57-1148
HEUSSNER, Charles	24	Rinteln	57-0961
HEUSSNER, Rudolph	19	Hainebach	59-0048
HEVERMANN, John	25	Louisville	57-1192
HEXTER, Regina	24	Homberg a/Ohm	57-0924
Friederike 19			
HEYDANK, Anna	20	Boehmen	61-0930
HEYDE, Gustav	19	Cassel	60-1141
HEYDE, Joh.	17	Hildesheim	59-1036
HEYDOLPH, Bertha	26	Muenchen	57-0961
HEYE, Ferdinand	20	Bremen	58-0815
HEYE, Julius	23	Bremen	57-0447
HEYER, C.F.	64	Madras	57-0961
HEYMANN, Lina	22	Essen	59-0477
Branette 20, Friedericke 20			
HEYN, Christ.Fr.	21	Scharmbeck	57-0436

NAME	AGE	RESIDENCE	YR-LIST
HEYN, Elisabeth	31	Coburg	62-0608
HEYN, Heinrich	31	Treysa	60-0533
Anna B. 35			
HEYRAND, Jean	26	Leige	59-0613
HEYROTH, Alwin	18	Bolmerswerdt	56-0589
HEYSE, EHler	19	Hoya	59-1017
HEYSE, Paul	24	Dresden	61-0682
HEYSER, Johann	17	Mainz	60-0334
HEYSING, Elis.	30	Hech	62-0232
HICKENTHIER, Joh.	36	Branderode	55-0812
Samuel 38			
HICKETHIER, Fr.Aug	34	Cracau	55-0812
Chris. Aug. 31, Gustav 7			
HIEKEL, Ignatz	51	Guentersdorf	57-1148
Th. 51, Fz. 28, Marianne 21			
HIERSGEN, P.J.(m)	35	Stongton	61-0804
Heinrich 9, Joh. 7			
HILBERG, Johannes	15	Bohnhausen	57-1067
HILCHENBACH, A.	31	Gonaives	62-1042
HILCKE, Henry	39	Frag	62-0938
HILD, Louise	34	Magdeburg	60-0334
HILD, Paulus	42	New York	61-0804
HILDEBRAND, Elise	21	Neuenkirchen	57-0850
HILDEBRAND, Ferd.	34	Schwesdnitz	58-0604
HILDEBRAND, Herman	27	Kuehrstedt	56-1260
Catharine 58, Charlotte 28, Anna 6			
Martin 3, Heinrich 9m			
HILDEBRAND, J.H.	25	Hannover	59-0477
HILDEBRAND, Johann	25	New York	58-0815
HILDEBRAND, Meinhd	27	New York	60-0622
Catharine 30, Catharine 4, Elise 9m			
HILDEBRANDT, Adam	14	Hersfeld	55-0634
Margaretha 7			
HILDEBRANDT, Carl	22	Schlesien	58-0399
HILDEBRANDT, Dora	28	Hovelworks	59-0613
Henry 3, AUgust 2, Howard 11m			
HILDEBRANDT, Felix	17	Stadthaide	56-0589
HILDEBRANDT, Fr'dr	36	Deissel	56-0527
Barbara 44			
HILDEBRANDT, Franz	28	Eplerode/Hess	55-0538
Elisab. 30, Caroline 4, Peter 2			
HILDEBRANDT, L.(m)	16	Baltimore	62-0232
HILDEBRANDT, M.(m)	21	New York	62-0467
Fabian 25			
HILDEBRANDT, Mart.	30	St.Francisco	59-0477
HILDEN, Franz	51	Oberinge	59-0477
HILDENBRAND, Paul	25	Ludwigsburg	59-0214
HILDINGER, Jacob	50	Muenchingen	61-1132
Anna 55			
HILDNER, J.G.	22	Basel	50-1017
HILDT, Gustav	22	Neuss	59-0951
Elise 18			
HILFEBRAND, Theres	20	Borgentreich	56-1216
HILGE, Georg	33	Baltimore	62-1169
HILGE, Helene	39	Baltimore	60-1196
Henry 2, Georg 31			
HILGENBERG, Heinr.	49	Jensungen	58-0576
Anna 41, Johann 20, Anna 16, Adam 8			
Jacob 6, Martha by			
HILGER, Joseph	29	Nassau	57-0606
Christine 27			
HILKE, Johann	37	Landechau	57-0704
Ernst 26			
HILKEN, Agnes	20	Boehmen	61-0716
HILKEN, Friedrich	23	Preussizie	61-0682
HILKER, Aug.	21	Berlin	59-0990
HILL, Ernst	29	Neubronn	56-0413
Wilhelmine 27			
HILL, Friedr.Gottf	25	Balstedt	62-0306
HILL, Gustav	21	Otterburg	59-0372
HILL, Nicolaus	18	Niederofladen	57-0776
HILL, William	21	England	56-1216
HILLE, Anna	24	Dresden	61-0897
HILLE, Carl	37	Carlshoff	57-0776
Wilhelmina 36, Friedrich 7, August 5			
Maria 3			
HILLE, Caroline	25	Sdt.Oldendorf	57-0850
HILLEBRAND, Otilie	54	Hermannsfeld	56-0413
Wilhelmina 59			
HILLEBRAND, Wilh.	31	Minden	56-0512
Johanna 30, Ida 3, Doris 1			
HILLEBRANDT, Jac.	25	Chicago	62-0730
HILLEBRECHT, Herm.	28	New York	62-0730
Nanny 22			
HILLEBRENDER, F.W.	50	Westhoyel	58-0604
Marie 50, Friderike 22, Margarethe 12			
Anna Marie 9			
HILLEKES, Lisette	23	Kirschweische	58-0306
HILLER, Anna Cath.	22	Schoenberg/He	55-0628
HILLER, Franziska	32	Schoenau/Aus.	55-1238
Carl 6, Lambert 2, Johann 9m			
HILLER, G.A.	41		61-0804
Julie 38, Emma 10, Louise 4			
HILLER, Gottliebe	98	Heiserb(died)	59-0951
HILLMANN, Cath.	47	Hartrup	62-0836
B.(m) 13, Therese 9			
HILLMANN, Christ.	29	Hannover	55-0628
HILLMANN, F.	22	Schweinsdorf	56-0512
HILLMANN, Heinr.	22	Hoya	55-0634
HILLMANN, Heinr.	38	California	60-0521
HILLMANN, Johanna	32	Stockheim	56-0951
Therese 22			
HILLMER, Helena	22	Weener	61-0682
HILPERT, Barbara	22	Blaufelden/CH	60-0622
HILSMANN, Heinrich	24	Ostenbruch	58-0563
HIMMELSTERN, H.H.	17	Beverungen	59-0951
HIMMER, Cath.	25	Stetfeld	62-0836
HIMMSEL, Anna	26	Gubitzmoos	61-0520
HIMSEL, Johann	31	Bettendorf	61-0520
HINDEL, Aug.	33	Philadelphia	60-0521
HINDERER, Babette	17	Rudersberg	59-0535
HINEKE, Caroline	20	Widerwarden	55-1048
HINER, Mariano (m)	25	Herstein	60-0334
HINGELHAUPT, Augta	18	Celle	60-1161
HINK, Georg Heinr.	17	Bremervoerde	58-0563
HINKE, J.G.	49	Germany	56-0550
HINKEL, Cathrina	46	Breitenbach	60-0371
Elisabeth 23			
HINKEL, Fr.(m)	36	Wetzlar	61-0482
HINKEL, H.	28	Echzell	59-0990
HINKEL, Jette	20	Hainchen/Hess	62-0608
Friedrich 17			
HINKEL, Johann	27	Oebergoenns	59-0535
Elisabeth 25			
HINKEL, Margaretha	16	Heinken	60-1141
HINKEL, Margaretha	14	Marburg	57-1407
HINKEL, Susanne	22	Eichen	61-0897
Augusta 17, Mary 9			
HINKHAUS, Bernhard	28	Hieter	57-1407
HINNERSEN, Marie	19	Sandstetermor	62-1112
HINRICHS, Albert	19	Jever	62-0730
Nanny 22			
HINRICHS, C.F.A.	22	New York	58-0604
HINRICHS, Christ.	34	US.	59-0951
Anna 24, Emma 4, John 3			
HINRICHS, G.	40	Uptloh	62-0938
HINRICHS, H.	34	Barnsen	62-1042
Cath. 32, Doroth. 9, Heinrich 7, Cath. 5			
Wilhelm 3			
HINRICHS, Herm.	33	Husum	56-0527
Lina 25			
HINRITZ, Anna Cath	18	Spanik/Bav.	55-0628
HINTE, Luder	25	Meyenburg/Han	60-0622
HINTE, Meta Marg.	20	Meyenburg	62-0401
HINTEN, Carol.	17	Clausthal	59-0990
HINTERTHIN, Wlhmne	16	Sassenhausen	56-0512
HINTERTHUER, H.	30	Harste	57-0578
HINTERTHUER, Marie	21	Bremen	62-1169
HINTZ, Georg Alb.	28	Duben	58-0815
HINZE, Franz	33	Deetz	62-0730
HINZE, Heinr. Chr.	32	Lindhorst	56-0589
Heinrich 3			
HIPP, August	21	Vlotho	57-1407
HIPP, Heinrich	32	Braunschweig	57-1407
HIPPEN, Anna	15	Aurich	57-0422
Marie 49			

NAME	AGE	RESIDENCE	YR-LIST
HIPPEN, Ulrich	48	Aurich	57-0422
Anna 40			
HIRDLER, Karl	32	Verden	60-1053
Martha 33, August 8, Karl 6, Wilhelm 4			
Theodor 2, Samuel by			
HIRSCH, Abraham	35	New York	56-0819
HIRSCH, B.(m)	16	Aberkochen	62-0730
HIRSCH, Babette	52	Muehringen	57-1148
HIRSCH, Bernh.	16	Hummelburg	60-0521
Lina 19			
HIRSCH, Catharina	19	Laufach	60-1053
HIRSCH, Clarissa	31	Leipzig	57-1192
Elisabeth 4, Charles 3, Clarissa 1			
HIRSCH, Emma	36	Gambach	60-0785
David 6			
HIRSCH, Hermann	30	Berlin	58-0885
HIRSCH, Louis	30	Trzmieszo	57-1192
Emilie 21			
HIRSCH, Moritz	19	Kuttenberg	61-0779
HIRSCH, Moses	38	Aschaffenburg	61-0770
HIRSCH, Nanni	18	Frankenbernhm	56-1216
HIRSCH, Wilhelm	26	Klein Kleden	62-0879
Ernst 22			
HIRSCHBERGER, Been	54	Geroldshofen	59-0214
Caroline 19, Bernhard 18			
HIRSCHEIDTER, Cily	15	Kunreuth	60-0521
HIRSCHFELD, Cath.	46	Treysa	60-0533
Elisabeth 8, Gerhard 9, Margarethe 4			
HIRSCHFELD, Elwina	18	Lauphausen	59-0477
HIRSCHHAUER, Lob.	29	Nuernberg	56-1260
Rosa 16			
HIRSCHLING, Johann	16	Zella	56-0279
HIRSCHMANN, Ad.	50	Cumreuth	61-0897
Caroline 30			
HIRSCHMANN, Ernst	19	Hagenbichach	55-0628
HIRSCHMANN, Julie	25	Koenigswart	61-0716
Carl 4, Anna 3, Mathilda 9m			
HIRTUNG, Jacob	49	Steinbach	56-0819
HITTER, Heinrich	23	Goeppingen/Wt	60-0622
HITZEMANN, Conrad	51	Bierde	55-0812
Sophie 50, Carl 23, Louise 15, Heinrich 9			
HITZEMANN, Engel M	23	Vornhagen	56-0589
HITZEMANN, Gottl.	21	Habichthorst	56-0589
HITZEMANN, Maria	24	Lindhorst/Lip	55-0628
HITZERODT, Berhnd.	13	Curhessen	58-0399
HOBAENS, Babette	40	Melrichstadt	58-0885
Pauline 16			
HOBERICH, Bertha	16	Geschwind	60-0411
HOBIGAND, Max	40	France	62-1042
Jeanette 34, Guilt. 14, Fanni 12			
HOCHLEITNER, Carl	50	Wien	57-0365
Anna 29, Carl 1			
HOCHREIN, Joseph	28	Kleinwenkheim	58-0881
HOCHSTAETTER, Chr.	34	Buffalo	62-1112
HOCHTOENS, Otto	37	Neunkirchen	59-1036
HOCHWEBER, Th.	28	Leustetten	59-0990
HOCK, J.	45	New York	62-0938
HOCK, Joh.G.	30	Degerschlacht	57-1067
HOCK, Martin	29	Mainaschaff	60-1053
HOCKEMEYER, Betty	50	New York	58-0885
HOCKEMEYER, Charlt	43	Rehburg	59-0951
Bertha 15, Marie 13, Hermann 9, Emilie 8			
Augusta 7, Louise 6, Friedrich 9m			
Wilhelm 9m			
HOCKER, Ludw. W.	30	Buer	55-1082
Clara 33, Fr. Wilh. 3			
HOCKMANN, Wilhelm	50	Burghoven	57-0776
Elisabeth 41, Heinrich 9m			
HODANK, Jacob	39	Guhra	56-0951
Elisabeth 41			
HODEL, Michael	27	Knopfhof	59-0613
HODERLIN, Carl	20	Deckenpfrod	60-0334
HOEBEL, Wilhelm	31	Stadtoldendrf	56-0629
HOEBER, Simon	50	Lippe	58-0399
Dorothea 50, Sophie 27, Jette 3			
HOECHSTEDTER, Marg	30	Kreisdorf/Bav	60-0371
Barbara 5, Dorothea 2			
HOECHSTER, K.(m)	18	Angeroth	56-0951

NAME	AGE	RESIDENCE	YR-LIST
HOECHSTER, Reiss	25	Angenroth	59-0214
HOECKE, Heinrich	28	Stemmen	56-1260
Sophie 28, Marie 9			
HOEDE, Wilhelmine	30	Teschendow	61-0716
HOEFER, August	21	Rosswein	61-0478
HOEFER, Carl	28	Hildburghsn.	62-0712
HOEFER, Carl	16	Plauen	62-1112
HOEFER, Ernst Max	13	Roemhild/Mein	62-0342
HOEFER, H.A.	25	Dresden	62-1112
HOEFER, Heinrich	19	Meiningen	61-0478
HOEFLEIN, Sara	21	Wustensachsen	62-0608
Caroline 17			
HOEFLER, Anna Barb	17	Ebersdorf	55-0812
HOEFNER, J.(m)	28	Stetfeld	62-0836
HOEFNER, J.(m)	28	Stetfeld	62-0836
HOEFT, Aug. Fr.	42	Berlin	59-0048
HOEGER, Dorothea	18	Waldstetten	60-0371
HOEGG, (f)	40	New York	57-1150
Chas. 3			
HOEHDE, Amalie	47	Frankfurt/Hes	56-0819
Therese 17			
HOEHL, Amalie	22	Weiers	60-0398
Friederike 16			
HOEHMANN, A.Cath.	25	Lohne/KH.	62-0342
HOEHN, Catharina		Weilers	58-0563
HOEHN, Conrad	17	Mariengardt	57-1113
HOEHN, Max	28	Coburg	62-0712
HOEHNE, H.J.	19	Petershagen	59-0477
HOEKE, Friedrich	19	Buende	56-1011
HOEKE, Ilse	23	Moordorf	62-0232
HOEKELTHAL, Jos.	18	Mengelrode	61-0167
HOEL, Ph.	28	Griesheim	56-1216
HOELENBERG, John	26	Wengsel	57-1148
HOELING, Carl	27	Petershagen	57-1122
Sophie 40			
HOELL, Heinr.	27	Homberg	61-0167
HOELLE, August	30	Heisebeck/Han	61-0770
HOELLE-PFORTNER, m	28	Berlin	61-0716
HOELLENSTEIN, Abr.	26	Beverungen	56-1011
HOELSCHER, Friedr.	15	Hille	56-0411
HOELSTE, Maria	20	Bremen	59-0951
HOELTER, Heinrich	18	Suhlingen	56-1044
HOELTER, Heinrich	42	Paderborn	57-0606
Helene 40, Christine 13, Elisabeth 5			
Anna 1			
HOELTER, Sophie	18	Siedenburg	58-0925
HOELZ, Johannes	25	Lorfeld/Hess.	61-0770
Catharine 24			
HOELZCHEN, Gerhard	30	Osnabrueck	56-1117
HOENE, Hermann	18	Osnabrueck	56-0411
Johanna 57, Henriette 23			
HOENNEKE, Carl	32	Buchholz	57-0447
Friederike 34, Carl 9, Maria 5			
HOENS, Conrad	22	Nartum	57-0961
HOEPFNER, Chr.	35	New York	62-1042
HOER, Johann	37	Grossachsen	62-1169
HOERCH, Bernhard	30	Schwappach	57-1067
HOERCHE, Gottfried	30	Neuhammer	56-0411
HOERCHELMANN, Elis	18	Kieselbach	57-1026
HOEREL, v. R. (m)	30	Stuttgart	62-0111
HOEREN, v.Ilsabein	16	Schwarzenmoor	56-0723
HOERISCH, Louise	32	Annaburg	62-0730
HOERLE, Justus	15	Moescheid	57-0754
HOERLEIN, Amalie	20	Unnerstadt	61-0716
HOERLEIN, Wilh'mne	20	Dorum	60-1141
HOERNER, Josepha	21	Neuenbrunn	59-0384
HOERNER, Michael	37	Montbertheim	59-0047
Dorothea 31, Michael 7, Burchard 5			
Georg M. 1, Michael 69			
HOERNLEIN, Geo. C.	65	Veilsdorf	55-0413
Louise 24			
HOERR, Philipp	23	Heuschelheim	56-0629
HOERTZ, C.	17	Denkendorf	59-0990
HOESBACHER, Johann	57	Winzenhohl/Bv	60-0429
Eva 32, Anna Maria 25, Christina 9			
Maria Eva 2			
HOESEL, August	32	Wallesforth	57-0654
HOESER, August	21	Rosswein	61-0478

NAME	AGE	RESIDENCE	YR-LIST
HOESSLER, Augusta	7	Walperndorf	61-0482
HOETZEL, Barbara	26	Unt.Nesselbch	61-0770
HOETZLE, Jalie	36	Jurich	59-0384
HOEVENER, John	30	Bersen	57-1192
HOEWE, J.H.	40	Cincinati	62-0836
HOEWELMANN, Edward	16	Detmold	56-0629
HOF, Christ.	46	Deidenshausen	56-0723
Catharine 20			
HOF, Johann H.	44	Ebernhuetz	57-1113
Marie 34, Anna 18, Marie 15, Heinrich 13			
Carl 8, Wilhelm 3			
HOF, Johannes	43	Wimme	57-1113
Wilhelm 30, Johannes 13, Friedrich 8			
Conrad 6, Heinrich 1, Marie 59			
HOFACKER, Joseph	32	Ueberlingen	61-0779
HOFEDITZ, Mar.Soph	18	Deissel	58-0563
HOFER, (f)	30	France	57-1150
HOFER, C.F.(m)	29	Reichenbach	62-0730
HOFER, Theo.	24	New York	60-0785
HOFF, August	26	Prellwitz	56-0819
Caroline 28			
HOFF, Catharina	18	Trier	61-0682
HOFF, Elisabeth	30	New York	61-0804
HOFFELD, Fr.Heinr.	55	Bramsche	56-1117
Amalie 16, Alfred 13			
HOFFEN, Catharine	47	Sprenge	57-1026
HOFFMANN, A.	50	Arnstadt	62-0993
F. 55, A. 17			
HOFFMANN, A.M.	18	Baiern	58-0399
HOFFMANN, Adolph	24	Berlin	56-0632
HOFFMANN, Adolph	35	Ober Odowitz	58-0885
HOFFMANN, Agnes	30	Wiesbaden	62-0836
HOFFMANN, Anton	45	Gablonz	56-0847
HOFFMANN, Anton	24	Meschede	58-0576
HOFFMANN, Aron	26	Langsdorf	59-0477
HOFFMANN, Aug.	54	Weinberg	55-0413
Louise 24			
HOFFMANN, August	48	Springe	57-0436
HOFFMANN, Bernhard	50	Schlottau	59-0951
Amalie 56, Hildegard 17			
HOFFMANN, C.	31	Wogau	56-1044
HOFFMANN, Carl	30	Eltersdorf	56-0632
HOFFMANN, Carl	23	Osnabrueck	60-0785
HOFFMANN, Carl	19	Euskirchen	61-0716
HOFFMANN, Carl	29	Colberg	62-0758
Caroline 28, Franz 2, (baby)(died) bob			
HOFFMANN, Carl Fr.	23	Nussbaum/Bad.	60-0429
HOFFMANN, Carl Ge.	32	Ober Eschbach	55-1082
HOFFMANN, Caroline	25	Tapfheim/Bav.	55-1238
HOFFMANN, Christ.	32	Peterlist	57-0704
HOFFMANN, Christof	50	Streitau	59-0535
Christine 55			
HOFFMANN, Conrad	34	Muenster/Hess	61-0770
Catharine 32, Elisabeth 9, Conrad 9m			
HOFFMANN, Conrad	45	Mistelgau	61-0520
Margaretha 22, Anna 17, Conrad 15			
HOFFMANN, David	58	Froenestedt	60-0521
HOFFMANN, E.(f)	25	Gessmold	57-0555
HOFFMANN, Ed.	21	Linsheim	62-0730
HOFFMANN, Elisab.	35	Wittelsberg	60-0334
HOFFMANN, Emil	21	Dresden	62-0608
HOFFMANN, Ernest	20	Biensen	57-1192
HOFFMANN, Ernst	41	Ilbeshausen	59-0990
HOFFMANN, Eva	24	Goldmil/Bav.	55-0628
Margaretha 21			
HOFFMANN, Ferdin.	19	Hildesheim	56-0819
HOFFMANN, Ferdin.	15	Wiedersbach	57-0924
HOFFMANN, Francois	35	Bremen	59-0477
Cintra 28			
HOFFMANN, Franz	24	Reisch	61-0770
Pauline 37, Louise 16, Marie 9, Selma 5			
Rosa 1			
HOFFMANN, G.Michel	18	Bartenstn./Wt	60-0622
HOFFMANN, Georg	18	Waldau	57-0924
HOFFMANN, Georg	23	Weidnitz	62-0232
HOFFMANN, George	19	Rodach	56-1011
HOFFMANN, Gottfr.	24	Liegnitz	56-0819
HOFFMANN, H.(m)	38	Hamburg	62-0232
HOFFMANN, Heinr.	16	Carlshafen	55-1082
HOFFMANN, Heinr.	34	Lippstadt	60-1053
HOFFMANN, Heinr.	40	France	61-1132
HOFFMANN, Heinrich	52	Wippenbach	58-0576
Catharine 21, Caroline 19, Minna 8			
HOFFMANN, J.Gottl.	28	Schoenwalden	57-0754
HOFFMANN, J.L.	34	Mkt.Brandenba	59-0477
HOFFMANN, J.Nic.C.	24	Pethen	59-0372
HOFFMANN, Jean	40	Baden	61-0107
Eugenia 50			
HOFFMANN, Joh. Chr	18	Wellen	56-0629
HOFFMANN, Joh.G.	47	Militz	57-1067
HOFFMANN, Johann	21	Gr. Buseck	56-0527
HOFFMANN, Johann	27	Bernreuth	60-0533
Catharine 27, Anna 2, Johann 32			
Margaretha 32, Friedrich 8, Margaretha 6			
Georg 11m			
HOFFMANN, Johann	32	Oberfranken	58-0399
HOFFMANN, Johannes	25	Oberlais	62-0712
HOFFMANN, John	21	Niedersumen	61-0107
HOFFMANN, John	34	San Francisco	62-1169
Mary 30			
HOFFMANN, Joseph	25	New York	59-0951
Heinrich 3, Elise 9m			
HOFFMANN, Josepha	29	Konigswart	59-0613
HOFFMANN, Julie	31	Finisterre	62-1042
HOFFMANN, Justus	27	Giessen	57-0606
Louise 22, Marie 1			
HOFFMANN, Kunigund	37	Neuses	60-0533
HOFFMANN, Magd.M.F	17	Doerzbch	62-0730
HOFFMANN, Otto	20	Friedberg	59-1036
HOFFMANN, P.Chr.	30	Bayreuth	59-0535
Johanna 22			
HOFFMANN, Peter	56	Frankenbrunn	59-0990
(f) 31, (baby) by			
HOFFMANN, Reinhard	34	Giessen	57-0606
Margarethe 24, Catharina 6, Johannes 3			
Elisabeth 9m			
HOFFMANN, Rosa	20	Rodenburg	59-0412
HOFFMANN, Wilhelm	26	Haine	56-0413
Anna 49			
HOFFMAYER, Carl	30	Babbenstedt	60-1053
HOFFMEIER, Louis	15	Meinburg	61-0682
HOFFMEIER, Sophie	23	Messlingen	61-0897
HOFFMEISTER, Andr.	18	Querum/Braun.	55-0628
HOFFMEISTER, Carl	23	Muenden	57-0422
HOFFMEISTER, Henry	22	Wilmershaim	56-0512
Amalie 24			
HOFGARTEN, Engelb.	23	Stockhausen	56-0819
August 20			
HOFHEINZ, C.	24	Spoeck	62-0730
C.H. 28			
HOFHERR, E.	16	Berlichingen	62-0993
HOFHERR, Fridolin	36	Baden	60-0371
HOFHERR, William	19	Berchlingen	57-1148
HOFMANN, Andreas	35	Kirchlaute	61-0682
HOFMANN, C.F.Dr.	29	Poughkeepsie	61-0716
HOFMANN, Gottlieb	29	Wiesenthal	57-0754
HOFMANN, J.C.(m)	27	Thuisbrunn	61-0482
HOFMANN, Joh. Frd.	40	Neuseifer/Sax	60-0622
Christiane 36, Friedrich 13, Amalie 11			
Emilie 8, Bertha 6, Ernestine 4, Maria 9m			
HOFMANN, Johann	20	Mistelgau	61-0520
HOFMANN, Michael	34	Roettingen	58-0885
HOFMANN, Wolfgang	23	Wesphalen	61-0682
HOFMEIER, Georg	30	Weidenwang	57-0754
HOFMOKEL, Anna D.	25	Steinbach	62-0467
Johann 2			
HOFSFELD, Charles	19	Meiningen	57-1192
HOFT, Joh.D.	59	Waldstetten	60-1196
Marg. 58, Marg. 22			
HOFTIETZ, Wilhelm	46	Hessen	61-0682
HOGEN, M.(m)	36	England	62-0401
HOGREFE, Charlotte	16	Verden	61-0482
HOGREFE, Louis	24	Wallrode	59-1036
HOGREFE, Wilhelm	48	Schweringen	56-0723
Anna 24			
HOGREVE, Franz	26	Hannover	57-0847

NAME	AGE	RESIDENCE	YR-LIST
HOGSTERT, Caroline	22	Sondermuehlen	61-0482
HOHBERGER, E.	33	Foesbau	59-0990
HOHE, Clementine	22	New York	62-1042
HOHE, Fr.(m)	20	Wuertemberg	57-0555
E.(f) 23			
HOHEDER, Joh.	40	Stoeheder	60-0785
Agatha 24			
HOHENDORF, Charl.	43	Muenster	57-1113
Sophia 17, Bertha 15, Franz 13			
Bernhard 8, Lina 6			
HOHENKAMP, Jos.	30	Stave	59-0951
Elisabetha 62			
HOHENSCHILD, Wm.	35	Buttenwiesen	62-0938
HOHENSTOCK, Doroth	24	Lautenberg	56-1117
HOHENTHAL, Johanna	19	Goslar	60-1141
HOHLBERG, Jacob	19	Gitzen	57-1148
HOHLER, Hermann	28	Adelhausen/Bd	60-0622
HOHMANN, Friedrich	20	Volmerdingsen	57-0021
HOHMANN, Henning	32	Katinsen	57-0447
HOHMANN, Sophia	25	Bavaria	60-0371
HOHMEYER, W.(m)	30	Motzenrode	56-0723
Adelheid 58			
HOHN, Adam	23	Germany	61-0167
HOHN, Jenz Christ.	18	Scherbeck	55-0812
HOHN, MAry	25	Stuttgart	57-0654
Sophia 20, Heinrich 19, August 16			
HOHNOLD, J.F.	16	Kirchheim	59-0990
HOISCHEN, John	24	Schwanei	57-0422
Gertrude 19			
HOISS, Vitorin	25	Boehmen	61-0930
Catharina 18			
HOLBE, Friedr. Ed.	27	Goldlauter	55-0932
Joh. Elise 46, Catharine 13			
HOLBECK, Mathias	26	Waldmuenchen	56-0847
HOLCH, Christiane	21	Horningstof	60-0334
HOLCH, Georg	21	Hall/Wuertt.	60-0429
HOLDMANN, Friedr.	16	Luetjenburg	57-0422
HOLGER, Joh.	18	Rheinbach	60-0521
HOLL, Catharine	19	Roswaelden	62-0467
HOLLAND, Conrad	25	Marburg	62-0712
HOLLE, August	59	Foerste	62-0938
Heinrich 33, Louise 34, Louise 7			
HOLLE, Eman.	33	Wohlau	56-0512
HOLLE, G.(m)	19	Aurich	61-0482
HOLLENBACH, Theod.	23	Ansbach	59-0214
HOLLENBECK, Aug.	22	Bramsche	61-0669
HOLLENBERG, Benno	20	Osnabrueck	60-0785
HOLLER, Elisab.	25	Steppach	61-0478
HOLLER, Johann	38	Offenbach	60-0521
Johann 34, Louis 9, Wilhelm 7			
Catharina 5, Heinrich 2			
HOLLER, Johann	20	Varel	59-0951
HOLLERBACH, J.A.	16	Altheim	58-0881
HOLLING, Albert	10	Brooklyn	59-0613
HOLLINGER, B.H.(m)	41	Charleston	60-0785
Henry 9			
HOLLMANN, Ann Cath	61	Oldenburg	57-0754
HOLLMANN, Bernard	19	Jever	57-0654
HOLLMANN, Hermann	23	Ottersberg	58-0306
Gesine 29, Margaretha 27			
HOLLMANN, Ludwig	24	Dortmund	59-0372
HOLLNER, Friedrich	50	Nandershausen	57-1416
Kath.Elisab. 19			
HOLM, D.R.	29	Hagerstown	59-0048
HOLM, Thomas	30	Scherbeck	55-0812
HOLMCKE, L.	41	Louisville	62-0938
Marie 23, Anna 3, Elisa 2			
HOLMS, Friedrich	28	Siedenburg	58-0925
HOLPP, Georg	63	Narbern	62-0001
HOLPUCH, Johann	26	Chlum	61-0779
HOLSCHBACH, Joh.	30	Kirchen	57-0578
HOLSCHER, Diedrich	44	Braacke	59-0372
HOLSCHER, Gertrude	60	Sandbeck	56-0512
Therese 30, Xaver 18			
HOLSTEIN, Cath.	23	Triemen	56-1117
HOLSTEN, Johann	32	Hatten	57-1280
HOLSTER, C.(m)	21	Ottersberg	57-0555
C.(f) 17			

NAME	AGE	RESIDENCE	YR-LIST
HOLT, John	17	Fuerth	60-0785
HOLTHANS, A.	20	Hamburg	59-1036
HOLTHAUS, (m)	28	Bremen	58-0306
HOLTHAUS, Carl	35	St.Louis	62-1169
HOLTHAUS, F.A.	34	Baltimore	57-1148
Sophia 13			
HOLTMANN, Bernhard	47	Aschberg	57-0422
Fanny 28, Bernhard 7			
HOLTMANN, J. Bernh	32	Burgsteinfurt	55-0634
Catharine 21			
HOLUP, Johann	52	Boehmen	61-0930
Maria 40, Maria 19			
HOLY, Marie	28	Cigu	61-0779
HOLYES, Johann		Bremen	57-1148
HOLZ, Heinrich	26	Schwerin	57-1280
HOLZ, Herm. Th.	48	Westerengen	55-0932
HOLZBERGER, Conr.	38	Columbus	59-1036
HOLZBORN, Christ.	59	Duderstadt	61-0897
Dorothea 30			
HOLZE, Martin	16	Bramstedt	56-0589
HOLZE, Sophie	23	Westen	57-1067
HOLZEN, Friedrich	36	San Francisco	59-0951
Anna 22			
HOLZFORTNER, A.Cat	21	Kirchberg	57-0754
Anna Christ. 19			
HOLZHAUSEN, Anna	44	Woelferbot	56-0723
Anna Cathar. 27			
HOLZHAUSEN, August	24	Kannawurf	57-0776
HOLZHEM, Georg	34	Baiern	58-0399
HOLZINGER, Gerhard	27	Rothenburg/Bv	55-0628
HOLZINGER, Jos.	23	Boehmen	62-0938
HOLZKORN, Adolph	27	Duderstadt	57-0924
Hermann 22			
HOLZMANN, Chr.Ludw	26	Tengedorf	59-0384
HOLZMANN, Fanny	44	Deggingen	60-0521
Jacob 17			
HOLZMANN, Jacob	18	Bingen	60-1053
HOLZMANN, Ludw.	19	Offenbach/H-D	60-0622
HOLZMANN, Therese	20	Deggingen	60-0521
Helene 18			
HOLZMEISTER, Alia	36	Trubau	57-0654
HOLZSCHEN, Isab.C.	16	Untersenzbach	57-0436
HOLZSCHMIDT, Elis.	22	Rothenhusen	61-0047
HOLZSCHNEIDER, Ch.	41	Burgsteinfurt	58-0885
Regina 32, Catharina 14, Adelheid 2			
HOLZSTADLER, Maria	22	St. Nicolai	55-0413
HOLZWERTH, Friedr.	15	Wieneshausen	60-1032
HOMANN, Diedrich	54	Hohenaverberg	57-0924
Margaretha 42, Elisabeth 20, Marie 17			
Fritz 13			
HOMANN, Heinr.	17	Regensburg	60-0521
HOMANN, Lorenz	24	Randenhausen	57-1113
HOMANN, Robert	18	Koethen	60-1053
HOMBERGER, Elisab.	19	Mouischeid	59-0535
HOMBERGER, Johanes	23	Morscheid	60-0398
Heinrich 15			
HOMBERT, Wilhelm	21	Gissen	62-0758
HOMBRUCK, J. Ferd.	35	Osnabrueck	60-0371
HOMBURG, Martin	30	San Francisco	57-0365
HOMEYER, Fr.	24	Lahde	61-0167
HOMEYER, Friedr.	15	Hofgeismar	60-1032
HOMEYER, Johanna	16	Bederkesa	62-0758
HOMMEL, C.A.	20	Spiegelberg	59-0990
HOMMER, Fr.	9	Cincinnati	62-0938
HOMPE, Jos.	26	Garthe	59-0951
HONECKER, Wilhelm	32	Iburg	62-0879
HONIG, Adreas	25	Handschukshm.	61-0770
HONIGMANN, Heinr.	28	Allendorf/Pr.	55-0538
Helena 28			
HOOP, Johannes	31	New York	61-0682
Adelheid 25			
HOOPS, Mary	24	Iselersheim	61-0897
HOOSE, Friedr. Jr.	30	New York	60-0785
HOOSE, Therese	21	Niederurf	57-0850
HOPF, Georg	18	Oberkutz	56-1044
HOPF, Georgia	50	Eisfeld	59-0951
Bertha 18, Friederike 15			
HOPP, Francis	24	Pesth/Hungary	57-0422

NAME	AGE	RESIDENCE	YR-LIST
HOPPACH, Chr. H.	18	Rittermanshsn	62-0401
HOPPE, Aug.	22	Nassau	61-0804
HOPPE, Carl	23	Oberglogau	56-0589
Christine 16			
HOPPE, Carl	27	Leipzig	56-0527
HOPPE, Emilie	21	Hextor	57-1407
HOPPE, Friederike	50	Nordhausen	57-0924
HOPPE, Hermann	26	Altstaedte	60-0334
HOPPE, Lewis	26	Kolpin	57-0422
Wilhelmine 24			
HOPPE, Maria	20	Rheinland	60-0371
HOPPENBROCK, Carl	29	Gehrden	57-1113
HOPPENSTEDT, Louis	20	Woeltingerode	57-1148
HOPPMANN, Wilhelm	20	Hille	58-0576
HORACK, Johann	22	Boehmen	62-0758
HORAZECH, Xaver	23	Mindelheim	59-0048
HORMANN, Christian	20	Eldagsen	57-1122
HORMANN, Doris	17	Petershagen	60-0371
HORMANN, F.W.	28	Heuerkamp	59-0951
HORMANN, Fr.	18	Dummerlahsn.	57-1148
HORMANN, Heinrich	28	Diersdorf	60-1161
HORMANN, Marie	18	Wittorf	57-0847
HORMANN, Marie	23	Essern	62-0938
HORMS, Eibert	23	Horsten	57-0850
HORN, Augusta	14	Bremen	62-0836
HORN, Carl	64	Battenberg	58-0925
HORN, Carl	32	New York	62-0467
Albertine 33, Anna 1			
HORN, Caroline	23	Bramsche	56-1117
HORN, Cornelia	14	Stechwitz	60-0521
Pauline 8			
HORN, Ernst	12	Goslar	59-1036
Carl 9			
HORN, Georg	37	New York	57-0578
HORN, Gottl. Fr.	58	Lobenstein	55-0932
Caroline 59, Henriette 14, Carl 15			
HORN, Heinrich	39	Ebern	62-0001
Marie 30			
HORN, J.	46	Osteritz	62-0993
A. 14, A. 12			
HORN, J.C.	41	Wiederstein	55-0413
Louise 24			
HORN, Joh. Valt.	36	Oberhuelsa	55-0812
Anna Cath. 40, Johannes 13			
Joh. Heinr. 11, Paul Albr. 9, Johannes 4			
Hermann by			
HORN, Johanna Fr.	30	Roda	62-0712
HORN, John	20	Frankfurt/M.	60-1141
HORN, Wilhelm	53	Stechwitz	60-0521
Margaretha 53, Henriette 23, Francisca 18			
HORNBACH, Marie	19	Schiebach	60-1032
HORNBERGER, Chr'ne	24	Giessen/Darm.	60-0622
HORNIG, Christine	58	Gr.Glogau	59-0384
HORNSCHUCH, J.Edw.	24	Loebejuin/Pr.	60-0429
Pauline 23, Wilhelmine 11m			
HORNSTEIN, Louise	22	Celle	57-0847
HORNTHAL, Helena	17	Pahres	56-0629
HORNUNG, Ernst	30	Hartschwiedau	61-0716
HORNUNG, Max	25	Friedrichstal	62-0938
Ern. 20, Max 9m			
HORNUNG, Minna	20	Cassel	57-0365
HORNUNG, Philip	50	Friedrichstal	62-0938
Caroline 44, Ludwig 23, Friedrich 13			
Pauline 11, Max 9			
HORNUNG, Wilh.Fr.	27	Friedrichstal	62-0938
Marie 29, Emilia 1			
HORRE, Agnes	18	Laufen	59-0384
HORRE, Wilhelm	16	Markoldendorf	60-0533
HORRSTADT, Heinr.	17	Hannover	60-0785
HORST, Arnold	27	Huntlosen	60-0521
HORST, Carl	37	Lora/Hess.	61-0770
Elisabeth 34, Johann 10, Anna 6, Johann 4			
Wilhelmine 1			
HORST, F.H.(m)		Quakenbrueck	58-0925
HORST, Georg	38	Hesse-Darm.	62-0712
Margaretha 34, Elisabeth 13, Georg 7			
Lena 2			
HORST, Heinrich	34	Hannover	56-1044

NAME	AGE	RESIDENCE	YR-LIST
HORST, van der W.	32	Wetzlar	61-0716
HORSTER, Christine	22	Giessen	57-1067
HORSTKEMPEN, Arnld	17	Wiedenbrueck	59-0951
HORSTMANN, August	22	Vaiel	57-0654
HORSTMANN, Elise	26	New York	62-0467
Heinrich 2			
HORSTMANN, Heinr.	23	Hille	55-0411
HORSTMANN, Heinr.	27	Gronbach	57-0447
Maria 33, Caspar 25			
HORSTMANN, Marg.	22	Brackswalde	59-0951
Bertha 19			
HORSTMANN, Marie	22	Suedfelde	57-1122
HORSTMANN, N.(m)	38	Cincinnati	62-0730
HORSTMEIER, Marie	22	Wendthagen	58-0576
HORSTMEYER, Carl	17	Hille	56-0411
HORSTMEYER, Louise	19	Hille	56-0411
HORSTREITER, (m)	23	Behem	57-0555
HORT, Georg	33	Kreuzburg	57-0606
HORTEN, Hub.	25	Wallenborn	56-0951
HORVE, Wilhelm	48	Rueden	57-0555
HORWITZ, Malina	21	Berlin	57-0654
HOSMAN, Augusta	20	Hannover	55-1048
HOSSFELD, Elis.	24	Wailar	59-0990
HOSTAK, Franz	38	Cittow	57-0850
Marie 31, Wenzel 8, Catharine 4, Anna 2			
HOTHAN, August	20	Deckbergen	58-0563
HOTHAR, Christian	29	Rehren R.O.	57-0847
HOTHAR, Christian	29	Rehren/Hess.	57-0847
Caroline 18			
HOTTENDORF, A.(m)	23	Achim	62-0730
HOTTENDORF, Carl	15	Achim	57-1148
HOTTLER, Kunigunde	24	Iphofen	60-1141
HOTTUM, Philipp	18	Wolfsheim	56-1117
Eva 21, Elisabeth 31			
HOTZE, Wm.	43	Germany	62-0166
(f) 32			
HOUBEN, Eliza	25	Uelzen	56-1011
Emily 22			
HOVEMEYER, H.(m)	24	Bueckeburg	60-0785
HOWARD, W.	48	England	56-0550
HOWERKA, Joh.	24	Boehmen	62-1042
HOWIND, Ed.	15	Gronau	55-0932
HOYER, Aug.	26	USA.	56-0550
HOYER, Augusta	3	Leipzig	59-0384
HOYER, Emma	14	Schletingen	56-0819
HOYER, Geo.Leo.Rud	15	Culm	56-1044
HOYER, Louise	18	Halden	56-0951
HOYERMANN, Carolne	29	Bisendahl	59-0047
HOYERMANN, Eduard	38	Spandau	59-0047
Caroline 29			
HRIBECK, Anton	27	Boehmen	62-0758
HUBBERT, Maria	18	Gimbsheim	60-0398
HUBEL, Joh.Caspar	27	Kirchheim	57-0754
HUBENTHAL, Adam	36	Pfaefe	57-1407
Marie 32, Carl 6, Georg 4			
HUBER, Ant.	34	Nendingen	61-0482
HUBER, Anton	30	Aufhausen	59-0951
HUBER, Ed.	26	Wallenstadt	59-0951
HUBER, J.	32	Rock Island	57-1192
Catharine 24, Emily 4			
HUBER, Joh.Jacob	34	Enzweihingen	62-0712
Christine 39, Carl 3, Marie 1			
Caroline 2m			
HUBER, Johann	31	Pipping	59-0214
HUBER, Michael	30	Sattelpeilnst	55-0630
HUBER, Otto	22	Eisenach	57-1192
HUBERS, Moritz	24	Esensheim	55-1082
Louise 24			
HUBERT, Michel	31	Baiern	57-1280
HUBERT, Valentin	24	Ohresfeld	60-0521
HUBERT, Wilhelm	20	Hausen	59-1036
HUBERTSHAUSEN, Ph.	58	US.	59-0047
HUBNER, Adolph	23	Schleid	60-1161
Cath. 26			
HUBNER, Anton	34	Reuhearmming	56-0951
Marg. 21			
HUCHT, Theodor	29	Paderborn	57-0606
HUCHTHAUSEN, Alwin	18	Mainholzen	59-1036

NAME	AGE	RESIDENCE	YR-LIST
HUCHTING, Adeline	25	Bremerhaven	62-0836
HUCK, Johanne	40	Bremen	56-0847
Heinrich 3			
HUCK, Leonhard	32	Sinzheim	59-0384
HUCK, Wilhelmine	24	Falkenhausen	56-0512
HUCKE, Heinrich	20	Rothenburg	56-0411
HUCKEL, Jos.	19	Cassel	61-0107
HUCKLEL, Jos.	19	Cassel	61-0107
HUDELMAIER, James	28	Monhofweiler	57-0422
HUDTWALKER, Maria	18	Luedingworth	60-0622
HUE, Hermann	17	Rodenberg	59-0384
HUEBEL, Mathias	56	Herbstadt	62-0712
HUEBENTHAL, Georg	54	Reichensachse	55-0628
HUEBER, Joh.	16	Affalterbach	60-1161
HUEBNER, Andreas	17	Weener	56-0632
HUEBNER, C.A.(m)	17	Posen	57-0555
HUEBNER, Florian	21	Lusdorf	62-0879
HUEBNER, Johann	29	Schlesien	62-0758
HUEBNER, Max	18	Berlin	61-0167
HUEBRIG, Johann	30	Steindorf	56-0847
Heinrich 3			
HUEBSCH, Joseph	36	Volkmarsen/He	61-0770
HUEBSCH, Sophie	18	Graefenberg	59-0214
HUECKER, Christine	27	Lemke	59-0047
HUEFFETH, Johann	25	Neuenhaus	55-0634
HUEHNDEL, Maria	18	Berlin	59-0384
HUEHNER, Louise	18	Buchholz	59-0951
HUEHNERBEIN, v.Geo	29	Berlin	60-0533
Albertine 25			
HUEHNS, Joh.	18	Narlum	60-0521
HUELS, Elisabeth	37	Salz	59-0047
Nicolaus 13, Wilhelm 11, P.Georg 3			
HUELSEBERG, Anna	31	New York	60-0521
HUELSHOFF, C.(m)	30	New York	61-1132
Friederike 27, Heinrich 6, Augusta 36			
HUELSKAMP, Lisette	26	Bertmanstulfe	62-0938
HUELSMANN, J.	19	Philadelphia	62-0938
HUELSWEDER, Heinr.	28	Klaro	59-0535
HUELZ, August	21	Hesse-Darmst.	60-0371
HUEMANN, Peter	60	Hirten/Pr.	55-1238
Louise 24			
HUEMER, Carl	26	Geboltskirche	56-0951
Maria 6			
HUEMME, Fr.W.	39	Holtensen/Han	62-0608
Wilhelmine 27, Amalie 14, Heinrich 9			
Caroline 9m			
HUENCKEN, Elisab.	30	Rothenburg	57-0606
HUENCKEN, Johann	16	Brinkum	58-0881
HUENE, Heinrich	16	Natzungen	56-1204
HUEPER, A.M.(f)	20	Varel	59-0477
HUEPKEN, L. (m)	30	Bremen	62-0467
HUERZTHAL, Richard	18	Remscheid	57-1148
HUESCHEN, Henry	27	Coeln	60-0411
HUESING, Heinrich	15	Loxstedt	61-0520
Martina 20			
HUESTER, Bernhard	24	Osterwick/Pr.	60-0622
Anna 26			
HUET, W.G.(m)	42	Lorain	60-0785
(f) 30			
HUETER, Adam	26	Salzungen	56-0847
Joseph 2			
HUETSCHLER, Fr.	24	Bremen	57-1148
HUETTER, Wilhelm	38	Solz	56-0819
Eva Maria 34, Elise 13, Eva Christ. 11			
Georg Heinr. 8, Augusta 3			
HUETTEROTH, C.(m)	38	New York	62-0111
HUEWE, C.(m)	24	Muenster	62-0836
HUEWE, C.(m)	24	Muenster	62-0836
HUFBAUER, Cathrina	17	Pemfling	55-0630
HUFMANN, Casp.	36	Niedersumen	61-0107
HUFNAGEL, Ant.	31	Schonholthaus	57-0422
Francis 25, Theresa 20			
HUFNAGEL, Julius	19	Steinau	59-0047
Bernhard 23			
HUFNAGEL, Marg.	19	Leonrod	59-0535
HUFSCHMIDT, Matias	14	Rothenburg	56-0411
HUGO, Celestin (m)	30	Nizio	60-0785
HUGO, Joseph	28	Hoesbach/Bav.	60-0429

NAME	AGE	RESIDENCE	YR-LIST
HUGO, Lorenz	20	Erdmannsrode	60-0622
HUHN, Anna	22	Roeddenau	57-0754
HUHN, Marie	22	Frankenberg	56-0847
HUHN, Veronica	24	Ulrichsberg	55-0413
Louise 24			
HUHS, Joseph	29	Lannhausen	57-0021
HUIS, Mathias	49	Rodemichl	57-1026
Franziska 46, Theresia 17			
HUITTEN, Henriette	35	Gruenberg	58-0881
HULENA, Gustav	36	Jena	55-0845
HULET, Meta	17	Hoenau	60-0334
HULL, G.M.(m)	19	Burbach	60-0334
HULLER, Henriette	23	Schmilowo	57-0654
Charles 9m			
HULLMANN, Louise	20	Vare	59-0951
HULLMANN, Theodor	21	Java	59-0951
HULSBERG, H.	34	New York	59-0951
HUMANN, C.(m)	24	Gessmold	57-0555
HUMANSDOERFLER, An	20	Azurdorff	60-0521
HUMBERG, Bernh.	21	Cassel	59-0951
HUMBERT, A.M.	23	Elbergen	62-0993
HUMBERT, Johann	34	Nassau	57-0606
Anna 25			
HUMBERT, Maria	24	France	62-1112
HUMFELDT, H.(m)	16	Lunsen	61-0482
HUMMEL, A.	26	Kalefeld	56-0512
HUMMEL, Gottlob	29	Stuttgart	57-0924
(baby)			
HUMMESHAGEN, C.M.	18	Walldorf	59-0477
HUNCOCK, Edward	26	Southampton	59-0477
HUND, Steph. Franz	47	Attendorf	57-0606
Elisabeth 47, Franz 21, Stephan 19			
Eberhard 17, Adolphine 15, Friedrich 13			
Maria 11, Wilhelm 7, Johann 6			
HUNDERTMARK, Louis	23	Oesdorf	59-0384
HUNDESHAGEN, Georg	18	Walldorf	59-0535
HUNEROTH, Henr.	23	New York	59-0990
HUNGARLAND, A.(m)	28	Jersey City	60-0785
Augusta 20			
HUNGER, Ana Sophia	34	Hof	57-1148
HUNGER, Gottlieb	44	Posen	57-0776
Juliane 32, August 7, Mathilde 2			
HUNKE, Catharine	30	Husfeld	60-0521
HUNNEL, Anna	23	Kemminden	58-0576
HUNZINGER, Theod.	25	Luzern	60-0521
HUPE, Christ.	52	Welsede	58-0306
HUPHAUF, Margareta	42	Baiern	59-0412
Margaretha 15, Georg 10, Louise 8			
Rosina 5			
HUPPERS, Derric	21	Kapellen	57-0422
HUR, Anna Elis.	55	Cassel	57-0654
HURKHEYMER, Heinr.	50	Wuerttemberg	55-0634
Catharine 42, Christiane 17, Pauline 8			
August 3			
HURY, Frederic	32	France	61-0107
HUSAF, H.J.	52	Bederkesa	59-0477
HUSCH, Mary	30	Graetz	57-0654
Armand 4			
HUSCHBACH, Rob.	39	Gr.Gathern	60-0785
Johanne 36, Maria 7, Robert 5, Richard 9m			
HUSCHKE, Gottlieb	18	Sachsenberg	56-0589
HUSCHMANN, Fried.	41	Werden	59-0384
Clarchen 9			
HUSE, Heinr.	33	Hennemsdorf	57-0447
HUSEMANN, Wilh.	24	Merkhausen	57-0850
HUSERICH, Julius	50	Berlin	57-0021
Catharine 30, Johannes 30			
HUSMANN, Catharine	21	Borgfeld	57-0654
HUSSA, Oscar	16	Boehmen	62-1169
HUSSA, Zdenka	14	Boehmen	62-1042
HUSTIG, Friedrich	28	Schoenau	57-0754
HUT, Elis.	17	Liebloss	60-0785
HUT, John	17	Fuerth	60-0785
HUTAFF, Joh. D.	49	Neukirchen/Ha	60-0622
Magdalena 48			
HUTER, Ernst	50	Messlingen	57-1122
George 17, Augusta 14, Friedrike 12			
HUTER, Georg	35	Henneberg	57-1122

NAME	AGE	RESIDENCE	YR-LIST
HUTER, Lisette	57	Messlingen	57-1122
HUTH, Albert	26	Rossla	62-0730
HUTH, Alwine	17	Altenburg	59-0372
HUTH, David	27	Mangen	55-0845
HUTH, Dorothea	27	Seege	55-0932
Minna 21			
HUTH, Friedrich	25	Schleesen	56-0819
HUTH, Julius	33	Magdeburg	60-0371
HUTH, L.	32	Meiningen	62-1042
Emma 30			
HUTH, Therese	22	Kobilin	57-0578
Wilhelmine 19			
HUTOF, Joh.	20	Bederkesa	60-0521
Nic. 25			
HUTT, Jacobine	46	Schluchten	61-0669
HUTWALKER, Henr´tt	17	Franzenburg	62-1042
HUVERT, Louise	34	Breslau	57-1122
HUXHOLD, Conrad	23	Hohnhorst	55-0630
HUXOT, Aug.	25	Almena	58-0306
HYERONIMUS, Chs.	38	Montverene	60-0521
HYRONYMUS, C.	38	New York	61-0482
Wilhelmine 40, Philippine 15, Sophie 2			
HYSECK, Franz	37	Boehmen	60-0785
Marie 43, Anna 9, Cathar. 8, Barbara 4			
Johann 37			
IBEL, Conrad	30	Heid	60-1032
IBNERTL, Johann	43	Zant	62-0730
Anna 24, (dau.) 9m			
IDOLSKY, Louis	17	Samter	57-0509
IFFLAND, Catharine	35	Bebra	56-1260
IGEL, Theodora	46	Breslau	58-0399
IGLER, Catharine	25	Oberlind	56-1011
IHDEN, Joh.	18	Leeste	62-0938
IHLE, Jacob	28	Lennack	57-0924
Wilhelmine 28, Friedericke by			
IHLEFELD, Conrad	25	Gelnhausen	62-0401
IHLING, Georg	70	Tiefenort	56-1044
Friedrike 72, Emilie 18			
IHLVEN, Died.	18	Ottersberg	55-0413
IKEN, Herm.	29	Paderborn	61-0897
IKEN, Louis	25	New York	62-0836
ILGEN, Catharine	18	Montreal	62-0467
Magdalena 17			
ILKEMANN, Bernhard	16	Wessum	59-0951
ILKERMANN, Heinr.	21	Wessum	59-0951
ILLE, J.A.	29	Cathrinenberg	62-0993
E. 28, M. 2, M. 1, Joh. 62, J. 32			
ILLE, Rudolph	32	Weida	59-0613
(wife) 30, Lin 5			
ILLING, Grace	19	Germany	62-1112
ILLMANN, Johannes	45	Mertendorf	56-0951
Albert 10			
ILSLEIB, Heinrich	15	Frauensee	57-1026
ILSLEIB, Martha	17	Tiefenort	57-1026
ILSLIG, Catharine	18	Pfordt	59-0214
IMBROCK, Christian	54	Bomersen/Hess	57-0847
Catharine 19, Friedr. 24			
IMHOF, Rudolph	23	Augsburg	59-0214
IMHOF, Theresia	42	Brueckenau	57-0021
Pauline 18			
IMHOFF, Carl Fed.	50	Schoenburg	60-1141
Caroline 37, Ottilie 17, Herman 14			
Louise 12, Mathilda 7, Eduard 4			
IMHOFF, George	25	Sendelbach	60-1141
Rosina 28			
IMIG, Valentin	24	Louisendorf	57-0422
IMLAUBE, Annette	17	Damme	57-0961
IMMEL, Amalie	27	Marburg	61-0482
IMMEL, August	22	New York	62-0342
IMMEL, Johannes	24	Nieder Dieten	60-0371
IMMEL, Peter	26	Kirschheim	58-0399
Elisabeth 30, Elisabeth 3, Catharine 9m			
IMMEN, Henry	32	Dorum	60-1141
Mary 28, Henrietta 3			
IMMENDORF, Joh.	49	Lembach/Hess.	55-0538
Anna 47, Christian 13, Georg 8, Conrad 2			
IMMETHUN, Gerhard	26	Illinois	62-0938
IMMIG, Catharine	20	Elfertshausen	58-0576

NAME	AGE	RESIDENCE	YR-LIST
IMMIG, Peter	24	Louisendorf	58-0306
Carl 54, (f) 50, Jacob 23, Wilhelmine 21			
Catharine 18, Heinrich 16, Elisabeth 13			
Carl 6, Friedrich 7			
IMMIG, Valentin	25	Louisendorf	58-0306
(wife) 23			
IMMLER, Elis.	24	Coburg	56-0723
IMMOHL, Doris	24	Olsberg	57-0447
INDERS, Mar. Cath.	19	Abhenruh	61-0478
INGERL, Magdalena	36	Holfen	59-0951
INGERL, Mart.	31	Hoefen	60-0521
INGULD, A.Fr.	24	New York	61-0716
INNSIEKE, Jos.	25	Reselage	59-0951
INSELMANN, Peter	19	Klenkendorf	62-0712
INTERLE, Johann	25	Muenchhausen	61-0520
INTERMANN, Heinr.	16	Eversen	56-0951
IRIS, Friedr.	25	Bohemia	60-1161
Anna 24, Marie 2			
IRWIN, John W.	16	Pittsburg	62-1112
ISE, Johann Carl	59	Arolsen	60-1141
ISENSEE, G.(f)	48	Bremen	55-0544
Dorothea 16			
ISENSEE, Wilhelm	48	Sershausen/Ha	61-0770
ISER, Christ.	22	Oberg	62-0712
ISERMANN, Carl	42	Minden	57-0447
ISERMANN, Louise	22	Minden	57-0776
ISIDOR, Henriette	58	Muenchen	59-0613
Therese 18			
ISKE, Ma.Elise	36	Hannover	59-0412
Anna 10, Heinrich 7, Maria 5			
ISKENIUS, Fr.	21	Briedermarsbg	61-0167
ISKER, Peter	40	Danzig	62-0758
Agnes 39, Ignatz 16, Marianne 14, Anna 9			
Johann 5, Pauline by			
ISLET, de la John	16	Unterohm	57-0654
ISPHORDING, F.	45	Attendern	62-1112
ISRAEL, C.G.(m)	48	Zittau	61-0804
F.A.C.S.(f) 18, Franziska 16, C.G.(m) 15			
ISRAEL, Julius	27	Waldcappel	59-0951
ISRAELISON, Minche	20	Voerden	56-0629
ISSING, Carl	28	Zell	59-0990
ISSLEBER, Georg	34	Friedlos	56-0819
Marie 35			
ISSLEIB, Heinrich	15	Frauensee	57-1026
ISSLEIB, Martha	17	Tiefenort	57-1026
ISSLEIB, Valentin	49	Ndr.Ingelheim	60-1053
ISWALD, Ed.	28	Isweil	56-0723
Albertine 20			
ISZEYMANSKY, Amal.	28	Posen	61-0716
ITSCHNER, Chr.	38	Barel	62-0836
ITTNER, Bernhard	22	Frohnsdorf	61-0482
ITZEN, R.P.	30	Westermarsch	58-0306
ITZIG, Moritz	18	Snyen	56-0629
ITZIG, Wolff	16	Zuin	59-0477
JABORG, Roelf	47	New York	58-0576
JACHENS, Lueder	35	Bremen	57-1148
JACHHEIM, Anton	38	Schreckhausen	59-1036
JACKEL, Cath.	27	Lissberg	56-1216
JACKEL, Johann	32	Cassel/Hessen	55-0628
Anton 28			
JACKELL, Jacob	19	Duerrenmettst	60-0334
JACKELN, Franziska	26	Friedland	57-0654
JACKER, Fr.	22	Ellenwangen	59-0990
W. 19			
JACOB, Cacilia	20	Klosterboeren	56-0512
JACOB, Christian	48	Messlingen	57-1122
JACOB, Friedrich	19	Philippsthal	60-1032
JACOB, Friedrike	19	Briesen	62-0938
Salomon 10m			
JACOB, Johann	55	Griebnitz	58-0576
Marie 55			
JACOB, John	46	Saxe-Coburg	56-0512
Dorothea 34, Elisabeth 16, Lorenz 13			
Johann 9, Kasper 5, Adam 2			
JACOB, John	24	Ersdorf	61-0482
Heinrich 37, Catharine 38, Heinrich 9			
Elise 3, Johannes 11m			
JACOB, L.(m)	26	Gneesen	57-0555

NAME	AGE	RESIDENCE	YR-LIST
JACOB, Moses	45	Sachsenhausen	58-0604
(wife) 40, Jacob 16, Friedericke 12			
Johanne 9, Amalie 7, Michael 5			
JACOB, Samuel	17	Niedergemuend	62-0879
JACOBI, Anna M.	18	Albig	62-1042
JACOBI, Friedrich	40	Rinteln	56-0279
JACOBI, Guiseppe	32	Italy	61-0167
JACOBS, Abrah.Ph.	35	Amsterdam	59-0477
JACOBS, Ahr. A.	28	Wayens	57-0422
JACOBS, Andreas	25	Hannover	56-0819
JACOBS, Annette	34	England	62-0938
JACOBS, Carl Fr'dr	26	Elbrinksen	56-0411
Louise 25			
JACOBS, Sam.	16	Devonshire	59-0384
JACOBSEN, Herm.	19	Schweringen	56-0723
JACOBSEN, Mag.	22	Copenhagen	62-0467
JACOBSOHN, Pauline	19	Rodenberg	58-0885
JACOBUS, Nath.	17	Lypniewo	59-0477
JACOBY, Edw.	41	New York	60-1161
Marg. 27, Gust. 15, Anna 4			
JACOBY, Philippine	21	Bremen	62-0938
John 15			
JACOPO, GeorgBatto	14	Italy	62-0166
JACOT, M.(m)	58	France	62-0232
JAECK, Babette	50	Bamberg	62-1112
JAECKEL, Anna	28	Schoenwalden	57-0754
JAECKEL, Maria	22	Irmerode	57-0776
JAECKELE, Joseph	15	Muenchweiler	60-0622
JAECKLE, Dorothea	15	Aspach	60-0521
JAECKLE, Johann	18	Schussenried	56-0847
JAEGER, A.	34	Louisville	59-0613
Emma 26, Fritz 8, Albert 6, Henny 5m			
JAEGER, Conrad	34	Villingen	57-1067
JAEGER, Friedrich	32	Goslar	55-0630
JAEGER, Gottl.	30	Walheim	60-0334
JAEGER, Joh.	24	Brooklyn	62-0608
JAEGER, Johann	59	Muetzenberg	56-0847
JAEGER, Joseph	29	Zorngriesbach	57-0754
JAEGER, Louis	17	Stordorff	56-0847
Rosine 8			
JAEGER, Maria	19	Hirtenheim	60-1161
JAEGER, Theodor	21	Effien	56-1044
JAEGGI, Marg.	28	Obergerlofing	59-0990
JAENICK, Robert	23	Geithagen	57-0961
JAEPP, G.H.	30	Nordheim	59-0477
Minna 26			
JAFESDORFER, John	27	Koenigshafer	57-1407
JAFFT, Christine	63	Pommern	58-0399
JAGELER, Chr.	22	Hagen	60-0785
JAGER, H.A.(m)	22	Tuebingen	60-0785
JAHN, Adolph	45	Markranstaedt	57-0850
Erdmuthe 35, Gustav 11, Franz 9			
Reinhold 7, Ernst 5, Liberta 3			
JAHN, Augusta	30	Preussen	57-0606
Augusta 6			
JAHN, Elisabeth	17	Grossensebach	60-0521
JAHN, Emilie	19	Suhl	56-1260
JAHN, Gertrude	26	Goettingen	56-1117
JAHN, Heinrich	36	Bohlscheiben	60-0429
JAHN, Johann	27	Schwansee	57-0776
JAHN, Johann	44	Meiningen	58-0881
Christiane 44, Augusta 14, Emma 12			
JAHN, Johann W.	29	Grossbockedra	56-0589
JAHNKE, Louis J.	57	Neuendorf	57-1192
Louise 58, Wilhelmine 21, Louis 17			
William 1			
JAHNSEN, Julia	14	Doese	62-0758
JAHREIS, G. (m)	25	Stetfeld	62-0836
JAHREIS, G. (m)	26	Goetschnitz	62-0836
JAHRES, Christoph	32	Darmstadt	58-0885
Friederike 31, Minna 7			
JAKOBI, August	18	Beverungen	57-1280
JAKOBS, A.G. (m)	45	Aurich/Ostfr.	55-0544
Marie 46, Henriette 20, Marie 16			
Hermann 12, Anton 9, Margarethe 7			
Catharine 5			
JAMES, J.E.	42	England	62-1042
JAMES, Otto	45	US.	62-0938

NAME	AGE	RESIDENCE	YR-LIST
JAMLER, Aug.	49	New York	59-0951
Emilie 44			
JANBY, N.	32	Ofen	62-0730
Catharine 29			
JANDA, Wenzel	43	Ziniwes	56-0629
Rosalie 20, Minna 43, Anna 9, Marie 7			
Elisabeth 2, Joseph 47, Anna 49, Maria 21			
Joseph 9			
JANDA, Wenzel	45	Kastenblad	56-0819
Catharina 26			
JANDER, August	46	New York	58-0815
Gottlieb 9			
JANDER, Christ.	52	Erfurt	60-0334
JANDERFOREL, (f)	18	Paris	62-1042
JANECKE, Heinz	30	Trexen	58-0815
JANISCH, Juliane	22	Malerneustadt	58-0925
Johanna 15			
JANKE, H.	30	Posen	59-0412
Wilhelmine 25, Ludwig 5m			
JANN, Georg	24	Greifswald	56-0819
JANSEMANN, Ferd.	46	Drensteinfurt	56-0723
Hinricka 42			
JANSEN, Fr.W.	26	Bremen	57-0606
Marie Marg. 25			
JANSEN, Gerhard	57	Jennelt	58-0563
Anna 55, Wilhelm 23, Anna 12			
JANSEN, Janje	22	Tergast	60-0398
JANSEN, Joh.	17	Bohrdum	56-0527
JANSEN, Joh.Friedr	19	Oyten	55-0932
JANSEN, Joh.Marten	28	Terborg	60-0398
JANSEN, Johann	54	Tergast	60-0398
Welke 54, Feutche 17, Thereschen 15			
JANSING, J.B.H.(m)	38	New York	60-0533
JANSON, Marie	24	Hofgeismar	62-0342
JANSSEN, Anna B.	16	Uphusen	55-0413
JANSSEN, Frerk	58	Aurich	57-0422
JANSSEN, Heinr.	16	Walsdorf	60-0785
JANSSEN, Margaret	24	Wrisse	57-0422
JANTZEN, Elise	24	Ruttel	57-1148
JAOCHNER, Jac.Fr.	28	Minzingen	59-0412
JAPFET, Johannette	26	Breitenbach	56-0411
JAQUET, Jos.	30	France	62-1042
JARRE, Louise	23	Hamburg	60-0622
JASPER, H.	39	Bremen	62-1169
JASPER, Hermann	51	Assendorf	61-0478
Wilhelm 36, Friedrich 15, Wilhelmine 11			
Charlotte 9, Henriette 7, August 5			
Caroline 11m			
JASPER, Theodor	20	Warendorf	62-1169
Heinrich 18			
JASZEK, Ambrosius	36	Petznik	57-0924
Marianne 20, Jacob 9, Eva 7, Theophil by			
JAUTZ, Joseph	30	Bibrach/Wuert	55-1238
JEHLE, Johanna	18	Cannstadt	60-0334
JEHN, Valentin	29	Breitenbach	61-0779
JEITTER, Friedr.	33	Wuertemberg	59-0535
JELLINGHAUS, W.	45	New York	58-0604
JENCHICK, Joseph	32	Radwanow	56-1011
Barbara 28, Katharina 6			
JENERT, J.(m)	33	New York	62-0730
JENNY, Jost	38	Glarus	61-0167
JENRICH, Gottlieb	49	Carlshoff	57-0776
Wilhelmina 59, Hinrich 30			
JENTH, Robertine	43	Burg	59-0990
JENTSCH, Bruno	30	Bavaria	62-1169
JERGEN, L.(m)	26	Georgia	59-0951
JERKEL, Joh.Eleon.	57	Dresden	57-1026
JESBERGER, Euseb.	33	Rottbach	62-0879
JESKE, Jules	31	Preussen	62-1112
Elisabeth 28, Sophie 3, Catharina 1			
JESSELSOHN, Salomn	21	Baden	59-0477
JESSING, Paul	24	Borchhorst	59-0412
JEUDE, Joseph	22	Ober Assber	61-0478
Johannes 15			
JOBST, Michael	48	Unterimmendrf	61-0770
JOCHEM, Heinrich	21	Ulfa	59-0214
JOCHENS, Marie	21	Osnabrueck	61-0716
Georg 1			

NAME	AGE	RESIDENCE	YR-LIST
JOCHIM, Friedrich	43	Eimbeckhausen	55-0845
Sophie 23, Justine 7, Fritz 4, Louise 3			
Caroline by			
JOCKLE, Joseph	21	Ulmbach	60-1141
JOECKEL, Catharine	39	Neudiskendorf	56-0629
JOECKEL, Catharine	33	Giessen	57-1067
Louise 2			
JOECKEL, Emily	24	Gruenberg	57-1148
JOECKEL, H.	44	Darmstadt	57-1067
JOECKEL, Herm.	17	Gruenberg	61-0897
JOECKEL, Joh.Fr.C.	14	Giessen/Lippe	62-0608
Carl 13			
JOELLNER, J.Friedr	23	Essen	56-0589
JOENYES, Helena	22	Dorum	60-1141
JOERG, Joseph	44	Oettingen	58-0815
Alvis 13, Georg 14			
JOERG, Mich.	58	Augsburg	55-0932
Anna 50, Josepha 30, Josepha 2			
JOERGENS, Aug.Ed.	44	Loembfoerd/Ha	62-0342
JOERGENS, Bernh.	36	Foehr	61-0478
JOERNS, Johann	26	Aurich	61-0520
JOHAENNING, Carlne	25	Natingen	61-0478
JOHANN, Peter	24	Steinberg	59-0384
JOHANNES, Mariane	20	Cloppenburg/O	60-0371
JOHANNING, Florenz	29	Bielefeld	57-1148
JOHANNING, Herm.	27	Holdorf	62-0401
JOHANNING, Theres.	18	Burgholz	60-0398
JOHANNINGMEYR, Flo	20	Buende	56-1011
JOHANNINGSMEIER, F	26	Faulensick	57-0422
JOHANNINGSMEYER, J	17	Ennigloh	60-0334
JOHANNSEN, D.(m)	24	Holstein	60-0785
JOHL, Carl Wilhelm	39	Muencheberg	61-0779
JOHLER, Jos.	27	Linden	57-0422
JOHN, David	59	Erfurt	62-0467
Dora 57, Therese 21			
JOHN, Ph.	20	Schluechtern	59-0990
JOHNE, Elisabeth	22	Wien/Aus.	55-0538
JOHNE, Joh.	30	Dresden	62-0166
JOHNSTON, John	32	USA.	60-0785
JOLSON, G.	34	Berlin	62-1169
JONAINIGG, Martin	15	Klagenfurt	62-0166
JONAS, Johann	23	Strelitz	57-0776
JONAS, Jos.	22	Duesseldorf	60-1196
JONG, Robert	18	Wernhausen	60-0334
JOOST, Carsten	14	Koehten	58-0815
JOOST, Elisabeth	29	Kaehlen	61-0716
Martin 9			
JORDAN, Carl	17	Storndorf	62-0879
JORDAN, Fried.	26	Hannover	59-0214
Friederike 26			
JORNS, Lina	17	Brunswick	57-0422
Henrietta 49			
JORNS, Wilhelm	35	Wolfenbuettel	57-1407
Wilhelmine 34, Johanna 23, Heinrich by			
JOSEPH, C.	24	Erlangen	62-0993
JOSEPH, Jonas	14	Pfingstadt	61-0482
JOSEPH, Wilhelm	22	Teubenhausen	56-0723
JOSEPHSON, Julchen	20	Alt Luneberg	60-0521
JOST, Cathar.	19	Niederweisel	59-0384
JOST, Elis.	18	Oberkalbach	62-1042
JOST, Elisabeth	25	Quickborn	62-1169
JOST, Geo.Friedr.	47	Niedereschbch	55-1082
Louise 24			
JOST, Johann	26	Koehlen	56-1117
JOST, Margaretha	22	Dieburg	59-0214
JOST, Philipp	19	Schluechtern	60-0521
JOSTING, Heinrich	15	Brochhausen	56-0951
JOUNERANDOT, Luise	53	France	62-0166
Augustina 6			
JOUNG, Jean	35	France	62-0938
(f) 21			
JUDAE, L.	19	Hildburghause	62-0993
JUEHLING, Hugo	24	Geringswalde	62-0467
JUELFS, Juelf Jac.	51	Hohenkirchen	57-1148
Mary 32, Jac. 12, Hillerich 10, Eva 9			
Antonie 7, Julius 2			
JUENGLING, G.	56	Pottsville	62-0938
JUENGLING, Johann	18	Eulenbach	57-1407

NAME	AGE	RESIDENCE	YR-LIST
JUENNEMANN, Joseph	24	Flinsberg	61-0669
Marg. 23			
JUERGENS, J.H.	19	Bremerhaven	57-1067
JUERGENS, J.H.(m)	18	Drangstedt/Ha	60-0622
JUERGENS, Ludwig	22	Wrexen/Wald.	60-0622
Carl 16, Caroline 23			
JUERGENS, Rika	21	Fuerstenberg	57-0776
JUERGER, Heinrich	33	Noepke	59-0535
JUERTJEN, B. (m)	29	Duesseldorf	59-0951
JUETLING, Fenna	24	Holtland	61-0716
JUETZUR, Stephan	27	Posen	57-0776
JUHR, Gustav	26	Charbruch	57-0704
JULFS, Christ.Rud.	32	Wayens	57-0422
JULIS, Joseph	31	Podolitz	55-0845
JULKE, Caroline	20	Schoeneberg	57-0704
JUNG, Anna	19	Habelschwerdt	59-0477
JUNG, Balthasar	23	Gelnhausen	60-0622
Juliane 20, Conrad 21			
JUNG, Carl	36	Possow	57-0704
JUNG, Conrad	16	Fauerbach	59-0384
JUNG, Elis.	16	Oes	62-0111
JUNG, Elise	28	Coeln	59-0477
JUNG, Emil	15	Biedenkopf	57-1067
JUNG, F.H.(m)	25	Mannebach	61-0682
JUNG, Fr. Casp.	18	Cloppenburg	55-0932
JUNG, Friedr.	39	Baltimore	61-0897
JUNG, G.S.	34		59-0477
Dora 28, Georg 5, Theodor 3			
JUNG, Georg	26	Bremen	62-0879
Jacob 33			
JUNG, Heinrich	49	Treysa	55-0812
Maria Cath. 18			
JUNG, Jacob	18	Hackenheim	60-0334
JUNG, Joh. Jac.	32	Rhein Baiern	55-0634
JUNG, Johannes	23	Baltimore	62-0401
Carl 26			
JUNG, Joseph	31	Dettmang	57-1280
JUNG, Marg.	19	Mitwitz	57-1148
JUNG, Marie	19	Ziegenberg	56-1216
JUNG, Otto	14	Elberfeld	59-1036
JUNG, Panratz	49	Grub	55-0630
Barbara 49, Anna 26, Margaretha 20			
Anna Marg. 18, Rosine 14, Hanne 12			
JUNG, Samuel	59	Sahl	62-0938
Henriette 42, Albert 19, Theod. 13			
JUNG, Wilh.	16	Gemuenden	58-0604
JUNGEL, Balth.	30	Giessen	56-0589
JUNGEN, Caroline	25	Ottendorf	57-0578
Friedrich 56			
JUNGERMANN, Mich.	32	Zeil	57-0654
Franziska 24			
JUNGHEIM, Elisab.	27	Rittenau	57-0924
JUNGK, August	20	Oberneuwark	56-0629
JUNGK, Franz	29	Seulingen	58-0399
JUNGMANN, Wilhelm	30	Sachsen	59-0412
JUNGMEYER, Paul	57	Freiburg/Pr.	55-1238
Louise 24			
JUNK, Anna C.	22	Ruderdorf	55-0413
JUNK, Georg	15	Bechtolsheim	60-1032
Elisabeth 16			
JUNKEL, Pauline	45	Giessen	57-0606
Wilhelm 7, Johanna 6, Julius 4, Augusta 3			
Minna 9m			
JUNKER, Joh.	26	Nordenberg	59-0613
JUNKERT, Jos.	24	Mies	61-0669
Ther. 23, Joseph 3, Sus. 10m			
JUNKOWSKY, Michael	34	Budzin/Pr.	62-0342
Rosalia 30, Agnes 7			
JURHELLE, Johanna	32	Lippstadt	57-0704
JUST, Francis	18	Hellefeld	57-0422
JUST, Georg	25	Fulda/Prussia	57-0847
JUST, Gottfr.	40	Hildburghsn.	55-0413
KABALIK, Franz	37	Solopitz	55-0845
Rosalie 38, Franz 7, Franziska 2			
KABATH, Joseph	47	Popowitz	56-1011
Anne 37, John 18, Joseph 16, Francis 14			
Wenzel 10, Antony 10, Anne 4, Charles 9m			
KABEL, Louise	30	Archenroth	61-0930

NAME	AGE	RESIDENCE	YR-LIST
KABISCH, Carl Hch.	32	Wetterwitz/Sx	60-0622
KABITZKY, Johann	60	Ostrau	55-1082
KABSCH, Johann	36	Rosanth	57-0436
KACH, August	24	Carlshafen	61-0520
KACKL, Caroline	46	Breslau	61-0897
KAEFER, Sophia	19	Muenster	59-0613
KAEFRICH, Cath.M.	20	Westercappeln	57-1192
KAEFTER, Franz	20	Bierden	59-0951
KAELBER, Egidius	21	Meiningen	62-0758
KAEM, Kihair	25	Churhessen	55-0634
Eva 23, Adam 19			
KAEMMERER, August	28	Weissensee	58-0576
KAEMMERER, Elisab.		Hohenberg	56-1117
KAEMMRER, Jacob	14	Lich	60-1053
Heinrich 21			
KAEMNER, Mary	27	New York	59-0951
Joh. 10m			
KAEMPER, Joh.	19	Eininghausen	60-0398
Heinrich 16			
KAEMPFF, Samuel	30	Bromberg	56-1044
Juliane 28, Julius 11m			
KAERCHELL, Chr.	20	Owen	60-0785
KAES, Franz	29	Wien	55-0812
KAESSLER, Eva Chr.	43	Bosserode	57-1026
Martha Lisa 20, Heinrich 14, Johannes 10			
Anna Marg. 8, Magdalena 5, Elisabeth 2			
KAESTER, Caroline	30	Strelitz	59-0047
KAESTNER, Bernhard	25	New York	57-1407
KAESTNER, Carl	35	Leipzig	61-0478
KAESTNER, P.W.	29	Ritnordhausen	58-0576
KAETHE, Severin	20	Muehlhausen	56-0527
KAEUFLER, Carl	30	Roemersberg	55-0932
KAGSEL, Rosine	44	Widden	60-0521
Wilhelm 14			
KAHAPKA, Anna	21	Waldau	55-0630
KAHL, Charles	27	Wiesbaden	62-0111
KAHL, G.A.	44	Liegnitz	56-0629
Clara 9			
KAHL, Henriette	19	Oels	57-0754
KAHLE, Henriette	20	Andreas Berg	59-1017
KAHLE, Sophie	18	Woelpe	58-0885
KAHN, Fanny	23	Gleicherwiese	62-0467
KAHN, Friederike	32	Hochheim	58-0815
KAHN, Isaac	28	Missouri	61-0897
KAHN, Isidor	23	Bergheim	56-1117
KAHN, Jeanette	25	Muenster	60-0521
KAHN, Kaethe	55	Hermannstein	60-1196
Seligmann 9, Bertha 7			
KAHN, Trommel	19	Fruehlendorf	62-0712
KAHNT, Bernh.	22	Medewitz	59-1036
KAHRMANN, Friedr.	23	Walthersleben	57-0422
KAHRS, Armand	28	New York	57-0654
Anna 28, Catherina 4, Henry 11m			
KAHRS, Heron.	35	NY.	55-0413
Louise 24			
KAIBE, Rud.	41	Bergen	57-0654
KAIFER, Marg.Chrst	51	Muehlhausen	57-1192
KAIL, Hermann	25	Livotschau	56-1044
KAIN, Amalie	16	Krupa	62-0401
KAISEMANN, Jacob	56	Eisenach	56-0723
Maria 6			
KAISER, August	60	Zittau	62-0712
Juliane 17, Caroline 15			
KAISER, Barbara	24	Hohenwart	62-0879
KAISER, Catharina	56	Bamberg	61-0682
Barbara 21, Nanny 8, Georg 14			
KAISER, Christiane	27	Ruggell	60-0533
KAISER, Franz	29	Arnsberg	59-0412
KAISER, Friedr.	27	Preussen	58-0399
KAISER, Friedrich	24	Rudersberg	55-0845
KAISER, Georg	20	Sievershausen	57-0555
KAISER, Heinr.	36	Washington	62-0836
Henr. 36			
KAISER, Heinr.Chr.	24	Ganste/Gotha	56-0819
KAISER, Heinrich	19	Pleichenbach	57-1407
KAISER, Hermann	33	Braunschweig	58-0925
KAISER, J.(m)	18	Singlis	62-0836
Sabine 17, Martha 19			
KAISER, J.G.	35	New York	56-1216
KAISER, Jacob	41	Kusterdingen	61-0482
Catharine 41, Jacob 13, Martin 9			
Caspar 7, Conrad 2			
KAISER, Johann	31	Vaduz/Lichten	60-0533
KAISER, Johannes	22	Kleinensee	57-1067
KAISER, Louise	22	Lauterbach	60-1053
KAISER, Marie	17	Kengingen	61-0482
KAISER, Philipp	19	Bleichenbach	58-0576
Marie 25			
KAISER, Valentin	23	Laimbach	61-0478
KAKIERSHING, Wm.	45	Buddissen	59-1036
KALB, Franz P.	25	Frankenberg	60-1053
KALB, Suzann Marg.	53	Graefenberg	58-0563
Margaretha 18			
KALBFLEISCH, John	26	Schoenberg/He	55-0628
KALEMANN, Christne	23	Hoevebach	56-0279
KALEMANN, Eva Elis	17	Hoevebach	56-0279
KALINA, Elisabeth	44	Zinken	56-0629
Katharina 40			
KALKHORST, Wmne.	19	Roden	59-0412
Wilhelm 21			
KALKMANN, Louis	19	Bremen	59-0951
KALKMANN, Wilhelm	15	London	59-0477
KALKOFF, Wilhelm	19	Trauensen	56-0512
KALL, Franz P.	25	Frankenberg	60-1053
KALLENBERG, Joh.W.	28	Erfurt	62-0758
KALLIGECK, Elisab.	16	Barrau	57-0961
KALLSTEDE, Carl	20	Delmenhorst	59-0048
KALTEBORN, Pet.Wm.	40	Altona	59-0372
KALTENBACH, Gottf.	16	Allendorf	55-0413
KALTENBACH, Loon	37	Schebingen	62-0111
KALTENBRUN, Marie	29	Reiselsfinger	59-0214
KALTENBRUNN, Gust.	18	Brieg	55-0932
KAMANN, Therese	29	Frankfurt	60-0785
KAMARATH, Friedr.	51	Falkenburg	57-0654
William 37, (f) 14, Charles 11, August 5			
Friederike 2			
KAMBRY, Albrecht	18	Zuerich	61-0930
KAMENA, Adelheid	23	Schopphausen	57-1148
KAMIATH, Elisabeth	15	Winterlingen	59-0477
KAMING, Marie	25	Lemke	58-0563
KAMKE, Maria	by	Pouschitz	55-0845
KAMM, Anna	25	Breidenbach	60-0371
KAMM, August	28	Detroit	60-0429
KAMM, Johannes	49	Heimershausen	57-1280
Elisabeth 45, Elisabeth 18, Jakob 12			
KAMMAN, Heinrich	20	Hannover	62-0758
KAMMELMEYER, A.Mar	24	Treuchthagen	55-0812
KAMMERLANDER, Geo.	32	Riedenburg	56-1117
A.(f) 27			
KAMMETTER, Adam	19	Meschede	62-0879
KAMMEYER, Heinrich	22	Brinckum	55-1048
KAMMING, F.W.	43	Stemmen	61-0482
Johann 14, Heinrich 4, Friederike 16			
Marie 19			
KAMP, Marianne	35	Lingen	56-1117
Elise 9			
KAMP, Pet.Jos.	45	Arweiler	62-1169
KAMPE, J.H.(m)	17	Wersage	60-0521
Anna 16			
KAMPE, Marie	65	Wille	60-0521
Louise 26			
KAMPEN, Sophie	20	Lueneburg	56-1260
KAMPF, Louise	19	Bremschede	59-0477
KAMPFMUELLER, Carl	23	Cassel	59-0477
KAMPHASSE, Marie	20	Holdorf	59-0951
KAMPHOEFNER, J.Fr.	16	Enniglohe	56-0723
KAMPING, Johann	36	Burgsteinfurt	57-0509
KAMPMANN, Heinrich	32	Iserlohn	57-1150
KAMPMANN, John	32	Ostercappeln	56-1204
KAMPMEIER, Fr.	21	Rheine	57-1192
KAMPS, Margar.	21	Luedingworth	56-0413
KAN, Jacob	59	Liegnitz/Pr.	62-0342
KANDLER, Joh.Georg	26	Bettstadt	57-1416
KANEIDER, Franz	60	Wien	60-1053
KANNE, Minna	22	Bovenden	60-0334
KANNGIESSER, Danl.	75	Lisbenhausen	58-0545

NAME	AGE	RESIDENCE	YR-LIST
KANNGIESSER, Wm.	36	Versmold	57-1026
KANNKE, Elisabeth	32	Gitter	55-0845
Christine 20			
KANNSTEIN, Wilhelm	24	Bielefeld	58-0576
KANT, Ernestine	19	Carzig	57-0776
KANZ, Lorenz	30	Siedingen	61-0047
KANZE, Minna	17	Bremen	59-0951
KANZELEITER, Rosa	29	Wuertemberg	61-0682
KAPER, Jos.	36	Ernsteck	59-1036
KAPERSCHMIDT, Wm.	27	Elbelingen	59-0048
KAPF, August	16	Stuttgart	56-0589
Elisabeth 47			
KAPP, Anna	21	Riegelsdorf	56-0512
KAPP, Ernst Heinr.	44	Luedingworth	56-0413
Heinrich 3			
KAPP, Herm.	27	Bettehausen	60-0785
KAPPELHOFF, Joseph	30	Burgsteinfurt	57-0509
KAPPELMANN, Carl	18	Wildbach	56-0589
Heinrich 3			
KAPPELMANN, Wilhm.	36	Suhlingen	62-0712
Dorothea 37, Heinrich 9, Anna 7, Marie 3			
Wilhelm 9m			
KAPPERS, Conr.	17	Ndr.Wellstadt	57-0422
Louisa 22			
KAPPES, Hartmann	52	Ndr.Wollstadt	58-0563
Eva 45, Georg 20, Elisabeth 16			
Catharina 13, Johann 11, Wilhelm 7			
Maria 1			
KAPPLER, Joh.Jac.	20	Bamberg	57-1148
KAPSCH, Heinr.	52	Bremen	60-0334
KARA, Adalbert	33	Cholka	57-0850
Josepha 24, Joseph 2			
KARCHNER, Carl	20	Frankenthal	59-1036
KARDENKOPF, F.W.	29	Lindhorst	60-0785
Anna 23, (child)			
KAREL, Wenzel	19	Nadrub/Boehm.	57-0924
KARELS, Johanna	5	Oldenburg	62-1169
KARG, Walburga	29	Litterzofen	57-0754
KARL, Anna	27	Mertesdorf	57-0654
KARL, August	35	Molzdorf/Goth	55-0538
Christiane 35, B-aete (f) , Eduard			
Therese 6m			
KARL, Louis	26	New York	59-0214
KARL, Marg.	15	Speyer	60-0521
KARL, Peter	25	Bamberg	59-0214
KARL, Wilhelmina	27	Altenstadt	57-0422
KARNATH, August	31	Jarischau	56-0819
Wilhelmine 33, Caroline 6			
KAROLEWSKY, M.	46	Romanshof	58-0576
Brigitte 37, Marie 16, Franziska 13			
Joseph 13, Johann 8, Julie 4			
KARPE, Andr.	59	Gr.Brembach	62-0730
KARR, Margarethe		Elbingen	59-0613
KARST, Andr.	32	New York	59-0384
Elisabeth 43, Johanna 9			
KARTHAUSER, Wlhmne	57	Halle	57-0422
KASANDA, Mathias	40	Bohemia	60-1161
Anna 23, Anna 2			
KASPER, Matthias	21	Kleinschiska	55-0845
KASSEBARTH, J.W.AF	25	Bremen	55-0634
Wilhelmine 26			
KASSEL, Mar.(f)	26	Linne	61-0669
KASSEL, Marcus	57	Schmugel	55-0845
KASSEL, Wenzel	31	Strigowitz	57-1113
Catharina 38, Maria 14, Johann 10			
Albert 7, Wenzel 5, Joseph 3, Math.(m) 6m			
KASSELMANN, Friedr	25	Maschen	60-1161
KASSER, Friedrich	24	Niederhipp	62-0467
Elisabeth 27, Marie 20			
KAST, Christ.	43	Coelln	59-0048
KASTEN, Johann	9	New York	62-0730
KASTENBEIN, Carl	15	Hardenburg/Ha	60-0622
KASTENDICK, Anna	18	Morsum	61-0478
KASTENS, August	18	Thedinghausen	57-0606
KASTENS, Heinr.	20	Ottersberg	55-0413
KASTNER, Lorenz	26	Wunsiedel	56-0632
Catharine 42			
KATER, Conrad	32	Rentdorf	61-0478

NAME	AGE	RESIDENCE	YR-LIST
KATL, Joachim	42	Weschnitz	62-0712
KATLE, Ernst Chr.	28	Lueneburg	59-0214
KATTEIN, Heinrich	30	Reuthen	59-0384
KATTENHORN, C.H.	25	Scharmbeck	62-0401
KATTENHORN, Herm.	35	New York	62-0401
KATTENHORN, J.	27	Cincinnati	59-1036
KATTENHORN, Martin	17	New York	59-1036
William 15			
KATTWINKEL, O.	30	Burtscheid	62-0993
KATZ, Amalie	16	Dodenhausen	62-0712
KATZ, Anna	42	Oppotschna/Bo	57-0924
Joseph 15, Bernhard 13, Allois 11			
Pauline 10, Julius 8, Leopoldine 6			
Anton 6, Anastasia 4			
KATZ, Emanuel	20	Mannsbach	60-1161
KATZ, Ernst	22	Dremsen	57-1148
KATZ, H.(m)	17	Steinbach	62-0467
KATZ, H.L.	42	Holtensen	59-0384
Caroline 41, Henry 17, Louis 11			
Caroline			
KATZ, Helene	38	Cassel	61-1054
Albert 17, Eva 10, Rosalie 9, Leontine 8			
Richard 6, Josephine 5, Joseph 3			
Rudolph 1, Siegfried 1			
KATZ, Joseph	50	Adelsberg	56-0692
KATZ, Lina	21	Rockenheim	60-0785
KATZ, Malchen	12	Dillieh	57-1067
Sara 36			
KATZ, Marcus	50	Zueschen	61-0478
Amalie 17, Abraham 13, Louis 5, Jacob 15			
KATZ, Meyer	18	Zischen	61-0682
Caroline 19			
KATZ, Philipp	41	Rauschenberg	60-1161
Catharina 36, Catharina 23, Marie 15			
Johannes 9, Georg 7, Catharina 3			
Wilhelm 9m			
KATZ, Rebeca	22	Valperz	60-0521
KATZ, Samuel	23	Steinbach	60-0334
KATZ, Sophie	19	Beckedorf	56-0589
KATZ, Suessmann	21	Schwarzenborn	61-0897
KATZENBERGER, Joh.	53	Hermannsfeld	56-0413
Elisab. 47			
KATZENMEYER, Joh.	26	Schierbach	59-1036
Agnes 9			
KATZENSCHWANZ, C.	36	New York	56-1216
KATZENSTEIN, Carl	15	Nieheim	62-1169
KATZENSTEIN, Gers.	44	Jesberg	56-0589
Stina 18			
KATZENSTEIN, Isaak	23	Altona	56-1260
KATZENSTEIN, J.	26	Hennyhausen	56-0512
KATZENSTEIN, Jette	41	Flieden	56-1216
Salomon 8, Bertha 6, Joseph 3			
KATZUNG, Valentin	45	Schmalkalden	58-0576
Elise 27			
KAUFELS, Friedrike	20	Waiblingen	55-0845
KAUFES, Heinrich	18	Makenzell	59-0047
KAUFFELD, Ernst	56	Minden/Pr.	62-0608
Marie 47, Marie 18, Amalie 17, Anna 16			
Ida 12, Peter 9, Pauline 6, Valesca 4			
Alexander 10m			
KAUFFELD, T.	19	Cassel	55-0932
KAUFFMANN, Joh.Chr	46	Sudenberg	62-1042
Minna 10, Otto 8, Ida 6, Bertha 5			
KAUFHUNGER, Maria	18	Gutenberg	57-0436
KAUFMANN, Albert	37	New York	58-0815
Janette 55, Catharina 30, Alex 3			
KAUFMANN, Amalia	26	Muenden	50-1017
KAUFMANN, Caroline	38	Rohrbach	56-0550
Angel.Marg. 60			
KAUFMANN, Catarina	15	Homberg	57-0776
KAUFMANN, Catharin		Elbingen	59-0613
KAUFMANN, Dora	37	Baltimore	60-0785
Catharine 5, Conrad 2			
KAUFMANN, Franz'ka	17	Worms	57-0918
KAUFMANN, Friedr.	34	Veckenstedt	57-0654
Anna 1, August 22, Ernest 15			
KAUFMANN, Heinr.	50	Schlei	59-1036
Cathar. 24			

NAME	AGE	RESIDENCE	YR-LIST
KAUFMANN, Joh.Geo.	24	Walduern	60-1053
KAUFMANN, Johann	37	Vormeln	60-0533
Louise 41, Louis 14, Wilhelm 2			
Heinrich 9, Minna 5, Fritz 2			
KAUFMANN, Johanna	33	Gettnau	57-1280
KAUFMANN, Johannes	23	Gudensberg	57-0754
KAUFMANN, Jos.	27	Grossachsen	62-1169
KAUFMANN, W.	64	Perleberg	62-0993
KAUFMANN, Wilhelm	16	Helsen	58-0576
KAUL, Franz	41	Gnadenfels	56-1044
KAULA, M.	25	Mniekowic	62-0993
KAUMANN, Henriette	20	Neuenschmiten	60-0521
KAUNHOFF, Fritz	27	Goslar	57-0606
Fridricke 23			
KAUTER, Anna	29	St. Gallen	60-0533
KAUTZ, W.	15	Reichelsheim	57-1192
Carolina 20			
KAWACK, Franz	32	Nischwalitz	55-0845
J.U. 25, Petroline by			
KAWI, Ferdinand	21	Hachen	56-0632
KAYSER, Adam	23	Klein Auheim	61-0779
KAYSER, Catharina	18	Hierbach	61-0779
KAYSER, Dorothea	19	Lerde	57-1407
KAYSER, Friedrich	34	Erfurt	55-1082
Louise 24			
KAYSER, Friedrich	27	Schwarzennach	57-1122
KAYSER, Gottl.	20	Kieselbach	60-0334
KAYSER, Hr.(m)	18	Gehrde	62-0467
KAYSER, J.W.	13	Torgau	62-0993
KAYSER, Rebecca	18	Niederhof	58-0563
KAYSER, Theodor	40	Kraehlingen	59-0477
KAZDA, Therese	25	Boehmen	61-0897
KEBEL, Johann	33	Coburg	57-1122
KEBERLE, Jos.	30	Bremen	59-0214
KECKEISER, Heinr.	34	Duggingen/Sil	60-0622
KECKNAGEL, A.	19	Cassel	55-0932
KEERE, A.E.	41	Washington	62-1042
KEFFEL, Gottfr.	33	Dingelstedt	56-0629
Sophia 33, Sophia 7, Christine 9m			
KEGEL, Louise	16	New York	60-0334
KEHL, Casp.Flor.	22	Poppenlauer	57-0422
KEHLENBECK, Heinr.	17	Insche	60-1161
KEHR, Barbara	17	Landigshoff	57-1026
KEHR, Carl Aug.	32	Zeitz	62-0836
KEHR, Heinrich	48	Hachborn	55-0630
Elisabetha 47, Philipp 23, Heinrich 16			
Sebastian 8, Elisabetha 18, Catharina 14			
Elisabetha 5			
KEHRS, Valentin	56	Wilshausen	60-0785
KEIBBAL, Susanna	25	Schwarzenbach	61-0930
KEIBSAM, Amadeus	28	Spal	56-0279
Elisabetha 43			
KEICH, August	24	Carlshafen	61-0520
KEIDEL, Margareth	9	Gemuend	59-0214
KEIL, Bertha Emily	19	Rattay	58-0815
KEIL, Catharina	24	Ettinghausen	62-0712
KEIL, Georg	25	Giessen	57-0961
KEIL, Heinrich Wm.	21	Ruedinghausen	58-0925
KEIL, J.G.(m)	26	Ellenbach	61-0482
KEIL, Johanna	22	Rubrechtsreit	57-1280
KEILBAL, Heinrich	40	Schwarzenbach	61-0930
Catharina 30, Georg 14, Henriette 19			
Catherina 2			
KEILHOFER, Felix	42	Lueftenegg/Bv	62-0608
KEILIG, Wilh.	73	Wien	59-0951
KEILING, Conrad	22	Stralenfels	56-0632
KEIMEL, Rich	11	Berlin	56-1216
KEINE, Doris	24	Bremen	60-0334
KEINER, Fr.(m)	24	Meiningen	56-0723
KEINER, Ludwig	41	Pittsburg	59-0214
Henriette 41			
KEIP, Matthias	30	Washington	61-0482
KEIP, Valent.	22	Wallenrod	55-0413
KEISCHEN, Cathar.	65	Burgsteinfort	56-0512
KEISER, Caroline	19	Mortorf	60-1032
KEISSER, Johannes	22	Sepa	56-0413
KEITEL, C.A.(m)	19	Berge	62-0879
KEITEL, Heinrich	23	Altenburg/Hes	62-0608
Catharine 20			
KEITEL, K.(m)	35	Rockwell	61-0897
Mary 42			
KEITH, John	18	Baechlingen	57-0422
KEITZ, Joh.	45	Fulda	57-1113
KEITZER, Marie	17	Uttenhausen	62-0342
KELLER, Andr.	40	Masbach	61-0482
Christiane 41, Barthold 12, Christine 9			
Cath. 7, Anton 4, Christiane 6m			
KELLER, Anna Mary	19	Bavaria	60-0411
KELLER, Anton	24	Emmingen/Egg	57-0080
KELLER, Antonia	44	New York	59-1036
Augustine 11			
KELLER, Augusta	17	Altenburg	60-0411
KELLER, Augusta	17	Rohden	60-0521
Carl 18, Wilhelm 14			
KELLER, Barbara	46	Burgpreppach	60-0533
KELLER, Catharine	26	Hemsbach/Bad.	60-0429
KELLER, Elisabeth	28	Unterhollau	62-1112
KELLER, Friedr.Aug	29	Heitersbach	57-0704
Chrstne.Ern. 26, Fr'ke.Carol. 5			
Carol.Amalie 3			
KELLER, Georg	33	Wetzlar	59-0477
KELLER, Gottfr.	20	Denkendorf	59-0990
KELLER, J.H.	32	New Orleans	62-0836
Christine 36, Caroline 15, Julia 9			
Emilie 6, Mathilde 3, Albert 1			
KELLER, Joseph	64	Waldernbusch	58-0925
KELLER, Martin	24	Hammelberg	62-0401
KELLER, Michael	26	Ueberlingen	61-0779
KELLER, Paul L.	31	St.Louis	62-0836
KELLER, Wildem.	22	Neuenhaus	57-0961
KELLERMANN, Friedr	29	Lintorf	56-0951
Adelheid 27			
KELLERMANN, Heinr.	16	Lohne	58-0306
KELLERMANN, J.Aug.	40	Nordhausen	55-0413
KELLERMANN, Marie	19	Meiningen	62-0758
KELLINGHAUSEN, Aug	18	Iburg	59-1036
KELLMER, Jacob	28	Altendorf	57-0754
KELLNER, Caroline	42	Philadelphia	58-0815
KELLNER, Elis.	59	Cassel	62-0836
KELLNER, Friedr.	54	Elderich	56-0629
Henriette 48, Wilhelmine 24, Friedrike 18			
August 9			
KELLNER, Fritz	28	Hedemuenden	62-0879
KELLNER, Joh.	24	Velmeden	60-1053
KELLNER, Joseph	34	Wolfenbuettel	60-0334
KELLNER, Sophia	22	Hann.Muenden	58-0399
KELLY, Mary	20	Baltimore	62-1042
KELLY, Miss	26	Southampton	59-0477
KELTEI, Andrea	77	New York	59-1036
KELTERBORN, Eugen	34	Stettin	61-0930
KEMMER, Dorothea	27	Neuenbrunn	59-0384
KEMMERN, Caroline	16	Alsfeld	59-0412
KEMNITZ, C.G.	24	Eisenberg	62-0836
Henriette 26, (baby) 1m, Louise 49			
Bertha 11			
KEMNITZ, F.A.(m)	30	Schoeneberg	57-0555
M.E.(f) 30, C.F.(m) 8, W.(m) 6, F.(m) 1			
KEMPEN, Heinr.	50	Cincinnatti	58-0815
KEMPER, Ad.	30	New York	62-0730
KEMPER, Elise	20	Garrel	60-0533
KEMPER, Ernst	32	Gehlenbeck	62-0100
KEMPER, Wilhelm	27	Duesseldorf	62-1112
KEMPERMANN, Wilh.	33	Hadamer	60-0334
KEMPF, C.W.	18	Hesse-Cassel	55-1082
KEMPF, Conrad	21	Hungen	57-1122
KEMPF, Georg	19	Hausen	60-0533
Marie 14			
KEMPF, Huber	23	Walheim	56-1117
KEMPF, Joh.Niclaus	17	Grub	55-0630
KENK, Leonhard	22	Ziegelbrunn	59-0951
KENKAM, Marie	14	Trendelburg	56-0723
KENNER, Georg L.	30	Esslingen/Wrt	60-0622
KENNING, Heinrich	17	Alfhausen	56-1117
KENTER, August	26	Herfurt/Pr.	60-0622
KEP, Friedrich	15	Koenigsberg	60-0334
KEPPERMANN, Janett	25	Niederamstadt	56-0847

NAME	AGE	RESIDENCE	YR-LIST
KERLE, G. M.	29	Salzburg	55-0845
Christian 21			
KERLING, Lorenz	21	Philadelphia	59-0214
KERN, Alexander	19	Eppingen	60-1196
KERN, Barbara	27	Hauendorf	56-1117
KERN, Friederike	23	Eisenach	62-0758
KERN, Jacob	58	Prachatetz	57-1026
Catharina 57			
KERN, Joh.Jacob	24	Basel	50-1017
KERN, Marg.	28	Wolfenbuettel	61-0804
KERN, Pulcherika	34	Neusatz	61-0930
Stephan 13, Maria 4			
KERN, Reinhard	63	Nordeck	60-1161
KERNER, Michael	25		57-1026
KERNKAMP, Anna	20	Hoya	60-0334
KERS, Sebastian	17	Kalzenheim	57-1113
KERSCHNER, Marie	17	Coburg	62-0712
KERSTE, Christian	23	Spangenberg	60-1032
Catharina 52, Christine 19			
KERSTEN, Heinrich	17	Machtlos	61-0520
Anna Martha 20			
KERSTING, H.J.(m)	24	Wehlheiden	62-0401
KERSTING, J. Heinr	26	Hombressen	56-0629
KERTGIR, F.W.		New York	59-1036
KERTWIG, Jos.	37	New York	60-0785
KERZELE, Jos.	32	St.Peter	62-0166
KESEL, Geo.	28	Hitzbach	61-0716
KESSE, Herm.	22	Alfhausen	56-1117
KESSEL, Georg	27	Taubenbach	56-0819
KESSEL, Wenzel	36	Nebellau	57-1113
Maria 26, Wenzel 10, Joseph 7, Martin 11m			
KESSEL, William	35	Konigsberg	60-0411
KESSEMEIER, Luisa	19	Hiddessen	57-0422
KESSENS, Herm.	28	Cincinati	59-0214
KESSINGER, Leo	18	Gottmadingen	61-0779
KESSLER, Anna Elis	20	Vohra	56-0723
KESSLER, Anton	37	Weimar	61-0682
Bertha 34, Hedwig 9m			
KESSLER, Augusta	25	Nienburg	55-1082
KESSLER, Carl	19	Oggesheim	60-1141
KESSLER, Eliza	13	Oggesheim	60-1141
KESSLER, Georg Nie	48	Kraehwinkel	59-0613
KESSLER, Jacob	23	Pyrmont	57-1122
KESSLER, Joh.	36	Oberlaichbach	62-1042
KESSLER, Justus	21	Roeddenau	57-0754
KESSLER, Margr.	20	Hochwedel	59-0384
KESSLER, Marie	16	Ulfeld	62-0938
KESSLER, Michael	22	Russdorf/Darm	62-0342
KESSLER, Peter	49	Nassau	55-0628
Louise 45, Wilhelmine 18, Theodor 15			
Eduard 13, Helene 11, Carl 7			
KESSLING, August	26	Limbergen	58-0604
KESSPOHL, Heinr.	19	Dissen	59-1036
KESTEL, Georg	9	Suhl	55-0630
KESTING, Ph.	46	Leiderode	62-0938
KESTLER, Heinrich	15	Hlalefeld	57-1416
KESTLER, Marie	16	Ulfeld	62-0938
KESTNER, Franz	22	Allerstadt	57-0447
KESTNER, Heinr.	29	Waltershausen	55-1238
Louise 24			
KETTELBERGER, Xav.	18	Riedlingen	56-0819
KETTELER, Engelb.	24	Munster	57-1416
KETTEMANN, Eva M.	25	Oberspeldach	57-0606
Catharine 17			
KETTLER, Caroline	33	Seesen	57-1148
KETTLER, Heinrich	27	Oldendorf/Han	55-1238
Carolina 34, Dorothea 5, Carolina 3			
Diederich 6m			
KETTNER, Christ.	31	Haransberg	60-0521
Barbara 9			
KEUN, C. Friedrich	18	Quackenbrueck	60-0533
KEUPP, Joseph	33	Guentersleben	56-0632
KEUTE, Henry	22	Frankenau	56-0692
KEUTHAN, Fr. Hch.	29	Jacobidrebber	60-0622
KEYSER, Heinr.Chr.	24	Ganste/Gotha	56-0819
KICK, Anna	25	Leuchtenberg	60-0429
Margaretha 16			
KIEF, Gustav	21	Remscheid	59-0951

NAME	AGE	RESIDENCE	YR-LIST
KIEFER, Ernestine	24	Blankenloch	62-1112
Benjamin 16			
KIEFER, Georg	29	Louisville	61-0897
KIEFER, J.(m)	12	Blankenloch	62-0730
KIEFER, Johann	29	Nuernberg	58-0576
KIEFER, Louis	25	Wittelsburg	60-0334
KIEHL, Ernest	37		57-1148
KIEHL, Joh.Heinr.	50	Bremen	59-0412
KIEHL, Ludwig	32	Darmstadt	59-0412
KIEHNE, Emil	25	Wilsdruff	58-0563
KIELBERGER, Adalb.	42	Nebylan	61-0779
Barbara 38, Barbara 17, Wenzel 12			
Therese 15, Adalbert 7, Martin 5			
Joseph by			
KIEMER, Therese	31	Baiern	57-1280
KIENE, Georg	58	Einbeck	55-0630
Georg 16, Fritz 11			
KIENE, Louise	18	Estorf	62-1042
KIENLE, Joh.Mich.	21	Magstadt	59-0613
KIEP, G.	45	Altenbruch	56-0413
Anna 22			
KIEPKER, Lisette	24	Westerkappel	60-1032
KIESEL, Christian	23	Cincinati	59-0214
KIESEL, Christine	25	Neu Schonewld	57-0704
KIESEL, Joh.Mich.	22	Verbau/Bav.	62-0342
KIESEL, Wilhelm	23	Philadelphia	56-1216
Maria 19, Carl 20			
KIESER, Carl	15	Muehlhausen	56-0847
KIESER, Christian	22	Menterode	56-1044
KIESER, Friedrich	15	Gr.Ingersheim	57-0924
KIESEWALTER, Ehren	28	Harmsdorf	62-0983
KIESLING, Elisab.	17	Verbau/Bav.	62-0342
KIESLING, Joh. A.	36	Quellenreuth	60-1053
KIESLING, Rosine	28	Grafenrath	56-0819
KIESS, Maria	20	Coburg/Sax	55-0628
KIESSLING, Carl	35	Reichenbach	57-1026
Chr. Frd'ke. 59, Geo. Friedr. 59			
KIEVIT, Johann	47	Aurich	61-0520
Foike 48, Richste 18, Jacob 13			
KIEWITSCH, August	56	Liebstadt	56-0279
KIHN, Valentin	36	Cincinati	59-0214
Anna Maria 29, Peter 5, Alexander 3			
KIJZA, Aloya	38	Poderpitz	55-0845
Franziska 37, Franz 4			
KILIAN, H.(m)	30	Ndr.Muellrich	62-0879
KILIAN, Johann	48	Washington	62-0836
KILIAN, Josephine	20	Bremen	56-1117
KILIAN, Mart.	36	Liederbach	61-0669
KILLINGER, J.G.(m)	27	Muenchingen	61-1132
KILLLAUS, Rud.	30	Sommerfeld	55-0413
KILMER, Anna	26	Oberhone	61-0478
KILMER, Mary	21	Quentel	60-0411
KILO, Ph. H.	34	Loehnberg	55-0413
Louise 24			
KIMPEL, Elisabeth	23	Keblos	62-0879
KIMPEL, Marie	17	Grebenau	56-1117
KIND, Adam	18	Grossenmoor	56-1117
KIND, George	35	Altona	61-0669
Wilhelmine 25			
KINDEL, Andreas	17	Falkenau	56-0847
KINDERMANN, R.(m)	33	Zeitz	62-0836
KINDERMANN, Ther.	33	Zeitz	62-1112
August 4			
KINDERVATER, Carl	20	Bleicherode	59-1036
KINDL, Josepha	30	Wien	56-0629
Joseph 9, Carl 3			
KINDLER, Fr.J.	38	Schreiberhaus	62-0993
H. 41, C.A. 9			
KINDT, Joseph	23	Witschau	60-0521
KING, Robert	24	Dresten	59-0412
KINTZLE, Maria	36	Alt-Simonswal	60-0398
Georg 15, Pauline 13, Victoria 9			
Anastasia 5			
KINZLE, Louise	21	Leonberg	62-1169
KIPFER, Friedrich	29	Bern	56-1044
KIPP, Johannes	29	Obervorschutz	57-0754
KIPP, Luis	15	Carlsruhe	57-1113
KIPP, William	40	France	62-1042

NAME	AGE	RESIDENCE	YR-LIST
KIRBACH, Carl Fr.	31	Bittdorf/Sax.	60-0622
KIRCH, Conrad	26	Grottheim	58-0399
KIRCHBERGER, Josef	36	Lengendorf/Bv	61-0770
KIRCHEN, Magdalena	23	Bivir	62-0100
KIRCHER, Johann	24	Seusswark	61-0482
KIRCHGEPNER, Ludw.	15	Damm	60-0785
KIRCHGESSNER, Jos.	24	Neusass/Baden	60-0371
KIRCHGESSNER, Plne	26	Hettingen	60-0429
KIRCHHAIN, Conrad	32	Langenstein	59-1036
Georg 14			
KIRCHHOF, Bernhard	20	Hastedt	57-1192
KIRCHHOF, Charles		Neuenbrunslar	59-0214
KIRCHHOFF, Aug.	19	Prussia	59-0951
KIRCHHOFF, Carl	32	Muenchberg	59-0048
KIRCHHOFF, Conrad	24	Wittgenstein	57-1407
KIRCHHOFF, Diedr.	19	Hemir	57-1026
Augusta 23, Emma 21			
KIRCHHOFF, Eleonor	25	Trille	61-0897
KIRCHHOFF, Joh.	62	Preussen	59-0951
Wilhelmine 62			
KIRCHHOFF, Wilhelm	28	Luets	57-0447
KIRCHNER, Elisabet	22	Alsfeld	59-0412
KIRCHNER, Elise	20	Meiningen	55-0634
KIRCHNER, Joh.	26	Pleningen	60-1053
KIRCHNER, Johann	31	Meiningen	55-0634
KIRCHNER, Lothar	18	Liebenstein	58-0881
KIRCHNER, Marie	20	Ziegelleumann	56-0723
KIRCHPERSLEY, Jos.	23	Daubleb	59-0951
KIRKELBACH, Heinr.	20	Stockheim	55-0812
KIRN, Jos.	41	France	62-1042
KIRSCH, Franz	32	Bonnville	59-0384
KIRSCH, Johannes	40	Hermannsfeld	56-0413
Ernst 3			
KIRSCH, Michael	32	Ellweiler	59-0384
Philippine 28, Elisabeth 24, Catharine 20			
Peter 18, Carl 20			
KIRSCHBAUM, Peter	28	Hessen	60-1161
KIRSCHT, G. C. (m)	20	Hohenfelden/W	55-0538
KISBERT, Wilhelm	26	Fischbach	62-0001
Eugenia 17			
KISSEL, Heinrich	33	Wiesbaden	57-1026
KISSEL, Joh.	33	Pohlgoens	55-0413
KISSLING, Jacob	22	Plauen	56-0819
Peter 14			
KISSNER, Joh.	39	Baltimore	60-0785
KISTEMACHER, Waldm	22	Sprottau	57-1113
KISTER, Martha	20	Eisenach	62-0467
KITTEL, Gustav	21	Jena	60-0334
KITTEL, Wilhelmine	24	Polichno	60-0533
KITTELMANN, Sophia	55	Braunschweig	55-1048
KITZ, Catharina	26	Fulda	57-1026
KIVEISER, Gottlieb	35	Posen	58-0399
Juliane 34, Adam 3, Gottlieb 9m			
KLAAS, Aug.	15	Lippe-Detmold	57-0447
Wilhelmine 26			
KLAAS, Wilhelm	30	Lippe-Detmold	57-0447
Wilhelmine 32, Wilhelm 9m			
KLAESPER, Augusta	28	Elberfeld	55-0634
Louise 24			
KLAG, Marg.	26	Bolanden	62-0401
Cath. 15			
KLAGEN, Johann	58	Bluack	56-0512
Josepha 54, Josepha 26			
KLAGER, Bd.H.	51	Hilter	62-0467
KLAGES, F.	50	Dorste	62-0993
J. 43, K. 19, Frd. 16, F. 12			
KLAHOLD, Anton	36	Altenbecken	58-0881
KLAMEYER, Hern.	25	Reher	60-0521
KLAMM, Johannes	25	Rheingoennhm.	62-1169
Margaretha 23			
KLAMMER, Georrg	50	Bavaria	60-1161
Elisab. 47, Wilhelm 18, Gottfried 16			
KLANDER, Joh.	19	Fressdorf	59-0535
KLANKE, Ludw.	23	Luebbecke	60-0398
KLAPP, Johannes	22	Ndr.Ofleiden	62-0712
KLAPPER, Carl	30	Mensfelden	61-0482
Wm. 9			
KLARNSMAYER, Phil.	32	Detmold	57-0365

NAME	AGE	RESIDENCE	YR-LIST
KLASING, Carl	15	Frille	57-1067
Augusta 25			
KLASSERT, Eduard	20	Gr.Klotzenbur	60-0398
KLASSERT, Eduard	20	Gr.Klotzenbur	60-0398
Anton 18			
KLATT, Carl	33	Griebnitz	58-0576
Friedricke 33, Heinrich 7, Therese 5			
Franz 2			
KLATT, Wilhelm	25	Alt Paleschke	61-0779
KLATTHAAR, J.Heinr	17	Oberholzhsn.	60-0533
KLAUBER, Anna	19	Tueschau	60-0521
KLAUENBURG, Alwine	37	Baltimore	59-0951
Albert 8			
KLAUERK, Fr.	33	Spadowitz	57-0961
Mary 37, Joseph 12, Charles 9, Wenzel 7			
Anton 11m			
KLAUSER, Barbara	20	Hechingen	57-1192
KLAUSSNER, Ursula	11	Guttenberg	57-0924
KLAWON, C.(m)	27	Dreidorf	62-0836
Ed.(m) 22			
KLEBART, Carl Herm	33	Reichenbach	57-1026
KLEBART, Erdmann	18	Reichenbach	57-1026
KLEEBERG, Meier	17	Borgentreich	60-0533
KLEEMANN, Joh.Geo.	39	Neuses	56-0632
Louise 24			
KLEFFMAN, Charlt.L	21	Luebbecke	57-0754
KLEIER, Catharine	22	Halessitz	57-1067
KLEIHANS, Wm.	21	Rondorf	57-1416
KLEIM, Georg	18	Ratzewinden	57-0447
Wolfgang 24			
KLEIM, Melchior	34	Obersinn	61-0520
KLEIMEYER, Hern.	25	Reher	60-0521
KLEIN, Adolph	26	Hungary	60-1161
KLEIN, Andreas	18	Capel	59-1036
KLEIN, Anton	47	Arnsberg	62-0879
KLEIN, Antonia	26	Netschetin	59-1036
KLEIN, Barbara	24	Altershausen	59-0535
KLEIN, Caroline	21	Hornbach	62-0467
KLEIN, Catharina	17	Oese	57-0850
KLEIN, Catharine	35	Lobenfeld	59-0372
Charlotte 10			
KLEIN, Christoph	27	Guxhagen	57-0754
KLEIN, Friedr. M.	19	Frohnsdorf	59-1036
KLEIN, Henry	21	Lengsfeld	60-0411
KLEIN, Jac.	15	Hagenbach	57-1148
KLEIN, Joh.	27	Lutterscheid	56-1216
KLEIN, Joh.Michael	23	Thalmassing	56-0819
KLEIN, Lisette	19	Bicken	62-0467
KLEIN, Ludwig	25	Bremen	61-0770
KLEIN, Maria	19	Amoneberg	56-0413
KLEIN, Marie	17	Selters	58-0576
KLEIN, Mathias	34	Neuenkirchen	60-0521
KLEIN, Sabine	25	Stockheim	56-0629
KLEIN, Sophie	22	Hoylen	59-0951
(dau.) 2m			
KLEIN, Theodor	31	Philadelphia	61-0897
Wilhelmine 49			
KLEINE, Sophie	26	Ostenholz	57-0847
Heinrich 6			
KLEINEKORTH, Conr.	58	Neuenkirchen	59-1036
Heinrich 8			
KLEINER, Aug.Fr'dr		Heitersbach	57-0704
KLEINER, Fanny	23	Scheinfeld	62-0467
KLEINFELDER, Barb.	28	Cassel/Bav.	62-0608
KLEINFELDER, Mich.	28	Cincinnati	57-1192
Elisa 26			
KLEINHANS, J.	45	Heimenkirch	56-0951
KLEINHANZ, Caspar	19	Weichersbach	60-0429
KLEINJOHANN, Veron	19	Prussia	60-1161
Elis. 15			
KLEINLEIN, Peter	25	Bayern	61-0682
KLEINSCHAEFER, Con	60	Langenholz	59-0535
Catharine 50, Amalie 20			
KLEINSCHAFER, Soph	23	Holzhausen	56-1117
KLEINSCHMIDT, Alb.	22	Neudorf	58-0881
KLEINSCHMIDT, Carl	23	Washington	62-1169
KLEINSCHMIDT, Chlt	22	Mensfelden	59-0384
KLEINSCHMIDT, Edu.	24	Fuerstenberg	56-0819

NAME	AGE	RESIDENCE	YR-LIST
KLEINSCHMIDT, H.	19	Minden	62-0836
KLEINSCHMIDT, Lou.	21	New York	59-0613
Lisette 21			
KLEINSCHMIDT, Ulr.	34	Aurich	60-1141
KLEINSCHMIDT, Wilh	34	Wismar	57-1026
KLEINSORGE, Gottl.	24	Witzenhausen	57-0436
KLEINSTAEUBER, C.	23	Gotha	57-0850
KLEISS, Johanna	24	Lech	58-0563
KLEMM, F.T.(m)	35	Vreden	60-0521
KLEMMER, David	38	Berlin	56-0629
KLENCK, Rosina	14	Wuertemberg	57-0555
KLENEN, Cath.	50	New York	59-0951
Marth. 14, Henry 50			
KLENK, Georg	33	Rothenburg/Bv	55-0628
Charlotte 21			
KLENKE, Wilhelm	27	Detmold	56-1044
Louise 29			
KLENZE, W.(m)	33	Landshut	62-0730
KLESS, Maria Cath.	17	Nuernberg	58-0604
KLEY, Andreas	29	Weilar	57-0447
KLEYER, J.C.(m)	24	Vistrup	61-0482
KLICK, Paul	56	Sarbske	58-0881
KLICKE, Martin	50	Sarbske	58-0881
Caroline 42, Justine 18, Carl 16			
Franz 14, Gustav 12, Friedrich 10			
Johann 8, Caroline 4, Charlotte 2			
KLIE, August	59	Doerigsen	60-0533
Hanchen 53, Minchen 23, August 17			
Amalie 16, Georgine 10			
KLIMESCH, Joseph	31	Boehmen	61-0716
KLIMM, Luise	30	Backnang	57-1113
KLING, Henry	34	Haan	60-0411
Elise 34, Catharine 17, Elisabeth 8			
Julie 2			
KLINGBERG, Charles	32	Perfschaw	57-0654
KLINGE, Caspar	17	Wilhelmsfeld	59-1036
KLINGE, Ludwig	51	Triemen	56-1117
Carl 11, Anna 48, Elise 15, Sophie 9			
KLINGE, Maria	17	Linfort	57-0447
Wilhelmine 16			
KLINGELHOEFER, Joh	30	Niederwetter	57-0447
Catharina 33, Elisabeth 54			
KLINGELHOEFF, Jos.	16	Alefeld	59-0951
KLINGENBERG, Edw.	39	Bremen	62-0608
Friedricke 33, Susanne 15			
KLINGENSPOHR, L.	38	Otterode	59-0990
(m) 14, (f) 5, (f) 3			
KLINGER, Catharine	10	St.Louis	59-0951
KLINGSIECK, Anna	58	Ennigloh	60-0334
Johann 18			
KLINK, Christine	23	Cornweiler	60-0398
KLINKE, Gerhard H.	27	Lengerich	55-0634
KLINKE, Johannes	35	Harbach	56-0819
Elisabeth 14, Appolonia 12			
KLINKER, Henry	23	Eitzendorf	57-1148
KLINKER, John	27	New York	58-0604
KLINKERT, H.(m)	26	Leipzig	62-0467
KLINKWORT, Fr. (m)	21	Ottersberg	55-0413
KLINTWORTH, Caspar	24	Kl.Meckelsen	59-0990
Marie 22			
KLIPP, Otto	25	Colberg	56-0723
KLIPPERT, Johannes	26	Riebelsdorf	60-0429
KLOCKE, Clementine	35	Bensdorf	56-0632
Dorothee 22			
KLOCKE, Franz	26	Hampenhausen	61-0482
KLOCKPETER, (m)		Vegesack	61-0804
KLOEBER, Elisabeth	22	Steinau	60-0429
KLOEBER, Georg	29	Hohl	62-0730
KLOEFFLER, Friedr.	19	Melsungen	61-0478
KLOEPP, Johann	39	Niederurf	57-0754
Anna Eva 41, Johannes 12, Friedrich 4			
KLOERLE, Ann El.	30	Steinau	57-1113
KLOES, Joest	27	Monshausen/He	62-0342
KLOESS, Christ.	20	Herzenheim	62-0730
KLOETZER, Otto	22	Neuhaus	57-0754
KLOIDT, Joseph	18	Bergheim	59-0214
KLOPFER, Charles	21	Gleithagen	57-0961
Emily 23			

NAME	AGE	RESIDENCE	YR-LIST
KLOPFER, Fried.A.	24	Geithain	59-0477
KLOPP, Ernst	31	Solingen	60-1141
KLOPPENBURG, Cath.	19	Worpswede	59-0951
KLOPPENBURG, Dan'l	53	Binrod	55-0845
KLOPPENBURG, Fr.	35	Worbswede	61-0804
Meta 26, Anna 3, Heinr. 11m			
KLOPPMANN, Friedr.	20	Deissel	61-0779
Gottlieb 30, Amalie 25			
KLOR, Adam	33	Mussen	56-0512
Anna 34			
KLOS, Johannes	31	Nohfelden	56-1216
KLOSE, Marie	17	Breslau	56-0847
KLOSE, Paul	21	Breslau	62-1112
KLOSS, Heinr.	25	Harzfeld	56-0413
KLOSS, Michael	34	Butzing	57-0776
Magdalena 23			
KLOSS, Reinhard	14	Curhessen	58-0399
KLOSTER, Wm.	19	Meerane	61-0482
KLOSTERMANN, J.H.	40	Bremen	57-0080
KLOTZ, Christian	14	Marburg	57-0961
KLOTZ, G.(m)	18	Piestritz	60-1161
KLOTZBACH, Dora	17	Wufferode	58-0399
KLOTZSCHE, F.M.	22	Starbach	59-0990
KLUCK, Johann	42	Danzig	62-0758
Anna 38, Maria 10, Anna 8, Johann 5			
Franz 3, Leonhard by			
KLUCK, Leonard	32	Danzig	62-0758
Magdalena 28, Franz 9, Franziska 7			
Pauline 3, Anna 64, Jula 37			
KLUCKE, Helene	23	Lehe	62-0879
KLUEBENSPIES, Carl	22	Bavaria	61-0482
KLUEBER, Damina	35	Fulda	57-1192
KLUEBER, Georg	29	Neiswurz/Bav.	55-0628
KLUEBER, Joseph	36	San Francisco	59-0951
Marianne 24, Barbara 21, Therese 19			
Scholastika 22			
KLUEBERT, Cathrina	29	Breitenbach	61-0779
KLUEGEL, August	40	Meissen	55-0630
August 21, Sophie 38, Gustav 10			
Wilhelm 6			
KLUEHE, Peter	23	Ndr.Wellstadt	57-0422
KLUENDER, Carl Aug	39	Minden	57-0924
KLUENGLER, Eva	27	Bueckelberg	60-0334
KLUENKER, Augusta	18	Haehlen	60-1141
KLUEPPERT, (m)	30	New York	58-0881
August 7			
KLUG, Heinrich	15	Poplob	56-1260
Christian 28, Albertine 19			
KLUG, Marie	30	Philadelphia	62-0938
KLUGE, Johanna	30	Lilbenhausen	57-0447
KLUGHERZ, Rupert	19	Weissenfels	57-0704
KLUMKER, Ana Elis.	29	Lech	58-0563
KLUMP, Louis	39	Altentown	59-0477
Charlotte 9, Charles 8			
KLUMP, Louis	39	Allentown	59-0477
Charlotte 9, Charles 8			
KLUMP, Nicolaus	28	Meklar	56-1260
KLUMPER, Ferd.	56	Baltimore	62-0467
Bernhardine 57			
KLUSEMANN, Fr.(m)	26	Prussia	57-0555
KLUSSMANN, Eliza	18	Esrod	56-1011
KLUT, Wilhelm	40	Carlshoff	57-0776
Ludwig 33, Emilie 26, Emilie 10			
KLUTE, Heinr. Wm.	38	Westercappeln	57-0924
KLUVER, Gott.	29	Koenigsberg	60-0785
KNABE, Adolph	23	Berlin	56-1044
KNABE, Diedr.	22	Gehrde	60-0521
KNABE, Elise	30	Philadelphia	62-0836
Anna 9m			
KNABE, Godfrey	46	Gross Furra	56-1011
Maria 44, Hariot 16, Frederick 14			
Ernestine 9, Herman 2			
KNABESCHUH, A.Cath	50	Nentershausen	56-0819
KNACK, Sophie	22	Sorau	57-1416
KNACKSTEDT, Heinr.	39	Braunschweig	59-0613
William 13, Marie 8, Ida 4			
KNAECK, Louis	39	Pittsburg	60-0521
KNAPHE, J.H.F.(m)	59	Werder	60-0998

NAME	AGE	RESIDENCE	YR-LIST
Catharine M. 57			
KNAPP, Michael	46	Wuerttemberg	60-0411
Catharine 42, Michael 16, John 14			
Georg 12, Gottlob 5, Anna Mary 1			
Dorothea 6m			
KNAPPE, Wilhelm	21	Breslau	57-1407
KNAPPER, Christine	15	Enzweihingen	56-0512
KNAPPER, Georg	52	-iznafingen/W	55-0538
Marie 9			
KNAU, Jacob	41	Renschade	60-0521
KNAU, Maria	21	Muenchberg	55-0630
KNAUER, G.	39	Gestungshause	56-0512
Eva 44, Elise 15, Ludwig 10, Johanna 7			
Margaret 4			
KNAUF, J.H.	34	Weisselbach	56-0589
KNAUR, Heinr.	26	Kirchhusen	61-0047
KNAUS, Jacob	24	Kurnbach	57-1148
KNAUSS, H.	18	Heidenheim	59-0990
KNEBEL, Peter	34	Schwalenberg	62-1112
KNECHT, Th.	32	Mimmenhausen	59-0990
KNEDEISEN, Johann	24	Lugde	62-1112
KNEES, Caspar	32	Leina	60-1161
Marie 32			
KNEFF, Michael Jos	32	Bischofsheim	62-0608
Anna 24			
KNEIFEL, Johann	23	Liegenhals	55-0413
KNEISEL, Elisabeth	21	Bieden/Hessen	62-0608
Ludwig 19			
KNEIVKOFSKY, Prok.	36	Prag	55-0812
KNELL, Georg	24	Wolfsheim	56-1117
KNELL, Philipp	27	Wolfsheim	57-0422
Barb. 23, Charlotte 21			
KNEMEYER, Marie	30	Kloster Oesch	57-1407
Clemens 14, Marie 8			
KNETE, Th.W.(m)	19	Scharmbeck	61-0804
KNETSCH, Charlotte	27	Beilstein	57-1280
KNEWKOSSKY, Prokap	36	Prag	55-0812
KNICKENBERG, Fr'ka	24	Minden/Pr.	62-0608
KNICKMANN, Chr.	46	Bevesen	62-1042
KNIEF, Anna	28	Kirchweiher	59-0951
KNIEF, Georg	29	Apelern	56-0629
KNIEL, Michel	27	Schmitzdorf	55-0630
Ann 26, A.Maria 9m			
KNIEP, Christian	17	Boeken	61-0682
Margaretha 18			
KNIERIEM, Elisab.	26	Bimborn	59-0535
Johannes 9m			
KNIERIEM, Gustav	19	Bielefeld	57-0447
KNIESS, Marie	21	Buedingen	56-1117
KNIG, Julius	32	Braunschweig	55-0932
KNIPE, Bertha	26	Dresden	56-0629
KNIPPENBERG, F.H.	43	Rabber	56-0951
Justus 14			
KNIPPENBERG, Fr.	28	Cappeln	60-0998
KNIPPING, Marie	21	Dondorf	60-0785
KNIPPLER, Anton	26	Wernborn/Nass	60-0429
KNISPEL, H.	21	Schlitz	59-0214
KNISS, Lina	22	Budingen	61-0047
KNISS, Margarethe	26	Zeilitzheim	59-0613
KNIZICK, Barbara	37	Carlsbad	59-0951
KNOBELAU, Mathias	19	Wullings	60-1161
KNOBLACH, Barbara	65	Gebhardsreuth	60-0622
KNOBLACH, Joh.	24	Trebes/Bav.	60-0622
KNOBLAUCH, Barb.	35	Nack	59-0990
(f) 8, (m) 6, (f) 3			
KNOBLAUCH, Carl	25	Schlesien	62-0758
KNOBLOCH, Johannes	18	Steinau	60-0429
KNOBLOCH, Paul	22	Neudorf	62-0111
KNOBLOCH, Wilhelm	45	Marklesa	61-0930
Lisbeth 40, Alwine 13, Wilhelm 9, Carl 3			
KNOCHE, F.H.G.	33	Aigendorf	59-0535
KNOELCKE, Staats	27	Steinhuden	57-0606
KNOELKE, Caroline	15	Aplern/Curh.	60-0429
KNOELKE, Heinrich	20	Aplern	61-0520
KNOELKE, Staats	47	Steinhude	57-0578
KNOELLER, Louise	20	Schwan	60-0398
Jacob 18			
KNOENER, J.H.J.	16	Lehe	59-0477

NAME	AGE	RESIDENCE	YR-LIST
KNOEPFE, Andr.	19	Graitschen	55-0413
KNOEPFEL, Heinrich	17	Curhessen	60-0371
KNOETTCHE, Cath.	24	Kaltenborn	58-0563
KNOLL, Jac.	30	Duermentingen	61-0107
KNOLL, Johannes	43	Stamheim	57-1067
KNOLL, Sebastian	19	Obergeis	56-0819
KNOLL, Sebastian	38	Zaubach	61-0167
KNOOP, Augusta	17	Stadtoldendrf	62-1042
KNOOP, Gottfried	22	Bremen	57-0961
KNOOP, Heinrich	24	Hinterpommern	58-0399
KNOOS, H.	34	Markgroningen	59-0990
KNOPF, Carl	47	Anger	56-1044
Elisabeth 47, Dorothea 20			
KNOPF, F.M.	30	Oedenburg	59-0477
KNOPF, F.M.	30	Oedenburg	59-0477
KNOPP, Conr.	26	Eckartsborn	55-0932
KNORR, Amalie	14	Eisfeld	59-0951
Caroline 13			
KNORR, Carl	36	Oppeln	59-0047
KNORRER, Joh.	59	Louisville	60-1196
KNOSPE, Franz	52	Blockendorf	57-0654
KNOSTMANN, Marg.	28	New York	59-0951
Wilh. 6, Emilie 18			
KNOTH, Andreas	13	Hofaschenbach	61-0779
KNOTH, Elisabeth	23	Guetersdorf	57-0704
KNOTTE, Ida	22	Solingen	59-0412
KNUEBEL, J.	15	Wurfleth	59-1036
KNUECK, John	55	Louisendorf	57-0422
Catharina 55, Peter 26, Lembert 18			
John 8, Theodora 14			
KNUEPFER, Albine	13	Rothenitz	61-0804
KNUEPPELN, Henr'tt	28	Loedingsen/Ha	55-0628
Wilhelmine 14			
KNUFF, Armand	32	Millen	57-1148
KNURN, Philipp	25	Nienburg	55-1082
KNUSE, John	17	Achim	60-0334
KNUSEMUELLER, Fr'd	18	Citter	59-1036
KNUSTMANN, Julia	29	Fuerth	59-1036
KOBATZ, Mathilde	20	Detmold	57-1192
KOBBEN, Adelheid	16	Amt Hagen/Han	62-0608
KOBELTIZH, Jacob	28	Petersdorf	57-0436
KOBER, Elise	22	Bamberg/Bav.	60-0429
KOBER, Elise	19	Bamberg	61-0520
KOBLENGER, Carolne	25	Kieselbronn	62-0879
KOBOLD, Christiane	24	Itzhofen	61-0716
KOCH, (f)	54	Bremen	59-1036
KOCH, Adam	19	Rothenburg	60-0521
KOCH, Andrew	36	Sondershausen	57-0422
KOCH, Anna	27	New York	57-1148
Henny 3			
KOCH, Anna	18	Altershausen	59-0535
KOCH, Anton	35	Halle/Pruss.	55-1238
KOCH, August	25	Berlin	56-1044
Rosalie 25, Franz 8m			
KOCH, August	28	Quincy	59-0477
KOCH, Augustus	28	Beuthagen	57-0422
KOCH, Bernh.	46	New York	58-0604
KOCH, C.F.(m)	31	Reinsdorf	61-0482
KOCH, C.P.	43	Maryland	62-0836
KOCH, Carl	28	Eisleben/Pr.	62-0608
KOCH, Carl	51	Wilsnack	59-0990
(f) 41, (m) 10, (f) 8, (m) 2, (baby) by			
KOCH, Carl Wilhelm	22	Widdern	62-0879
KOCH, Catharine E.	19	Bramsche	59-1036
KOCH, Chris.(m)	18	Buchenau	56-0723
KOCH, Christian	23	Sachsenhausen	56-0819
KOCH, Christoph	27	Hochheim	57-0606
KOCH, David	28	Ortburg/Hess.	62-0608
KOCH, Dorothea	15	Thedinghausen	62-0730
KOCH, Elias	42	Salzungen	61-0478
KOCH, Elisabeth	24	Niederurf	57-0754
KOCH, Elisabeth	17	Niederweimar	62-0730
KOCH, Ernestine	25	Friedrichshde	62-0938
KOCH, F.J.	54	Lachen	62-0993
C. 26, M. 11, E. 8			
KOCH, Fr.(m)	33	Langelsheim	56-0723
KOCH, Fr.(m)	31	Eickeloh	57-0654
Gertrude 20			

NAME	AGE	RESIDENCE	YR-LIST
KOCH, Friedr.	23	Lundshausen/H	60-0622
KOCH, Friedrich	41	Luebke	57-1280
Louise 19			
KOCH, Georg Lorenz	38	Ferrenbach	60-1117
Josephine 38			
KOCH, Gottlieb	41	Sachsen	58-0399
C.R. 42, Friedr. 15, Eduard 13, Karl 11			
Louis 8, Ernestine 6, Franz 2, Bertha 6			
KOCH, Guenther	21	Jecha/Schwrzb	56-0819
KOCH, Heinr.	33	Leiderode	62-0938
Rosalie 38, Anna M. 59, Josephine 9			
Friederike 8, M. 6, Anna Marie 9m			
KOCH, Heinr.Rud.	22	Groehndenberg	57-0606
KOCH, Heinrich	19	Gandersheim	62-0342
KOCH, Henry	26	Schwanei	57-0422
KOCH, Herm.	44	Wadersloh	61-0897
Anna 30, Catharine 6, Elisabeth 5			
Angela 3, Heinr. 11m			
KOCH, Innocentia	21	Aachen	62-0111
KOCH, Jac.	27	Waldstetten	60-1196
KOCH, Jochim	21	Tueschau	60-0521
KOCH, Joh. E.	27	Erdmansdorf	57-0578
KOCH, Joh. Ernst	21	Herbsleben	55-1082
Joh. Gottf. 18			
KOCH, Joh. Heinr.	15	Thedinghausen	57-1150
Anna 20			
KOCH, Johann	29	Rudendorf	60-1053
Barbara 29, (baby) by			
KOCH, Johann	31	Schwarza	57-0847
Julius 8			
KOCH, Johann	20	Cronberg	57-1026
KOCH, Johann	55	Bracht	61-0482
Cath. 33			
KOCH, Johanna	25	Erdmannsdorf	57-0578
KOCH, Jos.	30	Weisenbonn	62-0938
Bernh. 28			
KOCH, Jost	19	Ahlsfeld	61-0478
KOCH, Lina	17	Achim	55-0634
KOCH, Louise	24	Philadelphia	61-0897
Emil 4			
KOCH, Louise	26	Wrescherode	62-0730
Willy 9			
KOCH, Margaretha	18	Wengershausen	62-0879
KOCH, Michael	27	Semmd/Hessen	60-0622
KOCH, Otto	16	Hildesheim	62-0111
KOCH, Paul	23	Wiernsdorf	57-1407
KOCH, Pauline	19	Lippersdorf	56-0589
KOCH, Peter Ign.	35	Elben	62-0730
Josepha 26			
KOCH, Rud.	24	Halle	59-1036
KOCH, Simon	45	Steinfichter	61-0520
KOCH, Susanne	23	Friedberg	56-1260
KOCH, Th.	46	Heidelberg	59-0990
(f) 46, (son) 8			
KOCH, Therese	21	Lachen	60-0411
Jacob 15			
KOCH, Wm.	18	Schluechtern	62-0730
KOCHE, Hermann	28	Grothe	62-0879
KOCHEL, Marie	23	Plauen	56-0411
KOCHEMUSS, Georg	24	Anger	56-1044
KOCHENDOERFER, Car	25	Derdingen	59-0412
KOCHENDORFER, Fr.	26	Wuerttemberg	61-0716
KOCHENTHALER, Jete	20	Ernstbach	61-0682
KOCHER, Christ.	24	Krefeld	60-1196
KOCHER, Philipp	30	Haram	56-0847
KOCHLER, Marie	21	Wassungen	62-0938
KOCHLOWISKY, Mich.	42	Reinersdorf	55-0812
Johanna 24, Susanna 14, Carl 12			
Johanna 5, Maria 11w			
KOCHNEN, Jos(died)	59	Winterich	61-1132
Marie 40			
KOCHT, Tenne	26	Lahr/Hannover	56-0692
KOCHZIG, Johann	22	Neuwerder	56-0632
KOCK, Anna K.	20	Wallersdorf	57-1113
KOCK, Christiane	26	Bramsche	57-1192
Johanne 24			
KOCK, Friedrich	28	Gelbra	60-0533
KOCK, Gustav	23	Prussia	57-0555
KOCK, Ham.	24	Lauterbach	60-0998
KOCK, Heinrich	19	Diepholz	59-0214
KOCK, Johannes	26	Dens	56-1204
KOCK, Jos.	9	Duesseldorf	62-0730
KOCOCINSKY, Anton	40	New York	62-0712
KODE, Anna	16	Flitzla	57-0776
KODIT, Wenzel	39	Kmonertz	55-0845
Josepha 40, Aloys 9, Agnesa 5			
KODYM, Joseph	42	Oberstupno/Bo	57-0924
Anna 32, Anna 12, Maria 10, Josepha 8			
KOEBERLEIN, Georg	26	Bischwind/Bav	60-0622
KOEBLITZ, Mich.	25	Thiergarten	61-0482
KOEBMANN, Tiebke	39	Weena	58-0885
KOECHERT, Pauline	24	Weimar	62-0758
KOECHIG, Georg	37	St.Louis	58-0925
Dorette 28			
KOEGEL, Mich.	27	Baiern	57-0606
Sophie 24			
KOEGELMEYER, Simon	43	Hausen	56-0632
KOEHL, Clara	21	Salzschlief	56-0629
KOEHL, Friedr.	21	Meisenheim	56-1216
KOEHLER, Adam	28	Kirchberg	57-0754
KOEHLER, Anna	23	Ottenau	60-0521
KOEHLER, August	30	Forenberg	56-0819
KOEHLER, C.J.	52	New York	62-1042
KOEHLER, Carl	19	Elmshorn	56-1117
KOEHLER, Christian	39	Kiselbach	58-0545
Joh.Dorothea 33, Johannes 10, Balthasar 8			
KOEHLER, Dorothea	43	Berlin	56-0629
KOEHLER, Elisab.	21	Maar/Curhess.	60-0622
KOEHLER, Friedrike	19	Wasungen	62-0401
KOEHLER, G.G.	43	Welsbach	56-0629
KOEHLER, Georg	22	Wenjes	55-0413
Louise 24			
KOEHLER, Georg	31	Kreuzburg	60-0429
KOEHLER, H. (m)	27	New Brock	56-0723
KOEHLER, Heinrich	29	Politz	55-0845
KOEHLER, Henry	34	Uder	57-0422
A.Mary 27			
KOEHLER, Henry	36	Wenzwig	58-0545
Mar.Elisab. 34, Conrad 6, Hinrich 3			
Georg 9m			
KOEHLER, J.F.(m)	12	Lenkershausen	62-0836
KOEHLER, Johann	17	Allendorf	56-0589
KOEHLER, Johann	78	Irmerode	57-0776
KOEHLER, Johann	18	Irmerode	57-0776
KOEHLER, Lorenz	31	Versbach	60-0521
Margtha. 26, Elisabeth 5			
KOEHLER, Louis	20	Steinhude	60-1053
KOEHLER, Ludwig	39	Bomte	59-0412
KOEHLER, Marg.	20	Radmuehl	59-0990
KOEHLER, Margareth	21	Steinbach/Bav	55-0628
KOEHLER, Maria	23	Kirchberg	57-0754
KOEHLER, Marie C.	18	Huettengesaes	62-0730
KOEHLER, Melcher	36	Diedorf	57-1280
Anna 35, Nicolaus 12, Johannes 9, Ernst 7			
Georg 5, Elisabeth 2			
KOEHLERN, J.E.	34	Koenigshain	62-0836
KOEHLING, Louise	27	New York	62-0938
KOEHLMES, H.(m)	38	Eyssel	61-0804
Anna 24			
KOEHN, Doris	55	Kakstedt	60-0785
Catharine 14, Heinrich 10			
KOEHNE, Ad.	36	Salzburg	61-0167
KOEHNE, F.	21	Hannover	57-1150
KOEHNE, Friedrich	54	Oberlethe	57-1113
Cathar.Soph. 45, Diedrich 23			
Catharina 19, Sophie 13, Johann 9			
Marie 5			
KOEHNE, Helene	33	Osnabrueck	56-0413
KOEHNE, Joh.	48	Wucharir	62-0401
Caroline 31, Marie 16, Louise 14			
Johanna 13, Helena 9, Augusta 7, Ernst 4			
August 10m			
KOEHNEN, Fritz	19	Bremerhaven	56-0847
KOEHNEN, Henry	26	Louisendorf	57-0422
KOEHNLEIN, Wlh'mne	20	Buckstadt	60-0334
KOEHRING, B.	31	Blomberg	56-0512

NAME	AGE	RESIDENCE	YR-LIST
Elise 25			
KOEHRING, Chr. (m)	46	Gr. Lafferde	57-1067
KOEHRING, Mathias	19	Koblenz/Main	56-0632
KOELEMANN, Tiebke	39	Weena	58-0885
KOELER, Robert	19	Pyrmont	61-0482
KOELKBECK, Betty	24	Vegesack	59-1036
KOELLE, Ernst	18	Widderstadt	56-0951
D. 30			
KOELLE, Friedrich	56	Winzlar	56-1011
Dorothy 58, Dorothy 22, Maria 20			
KOELLING, Elisab.	30	Mindneheide	56-0411
Carl Heinr. 13, Friedr.Wilh. 7			
Carl Heinr. 5, Louise Maria 50			
KOELLING, Heinr.	24	New York	59-0048
KOELLING, Heinrich	24	Eichhorst	56-0411
KOELLNER, Charlott	58	Han. Muenden	60-1032
KOELLNER, Johannes	57	Rossdorf	56-0723
Anna 34			
KOENCK, Rud.	36	New York	62-1169
KOENECKE, Wilhelm	25	Hameln	62-0879
KOENEMANN, A.	29	Sacramento	56-1216
Cath. 22			
KOENEMANN, Victor	49	Bogonsdsz	57-1192
Helene 49, Sophie 17, Helena 15, Olga 13			
KOENIG, Anna	24	Baiern	57-0606
KOENIG, Anna	20	Merseburg	61-0482
KOENIG, Anna	20	Reichenberg	59-0951
KOENIG, Antonia	35	Rappach	61-0482
KOENIG, Arm.H.	24	Westercappeln	57-1192
KOENIG, Beta	20	Jueringen	56-1260
KOENIG, Carl	21	Unterfarnstdt	60-0334
KOENIG, Carl	26	Zempelburg	56-1260
KOENIG, Carl	16	Blankenburg	59-0372
Therese 8			
KOENIG, Carl	25	Langwedel	62-0712
August 17			
KOENIG, Catharine	20	Henner	62-0879
KOENIG, Celestin	22	Kammerzell	62-0712
KOENIG, Fr.	37	Cincinnati	62-0938
KOENIG, Friedrich	32	Luebbecke	56-1011
KOENIG, Georg	55	Schwarzenreut	55-0812
Therese 20			
KOENIG, H.	23	Bossel	59-0477
KOENIG, Joh.	32	Stockau/Bav.	62-0608
Marie 25, Lorenz 10m, Marie 19, Rosina 22			
KOENIG, Joseph	33	Buffalo	62-0232
KOENIG, Louise	17	Obermoerte	62-1042
KOENIG, Ludwig	23	Neustadt	55-0630
Emma 19			
KOENIG, Maria	42	Blankenburg	59-0372
KOENIG, Mathilda	24	Volkmarsen/He	62-0608
KOENIG, Rudolph	25	Brilow	61-0482
KOENIG, Theodor	26	Aslan	58-0925
KOENIGS, Christine	22	Quetzen	57-1067
KOENIGSMARK, Cath.	28	Cigu	61-0779
KOENIGSREICH, Mar.	20	Stubach	62-0938
KOENKER, Carolne.M	24	Osnabrueck	56-0411
KOEPER, Anna	14	Fehr	56-0819
KOEPER, Joh.	26	Bremen	61-1132
KOEPFLE, Mich.	40	Lechthal	57-0578
KOEPFLER, Johann	24	Remetschwyl	58-0881
KOEPKE, T.(m)	57	Prussia	57-0555
Maria 27			
KOEPPE, Adolph	23	Coelln	59-0048
KOEPPNER, Gottfr.	59	Goslar	59-1036
Augusta 59, Herrm. 27			
KOERBER, G.(m)	48	Goerlitz	62-0111
KOERBER, Georg	31	Zugenreite	57-1280
KOERBER, H.	31	Quackenbrueck	57-1192
KOERING, Wilhelm	23	Blomberg/Prus	57-0847
Carl 21			
KOERLING, Peter	32	Vaterode	57-1067
KOERNEMANN, Friedr	22	Osterode	57-0447
Johanna 52, Caroline 13			
KOERNER, Adam	27	Meiningen	55-0634
Elisab. 21			
KOERNER, Bernhard	19	Paderborn	56-0819
KOERNER, Edw.	22	Muenster	55-0413
KOERNER, H.(m)	21	Saxony	57-0555
KOERNER, Peter	36	Rodach	62-0166
KOERNIG, Carl	26	Zempelburg	56-1260
KOERPER, Anna	20	Resulow	62-0836
KOESELITZ, Philip	40	Dessau	62-0342
KOESTER, Ferd.	35	Essen	59-1036
KOESTER, H.	33	San Francisco	62-1042
Minna 29			
KOESTER, Heinrich	30	Alsfeld	57-0447
Elisabeth 40			
KOESTER, Herm.	28	Lafayette	62-1112
KOESTER, Justine	24	Dingolfing	60-0521
KOESTER, Susanne	39	New York	62-1042
KOETHE, Paul	42	Cassel	55-0812
Sophie 43			
KOETHER, Julius F.	25	Schlettfingen	57-1113
KOETZEL, August	40	Koenigsberg	61-0897
KOETZELEIN, Bened.	24	Oberehrenbach	56-0632
KOGELSBERGER, Seb.	29	Deining	57-1026
KOHL, Carl	20	Han. Muenden	60-1032
KOHL, Edward		Wippen	57-1192
KOHL, Georg	52	Menderferbach	62-0730
Maria 57, Johann B. 15, Marg. 9, Georg 7 (son) 9m			
KOHL, Johannes	33	Siegel	57-0754
KOHL, Mich.	53	Windheim	61-0669
KOHL, Michael	30	Weissenberg	62-0608
KOHLBACHER, Adam	25	Koenig/Hessen	62-0608
KOHLBECK, Cat.(m)	25	Muenster	61-0682
KOHLBECK, Philomne	21	Bleibach	60-0334
KOHLE, Charlotte	69	Vilsen	56-1044
KOHLE, Friedrich	39	Berghausen	56-1044
KOHLE, Julius	7	Stuttgart	56-0512
KOHLEIN, A.Barbara	22	Kalferbach	57-0654
KOHLEN, Gerhard	28	Moers	62-0938
KOHLER, Elisabeth	37	Curhessen	57-1122
KOHLER, Georg	41	Huln	57-1416
Anna Cath. 38, Ernst Heinr. 18			
Georg Conrad 14, Georg Wilhm. 10			
KOHLHEPP, Elisab.	30	Oberzell/Bav.	62-0608
KOHLHORST, Heinr.	24	Barnbossel	57-1026
KOHLMANN, Carl	15	Ritterheide	56-0723
KOHLMANN, Herm.	23	Meyerdamm	56-0951
KOHLMANN, Joh.Geo.	29	Weingratz	56-0632
KOHLS, Ant.	18	Oetheim	59-0951
KOHLSDORF, Johann	12	Muehlsdorf	56-0413
KOHLSDORFF, Bertha	39	Breslau	57-0654
Robert 8, John 7, Armand 4			
KOHLSTEDT, Carl	4	Hoexter	56-0723
KOHN, Anna	31	Boehmen	62-0938
KOHN, B.(m)	33	Foerste	59-1036
KOHN, H.	30	Bromberg	56-0550
KOHN, Isaac	40	Buchau	60-0521
KOHNE, Anna	20	Sandstedt	60-0521
KOHNER, Sara	28	Petzschau	61-0716
Max 6, Rosalie 4, (daughter) 10m			
Babette 28			
KOHRS, Jacob	25	Buelstedt	60-0334
Claus 20, Johann 16, Marie 25			
KOHTE, Johann	16	Achim	55-0634
KOLAR, F.	47	Nemschuetz	62-0993
E. 48, C. 21, H. 19, Fr. 15, J. 5			
KOLASCHECK, Anna	54	Langensalza	62-0712
KOLB, Barb.	31	Langenfeld	60-0785
KOLB, Catharine	24	Wien	57-0961
KOLB, Henriette	46	Ndr.Dresseln	57-0850
Bertha 17, Eduard 12, Emma 10			
Adolphina 8, Lina 3			
KOLB, Michael	20	Pfersdorf	60-0533
KOLB, Sophie	9	Weitheim	61-0482
KOLBE, Friedr. Ed.	27	Goldlauter	55-0932
Joh. Elise 46, Catharine 13			
KOLBE, Friedrich	22	Braunschweig	55-0932
KOLBE, Gustav	25	Landeshut	57-0961
KOLBE, Johann	21	Thuerfeld/Sax	55-0538
KOLBE, Martin	26	Niedergute	59-0535
KOLBES, August	20	Gressendorf	59-0535
KOLBY, Christiane	23	Bremen	61-0520

NAME	AGE	RESIDENCE	YR-LIST
KOLH, Mich.	53	Windheim	61-0669
KOLIBA, Philippine	26	Wien	60-1053
KOLKMANN, Louise	21	Schwagsdorf	60-1053
KOLLE, Ernst	20	Muehlhausen	57-1192
KOLLER, Anton	48	Hollerwaus	57-1150
KOLLER, Louise	18	Probsthagen	60-0785
KOLLER, Sophie	18	Probsthagen	60-0785
KOLLMANN, Charles	40	Hannover	57-1148
Helene 30, Lisette 9, August 9m			
KOLLMANN, Marie	40	Kenneci	60-0521
KOLLNER, Heinrich	28	Schnellenbach	57-1122
KOLLNER, Michael	22	Hungen	57-1122
KOLMEYER, Hch.Fr'd	30	Weener	58-0881
KOLROSS, Magdalena	60	Boehmen	62-0758
Maria 4			
KOLSBACH, Minna	18	Lengsfeld	61-0478
KOMMER, Valentin	19	Hinternach	62-0879
KOMRS, Matthias	59	Boehmen	62-0001
Eleonore 57, Franz 20			
KONBECK, Rosalie	58	Boehmen	62-0467
KONE, Julius	27	Stadtlohn	61-0482
KONEMANN, P.	30	Hamerich	55-0413
Louise 24			
KONIG, Amalia	59	Blomberg/Lipp	57-0847
KONTHEIM, Conr.	28	Wildfleggheim	55-1082
KONZE, Johann	34	Steindorf	56-0413
Maria 6			
KOOF, Johann	31	Schwarza	57-0847
Julius 8			
KOOP, Georg	23	Riglashoff	55-0413
KOOP, John	27	New York	57-0654
KOOPER, Jacob	27	Louisville	59-0214
KOOPMANN, Bernhard	35	Charlotte/NC	58-0885
Johanne 19			
KOOPMANN, Moritz	33	Charleston	58-0885
KOOPS, C.A.L.(m)	25	Bremen	62-0166
KOPF, Crescentia	15	Muenchen	62-0938
KOPF, Heinrich	19	Gontershausen	56-0847
KOPF, Johanne	19	Eisfeld	59-0613
Friedr. 15			
KOPFF, Theodor	27	Helmstedt	56-0411
KOPFMANN, Magdal.	22	Nienburg	61-0682
KOPLICH, Joseph	27	Neisse	55-0845
KOPP, Friedr.	24	Tessen	60-1161
Lina 24			
KOPP, Louise	28	Melsungen/Wrt	60-0622
KOPP, Wilh.	19	Mannheim	59-1036
KOPPCHEN, August	30	Brachbach/Hes	62-0608
KOPPE, Joseph	37	Hohenwessel	62-0342
KOPPEL, Maria	40	Hessen	60-0371
KOPPES, Hartmann	52	Ndr.Wollstadt	58-0563
Eva 45, Georg 20, Elisabeth 16			
Catharina 13, Johann 11, Wilhelm 7			
Maria 1			
KOPPLIN, Carl	24	Prosekel	56-0819
KOPPLINGER, Leop.	44	Borndorf	57-0850
Anna 35, Therese 10, Leopold 6, Franz 4			
KORB, Adam	24	Helfenberg	62-0879
KORCK, Clara	23	Bremen	57-1192
KORELL, Johannes	26	Schependorf	62-1112
Anna 26			
KORF, Henry	18	Todenmann	59-0384
KORMANN, Joh.	50	Runsdorf	60-0398
Babette 48, Elisabeth 8			
KORN, Charles	34	Lueneberg	57-0654
KORN, Ferd.	30	Missouri	62-1169
Lina 7			
KORNDER, Jacobine	22	Wetzlar	57-0704
KORNDER, Johanette	22	Herborn	58-0925
KORPPEL, Ewald	30	Steinseifersd	62-0879
KORTE, Joh. Derric	56	Bremen	57-0422
KORTEN, August	21	New York	60-0785
KORTEN, Fr.Wm.	29	Solingen	59-0412
KORTENHAUS, Fr.(m)	46	Hohn	62-0467
KORTH, F.W.L.	18	New York	61-0716
KORTHAUER, Diedr.	27	Hagenburg	57-0606
KORTSCH, Ferd.	34	Magdeburg	56-0847
KORTSCH, Minna	28	Berlin	56-0847
Anna 7			
KORTSCHEINER, B.	25	Praschka	56-0951
KORTTYOKER, Heinr.	22	Hagen	57-0776
KORTUEME, Anton	27	Westhellen/Pr	60-0622
KOSACK, Barbara	20	Nebillan	57-1113
Martin 34, Maria 28, Joseph 4, Franz 4m			
KOSCHLAND, Albert	56	Philadelphia	58-0815
KOSCHWITZ, E.	35	Berlin	56-0527
KOSER, Chr.(m)	25	Niederweden	62-0836
KOSHATKO, Jacob	40	Boehmen	60-0785
KOSSLOSSKY, Marie	32	Nabfell	57-1407
Anna 18			
KOST, C.	23	Heerden	57-0850
KOST, Gottlieb	17	Vetesheim	59-0613
KOSTAMLUTZ, Rosaly	23	Ziniwes	56-0629
KOSTER, G.	22	New York	59-0990
KOSTER, Jacob	16	Bockeln	55-1082
KOSTER, Joh.	17	Fressdorf	59-0535
KOSTER, Marg.	34	Vegesack	61-0482
Henry 6, Johann 5, Edw. 2			
KOTBINGER, Carl	36	Hachstuhl	55-0812
Theresa 26			
KOTHE, Catharina	24	Ndr.Vorschutz	57-0847
KOTHE, Emil	14	Cassel	58-0815
KOTHE, Georg	15	Reckwarte	60-1141
KOTTE, Gerh.	23	Eber	60-0785
KOTTEMANN, Wilhelm	26	Ibbenbuhren	60-1032
KOTTER, Chr.Heinr.	24	Einighausen	56-1117
KOTTKE, Ludwig	21	Strozewo	56-0819
KOTTMANN, Bertha	24	Salzuffeln	60-0521
KOTTMEIER, Julius	20	Scharmbeck	56-0819
KOTTWITZ, Susanne	46	Posen	57-0654
Rosalie 16, Henriette 12, Armand 9			
Caroline 3			
KOTZELL, Wenzel	20	Budweis/Boehm	62-0608
KOTZENEVAR, Johann	33	Neschopesdorf	56-1260
Peter 28			
KOTZER, Gottlieb	54	Wittenburg	55-0845
Christiane 53			
KOVAR, Anton	38	Boehmen	62-1042
Anna 34, Wenzel 8, Anton 5, Barbara 3			
Johann 9m			
KOVAR, Joh.	33	Boehmen	62-1042
Barb. 30, (daughter) 2, Anna 7m, Jos. 59			
Catharine 58			
KOVARZICK, Gustav		Schweidnitz	59-0048
KOVERT, Bernhard	28	Quendorf	57-1148
KOWALSKY, August	24	Zerniem	56-0723
KOWANDA, Martin	29	Barrau	57-0961
Catharina 27, Matthaeus 10m			
KOWAR, Mathas	35	Boehmen	61-0897
Johanna 32, Adalbert 5, Johanna 3			
Franz 25			
KOZHUSAR, Johann	40	Nestoplsdorf	57-0436
KOZISBECK, Bernh.	39	Austria	62-0712
Josepha 44, Franz 17, Anna 11			
Catharina 6			
KRAAS, Wilhelmine	15	Linsburg	59-0535
Louise 15			
KRABITZ, Mar.Luise	20	Leipzig	55-0630
KRACH, Joseph	19	Bremen	55-0845
KRACH, Josepha	28	Ellingen	61-0482
KRACHT, Conrad	35	Hohenhausen	61-0478
Anna Marie 33, Conrad 10, Wilhelmine 7			
Friedricke 3			
KRACHTER, Barbara	27	Sulzheim	62-1042
Joh. 5			
KRACK, J.A.	27	Weichersbach	59-0990
KRACKE, Fritz	22	Scharmbeck	56-1117
Doris 19			
KRACKER, Jos.Ant.	27	Oestereich	57-0606
KRAEMELBEIN, John	24	Rautenberg	61-0779
KRAEMER, Carl	27	Lengfeld	57-0704
KRAEMER, Heinr.	22	New York	62-0232
KRAEMER, Joseph	36	Hoechst	61-0047
KRAEMER, Marie	29	Gr.Buseck	62-0467
KRAEMER, Sophie	28	Helpsen	57-1150
KRAEMER, Wilh'mine	24	Alnzefahr	62-0467

NAME	AGE	RESIDENCE	YR-LIST
KRAEMER, Wilh.B.	72	US.	57-1113
Bertram 16			
KRAFFT, Augusta	46	Jena	59-0951
KRAFFT, Christiane	16	Fraurombach	57-0654
KRAFFT, Elisabeth	19	Curhessen	58-0399
KRAFFT, John	16	Pfordt	57-0654
Valentin 18, Conrad 22, Marg. 24			
Valentin 14			
KRAFFT, Sebastian	41	Ob.Schrambach	57-1026
KRAFT, Adam	25	Roehrach	61-0897
KRAFT, Anna	30	Niederlindach	56-1117
KRAFT, Eva Elisab.	19	Sachs.-Weimar	55-0634
KRAFT, Fr.	26	Koenig	62-0836
Eva 36, Elise 9, Fr.(m) 16			
KRAFT, Fr.August	33	Haselbach	58-0576
Emilie 26, Hedwig 3, Hugo 2, Anna by			
KRAFT, Friedrich	45	Stantenberg	55-0812
Elisabeth 47, Regina 21			
KRAFT, Jacob	34	Philadelphia	62-1169
Mrs. 31			
KRALIK, A.(m)	36	Boehmen	62-0730
Marie 28			
KRALL, Carl	28	New York	58-0306
Mrs. 20			
KRAMASZ, Franz	34	Prag	58-0576
Marie 27, Franz 7, Louis 4, Marie by			
KRAMER, Carl	31	Husum	56-0527
KRAMER, Daniel	24	Biedenkopf	56-0951
KRAMER, Ernst Chr.	16	Wiederschall	56-1117
Louis 14			
KRAMER, Fr.	30	Rhoden	62-1042
KRAMER, Georg	33	Hochberg	56-1117
KRAMER, Georg	23	Linsc/Drauns.	57-0924
Caroline 20			
KRAMER, Hanna	22	Giebelstadt	62-0730
Regina 20			
KRAMER, Hermann	21	Hochstadt	61-0047
KRAMER, Isla	38	Potsdam	61-0716
KRAMER, J.H.	54	Damme	59-0951
Anna 50, Bernhard 16, Therese 18			
Dener (f) 12, Cath. 9, Caroline 7			
KRAMER, Joh.Heinr.	24	Gerde	56-0413
KRAMER, Johanne	23	Braunschweig	56-1044
KRAMER, Joseph	40	Coesfeld	61-0482
Heinrich 9, Franz 7, Catharine 2			
KRAMER, Ludwig	30	Volkmarsen/He	62-0608
Therese 27, Leopold 1, Hermann 3m			
KRAMER, Max	18	Wierup	59-0951
KRAMER, Rud.	16	Altenmuhr	62-0730
KRAMER, Sophia	16	Bodungen	57-1192
KRAMM, Helene	24	Paddingmittel	58-0306
KRAMP, Ludwig	47	Pommern	57-0776
Wilhelmine 39, August 17, Johanna 9			
KRAMPERT, Andreas	30	Luneburg	61-0478
KRAMPF, Caspar	23	Baiern	55-0634
KRAMSCHUSTER, Mich	42	Raitenbuch/Bv	57-0924
Anna Maria 35, Walburga 8, Anna Marie by			
KRANBERG, Bernhard	40	Muenster	59-0214
KRANEFUSS, Rud.	19	Haesewinkel	59-1036
KRANICH, Christian	33	Altenfeld	58-0399
Christiane 32, Franz 9, Amanda 7			
Hermann 3, Irene 11m			
KRANITZKY, Marie	26	Kratzow	57-0606
Anna 3			
KRANSTOEVER, J.Frd	32	Linde/Hann.	57-0754
Elise 32, August 2			
KRANZ, Christian	29	Erbsen	56-0632
KRANZ, Conrad	20	Felsberg	56-0847
KRANZLEIN, J.G.	22	Atha	57-1192
KRAPF, Caroline	50	New York	60-0371
Susanne 19			
KRAPPOWITZ, Jos.	28	New York	61-0716
KRASMY, Andrew	42	Prag	57-0654
KRASS, Catharina	20	Brike	57-1067
KRASTEL, Fritz	38	Fuerth	60-1032
KRATKY, Wenzel	29	Stelcowes	57-1148
Johanne 27, Agnes 5, Florian 3			
KRATOSCHWILL, A.	38	Posen	62-0166
KRATSCHMANN, Heinr	28	Eisberg/Alt.	62-0608
Louise 30, Richard 4			
KRATT, Martin	22	Wuertemberg	58-0925
KRATZ, Christian	20	Rauscheberg	62-0342
Elisabeth 39, Charlotte 14, Johannes 9			
Catharina 7, Marie 8m			
KRATZ, Diedrich	42	NYC.	55-1238
KRATZENBERG, C.(m)	33	Bischhausen	57-0555
E.(f) 32, A.(m) 6m, H.(m) 5, R.(m) 4			
H.(m) 3, L.(m) 2			
KRATZENSTEIN, Jo'a	28	Hemingerode	55-0932
Louise 52			
KRAUER, Marg.Barb.	27	Schoenweissa	57-0704
KRAUL, Jacob	24	Ndr.Ingolheim	60-0785
KRAUS, Friedr.	30	Esslingen/Wrt	60-0622
Catharine 25			
KRAUS, Georg	28	Flossenburg	55-0812
KRAUS, Georg	21	Berkau	59-0477
KRAUS, Helene	17	Homberg/Hesse	57-0924
KRAUSCHAAR, Clara	26	Leitmar	57-1067
KRAUSCHE, Heinrich	22	Bircklar	57-1067
KRAUSE, August	40	Kluetzkon	56-0629
Caroline 33, Bertha 8, August 2m			
KRAUSE, Carl	44	St.Louis	58-0925
KRAUSE, Caroline	19	Zadro	56-0512
KRAUSE, Fr.	23	Althuttendorf	61-0482
Malvina 24, Ernst 2			
KRAUSE, Fr.(m)	23	New York	61-0804
KRAUSE, Joh.	35	Than	56-0723
Emma 20			
KRAUSE, John	44	Frankenhausen	56-0512
Mary 37, Louis 17, Justus 14, Cha. 10			
Rieke 8, Heimann 5, Christel 2			
KRAUSE, Maria	24	Niederheim	62-0938
KRAUSE, Marie	22	Frankfurt a/M	61-1132
KRAUSE, Pauline	40	Halle	57-0422
KRAUSE, Wilhelm	45	Holzminden	55-0845
KRAUSE, Wilhelm	28	Kroegelstein	60-1053
KRAUSEN, Catharine	34	Margreiz	55-0630
KRAUSER, Louis	40	Fuerth	57-1148
KRAUSHAAR, Ernst	21	Niederaula	56-1117
KRAUSHAAR, Ludwig	18	Schmalkalden	61-0779
KRAUSMEIER, Mar.An	27	Prussia	60-0371
KRAUSS, Barbara	21	Heumade/Bav.	60-0622
KRAUSS, Barbara	11	Wilhelmsdorf	61-0478
KRAUSS, Daniel	41	Gabel	59-0951
Therese 21, Adolph 5, Peter 1			
KRAUSS, Elisabeth	22	Ellingrode	57-0447
KRAUSS, Mary	68	Schrabach	56-0512
KRAUSS, Wilh.	38	Wien	59-0951
KRAUSS, William	20	Backnang	56-0512
KRAUT, Carl	27	Linnep	59-1036
Louise 23			
KRAUT, Elis.	23	Tennelohe	60-0785
KRCH, John	44	Lomma Krchwa	56-1011
Antonia 33, Anne 14, John 10, Francis 8			
Antonia 4, Anthony 3m			
KREB, Carl	23	Langen	60-0785
KREBS, Carl	32	Spornitz	57-0754
Susanne 42, Carl 11, Julius 7, Louise 5			
Caroline 1			
KREBS, Godfrey	19	Fakelstedt	57-0422
KREBS, Wilhelm	25	Pittsburg	60-0334
KRECK, Carl	36	Tennstedt	59-1036
Sophia 35, Carl 7, Hugo 5, August 4			
Dorette 2, Pauline 11m			
KRECK, Josephine	40	Baltimore	60-0785
KRECKEL, Friedrich	50	New York	58-0604
KREGER, Johanna	21	Rothleben	59-1036
KREHE, Friedrike	25	Tromelshein	55-0845
KREHFUSS, Heinrich	21	Hainsdorf	57-1407
KREIBOHM, Clemens	17	Gronau	58-0563
KREIBOHM, Wilh'mne	19	Gronau	58-0563
KREICHER, Carl	20	Laubach	57-1067
KREIE, August	26	Sachsen	58-0399
Wilhelmine 23, Hermann 2, Marie 6m			
Wilhelm 28, Wilhelmine 16			
KREIG, Anna Marie	20	Sarsheim	59-0372

NAME	AGE	RESIDENCE	YR-LIST
KREILING, Ludw.	24	Heuchelheim	60-0521
Elisabeth 50, Anna 19, Heinr. 9			
KREIMER, Cath.	14	Oldendorf	60-0521
KREINER, Anna	30	St.Andrae	59-1036
KREISELMEIER, Anna	27	Rodenburg	55-0932
KREISER, Pauline	21	Heilbronn	60-0785
KREITLER, F.(m)	18	Achern	59-0951
KREITMAYER, Chs.	38	Philadelphia	60-0785
Anna 22			
KREIZI, Anton	28	Wieseck	57-1113
Marie 25, Marie 3			
KREIZL, Joseph	39	Latzicht	56-0413
Johann H. 20			
KREIZMANN, Franz	54	Egeln	57-0447
Dorothea 55			
KREKEL, Christian	20	Nassau	55-0628
KRELING, Elisabeth	16	Darmstadt	57-0447
Anna 7, Johann 13, Johannes 10			
KRELL, August	24	Quedlinburg	57-0447
KRELL, Joh. G.	50	Neuseifer/Sax	60-0622
Joh. Rosina 42, Eduard Herm. 15			
Ernst W. 13, Amalia Henr. 11			
Ehrgt. Ferd. 8, Emma Ida 7, Amalia Aug. 4			
KRELL, Joh.Cathar.	25	Meiningen	61-0478
KRELLER, Catharina	18	Bieber	60-1053
KRELLWITZ, Wilhelm	36	Olbersleben	59-0535
KREMER, Anna	18	Montabaur	59-0535
Josepha 10			
KREMER, Clara	25	Horn/Lippe	55-0628
KREMER, John	16	Obertiefenbch	57-0422
KREMER, Philippine	28	Perleburg/Pr.	60-0371
Wilhelm 10			
KREMER, Wilhelmine	24	Alnzefahr	62-0467
KREMLING, Rud.	18	Gr. Vahlberg	60-0785
KREMM, Aug.	16	Puttingen	61-0047
KREMPEL, Friedr.	36	Eckartsborn	55-0932
Johanna 32, Heinr. 14, Friedr. 12			
Emilia 11, Caroline 6, Cath. 2			
KRENDEL, Aug.	28	Wolfenbuettel	56-0723
KRENKEL, Catharine	59	Semd/Hessen	60-0622
Elisabeth 15			
KRENTZER, Marg.	21	Udenhausen	56-1117
KRENZ, Gott.	46	Prossekel	57-1148
Carolina 46, August 19, Louis 14			
KRENZ, Gottlieb	22	Jankendorf	56-0819
KRENZER, Vincens	26	Baiern	57-0776
KREPF, Andreas	38	Buchs	60-0785
KREPP, Adam	24	Elm	62-1042
KRESS, Joseph	24	Curhessen	58-0399
KRESS, Rosalina	25	Magdlose	60-1141
KRESSIN, Friedrich	36	Altborck	56-0723
KRETCHMANN, J.(m)	55	Hamburg	62-0232
KRETSCHMAR, Andrew	31	Lodz	56-0589
KRETSCHMAR, Carl M	27	Hermesdorf	61-0520
KRETSCHMAR, Emma	17	Altenburg	57-0606
KRETSCHMAR, Joh'a.	55	Leipzig	59-0384
KRETSCHMAR, Johann	24	Vegesack	60-0334
KRETZ, Emma	17	Heilbronn	58-0885
KRETZE, Johanne	22	Stockheim	56-0951
KRETZER, Gottlieb		Unterdiederst	56-0589
KRETZMER, Johann	24	Vegesack	60-0334
KRETZSCHMAR, Ferd.	30	Prussia	56-1044
KREUDER, Elisabeth	17	Oberofladen	57-0776
KREUEL, Heinr.J.	71	Wesecke	62-0983
Johanna 69, Johann 34, Helena 36			
Johanna 7, Catharina 5, Bernhard 3			
Gertrude 1			
KREUTLEIN, Margret	23	London	60-1032
KREUTZBERG, Franz	23	Ahrweiler	56-1117
KREUTZBERG, Simon	20	Goldbeck	59-0412
KREUTZER, Cathrina	24	Gernau	57-0847
KREUTZER, Charles	17	New York	57-0961
KREUTZER, Elise	24	Wiesenthan	57-1026
Burchard 19			
KREUTZER, J.(m)	37	Philadelphia	62-0836
KREUTZMANN, Carl	28	New Brock	56-0723
KREUZBURG, Casper	45	Gotha	56-0847
Anna Elisab. 15			
KREUZER, Sebastian	26	Kleinlongheim	60-1141
Lucia 24, George 9m			
KREY, Constantia	71	Lienczewo	61-0779
Carl 30, Augusta 25, Johann 27			
Charlotte 22			
KRIBANEK, Joseph	28	Boehmen	61-0930
Catharina 30, Carl 3, Maria 11m			
KRICK, Johann	27	Haibach/Bav.	60-0429
KRIEF, Johann	17	Zeven	61-0682
KRIEFT, Caroline	27	Glandorf	60-0334
KRIEG, Ernst	20	Neubronn	56-0413
KRIEG, Heinrich	19	Munchhausen	61-0520
KRIEG, Philip	18	Muenchhausen	57-0924
KRIEG, Theodor	28	Lobschuetz	56-0589
Anna 30			
KRIEGER, Friedrich	19	Spradow	56-1011
KRIEGER, Heinrich	15	Gartha	59-0951
KRIESCHE, AUg.	25	Phildelphia	59-0613
KRIESEL, H.(m)	15	Kurhessen	57-0555
KRIETE, August	31	Messlingen	57-1122
Christian 23, Sophie 9m			
KRIETE, Heinrich	52	Eisbergen	56-1117
Cathrina 45, Sophie 18, Wilhelm 13			
Christine 9, Caroline 7, Carl 5			
KRIETEMEIER, Luisa	16	Hille	56-0411
KRIETENSTEIN, Sim.	50	Calldorf	59-0535
Sophie 50, August 18			
KRIEWITCH, F.(m)	59	Kurhessen	57-0555
A.(f) 25			
KRIGH, Johannes	28	Echzell	61-0779
Maria 26, Catharina by			
KRILL, Gustav	24	Siefershausen	57-1407
KRIM, Saleine	16	Lohr	58-0885
KRIMER, Math.	22	Philadelphia	61-0047
KRIMM, Johann	23	Partenstein	60-1196
KRIMMEL, Elise		Elbingen	59-0613
Maria 14			
KRINKMEYER, Fritz	20	Vahrenholz	56-1260
KRINS, K.M.	33	Neermoor	55-0413
Louise 24			
KRISCHE, Sophie	23	Riessen	57-0447
KRIWANECK, Charles	39	Gr.Hirschau	56-1011
Maria 32, Anthony 10, Anne 9, Maria 6			
Antonia 3, Charles 6m			
KRIWEGAN, Wm.Arm.	32	Glauchaw	57-0654
KROA, Barbara	25	Hofheim	57-0606
KROB, Johann	46	Mutiowitz/Boh	57-0924
Anna 36, Franz 16, Marie 13, Josepha 10			
Joseph 8, Anna 6, Veit 3			
KROCH, J.F.	58	Fennstadt	59-0951
KROECKEL, G.(m)	33	Kreinitz	62-0467
KROEGE, Adolph	30	Brockeloh	56-1044
KROEGEL, Sophie	30	Brockeloh	56-1044
Maria 40, Heinrich 40			
KROEGER, B.	24	Cloppenburg	57-0578
KROEGER, C.A.(m)	28	Vechta	61-0897
KROEGER, Christ.	17	Westphalen	57-0606
KROELL, Peter	58	Radheim	59-0214
KROENCKE, A.(m)	27	Posen	57-0555
KROENERT, Barb.	58	Grosselbstadt	61-0482
Mich. 24, Barb. 27, Marg. 20			
KROENLEIN, Franz	30	Rottenburg	62-0879
KROENNIG, Johann H	45	Colberg	56-0723
Elisabeth 27			
KROER, Johann	21	Vlotha	57-1067
KROGE, v. Marianne	26	Hechthausen	60-1032
Marie 9			
KROGER, Carl	27	Messlingen	57-1122
KROGER, Joh.	19	Hastedt	60-1161
KROHN, M.(m)	29	Luebeck	62-0111
KROIS, Anton	50	Lippstadt	60-0998
KROLL, Catharine	22	Wangen	57-0447
KROLL, Elisabeth	26	Selchow	57-1148
KROLL, Theodore	29	Budzyn	56-0632
Agnes 32, Anton 10m			
KROLLMANN, Seb.	28	New York	60-0521
Anna M. 26			
KROME, Christian	42	Oerlinghausen	56-1260

NAME	AGE	RESIDENCE	YR-LIST
KROMER, Christine	18	Wien	62-0836
KROMER, Hermann	46	Askendorf	61-0478
Helene 44, Helene 21, Johann 20			
Hermann 18, Mathias 15, Bernhard 13			
Margaretha 10, Marie 8			
KROMER, Joh.Georg	28	Enningen	62-0712
KRON, Ezechiel	17	Niederstetten	57-1148
KRONE, Dorothea	30	Blomberg/Lipp	57-0847
KRONE, Ferdinand	16	Roldisleben	61-0779
KRONE, Fr. Wilhelm	25	Stolzenau	55-0932
KRONE, J.	29	Nackel	56-0512
Friederike 24, Anna 2, Male 59, Anna 57			
Mathilde 27, Bertha 3, Ottilie 1			
KRONEBERG, Emilie	21	Solingen	60-1141
Edward 17			
KRONEMANN, Carl	19	Bielefeld	57-0447
KRONEMULLER, Phpne	25	Hessenthal	60-1141
KRONENBERG, v. F.	38	Dortmund	61-0167
Caroline 24, Marie 4			
KRONENBERGER, B.	45	Bayern	62-0712
Theresia 46, Barbete 20, Emma 18			
Benedict 15, Fritz 14, Lina 12, Otto 11			
Margareta 3			
KRONENBERGER, Bety	21	Darmstadt	61-1054
KRONENBERGER, Em.	21	Oldenburg	61-0897
KRONER, J.	32	Grosskrausche	62-0993
KRONERT, Eduard	22	Prussia	62-0758
KRONLAGE, H. (m)	22	Cincinnati	61-0804
KRONSBERG, Dorette	23	Rodenberg/Hes	57-0924
KROOG, Carl A.	34	Arnsberg	60-1053
Bertha 25, Carl by			
KROOME, Franz	23	Ottenhausen	57-1280
KROOS, Johanna	38	New York	62-0836
KROOS, Thomas	40	Zoudkamp	56-1117
KROOSE, Carl	16	Flegeln	57-1026
KROP, Nicolas	26	France	61-0482
KROPF, A.	52	Asch	62-0993
E. 52, M. 19, E. 17, C. 13			
KROPF, G.	42	Philadelphia	62-1112
KROPFF, v. O.	34	Berlin	62-1042
KROPP, Franz	36	Hundsgiebel	57-0578
KROSS, Elisabeth	17	Flensungen	62-0467
KROTZ, Joseph	36	Krisek/Boehm.	57-0924
Josepha 32, Joseph 13, Anton 11, Maria 7			
Johann 3			
KROTZ, Maria	21	Krisch/Boehm.	57-0924
KROTZ, Mathias	28	Oberstupno/Bo	57-0924
Anna 26, Joseph 6			
KROTZ, Wenzel	24	Oberstupno/Bo	57-0924
Catharina 24, Barbara by			
KRSCHK, Johann	30	Altwozik	57-1067
Rosalie 24, Hermann 3, Johann 6m			
KRUDNER, de H.M.	21	Neukirchen/Ha	60-0622
KRUDOP, Johann	30	Fortwaerne	59-0613
KRUECKEBERG, Conr.	21	Dielemissen	57-0447
KRUEGELE, Cathrina	23	Wuertemberg	57-0606
KRUEGER, Aug.	19	Nassau	58-0885
KRUEGER, August	25	Pommern	56-1044
KRUEGER, Augusta	28	New York	61-0482
Willi 4, Catharine 1, Lina 20			
KRUEGER, Caroline	24	Finkenhausen	56-0819
KRUEGER, Caroline	39	Nalencza	62-0100
Hermann 3, Carl Gust. 16			
KRUEGER, Christian	58	Hannover	56-1011
KRUEGER, Christian	13	St.Louis	59-0613
KRUEGER, Daniel	26	Pommern	62-0758
KRUEGER, Dorothea	15	Frehlsdorferm	61-0478
KRUEGER, Franz	18	Calveslage	59-1036
KRUEGER, Friedrike	40	Lingen	56-1117
Minna 19, Louise 15, Henriette 12			
Rudolph 10, Ernestine 5			
KRUEGER, Herm.	26	New York	62-0730
KRUEGER, Hugo	35	Schweidnitz	58-0399
KRUEGER, J.C.(m)	28	Prussia	57-0555
F.(f) 24, Johann 6m			
KRUEGER, Joh Gottl	53	Schoenwalde	56-0632
M.Soph.Elis. 52, Joh.Gottlieb 19			
Ferd. Gustav 15, Wmne.Augusta 25			
Fr'ke Charl. 11, Augusta C.			
KRUEGER, Johann	26	Mohron	56-0723
KRUEGER, Louise	53	Carzig	57-0776
KRUEGER, Rob.	43	New York	62-0232
KRUEGER, Th.(m)	19	Bernhausen	62-0467
KRUEGER, Wilhelm	27	Benz	59-0477
KRUEGER, Wm.	22	Treuenbritzen	62-0467
KRUEGGERS, Elise	15	Braunschweig	59-0384
KRUEPER, A.	42	Luhnill	59-0951
KRUEPER, August	20	Hildesheim	62-0730
KRUEPPENBERG, Geo.	44	Cincinnati	58-0815
KRUG, Anna Elisab.	21	Ndr.Dieten/He	60-0371
KRUG, Christian	52	Goldlauter	61-0520
Pauline 47, Rosamunda 18, Gottgetren 13			
Ernst Emil 11, Heinr.Bernh. 9			
Ernst Friedr 7, Augusta 5			
KRUG, Ernestine	16	Goldlauter	57-1280
KRUG, Fr.(m)	24	Luezelbusch	62-0166
KRUG, Georg	15	Uttenhausen	57-0606
KRUG, Heinrich	55	Ndr.Dieten/He	60-0371
Adam 28			
KRUG, Heinrich	28	Alsfeld	57-0606
Catharina 34, Elisabeth 9m			
KRUG, Heinrich	25	Niederamstadt	59-0477
KRUG, Jacob	18	Niederweren	55-0630
KRUG, Joh.	17	Metze	56-0411
KRUG, Johannes	58	Curhessen	55-0634
Carl 35, Martha Elis. 28, Martha 6			
Caspar by			
KRUG, M.	18	Suhl	56-0512
Louise 20			
KRUG, Marsell	28	Weissenbach	57-0654
KRUGER, Henry	59	Darmstadt	57-0654
A.Mary 40, Andrew 13			
KRUGER, Herm.	25	Coesfeld	61-0482
KRUGER, John Gotfr	25	Cradifeld	57-0654
KRUKENBERG, Johann	26	Milwaukee	57-1280
Catharine 23, Johann 18			
KRULL, Julius	23	Bremen	60-0334
KRUM, Catharine	44	Cassel	59-0047
Friedericke 21, Carl 19			
KRUMB, Adam	17	Pfingstadt	61-0482
KRUMDICK, Marg.	58	Estorf	62-1042
KRUMHOLZ, Mich.	39	Haransberg	60-0521
KRUMLAND, Joh.	30	Dahlen	60-0521
KRUMMDIECK, H.	18	Buchel	59-0535
KRUMMER, Heinrich	35	Kalbe	57-1280
KRUMMREY, Wilh'mne	45	Curhessen	60-0371
Heinrich 16, Emil 13			
KRUMPHOLZ, Joh.G.	24	Erdmannsdorf	57-0578
KRUMSIEG, Theodor	24	Neuhaldensleb	60-1141
Helene 25, Hugo 3			
KRUMSVIEHL, Heinr.	23	Reversen	58-0881
KRUSE, Arthur	17	Holle	60-0785
KRUSE, Caesar	23	Luegde	60-0521
KRUSE, Carl	51	New York	61-0897
Louise 25			
KRUSE, Caroline	21	Rahden	56-0819
KRUSE, Diedrich	17	Wansdorf	59-0990
KRUSE, Friedrich	25	Rentdorf	61-0478
KRUSE, Friedrich	37	Suedfelde	57-1122
Caroline 30, Catharine 3			
KRUSE, Hermann	23	Garrel	60-0533
KRUSE, Lina	40	Goslar	61-0804
KRUSE, M.(m)	36	New York	61-1132
KRUSE, Margaretha	14	Ellerbruck	61-0779
KRUSE, Marie	16	Stemmen	61-0482
Caroline 16			
KRUSE, Mathias	27	Swiebnitz	57-0436
KRUSE, Sophia	21	Brinkum	57-0654
Mary 18			
KRUSE, Sophie	42	Messlingen	57-1122
Christine 38, Dorethe 30, Minna 5			
Oliesa 3, Hermann 4m			
KRUSE, W.J.	32	Wolstein	55-0932
KRUSE, Wilhelm	47	Stolzenau	62-0712
KRUSELIS, Chr.	27	Frankfurt	62-0730
KRUSEMARK, Fr'dke.	50	Wittenburg	57-1148

NAME	AGE	RESIDENCE	YR-LIST
KRUTHAUPT, Fd.	40	Cincinnati	57-1192
Bernhardine 35			
KRUTZ, Carl	56	Vitzig	57-0704
Eva Charlote 49, Caroline 20			
Ernestine 18, Carl Adam 4			
KSYCKY, Georg	29	Bromberg	57-0776
KUBACH, Friedricka	23	Niedernhall	59-0412
KUBE, Martin	30	Mannheim	57-1407
Emilie 30, August 5, Johann 3			
KUBELE, Emil	21	St.Gallen	62-1112
Heinrich 18			
KUCERA, Jacob	24	Strigowiz	57-1113
Anna 25, Maria 4, Joseph 2, Adalbert 3m			
KUCERA, Jan.	58	Boehmen	62-1042
Cath. 58, (daughter) 20, Rosalie 13			
Franz 33, Anton 19, Joseph 17, Vincent 15			
KUCH, Elise	38	Frieburg/Darm	60-0371
KUCHER, Joseph	28	Wittenberg	57-1067
Cathrine 28, Cathrine 9m, Joseph 3			
Marianne 4			
KUCHINKA, Math.	25	Nebellau	57-1113
Catharina 24			
KUCHTELL, Rob.	36	Austria	60-1161
KUCK, Daniel	27	Midlingen/Wrt	62-0608
KUCK, Louis	15	Worpswede	56-0723
KUCK, Wilhelmine	27	Ledde	57-1026
Sophie 17			
KUCKLEL, G.Ph.	38	Ingenheim	61-0107
KUCKS, Eilert	38	Oldenburg	60-1196
KUCKUCK, Heinr.	48	Louisiana	60-0334
KUDDER, Johann	22	Heilbronn	57-1280
KUDER, Carl	43	Lignitz	56-0847
Betty 51			
KUEBLER, August	18	Heringen	61-0482
KUEBLER, Chr.	24	Hahnberg	56-0847
Heinrich 3			
KUEBLER, Christian	28	Elvershausen	56-0847
KUECHENDAHL, Sidon	26	Magdeburg	60-0521
Herm. 4, Louise 5m			
KUECHER, Friedrich	58	Gaudesbuenden	61-0930
Louise 56			
KUECHERER, Johann	19	Noertingen	59-0214
KUECHLE, Philip	44	Muenchingen	59-0613
Margarethe 30, Caroline 5			
KUECHLER, Ernst	20	Muehlhausen	59-1036
KUECHLER, Johann	24	Schweitz	58-0925
KUECK, Johann	28	Meinertshagen	58-0815
KUECK, Meta	24	Beverstedt	56-1117
KUECK, Meta	15	Scharmbeck	59-0990
KUECKEN, H.H.	36	Hannover	56-0354
KUECKER, J.H.	22	Empede	57-0422
KUECKS, Catharina	27	Oldendorf/Han	60-0429
Anna Cath. 22, Claus Heinr. 18, Peter 16			
KUEFER, Joh.Heinr.	30	Herringhausen	56-1117
A.Marie 33			
KUEGELCHEN, Barbra	28	Mainz	57-1150
KUEGELER, Anna	18	Dorum	60-1141
KUEGELGEN, Babette	27	New York	59-0477
Louis 8			
KUEHL, Dora	28	New York	62-0467
KUEHL, Emilie	24	Dorndorf	57-0447
KUEHL, Godfrey	25	Ziethen	57-0422
KUEHL, William	25	Schoenwalde	57-0422
KUEHLKEN, Joh.	35	New York	60-0521
KUEHLSCHMIDT, Hch.	21	Frotseim	60-0429
KUEHN, Alb.	32	Lissen	61-1132
KUEHN, Amalia	22	Grafenrode	57-0924
KUEHN, C.	22	Darmstadt	62-0993
KUEHN, Dina	16	Erdmanrode/He	55-1238
KUEHN, F.J.	26	Ahrenstadt	59-0990
KUEHN, Ferdinand	3	Nordhausen	62-0836
KUEHN, G.(m)	24	Posen	57-0555
KUEHN, Gottlieb	24	Posen	57-0776
KUEHN, Lina	34	Tiefenort	60-0411
KUEHN, Wilhelm	40	Posen	57-0776
Wilhelmine 30, Johann 6, Friedrich 3			
Ottilie 6m			
KUEHN, Wilhelm	32	Behle	62-0100

NAME	AGE	RESIDENCE	YR-LIST
Rosina 27, Adolph 6, Juliane 1			
KUEHNE, Elise	26	Nofels	60-0533
KUEHNE, Theodor	28	Jever/Oldenbg	60-0622
KUEHNLE, Catharina	21	Benningen	57-1407
KUEHNREIEN, Aug.	28	Coburg	57-0422
KUEHORN, Andreas	28	Steppach	61-0478
KUEKEL, Heinrich	38	Gaudesbuenden	61-0930
Maria 16			
KUEKEN, Meta	24	Lesum	55-0634
KUELITZ, Charles	33	New York	56-1216
KUELKEN, Louise	26	New York	61-0520
Alfred 3, Josephine 10m			
KUEMEL, Rich	11	Berlin	56-1216
KUEMMEL, F.	41	Wiesbaden	62-0993
KUEMMEL, Georg	41	Sorga	61-0779
KUEMMEL, Wm.	23	Cassel	60-1161
KUEMMERLE, Philipp	21	Wuertemberg	57-0606
Joh.Georg 26			
KUEMPEL, Fr.	21	Wernshausen	62-0993
A.E. 24			
KUENECHEL, Heinr.	59	Ebenhausen	60-0521
KUENECKE, G.(m)		Vegesack	61-1132
KUENEMUND, Anna E.	23	Hessen	57-0606
KUENFER, Wm.	34	Nienburg	60-0785
KUENHOLZ, Anna	24	Busserode	55-1082
KUENMANN, John	37	California	59-0214
KUENNE, Conrad	33	Tuemmelsee	57-1148
KUENNE, Friedrich	20	Fakelstedt	57-0422
KUENNETH, Joh.A.	50	Goldkronach	62-0608
Catharine 20, Franziska 17			
KUENSEL, Gottlieb	18	Boehmen	58-0399
KUENSLE, Gottl.	48	Hardhoff	57-0422
KUENTZEL, Heinrich	35	Germany	61-0482
Ludwig 26, Augusta 21			
KUENZEL, Chr.	15	Asche	55-0413
KUENZEL, Th.E.(m)	20	Heilbronn	62-0467
KUEPER, August	34	Derby	59-0048
KUEPLER, Wilh.	30	Easton	57-1150
KUEPPENS, Dora	23	Kosfeld	59-0477
KUEPPER, Julius	24	Barmen	56-0589
Marie 27			
KUERGNER, Otto	24	Zensburg	59-1036
Oscar 26			
KUERK, Joh.	19	Fullerrode	59-0951
KUERSEMUELLER, C.	48	St.Louis	60-0334
Heinr. 20			
KUESERMANN, Ernst	33	Wimmer	59-1036
KUESSNER, Friedr.	29	Philadelphia	58-0881
KUESSNER, Heinrich	17	Pennsylvania	59-0372
KUESTER, August	42	Luedhorst	56-0527
Bertha 11			
KUESTER, Catharine	35	Eimelrod	60-0521
Caroline 9			
KUESTER, Friedrich	29	Schlingen	59-0214
KUESTER, Heinrich	30	Philippsthal	60-1032
Dorette 58, Eduard 58, Georg 20			
KUGELMANN, Wilhelm	25	Wartdorf	57-1407
KUGELSCHATZ, Heinr	29	Ankerslin	57-1122
August 15			
KUGLE, Barbara	23	Oberwindenbch	59-0535
KUGLER, Franz	21	Wien	61-0047
Carl 19			
KUGLER, Heinrich	36	New York	57-1148
Anna 39, Mathilde 4, Louise 11m			
KUGLER, John Nicl.	39	Dorum	57-0422
Mary 6			
KUGLER, Lorenz	17	Burkau	60-0521
KUHFALL, Ernst	24	Berlin	59-0047
Wilhelmine 19			
KUHL, Bernh.	53	Schall	61-0669
Anna 15, Gesine 13, Joh. 11			
KUHL, Heinrich	82	Schale	56-0819
KUHLAND, Ch.	57	Dingen	59-1036
Cath. 58, Friedr. 18, Aug. 13			
KUHLBARS, Aug.Fr.W	38	Potsdam	61-0779
KUHLENKAMPF, Anna	53	Kroge	56-0632
Elise 21			
KUHLER, Conrad	17	Roemershausen	57-0924

NAME	AGE	RESIDENCE	YR-LIST
KUHLMANN, Doris	43	Hannover	62-0758
Arend 13, Friedrich 9, Melchior 7, Anna 4			
Lueder by			
KUHLMANN, Ernst	18	Bremen	60-1117
Heimann 22			
KUHLMANN, Fr.Aug.B	15	Detmold	62-0608
KUHLMANN, Georg	31	Struek	58-0815
Jacob 35			
KUHLMANN, Jane	29	Lieme	57-0422
Lizy 17			
KUHLMEYER, Joseph	25	Schlat	56-1117
KUHLUS, Joseph	30	Horoseel	56-0411
Barbara 34, Albert 8, Joseph 6, Franz 4			
Johann 18			
KUHN, Catharina	27	Hanau	57-0606
Philipp 18			
KUHN, Fanny	17	Bavaria	59-0214
KUHN, George	18	Friedewald	56-0279
KUHN, Gustav	19	Hersfeld	56-1044
KUHN, Johann A.	24	Platz	60-0533
Magdalena 24, Margaretha 11m			
KUHN, Meta	17	Achim	60-0521
KUHN, Sophie	42	Marburg	56-0692
Michael 27			
KUHNE, James	25	Veckenstedt	57-0654
KUHNLE, A.	14	Rothwail	62-0993
KUKUK, Caroline	22	Demke	56-0819
KULB, Christian	18	Sicherhausen	57-1280
KULINSKI, J.	34	France	62-0938
KULLE, Heinrich	23	Holzerode	57-1280
KULP, Henry	27	Hettersen	57-0422
Amalia 25, Augustus 7, Charles 5			
William 10m			
KULSCHEN, Marg.	16	Fischerhude	62-0938
KULZ, Sophie	28	Markt Degging	61-0804
KUM, R.		Germany	59-1036
(f)			
KUMBEL, Paul	25	Albrecht	56-0847
KUMLE, Alois	20	Waldshut	62-1112
KUMLE, Augusta	36	Waldshut	62-1112
KUMLE, L.B.	32	Waldshut	62-1112
Margaretha 9			
KUMMER, Louis	17	Schmolze	59-0951
KUMMER, v. U. (m)	20	Schoenbeck	62-0166
KUMPF, Mar.	24	Hirschhorn	59-0384
KUNDER, Cath.	26	Hammelberg	62-0401
KUNDI, Emil	22	Berlin	60-1161
KUNDMUELLER, Anna	35	Zettmannsdorf	61-0478
KUNDMUELLER, Anna	20	Broelsdorf	61-0478
Barbara 25			
KUNERT, Franz	17	Dobern	57-1148
KUNIG, Wilhelmine	30	Hainchen	59-0990
(m) 9, (m) 7, (m) 2			
KUNITZ, Carl	18	Hohennoelzen	55-0845
Henriette 41, Louise 16, Gustav 14			
Julius 12, Emilie 11, Alwine 5, Lina 3			
KUNKEL, Gabriel	30	Neustaedten	60-0334
KUNKEL, Rudolph	28	Stettin	57-1150
KUNSCH, Carl	23	Magdeburg	59-0047
KUNTE, El.	26	Mecklenburg	55-0845
Friedrike 24			
KUNTERMANN, Laura	15	Sachs.-Mein.	57-0606
KUNTZ, Christian	19	Petershagen	60-0371
KUNZ, Anna	20	Rolshausen/He	55-0628
KUNZ, Burchhard	55	Reelshausen/H	55-0628
Anna Cath. 42, Elisabeth 20			
Joh. Heinr. 15			
KUNZ, Carl	24	Chicago	59-0613
KUNZ, Catharine	57	Winzeln	62-0879
Louise 20, Charlotte 17			
KUNZ, Conr.	30	Wetzikow	62-1112
KUNZ, Elisabeth	18	Hofheim/Nass.	55-0628
KUNZ, Wm.	18	Niederklein	59-0951
KUNZE, August	22	Thierfeld	55-0538
KUNZE, Johann	35	Thuerfeld/Sax	55-0538
KUNZE, Michael	42	Oetisheim	62-0879
Christine 35, Friederike 16, Jacob 11			
Carl 9, Caroline 8, Christiane 2			
Friedrich 3m			
KUNZE, Otto	33	Altenburg	62-0467
KUNZE, Pauline	20	Liegnitz	60-0533
KUNZEL, Christina	27	Eger	56-1044
KUNZIG, Clara	38	Berndeel	60-0411
Mechtilda 7			
KUP, Math.	24	Washington	60-0785
KUPFER, Albertine	22	Werssels	60-0521
KUPFER, Sophie	21	Burgkundstadt	61-0482
KUPFERSCHMIDT, Wm.	27	Elbelingen	59-0048
KUPHAL, August	31	Callberg	61-0716
KUPKA, Barbara	22	Krisch/Boehm.	57-0924
KUPNART, Wm.	14	Mohrenbach	60-0521
KUPPEL, Margarethe	34	Kieferndorf	55-0845
KURRASCH, Carl F.	26	Vangersk	57-1192
Joh. C. 21, Mary 56, Emily 5			
KURRE, Dor.	25	Goettingen	62-1112
KURRE, Martin	22	Unterwald	56-0819
KURRELS, Gerard	38	Campen	57-0422
KURS, Hermann	17	Bremen	62-0758
KURT, Josephine	67	Seligenstadt	60-0521
Josephine 22			
KURTH, August	37	Kaikow	56-0723
KURTH, Joh.	21	Schaptauen	59-0951
KURTZ, Martin	20	Betzingen	60-1141
KURVE, Heinr.	21	New York	58-0306
KURZ, Babette	31	Reidern	60-0785
KURZ, Christ.	26	Moringen	61-0897
Gottl. 24, August 19			
KURZ, Christian	50	Schoedorf/Wrt	55-1238
KURZ, Henriette	26	Lengsfeld	55-0845
KURZ, Johann	28	Aschaffenburg	60-1032
KURZ, Ludwig	26	Brechthausen	62-1112
KURZ, Maria	16	Gellenhausen	59-0951
KURZWEG, G.(m)	24	Neuenburg	57-0555
KURZWEG, Martin	50	Briesenhorst	60-0429
Marie Elisb. 58, August 23, Wilhelmine 19			
KURZWEG, Wilhelm	31	Zorndorf/Pr.	60-0429
Caroline 30			
KURZWEIL, Joseph	50	Wien/Aus.	55-0538
Josepha 40, Johanna 18, Marie 15, Rosa 8			
Adolph 5, Joseph 4			
KUSCHEL, Anton	19	Albersdorf	59-0477
KUSENBERG, W.A.	33	Prussia	57-1148
KUSKE, Wilhelm	39	Soldin	57-0704
Justine 38, Wilhelmine 16, Carl Fr.Wm. 14			
Julius Fr. 13, Carl Friedr. 11			
Carl August 8, Ernestine A. 6			
Marie Louise 4, Joh.Friedr. 2			
Carl Ludwig 11m			
KUSSMANL, Ernestin		Heidelberg	56-0629
KUSTER, Creszentia	21	Starzeln	61-0482
KUTCHAT, Catharine	18	Nimmerfried	61-0107
KUTSCHE, Paschalis	38	Warendorf	58-0885
KUTSCHER, Heinrich	24	Varrel	60-1161
KUTSCHERA, Jacob	24	Strigowitz	57-1113
Anna 25, Maria 4, Joseph 2, Adalbert 3m			
KUTSCHKE, Friedr.	39	Soehland	60-0334
KUTTRUP, Helene	35	New York	62-0938
Marie 14, Louise 8			
KUTZELMANN, Lorenz	17	Grossteinheim	56-1216
KUWITZKY, Johann	42	Marienburg	59-0372
Josephine 33, Gustav 10, Johann 7			
KUWTE, El.	26	Mecklenburg	55-0845
Friederike 24			
KUZREWSKY, M.(m)	27	Jarotschin	56-0723
Anna 18			
KWEISER, Gottlieb	35	Posen	58-0399
Juliane 34, Adam 3, Gottlieb 9m			
LABOURISIERE, (m)	34	France	61-1132
(f) 26			
LABUDDA, Franz	29	Karwenbruch	55-1082
LABUSEUR, Aide H.	21	Dorum	56-1044
Elise 18			
LACHANT, Franz	36	Solopiske	55-0845
Magdalena 36, Anna 10, Franziska by			
Maren 7			
LACHEMEYER, Xaver	35	Hochstadt	56-0527

NAME	AGE	RESIDENCE	YR-LIST
LACHMANN, Cath.	38	Fraurombach	57-0654
LACHMANN, Joseph	22	Westendorf	60-0334
LACHMEIER, Michel	28	Kroegelstein	60-1053
LACHMUND, Wilhelm	18	Braunschweig	58-0881
LACHNER, Georg	41	Buffalo	58-0306
(wife) 42			
LACHNER, Mart.	32	Balmbrack	59-0990
LACHNER, Peter	34	Mannheim	62-1112
LACKMANN, Henry	21	Thedinghausen	57-0654
LADEBACH, Julius	28	Bambersrode	57-0704
LADEBOCK, Michael	28	Waldau	60-1032
LADENSACK, Henry		Querfurt	57-0961
LADEWIG, Otto	26	Danzig	56-0819
LADEWIG, William	40	Strassburg	57-0961
Wilhelmine 30, Friederike 9, Charles 4			
LADI, Henry	30	Tarmstedt	57-1148
Anna 28, Mary 11m			
LAEFTLER, Wilh'mne	17	Salzbach	60-0334
LAEMMER, Johann	35	Niederndorf	56-1204
LAEMMERER, Anna	24	Niederurf	57-0754
LAEMMERHIRT, Ana C	23	Mohra	55-0932
Elise M. 21			
LAEMMERHIRT, Georg	20	Salzungen	55-0932
LAENGER, Catharina	38	Giessen	57-1067
LAEUCHLI, Heinrich	20	Aarau/Switz.	60-0371
Joh.Heinrich 18			
LAGE, Henry	25	Probstei	57-0654
LAGEMANN, Cord	41	Sudwalde	62-1112
LAGES, Johann	27	Kreuz Riehl	55-0630
LAGOMARTINO, Loren	26	Italy	61-0716
LAHEROTTI, Ursula	36	America	56-1216
LAHEYDE, Elisabeth	30	Cincinnati	58-0815
LAHM, Johannes	33	Muenster	59-0384
Cath. 30			
LAHM, M. Ma.	17	Muenster	59-0384
LAHMANN, Hermann	14	Emsen	58-0925
LAHNSEN, Johanna	18	Lienen	60-1196
LAHNSTEIN, Emanuel	20	Ruedingen	59-0951
LAHR, Johann	22	Weinheim	62-0879
LAHR, Michael	30	Gebhardsreuth	60-0622
Madgalena 26, (boy) bob			
LAHRS, Margaret	27	Arsten	59-0951
LAIBER, Albert	21	Carlsruhe	57-0422
LAICH, Sophie	17	Vaihingen	62-0879
LAIME, Francois	32	Rouen	62-0836
LAINE, J.(m)	24	England	60-0521
LAINZ, Angnette	17	Damne	58-0815
LAINZ, Val.	21	Marschau	60-0334
LAITIG, Caroline	26	New York	62-1169
LAKEMACHER, J.Jac.	39	Magdeburg	57-0606
Dorothea 39, Louise 5, Anna Doroth. 3			
Marie 1			
LALLMEYER, Benno	35	Muenchen	59-1036
LAMBERT, Charles	15	Meimbressen	60-0411
LAMBERT, Reinh.	21	Kansas City	58-0604
LAMBKE, Christian	28	Marienwerder	57-0704
LAMERIN, Marie	26	Londorf	57-0606
LAMEYER, J.D.(m)	35	New York	62-0730
LAMGART, Carl	21	Hildesheim	60-1141
LAMMANN, Wilhelmne	20	Gerden	56-0847
LAMMERMANN, Lueder	20	Lockstedt	59-1036
LAMMERMEYER, Cath.	58	Groneberg	56-1011
Frederick 24			
LAMMERS, Anna Mary	24	Luetten	57-0961
LAMMERS, Charlotte	34	Rothenfelde	56-0847
LAMMERS, G.	19	Cloppenburg	58-0881
LAMMERS, Jacob	18	France	61-0482
LAMMERS, Rebecca	20	Holsel	61-0897
LAMMERT, Jacob	33	New York	57-1192
LAMPARTER, Elisab.	24	Wittenberg	62-0758
LAMPE, Albert	38	Ndr.Bessingen	61-0047
Carl 19			
LAMPE, Christ.	24	Minden	60-0785
LAMPE, Eduard	20	Halle	59-1036
LAMPE, Ernst	32	Ottensen	62-0836
LAMPE, F.C.H.	28	Labourland	58-0885
Emily 18			
LAMPE, Friedrich	22	Lachenhorst	56-0411

NAME	AGE	RESIDENCE	YR-LIST
LAMPE, Friedrich	56	Luetjenburg	57-0422
Ida 33, Sophia 25			
LAMPE, Heinrich	18	Osterhausen	60-0533
LAMPE, Heinrich	26	Gr.Berkel	59-0384
LAMPE, Jacob	18	Eilge	59-0951
LAMPE, Joh.	27	Haldorf	59-0951
LAMPE, Ludwig	29	Wolfenbuettel	62-0342
LAMPE, Wilhelm	19	Bernstrupp	60-0334
LAMPE, Wm.	59	Balsehle	60-1196
LAMPRECHT, Gottl.	22	Prussia	62-0758
LAMPRENT, Johann	16	Schwarzennach	57-1122
LANDEFELD, J.(m)	35	Breitzbach	62-0401
LANDER, Carl H.	24	Posen	56-1044
LANDER, Dorothea	15	Wagenfeld	60-0334
LANDES, Jacob	25	Zuzenhausen	59-0613
LANDESVATER, Carln	17	Widden	60-0521
LANDGRAF, Wil.	23	Danhausen	56-0527
LANDICKER, Will.	27	St.Louis	57-1192
LANDMANN, Ad.	53	Oberschmitten	62-0730
Christine 34, Emil 9, Antonia 8, Julius 7			
Heinrich 6			
LANDMANN, F.C.	36	Leipzig	59-0535
LANDVOGT, Anton	43	New York	62-1112
LANDWEHRMEIER, Mar	22	Eelstedt	56-0951
LANE, David	36	London	62-0401
LANEMANN, H.(m)	31	Quackenbrueck	59-0951
Adelheid 58, Gerhard 16			
LANG, Anna Maria	17	Pfarmsche	57-0847
LANG, August	22	Spoeck	62-0730
LANG, Bernhard	18	Demme	57-1192
LANG, Cath.D.	26	Utphe	62-0467
LANG, Catharina	16	Eichelsdorf	59-0214
LANG, Christoph	16	Meimsheim	62-0879
Wilhelmine 17			
LANG, Eduard	27	Stockach	61-0779
LANG, Elisabeth	21	Schoenlind	56-0951
LANG, Elisabeth	40	Kleintreubach	60-0521
LANG, Franz	34	Pelitschud	55-0932
LANG, Friedr.	24	Allenbach	56-1216
Charl. 20			
LANG, Friedrich	17	Dietzhausen	55-0630
LANG, Friedrich	31	Muencherndorf	57-0776
LANG, Georg	28	Moenchsambach	56-0512
Anna 28, Adam 7, Margaret 4			
LANG, Georg	17	Bayern	56-1044
LANG, Georg	51	Baltimore	59-0214
LANG, Georg Friedr	23	Dietfurt	57-0422
LANG, Heinrich Ph.	15	Alsfeld	57-0606
LANG, Helene	29	Hadamar	57-1148
LANG, Jacob	33	New York	61-1132
Cath. 30, M.M.(m) 9, Jacob 11m			
LANG, Jacob	29	Hermsdorf	59-0535
Marianne 23			
LANG, Joh.J.	22	Obertharheim	62-1169
LANG, Johanna	22	Ottersweier	62-0938
LANG, Joseph	20	Hanau	59-0951
LANG, Josephine	23	Pesth/Hungary	57-1148
Charlotte 27			
LANG, Leop.	33	Pesth/Hungary	57-1148
Theresia 35, Siegismund 6, Amalia 1			
Josephine 4m			
LANG, Magd.	29	Ahornberg	62-0401
LANG, Marie C.	23	Bieden/Hessen	62-0608
LANG, Sara	25	Muenchen	60-0521
LANG, Therese	26	Ahornberg	56-0723
LANG, Therese	25	Tirschenreuth	57-0754
LANG, Therese	20	Buttenwiesen	59-0214
LANGBEIN, Eva	28	Steinfeld	55-0413
LANGBEIN, J.C.	20	Hopfgarten	58-0881
LANGE, (m)	44	Barmen	56-0589
LANGE, A.(m)	22	Oldenburg	62-0730
LANGE, A.Ges.	37	Delmenhorst	59-0477
Bertha 8, Herm. 4, Aline 2			
LANGE, Alwine	30	Goettingen	59-0951
LANGE, Amalie	36	Prussia	57-0847
Franziska 7, Bertha 4			
LANGE, Amalie	23	Bartshausen	62-0608
LANGE, Anton	21	Bremen	56-0413

NAME	AGE	RESIDENCE	YR-LIST
LANGE, August	31	Bensen	56-0589
Anna 24			
LANGE, Carl Gottl.	39	Buchwalde	55-0812
Christiane 33, Anna Maria 7			
Friedr. Otto 2, Carl Paul 4m			
LANGE, Christian	27	Luepke	58-0399
LANGE, Eckhard	43	Bessel	56-0512
Anna 33, Eckhard 15, Elisabeth 6, Anna 3			
Gertrud 18, August 1			
LANGE, Elisabeth	24	Loshausen/Hes	55-0628
LANGE, Elise	20	Pfaffenries	56-0527
LANGE, Emanuel	24	Neisse	58-0399
LANGE, Emily	18	Fritzlar	57-0961
LANGE, Francis	39	Goettingen	59-0951
LANGE, Franz Conr.	19	Dessen	56-0411
LANGE, Fried.	18	Winsebeck	59-0214
LANGE, Friedrich	25	Oldenburg	60-0334
LANGE, Friedrich	65	Braunschweig	57-0422
Jane 48			
LANGE, Friedrich	22	Frankfurt	57-1148
LANGE, Gustav	15	Darmstadt	62-0401
LANGE, Heinrich	32	Eifahr	61-0478
Elisabeth 32, Jacob 3			
LANGE, Henry	37	Sachsenburg	58-0545
LANGE, Herm.	34	Nordhausen	62-0467
Emilie 30			
LANGE, Herm.	42	Delmenhorst	59-0477
August 31			
LANGE, Hermann	20	Goettingen	61-0682
LANGE, Joh.	32	Almenhausen	57-1067
LANGE, Joh.H.	22	Hannover	56-1044
LANGE, Johann	26	New York	60-0334
LANGE, Johanna	18	Rothenstein	55-0413
LANGE, Jurgen	38	Hannover	57-0847
Sophie 32, Heinrich 4, Catharina 11m			
LANGE, Louis	20	Holzminden	57-0654
LANGE, Louise	32	Zeitz	62-1112
Friedr. 6, Helene 5, Bertha 36, Otto 9			
Hermann 7, Anna 4, Bertha 11m			
LANGE, Maria	24	Langenbrueck	57-0847
LANGE, Mary Berthe	18	Zwenkau	57-0654
LANGE, Mathilde	22	Eldaxen	57-1122
LANGE, Max	22	Klost. Ebrach	59-1036
LANGE, Otto	25	Salzwedel	60-0334
LANGE, V.	46	Birkenride	62-0993
J. 32, L. 13, Th. 10, H. 5, J.N. 6m			
LANGE, W.(m)	22	Musingen	61-0897
LANGE, W.C.	36	St.Louis	62-1042
LANGEBARTELS, Aug.	34	Bremen	58-0576
LANGEFELD, Cathar.	30	Battenhausen	57-0924
LANGEFELD, Heinr.	25	Battenhausen	57-0924
LANGEN, Helena	21	Trier	62-0758
LANGENBERG, Const.	27	Blankenheim	56-0629
Dorothea 33			
LANGENBERG, Fritz	28	Schoettmar	56-0629
LANGENDOERFER, Dor	28	Meiningen	58-0815
LANGENER, Rudolph	26	Auras/Silesia	55-0628
LANGENHAHN, Bernh.	16	Wichthausen	55-0630
LANGER, Henriette	38	Quedlinburg	57-1192
Otto 9, Anna 8, Martha 6, Clara 4			
Rudolph 2			
LANGERER, Georg	38	Vitzerode	57-1026
Gertruth 38, Georg 9, Johannes 6			
LANGEWALD, Fd.	22	Peitz	57-1148
LANGFELDER, Babett	24	Zeckendorf	60-0521
LANGGUTH, H. (m)	18	Wertheim	61-1132
LANGGUTH, H.W.(m)	60	Gr.Breitenbch	60-0521
Catharine 56, Emil 20, Caroline 16			
LANGHOF, C.	27	Berlin	59-0990
LANGHOFF, Ant.	40	Coburg	57-0654
LANGHORST, Sophie	19	Rahden	59-0412
LANGHORST, Wilh.	27	Luedersfeld	59-0951
Doroth. 22			
LANGKNECHT, Anna M	26	Schifferstadt	62-0232
LANGLETT, Diedrich	35	Bechholz	61-0520
LANGLITZ, Heinrich	16	Steinberg	62-0730
LANGNER, Carl	43	Waldenburg	57-1407
Augusta 32, Johanna 53, Marie 5, Fritz 6			

NAME	AGE	RESIDENCE	YR-LIST
Anna			
LANGOLD, Barbara	32	Kronach	57-0961
LANGSCHMIDT, C.Fr.	31	New York	58-0815
Marie Cath. 25			
LANGSDORF, Maria	47	New York	59-0384
LANGSTRUSTER, Pet.	19	Osterode	57-1407
LANKENAU, J.F.	32	Dorum	56-0512
LANKENAU, Louise	25	Bremen	60-1053
LANTGEL, Maria	25	Steiereck	55-0812
M. (f) bob			
LAPFGEER, W.A.	38	Bremen	62-0938
LAPP, Christina	25	Wolfenrod/CH.	60-0429
LAPP, Theodor	30	Herbrum	60-1032
LAPPE, Dorette	17	Schmalkalden	58-0576
LAPPE, Fr.Will.	39	Osnabrueck	57-1148
Carolina 30, Julius 4, Johanne 9m			
LAPPE, Franz Chris	19	Roden	59-0412
LAREDAG, Wm.	34	Ladbergen	62-0836
Christine 30, Marie 7, Johann 4, Paul 2			
LARGES, Lucie	24	Germany	59-0951
LAROCHE, Anton	28	Wheeling	60-0334
LASBE, August	23	Brackwitzhsn.	56-0819
LASCH, Johann	44	Thierfeld	55-0538
LASCHLAFKA, Joseph	36	Zielhof	56-0819
Anna 42			
LASKY, Jos.St.	42	England	56-1216
LASTILLER, Joh.	30	Celle	60-0785
Elise 26			
LATTE, Samuel			56-0279
LATTE, Samuel	32	Schwenteinen	56-0279
LATZ, Fr. Wilhmine	18	Westercappeln	56-0723
Maria 40			
LATZ, Martha	21	Spiescappeln	55-0812
LATZKE, Gottfried	50	Rolmohrdorf	55-0932
Christiane 45, Marie 17, Christian 16			
Emil 6			
LAUBACH, (f)	40	Muehlheim	62-1112
LAUBE, August	23	Brackwitzhsn.	56-0819
LAUBENBERGER, Jac.	8	Emmingen/Egg	57-0080
Gottlieb 6			
LAUBENGEIGER, Jos.	41	Grafenberg	59-1036
Marie 37, Johannes 13, Johann 9m			
LAUBENHEIMER, Ad.	28	New York	56-1216
LAUBER, Christiane	23	Bechtheim	57-0422
LAUCHSEN, Peter	24	Otterndorf	60-1032
LAUENROTH, Nanny	30	Nordhausen	58-0563
LAUENSTERN, Moritz	23	Hannover	57-0422
LAUER, J.	50	Hauswurz	62-0993
LAUER, Joh.	27	Bayern	56-1044
LAUER, Peter	26	Sarodt	59-0047
Sybilla 29			
LAUER, Sophie	25	Burgkundstadt	61-0482
LAUFER, Joh.Andres	28	Hochstedt	57-1067
LAUFFER, C.C.	27	Eisenach	62-0836
LAUGLOTZ, Johannes	25	Gerstungen/CH	60-0622
LAUHARD, Camille	36	Rouen	62-0836
LAUHOFF, Alex	33	Brackel	56-0512
D. 30, Joseph 9, Maria 7, William 5			
Engelbert 3, Anna 3m			
LAUKEMPER, Hermann	30	Muenster/Pr.	62-0342
LAUKES, Peter	18	Singendorf	62-1042
Rosalie 27			
LAUN, Catharine	18	Kurhessen	57-0555
LAUN, Conrad	17	Obermoellrich	60-0411
LAUNEMANN, Cathar.	18	Osnabrueck	59-0951
LAUNSBACH, Carl	25	Hessen	58-0399
LAUPFUSS, Helene	21	Crefeld	58-0885
LAUR, Dorothea C.	22	Blankenbach	62-0608
LAURENZ, H.	32	Frischenmoor	59-0951
Johann 18			
LAURINGER, Oswald	30	Baden-Baden	62-0758
Wendelin 41			
LAUS, John	59	Herpersdorf	60-1141
LAUSER, Johann	30	Kestran/Boehm	57-1067
Anna 24			
LAUSER, Mathias	54	Kestran/Boehm	57-1067
Anna 50, Anna 23, Catharina 22, Franz 14			
Wenzel 13, Simon 9, Joseph 7			

NAME	AGE	RESIDENCE	YR-LIST
LAUSING, Franz	39	Sandstedt	62-0467
Dorothea 20			
LAUSMANN, Anna	21	Ottersberg	55-0413
LAUT, Anna Mary	20	Godamstein	60-1141
LAUT, Christine	56	Weihe	62-0730
Minna 17			
LAUT, Georg	28	Neuenmuhr	60-0334
LAUTENBACH, Chstne	53	Lauffen/Wurtt	60-0429
Louise 18, Gottlob 12			
LAUTENSCHLAGER, A.	27	Lehrenscheinf	59-1036
LAUTER, Amandus	18	Berlin	60-1053
LAUTERBACH, Christ	23	Weidness	57-0754
LAUTERBACH, Elise	23	Uttershausen	57-1067
LAUTERBACH, Jac.	27	California	62-0938
LAUTERBACH, Lena	22	Burgkundstadt	61-0482
LAUTERBACH, Wilh.	28	Altershausen	62-0879
LAUTIN, Lorenz	24	Kelmunz	60-0398
LAUTNER, Cath.	21	Gottsfeld	59-0990
LAUTNER, Friedr.	59	Doberschuetz	60-0521
Marg. 59, Johanna 33, Anna 32, Anna 24			
Marg. 33, Johann 23, Friedrich 30			
Lorenz 17, Johann 18, Cath. 20			
LAUTNER, Jacob	43	Lautner	59-0990
(f) 39, (f) 9, (m) 2			
LAUX, Catharine	26	Rottenburg	57-0021
LCKEMEIER, Max	19	Steinheim	59-0214
LEBENBAUM, Fanny	26	Borgentreich	58-0815
LEBENBAUM, Sally	18	Borgentreich	58-0815
LEBER, Peter	43	Obertiefenbch	57-0422
LEBERICH, Johann		Sternheim	59-0047
LEBERMANN, Adam	58	Wuertemberg	57-0606
Susanne 19			
LEBERT, Joh. Georg	28	Krumwaelden	57-0021
Nicolaus 17			
LEBRUN, (m)	34	Bordeaux	62-0401
(f) 31, George 6, Albert 14			
LECH, Friedrich	28	Vienna	55-0845
Johann 32			
LECHNER, Barbara	28	Bayern	56-1044
LECKER, Herrm.A.	16	Foelkinghsn.	59-1036
LEDEKUGEL, Gottfrd	38	Anger	56-1044
Dorothea 37, August 13, Friedrike 8			
Anna 5			
LEDEL, Caspar	51	Neudorf	58-0399
Sabine 44			
LEDERER, Jacob	58	Freiburg	58-0604
LEDERER, Theresia	19	Rilsen	60-1117
LEDERMANN, Barbara	50	Muennerstadt	58-0881
LEDERMANN, Cath.	23	Minnerstadt	61-0682
LEDERMANN, Jette	4	Bavaria	55-0845
LEE, Rich.	28	Cincinnati	60-0334
LEEP, Heinrich	27	Schlitz	57-0704
LEESEMANN, H. (m)	31	Cincinnati	62-0836
LEESER, Adelheid	35		59-0477
LEFERT, Aug.Grosse	21	Hollich	60-0398
Heinr. Gross 17			
LEFFLER, Jacob	23	Horzakoff	59-1036
LEGAY, C.	22	US.	62-1042
LEGDORF, Marie H.	29	Eisrode	56-0723
LEGELER, Heinrich	11	Coelln	59-0372
LEGENS, Anna Elis.	16	Lenkens/Hess.	61-0770
Christine 14			
LEGONGE, P.	22	France	59-0613
LEHE, Charlotte	28	Kuenig	59-0951
LEHM, Elise	20	Preiss	57-0776
LEHMAIER, Georg	31	Forst	57-1026
LEHMANN, A.	25	Wurtemberg	56-0550
LEHMANN, A. Alwina	17	Dresden	56-0629
LEHMANN, Amalie	19	Lehe	62-0467
LEHMANN, Armia	17	Frankfurt a/M	61-0482
LEHMANN, Carl	16	Prussia	62-0758
Franz 14			
LEHMANN, Carolina	21	Obersenn	57-1148
Th. 20			
LEHMANN, Ernst	28	Dresden	59-0477
LEHMANN, Gottlieb	32	Gohau	56-1044
LEHMANN, H.(m)	32	New York	62-0836
Louise 24			

NAME	AGE	RESIDENCE	YR-LIST
LEHMANN, J. Friedr	36	Ziethen	56-0629
Christine 26			
LEHMANN, J.(m)	17	Osterfeld	61-0804
LEHMANN, M.	29	Wen	62-0938
LEHMANN, Mary	20	Verden	57-1148
LEHMANN, Th.	22	France	62-0938
LEHMANN, Therese	28	Berlin	55-1082
LEHMEYER, Friedr.	23	Gastrup	57-0422
LEHMEYER, Friedr.	24	Gastrup	59-0477
LEHMKUHL, Anna	17	Hatten	57-1192
LEHMKUHL, Joh.	30	Hasserd	60-0521
LEHMKUHL, Sophia	58	Verden	57-1148
LEHNER, Matthias	29	Schwaig	57-1122
LEHNERT, Ch.	37	Walternburg	59-0951
LEHNING, Wilhelm	20	Laubach	59-0214
LEHR, Samuel	60	Philadelphia	55-0812
LEHRBERGER, Helene	19	Bottenheim	60-0521
LEHRHARD, Chrstine	59	Mainz	62-0938
Anna Louise 26, Barb. Joh. 23			
LEHRNICKEL, Mary	25	Sprendlingen	57-1148
Catharina 18			
LEIBER, Wm.	25	Hemstadt	61-0669
LEIBERMANN, Mathil	26	Bietigheim	59-0214
LEIBGRIES, Charles	33	Danzig	56-1011
LEIBOLD, Mich.	25	Grossenwinkhm	57-0422
LEIBOLD, S.(m)	32	Elters	59-0951
C.(f) 26			
LEICHT, Marg.	18	Baiern	57-0606
LEICHTAUER, Anna	32	Baiern	58-0399
LEICHTER, Sylvestr	17	Wagenfort	57-1280
LEIDERT, Wilhelm	30	Etzdorf/Sax.	60-0622
Pauline 22			
LEIDHEISER, Cath.E	19	Gutenburg	58-0545
LEIDICH, Elisabeth	57	Grueningen	57-1067
LEIDISCH, Cath.	16	Grueningen	62-0111
LEIDL, Johann	59	Michigan	62-0467
LEIDOLF, Carl Ad.	46	Hassenhausen	61-0482
Christine 44, Theodor 14, Wilhelm 9			
Herm. 6, Lina 8, Emma 7			
LEIFTEIS, Dorethe	25	Muehlrarlen	60-0785
Eleonore 20			
LEIMHORST, B.	29	Weiner	56-0723
LEINAUER, Martin	30	Westheim	59-0214
LEINBERG, C.A.	34	Pennsylvania	59-1036
Ferd. 7, Wm. 6, Alb. 3			
LEING, Maria	51	Damme	59-0477
Friedrike 14, Augusta 9			
LEINHOLZ, Anna	53	Datterode	62-0938
Marie 19			
LEINKER, Heinrich	19	Lockhausen	56-0589
LEINTER, William	18	Lueneburg	57-0654
LEIPENGUT, Georg	30	Worsten	57-0578
LEIPOLD, Anna M.	23	Schluechtern	59-0990
LEIPOLD, Barb.	24	Sondershausen	57-0422
LEIPOLD, Susanne	17	Hessen	57-0847
Alwine 7			
LEIRER, Joh.(m)	25	Climbach	55-0630
LEISBERGEN, Aug.C.	18	Lich	57-0924
LEISENTRITT, Georg	29	Zeil	56-0951
George 18			
LEISIG, H.O.(m)	20	Hirschfeld	62-0232
LEISNER, Anna Cath	24	Leer	61-0478
LEISS, August	29	Heestlingen/H	55-0628
LEISSLER, Margar.	24	Schehenmuehl	56-0632
LEIST, Eckard	19	Meckbark	56-1044
LEIST, Otto	24	Hessen	58-0925
LEISTER, Anna	22	Koenigswald	60-1032
LEISTIKOW, William	27	Succow	57-0961
Johanne 26			
LEITENBERGER, Mich	29	Weilersteissl	57-0924
Dorothea 29, Michael by			
LEITNER, Barbara	30	Bojan	55-0845
Anna 4, Franz 2			
LEITNER, Conrad	45	Brueck	60-0533
LEITNER, G.	20	Hannover	59-0990
LEITNER, Wenzel	32	Bojan	55-0845
Wilhelmine by			
LEITSCH, Veronika	15	Burgham	56-0847

NAME	AGE	RESIDENCE	YR-LIST
Catharine 40			
LEIV, Catharine	24	Husede	56-0951
LEIVALLING, Heinr.	52	Cosfeld	55-0932
LEIVE, Joh.	43	Wendorff	60-0521
Gertrud 44, Cath. 71, Johann 16, Carl 13			
Cath. 9, Joh. 5, Ernst 4			
LELLEVER, David	18	Lissa	61-0482
LEMAIN, Anatole	22	Paris	62-0938
LEMBACH, Anna	31	Koenigshofen	56-0847
Meyer 27			
LEMBACH, Margareta	24	Lohr	60-0533
Theresia 19, Anna 4			
LEMBKE, Dan.	28	Prussia	57-0555
W.(f) 30, M.(f) 6m, C.(m) 2			
LEMBKE, Fr.	26	Ehrenberg	57-0606
LEMBKE, Sophie	34	Ehrenburg	57-0606
LEMKE, Christian	52	Latzen/Hann.	56-0819
Dorothea 34, Hinrich 17, Wilhelm 15			
Friedrich 7, August 4, Dorothea 11m			
LEMKE, Claus	20	Nordsohl	57-0422
LEMKE, Wilhelm	32	Detmold	62-0938
LEMM, Bernard	26	Grefenhausen	62-0111
LEMME, F.	28	San Francisco	59-0951
LEMMER, Elisabeth	21	Grossenbuseck	60-0398
LEMMERHEIT, Dorot.	20	Ettenhausen	60-0398
LEMMERMANN, Diedr.	16	Loxstedt	61-0520
LEMMERMANN, Friedr	27	New York	58-0885
Charlotte 29			
LEMMERMANN, Meta	28	Bremen	56-0951
LEMMING, John	34	Lage	57-1148
John 65, Gerhard 26, Johann 38, E. 19			
LEMON, Friedr.	29	Eringhausen	60-0521
LEMP, Margarethe	23	Frais	59-0613
Johannes 12			
LENDE, Dorothea	22	Neustadt/Hann	60-0371
LENDEL, Philipp	24	Rompenheim	59-0613
LENDEROTH, An.Elis	25	Frankenhain	60-0429
LENK, Carl	43	Tremen	56-1216
LENK, Friederike	49	Greiz	62-1169
Maria 19, Friederike 15, Franz 9			
Hermine 8			
LENKENSCHMIDT, Lse	18	Noertingen	59-0214
LENKERSDOERFER, G.	28	Steinau	60-0429
Sophie 21			
LENNLIG, Johann	43	Gr.Woelwitz	56-1260
Christine 41, Paul 23, Louise 21			
Johann 19, Henriette 17, Wilhelm 13			
Justa 7, Gottlieb 6, Carl 4, Adoline 2			
Gustav 6m			
LENTGRAF, John	38	Lahrbach	60-1141
LENZ, Anna Cath.	20	Bernsburg/Hes	60-0371
LENZ, Christian	59	Kartnow	61-0779
Constantia 57, Eva 17, Louise 9, Carl 7			
LENZ, Georg	40	Brooklyn	59-1017
LENZ, Heinrich	27	Schlitz	57-0924
LENZ, Jacob	20	Unbriken	55-0413
LENZ, Maria	45	Sachs.-Coburg	55-0630
LEO, Bertha	39	Bonstadt	61-0482
Emma 9, Nathan 7			
LEONHAEUSER, Conr.	19	Halsdorf/Hess	62-0608
LEONHAEUSER, Conr.	46	Curhessen	58-0399
Elisabeth 42, Carl 14			
LEONHARDI, Augusta	50	Mengeringhsn.	57-1192
Augusta 18			
LEONHARDT, Fr'dke.	35	Naumburg	62-0608
Emil 9, Adelbert 7, Louis 5, Julius 3			
Otto 10m			
LEONHARDT, Fr.(m)	36	Naumburg	61-0897
Therese 34			
LEOPOLD, Heinrich	31	New York	58-0925
LEOPOLD, Louise	47	Deutz	57-1148
Mary 19, Mathilde 9, Charles 15			
LEPPEIN, John	26	San Francisco	60-0785
LEPPER, A.E.(m)	50	Heuchelheim	62-0467
Elisabeth 21, Georg 18, Caroline 15			
Ludwig 9, Carl 7			
LEPPER, Cath.	28	Heuchelheim	60-0521
LEPPER, Christine	57	Hundelshausen	60-0429

NAME	AGE	RESIDENCE	YR-LIST
Apelius 27, Peter 25			
LEPPER, Johann J.	42	Koenigsberg	59-0214
Margaretha 38			
LEPPER, Wm.	18	Alten Busieck	62-0836
LEPS, Gottfried	24	Zerbst	60-1032
LERCH, Elisabeth	35	Wallersheim	56-1260
Margarethe 17, Balthasar 13, Heinrich 10			
Conrad 7, Georg 13			
LERICH, Maria	23	Washington	57-1148
(baby) 1			
LERNER, Marg.	24	Bayern	61-0669
Magda. 32, Anna 3			
LERNER, Ursula	25	O.Dannlach/Bv	55-0628
LESCARILL, Jean	42	Spain	61-0482
LESCH, Anton	37	Lischin	58-0881
Barbara 38, Catharina 7, Johann 3			
Maria 6m			
LESCH, Casper	30	Dudelsheim	57-1026
Margaretha 26, Catharina 1, Maria 6m			
LESCHIER, Heinrich	17	Hainchen/Hess	62-0608
LESEBERG, Heinrich	20	Raderholz	58-0881
LESKER, Bernh.	22	Schwerin	61-0167
LESSER, Minna	25	Schoenlanke	56-0819
LESSING, Albrecht	18	Goeppingen	59-0613
LETCHER, Ad.	31	Baltimore	57-1150
LETTAU, Johannes	43	Grunau/Pruss.	57-0924
A.Elisabeth 36, Carl 17, Johann 13			
Gustav 10, Ferdinand 8, August 6			
Justine 2, Augusta by			
LETTMANN, Sophie	30	New York	59-0477
Heinrich 2, Wilhelmine 5			
LETZCUSS, Clemens	33	Rottenberg	62-0938
Wilhelm 27			
LETZKUS, Wilhelm	21	Engen	59-1036
LEUBOLT, John Gotl	47	Obelsdorf	57-0654
Jane 37, Julie 12, Ernest 8			
LEUCHS, Wilhelm	36	Augsburg	57-1280
LEUR, M. Charlotte	21	Legden	62-0232
LEUSEMANN, Henry	18	Louisville	57-1192
LEUSING, Carl	17	Heinersdorf	56-0629
LEUTBECHER, Josfne	35	Baltimore	62-0938
Marg. 6			
LEUTE, Heinrich	30	Baden	60-1161
LEVE, August	41	Barmen	62-0879
Helene 32, Walter 8, August 6, Herrmann 3			
Ernst 1			
LEVERING, Gesine	23	Groes	60-0334
LEVERMANN, Lisette	35	Muenster	58-0306
LEVEZAU, Nicolai	25	Copenhagen	57-1148
LEVI, Dora	17	Prussia	57-0654
LEVI, Isidor	35	Wolstein	55-0932
LEVIN, Ellen	19	Russia	60-0334
LEVIN, Julius	30	Wien	59-0613
LEVING, Heinrich	36	Granau	59-0951
Gerhard 30			
LEVIS, Eugene	30	Havre	57-0578
LEVIT, S.	17	Thoren	59-0477
LEVIUS, M.(f)	30	US.	57-0578
LEVY, Carl	24	Camen	59-0477
LEVY, H.	33	Putglotz	62-1112
LEVY, Johanna	22	Huemme	62-0467
LEVY, Julius	35	Massachussett	61-0897
LEVY, Lewis	38	England	56-0550
Nicolaus 20			
LEVY, Louis	66	Texas	58-0815
LEVY, Moritz	42	Radwitz	62-1112
Catharina 9, Chr. 8, Alex 7, Regine 5			
Simon 6, Bertha 3, Margaretha 9m			
Margaretha 9m			
LEVY, Nathan	49	Tesnus	62-1112
Betty 45, Fanny 17, Illina 15, Anna 6			
Emma 3, Max 9, Simson 8, Jacob 6			
Josephia 3m			
LEVY, Sara	24	Volkmarsen	61-0482
LEVY, Sophie	48	Winschofen	61-0716
Louise 9, Julie 8			
LEWEKING, Conrad	20	Bockel	59-1036
LEWIN, Ernestine	22	Thorn	62-0730

NAME	AGE	RESIDENCE	YR-LIST
LEWINSCHEN, Hannah	17	Heinum	56-0629
LEWITOCK, Marie	19	Caladei	60-0521
LEWY, Samuel	18	Heubach	56-0629
LEXA, Ferd.	15	Pilsen	57-0578
LEY, Jul.	26	Gellenhausen	59-0990
LEYA, Adolph	40	Stockholm	61-0482
LEYH, Adam	21	Altenbreitung	58-0576
LEYH, Fed.	19	Gellenhausen	60-1141
LEYRER, Genoveva	27	Steisslingen	56-0629
Carl 15			
LHATKA, Joseph	35	Boehmen	61-0930
Franziska 29, Marie 9, Matthias 6, Anna 4			
Antonia 2			
LHOTO, Joseph	27	Boehmen	62-0758
LIBERUM, Valentin	27	Hitzerode	56-0723
LIBOLL, Matthias	40	Liboll	57-0850
Rosalie 39, Anna 12, Pieta 10, Rosalie 6			
Marie 4, Julie 1			
LICH, Philipp	17	Londorf	57-0606
LICHTEN, Anna	19	Loxstedt	61-0520
LICHTENBAHN, Gg Ph	25	Sachs.-Weimar	55-0634
Heinrich 20, Joh. G. 21			
LICHTENBERG, J.W.H	24	Australia	55-0538
LICHTENBERGER, Chr	26	Chicago	61-0804
LICHTENFELD, Ed.	16	Meisselbach	59-0951
LICHTENSTERN, Ludw	22	Pesth/Hungary	58-0881
LIEB, E.	27	Coburg	62-0993
LIEBAU, Fritz	29	Frankenhausen	60-0533
Amalie 29, Augusta 6, Anna 5, Emilie 3			
Bertha 11m			
LIEBE, Ester	30	Westiken	57-1067
LIEBENAU, Anna	50	Helzerved	57-1122
Johann 34, Anna 15, Louise 13, Anna 34			
Louise 11m			
LIEBENGUT, Georg	30	Worsten	57-0578
LIEBENTHAL, J.Gust	52	Lippene	56-0819
Carmin 20			
LIEBER, Babette	21	Bechtolzheim	62-0938
LIEBER, Christine	30	Liegnitz	60-0533
LIEBERMANN, Emilie	23	Bietigheim	59-0214
LIEBERMANN, Martha	27	Reichenbach	55-1082
LIEBICH, Oscar	25	Warendorf	56-1044
LIEBICH, Sophie	20	Bremen	58-0563
LIEBL, Carl	23	Muenchen	58-0815
LIEBL, Maria	24	Sauberieth/Bv	60-0429
LIEBRAND, Fr'drke.	24	Thuringenhsn.	61-0930
LIEBRECHT, Ernst	25	Lauenfoerde	59-0214
LIEBRECHT, Friedr.	15	Wagenfeld	60-0334
LIEBRECHT, Johann	32	Protzen	56-1044
LIEBST, Elisabeth	39	Usleben	56-0847
Heinrich 3			
LIEBZEIT, Chr.	48	Schertendorf	57-0555
E. 40, Paul 18, Ernst 8			
LIEGL, Johann	32	Schefferey	55-0630
Franziska 25			
LIELZ, Wm.	27	Werdorf	60-0521
LIENHARDT, Friedr.	22	Sparreck	60-0521
LIER, Georg	30	Leiderode	62-0938
LIESENER, Geo.Pet.	14	Arnsheim	56-0413
LIETZ, Peter	54	Buden/Posen	57-0654
Louise 54, Wilhelmine 18, Augustin 16			
Louis 14, Gottlieb 12			
LIETZ, Wm.	27	Werdorf	60-0521
LIETZE, E.L.	22	Berlin	59-0477
LIEVERS, Martin	22	Hannover	62-0758
LILIENDAHL, Ernest	50	Neudietendorf	57-1148
LILIENHOF, v.Oscar	31	Scharley	61-0779
LILIENTHAL, Jan	17	Osterholz	55-0634
LILIENTHAL, Marie	9	Berlin	62-0730
LILIENTHAL, Solom.	19	Brakel	56-1011
LILL, Jac.Remigius	30	Radelsheim	59-0214
LILLICH, Joh.	33	Schwann	60-1053
LIMBACH, Anna	25	Lohr/Bav.	60-0622
LIMBERG, Franz	37	Rheime	58-0545
Julia 46, Maria 13, Otto 9			
LIMMERICH, Joseph	31	Kreuznach	55-0932
LIMMERMANN, Trina	22	Achim	58-0563
Sophie 21			

NAME	AGE	RESIDENCE	YR-LIST
LIMPER, Elisabeth	27	Unglinghausen	61-0779
LINALE, Guiseppe	40	Italy	62-0111
Marie 30, Joseph 9, Amanda 7			
LINCK, Ths.(m)	28	Saetzkirchen	60-1196
LINCKE, Carl	25	Bilitz	56-0847
LIND, C.M.	18	Walldorf	59-0477
LINDAU, Henry	48	New York	62-0467
LINDAUER, Salomon	23	Zebenhausen	59-0613
LINDDE, Louise	35	Hohenfels	56-0723
P. (m) 23			
LINDE, Andreas	29	Rittenhausen	61-0682
LINDE, Johann	34	Badbergen	60-1032
LINDEMANN, Ad.	22	New York	60-1196
LINDEMANN, Caspar	20	Empfertshsn.	61-0482
LINDEMANN, Helene	35	Ruhort	59-1036
Anna 6, Marie			
LINDEMANN, J.Georg		New York	58-0815
LINDEMANN, Joh. H.	18	Hahlen/Hann.	60-0622
LINDEMANN, Max	14	Osnabrueck	57-0422
LINDEMANN, Nic.	24	Oberkatz	56-1044
Sophie 22, Johannes 18			
LINDEMANN, Theresa	20	Habbicke	57-0422
Betti 20			
LINDEMANN, Wilh. C	28	Campen	55-1082
Olbe (m) 5			
LINDEN, Anna	31	Danzig	62-0938
Eddy 9, Otto 2, Wilhelm 42			
LINDEN, Johann	25	Lusenich	60-0785
LINDEN, v.Caroline	1	Ludwigsburg	61-0482
LINDENBAUM, Rosa	17	Oberlistingen	56-0589
LINDENBERG, August	25	Eitzum	58-0563
LINDENBERGER, Mary	24	Wuertemberg	57-0606
LINDENFAELSER, Jac	30	Lahr	60-1053
LINDENKOHL, Friedr	17	Cassel	58-0885
LINDENLAUB, E.A.	39	Gera	56-1117
LINDENMANN, Eduard	22	Toelkau/Prs.	61-0770
LINDENSCHMIDT, J.H	25	Rheinland	60-0371
LINDER, Caroline	20	Wallenstadt	59-0412
LINDERS, Christian	42	Hoenze	56-0629
LINDESTROM, Aug'ta	15	Bovenden	61-0482
LINDEWERTH, Anna	19	Bielefeld	57-0447
LINDL, Barbara	20	Hohenfelsen	59-0412
LINDLAU, Wenzel	27	Coeln	60-0411
LINDLOW, Catharina	27	Coeln	60-1141
Margaretha 5			
LINDNER, Carl	26	Reuth	61-0779
Barbara 59			
LINDNER, Caroline	44	New York	60-0785
LINDNER, G.L.(m)	7	Billigheim	62-0836
LINDNER, Georg	18	Hampton	59-0613
LINDNER, Gottl.	31	Prussia	57-0555
Dorothea 26			
LINDNER, Moritz	25	Doebeln	60-0398
Bertha 21			
LINE, George	22	England	60-0334
LING, Caroline	22	Cassel	59-0951
LING, Maria	17	Hessen	56-1044
LINGE, Adam	29	Wollstein	57-0776
LINGE, Christoph	45	Hetzerode	57-0776
Anna 35, Heinrich 9, Carl 7, Justus 5			
Anna 2			
LINING, Marie	20	Hecke	59-1036
LINK, Adam	26	Oberhildershe	59-0613
LINK, Barbara	19	Gemeinfeld	61-0520
LINNEMANN, Bernh.	22	Lohne	59-1036
LINNEMANN, C.A.(m)	20	Lehne	60-1196
LINNEMANN, Engel	35	Cincinnati	61-0167
Joh. H. 9			
LINNEMANN, G.Otto	19	Ehrdissen	59-0477
LINSE, Gottlieb	20	Erfort	59-0412
LINSE, Johanna	24	Crosswitz/Sil	60-0622
LINSENBAERT, Ther.	32	Philadelphia	62-0730
LINSMEYER, Maria	54	Froschmuehlen	59-0384
Theresia 22			
LINSMEYER, Michel	45	Schachenbach	59-0384
Maria 18			
LINTOPP, Heinrich	24	Rechesbuettel	56-0411
LINZ, Georg	28	Schaalfeld	62-0712

NAME	AGE	RESIDENCE	YR-LIST
Barbara 30, Anna 6			
LINZ, Heinrich	20	Oberzell/Bav.	60-0429
LINZ, Johannes	17	Curhessen	55-0634
LINZ, Johannes	57	Heiligenstadt	57-0606
Margarethe 56, Martin 27, Elisabeth 25			
Dorothea 23, August 21, Anna Elisab. 19			
LINZENBART, Theres		Frankenhausen	56-0512
LINZMEYER, Joseph	40	Boehmen	62-0758
Anna Maria 32, Johann 7, Barbara 5			
Margaretha 3, Maria by			
LION, Henry	20	Goettingen	60-1141
LIPINSKI, Carl	34	Kalbe	57-1280
LIPP, Carl Wilhelm	47	Weibelingen	59-0048
LIPP, Dominicus	21	Freiburg	57-0606
LIPP, Johannes	32	Bueckeburg	57-0654
LIPP, Rozine	16	Ulm	55-0932
LIPPART, Anna Marg	59	Lingelbach	57-0704
LIPPE, Heinrich	28	Freienhagen	57-1067
LIPPEL, Heinrich	38	Braunschweig	59-0613
LIPPELMANN, Anna	20	Wallenbruecke	57-1113
Marie 24			
LIPPELT, Carl	41	Rogaetz	57-1067
LIPPELT, Dorette	24	Koenigslutter	57-0850
LIPPELT, Emil	29	Braunschweig	57-1192
LIPPERT, Johann	30	Bayreuth	56-0527
LIPPERT, Peter	17	Heimertshsn.	60-0533
LIPPHARDT, Franz	16	Friedland	55-0845
LIPPIGHAUS, Carl	26	Kirnborn	57-1067
Catharine 27, Heinrich 5, Ernst 3			
LIPPMANN, Lippmann	19	Pinne	57-0961
LIPPOLD, Jacob	28	Berlin	60-1053
LIPPOLD, Leonhard	34	Baiern	59-0412
LIRBEL, Carl	24	Minden	57-0924
LISBERGER, Marie	24	Bromberg	56-0550
LISCHKA, Catharina	33	Lischin	58-0881
LISCHKA, Joseph	37	Bobschuetz/Bo	57-0924
Anna 35, Maria 7, Wenzel 5			
LISCHOW, Joh.Fr.	34	Zerrenein	57-1192
LISKAR, Julius	23	Roda	61-0770
LISKOREN, Serena	34	Aachen	62-1042
LISS, Fr.	28	New York	62-1042
LISSAUER, Michaels	24	Neidenburg	59-0412
LISSEMER, Conrad	14	Albrehm	61-0478
LISSER, Friedrich	26	Schloben/Alt.	57-0924
LIST, Adolph H.	22	Marburg	61-0682
LISTMANN, Andr.	22	Almenrod	56-0527
LITTELNOTH, Max	18	Ikentant	58-0815
LITTHAUER, Fr'dke.	22	Neustadt	59-0951
LOB, Ann Christina	35	Beerfelden	61-0779
LOBCKE, Fritz	18	Sorsum	56-0629
LOBENBERG, Aurelia	21	Willebadessen	60-0521
LOBER, John	31	St.Peter	62-0166
LOCH, Johann	34	Ludwach	61-0478
LODESCHER, Joseph	54	New York	59-0384
Marianne 24			
LODL, Anna	21	Hadacke	61-0779
LODTMANN, Heinrich	17	Diepholz	59-0214
LOEB, Malch.	15	Obertiefenbch	57-1148
LOEB, Moses	19	Wrexen	60-0533
LOEBE, Bennchen	21	Hohenlohe	60-0785
LOEBELL, Mon.	46	Berlin	57-0961
LOEBENFELDER, Hch.	47	Bayern	56-1044
Dorothea 17, Christine 10, Elisabeth 7			
LOEBENS, Elisabeth	58	Bausendorf	59-0214
Margarethe 30, Marie 25			
LOEBER, Altm.	15	Leidhecken	57-1192
Fred. 18			
LOEBER, Charlotte	24	Staufenberg	59-0412
LOEBER, Johannes	50	Teubenhausen	56-0723
Jacob 9			
LOEBER, Just.	23	Neuhof	57-0578
LOEBHARAT, Lippel	37	New York	56-1216
LOEBNER, Johann	52	Wien	62-0730
LOECHEL, Julius	29	Giessen	57-1067
Marie 24			
LOEFFELHARDT, Frdr	15	Wuestenroth	60-1053
LOEFFELHOLZ, J.Con	24	Heuthen	57-0606
LOEFFELHOLZ, Jos.	23	Heuthen	61-0669
Johannes 25			
LOEFFELMACHER, Joh	54	Grunau	57-0924
Christine 40, Franz 15, Hanne 10			
Louise 6, Wilhelm 3			
LOEFFELMANN, Herm.	17	Halle	56-1216
LOEFFLER, Emil	22	Connecticut	62-0111
LOEFFLER, Friedr.	26	Grosshebach	61-0520
LOEFFLER, Jacob	17	Bessungen/Hes	62-0608
LOEFFLER, Johannes	29	Landenhausen	57-0924
Catharine 30, Johannes by			
LOEFFLER, N.	42	Boll	62-0993
Fr. 28, J. 7, F. 4, W. 2			
LOEHL, Joh. H.	16	Beckedorf	56-0589
LOEHLEIN, M.(m)	19	Doerznack	62-0836
LOEHMANN, Anna	20	Achim	60-0785
LOEHN, Andreas	26	Neubronn	56-0413
J. 30			
LOEHNHOLZ, Cathar.	23	Krehlingen	57-1148
LOEHNING, J.E.(m)	19	Coburg	61-0804
LOEHR, Carl	20	Weilburg	56-0819
LOEHR, Joh.	23	Pommersfeld	60-1032
LOEHRER, Rosine	28	Duerrenmettst	60-0334
Christine 20, Wilhelm 19			
LOEHRS, L.	37	Doerste	62-0993
LOEHRSEN, Joh.	25	New York	59-1036
LOELL, Helene	20	Asslar	59-0214
Wilhelm 14			
LOENINGER, Peppi	24	Laupheim	60-0521
Sophie 18			
LOESCHER, John	58	Wellingen	57-1122
LOESCHIGK, W.Gottl	21	Schweinfurt	57-1416
LOESEKANNE, Elisa.	25	Speckwinkel	57-0754
Anna Elisab.			
LOESEMANN, Otto	21	Linge	58-0563
LOESER, Lazarus	32	Washington	57-0961
LOESKE, Leiser	27	Miasteko	57-0704
LOEVY, Ludw.	17	Kommotau	61-0716
LOEW, Adelheid	24	Lutzbuerg/Bv.	55-0538
LOEWE, Henry	20	Goettingen	60-1141
LOEWEL, Carl	19	Gotha	62-0993
LOEWENBEIN, Nath.	58	Libeschig	61-0482
LOEWENBERG, Selig	20	Brilon	56-0632
LOEWENSTEIN, Babet	23	Muehlhausen	60-0521
LOEWENSTEIN, Berta	18	Lichtenstadt	61-0716
LOEWENSTEIN, Elis.	21	Wieseck	59-0990
LOEWENSTEIN, J.	30	New York	60-0785
LOEWENSTEIN, Levi	25	Bueckeburg	55-0634
LOEWENSTEIN, Marie	56	Wolpshagen	57-1122
LOEWENSTEIN, Noah	37	Remagen	56-1117
LOEWENSTEIN, Phil.	17	Lichtenstadt	59-0477
LOEWENSTEIN, Selig	20	Gudensberg	60-0411
LOEWENTHAL, Jul.	18	Magdeburg	57-1148
LOEWENTHAL, Minna	25	Adelebsen	58-0399
LOEWENTRAM, Louise	23	Bremen	59-1036
LOEWI, Lea	20	Hischaid	57-1148
Caroline 20			
LOGEFELD, Albert	21	Flatow	57-0704
LOGES, Friedrich	26	Grossberkel	56-0819
Wilhelmine 30			
LOHAUS, Ernst Aug.	18	Bagenfeld	58-0604
LOHAUS, Joseph	29	Coesfeld/Holl	60-0622
LOHBERGER, Adam	35	Reifberg/Bav	62-0608
Catharine 28, Hermann 3, Lorenz 6m			
LOHE, Herm.	33	Barmen	57-0606
LOHIS, Garith	22	Holland	61-0478
LOHMANN, Adolphine	20	Westphalia	60-0411
LOHMANN, Caroline	26	Riessen	57-0447
LOHMANN, Diedrich	19	Bremen	55-0634
LOHMANN, Elisabeth	26	Hohenaverberg	57-0924
LOHMANN, Ernst	23	Muenden	59-0613
LOHMANN, Martha	24	Hollenburg	61-0047
LOHMANN, Math.	29	Repellen	57-0422
Catharina 23, John 10m			
LOHMANN, R.	53	England	62-1112
Anna 40, Maria 29, Augusta 10, Charles 4			
(son) 9m			
LOHMANN, Wm.	37	Luedinghausen	60-1141
Amalie 42			

NAME	AGE	RESIDENCE	YR-LIST
LOHMEYER, Aug.	23	Stemmen	58-0306
Simon 17			
LOHMEYER, Conr.	54	Holthausen	55-0413
LOHMEYER, Diedrich	26	Botenberg	61-0520
LOHMEYER, Louise	18	Buende	60-0334
LOHMEYER, W.H.	26	Bramsche	62-0730
LOHMEYER, Wilhelm	29	Stemmen	58-0306
Henriette 20			
LOHMUELLER, J.(m)	59	Pleystein	62-0836
LOHNSTEIN, Josh.	16	Rudingen	57-0654
LOHR, Henriette	36	Braunheim	61-0520
LOHRBACH, Apolonia	24	Beblis	60-1141
LOHRE, Catharine M	15	Bederkesa/Han	60-0622
LOHRMANN, Joh. Wm.	19	Dorum	60-0429
LOHRMANN, M.(m)	59	Gmuend	61-0897
LOHSE, Amalie	25	Ibbenbuehren	60-0521
LOMKE, Herm.	32	New York	61-0804
LONA, Barbra(Hahn)	22	Germany	61-0167
LONNEMANN, Hch.	26	Selm	56-1117
Elise 27, B. 4			
LOOCK, Heinrich	55	Salzdetfurth	58-0885
LOOF, Heinrich	63	Malsum	55-1048
LOOKMAN, Friedrike	38	Wollfede	57-1122
LOOSE, Cathar.	22	Melle	57-1113
LOOSE, Charlotte	58	Minden	61-0482
LOPPLER, Julius	24	Burgsteinfurt	60-0785
LORE, Bartholomeo	28	France	59-0613
LORENGEL, John	23	Gross Warzula	56-1011
LORENTZ, Gustella	28	Italy	61-0167
LORENZ, Adam	39	Dickelhaus	55-0845
LORENZ, Carl Hch.	21	Technitz/Sax.	60-0622
LORENZ, Carl Jos.	28	Marbach/Sax.	60-0622
LORENZ, Caroline	16	Philadelphia	62-1112
LORENZ, Charles	58	Rothenburg	57-0961
Augusta 22, Ernest 25			
LORENZ, Franz	23	Wuerzburg	59-0372
LORENZ, Frieda	36	Hew York	60-1196
LORENZ, J.F.	9	Bremen	62-1112
LORENZ, Joh.H.	19	Luetringhause	59-0477
LORENZ, Joseph	27	Brockendorf	56-0413
LORENZ, L.	49	New York	57-0422
LORENZ, M.	28	Fuerth	62-0993
G. 1			
LORENZ, Margaretha	23	Germany	61-0167
LORENZ, Pauline	32	Wartenberg	62-0730
LOREY, Heinrich	36	Meiningen	55-0634
LOREY, Marie	21	New Isenburg	59-0990
L. 19, H. 17			
LOSE, Emil	19	Habelschweidt	60-0785
LOSER, Jacques	56	Luxemburg	61-0482
Angelica 40, Pierre 11			
LOSIN, Henriette	18	Luebeck	57-1407
LOSSMEYER, Michel	27	Pfaffenburg	57-1407
LOTH, Ludwig	18	Giessen	57-0606
LOTTMANN, Anna	14	Norden	60-0785
LOTZ, Georg	30	Kruspis	55-1082
Louise 24			
LOTZ, H.	38	Arnshain	61-0478
Susanne 36, Johannes 15, Jacob 13			
Elisabeth 9, Marie 6, Conrad 3			
LOTZ, Joh.	14	Ranstadt	59-0990
LOTZ, Jost	18	Heidelbach	61-0478
Elisabeth 21			
LOTZ, Maria	22	Rumpenhein/He	57-0924
LOTZ, Valentin	19	Weimarschmidt	57-1067
LOTZ, Wilh.	50	Haitz	58-0563
Elisabetha 25, Heinrich 16, Margaretha 2			
LOTZE, August	28	Weingassen	60-1053
LOTZGESELL, A.Cath	17	Wattenbach	57-0924
LOUIS, A.(f)	46	New York	60-0521
LOUIS, Eva	28	Neufels	60-0334
LOUIS, Friedrike	33	Emden	62-0879
LOUIS, Joh.Mart.	50	New York	58-0815
LOUIS, Rosalie	28	Cassel	61-1054
Eduard 5, Heinrich 2			
LOWA, Jac.Friedr.	23	Laufen/Wuertt	60-0429
LOWENSTEIN, Betty	23	Moellerich	57-1148
LOWENSTEIN, Helene	20	Kuttenfalau	60-0334

NAME	AGE	RESIDENCE	YR-LIST
LOX, Nicolaus	23	Weiler/Pr.	55-1238
LUBESKY, Joseph	28	Berent	58-0881
Josephine 25, Mariane 2, Joseph 5m			
LUBKEN, H.E.(m)	17	Bremen	56-0819
LUCAS, Georg	37	London	59-0477
LUCAS, Heinrich	28	Garlebsen	56-0413
Barbara 38			
LUCAS, Henry	30	Gilsa	60-0411
Anna Elis. 30, Ch. Henry 9m			
LUCAS, Nicolaus	33	Salzungen	57-0447
LUCCAS, An.Rebekka	23	Illienworth	62-0608
LUCE, Magdalena	20	Bremen	57-1148
LUCE, Magdalene	29	Bremen	60-0521
LUCHARDT, Just.	54	Cassel	56-0589
Louise 26			
LUCHBUECHLER, Phlp	18	Grosssachsen	62-1169
LUCHT, Wm.	39	Makenheide	62-0401
Sophie 39, Christiane 10, Henriette 7			
Albert 2, Carl 37			
LUCHTING, Wm.	21	Bremen	62-0730
LUCK, August	24	Preuss.Minden	57-1416
LUCK, Johann	28	Salzbruch	56-0512
Catharine			
LUCKE, John	16	Martuon	57-0654
LUCKENBACHER, Rud.	32	Nuernberg	57-1192
Augusta 20			
LUCKHARD, A.B.	27	Nassenerfurt	57-0850
LUCKHARDT, Julie	19	Mingshausen	59-0372
LUCKHARDT, Marie	21	Mengshausen	58-0576
LUCKMANN, Salome	20	Heina	56-0819
LUDEMANN, Heinrich	17	Dressel/Hann.	57-0847
LUDEN, J.B.	49	Huntingdon	57-1148
Sarah 36			
LUDEWIG, Heinrich	30	Wollmar	59-0535
LUDNER, Johann	28	Bettstadt	57-1416
LUDWIG, Andreas	30	Tams	57-1416
LUDWIG, Heinrich	17	Wolfenrod/CH.	60-0429
LUDWIG, Johann	55	Neuenheerse	55-0812
Philipp 13			
LUDWIG, Johann	36	Auerbach	56-0819
LUDWIG, Johann	14	Kurhessen	56-1044
LUDWIG, John	48	St.Louis	60-0785
LUDWIG, M.	43	Birkenride	62-0993
M. 37, J. 16, H. 14, Fr. 12, C. 10, C. 8			
J. 6, A. 4, J. 1			
LUDWIG, Phil.	32	Lorsen	60-0785
LUDWIG, Philipp	23	Wihersrode	56-0847
LUDWIG, V.	36	Birkenride	62-0993
LUEBBE, Diedrich H	39	Steinhude	57-1067
LUEBBE, Friedrich	34	Heithoefen	57-0754
Joh.Heinrich 4			
LUEBBEKE, Hermann	40	Luets	57-0447
LUEBBEKE, Wilhelm	18	Barsenhausen	57-0447
LUEBBEN, H.	36	Wisconsin	62-0938
Amalie 28, Mary 4, Melchior 2, Hinr. 6m			
Hugo 6m			
LUEBBEN, Loehr	16	Emsen	58-0925
LUEBBERS, Anna	22	Wardenburg	57-1113
Maria 14			
LUEBBERT, H. (m)	23	Schweringen	56-0723
LUEBBERT, Marie	21	Lockhausen	56-0951
LUEBBERT, Wm.	33	Quincy	62-0166
Friedricke 28			
LUEBBESMEYER, Ludw	40	Oringhausen	57-0961
LUEBKE, Gottlieb	32	Neu Schonewld	57-0704
Friederike 28, Carl 3, Anna 6m			
LUEBKEMANN, Lucia	20	Estorf	59-0384
LUEBKEN, Louis	27	Dedersdorf	61-0107
LUEBKING, Charl.	26	Duetzen	55-0413
LUECK, August	45	Senna/Pr.	60-0371
Friederike 38, August 15, Carl W. Hch. 12			
Wilhelm Carl 1			
LUECKE, Armand	28	Engter	57-0422
LUECKE, Cath.	18	Fachinghausen	60-0521
Joh. 15			
LUECKE, Catharine	23	Fressen	57-1067
LUECKE, Fr.	46	Neuenkirchen	56-1216
LUECKE, Franz	35	Wiedenbrueck	60-0334

NAME	AGE	RESIDENCE	YR-LIST
LUECKE, Heinrich	21	Ostercappeln	56-1204
LUECKEMEYER, A.H.	18	Schellenburg	59-1036
LUECKEMEYR, Louise	21	Luebbecke	57-0606
LUECKEN, Heinr.	19	Duderstadt	60-0334
Johann 17			
LUECKEN, Joh.	21	Kloster Holte	59-1036
LUECKEN, Johann B.	40	Cloppenburg	59-0047
LUECKER, Anna	24	Geckhausen	60-1141
LUECKERT, Andreas	51	Lendershausen	56-0723
LUECKERT, Franz	58	Hundelshausen	60-0429
Margaretha 59, Liberius 17, Catharina 20			
LUECKING, Anton	27	Gehrden	57-0021
Wilhelmine 27			
LUECKMANN, G.	50	Cincinati	62-0467
Engel 42, John 9, Elise 5			
LUEDECKE, Anna	28	Oelshausen	57-1407
LUEDEMANN, Johann	18	Zeven	61-0682
LUEDER, Magnus	25	Mainzlar	57-0924
Elisabetha 26			
LUEDER, Wilhelm	58	Bremen	57-1026
LUEDERS, Ernst	51	Holtensen	57-0924
Louise 40, Wilhelm 21, Minna 12			
LUEDERS, Heinrich	28	Dushorn	57-1113
LUEDERS, J.	31	Hannover	62-1042
Mrs. 27			
LUEDEWING, Wilhelm	19	Aplern	61-0520
LUEDKE, Carl	50	Ostrovo	60-1117
Julius 19			
LUEDKE, Wilhelm	24	Kraczke	58-0881
LUEHMANN, Louise	26	Esebeck	59-1036
LUEHNGEN, Ph.	45	Wetzlar	60-0334
Augusta 28			
LUEHRING, Christ.	39	Fallingbostel	57-0847
Maria 39, Fritz 13, Maria 12, Heinrich 7			
Wilhelm 11m			
LUEHRS, Cath.	20	Lilienthal	57-0606
LUEHRS, Cath.	21	New York	61-1132
LUEHRS, Heinrich	30	New York	62-0758
LUEHRS, Hinderika	23	Bracke	57-0021
LUEHRS, Joh. F.	28	Astaedt	57-0850
LUEHRS, John	28	New York	61-0482
LUEHRS, Lina	28	Heiligenlohe	56-0847
LUELING, (m)	33	Paris	61-0804
(f) 24, Herm. 1			
LUELLAU, Becka	24	Syke	59-0613
LUELLMANN, D.	35	Pesth/Hungary	62-0993
LUEMMEL, Anna	30	Aschaffenburg	60-0398
LUENDERMANN, Beta	23	Achim	56-1044
LUENEBURG, Maria	11	Stettin	59-0214
Anna 9			
LUENZMANN, Betty	24	Bremen	57-1192
LUEPENHOF, Fr.(m)	17	Harste	61-0482
LUEPKE, Henriette	22	Prellwitz	56-0819
LUEPKE, Joh.Heinr.	17	Riehe/Curhess	60-0429
LUEPKEMANN, Doroth	22	Nienburg	55-0634
LUEPS, Barbara	24	Walldorf	59-0477
LUERDING, John D.	32	Louisville	59-0951
Elise 23, Ilse 60			
LUERMANN, J.H.	26	Bremen	61-0482
LUERSSEN, August	44	Stollbaum	62-0730
LUERSSEN, Friedr.	16	Stubben	59-0384
Anna 18			
LUERSSEN, J.(m)	26	Ndr.Blockland	61-0804
LUERSSEN, Pet. Hch	39	Luedingworth	56-0413
Pauline 15			
LUESCHEN, Heinrich	25	Wardenburg	57-1113
LUESCHEN, Marg.	20	Embsen	57-1148
LUESSEN, Gesche	28	Emsen	58-0925
LUESSENHOF, Fr.(m)	17	Harste	61-0482
LUESSING, Reinhard	30	Harksbergen	59-0951
LUETGENS, Diedr.	24	Sottrum	62-0111
LUETHWITZ, v. Ad.	27	Triest	61-1132
LUETJENS, J.H.	50	Stapelmorheid	55-0413
Louise 24			
LUETJENS, Jacob	18	Weener	61-0682
LUETKE, Martin	60	Guetzlowhagen	57-0704
Martin 35, Dorothea 35, August 8			
Wilhelmine 6, Albert 4, Emilie 1			

NAME	AGE	RESIDENCE	YR-LIST
LUETMANN, Carl	26	Riesenbeck	59-0613
Cath. 24, Heinrich 9m			
LUETTGE, Julius	28	Wolfenbuettel	55-0845
LUETTIG, Jos.	50	Wewelsburg	62-1042
Franz 24, Lisette 26			
LUETTJEN, Joh.	28	Wilmington	58-0815
LUETTKE, August	23	Ossowo	57-0924
LUETTMANN, August	24	Wittgenstein	57-1407
LUETZ, Anton	26	Sand	57-0754
LUFT, H.(m)	24	Noesberts	61-0669
LUFT, Marie	17	Isenburg	60-1032
LUGARD, M.	30	California	59-0214
(son) 11			
LUHM, Christoph	58	Jankendorf	56-0819
(son) 13			
LUHMANN, Christine	21	Messlingen	57-1122
LUHN, Louis	8	Vacha	59-0477
LUHNE, Carl	30	Berleburg	61-0930
Louise 30, Otto 2, Carl 10m			
LUHR, Anna	16	Benskamp	62-0730
LUIGG, Alois	38	New York	62-0401
LUKESCH, Johann	34	Boehmen	62-1112
Johanna 27, John 11m			
LULOF, Friedrich	41	Sachsa/Pruss.	57-0924
LUMM, Georg	23	Malsfeld	57-0436
LUMPER, Ant.	32	Elbingenalp	55-0413
LUND, (f)	30	Gothenburg	62-0730
LUNDS, Marg.	22	New York	62-0836
LUNEBERG, Meyer	28	Gutenholz	56-1260
LUNECKE, Alexander	23	Missouri	62-0342
LUNKAN, Friedr.	23	Hannover	58-0925
LURGENSTEIN, Otto	25	Leipzig	58-0399
LUSALL, Justus	19	Roeddenau	57-0754
LUSCHNER, Louise	32	Leipzig	56-0550
LUST, Friedr.	31	Ringleben	61-0482
Augusta 31, Friedericke 7, Franz 11m			
LUTE, Christiane	56	Weihe	62-0730
Minna 17			
LUTH, Jacob	28	Amerika	56-1216
LUTHER, Hermann	20	Strunpfede	57-1122
LUTHER, Joh.Valent	27	Geestendorf	62-0712
LUTHER, Pauline	41	St.Louis	62-1112
Ernst 4			
LUTKEHALBEN, Ther.	21	Beelen/Pr.	62-0608
LUTSCH, Margarethe	21	Bischwind	60-0533
LUTSCHA, Joseph	25	Boehmen	62-0758
LUTTER, Bertha	18	Bremerhaven	62-1112
LUTTER, G.M.	28	Salzungen	56-0354
LUTTER, Georg	35	Wettesingen/H	55-0628
Christine 34, Friederike 21, Augusta 14			
Christine 52, Anna 2			
LUTTER, Jacob	24	Hailbach	56-0951
LUTTER, Johann	51	Wiersen	59-0384
Sophie 43, Louise 17, Justine 15			
C. Friedr. 9, Caroline 8, Wilhelm 6			
John Henry 3, Carl 10m			
LUTTERCORD, F.H.	28	St.Louis	57-1148
Sophia 40			
LUTTGEN, F.	15	Scharmbecksto	56-0512
LUTTGER, Henrich	20	Homberg/Hann.	57-0847
LUTTMANN, Helene	20	Walle	62-0712
LUTZ, Adam	28	Linden/Nassau	62-0608
Marie 23			
LUTZ, Anna	33	Kreisdorf	60-1032
LUTZ, Catharina	22	Holzingen	57-0754
LUTZ, Christine	20	Vaihingen	60-0398
LUTZ, Jacob	36	Germany	60-0411
Catharine 41, Friedrich 11, Joh. Georg 9			
Regina 40, Jacob Fr. 12, Cath. 10			
LUTZ, Joh.M.	22	Millestadt	62-0730
LUTZ, John A.	43	Philadelphia	62-0836
Friedricke 30, Georg 6, Anna 4			
LUTZ, Lisette	21	Gruessen	60-0533
LUTZ, Marie	18	Sersheim	62-0836
LUTZ, Mary	26	Tuebingen	60-0411
LUTZ, Wm.	27	Werdorf	60-0521
LUTZENBERGER, Dim.	27	Bavaria	61-0770
Bernhardt 32			

NAME	AGE	RESIDENCE	YR-LIST
LUY, Elisabeth	18	Nirenlingen	60-0521
LUYTIES, Dn.	34	St.Louis	58-0306
(wife) 30, (baby) 1			
LePAGE, J.(m)	26	England	60-0334
MAACK, Albecka	40	Bassum	57-0606
MAAG, Fermus	28	Oberhausen	61-0682
MAAPER, Richard	23	Elberfeld	57-1416
MAAR, Clemens	20	Beverungen	56-1044
MAAR, Heinrich	21	Kirtorf/Hesse	57-0924
MAAS, Carl	16	Hildesheim	56-1216
MAAS, Cath.	33	Hammel	60-0334
Engel 26			
MAAS, Catharine	52	Niederweisel	62-0730
Juliane 20, Conrad 16, Marie 9			
Christoph 13			
MAAS, Claus	24	Berne	60-0998
MAAS, Henriette	21	New York	58-0815
Caroline 1			
MAAS, Hubert	20	Natzungen	57-0555
MAAS, Johann	24	Zickerk	58-0881
MAAS, Jos.	16	Erich	62-1112
MAASNER, Michael	39	Emskirchen	62-0306
MAASS, G.B.	38	Pinnow	62-0401
Rosalie 26, Marie 7, Joh.Louise 4			
MACHLET, Elisabeth	23	Volkershausen	62-0879
MACHMERDT, G.(m)	25	Oerlenbach	61-0482
MACK, Cath.	24	Wertheim	60-0334
MACK, Fritz	40	Braunschweig	62-1169
Heinriette 35			
MACK, Ludwig	19	Wuertemberg	57-0436
MACKENRODT, Joh.J.	30	Baehrheim/Hes	62-0608
MACKENTIP, Bernh.	39	Cincinnati	59-1036
Maria 32			
MACKSAN, Caroline	28	Langenselbold	62-0730
Peter 5			
MADER, Adam	18	Bonsweiler	62-0730
MADER, Barbara	23	Schauerberg	56-1117
MADER, Elise	20	Neustadt	60-0521
Mag. 16			
MADER, Georg	24	Bern	60-0521
MADER, Jos.	29	Simonswald	62-0166
MADERA, Vincent	40	Naples	60-0785
Prosper 15			
MAEHLMANN, Herm.B.	42	Sandleimers	56-0527
Joseph 15			
MAENDLER, Christne	21	Bayreuth	57-0422
MAENICKE, Charles	35	Pelleben	57-0961
MAERKEL, Heinrich	30	Logisch	58-0881
MAERKELER, August	32	Brunhausen	56-0723
MAERKER, Peter	15	Ellweiler	59-0384
MAERSHAUS, Elisab.	27	Langenberg	61-0804
Anna 11m			
MAERZ, Ernst	32	Forstmutt	60-0334
MAERZ, Wilhelm	18	Hessen	60-0371
Helene 21			
MAEUSGEIER, Marg.	20	Hain	61-0779
MAGEL, Elisab.	16	Gruenberg	60-0785
MAGENROH, E.(f)	24	Rodach	57-0555
MAGES, Wm.	49	Rodwald	61-0716
MAGETTI, E.	17	Switz.	62-0467
MAGNUS, Justine	24	Rotenuffeln	56-0819
MAGNUS, Simon	52	Albany	57-1148
MAGOLD, Henriette	23	Heldburg	57-0654
MAHERT, Anna Cath.	20	Dessen	56-0411
MAHL, Christiane	59	Marburg	61-0482
MAHLE, Friedrich	29	Backnang	57-0422
MAHLE, Johann	32	Huntlosen	60-0521
MAHLER, Anna	24	Hambuehl	60-0334
MAHLER, Gust.	35	Beverstedt	56-1117
Anna 24, Hermine 9, Gustine 8, Elise 3			
MAHLER, Joh.Herm.	18	Langenhausen	61-0478
MAHLER, Josepha	28	Willazhufen	61-0107
MAHLMANN, Johanna		Quakenbrueck	58-0925
MAHLSTAEDT, E.	40	Dyckhausen	57-0850
Henriette 9, Henrich 6, Christoph 3			
MAHNKE, Heinr.	27	Nordsode	58-0815
MAHNKEN, D.(m)	29	New York	60-0334
MAHNKEN, Died.	29	New York	60-0334
MAHNKEN, Heinrich	18	Worpswede	56-0723
MAHNKEN, Henry	26	Buckholz	57-0654
MAHNKEN, Herm.	20	Ottersberg	55-0413
MAHNKEN, John	26	Buckholz	57-0654
MAHNKEN, Marg.	16	Lehe	60-1161
MAHNKEN, Marg.	29	New York	62-0938
MAHNKEN, Trina	29	Worpswede	56-0723
MAHRET, Andreas	25	New York	58-0399
MAHRKE, Julius	8	Kalisch	58-0815
MAI, Adam	18	Gudenberg	57-0754
MAI, Anna E.	50	Hornel	60-0533
Anna 18, Catharina 15			
MAI, Eduard	22	Krotzenburg	62-1169
MAI, Francis	25	Obertiefenbch	57-0422
MAIBACHER, Philipp	32	Hochweissel	62-0608
Elisabeth 28, Elisabeth 3, Heinrich 6m			
MAIER, Adam	37	Curhessen	58-0399
Marie 35, Johannes 11, Wilhelm 4			
A.M. 11m			
MAIER, Anna M.	32	Eschelbronn	62-0836
MAIER, Barbara	20	Eichstaedt	60-0521
MAIER, Barbara	19	Merklingen	59-0214
MAIER, Caroline	22	Bavaria	61-0770
MAIER, Dor.	23	Melle	59-0990
Aug. 21			
MAIER, Elizabeth	22		61-0770
MAIER, Franz	48	Wall	60-0521
MAIER, Franz	48	Wall	60-0521
Elisabeth 37, Franz 11, Leonhard 9			
Marie 9, Franz 6, Johann 5, Joseph 8			
Elisabeth 12, Therese 2, Georg 1			
Barbara 2m			
MAIER, Geo.	35	Philadelphia	62-0730
MAIER, Isidor	30	Duningen	62-0730
Johanna 41, Sebastian 5			
MAIER, Jos.	17	Hechingen	57-1192
MAIER, Joseph	44	Dundsdorf/Wrt	61-0770
MAIER, Moris	21	Hoexter	60-0521
MAIICKSCHAH, L.	40	Armenia	62-1042
MAIKRANTZ, Cath.	26	Herrenbreitun	57-1067
MAIKRANZ, William	28	Ehrenbreitung	60-1117
MAIL, Lina	14	Braunschweig	59-0384
MAILE, Andreas	24	Frickhofen	60-1053
MAILL, Christine	28	Wuertemberg	59-0412
Rosine 8			
MAINHARDT, Aug.	21	Tauberbischof	62-1169
MAIRE, Louis	19	Breslau	62-0342
MAISCH, Caspar	31	Unteretzbach	62-0879
MAISON, Maria	59	Dittenheim	60-0334
MAIWALD, Wilhelm	27	Berlin	55-1238
MAIZ, Friedr.	34	Marienwerder	57-0704
Johanna 32, Henriette 9, August 7			
Albertine 2			
MAJEWSKY, Wolf	16	Hohensalza	61-0167
MAKOWSKY, B.	30	New York	62-1042
Louise 6			
MALDONER, Johann	38	Imst	57-0578
MALEMUS, Anton	18	Hinfeld	57-0704
MALER, Heinrich	15	Langenhausen	58-0563
MALEWSCHKA, Julius	38	Osterode	60-1141
MALI, Agnes	26	Boehmen	56-1044
MALKEMUS, Andreas	15	Mengshausen	61-0770
MALLE, Francoia le		Liege	59-0613
MALLENHAUER, Heinr	29	Brueggen	59-0214
MALLOT, Franz	20	Boehmen	60-1161
MALLSTEDT, Carl	20	Delmenhorst	59-0048
MALLWITZ, Rosalie	18	Eisfeld	59-0951
MALSCH, Emil	23	Marienthal	60-1161
MALTEREN, Ph. (m)	33	Germany	62-0467
MALZDORFF, Charles	22	Bergholz	57-0654
MALZOW, Henriette	24	Arnswalde	57-1192
MAMEKEN, Marie	28	Oettingen	57-0847
MANDEL, Julius	16	Schlesien	56-1044
MANDEL, Lipporn	26	Langepuern/Bv	55-0538
MANGDORF, Jacob	42	New York	61-0482
MANGELS, Elisa	24	Ringstedt	59-1036
MANGELS, M.	24	Kuhrstedt	58-0306
MANGELS, Peter	19	Abbenseth	60-0334

NAME	AGE	RESIDENCE	YR-LIST
MANGELS, W.	60	New York	59-0477
MANGER, Carl	21	Weitburg	60-0334
MANGOLD, G.C. (m)	23	Darmstadt/Hes	55-0538
MANGOLD, Henriette	23	Heldburg	57-0654
MANGOLD, J.C.	29	Spoeck	62-0730
MANGOLD, John	38	Philadelphia	57-0422
Mary 40, Mary 9, Anna 4, Margaret 3m			
MANKE, Carl	45	Schwerin	56-0951
Gertrude 34			
MANN, Anna	25	Heinrichsstad	55-0845
MANN, Elisabeth	15	Ekelsheim	60-0334
Catharine 18			
MANN, Ernestine	34	Gera	55-0413
MANN, Ernestine	27	Klingruegen	57-1026
MANN, Georg	22	Andernach/Pr.	57-0924
Margarethe 23			
MANN, Hironimus	26	Neisse	55-0845
Louise 15			
MANN, Johann	32	Marburg	57-0578
MANN, Levin	28	Kissingen	57-1148
Hanna 24			
MANNEBACH, Anna	29	Munstermaifld	60-1032
MANNEL, Georg	16	Wehrshausen	60-0334
MANNEL, Margaretha	25	Suislite	61-0520
MANNFELD, Marie	50	Walldorf	57-0924
Heinrich 13, Wilhelm 10			
MANNHEIM, Helene	23	Neustadt	59-0951
MANNHEIMER, Caroln	48	Mangberg	60-0521
Meyer 27, Sophie 19, Isaac 16			
MANNIG, Johannes	47	Heiligenstadt	56-0723
MANNING, Hermann	32	Meppen	58-0576
MANNS, Anton	25	Ob.Breitsbach	61 0520
MANNSBACH, v.J.C.A	25	Meiningen	61-0716
MANNT, Johanne	28	Berleburg	56-0847
MANSBACH, Heineman	16	Maden	56-0589
Elise 50			
MANSHALD, H. (m)	29	Holtland	61-0716
MANTANE, Jean Bte.	28	France	61-0167
MANTEL, Heinrich L	34	Harpenfeld	56-0951
Eleonore 35, Friedrich 6			
MANTHEY, Gottlieb	27	Tarnowo	56-1117
MANZ, Johann	33	Hellhausen	56-1117
Cathrine 23			
MANZELMANN, Heinr.	19	Granmow	56-1117
Ad. 17			
MANZER, Franziska	22	Carzig	57-0776
MAPHAUS, Heinrich	21	Buchenberg/He	57-0847
MAQUARD, Heinrich	39	Proebsten	57-0847
Dorothea 27			
MARA, Adam	17	Hutzdorf	56-1117
MARAND, P.	45	France	62-0938
(f) 45			
MARANGONY, Dominic	35	Venedig	58-0885
MARBACH, Henry	21	Leidhecken	57-1192
MARBACH, Jacob	54	Hattenbach	59-0047
Elisabeth 62			
MARBES, C.	20	Bremen	62-1169
MARBING, Margareta	21	Oldendorf	60-0521
MARCH, Joh.	47	Boehmen	60-0785
Eva 42, Maria 5			
MARCHALL, Marie	32	Cassel	59-1036
MARCHARD, Carl	19	Herfurt	57-1067
Augusta 16			
MARCK, Michael	36	Waldamorbach	58-0925
Adam 38			
MARCUS, Adolph	18	Glogau/Pr.	55-0538
MARCUS, Jette	50	Hoechst	60-0521
Marianne 18			
MARCUS, Rebecca	25	Strassburg	58-0306
Penny 2			
MARDERSTEIN, Georg	32	Gehra	59-0535
Anna 35, Anna 66			
MAREIS, Marie	26	Adling	59-0214
MARENSE, Meyer	39	Koenigsberg	62-0467
MARGGRAFF, Cath.	57	Weinweiler	59-1036
MARGRAF, Sophia	23	Niederdarla	56-1011
MARIK, Joseph	36	Boehmen	62-1112
Fran. 36, Anna 9, Franz 8, Josef 7			

NAME	AGE	RESIDENCE	YR-LIST
Anton 3, Joh.Bapt. 11m			
MARISSE, Julius	38	US.	59-0951
Caroline 30			
MARK, Julius	48	Fraurling	58-0881
MARK, Meier	18	Fritzlar	57-1148
MARK, Meyer	36	Fritzlar	60-0521
MARK, Moritz	18	Fritzlar	60-0334
MARKEL, Georg	58	Strebendorf	56-0951
Catharine 29			
MARKERT, Caroline	24	Moenchsroth/B	55-0628
MARKING, Johann	31	Freden	59-0951
Johanna 58			
MARKING, Wilh.	41	Eppe	59-0951
MARKOLF, L.	56	Otterhausen	59-0990
MARKOLF, Martha E.	28	Odershausen	58-0563
Marie 22			
MARKS, (m)	30	San Francisco	62-0836
(wife) 24			
MARKS, Agnes	25	Loebschuetz	62-0712
MARKS, Franz	23	Schneidemunch	60-0622
MARKS, Ludwig	26	Essen	59-1036
MARKS, Martin	56	Altriedwitz	57-0704
Maria 43, Sophia 23, Doro.Ottilie 8			
MARLING, Friedrich	19	Lohe	57-1122
MAROHN, Johannes	33	Goldziemitz	56-1011
Caroline 26, Reinhold 6, Albertine 2			
Augusta 3m, Pauline 23			
MARPE, Louisa	27	Lewera	57-0422
Lizy 22			
MARPE, Wilhelm	21	Schmillinghsn	57-1113
MARQUARD, Friedr.	25	Littlehagen	57-0704
MARQUARDT, Anna	30	Bremen	59-1036
MARQUARDT, Heinr.	39	Proebsten	57-0847
Dorothea 27			
MARQUARDT, Wm.	18	Iburg	59-1036
MARQUART, An.(f)	28	Troppstadt	61-0669
MARR, Margarethe	25	Meunich/Bav.	56-0632
Caroline 18			
MARSCHALK, Christ.	28	Reissendorf	57-0021
MARSCHALK, v. Dor.	22	Stade	57-0606
MARSCHALLEK, Chr.	36	Juliusberg	57-0754
Anna 41, Johanna 5, Carl 3			
MARSCHEU, Christ.	22	Gross Furra	56-1011
MARSCHNER, Friedr.	37	Goerlitz	60-0521
Rosalie 46			
MARSKY, Ernst	50	Kolmar/Posen	58-0881
Ernst 17			
MARTBURGER, Hartm.	20	Ramholz	59-0047
MARTEN, G.	40	England	62-0938
MARTEN, Henriette	27	Elberfeld	57-1192
Louis 3			
MARTEN, Jette	31	Calldorf	56-1260
MARTEN, Wilhelm	23	Stangenforth	56-0819
Johanne 24			
MARTENS, Anna	24	San Francisco	59-0951
Cath. 4, Betty 2, Anna 6m			
MARTENS, August	32	Badegast	57-1122
MARTENS, Claus	38	New York	56-1117
Anna 39, Johann 7			
MARTENS, D.	36	Elbersdorf	61-0897
Anna 32, Joh. 4, Nic. 7m, Elise 20			
MARTENS, Elise	35	Varel	62-1042
MARTENS, Fritz	28	Bremervoerde	59-0613
Charles 10			
MARTENS, Hermann		Decksdorf	59-0477
MARTERN, Jos.Mich.	18	Erfurt	57-0654
MARTH, Crecenz	32	Neresheim	56-0629
MARTH, Gottlieb	16	Gemuenden/CH.	60-0622
MARTH, Jos.	33	Dilingen	56-0629
MARTIN, Adam	18	Obervorschutz	60-0622
MARTIN, Anna Maria	21	Gutenburg	58-0545
MARTIN, Carl	22	Greussen	60-0533
MARTIN, Casp.	28	Helmstedt	59-0384
MARTIN, Caspar	26	Helmstedt	59-0384
MARTIN, Catharina	20	Leutenberg	56-0819
MARTIN, Christian	18	Alzey	59-0214
MARTIN, Elisabeth	24	Helmstedt	59-0384
MARTIN, Elise	22	Kurhessen	57-0555

NAME	AGE	RESIDENCE	YR-LIST
MARTIN, Friedr.	40	Havre	60-1196
MARTIN, G.H.	45	Eichelheim	55-1082
MARTIN, J.	25	Zeighorn	56-0512
MARTIN, Johannes	29	Scherka	56-1044
Caroline 27			
MARTIN, Marie	26	Tutlingen	59-1036
MARTIN, Martha	19	Kirchberg	57-0754
MARTIN, Miles	36	New York	62-0401
MARTINELLI, Lorenz	24	Switz.	62-0467
Igenio 17			
MARTINI, Joh.Heinr	18	Frendelburg	58-0563
Julius Fr. 17			
MARTINI, Nie.	30		59-0384
MARTINI, Wilh'mine	21	Freyburg	56-0411
MARTINKE, Ludwig	38	Roemerstadt/A	61-0770
Maria 33, Anna 11, Maria 10			
MARTINS, Andr.	30	New York	61-0897
Meta 29, Anna 3, Gesine 9m			
MARUSCHKA, Jan	24	Budweis/Boehm	62-0608
Catharine 23, Marie 20, Joseph 10m			
MARX, Lenchen	16	Duesseldorf	57-1067
MARX, Leopold	25	Leipzig	62-1112
MARX, Ludwig	24	Braunfels	60-0398
MARX, Mathilde	21	Wuerttemburg	61-0482
MARXER, Johann G.	36	Ruggell	60-0533
MARZ, Johann	19	Lippstadt	55-0634
MARZETTI, Joseph	32	France	62-0730
Gabrielle 20			
MARZETTI, Julie	28	New York	62-0730
Adele 13			
MARZINIUS, Franz	38	Kupferbach	57-1407
MASCH, Johann	41	Boehmen	62-0467
Elisabeth 34, Thomas 13, Franz 7			
MASCHEYER, Johanne	25	Minden	57-1407
Louise 4			
MASCHINK, Gus.Rud.	12	Eisleben	57-0021
MASCHKE, Heyman	20	Stargard/Pr.	60-0429
MASCHMEYER, Herman	21	Bremerlehe	62-0879
MASCHTALIN, Friedr	50	Mirowig	57-1113
Barbara 45, Johann 16, Franz 13, Marie 20			
MASON, D.G.	26	San Francisco	62-1169
MASOPUST, Joseph	35	Boehmen	62-0467
Catharine 22, Johann 11m			
MASS, zum Cath.	50	Werel	61-0804
Heinr. 18			
MASSAR, Magd.	35	Oppau	62-0730
Georg 11, Theobald 9, Susanna 5			
MASSMEYER, Eduard	44	Salz	56-0847
MASSOR, Chr.	31	Dresden	61-0047
Maria 48, Lena 10, Elisab. 7			
MAST, Heinr.	23	Wieda	62-1042
MAST, Theo.	20	Gruenenplan	62-1112
MATENAAR, (widow)	58	Louisendorf	58-0306
Maria 37, Christine 35, Johann 32			
Gerhard 48, Ida 26			
MATERN, Conrad	34	Villingen	57-1067
Marie 32, Marie 4, Heinrich 2			
MATERN, Wilhelmine	29	Washington	62-0938
Chr. 2			
MATHERN, Christine	24	Fielingen	57-0924
MATHES, Augusta	40	St.Gangloff	62-0879
MATHESIUS, Carolne	16	Herzenheim	62-0730
MATHESS, Johann	27	Michelbach	56-0527
MATHEUS, Emil	18	Cappeln	55-0932
MATHEY, v. Emil	18	Altenburg	61-0716
MATHIAS, Heinrich	22	Rethen	60-0533
MATHIAS, Paul	27	Vegesack	62-1169
MATHIES, Friedrich	53	Wendenbostel	58-0881
Catharina 48, Maria 28, Dorothea 23			
Friedrich 21, Louise 19, Wilhelm 14			
Heinrich 10, Dorette 7, Louise 1			
MATHIN, Christiane	24	Sarsheim	59-0372
MATHIS, Mariane	70	US.	60-0521
MATHWIG, Wilh'mine	20	Carlstadt	59-0372
Christine 24, Joh. Ludwig 25			
MATTER, Heinr.	21	Daschitz	59-1036
MATTER, Michael	27	Freeport	62-0232
MATTERN, Friedrich	29	Wolfsheim	57-0422

NAME	AGE	RESIDENCE	YR-LIST
MATTERN, Hermann	26	Alsfeld	59-0412
Christian 16			
MATTFELD, Louis	20	Celle	59-0477
MATTHAEUS, Amalie	32	Emskirchen	59-0477
MATTHAUS, Georg	17	Kurhessen	56-1044
MATTHEIM, Christne	20	Ehringdorf	56-0847
MATTHEUS, Aug.	17	Woltersdorf	59-0990
MATTHEUS, J.	42	Woltersdorf	59-0990
(wife) 41			
MATTHEWS, Th.	24	New York	61-0107
MATTHIAS, Anna	22	Bekedorf	55-0630
Dorothea 17			
MATTHIES, Fr.	29	Elstra Montra	61-0804
Caroline 26, Emil 3, Lina 11m			
MATTKE, Friedr.	19	Lipiarg	59-0214
MATZ, Carl	22	Stadtloesch	56-0847
MATZ, Caroline	26	Wildberg	57-1280
MATZ, Fr.	24	Stralsund	60-0411
MATZFELD, Friedr.	47	Behle	61-0930
Rosina 46, Emil 9, Theresia 7			
MAU, C.Chr.(m)	39	Prussia	57-0555
Anna 32			
MAU, Elisabeth	25	Hessen	59-0412
MAU, L.Chr.(m)	31	Prussia	57-0555
Caroline 28, Wilhelmine 4, Maria 2			
MAUE, Fritz	40	Braunschweig	56-0847
MAUER, Adam	37	Curhessen	58-0399
Marie 35, Johannes 11, Wilhelm 4			
A.M. 11m			
MAUER, Joh.Caspar	31	Gleicherwiese	57-0924
MAUER, Regina	17	Egushausen	60-0334
MAUER, Wm.	20	Emberg	61-0669
MAUKE, August	15	Vegesack	55-0634
MAUL, Anna	17	Groschenboste	62-0938
MAUL, Friederike	34	Baudenheim	61-0779
MAUMANN, Heinrich	28	Kefenrod	58-0925
MAURER, Auguste	42	Heilbronn,Wue	55-1238
Anne 18			
MAURER, Christian	22	Wennen	60-1032
MAURER, Hermine	32	Aurich/Hann.	60-0622
Antoinette 23			
MAURER, Johannette	25	Guntersblum	62-0879
Catharine 1			
MAURER, Joseph	31	Margoldsheim	58-0576
Elisabeth 29, Genoveve by			
MAURER, Joseph	28	Reifberg/Bav.	62-0608
Anna 24, Joseph 9m			
MAURUS, Joseph	27	Oberguntsburg	61-0520
Caroline 26, Anna 6, Barberle 6m			
MAURY, M.T.	54	Washington	60-1196
MAUS, Heinrich	59	Illinois	59-0613
MAUS, Hermann	33	Stamheim	57-1067
Elisabeth 34, Carl 4, (baby) bob			
MAUS, Julius	19	Amoeneburg/CH	60-0429
Gertrude 16			
MAUS, Lucas	16	Niederklein	60-0429
MAUS, Nicolaus	20	Breitenbach	57-0704
MAUSE, Heinrich	31	Duesseldorf	62-1112
MAUSER, Johann	26	Kl.Aspach/Wrt	60-0622
MAUSS, Fanny	17	Wasserloor	62-0836
MAUTEL, Heinr. L.	34	Harpenfeld	56-0951
Elisabeth 38			
MAVENKE, (f)	43	Scharmbeck	61-0804
MAY, Adam	18	Treysa	59-0613
Anna 23			
MAY, Catharine	26	Neuwied/Pruss	55-0628
MAY, Ephraim	29	Grossekarben	59-0214
MAY, Fr.	20	Bueckeburg	57-1148
MAY, Georg	36	Baltimore	59-0372
MAY, Heinrich	28	Kirchberg	57-0754
MAY, Helene	20	Trenzdorf	57-1148
MAY, Herm.	21	New York	60-0785
MAY, Lud.	25	Elkerhausen	62-0730
MAY, Meier	56	Billigheim	62-0467
Louis 16, Julia 15			
MAY, Moser	21	Raboldshausen	62-0712
MAY, Nich.	27	Kirchhausen	57-0422
MAY, Ottmar	46	Strassberg	61-0930

NAME	AGE	RESIDENCE	YR-LIST
MAY, Wiegand	18	Treysa	60-0533
MAYBERG, David	25	Loewen	59-0477
MAYER, Ad.(m)	32	Cleveland	62-0836
MAYER, Alexanderr	22	Ochsenberg	56-1011
MAYER, Carl	25	Bueren	58-0881
MAYER, Christoph	15	Kirchheim/Wrt	60-0429
MAYER, Friedr.	27	Lohr	60-0785
MAYER, Gust.	17	Ehnigen	56-0629
MAYER, Heinrich	25	Wittgenstein	57-1407
MAYER, Joh.	66	Bleurer	60-0521
MAYER, Johann	44	St.Louis	62-0730
MAYER, Johanna	17	Hextor	57-1407
MAYER, Johannes	27	Laufen/Wuertt	60-0429
MAYER, Louise	26	Minden	61-0482
MAYER, Moritz	17	Obenheim	58-0576
MAYER, Ph.D.	22	New York	62-1169
MAYER, Vincent	37	New York	61-1132
MAYFART, Hinrich	35	Sonneborn	59-0412
MAYHOEFER, Louise	15	Goeppingen	59-0613
MAYKRANZ, William	19	Herrenbreit	60-0411
MAYLAND, Dora	22	Rheine	59-1036
MAYR, Moritz	23	Zebingen	59-0613
Joseph 32			
MAYRAU, Georg	25	Heidelberg	59-0477
MAYROSS, S.	47	Storndorf	56-0527
MAYWALD, Gottlieb	38	Lugnitz	57-1026
Friedricka 34, Anna 9, Paul 5, Clara 3			
MAZEK, Joseph	20	Boehmen	61-0482
Maria 23, Johanna 2, Joseph 9m			
MEBES, Herrmann	31	Schoenebeck	62-0342
MEBUS, Christ.	45	Nauheim	61-0482
Maria 45, Wilhelmine 18, Adolph 9			
Christine 14, Wilhelmine 6			
MECHT, Elisabeth	21	Munschbach	62-0730
MECILER, Johanne	21	Meiningen	56-0527
MECKE, Wilhelm	26	Bardolffelde	58-0563
MECKERT, Wilhelm	27	Speckwinkel	57-0754
MEDER, Anna	18	Forchheim/Bav	60-0429
MEDICUS, Georg	49	Tuerkheim	59-0477
MEDRAZKE, Franz	23	Boehmen	62-0938
MEENEN, Michael	24	Marx	57-0436
Hilke Cath. 21			
MEESEGADE, Died.	25	Dondorf	60-0785
MEG, Maria	46	Kirchheim	62-0306
MEHDING, Friedrike	28	Berlin	56-0819
MEHL, Albert	25	Dellenhusen	61-0047
MEHL, Jonas	28	Offenbach	57-1067
Johanne 28, Johann 4, Robert 2			
Valentin 1			
MEHLER, W.(m)	27	Baltimore	61-0804
MEHLHASE, Friedr.	53	Gr. Mondra	56-0527
Anna 22			
MEHLHEIM, Emma	19	Sachsen	58-0399
MEHLHORN, Friedr.	58	Alberode/Sax.	55-0538
MEHLWITZ, A.(m)	37	San Francisco	62-0730
MEHRHOFF, Joh.Hch.	23	Hagen	55-0812
Mar. Elisab. 24, Mar. Elisab. 2			
MEHROFF, Heinrich	25	Osterkappeln	60-1053
MEHRTENS, Anna M.	15	Schiffdorf	62-1112
MEHRTENS, Cathrina	19	Hagen/Hann.	62-0342
MEHRTENS, Christne	24	Uthlede	60-0622
MEHRTENS, Conrad	54	Leese	56-0847
M. Ilsebein 29			
MEHRTENS, Friedr.	23	Ritterhude	60-0785
Betha 64, Sophie 30, Marg. 26			
MEHRTENS, Heinrich	18	Lorstedt	56-1117
MEHRTENS, Henry	22	Loxstate	60-1141
MEIDHOF, Jacob	42	Hoesbach/Bav.	60-0429
MEIENSCHEIN, Cath.	45	Altenkronau	61-0520
Peter 11, Conrad 7, Adam 4			
Anna Barbel 10m			
MEIER, August	36	Koenigsberg	57-0704
Wilhelmine 27, Bertha 6, Carl 3, Albert 2			
MEIER, August	35	Adelebsen	58-0881
MEIER, Balthasar	21	Zeilhard/Hess	57-0924
MEIER, Caroline	23	Linkelsbuehl	56-0527
MEIER, Catharine	18	Baiern	58-0399
MEIER, Elise	22	Soltau	56-0527
MEIER, Fritz	55	Emden	55-1240
Betty 43, C.Friedrich 19, Th. Edgar 17			
J. Henriette 13, R. Heinrich 15			
Caspar 11, Elisabeth 8			
MEIER, Gustav	26	Werl	59-0384
MEIER, H.J.Wm.	37	Braunschweig	59-0384
Hanne Mar. 44, Sophie 3			
MEIER, Heinr.	37	Billerbeck	56-0527
Anna 18			
MEIER, Heinr.	19	Huelshagen	62-0836
MEIER, Heinrich	55	Fuerstenau	56-0527
MEIER, Henry	23	Gestendorf	60-1141
MEIER, Herm.	23	Bothel	58-0399
MEIER, Hermann	16	Bremen	58-0399
MEIER, J.(m)	25	Musingen	57-0776
MEIER, Jacob	23	Fritzlar	56-0819
MEIER, Johann	22	Dedendorf	60-0533
MEIER, L.	42	Barnstorf	62-0993
MEIER, Ludwig	25	Grave	57-0606
MEIER, Marg.	14	Neuhausen	59-0990
MEIER, Theodor	22	Braunschweig	55-0932
MEIERHOFEN, Michel	55	Niuburg	60-1141
MEIERHOFF, Wm.	50	Wendthagen	61-0482
Catharine 50, Christ 16			
MEIERING, Bernhard	28	Rheina	60-0411
MEIERISH, August	26	Magdala	57-0436
Ida 26, Alwina 8, Caroilina 2			
Augusta 10m			
MEIJER, Christian	42	Rheden	59-0214
MEIKEL, Margaret	23	Muehlhausen	56-0512
Marg. 30			
MEIL, Georg	30	Kubert	55-0630
MEILE, Heinrich	21	Basel	50-1017
MEILER, Anton	50	Weiler/Pruss.	55-1238
Elisabeth 38, Theresia 25, Maria Elis. 22			
Helena 19, Margaretha 17, Maria 15			
Georg Bernh. 7, Johann 5, Joseph 3			
MEILER, Georg	28	Hemerleinsmue	61-0478
Marie 23			
MEINBERG, Johann	21	New York	59-0613
MEINDEL, Joseph	32	Tirschenreuth	57-0754
MEINECKE, Augusta	17	Braunschweig	59-0384
MEINECKE, Elisab.	30	Nassau	62-1042
MEINECKE, Ferd.	23	Helmstedt	59-1036
MEINECKE, Henriett	32	Braunschweig	59-0384
MEINECKE, Theod.	33	Braunschweig	59-0384
MEINEFELD, Emma	20	Erfurt	59-0951
MEINEN, Dierk	23	Strackholt	56-0629
MEINEN, Maria	24	Scherstens	56-0629
MEINER, Maria	4	Langweil	56-1260
Bertha 2, Catharina 16			
MEINERT, Christoph	27	Mehding	60-1141
MEINERTS, Gerhard	29	Denekamp	57-1148
MEINGON, Joseph	51	Finisterre	62-1042
MEINHARD, Elisab.	33	Breslau	55-1238
Louise 24			
MEINHARD, Theresia	28	Schoenau/Aus.	55-1238
MEINHARDT, Henry	38	Alsfeld	57-0654
Marg. 31, Louis 6, Helen 4, Henry 2			
Mary 6m			
MEINHARDT, Joh.	27	Schlackenau	60-0334
Johanna 26, Johann 5			
MEINHOLZ, Eward	29	Philadelphia	58-0815
Caroline 21			
MEINICKE, Conrad	23	Wunstorf	57-0606
MEINICKE, Heinrich	18	Forstfelde	57-1407
MEINIG, Adam	33	Ziegelheim	61-0482
MEININGER, Andr.	26	Gleichamberg	59-0951
Minna 22			
MEINKE, Friedrich	58	Luebsel	60-0533
Dorothea 59, Fritz 22			
MEINKEN, Catharina	18	Javerdenbruch	61-0482
MEINKER, Joh.	38	Osnabrueck	59-0951
Agnes 30, Heinrich 5			
MEINKOTH, Georg	46	Goslar	57-0606
Christine 47, Carl 18, Ernst 12			
Hermann 7, August 6, Julius 5			
MEINRAUS, Peter	15	Gadenheim	61-0047

NAME	AGE	RESIDENCE	YR-LIST
MEINS, Harms	27	Hohenkirchen	58-0604
MEINS, Siebers	30	Oldenburg	58-0604
Christiane 27			
MEINSCHIEN, Johana	19	Wersabe	61-0478
MEINTS, Chr. John	27	Suederneuland	57-0422
MEISEL, Aloys	26	Wallendorf	58-0604
MEISEL, Caeser	14	Wallendorf	58-0604
MEISLER, Therese	16	Sooden	56-1117
MEISNER, Rosalie	23	Breslau	60-1161
Henry 5, Anna 2			
MEISS, August	37	Singen	57-1122
MEISSBURGER, Elis.	39	Freiburg	60-0334
MEISSEL, Eduard	21	Meckern	55-0812
Wilhelmine 21			
MEISSEL, Margareth	58	Steindorf	56-0847
MEISSENBACHER, Jac	29	Schoenbergen	56-0847
MEISSNER, Carl	20	Treuen/Sax.	62-0608
MEISSNER, Gottfr.	50	Kirchscheidun	56-0411
MEISSNER, Nicolaus	28	Baiern	58-0399
Dora 25			
MEISSNER, Oscar M.	22	Halle	56-1044
MEISTER, Anna	33	Bayern	56-1044
MEISTER, Betty	23	Chlistau	59-1017
MEISTER, Ernst	9	Altenburg	62-0306
MEISTER, Freddi	30	Sondershausen	56-0692
MEISTER, Gustav H.	33	Gruz	59-0047
MEISTER, Joh. Wm.	21	Frankenhsn/Rd	55-0628
MEISWINKEL, August	43	Crefeld	56-1117
Julius 14, Margaretha 40, Richard 13			
August 11, Hugo 8, Alwine 6			
MEITNER, Joh.	26	Bohemia	60-1161
MEITZ, Elise	32	Selubbe	57-0654
Ernestine 8			
MEIWALD, Christian	28	Graditz	57-0447
MEIXNER, Peter	18	Malerneustadt	58-0925
Franz 16			
MELATA, Wenzel	32	Boehmen	60-0785
MELBER, Geo. Adam	42	Beiden	55-0812
Anna Maria 34, Babette 7, Joh. Friedr. 6			
Catharina 3			
MELCHER, Chr.	38	Cincinati	62-0166
MELCHER, Joh.	35	New York	57-1150
MELCHERS, Gust.	24	Soest	57-1150
MELCHERS, Heinr.	15	Dortmund	57-1150
MELCHING, Heinrich	19	Sievershausen	59-0214
MELETTA, Henry	25	Mainz	56-1216
MELHORN, Zacharias	22	Bandewitz	55-0845
Auguste 18			
MELIOR, Wm.	28	Gr. Buseck	62-0467
MELLE, Marie	25	New York	62-0730
Gustav 2, Marie 9m			
MELLINER, Pauline	26	St.Louis	62-0938
Alphons 2, Edmund 6			
MELLING, Ernst	28	Boffzen	59-0990
(baby) by			
MELLINGHAUSEN, L.	50	Osterbruch	55-0630
Johanna 15, Wilhelmine 7, Johanna 6			
MELTI, Francis	29	Naples	60-0785
Joseph 15, Francois 16			
MELZ, Ludwig	17	Germaheim	56-0629
MEMUT, Joseph	19	Eber	60-0785
Hannchen 22			
MENCKE, Carl Fr.	30	Altenburg	59-0477
MENCKE, Joh.	24	Bremen	57-0654
MENDEL, Conrad	27	Hesse-Cassel	56-0512
MENG, Carl		Calbach	60-0052
MENGE, Fr.	22	Herford	62-0938
MENGE, J.J.(m)	32	Alton	61-0897
MENGERS, Christian	29	Treffurt	55-0812
Wilhelm 31			
MENGES, Conrad	16	Oberselsbach	57-0436
MENGES, J.(m)	21	England	60-0521
MENIKE, Carl Fr.	30	Altenburg	59-0477
MENK, Chr.	43	Hohenroth	56-0951
Christine 48			
MENKE, Anna	20	Cloppenburg	62-0467
MENKE, Carl	21	Muenster	60-0533
MENKE, Helene	24	Buehren	59-0951
MENKEL, Blondine	20	Sachsenberg	60-0521
MENKHAUSEN, Carl	30	Menkhausen	56-0589
MENNE, H.	20	Kiesel	57-1192
MENNE, Helene	28	Raderborn	56-0411
MENNY, Julius	35	Minden	60-0785
MENSCHING, Sophie	18	Mathe/Curhes.	60-0429
MENSEL, Ant.	28	Zedechowitz	57-0961
MENSEN, Fr.B.	30	Hucksiel	57-1148
MENSING, Elise	25	Gronau	59-0951
MENSING, Friedrich	44	Woeltingerode	56-0629
Eleonore 36, Dorothea 18, Friedrich 15			
Christine 10			
MENSING, Heinr.Edw	21	Dorum	56-0589
MENSING, Maria	20	Sansteth	56-1011
MENSLAGE, Marg.	26	Essen	62-0938
MENTZEL, J.	23	Schweinsdorf	56-0512
MENZ, Carl	18	Wollstaedt	57-0776
MENZ, Catharina	19	Welzbach	56-1011
MENZ, Eva	28	Cassel	62-1112
MENZ, Pauline	26	Brix	61-0478
MENZEL, (m)	31	Schweinsdorf	56-0512
MENZEL, C.J.	43	Fulda	62-0938
MENZEL, Ferd.Gust.	18	Ofenstedt/Pr.	62-0608
MERCKEL, Ann Maria	43	Andernach/Pr.	57-0924
Therese 15, Carl 13, Margarethe 6			
MERER, Christ.	19	Hannover	57-1113
MERG, Anna Cathar.	19	Lauffen	56-1117
MERGEL, Louis	28	Goettingen	57-1280
MERGEL, Th.	30	Langenholzhau	62-0993
F.W.C. 29			
MERKAM, Wilhelmine		Trendelburg	55-0932
MERKEL, Anna	29	Muenchen	60-0785
MERKEL, Cath.	26	Hamberg	57-1067
MERKEL, Friedrike	31	Jever	57-1067
MERKEL, Georg	33	Auerbach	57-1067
MERKEL, J.L.	26	Sturth	56-0550
MERKEL, Mary	23	Niederod	59-0951
MERKEL, Philipp	24	Hassloch	59-0372
MERKER, Emilie	22	Heilbronn	59-0477
Fanny 18			
MERKSHIES, Carl	18	Berlin	50-1017
MERLAGE, Elise	24	Louisville	57-1192
MERLAN, Georg	16	Ramrod	55-0630
MERLE, Isidor	17	Brian-	62-0111
MERLE, Marie	17	Frankenberg	57-0924
MERREL, Louise	38	France	61-0716
Justine 28			
MERRSING, Joh.	26	Charleston	59-1036
MERSCHPETER, Marg.	30	Westerweihe	58-0925
MERSING, S. (Mrs.)	59	Badbergen	62-1042
MERSMANN, J.H.	40	New York	59-0951
MERTE, Johannes	54	Gennern	56-0723
Henriette 27			
MERTEN, Friedr.	42	Bischoffsrode	60-0398
Sophie 38, Adam 11, Elisabeth 7			
Christoph 2			
MERTEN, Her.	40	Driftsethe	59-1036
MERTENS, Adelheid	49	New York	58-0885
MERTENS, G.(m)	26	Amt Hagen/Han	62-0608
MERTENS, Johanna	18	Helmstaedt	57-0850
MERTENS, Martin	18	Hannover	62-0758
MERTENS, Sophie	30	Langenberg	60-0521
MERTHENS, Anna	21	Osterholz	62-0100
MERTING, Adolph	19	Minden	60-0785
MERTZ, Ad.	30	Berlin	61-0107
MERTZ, Catharine	50	Graefenberg	59-0535
Babette 17			
MERTZ, Louise	19	Hanau	60-0521
MERZ, Franz	26	Herbstein	60-0429
MERZ, Henry	35	Achatz	61-1132
MERZ, Joh. Georg	30	Stellau	57-1026
MERZ, Joseph	24	Dambach	61-0779
MERZ, Marianne	27	Knittelsbach	57-1026
MERZ, Nicolaus	28	Sackenbach	60-1053
MERZ, Philip	41	Baltimore	59-0214
MESCH, Gottlob	31	Nauendorf/Pr.	55-1238
Louise 24			
MESENBURG, Elise	20	Bremervoerde	61-0804

NAME	AGE	RESIDENCE	YR-LIST
MESER, Christ.	19	Hannover	57-1113
MESSER, Joh Friedr	22	Oldenburg	55-0634
MESSERSCHMIDT, J.	29	Hochelheim	55-0413
Louise 24			
MESSERSCHMIDT, Joh	25	Kotzenfurth	59-0214
MESSNER, Gustav	26	Oberndorf	61-0520
MESTERMACHER, Ludw	25	Bielefeld	57-0447
Hermine 17			
METAGER, Jacobina	18	Vaihingen	60-0398
METTER, Catharina	30	Hochdorf	57-0606
METZ, Adam	17	Koerle	57-0754
METZ, Aug.	18	Hersfeld	57-1148
METZ, Balthasar	29	Kl.Sendelbach	58-0563
METZ, Christian	19	Neubronn	56-0413
METZ, Elisabeth	24	Halbensachsen	57-0850
METZ, H.	16	Buergel	62-0993
METZ, H.L.	28	Ballhausen	58-0576
METZ, Ignatz	21	Spath	57-0447
METZ, Joseph	27	Steinach/Bav.	62-0608
Margaretha 27, Franz Jos. 6m			
METZ, Marie	26	Lissbing	60-0334
METZ, Wilhelm	38	Hildesheim	57-1416
METZ, Wilhelm	18	Hessen	61-0682
METZENER, Oskar	19	Daebeln	55-0845
METZER, Anna D.	60	Philippsthal	60-0622
Bernhard 24			
METZGER, Carl	18	Stuttgart	57-0776
METZGER, Cath.	25	Schweinsdorf	56-0512
METZGER, Catharina	25	Gimbsheim/Bad	60-0429
METZGER, Christina	20	Wieseth	57-1407
METZGER, Fr.(m)	43	France	61-1132
METZGER, Gottl.	20	Daunsheim	56-1216
Christ. 18			
METZGER, Rudolph	22	Gambach	57-1067
METZGER, Seligman	58	Ballersheim	62-0712
Jette 42, Frieda 15, Salmon 13			
METZGER, Therese	23	Ansbach	60-0785
Marie 31, Therese 6			
METZGER, William	14	St.Louis	60-0785
METZING, Caroline	51	Gera	59-0477
METZINGER, Chr.	22	Ottersweier	62-0938
METZKER, Fr.Henry	37	Suederneuland	57-0422
METZLER, August	39	Philadelphia	62-1112
METZLER, Barbara	27	Layfurth	60-0334
METZLER, Fried.A.	21	Dresden	59-0613
METZLER, Veronika	16	Memmingen	55-0630
METZNER, Herm.	27	Eckartsberga	61-0482
METZNER, Johann	27	Achthusen	56-1117
MEUB, Joh.H.	12	Obermoxstadt	62-0401
MEUEJUZY, Paul	45	New York	59-0477
MEUNER, Maria	19	Wuerges	62-1112
MEUNKE, Johann	23	Luebsee	57-1026
MEURER, Rosalie	25	Heinrichs	61-0520
MEUSEL, Barbara	28	Kippo	57-0704
Johann 2			
MEVENBROCK, D.	25	Wohlscheid	60-0334
MEVES, Chr.	47	Veckenstedt	57-0654
Louise 46, Jane 14, Christian 9			
MEVES, Fr.	29	Veckenstedt	57-0654
Jane 24			
MEY, E.J.	21	Goettingen	59-0477
MEYENBERG, Joh.	18	Dremen	60-0398
MEYER, A.	19	Austria	57-0961
MEYER, Ad. Christ.	16	Lobenstein	55-0932
MEYER, Adolph	33	Lesum	61-0682
Anna 38			
MEYER, Alb.Vocken	24	Suederneuland	57-0422
MEYER, Albert	20	Hoya	60-0334
MEYER, Albert	13	Blumenthal	59-0048
MEYER, Aloys	19	Wien	57-0961
MEYER, Andr.	24	Kieselbach	60-0334
Cath. 43, Cath. 19, Anna 23			
MEYER, Andr.	22	Oetzen	57-1150
Herm. 15, Hedwig 17			
MEYER, Andreas	27	Hochstedt	60-1032
MEYER, Andreas	35	New York	59-0613
MEYER, Anna	19	Bederkesa	58-0563
MEYER, Anna	43	Bremen	62-0467

NAME	AGE	RESIDENCE	YR-LIST
Minna 22, Enna 20			
MEYER, Anna	27	Oeldinghausen	59-0477
MEYER, Anna	3m	Luedersfeld	59-0951
MEYER, Anna	19	Hagen	62-0938
MEYER, Anna	15	Bevern	62-0938
MEYER, Anna Henr.	18	Wersabe	61-0478
MEYER, Anton	58	Boffsen	56-0550
MEYER, Arend	59	Fischelwarf	62-0608
Antje 50, Arend 18, Geppe 16, Jan 14			
Gretje 11			
MEYER, Armand	32	Heiligfuld	57-0654
MEYER, August	41	Wernfeld	57-1416
MEYER, August	23	Braunschweig	58-0604
MEYER, Augusta	38	Vacha	59-0477
MEYER, Augusta	38	Vacha	59-0477
Marie 8, Fritz 6			
MEYER, Barbara	28	Hohenlinden	61-0478
MEYER, Bernh.	21	Halle	56-1044
MEYER, Bernhard	19	Gruppenbueren	58-0925
MEYER, Bernhard	16	Schmilbe	59-0477
MEYER, C.	32	Basteve	59-0477
MEYER, Carl	27	Langericht/Bv	55-0628
MEYER, Carl	47	Beveringen	61-0047
MEYER, Carl	14	Cammer	57-1067
MEYER, Carl	5	Bofzen (died)	57-1407
MEYER, Carl	34	Bayern	61-0682
Margaretha 18			
MEYER, Carl	34	New York	62-1169
MEYER, Carl Friedr	17	Beber	60-1196
MEYER, Carol.	29	Radesdorf	62-1112
Sophie 5			
MEYER, Caroline	24	Meesdorf	56-1011
MEYER, Caroline	46	Minden	57-1407
MEYER, Caroline E.	22	Barkhausen	56-0951
MEYER, Cath.	28	New York	61-0804
Anna 9			
MEYER, Catharina	16	Langweil	56-1260
Bertha 2, Maria 4			
MEYER, Catharina	24	Koenigsberg	57-1067
MEYER, Catharina	32	Louisville	58-0885
MEYER, Catharine	34	New York	59-0214
MEYER, Charles	22	New Orleans	57-1192
MEYER, Charles	22	New York	56-1216
MEYER, Charles	40	Leopoldshagen	57-0654
Augusta 36			
MEYER, Charlotte	28	Neustadt	61-0716
MEYER, Charlotte	28	Halden	59-1017
MEYER, Chr.	22	Chemnitz	59-0613
MEYER, Chr.	52	Liesten	62-1042
Elisab. 53, Heinrich 24, Fr. 22			
Wilhelm 19			
MEYER, Christ.	18	Frillsdorf	56-1117
MEYER, Christ.	28	Gluckstein	57-0654
MEYER, Christ.	34	Luedenscheid	59-0951
Sophie 31, Christ. 7			
MEYER, Christian	20	Kirchberg	56-0589
MEYER, Christian	52	Salzderhelden	60-1053
Louise 47, Dorette 9, Carl 3			
MEYER, Christian	18	Lonstedt	56-1204
MEYER, Christian	44	New York	58-0815
(wife) 35			
MEYER, Christian	42	Rheden	59-0214
MEYER, Christoph	29	Cincinnati	58-0306
MEYER, Conrad	15	Ndr.Vorschutz	60-0622
Georg 14			
MEYER, Conrad H.	54	Harten/Hann.	57-0847
Dorothea 54, Maria 22			
MEYER, D.B.	15	Bremen	59-0477
MEYER, Diedrich	27	Altbucken	56-0819
MEYER, Doris	15	Stolzenau	60-0785
MEYER, Doris	26	Syke	59-0613
Johannes 6			
MEYER, Dorothea	22	Preuss.Minden	60-0371
MEYER, E.E.(m)	19	Leipzig	61-0804
MEYER, Edward	18	Osnabrueck	59-0477
MEYER, Eland	19	Bremen	60-0334
MEYER, Eleonore	46	Cathrinhagen	57-0847
Hinrich 19			

NAME	AGE	RESIDENCE	YR-LIST
MEYER, Elise	25	Verden	61-0804
MEYER, Engel	18	Sooldorf	60-0785
MEYER, Erich	28	New York	62-0836
MEYER, Ernst	30	Eldaut	56-0819
MEYER, F.W.F.(m)	17	Sondershausen	60-0622
MEYER, Felix	31	Taiskirchen	57-0021
MEYER, Ferd.	23	Bueckeburg	57-0654
Walpurga 18			
MEYER, Ferdinand R	25	Alt Paleschke	61-0779
MEYER, Fr.	21	Calle	57-1148
MEYER, Fr.	29	Drakenburg	61-0804
Eleanore 17			
MEYER, Fr. (f)	18	Preuschenstor	62-0836
Wilhelmine 20			
MEYER, Fr.(m)	40	Gehlenbeck	62-0401
MEYER, Franz	27	Altenheil	56-0629
MEYER, Franz	29	Osterdamme	59-0951
MEYER, Franziska	26	Rengersricht	57-0754
MEYER, Fried.	23	Leeste	62-1112
MEYER, Friedr.	22	Celle/Hann.	60-0052
MEYER, Friedrich	18	Ratzik	56-0723
MEYER, Friedrich	25	Licherode/CH.	60-0371
MEYER, Friedrich	17	Hannover	62-0712
MEYER, Friedrich	21	Rahden	59-0384
MEYER, Friedrich	19	Minden	59-0535
MEYER, Friedrich	18	Lehrte	59-1036
MEYER, Friedrich	23	Misselwerden	62-0879
MEYER, Fritz	18	Wellsdorf	60-0334
MEYER, Fritz	25	Muenster	61-0167
MEYER, Fritzz	25	Gotha	61-0482
MEYER, Frz.	19	Glueckstadt	62-0467
MEYER, G.C.	25	Bremervoerde	59-0477
MEYER, G.D.	25	Hofgeismar	58-0399
MEYER, G.F.	37	Quackenbrueck	57-1192
MEYER, G.J.	23	Heepen	59-0951
Lina 23			
MEYER, Georg	57	Wiersen	57-0578
Caroline 38, Caroline 12, Wilhelmine 8			
Wilhelm 5, Sophie 3m			
MEYER, Georg	18	Bayern	61-0682
Margaretha 16			
MEYER, George	30	Winsheim	61-1132
MEYER, Gerhard	27	Menslage	59-0951
MEYER, Gottlieb	18	Auhagen	62-0836
MEYER, Gretje H.	25	Fiebing	57-0422
MEYER, H.(m)	30	Rothenfleth	60-0521
MEYER, H.C.	32	Herford	56-0512
MEYER, H.H.(m)	19	Cloppenburg/O	60-0371
MEYER, H.J.	16	Langwedel	59-0477
MEYER, H.J.	28	New York	59-0477
MEYER, H.Wilhelm	29	Dissen	56-0279
MEYER, Heinr.	26	Wardenburg	62-0166
MEYER, Heinr. Aug.	29	Preussen	55-0634
MEYER, Heinrich	23	Coburg/Sax	55-0628
Christian 22			
MEYER, Heinrich	50	Hohdorf	55-0932
MEYER, Heinrich	17	Luebbecke	56-0847
MEYER, Heinrich	27	New York	56-1117
Cathrine 25			
MEYER, Heinrich	17	Inschide	57-0606
MEYER, Heinrich	17	Stadthagen	57-0606
MEYER, Heinrich	23	Braunschweig	57-1280
MEYER, Heinrich	23	Oldenburg	58-0881
Helene 27			
MEYER, Heinrich	25	Quackenbrueck	58-0563
MEYER, Heinrich	33	Halle	62-0232
MEYER, Heinrich	36	Otterndorf	62-0712
Louise 29, Wilhelm 3m			
MEYER, Heinrich	50	Messenkamp	59-0384
Wilhelm 47, Heuer 18			
MEYER, Heinrich	21	Otting	59-0535
Hermann 19			
MEYER, Heinrich	20	Buchel	59-0535
MEYER, Heinrich	23	Detfurth	62-0983
Minna 25			
MEYER, Heins	27	Huetthagen	60-0334
MEYER, Helena	24		62-1042
Carl 3			

NAME	AGE	RESIDENCE	YR-LIST
MEYER, Helene	20	Nienburg	59-0477
MEYER, Henriette	24	Posen	61-0779
MEYER, Henry	29	Westendorf	57-0422
MEYER, Henry	22	Oerthe	57-0422
MEYER, Herm.	17	Marsum	57-1150
MEYER, Herm. H.	6	Fallingbostel	57-0847
MEYER, Hermann	30	New York	59-0372
MEYER, Hermann	15	Stollhamm	59-0535
MEYER, Hermann	35	Chicago	59-0048
MEYER, Hinrich	23	Cathrinhagen	57-0847
MEYER, J.	45	Betznau	56-0512
MEYER, J. Werner	25	Bremen	61-0107
MEYER, J.A.(m)	29	Engten	61-0482
MEYER, Jacob	28	Wallau	57-0924
Catharine 22			
MEYER, Jacob	21	Stapelmoor	62-0232
MEYER, Jette	24	Polle	56-0819
MEYER, Joh.	52	Dichingen	60-0521
Cath. 55, Carl 14, Minna 17			
MEYER, Joh.	24	San Francisco	57-1150
MEYER, Joh.	30	New York	62-1169
Fr. 25			
MEYER, Joh.D.	28	New York	57-1148
MEYER, Joh.H.	15	Halste	59-1036
MEYER, Joh.Heinr.	29	Docktrop	58-0925
MEYER, Johann	27	Voerden	56-0629
Caroline 26, Joseph 57, Sophie 20			
MEYER, Johann	27	Emsen	58-0925
Diedrich 24			
MEYER, Johann	27	Goettingen	57-0924
MEYER, Johann	20	Hannover	62-0758
MEYER, Johann W.	18	Borkenheim	60-0533
MEYER, Johanna	30	Wunsiedel	56-0527
MEYER, Johanna	20	Offenbach	60-0371
MEYER, Johanna	19	Struek	58-0815
MEYER, Johannes	26	Vilsiek	57-1067
MEYER, John	38	Neuses	57-0654
MEYER, John	22	St.Louis	62-0938
Edw. 21			
MEYER, John Gottl.	22	Heinersberg	57-1192
MEYER, John Wilh.	24	Emden	56-0413
Henry 8			
MEYER, Jos.	23	Wangen	60-0334
MEYER, Joseph	28	Leitmar	57-1067
Lena 28, Philipp 6m			
MEYER, Joseph	23	Elberfeld	59-0613
MEYER, Julius	29	Bielefeld	56-0847
MEYER, Julius	30	Bremen	58-0815
MEYER, L.Aug.	28	Braunschweig	59-0535
Louise 28, Hermann 9m			
MEYER, Larine	20	Bremen	59-0613
MEYER, Leib	26	Westiken	57-1067
Anna 22, Zudel Leib 6, Hanne Leib 10			
Jankel Leib 20, Liebe 9, Sire Jankel 50			
MEYER, Leopold	39	Echte	61-0897
MEYER, Louise	25	Vahrenholz	56-1260
MEYER, Louise	22	Erle/Hannover	57-0847
MEYER, Louise	28	Elze	59-0214
Louise 8, Augusta 6, Friedr. 3			
MEYER, Ludw.	24	Stern	60-0334
MEYER, Ludwig	41	New York	59-1036
MEYER, M. (f)	24	Norden/Hann.	55-0538
MEYER, Magd.	32	Muehlheim	59-1036
Carl 8, Casm. 3			
MEYER, Margaretha	28	Moenchsheim/B	55-0628
MEYER, Margaretha	23	Zeven	61-0682
MEYER, Maria	28	Ostheim/Bav.	55-0628
MEYER, Maria	23	Marschkamp	58-0885
MEYER, Maria	19	Braunschweig	59-0384
MEYER, Maria	30	New York	56-1216
William 10m			
MEYER, Martin	29	Bramsche	59-0477
MEYER, Mary	10	Bremen	56-0512
MEYER, Mary	38	Peitz	57-1148
Arthur 6			
MEYER, Mathias	28	Deuzingen	56-0629
MEYER, Meta	20	Nesse	56-1117
MEYER, Meta	19	Schwarmbeck	57-1067

NAME	AGE	RESIDENCE	YR-LIST
MEYER, Paulus	25	Coburg	58-0576
MEYER, Ph.	36	France	61-0897
Christine 19, Phil. 10, Georg 24			
MEYER, Philippine	22	Wuerzburg/Bav	55-0628
MEYER, Rud.	32	Runlingen	60-0785
MEYER, Rudolph	36	Cincinnati	57-0365
MEYER, Rufine	28	Durmersheim/H	60-0052
MEYER, Sabina	25	Ob.Moenchshm.	55-0628
MEYER, Th.(f)	25	Bremen	60-1053
MEYER, Th.F.H.	16	Bremen	61-0482
MEYER, Theodore	17	Cloppenburg/O	60-0371
MEYER, Valentin	25	Louisendorf	58-0306
MEYER, Wilhelm	18	Auhagen	56-0411
MEYER, Wilhelm	22	Anhagen	60-0533
MEYER, Wilhelm	35	Regen	61-0682
Kunigunde 28, Eva 4, Rosa 9m			
MEYER, William	34	Janesville	57-1148
Friedrich 32			
MEYER, Wm.	29	Cloppenburg	62-0938
MEYER, Wm.	24	Dankelsheim	62-0938
MEYERHARD, G.L.	22	Millenberg	59-0477
MEYERHOFF, Wilh.	33	Wendhagen	59-0214
MEYERKORD, Friedr.	28	Billinghausen	59-1036
MEYERRING, J.B.(m)	22	Bremen	60-0052
MEYERSBERG, Ad.(m)	24	Einbeck	60-0521
MEYERSBERG, Carl	19	Coeln	61-0047
MEYERSFELD, Wilh.	20	Neustadtgoden	57-0436
MEYERSHOFF, Jurgen	27	Fischendorf	57-0422
MEYERSIEK, Alwine	25	Braunschwieg	59-0384
MEYFORTH, Valentin	42	Sachsen	58-0399
MEYNBERG, Joseph	28	Lippstadt	57-0509
Elisabeth 26			
MEYRATH, Wilh'mine	47	Creuznach	58-0306
MEYSENMEYER, Marie	25	Essenerberge	62-0730
MEYTLER, Alb.	52	Unt.Kartenbch	56-1216
MIBACH, Wm.	55	Bensberg	60-0521
MICHAEL, Cath.	48	Muenster	61-0669
Ch.(f) 9			
MICHAEL, D.	39	Bederkese	58-0925
MICHAEL, W.	26	Bavaria	62-1169
MICHAELIS, Bernh.	28	Muenster	59-0214
MICHAELIS, Carl	45	Zellerfeld	55-0932
Charlotte 50, Wilhelm 15, Augusta 20			
Carl Wilhelm 45, A. by			
MICHAELIS, Carolne	39	Berlin	57-0422
MICHAELIS, Fr.Wm.	38	Cartzig	57-0704
Marie 35, Carl Aug.Hm. 11, Caroline Wm. 9			
Julius Ferd. 4			
MICHAELIS, Gesche	24	Buelstedt	60-0334
MICHAELIS, Isidor	17	Flatow	57-0704
MICHAELIS, Johanns	39	Lichtenau	57-0654
Mary 38, Antony 6			
MICHAELIS, Selig	51	Fritzlar	61-0716
Minna 40, Heinrich 18, Julius 13			
Sophie 17, Julie 15, Caroline 9, Emilie 8			
Bernhardine 5, Johanna 4			
MICHAELSEN, C.	40	Bremerfoerde	59-1036
MICHAELSEN, Chr.	33	Milsum	62-0730
MICHAELSON, Sophia	26	Wenl	60-0998
MICHALICK, Antonia	30	Reichthal	59-1036
MICHALIK, Carl L.	24	Prag	60-1117
MICHEL, Albert	30	New York	62-1169
MICHEL, Ane Martha	48	Wetter/Hessen	55-0628
MICHEL, Anna Maria	51	Wutburg	57-1026
Caroline 13, Henriette 9, Johanna 7			
MICHEL, Arnold	32	France	61-0897
MICHEL, Barbara	23	Poppenhusen	58-0815
MICHEL, Carl	58	Muehlhausen	56-0527
Rebecca 21			
MICHEL, Caroline	32	Falkenburg	57-0776
Bertha 7, Heinrich 5, Albert 3, Otto 2			
MICHEL, Charlotte	19	Weilburg	56-0819
Wilhelm 14			
MICHEL, Elisabeth	32	Burgdorf	57-0606
MICHEL, Elisabeth	58	Riesenbeck	59-0613
MICHEL, Feist	30	Klatenbach	60-0398
MICHEL, Francisca	25	Warnsdorf	60-1141
MICHEL, Franz	40	Wien	60-0785

NAME	AGE	RESIDENCE	YR-LIST
Franciska 32			
MICHEL, Friedrich	22	Darmstadt	57-1407
MICHEL, Georg	21	Gintershof	55-1082
Margar. 12, Cathar. 9			
MICHEL, Jacob	46	Bierfelden	55-0932
MICHEL, Johann	26	Geismar	57-0850
MICHEL, Joseph	18	Borgholz/Pr.	60-0622
MICHEL, Marie	21	Muehlhausen	61-0478
MICHEL, Marie E.	20	Eppendorf	59-1036
Wilhelmine 20			
MICHEL, Philipp	46	Carlstadt	59-0047
MICHELE, Christoph	32	Beckum	61-0482
Gertrude 23, Franz 6, Anna 2, Carl 6m			
Franz 59			
MICHELS, Berthold	22	Brameln	56-0819
Claus 16			
MICHELS, Joseph	30	Erkeln	60-0398
MICHELS, Peter	14	Eicheln	56-0411
MICKEL, Geo.	38	Celle	60-0785
Israel 14			
MICKISCH, Otto	27	New York	62-0342
MICKSCHEL, Augustn	54	Wuestrow/Boeh	55-0538
Catharine 55			
MICKSCHEL, Mathias	47	Wuestrow/Boeh	55-0538
Elisabeth 46, Mathias 19, Thomas 16			
Joseph 14, Anton 11, Marie 9, Johanna 5			
Jacob 1			
MIDDELKAMP, H.H.	54	Borringhausen	59-0477
Bernhard 20, Friedrich 11			
MIDDENHOFF, Meta	20	Bremen	57-0654
MIEDENTHAL, Magdal	17	SUmberg	60-0398
MIEGEL, Heinrich	33	Falkenberg	56-1260
MIEGER, M.Cath.	15	Riedelback	62-0401
MIEHMS, Ludwig	15	Sorgenzell	60-0533
Helene 12			
MIEKSCHL, Prokop	36	Prochatitz	58-0306
(wife) 34			
MIELING, Bernhard	24	Ochtrup	60-0411
MIELKE, Adam	24	Oberdowo/Aust	56-1260
MIESSNER, Friedr.	22	Klitten/Pr.	55-0628
MIHM, Gustav	17	Sachun	57-1122
Carmin 20			
MIHR, Christ.	24	Griffte	57-0578
MIKULEWSKI, John	30	Mentour	57-0961
Catharina 33, John 12, Catharina 9			
Joseph 6, Franz 4, Wenzel 11m			
MILAW, Joach.	58	Strassburg	57-0961
Charlotte 42, Auguste 16, Ida 12, Otto 9			
Amand 6, Albert 4			
MILBRAT, Daniel	30	Grodmada	56-0411
Louise 22, Gustav 2			
MILCHLING, v.F.(m)	27	Marburg	62-0111
MILCHSACK, W.C.A.	19	Bielstern	60-1196
MILDBREDT, Maria	48	Berlin	59-0047
MILENZ, Fr.(m)	31	Rinitz	62-0401
MILIUS, Dorothea	49	Rodenberg	56-0589
Susanna 27			
MILLACHER, Emil	24	Neustadt	59-0613
MILLEG, Albert	27	Loewen	59-0477
Augusta 27, Maria 2, Charles 6m			
MILLER, Barbara	25	Steppack	60-1141
MILLER, George	25	Grossenlinte	60-1141
MILLER, Wm.	31	Haggen	60-0998
Elisabeth 41, Carl 9, Heinr. 8, Wm. 3			
Gin. (f) 6, Johann 5m			
MILLWILL, John	25	Bergholz	57-0654
Augusta 18, Wilhelmine 2			
MINCK, Conrad	20	Duchhausen	60-0334
MINDERER, Alois	45	Cleveland	59-0477
MINDERMANN, Marie	23	Ottersberg/Ha	62-0608
MINGST, H.W.(m)	37	New York	62-0401
MINGST, W.	27	Bremen	62-1042
MINKE, Catharine	19	Lohme	57-0754
MINKE, Johannes	17	Hadamar	57-0754
Engel Elisb. 23			
MINNER, Adolph	18	Breitenbach	60-0533
MINSEN, Dorothea	30	Hucksiel	57-1148
MINSEN, Friedrich	30	Hucksiel	57-1148

NAME	AGE	RESIDENCE	YR-LIST
MIRWITZ, Max	30	Bremen	62-0467
MISCH, Augusta	34	Gegensee	61-0669
August 9, Wm. 7, Wilhelmine 6, Fr. Aug. 4			
Augusta 6m			
MISDZIOL, Gregor	30	Oppeln	61-0930
MISSAMELIUS, Heinr	39	Marburg	60-0334
Elisabeth 36, Heinrich 12, Margareth 9			
Rudolph 7, Elisabeth 3			
MISSBARTH, Carolne	59	Jena	60-0521
MISSE, Johann	36	Rothenbergen	59-0951
Franz 30, Mathilde 9, William 8, Anna 5			
Francis 2			
MISSLITZ, C. W. A.	46	Goessnitz	55-0413
Louise 24			
MISSPAGL, Magdal.	20	Goettingen	57-1122
MITSCH, August	28	Unterauf	56-0527
MITSCH, Sebast.	35	Untertaufstet	55-0932
MITTELDORF, Louise	58	Wald	57-0924
MITTELKAMP, Heinr.	23	Damme	59-0214
MITTELMANN, Georg	38	Thomsenreuth	55-0845
Elisabeth 37, Magdalena 12			
MITTELSTEDT, Juls.	23	Osterowke	56-0819
MITTENBERGER, Edu.	20	Hobbach/Bav.	60-0429
Elisabeth 18			
MITTENEROTZWEI, C.	59	Glauchau	57-0850
MITTERREITER, John	33	Milwaukee	62-0712
Catharine 30			
MITTNACH, v. Max	26	Ellwangen	62-0111
MITTRACH, Elise	33	Worms	61-0897
Wilhelmine 8, Louise 6, Elise 3			
Wilhelm 1m			
MITTREITER, Wilhm.	23	Stargard	59-0477
MITZENHEIM, C.G.	25	Wailsdorf	62-0993
MITZENHEIM, Franz	24	Voilsdorf	61-0478
Agnes 32			
MITZLER, Elisabeth	1	Hesse-Darmst.	60-0371
MLEYNEK, Wenzel	31	Boehmen	61-0482
Hellna 28, Anna 9, Marie 8, Joseph 5			
Wenzel 2			
MOBIUS, Fr. (m)	47	Roedigast	55-0413
MOBUS, Catarina	14	Frankenberg	57-0776
MOCK, August	35	Holland	57-1148
Mary 26			
MOCKER, Wilhelm	55	Plauen	56-0411
Emilie 51, Christian 24, Antonia 19			
Maria 17, Rudolph 9			
MOCKOW, Carl	32	Wusterhausen	57-0776
MODE, Carl	21	Berlin	58-0604
MODEST, Johann	15	Tilsit	58-0881
MODICK, Franz	42	Vienna	55-0845
Eleonore 30			
MOEBERS, Rob.Gerh.	34	Fuerstenwald	59-0412
MOEBIUS, Adalbert	25	Pegau/Saxony	57-0754
MOEBIUS, Samuel	44	Wittenberg/Pr	62-0342
MOECKEL, Johann	24	Langenhain	59-1036
Elise 26			
MOEDDELMANN, Herm.	32	Louisville	56-1216
MOEGLICH, Geo.Phil	48	Schwalbach	57-0704
Maria Dorot. 46, Margaretha 12, Jacob 9			
MOEHE, Emil	25	Muehlheim	58-0885
MOEHLE, Herm.	45	New York	60-0334
Gertrude 45			
MOEHLE, Maria	20	Hille	56-0411
MOEHLENHOFF, Heinr	18	Triessel	59-0535
MOEHLMANN, F.	18	Binnen	59-0535
MOEHRING, Elisab.	24	Schwaebheim	58-0576
MOEHRING, Georg	28	Gatterhof	61-0478
Barbara 26, (baby) bob			
MOEHRING, Heinr.	16	Hueffen	60-0334
MOEHRING, Philipp	27	Baltimore	58-0925
MOEHRL, J.G.	51	Podelsatz	61-0669
Carol. 40, Ad. 8, Hugo 6, Gust. 4			
Franz 10m			
MOEHRL, Johann G.	48	Grossbockedra	56-0589
Wilhelmine 25			
MOEHRLE, W.J.	28	Unterschwands	55-1082
MOEHRLEIN, Joh.	31	Truppach	55-0932
Marg. 28, Barbara 5, Georg 2			

NAME	AGE	RESIDENCE	YR-LIST
MOELLENBERGER, M.	28	Melzungen	62-0993
MOELLER, Albert	24	Greven	57-1192
MOELLER, Anna M.	51	Enniglohe	56-0723
MOELLER, Anton	32	Hattendorf	56-1216
Agnes 29, Leopold 3, Florian 6m			
MOELLER, August	16	Sundhausen	61-0520
MOELLER, Auguste	18	Wuellen	56-1117
MOELLER, C.(m)	23	Krell	62-0836
MOELLER, Carl	57	Marburg	59-0384
MOELLER, Casper	17	Buende	56-1011
MOELLER, Chr.	28	Kreinitz	62-0467
MOELLER, Ernst	11	Mehle	61-0669
Louise 4			
MOELLER, Eva Barb.	16	Wilfershausen	57-0924
Cath.Elisab. 22			
MOELLER, Fr.	20	Loh	57-1067
MOELLER, Fr. Wilh.	19	Wiedersheim	57-0422
MOELLER, Fr.Jacob	42	Alperstedt	56-0589
August 14			
MOELLER, Heinr.	40	Bocke	62-0232
MOELLER, Heinrich	52	Silbeck	57-0850
Marie 52, Wilhelmine 25, Caroline 17			
Sophie 9, Friedrich 30, Heinrich 21			
Friedrich 13			
MOELLER, Johann	16	Kressenbach	56-1117
MOELLER, Rosine	21	Schleid	57-0447
MOELLER, Thielmann	22	Kieselbach	60-0334
Anna 45, Gottl. 17, Thielmann 4			
MOELLER, Valentin	33	Eiterfeld	57-0447
MOELLER, William	21	Deissel	57-1192
MOELLERS, Johann	15	Ahaus	62-0836
MOELLING, Amalie	61	Jever	58-0925
MOELLING, Geo.Fr.P	62	Oldenburg	59-0048
MOENCH, Catharine	25	Dens	56-1204
MOENCH, Georg	19	Arnstadt	56-0589
MOENCKE, Andreas	44	Moechst	60-0334
Catharina 39, Margaretha 8, Elise 7			
Ludwig 9m			
MOENKEMEYER, Fr'dr	51	Maltensen	55-0932
MOENNIG, Joh. H.	58	Ostercappeln	56-1204
Mag.Elisab. 54, Louise 12, Ludewig 15			
MOERECKE, W.C.	21	Braunschweig	59-0477
MOERWALD, Mich.	30	Birbach	57-0850
MOESER, Conrad	52	Leisenwald	58-0563
MOESER, Sophie	28	New York	62-0938
Sophie 5, Caroline 3, Wilhelmine 3m			
MOETINGER, Johanna	17	Strumpfelbach	62-1042
MOGGE, Anna	25	Pattensen	58-0925
MOGK, H.C.	22	Echzell	59-0990
Carl 18			
MOGK, Wilhelm	23	Echzell	58-0881
MOHMEN, Friederike	28	Wiersen	56-0589
MOHN, Anna M.	50	Bretthausen	62-1112
Henriette 18			
MOHN, C.	24	Saxony	57-0555
MOHN, Fried.	27	Peoria	62-1112
MOHN, Henry	26	Retthausen	58-0545
Friedrich 23			
MOHR, Carl	25	Wetzlar	57-0704
MOHR, Caroline	30	Schleid	62-0306
MOHR, Catharina	21	Rautenberg	61-0779
Elisabeth by			
MOHR, Charles	23	Stockhausen	57-0422
MOHR, Christoph	40	Richelsdorf	61-0520
Wilhelminc 34, Barberle 12			
Anna Martha 10, Conrad 6, Anna Liese 9m			
MOHR, Conrad	41	Astheim	62-0401
Elise 30			
MOHR, Elisabeth	16	Hesse-Darmst.	60-0371
MOHR, Franziska	24	Hameln	61-0682
MOHR, Friedrich	28	Pommern	62-0758
Louise 24			
MOHR, Isidor	24	Breslau	55-0634
MOHR, Johannes	14	Ruhlkirchen	56-0413
MOHR, Julius	33	Berlin	56-0951
Franziska 44			
MOHR, Ros.Car.	24	Mahr	62-0232
MOHRENSTECHER, Hch	18	Guetersloh	57-1192

NAME	AGE	RESIDENCE	YR-LIST
MOHRFELD, Friedr.	24	Vehlage	60-1053
MOHRHAUPT, Franz	54	Karolinenthal	55-0932
Ludmiller 50			
MOHRHOFF, Christ.	16	Rahden	59-0412
MOHRMANN, Rudolph	35	New York	60-0411
MOHRSTEDT, Christ.	30	Muehlhausen	57-1192
Cat. 28, Gg. 5, Amalie 3			
MOHRWEISS, Ph.	48	Gerstetten	58-0563
MOHWECKE, Friedr.	42	Hohenarstel	61-0770
MOLDSCHUKA, Ed.	25	Lyck	61-0804
Elise 22, Carl 9m			
MOLL, Richard	35	Elberfeld	55-0413
Louise 24			
MOLLENHAUER, Hente	50	Gadenstaedt	60-0398
Caroline 18			
MOLLENHAUER, Hm.C.	32	Liebenau	57-1026
MOLLER, Justus	27	Uslar	56-0819
MOLLIKOFF, Walburg	16	Dollingen	59-0477
MOLLIVADE, St.(m)	29	Corfu	62-0467
Alberta 29			
MOLLMANN, Derric	22	Budberg	57-0422
MOLLSUCH, Gottlieb	35	Blankendorf	56-0819
Wilhelmine 37, Ernestine 6			
MOLTHAN, Friedrich	32	St. Louis	55-0634
MOMBAUER, J.	48	Heyen	62-0993
E. 48, M. 21, F. 19, A. 17, E. 15, C. 9			
F. 7			
MOND, Aug.	18	Bretthausen	59-0047
MONKE, Heinrich	15	Poplob	56-1260
MONSEES, Anna	18	Hannover	58-0545
MONSEES, Meta	15	Altwistedt	59-0412
MONTAG, Charles	36	Cleveland	57-0422
MONTAG, Joseph	23	Martinfeld	57-0447
MONTANUS, Henriett	18	Ziegenhain	60-0429
MOOCK, Elisabeth	17	Alsfeld	57-0606
MOOG, Louise	21	Vaihingen	60-1053
Carl 14			
MOOG, Margaretha	23	Weidenhausen	60-0398
MOON, J.S.	38	England	59-1036
F. 27			
MOORMANN, Died.	30	Cincinnati	59-1036
Doris 28, (baby) 10m			
MOORMANN, Heinrich	26	Huede	62-0879
MOOS, Friedrich	18	Nassau	58-0885
MOOSBERGER, Magdal	26	Pittsburgh	62-0608
Marie 6			
MOOYER, J.(m)	24	Havana	62-0730
MOR, Johann	13	Schnei	62-0467
MORAST, Marie	24	Philadelphia	62-1169
MORCKEN, Trina	50	Fischerhude	55-0413
Louise 24			
MOREAU, Aug.	28	New York	57-1150
MORENZ, Ad.	53	Gruenau	57-1148
Christina 53, Charles 21, Friederike 13			
MORG, Elis.	28	Margelse	55-0413
MORGEL, Johannes	20	Oebergoenns	59-0535
Helene 45, Eva 19, Margaretha 16			
Helene 9			
MORGENBAUM, Carol.	20	Hildburghsn.	55-0845
MORGENROTH, E.(f)	24	Rodach	57-0555
MORGENWECK, Heinr.	28	Allendorf	61-0478
MORGENWEG, Friedr.	19	Kutendorf	57-0847
MORITZ, Carl	25	Berlin	62-0712
Louise 30			
MORITZ, Friedrich	37	Goellen	61-0779
MORLACH, Cresentia	20	Lehningen/Bad	60-0622
MORMICH, C. Engel	28	Stockum	55-0932
MORRO, Augusta	45	New York	57-0961
MORSCH, August	35	Colberg	56-0723
Barbara 27			
MORSE, Louise	24	Boston	62-0938
MORSPAHL, Bernh.	41	Borghorst	59-0951
Gertrude 38			
MORTEL, George	24	Willisdorf	57-1122
MORTITZ, Joh. Adam	28	Cuerdorf	55-0812
MORVISSER, Elisa	30	Kellen	61-0047
MOSCHENBACH, Rosa	24	Wunsiedel	60-0411
MOSCHENHEIM, Moriz	32	Cincinnati	56-0847

NAME	AGE	RESIDENCE	YR-LIST
MOSEL, Andrew	30	Helmstedt	57-0422
Eliza 23			
MOSEL, Heinrich	25	Uchte	58-0563
MOSEL, John	55	Maryland	62-0938
Barbara 55			
MOSELER, Ferd.	18	Freysen	60-0785
MOSER, Aron	30	Maxheim	56-0847
MOSER, Emilie	25	Ansbach	59-0047
Carl 9			
MOSES, Bernhard	38	Quincy	58-0604
MOSES, Jacob	27	New York	58-0399
MOSES, Koppel	58	Ndr.Gemuenden	62-1169
Jette 20, Rosa 18			
MOSES, Wolf	15	Lobsens	57-1148
MOSSET, John	21	Paris	62-0401
Fanny 26, Cecile 26, Louis 6, Charles 3			
Numa 6m			
MOST, August Heinr	18	Ohndorf	61-0520
MOTER, Carl	17	Bessungen	58-0881
MOTTA, Minna	30	Berlin	61-0716
MOTTER, C.H.	27	Woquard	57-0422
MOTTERER, Anton	49	Stauffen	62-0712
MOTTERSBACH, Henry	28	Emmerzhausen	57-1192
MOTZ, Christian	32	Roterode	60-0411
MOUSEES, Cath.	23	Wittorf	57-1113
MOUTOUX, Carl	18	Curhessen	58-0399
Wilhelm 14			
MOYON, Jacques	28	France	62-0467
MRAZEK, Joseph	40	Prague	60-0052
Rosalie 42, Joseph 18, Catharina 40			
Marie 7, Franz 3, Joseph 59			
MUCH, Carl	44	Sarboke	58-0881
Henriette 37, Ernestine 13, Anna 10			
Karl 8, August 2			
MUCH, Franz	28	Domattau	55-1082
Louise 24			
MUCKE, Carl	24	Jecha/Schwrzb	56-0819
MUDLING, August	33	Berne	57-1416
MUECKE, G.(m)	20	Oberschuetzen	62-0467
MUECKE, Georg	28	Beeskow	59-0477
MUEHE, Carl	31	Madison	59-0477
MUEHL, C.	51	Tielber	62-0993
A.D. 37, W. 17, C. 15, L. 13, W. 11, A. 8			
F. 2, D. 11m			
MUEHLBACHER, Anton	47	Zell	57-0850
Margaretha 46			
MUEHLECK, Philipp	43	Regardshausen	58-0576
MUEHLEISEN, Andrew	21	Wuerttemberg	60-0411
MUEHLENBERGER, Jos	36	New York	62-0401
MUEHLENBROCK, Died	19	Bierde	55-0812
Hanne 16			
MUEHLFATH, Johanna	17	Hessen	57-0606
MUEHLHAEUSER, M.	58	Milwaukee	62-1112
MUEHLHAUSEN, Heinr	21	Schemmern	60-1053
MUEHLHAUSEN, Peppi	20	Huerben	59-0951
MUEHLICH, Philipp	20	Giessen/Hess.	55-1238
MUEHLING, Adam	26	Fraurombach	56-1117
Marie 24			
MUEHLING, Cathrina	24	Neuenhof/Bav.	55-0628
MUEHLMEIER, Ernstn	28	Belle	61-0520
MUEHRER, Johann	44	Eichfier	56-0819
Marie 34, Henriette 11, Friedr. Rud. 6			
Wilhelmine 4			
MUELLE, Ernst	30	Markranstaedt	57-0850
Auguste 30, Augusta 7, Louise 5, Anna 4			
Otto 3, Marie 1			
MUELLER, (f)	44	New York	62-0467
MUELLER, A.(m)	9	Muenden	61-0482
MUELLER, Adalbert	46	Mutiowitz/Boh	57-0924
Marie 21, Anna 19, Paul 16, Antonie 14			
Catharine 11, Agnes 9, Cecilie 6			
MUELLER, Adam	22	Rodendorf	57-128[illegible]
MUELLER, Albert	38	Cincinnati	62-0100
Hanna 29			
MUELLER, Albertine	27	Kluetzkon	56-0629
MUELLER, Amanda	21		59-0477
MUELLER, Aneta	20	Ottersberg	55-0413
Louise 24			

NAME	AGE	RESIDENCE	YR-LIST
MUELLER, Ann Marie	18	Hesse-Darmst.	60-0371
MUELLER, Anna	23	Reisach	60-0533
MUELLER, Anna	24	Meiningen	60-0334
MUELLER, Anna	17	Koburg	57-0555
MUELLER, Anna Elis	16	Langgons	61-0804
MUELLER, Anna M.	22	Silbertshause	59-0613
MUELLER, Anna M.	40	Deisslingen	62-1112
MUELLER, Anton	29	Frikingen	56-0629
MUELLER, Arnold	24	Baden	58-0925
MUELLER, Aug.	20	Huxoll	57-1148
Fr. 31			
MUELLER, August	40	Colberg	56-0723
Helene 30			
MUELLER, August	24	Berlin	62-0608
MUELLER, August	27	Warndorf	59-0047
MUELLER, August	13	Bremen	59-0477
MUELLER, Barb.	25	Oberbimbach	62-1112
MUELLER, Barbara	25	Steppack	60-1141
MUELLER, Barbara	67	Stockstadt	59-0214
MUELLER, Bernardin	36	Bremen	57-0080
Rebekka 14, A.M. Magd. 12, Bernardina 8			
Eduard 5			
MUELLER, Bernhard	25	Bielefeld	58-0925
MUELLER, Bernhard	24	Billerbeck/Pr	62-0342
MUELLER, Bernhard	54	Rodebach	59-0613
Martha 52, Elisabeth 16			
MUELLER, Bertha	54	Koburg	57-1113
Anna 14			
MUELLER, Bonifacus	27	Laibach	61-0478
MUELLER, C.	58	Muender	59-0951
MUELLER, C.	63	Huxoll	62-0993
Ch. 63, S. 18, H. 11			
MUELLER, C. Fr.	24	Rudolstadt	57-1416
Elise 24			
MUELLER, Carl	28	Aschenbach	60-0334
MUELLER, Carl	33	Williamsburg	61-0779
Crescentia 40			
MUELLER, Carl	59	Wildberg	57-1280
Dorette 58, Wilhelm 29			
MUELLER, Carl	20	Nuernberg	58-0881
MUELLER, Carl	30	New York	61-0482
MUELLER, Carl	40	Zoerbig	62-0730
MUELLER, Carl	21	Altenfeld	59-0477
MUELLER, Carl	18	Diepholz	59-0214
MUELLER, Carl Fr.	59	Gahlenz	55-0812
MUELLER, Carl Fr.	43	Wiarden	61-0482
Marie 31, Diedrich 11, Teckla 9			
Adelheid 7, Wm. 3, Sophie 1			
MUELLER, Carl Herm	51	Leipzig	62-0712
Maria 33			
MUELLER, Caroline	29	Nassau	55-0628
MUELLER, Caroline	15	Wuertemberg	57-0555
MUELLER, Caroline	21	Sdt.Oldendorf	57-0606
MUELLER, Casten	37	Hannover	58-0399
Dora 30, Dora 5, Casten 3, Sophie 3m			
MUELLER, Cath.	20	Laufen	59-0384
MUELLER, Cath.	16	Braunschweig	59-0384
MUELLER, Cath.	33	Philadelphia	62-1112
MUELLER, Catharine	25	Messinghausen	59-0372
MUELLER, Catharine	25	New York	58-0885
MUELLER, Catharine	15	Groschenboste	62-0938
MUELLER, Chr.	34	Eupin	61-0669
MUELLER, Christ.	30	Riebau	55-0932
Elisabeth 26, Elisabeth 4, Dorothea 3m			
MUELLER, Christ.	17	Wuestenroth	60-1053
MUELLER, Christian	18	Waldeck	57-0606
MUELLER, Christian	26	Hammersleben	62-0608
MUELLER, Christoph	27	Gross Gera	57-0606
Margarethe 21, Marie 6m			
MUELLER, Christoph	41	Schmilowo	57-0654
Henriette 40, Friedrich 15, William 9			
Hulda 8, Emil 6, Augusta 1, Ottilia 6m			
MUELLER, Conrad	25	Wuertt.	55-0634
Catharine 24			
MUELLER, Conrad	16	Pohlgoens	55-0413
MUELLER, Conrad	26	Lauterbach	57-0606
MUELLER, Conrad	34	Mainz	59-0613
MUELLER, Conrad	58	Vanderla	59-0412

NAME	AGE	RESIDENCE	YR-LIST
MUELLER, David	28	Phildelphia	59-0214
Anna 31, Mary 2			
MUELLER, Diedr.Frd	22	Hilzendorf	61-0520
MUELLER, Donat	29	Neustadt	62-0879
Sybille 26, Nicolas 2			
MUELLER, Dorothea	21	Boeken	61-0682
Augusta 6m			
MUELLER, Dorothea	40	Braunschweig	59-0384
MUELLER, Dorothea	25	Baltimore	62-1169
MUELLER, Ed.(m)	18	Cassel	62-0111
MUELLER, Edmund Ed	17	Coburg	62-0608
MUELLER, Elisabeth	35	Watzendorf	55-0630
MUELLER, Elisabeth	36	Treffurt	55-0812
MUELLER, Elisabeth	28	Bremen	57-1148
MUELLER, Elisabeth	22	Giessen	58-0604
MUELLER, Elisabeth	23	Posen	58-0399
MUELLER, Elise	22	Kratzstadt	55-0413
MUELLER, Elise	24	Leipzig	57-1416
MUELLER, Elise	19	Sandstedt	62-0467
MUELLER, Ernestine	32	New York	62-0938
Caroline 5			
MUELLER, Ernst	37	Strelitz	57-0776
Maria 36			
MUELLER, Ernst	16	Wiederau	62-0836
Therese 22, Wm. 26			
MUELLER, F.W.(m)	37	New York	62-0730
MUELLER, Ferdinand		Radenauwalde	59-0477
MUELLER, Fr.	25	Vorwahle	59-0214
MUELLER, Fr.	9	Tortenhausen	62-0938
MUELLER, Fr.(m)	17	Zwingenburg	62-0232
MUELLER, Fr.(m)	19	Minden	62-0836
MUELLER, Fr.(m)	23	Muenchingen	61-1132
MUELLER, Franz	21	Cloppenburg	55-0932
MUELLER, Franz	28	Hesse-Darmst.	60-0371
Heinrich 17			
MUELLER, Friedr.	32	Preusen	61-0047
MUELLER, Friedr.	24	Herfurt	57-1067
MUELLER, Friedrich	20	Gotha	55-0634
MUELLER, Friedrich	56	Minden/Wald.	55-0538
MUELLER, Friedrich	36	Jarischau	56-0819
Euphrosine 34, Ludwig 9, Carl 7, Julius 4			
Hermann 11m			
MUELLER, Friedrich	14	Laufen/Wuertt	60-0429
MUELLER, Friedrich	26	Oberwohlsbach	60-1053
MUELLER, Friedrich	23	Schleusingen	56-1117
MUELLER, Friedrich	24	Weisenstadt	57-0847
MUELLER, Friedrich	24	Lagershausen	58-0881
MUELLER, Friedrich	22	Braunschweig	58-0881
MUELLER, Friedrike	24	Sansteth	56-1011
MUELLER, G.(m)	31	New York	62-0467
MUELLER, G.H.(m)	24	Chemnitz	56-0847
MUELLER, G.H.J.	27	Lehmden	59-0477
MUELLER, Gabriel	33	Wichthausen	55-0630
MUELLER, Georg	17	Stollberg/Sax	55-0538
MUELLER, Georg	17	Hamm/Pr.	62-0608
Gabriel 20			
MUELLER, Georg	32	Urach	60-0398
Louise 23			
MUELLER, George	26	Grossenlinte	60-1141
MUELLER, Georgine	61	Saal	57-1192
Mary 25, Bertha 22			
MUELLER, Gertrude	40	Bracht	61-0482
MUELLER, Gottfried	30	Henff	56-0629
MUELLER, Gottlieb	52	Endesdorf	57-0847
Anna Rosina 53, Ernst 22, Ferdinand 20			
Caroline 18, August 16, Carl 13			
Grambert 11			
MUELLER, Gustav	22	Chemnitz	56-1216
MUELLER, H.	23	Melle	57-0606
MUELLER, H.	29	Hucksiel	58-0306
MUELLER, H.	68	Havana	62-1112
MUELLER, H.	30	Berlin	62-0993
L. 30, L. 4, M. 2, H. 8m			
MUELLER, H.(m)	26	Magdeburg	61-0478
MUELLER, H.F. (m)	19	Uphusen	55-0413
MUELLER, H.J.	17	Wedel	59-0477
MUELLER, Hans Hch.	20	Horsten	61-0520
MUELLER, Harms	23	Achtelbur	62-0306

NAME	AGE	RESIDENCE	YR-LIST
MUELLER, Heinrich	20	Zellerfelde	55-0538
MUELLER, Heinrich	25	Hannover	60-0622
MUELLER, Heinrich	38	Winsen	57-0509
Sophie 34, Heinrich 7			
MUELLER, Heinrich	22	Buttendorf	57-1280
MUELLER, Heinrich	33	New York	58-0885
Anna 23, Marie 2m			
MUELLER, Heinrich	16	Dedesdorf	59-0613
MUELLER, Helena	22	Pyrmont	55-1048
MUELLER, Henry	37	Pulvermuehle	57-0422
MUELLER, Henry	39	St.Louis	57-1148
Catharina 39			
MUELLER, Henry	35	Roepke	59-0384
MUELLER, Henry L.	23	Washington	60-0521
MUELLER, Herm.	28	Leen	59-1017
MUELLER, Hermann	26	Lueneburg	61-0779
MUELLER, J.	25	Popitz	58-0885
Ernestine 22			
MUELLER, J.Friedr.	16	Glane	60-0533
MUELLER, J.G.	42	Baerenreuth	55-0413
Louise 24			
MUELLER, Jac.	29	St.Louis	61-0897
MUELLER, Jacob	36	Wunsiedel	59-0047
MUELLER, Jo.	24	Runau	56-0527
MUELLER, Joachim	32	Brok	56-0512
MUELLER, Joh.	43	Schikenhoff	55-0413
MUELLER, Joh.	44	Grattstedt	60-0785
Nicol 46			
MUELLER, Joh.	26	Bremen	61-0804
MUELLER, Joh.	42	Weissenbrunn	60-0398
Christina 39, Elfriede 3m			
MUELLER, Joh.	21	Bremervoerde	59-0990
MUELLER, Joh.Mich.	30	Doelsberg	58-0604
Margarethe 23, Louise 9m			
MUELLER, Johann	32	Sallstedt	60-0334
(wife) 32			
MUELLER, Johann	32	Glarnsee	57-0704
Emilia 30, Bertha 5, Wilhelmine 2			
MUELLER, Johann	14	Heidelberg	57-0776
MUELLER, Johann	31	Eifel	57-1280
MUELLER, Johann	56	Ob.Breitsbach	61-0520
Elisabeth 54, Anna Marg. 25			
Anna Cath. 16, Caspar 4			
MUELLER, Johann	23	Dunningen	62-0730
MUELLER, Johann	55	Memleben	59-0535
Andreas 24, Justine 22, Anna Louise 19			
MUELLER, Johann	58	Alsfeld	57-0776
Anna 34, Anna 7, Heinrich 29, Johannes 19			
Elise 17, Dorothea 9, Catharina 7			
Margaretha 5, Johannes 13, Elisabeth 16			
MUELLER, Johann	19	Breslau	57-1122
MUELLER, Johanna	17	Bremerlehe	57-0924
MUELLER, Johannes	56	Gunterstorf	55-0630
Wilhelm 31, Anna 59, Catharine 23			
MUELLER, Johannes	24	Buchenau	56-0723
MUELLER, Johannes	15	Gennern	56-0723
MUELLER, Johannes	28	Hesse-Darm.	60-0371
MUELLER, Johannes	17	Argenstein	57-1192
MUELLER, Johannes	25	Eilsdorf	62-0712
MUELLER, John	25	New York	57-0654
MUELLER, John Gg.	25	Philadelphia	57-1192
MUELLER, Jos.	21	New Orleans	62-1169
MUELLER, Juerg	24	Mittlum	55-0413
MUELLER, Juergen	37	Kiel	57-0961
MUELLER, L.(m)	30	Luebeck	57-0555
MUELLER, Leberecht	14	Ferrenbach	60-1117
MUELLER, Lenore	22	Bischhausen	56-0819
MUELLER, Lina	15	Bavaria	60-0371
MUELLER, Lina	18	Schaffheim	59-0613
MUELLER, Lisette	20	Nienburg	57-1148
MUELLER, Lisette	20	Nienburg	57-1148
MUELLER, Lorenz	26	Hamelburg	60-1032
MUELLER, Louis	23	Hamilton	57-1192
Jacob 9			
MUELLER, Louise	15	Lahr	61-0804
MUELLER, Ludw.	31	Leise	55-1082
Louise 24			
MUELLER, Ludwig	22	Oldendorf/Han	55-1238

NAME	AGE	RESIDENCE	YR-LIST
MUELLER, Ludwig	20	Gross Fehden	61-0779
MUELLER, Ludwig	29	Muehlheim	62-0758
MUELLER, Magd.	25	Hammelberg	62-0401
MUELLER, Marcus	19	Eiterfeld	60-0785
MUELLER, Marg.	24	Thuisbrunn	61-0482
MUELLER, Marg.	31	Buckarst	59-0535
MUELLER, Margar.	20	Velbel	59-0384
MUELLER, Margareta	25	Uslar	56-0819
MUELLER, Margareta	32	Redwitz/Bav.	60-0429
Joh. Adam 7			
MUELLER, Margareta	17	Freiensteinau	62-0879
MUELLER, Maria	19	Petershagen	59-0477
MUELLER, Marie	20	Kloster Oesch	57-1407
MUELLER, Marie	35	Gratterstadt	61-0478
Dorothee 48			
MUELLER, Marie	18	Stangenroth	61-0716
Rosalie 15			
MUELLER, Marie E.	24	Hollerbach	62-0467
MUELLER, Martin	20	Marburg	60-0052
MUELLER, Mathilda	29	New York	59-0951
Anna 6m			
MUELLER, Mathilda	27	US.	59-0951
Mathilda 7			
MUELLER, Meta Cath	26	Wattens	57-0961
MUELLER, Metta C.	27	Deedesdorf	62-0730
MUELLER, Michael	20	Birkenfeld	61-0478
MUELLER, Minna	21	Cassel	60-1032
MUELLER, Nicolaus	47	Obersinn	61-0520
Anna Margar. 47, Anna Maria 22			
Elisabeth 19, Catharine 16, Georg 11			
Anna Margar. 7, Christina 10m			
MUELLER, Otto	25	Altenburg	56-1044
MUELLER, Philipp	50	Meiningen	61-0478
Dorothea 50			
MUELLER, Philipp	34	Tiefenthal	61-0482
MUELLER, Philipp	47	Rendel	58-0881
Susanna 37, Susanna 15, Heinrich 13			
Philipp 10, Elisabeth 6, Catharina 3			
MUELLER, Simon Eng	35	Reuhearmming	56-0951
MUELLER, Sophie	20	Piesau	60-0521
MUELLER, Sophie	47	Bremen	61-0716
Johanna 9, Louis 6, Henriette 7			
Augusta 3, Heinrich 11m			
MUELLER, Stephan	37	Treviss	60-0533
Marie 30			
MUELLER, Therese	24	Bobstadt	59-0990
MUELLER, Valentin	40	Breitzbach	56-0279
MUELLER, Veronica	13	Maroldsweisac	56-1011
MUELLER, Walburga	22	Reisendorf	62-0467
MUELLER, Wilh'mine	21	Brohme	56-0819
MUELLER, Wilh'mine	23	Wangenstaedt	57-0850
MUELLER, Wilh'mine	27	Urach	58-0881
MUELLER, Wilh.	45	Illinois	62-1042
Anna 28, Maria 11, Harm 59			
MUELLER, Wilhelm	19	Hoexter	55-0845
MUELLER, Wilhelm	26	Teschendorf	60-0371
MUELLER, Wilhelm	49	Schierholz	57-1192
Eleonore 48, Dorothea 25, Elisabeth 15			
Maria 11, Eleonore 6, Mary 16			
Christian 18			
MUELLER, Wilhelm	42	Luebke	57-0447
Wilhelmine 42, Gottlieb 1, Heinrich 7			
Dorothea 14			
MUELLER, Wilhelmna	28	Neuhaus	57-0654
MUELLER, Wm.	22	Cassel	62-0166
MUELLERMEYR, Joh.H	42	Huesede	56-1117
Heinrich 16, Elisabeth 18, Friedrich 14			
MUELLERN, Wilh'mne	24	Wietzen	61-0482
MUELLING, Joachim	52	Rattig	57-0776
Dorothea 56			
MUELLMANN, Cath.	27	Louisville	57-1192
MUELVERSICK, Fr'dr	39	Keulen	56-0279
MUENCH, Georg Wm.	23	Issigau/Bav.	62-0608
MUENCH, Jacob	16	Wetzlar	59-0384
MUENCH, Joseph	47	New York	60-0521
MUENCK, Christoph	16	Grossenbuseck	61-0482
MUENDER, Caroline	15	Bremen	59-0048
MUENDER, Friedrich	57	Schwarzburg	58-0399

NAME	AGE	RESIDENCE	YR-LIST
Julie 44, Adelheid 13			
MUENDERLOH, Wolfg.	35	Weimar	55-0932
MUENDHEIM, Therese	30	Dransfeld	61-0804
MUENDLEIN, Marg.B.	19	Spielbach/Wrt	55-0628
MUENKE, Albert	18	Lehe	60-1161
MUENNICH, Carl	17	Boehmen	62-0758
MUENNINGER, J.Chr.	46	Schlesien	62-0306
Therese 36, Marie 12, August 5			
MUENSTERMANN, G.	23	Drensteinfurt	59-0990
MUENZ, J.F.	28	Muensingen	62-0993
C. 32, E. 14, M. 10, A. 6, J. 4, W. 7m			
C. 7m, E. 65			
MUENZ, Judas	17	Altengronau	59-0990
Fanny 18			
MUENZBERG, Joh.Fr.	28	Oels	57-0754
Louise 28, Henriette 6, Paul 5, Emil 11w			
Anna 11w			
MUENZEBROCK, Bern.	18	Brochstedt	62-0938
MUENZEL, Wilhelm	30	Buttelstedt	56-0589
MUETZE, Georg	26	Schmidtlothm.	57-0850
Heinrich 26			
MUETZENHEIM, Barb.	22	Meiningen	61-0478
MUHL, Henriette	16	Ilbeshausen	60-0622
MUHL, Julius	18	Hummelbeck	57-0422
MUHLE, Elisabeth	15	Damme	57-0961
MUHRING, Christine	38	Eicha	60-0334
Marie 15			
MUIKES, Joh.Gottl.	31	Gross Kroschi	55-0630
MULLER, Christian		Minden	57-0961
(wife) , (baby)			
MULLER, Gottlieb	43	Rochlitz	55-0845
August 43, Theo. 11, Mulda 15, Emil 13			
MULLER, Wilhelmine	21	Hebach	56-0512
MULLHAL, John	24	Roma	62-1169
MULROUX, Madl.	20	France	61-0167
MULSON, (m)	53	France	62-0467
Anna 52			
MUNCH, Christian	22	Schwarzennach	57-1122
MUNCH, Conrad	59	Gr.Buseck	62-0467
Gertrude 58			
MUNCH, Doroth.	28	New York	62-0938
Johannes 7m			
MUNCH, Joh.Adam	26	Messelhausen	57-0924
MUNCK, Friedrich	19	Gotha	56-0279
MUNDER, Wilhelm	34	Wahehausen	57-1407
MUNDERLOH, Wilhelm	25	Bremen	57-0447
MUNDHENKE, August	19	Hemelschenbrg	56-0819
MUNDT, Carl	25	Hameln	55-0634
MUNICHHAUSEN, F'ke	21	Herstelle/Pr.	55-1238
MUNK, Amalie	21	Burgkundstadt	61-0482
MUNK, Wm.	25	Meiningen	61-0167
MUNKE, Gustav	46	Falkenburg	57-0776
Caroline 36, Therese 19, Theodor 17			
Gustav 3, Louis 10m			
MUNKEWITZ, Johann	28	Lauchroeden	59-0047
MUNNEKOFF, Elise	23	Ochtrup	60-0411
MUNSCHEIN, Heinr.	37	Curhessen	55-0634
MUNSTERMAN, And.Ed	27	Malcha	60-0411
Andreas 28			
MUNTER, Ludwig	23	Haldensleben	58-0576
MUNTIGNON, J.G.	37	Bremen	59-0951
Marie 36			
MUNZ, Lud.Friedr.	28	Pluidershsn.	57-0924
MUNZ, Wm.	36	Deitz	60-0785
Georg 20			
MURAWEC, J.(m)	27	Boehmen	61-0897
MURCK, Hermann	18	Langenhausen	58-0563
MURCKEN, Gefert	16	Hannover	58-0545
MURKEN, Gewert	16	Nordsohl	57-0422
MURKEN, Heinrich	18	Worpswede	56-0723
MURKEN, Trina	29	Worpswede	56-0723
MURR, Gottfried	57	Noerdlingen	57-1192
Anna 52, Mary 22, Charles 9, Catharina 1			
MURRY, Elisabeth	29	Schwarzennach	57-1122
MURTEN, Wilhelm	45	Goettingen	57-1280
Magdalena 44, Amalia 23, Georgine 20			
Louis 18, Wilhelmine 14, August 11			
Marie 7			
MUSEMANN, Herm.	55	Mattfeld	60-0785
Marg. 14, Joh. 42			
MUSLER, Ant.	22	Weidenung	59-0384
MUSSBACHER, Betty	27	Gleicherwiese	62-0467
MUSSBACHER, S.(m)	24	Gleicherwiese	62-0467
MUSSHAKE, August	22	Offerwick	58-0576
MUSSINA, Fr'z Gust		Leipzig	57-1026
MUSSMACHER, Fr'zka	31	Atthausen	57-1416
Elisabeth 18, Balthasar 11, Catharina 5			
Regina 9m			
MUSTERMANN, J.H.	23	Gehrde	62-0836
MUTH, Andr.	23	Duerrenmettst	60-0334
MUTH, Ariette	17	Dresden	55-0630
MUTH, Frz.	20	Langenselbold	62-0730
MUTH, Martha	16	Wabern	62-0712
MUTH, Matth.	17	Ockerhausen	60-0334
MUTH, Rudolph	30	Unterriedenbg	60-0533
Michael 27			
MUVERSTEDT, Gottfr	19	Muehlhausen	56-0819
MUX, Fr.(m)	24	Gr.Drahnow	62-0836
Caroline 57, Henriette 21			
MYER, Dorothe	42	Carlshaven	57-1122
MYER, Johann Peter	26	Frankfurt a/M	57-1416
MYER, John Henry	18	Jeddingen	60-1141
NABER, Barbara	22	Kemnatheroed	61-0770
NABER, Gesine	20	Oldenburg	58-0576
NABER, John	24	Huntlosen	60-0521
NABORAD, Andreas	27	Margarethen	57-0850
Therese 27, Michael 2			
NACHAZEL, Johann	29	Boehmen	62-0467
Marie 24, Marie 4, Anne 6m			
NACHBAU, Ferd.	30	Giessen	55-0634
NACHTIGALL, Adelh.	20	Hildesheim	56-0723
NACHTMANN, Anton	33	Pemfling	55-0630
Josepha 39			
NACHTWEG, Bern.Leo	25	Sulingen	59-0613
NACHTWEG, Louise	22	Detmold	59-0613
NACHWEY, Nicolaus	23	Worbes/Pruss.	61-0770
NACIS, Johann	19	Hesperingen	62-0730
NACK, Johann	58	Germaheim	56-0629
NACKER, Adolph	30	Markoldendorf	62-1042
NADLER, Adolph	17	Tachau	58-0885
NADLER, Elisabeth	21	Rierenford	57-1280
NAEBELSIEK, Julius	20	Pyrmont	57-1280
NAEGEL, Henriette	21	Reichelsheim	62-1042
NAEGLER, Christine	37	Oberwesel	62-0879
NAESSEL, Mag.	20	Hechborn	60-0334
NAGEL, Anna	20	Untermimbach	56-1117
NAGEL, Anna M.	56	Rudenberg	56-0279
Anna 26			
NAGEL, Carl	18	Brueggen	59-0214
NAGEL, Cath.	22	Bavaria	62-1169
NAGEL, Conrad	23	Hessen	57-0606
NAGEL, Derrn	26	Asseln	57-0654
NAGEL, Ernst	16	Rheden	59-0214
NAGEL, Georg	25	Darmstadt	57-1407
Christina 25			
NAGEL, John	25	New York	62-0232
NAGEL, Nic.	16	Hettingen	60-0334
NAGEL, Ontars	43	Wesenthal	60-0998
Elisabeth 33, Albert 10, Caroline 8			
Wilhelm 4, Carl 2			
NAGELSTOCK, Helene	18	Chernowitz	56-1260
NAGENGAS, Maria	26	Hochstadt	61-0047
NAGL, Friedrich	19	Wernigerode	57-0654
NAGLER, Barb.	30	Gintershof	55-1082
NAHNAHOCH, Mathias	33	Morawith	56-1011
Anne 27, Frances 9, Francis 7			
NAHRWOLD, Ernst	30	Rosenhagen	57-1067
Sophie 29, Friedrich 14			
NAISKY, Franz	38	Boehmen	61-0478
Elisabeth 34, Catharina 10, Carl 8			
Theresia 7, Anna 5, Clara 2, Margaretha 1			
NALLE, Friedr.	17	Sulbach	61-0482
NALZ, Louis	22	Schlessingen	58-0815
NAMUTH, Julie	42	Eimen	57-0850
NANDRIE, Christian	52	Grueno	57-0776
Christian 26, August 17			

NAME	AGE	RESIDENCE	YR-LIST
NANZ, Sophia	32	New York	57-1148
NARMANN, Christine	31	Dresden	55-0845
NASBAUER, Fr.(m)	19	Eckartsberga	61-0482
NASH, James	45	New York	61-0107
NASSANN, Samuel	19	Volkmarsen	62-0306
NAST, Albr.	30	New York	62-0836
Magdalene 28, Josephine 8, Fanny 6			
NATH, Carl Fr.	24	Kapruf	59-0047
NATH, Marie	19	Gellenhausen	59-0990
NATHAN, Georg	21	Montabaur	62-0879
NATRUP, Johann	30	Westbevern	59-0214
NATUSCH, A.	55	Luckar	56-0512
Johanne 53, Johanne 26, Emily 10, Emily 1			
NAU, Andreas	25	Cappeln	60-0334
NAU, August	15	Frankfurt a/M	58-0815
Heinrich 14			
NAU, Heinr.	32	Cappeln	60-0334
NAUCK, F.W.(m)	23	Torgau	62-0467
NAUMANN, Catharine	25	Muenchhausen	57-0924
NAUMANN, Georg	31	Oberndorf	62-0879
Catharine 26			
NAUMANN, Johann	30	Stettin/Pruss	55-1238
Theresia 34, Hermina 1			
NAUMANN, Johannes	19	Wohra	57-0754
NAUMANN, Johs.	46	Gisselberg	60-0334
Elise 39, Heinr. 13, Elise 9, Johann 8			
Georg 7, Sophie 5, Marie 3, Anna 11m			
NAUSE, Friederika	33	Cheboygan	57-0422
Jane 5			
NEABUL, Wenzel	32	Posen	60-0785
Anna 28, Ambrose 11m			
NEANDER, Friedrich	28	Friedland	56-0819
Friederike 28, Augusta 3, Friederike 8m			
NEBEL, Christian	29	Hannover	58-0604
NEBMANN, Louise	23	Lesum	61-0482
NEDAMANN, Cath.	50	Haenburg	60-0785
Heinrich 10			
NEDELMANN, Albert	32	Aspe	60-0521
NEEBE, Caroline	24	Wahren	61-0478
NEEFE, Chr.Th.	41	Poelzig	59-0384
NEES, Jacob	58	Kleinostheim	60-0521
Elise 50, Marie 18			
NEESEN, Thomas	22	Logabirum	60-0533
Antje 20, Johann 17, Anton 15			
Volbrecht 47, Johanna 9			
NEFF, Caroline	24	Schlossau	57-1407
NEHMER, Johann	27	Carzig	57-0776
Caroline 26			
NEHREN, Fz.	19	Baltimore	62-0938
Ida 17			
NEHRING, Augusta	36	Milwaukee	57-0961
John 6			
NEHRING, E.	26	Pasewalk	59-0477
NEHRLICH, Heinrich	57	Appelstedt/Go	55-0538
Sophie 47, Wilhelm 19, Ernst 15			
Friederike 12, Emil 9			
NEID, E.	24	Birkenride	62-0993
NEIDERT, Leopold	15	Steinbach/KH.	60-0622
NEIDHARDT, J.G.	35	Langenselbold	62-0730
NEIER, Mar.Therese	22	Prussia	60-0371
NEILHARDT, Regina	22	Hohenberg	56-1117
NEISE, Jul.(m)	37	Hessen	60-1196
NEITERT, Franziska	19	Steinbach	56-1117
Lili 22			
NEITHARDT, Carl	17	Hessen	60-1161
NEIZNER, David	20	Praschka	56-0951
NELP, Friedr.	51	Cincinnati	60-0785
NELTMANN, Wilhelm	24	Metzhausen	59-0384
NENNSTIEL, Hinrich	27	Helmert	57-0847
NENNSTIEL, Nikolas	33	Berka/Weimar	60-0622
Christiane 30, August 6, Valentin 4			
Dorothea 2, Georg 4m			
NEPPE, E.(f)	20	Kurhessen	57-0555
NEPPUTH, Friedrike	29	Hersfeld	60-1053
Wilhelmine by			
NERMANN, Chr.	19	Cammer	57-1067
NESSEMANN, Heinr.	29	Emptinghausen	59-0613
NESSLAGE, Cathrina	17	Hatten	59-0951

NAME	AGE	RESIDENCE	YR-LIST
NESSLAGE, Marie	17	Andorf	59-0951
NESSLER, Eva	18	Koenigswartha	60-0521
NESSMANN, D.	30	San Francisco	59-0613
Lucille 23, Becka 58, Lina 31			
Margaretha 54			
NEST, Maximilian	22	Potsdam	60-0429
NETHING, Jacob	28	Esslingen/Wrt	60-0622
Margaretha 31, Bertha 6, Gustav 3			
NETTE, Friederike	28	Herstelle	56-0589
NETTLS, Heinrich	25	Leipzig	55-0630
NEU, Peter	56	Louisendorf	58-0306
(wife) 49, Heinrich 23, Hendrina 19			
Johannes 17, Wilhelm 16, Theodore 5			
Maria 6, Peter 7, Gerhard 6, Johanna 2			
NEUBAUER, Gust.	40	New York	62-0712
NEUBAUER, Gustav	34	Tanne	57-0924
NEUBAUER, Johann	22	Bronn/Bav.	60-0429
NEUBAUER, Johann	26	Mischbach	58-0399
NEUBAUER, Joseph	30	Schrotz	61-0930
NEUBAUER, Marg.	31	St.Louis	62-1112
Philippine 11m			
NEUBAUER, Rosine	40	Langendorfles	62-0712
NEUBAUER, Therese	47	Seligenstadt	60-0334
NEUBERGER, Carolne	26	Ruchheim	56-0550
NEUBERGER, R.	49	Umpfenbach	59-0990
NEUBERT, Pauline	21	Peitz	57-1148
NEUBERT, Therese	18	Hofheim	62-0730
NEUBURG, Alb.	32	Elberfeld	55-0634
NEUBURGER, Helene	17	Ruppel	59-0477
Therese 16			
NEUBURGER, Marg.	39	Winzenhohl	61-0478
NEUCHEL, Joseph	28	Waltershofen	59-0613
Anna 28			
NEUDAHL, Christ.	45	Griebau	62-0758
Caroline 44			
NEUDAHL, Johann	26	Colberg	62-0758
NEUDAL, Johann	45	Altbrock	56-0723
Louise 33			
NEUDOERFER, Casp.S	25	Ellingen	57-0754
NEUENDORF, Gustav	33	Gerswalde	56-1260
NEUHAEUSER, Caroln	36	Boehmen	61-0897
Anna 17, Adiah 9, Marie 8, Gustav 7			
Anton 6			
NEUHAEUSER, Gottlb	47	Metterzing	57-1192
Friedericke 33, Friedericke 13			
Gottlieb 5			
NEUHANS, Catharine	20	Albertloh	58-0604
NEUHAUS, Albert	19	Bremen	59-0214
NEUHAUS, Cath.	27	Bremen	62-1042
Friedr. 20			
NEUHOF, Mayer	18	Schluechtern	60-0785
NEUHOFF, Jo.Sophie	18	Dorum	56-1044
NEUHOFF, Maria	28	New York	58-0306
(baby) 1m			
NEUKIRCHNER, Chr.	45	Thuerfeld/Sax	55-0538
Frederika 40, Wilhelmine 20, Friedrich			
Christliebe 15, Ernestine 10			
NEUKS, Wilhelmine	28	New York	62-1112
NEUMANN, Bertha	26	Weisenstadt	57-0847
NEUMANN, Betty	23	Untersulzbach	60-0785
NEUMANN, Elis.	18	Niederommer	59-0990
NEUMANN, F.	24	Algeschuetz	62-0938
NEUMANN, Georg Hch	21	Bremervoerde	58-0563
NEUMANN, H.Georg	24	Richmond	60-1117
NEUMANN, Heinrich	35	Bederkesa	58-0925
NEUMANN, Joh.G.	24	Ulbsche	57-0578
NEUMANN, Joh.Gottf	29	Runau	56-0819
Albertine 20, Martin 75, Anna Rosine 56			
Auguste 22, Ernestine 20, Christoph 15			
NEUMANN, Marie	28	Neuendorf	61-0107
NEUMANN, Metta	23	Molsum	58-0563
Margaretha 19			
NEUMANN, Nicolaus	25	Than/Bav.	61-0770
NEUMANN, Samuel	15	Schildbeck	58-0545
NEUMANN, Sophia	20	Wiesenthan	57-1026
NEUMANN, Sophie	25	Muttersdorf	55-0932
NEUMANN, Sophie	18	Bremervoerde	61-0804
NEUMANN, Wilhelm	20	Calbe/Saale	58-0881

NAME	AGE	RESIDENCE	YR-LIST
NEUMANN, Wm.	17	Lehe	60-0521
NEUMANN, Wm.	17	New York	62-0401
NEUMARK, Bernh.	23	Krotoschin	57-0578
NEUMARK, Caroline	22	Wilhelmsdorf	57-0961
NEUMEISTER, Johann	41	Wien	57-0924
NEUMEYER, Barbara	24	Siefershaide	57-1407
NEUMEYER, Carl	23	Arolsen	57-0606
NEUN, Carl	59	Hoellrich	55-0630
NEUN, Wilhelm	24	Buedingen	59-0613
NEUNER, Barbara	21	Siglitzhof	61-0520
NEUNKEN, Cath.	62	Hornbach	62-0467
NEUPERT, Ed.	23	Potsdam	56-1216
NEUPERT, Eva M.	57	Coburg	57-0422
Adolphus 9, Charles 8			
NEURAD, Elisabeth	26	Niederursel	55-1082
NEURATH, Christine	23	Niederursel	60-1196
NEURAULER, Fr.Ant.	24		57-1416
NEUROTH, Anton	36	Colberg	56-0723
Louisa 28			
NEUROTH, Elisabeth	20	Rotenburg/Hes	55-0628
NEUSCHAEFER, John		Rennerthausen	56-1260
NEUSCHAEFFER, (f)	40	New York	58-0306
Hanna 27			
NEUSEL, Johann	45	Solingen	60-1161
NEUSER, Eberhard	51	Prussia	55-0538
Agnesia 41, Johann 22, Anton 18			
Wilhelm 14, Heinrich 9, Carl 8			
NEUSTADEL, Meyer	34	Pressburg	57-0422
NEUSTAEDTER, David	32	Muenchen	59-0951
NEUT, Michael	28	Springfield	58-0815
NEUVAHL, Isaac	20	Mischede	60-0334
NEUWEGER, Elisab.	26	Ingenhausen	57-0704
NEUYMANN, S.Sara	16	Wiesentau	59-0477
NEWCOMBE, George	19	London	62-1169
NICKEL, August	23	Schloppe	61-0779
NICKEL, Barbara	18	Esrod	56-1011
NICKEL, Eduard	31	Frankenstein	61-0770
Marie 24, Oscar 3, Rudolph 4m			
NICKLES, Urs.	32	Felsbrunn	59-0990
NICKOL, Carl	40	Lauterbach	60-0398
Marie 50, Johann 17, Johannes 15			
Heinrich 9, Marie 7, Sophie 4			
NICOL, Marg.B.	30	Ickelheim	62-0836
NICOLAI, Elisabeth	17	Niederweisel	62-0730
NICOLAI, Fr.	10	Muenster	62-1112
NICOLAI, Jacob	39	Springlingen	62-0001
Peter 14			
NICOLANDS, Fr'dke.	29	Netze	59-0535
Christine 9, Christian 5, Friedrich 3			
NIDA, v. Elis.	43	Mannheim	56-1216
Minna 9			
NIEBERGA, Wilhelm	40	Kiselbach	58-0545
Elisabeth 44			
NIEBERGALL, Elias	59	Kieselbach	57-1026
Christine E. 43, Elias 25, Johannes 22			
Elisabeth 19, Margaretha 16, Joh.Georg 14			
Christ.Elisb 9			
NIEBLER, Elisabeth	28	Buch	60-1032
NIEBLING, Christ.	30	Ulm	55-0932
NIEBUHR, Simon	19	Kirchheide	57-1407
NIEDABREMER, Anne	23	Bieren	56-1011
NIEDER, Friedrich	28	Wolfenbuettel	60-0429
NIEDERMEIER, John	54	Steinbeck	57-1148
Dor. 56, William 16			
NIEDERWINTER, Wm.	32	Haselbeck	61-0520
NIEDHOLD, Wilhelm	23	Eisenberg	61-0520
NIEGEL, Carl	27	Bladen	61-0167
NIEHAUS, B.(m)	18	Cincinnati	61-0804
NIEHAUS, H. (m)	20	Achtrup	62-0836
NIEHAUS, Marie	20	Bethen	59-0951
NIEHAUS, Meta	30	Berne	59-0613
NIEHL, Walburga	28	Balt	57-1113
Maria 4m, Antonia 56			
NIEHOFF, C.L.	33	Chicago	57-1192
NIEHRING, A.	47	Neise	56-0512
NIEHUES, Johann	59	Leipzig	55-0630
Rosine 45			
NIEHUS, C.(m)		Goettingen/Ha	60-0622

NAME	AGE	RESIDENCE	YR-LIST
NIEMANN, Anton	25	Cloppenburg/O	60-0371
NIEMANN, C.W.(m)	30	San Francisco	60-0785
Charlotte 21			
NIEMANN, Gertrude	28	Suedholz	59-0412
NIEMANN, Heinrich	15	Suedfelde	57-1122
NIEMANN, J.H.	29	Haltern	62-0401
M.Engel 25, Minna 2, Marie 3m			
NIEMANN, Marie	33	Friesoythe	59-0951
NIEMEYER, Heinr.	43	Hohe	59-1036
NIEMEYER, Louis	21	Braunschweig	55-0932
NIEMEYER, Ludwig	19	Deissel	62-0100
NIEMEYER, Sophia	20	Blomberg	56-0512
NIEMOELLER, J.Hch.	27	Huecker	61-0779
NIEMS, August	16	Colberg	56-0723
NIEMUTH, Georg	39	Karwenhof	55-1082
Louise 24			
NIENABER, Clara	21	Vechta	59-0412
NIENDICKER, Louise	27	Bochholt	62-0938
NIENHAEUSER, Henry	18	Markendorf	56-1011
NIENHARDT, Carl	20	Markoldendorf	57-1280
NIEPAG, Eduard	47	Calbe/Saale	58-0881
Maria 47, Minna 14, Otto 11, Louise 7			
Carl 2			
NIEPER, Ludwig	29	Neudorf	56-0411
Dorothea 25, August 4, Dorothea 6m			
NIEPORTE, Catharin	56	Buehren	56-1117
Elisabeth 22, Diedrich 25, Rudolph 17			
Heinrich 25			
NIER, Catharine	24	Teppenhausen	55-0845
NIERMANN, Caspar	27	Wellinghausen	57-0447
NIERMANN, Franz'ka	31	Muenster	59-0951
NIERMANN, Joseph	24	Essen	58-0545
Josepha 22			
NIES, Joh.Wilh.	18	Rossbach	61-0478
Joh.Peter 12, Anna Maria 4, Anna Elise 42			
NIES, Mary	17	Pouches	59-0990
NIESS, Anton	52	Georgenhausen	57-0924
Dorothea 47, Carl 19, Dorothea 22			
Anton 17, Geo.Heinrich 14, Maria 8			
Magdalena 4, Maria by			
NIESSEN, P.	34	Aachen	62-1042
NIESSLE, Wilhelm	4	Stuttgart	56-0512
NIEWEG, John B.	30	Lieme	57-0422
Julia 17, A. 40, Jane 26			
NIEWEGE, Christian	33	Lieme	57-1407
Florentine 23			
NIGGLE, Georg	22	Molenes	56-0951
NIGL, Therese	28	New York	56-1216
Emilie 5			
NIKOLASCHEFF, Jos.	32	Dublowitz	55-0845
Barbara 24, Marie by			
NIPPER, Ant.	34	Cincinnati	57-1192
NITSCHE, August	25	Gotha	56-0847
NITSCHKE, Chr. Fr.	36	Darmuetzel	62-0001
Christine Wm 36, Carl Friedr. 13			
Wm. Julius 4, Augusta Wm. 2			
NITSCHKE, Heinr.	35	Erfurt	56-0629
Martha 35, Heinrich 7, Elisabeth 4			
Caroline 9m			
NIX, Christian	30	Duesseldorf	60-0785
NOBIS, Daniel	44	Hessen	57-0606
Elisabeth 42, Anna 14, Louise 7			
Henriette 3			
NOCK, Joseph	32	Bavaria	62-0758
NOCKIN, Anna	31	Chicago	59-0477
Lina 3, Bertha 2, Amanda 6m			
NOEBEL, Ernst	22	Altenburg	60-0429
NOEDING, Martha	26	Kornfeld	56-0411
NOELKE, Jac.	15	Bremerfoerde	59-1036
NOELLMANN, Heinr.	23	Rothenfelde	59-0613
NOENEIR, Joseph	50	Alkosen/Aust.	55-1238
Louise 24			
NOESSLER, Eva Elis	32	Herrnbreitung	62-0001
NOETHE, (f)	35	America	56-1216
NOHARWITZ, Mathaus	31	Bemen	57-1280
NOHN, Margaretha	49	Sinsheim	62-0467
NOHR, Theod.	22	Greussen	61-0669
NOLD, Heinrich	56	Haussen	57-0847

NAME	AGE	RESIDENCE	YR-LIST
Maria 20			
NOLHARDT, Peter	20	Eimshausen	60-1032
NOLKEMPER, F.	45	Neuenkirchen	59-0990
(f) 42, (f) 16, (f) 14, (m) 10, (m) 4			
NOLL, Carl	40	Giessen	59-0951
Sophie 33, Sophie 6m			
NOLL, Jacob	31	Unterzuhl	57-1113
NOLL, Johann	32	Kl.Eichholzhm	62-0608
NOLL, John	23	Nachtillhsn.	57-0422
NOLL, Margaretha	15	Soden	60-1141
NOLLAND, Robert	32	Weimar	61-0167
NOLLE, Albert	23	Dresden	59-0951
NOLLE, Ernst	39	Rossleben/Prs	61-0770
Christiane 35, Charlotte 10, Friedrich 7			
Friedrich 4			
NOLTE, Anton	32	Grundsteinhm.	59-0372
NOLTE, Carl	46	Beverungen	56-1044
NOLTE, Christian	18	Niederwoehren	60-0533
NOLTE, G.	21	Freienhafen	62-1169
NOLTE, Georg	38	Mersenkamp/He	55-0628
Louise 24, David 11m			
NOLTE, Heinrich	33	Hessia	56-0847
NOLTE, Peter	25	Prussia	55-0538
Franziska 22			
NOLTE, Wilhelm	37	Dudensen	56-0589
Agnesia 41			
NOLTEN, Carl Ant.	58	New York	62-0712
NOLTING, Augusta	23	Guetersloh	57-0961
Anna 22			
NOLTING, Johann	23	Grissen	57-0447
NONNENKAMP, Henr´t	23	Bextehoevede	60-1141
NONNENMACHER, Crln	19	Breitenstein	60-0521
NONNENPREDIGER, J.	26	Grabbionne/Pr	62-0608
NOPPER, Joseph	34	Herbolzheim	62-0879
NORBOHM, Carl	20	Eiderfeld	57-1113
Julie 22			
NORDEN, Heinrich	27	Holtans	58-0925
NORDEN, Heinrich	26	Stelligt	59-0535
NORDEN, Henry	35	Wense	57-0422
NORDHAUS, John H.	43	Altenburg	60-0521
Anna 36			
NORDHAUS, Wilhelm	45	Osnabrueck	57-1407
Augusta 8			
NORDHOFF, Jos.	24	Damme	59-0951
NORDMEYER, F.H.	59	Buecken	59-0535
Sophie 15			
NORDMEYER, Wilhme.	17	Golbeck	58-0306
Ernst 15			
NORDSIECK, W.(m)	38	New York	62-0836
Cath. 33, Mathilde 4			
NORK, August	25	Berk	61-0478
NORMANN, Lina	20	Bremen	61-0478
NORMANN, v.Carolne	24	Ludwigsburg	60-0521
Josephine 20			
NORMANN, v.Josefin		Ludwigsburg	61-0482
NORTDORF, Caroline	40	New York	59-0048
Franzisca 19			
NORTHNAGEL, Wilh.	19	Barchfeld	58-0576
NOSSECK, Joseph	29	Boehmen	61-0930
Cathrina 21			
NOTHACKER, Anna B.	20	Wuerttemberg	60-0411
NOTHACKER, Joh.Geo	27	Oferdingen	59-0412
NOTTMEIER, Louise	25	Dankersen	57-1067
NOURVITT, (f)	24	Paris	62-0938
NOVOTNY, Joseph	43	Budweis/Boehm	62-0608
Anna 37, Johann 19, Martin 5, Norbert 10m			
NOWACK, Carl	17	Kallen	55-1082
NOWACK, Joseph	54	Belokozel	56-1260
Dorothea 55, Johann 18, Franz 15			
Joseph 5, Franziska 7, Maria 9m			
NOWAG, Carl	35	Leibel	57-1280
Elisabeth 26, Louise 6m, Herrmann 2			
Anna 60			
NOWAK, Gottlieb	38	Codleve	55-0845
Ferdinand 9, Robert 5, Elisabeth 39			
Louisa 3			
NOWAK, Johann	25	Buschowitz/Bo	57-0924
Ludmilla 26, Wenzel 3			

NAME	AGE	RESIDENCE	YR-LIST
NOWOTNY, Johann	23	Boehmen	62-0467
Anna 22			
NUECHTER, Nicolaus	38	Kothen	57-1026
Anna Mag. 39, Gertrud 10, Martin 7			
NUERGE, Chr.	18	Doehren	60-0533
NUERNBERG, Barb.	26	Ingolstadt	61-0669
NUERNBERG, S.	29	Aachen	62-1042
NUERNBERGER, Elis.	30	Grafenrath	56-0819
NUESS, Lewich	17	Haitz	60-1141
NUESSE, B.H.	24	Mehringen	62-0993
NUHLHENCH, R.	18	Cassel	56-0512
NUHU, Anna Eva	43	Hessen	56-1044
Adam 17			
NUHU, Michael	20	Niederaula	56-1044
Adam 18			
NUNNER, Andr.	24	Anspach	57-1416
NUNZ, Christian	23	Westhofen	59-0048
NURRE, Bernhard	50	Evansville	58-0815
Bernhardine 38, Joseph 6, Georg 2			
NUSSBAUMER, Elisab	30	Ihringer	58-0881
NUSSBICKEL, Carlne	44	Baltimore	61-0804
NUTH, Margaretha	40	Bavaria	60-1161
Christ 4			
NUTTELBURG, D.G.	28	Unthuisen	62-0306
Gesina 32			
NYSTEDT, O.	27	Stockholm	57-0961
O'BEIRNE, Ivan	42	England	62-0938
O'Neill, C.F.	25	England	59-0613
OBACHT, Franz	34	Baden	60-1032
OBERDIEK, John	24	Marssel	57-0961
OBERDORF, Andreas	36	Remlingen	60-1053
OBERENTA, Anna	20	Grossgarnstad	56-0512
OBERG, August	31	Meinbrexen	61-0930
OBERGFELL, Isidor	26	Klengen	62-0467
Marie 24, Marie 11m, Matthias 23			
Philipp 19, Paul 12			
OBERGFELL, Johann	27	Erdmannsweile	62-0467
Dominic 18			
OBERKAMP, Anna	18	Habern	57-0422
Theresa 21			
OBERKAMP, Armand	30	Cincinnati	57-0422
OBERLAENDER, Math.	25	Friedensdorf	60-0521
Carl 4, Louise 3, Oscar 11m			
OBERLAENDER, Th.	32	Blankenburg	57-0422
Sophia 28			
OBERLE, Jacob	34	Johlingen	62-0712
OBERLE, Johann	22	Hesse-Darmst.	60-0371
OBERLEIN, Conr.	27	Bremervoerde	59-0990
(f) 19			
OBERMARCK, H.(m)	30	Gessmold	57-0555
K.M.(f) 30			
OBERMARK, Caspar	18	Spradow	56-1011
OBERMEYER, Friedr.	27	Papenhausen	57-0422
OBERMEYER, Heinr.	47	Landshut	56-0819
OBERMEYER, Ilsbein	58	Nienhagen/Lip	55-1238
Louise 24			
OBERMOELLER, Peter	30	Buende	56-1011
Augusta 24			
OBERNDOERFER, Jac.	20	Furth	59-0048
OBERRENSLER, Marg.	55	Sonnberg/Pr.	55-1238
OBST, Friedr.Wilh.	50	Zulichau	57-1026
Caroline 56			
OBST, Selma	19	Eisenberg	57-0436
OCHS, Amalie	20	Hoechst a/M	59-0477
OCHS, Anna	42	Sollenberg	57-0447
OCHS, Fanny	14	Hoechst	59-0477
OCHS, Henry	26	Jesberg	60-0411
OCHS, Minna	21	Wenings	59-0990
OCHS, Rebecca	20	Ulmbach	58-0885
Jette 18			
OCHS, William	19	Niederzweden	59-0384
OCHSE, Gertrude	23	Rosenthal	61-0682
OCHSENFURT, Marie	22	Dankersen	57-1067
OCHSMANN, Wilhelm	18	Dainrode	56-0723
Pauline 16			
OCHTMANN, John	30	California	55-1238
Maria 28			
OCKEN, Sophie	56	Bremen	57-1148

NAME	AGE	RESIDENCE	YR-LIST
OCKER, August	24	Diepholz	59-0214
OCKERMANN, Heinr.	23	Veckerhagen	57-0924
OCKERT, Maria	26	Baden-Baden	62-0758
ODEN, Fried.A.Wm.	19	Berlin	59-0477
ODENWAELDER, Anton	28	Kranzberg	61-0520
Joh. Magdal. 35, (child) bob			
ODENWAELDER, Marg.	35	Ditzelbach	61-0520
Philipp 9, Elisabeth 4, Heinrich 2			
ODERSSEN, Margaret	22	Wulmsdorf	61-0478
ODEWALD, Carl	24	New York	56-0847
OEBBECKE, Anton	19	Jacobsberg	62-0879
OEBICKE, (m)	23	Warburg	58-0306
OECHSNER, Andreas	24	Tauberettersh	58-0925
Casper 31, Marie 1, Barbara 2m			
OECHSNER, Barbara	23	Tauberretters	58-0925
OECHSNER, Christ.	25	Kolba	61-0520
OECKERT, Louis	25	Oberfrohna	62-0712
OEFINGER, Chr.	36	Aldingen	62-0467
Anna 29			
OEHL, Eva M.	23	Lindflur	61-0897
OEHLER, Christian	21	Untereiseshm.	60-0429
Rosine 26			
OEHLER, Rob.	28	Zeitz	62-1042
OEHLERS, Marie	17	Braunschweig	57-1280
Caroline 19			
OEHLKE, Ernestine	24	Pitzerie	56-0632
OEHLKE, Gottfried	29	Glaskowo	57-0704
OEHLKE, Michael	57	Pitzerie	56-0632
Henriette 29, Henriette 14, Augusta 9			
Albertine 6, Emil 3, Julius 1			
OEHNS, Carl Julius	36	Jueterborg	59-0412
OELBERMANN, F.W.	26	Cologne	62-0111
OELFKE, Dorothea	21	Fallingbostel	57-0847
OELFKE, Heinrich	56	Fallingbostel	57-0847
Dorothea 35			
OELKER, Carl	30	York	58-0563
OELRICH, Carl	25	Berlin	57-0422
OENTRICH, H.(m)	29	Washington	62-0730
OENTRICH, J.H.(m)	18	Syke	62-0730
OERDING, Johann	23	Deimstadt	57-0776
OERTEL, Gustav	25	Freiburg/Prus	55-1238
OERTEL, Margaretha	26	Isling	55-0630
OERTEL, Minna	25	Marklesa	61-0930
OERTEL, Pauline	25	Leipzig	60-0334
OERTEL, W.	26	Leipzig	56-1044
Dorothea 27, Emilie 1			
OERTELS, Friedrika	24	Gensbach	57-0654
OERTLACH, An Cath.	20	Hettingen	57-0847
OERTREICH, Heinr.	23	Philadelphia	56-1216
OESER, August	32	Mellzen/Sax.	55-0538
Wilhelmine 30, Ida 8, Ernst 6, Augusta 4			
Emil 2			
OESER, Otto	18	Giessen	62-0879
OEST, Hch. Claus	25	Nordteda/Hann	60-0622
OESTE, W.	20	Eschenstruth	62-0993
OESTER, Andreas	23	Bavaria	62-0758
OESTEREICHER, Lina	19	Alzenau	60-1032
OESTREICHER, Joh'a	24	Alzenzau	59-0990
OETJEN, D.	18	St.Juergens	59-0951
OETTING, Wilh'mine	15	Bremen	62-0758
OETTINGER, Friedr.	21	Montverene	60-0521
OETTLING, Fr.	22	Herrenkamp	59-1036
OETZEL, Johannes	69	Wallburg	60-1053
Maria 55, Martha 12, Andreas 10			
OFENSTEIN, Johann	66	Thalau	56-1216
OFF, Friedrich	24	Wuertemberg	58-0925
OFFINGEN, Wilhelm	23	New York	62-1169
OFFNER, Juditha	54	Lichtenstadt	61-0716
OHLAND, Wm.	30	Bruchdorf	62-0401
OHLE, Fr. T.	18	Vesselhoevede	60-1196
OHLE, Hinr.	31	Baltimore	59-0214
OHLENDORF, Heinr.	33	Gross Heere	56-1260
OHLENKAMP, Diedr.	24	Lemke	58-0563
Dorothea 22, Joh.Heinr.W. 20			
Fr.Conrad 17, Marie 14			
OHLMANN, William	29	Fakelstedt	57-0422
OHLMEYER, Heinrich	7	Bremen	57-0606
OHM, Carl	27	Ottenstein	57-0606

NAME	AGE	RESIDENCE	YR-LIST
OHM, Catharina	28	Attendorn	57-0606
OHM, v. Johann	40	Bremen	62-0232
OHMERS, Henriette	36	Bremen	59-0477
Therese 2			
OHMICHEN, Mathilde	36	Dresden	57-0606
Edmund 7			
OHNEMUS, Andreas	39	Quincy	59-0613
OHNHAUSEN, Henry	49	Pfedebach	57-1148
Caroline 44, Caroline 9, Gustav 5			
OHSENFORT, Marie	22	Dankersen	57-1067
OKERT, Wilhelmine	44	Dessau	56-0411
Anna 34, Wilhelm 9, Otto 7, Anna 2			
OLAND, Nicl.	39	Steuren	59-1036
OLBACH, Caspar	46	Mengede	60-1032
OLBEN, Helen	28	U.S.	55-1082
Louise 24			
OLBERDING, H.H.	36	Emden	55-0932
Wilhelm 32, Agnes 6, Heinr. 4			
Elisabeth 2			
OLBERDING, Joh.	28	Steinfeld	61-0669
Wilhelmine 10, Caroline 8, Helene 6			
OLBERMANN, Peter	15	Beltheim	59-0613
OLBERMANN, Peter	30	Nedford	59-0613
OLDE, Friederike	18	Wuerttemberg	61-0682
OLDEMEYER, Theodor	22	Stolzenau	55-0634
OLDENDIECK, Joseph	21	Ellenstedt	59-0535
Elisabeth 56, Catharine 16			
OLDENHAGEN, Johann	46	Badbergen	60-1032
Margrete 44, Catharine 16, Hermann 20			
Heinrich 15, Anna 5			
OLDENHOFF, Carl	22	Bassum	60-0411
OLEDORF, Carl Hch.	20	Curhessen	55-0634
OLKER, Hanns	38	Atel	59-1036
OLPER, Otto	17	Beck	59-1036
OLPP, Carl Wm.	24	Merklingen	59-0214
OLRICH, Louise	21	Laumuehlen	60-1032
OLSEN, Sophie	20	Verden	56-0847
OLT, Barbara	21	Waldamorbach	58-0925
OLTHOFF, Aug.	16	Detmold	59-0613
OLTINGER, Louisa	24	New York	62-0938
Henry 6, Delia 4			
OLTINGER, M.	41	Baltimore	62-0938
OLTMANN, Ludwig	34	Ostfriesland	55-0413
Louise 24			
OLTMANN, O.S.	35	St.Georgiwold	55-0413
Louise 24			
OLTMANN, Wilh.	25	Emden	58-0925
OLTROGGE, H.C.	28	Horsten	59-0384
OLTROGGE, Soph.Chr	30	Hannover	59-0384
OMLAR, Jakob	28	Rh.Baiern	59-0412
OMMEN, Ammo	53	Alfensiel	56-1260
ONDE, Johanna	31	Breslau	61-0897
Julius 4m			
ONDEREICK, Tilm	36	Vluym	57-0422
ONESO, Guiseppe	31	Italy	61-0716
ONETO, Gerominne	21	Italy	61-0716
OPHULS, Carl	23	Crefeld	61-0107
OPITZ, Albert	36	Berlin	61-0520
Sophie 31, Louise 6, Helene 3			
OPPENHEIM, Anton	19	Pressia	60-0521
OPPENHEIM, Berndne	39	Hannover	60-0521
OPPENHEIM, Leopold	20	Offenbach/M.	62-0879
OPPENHEIMER, Aron		Oberzell	59-0951
Brenile 20, Mathilde 15, Moses 12			
OPPENHEIMER, Beta	20	Kleintreubach	60-0521
OPPENHEIMER, D.	52	New York	62-1169
OPPENHEIMER, Max	30	Baden	56-0847
OPPENHEIMER, Soph.	20	Baden	61-0107
OPPENLANDER, Gottl	25	Waldruems	62-0879
OPPER, Catharine	40	Aurich	57-0578
OPPER, Conrad	42	Schuckhausen	57-0606
OPPER, Georg	29	Elze	57-0578
OPPER, H.	34	Aurich	57-0578
OPPER, Heinrich	30	Oberseemen/CH	60-0622
Catharine 30, Catharine 15, Johannes 12			
Margaretha 2			
OPPERMANN, Christ.	22	Grobau	60-0521
OPPERMANN, Marie	20	Neukirchen	62-0879

NAME	AGE	RESIDENCE	YR-LIST
ORFKE, Heinrich	26	Fallingbostel	58-0399
ORLEMANN, Rosa	19	Oppenheim	60-0785
ORTEGEL, Margareta	18	Frauenaurach	60-0533
ORTEL, Carl	16	Eckartsborn	55-0932
ORTH, Catharine	23	Moellerich	57-1148
ORTH, Chr.	20	Bavaria	62-1169
ORTH, Ludwig	35	Kirtorf	55-0630
ORTHAUS, Jos.	36	New York	59-0477
Franziska 29, Joseph 3			
ORTHEY, Julius	24	Coblenz	59-0372
Bertha 36, Agnes 12			
ORTLAND, G.(m)	35	New York	62-0467
ORTLEB, A.W. (m)	24	Gotha	61-0682
Ida 24			
ORTMANN, Fr.	23	Halle	56-0951
ORTWEIN, Louise	21	Volkmarsen	62-0306
ORTWEIN, Valentin	33	Bramrode	55-0845
OSANG, Heinrich	30	Bothfeld/Pr.	55-0628
OSBERG, Franz	32	Berlin	61-0804
OSBORNE, W.	18	England	62-0938
OSBRINGHAUS, Heinr	40	Oldenach	59-0372
OSINERS, Fr. Hch.	24	Emsen	57-1148
OSMERS, Friedr.	25	Achim	61-0716
John 41, John 9			
OSMERS, Johann G.	23	Hastedt/Brem.	60-0622
OSSEFORTH, Johann	45	Rhede/Hann.	62-0608
Margaretha 28, Joseph 3			
OSSELN, H. (m)	21	Zetel	62-0879
OSSMANN, Maria	19	Dainrode	55-0630
OSSWALD, Dan.	22	Heppenheim	62-1112
OSTENDORF, Elise	17	Wremen	55-1082
OSTENDORF, Gerhard	26	Oldenburg	58-0576
Anna 27			
OSTENDORPH, L.H.F.	34	Reepshold	62-0993
H. 27			
OSTER, Carl	22	Lindheim	59-0372
OSTERART, Johann	21	Struek	58-0815
OSTERBIND, H.B.(m)	36	Pikway	61-0682
OSTERHAGE, S.	49	Rentorf	62-0993
C. 22			
OSTERHELD, Christ.	15	Neusesen	57-1280
Elisabeth 17			
OSTERHOLD, John	19	Sansteth	56-1011
OSTERHOLD, Margar.	19	Lotheim	56-0413
OSTERHUES, F.W.(m)	25	Osnabrueck	62-0401
Fr. Heinr. 22			
OSTERHUES, Lisette	42	Ahaus	61-0482
Marie 9, Wm. 5, Franz 3, Joseph 11m			
OSTERLOH, Christof	49	Bremen	60-1053
OSTERNDORFF, J.(m)	18	Sievern	62-0730
OSTHAUS, Arm.	22	New York	57-1192
Leonore 18			
OSTHEIM, Julius	20	Brake	59-0477
OSTHEIM, Rieke	40	Brakel	60-0533
Henriette 18, Julie 17, Joseph 16			
OSTLONGENBERG, G.H	50	Westfalen	60-0785
OSTREIN, Jac.	40	Gisselberg	60-0334
OSWALD, Ed.	28	Osweil	56-0723
Amalie 29			
OSWALD, F.	19	Kirchheim	62-0993
OSWALD, Gottfried	36	Muehlhausen	56-0629
Joh. Elisab. 26, Julius 2			
OTHEWEIN, Sophie	24	Kiselberg	59-0047
OTSCHIEK, Wm.	36	Michelwitz	61-0804
OTT, Jacob	35	Wuertemberg	57-0436
Jacob 29, Barbara 22			
OTT, Joseph	20	Ladenburg/Bad	60-0622
OTTE, Cath.	23	Hockenberge	60-0521
OTTE, Charles	38	New York	57-0080
OTTE, Claus	59	Berne	62-0467
Hedwig 58, Margaretha 33, Gerhard 28			
Diedrich 32			
OTTE, Friederike	18	Vilsen	56-1044
OTTE, J.H.	26	Fallingbostel	58-0399
Ilse 21, Marie 5, Engel 11m			
OTTE, Minna	22	Goettingen	60-0785
OTTEN, Fr.	19	Altlueneburg	57-1148
OTTEN, Friedrich	22	Garrel	60-0533
Angelika 25			
OTTEN, J.H.	27	Altlueneberg	57-1148
OTTEN, Marg.	26	New York	62-1112
OTTEN, Mary	22	Enger	57-1148
OTTEN, Otto Friedr	37	America	58-0815
OTTEN, Trinchen	20	Lanstedt	57-1407
OTTEN, Wilhelm	28	Delmenhorst	62-0938
OTTENDORF, Joh.Fr.	36	Iheringsfehn	58-0815
Gretje Marie 32, Gretje 13, Trientje 5			
Focke 3, Geert 1			
OTTENHAUSEN, Aug.	21	Kaldorf	57-0606
Amalie 48			
OTTENHEIMER, Jul.	30	New York	62-0836
OTTENSARNDT, Luisa	34	Steinhagen	60-0521
Johann 5			
OTTERBACH, Chrstne	18	Nassau	55-0628
OTTERBEIN, Barbara	25	Schleitz	59-0613
OTTERBEIN, Henr'te	19	Salzschlief	56-0629
OTTERSLACHER, Gotf	20	Spazenhof	57-1026
OTTERSTEDT, Died.	20	Ottersberg	55-0413
OTTILIE, C.(m)	26	Blankenburg	60-0785
OTTINGER, Julie	20	Moenchsroth	57-1148
OTTO, August	21	Arolsen	55-0634
Caspar 16			
OTTO, Augusta	19	Clausthal	57-0447
OTTO, Barbara	19	Ostheim	56-0951
OTTO, Bernhardine	28	Carolinensiel	57-0961
Emil 9, Charles 7			
OTTO, Carl	17	Lichtenstein	57-1280
OTTO, Carl	19	Osterfeld	61-0682
OTTO, Conrad	29	Dissen	57-0754
Anna Cathar. 27, Gertrud 9m			
OTTO, Erich F.	14	Wernhausen	62-0879
OTTO, George	58	Reichensachse	56-1011
Ernestine 15, Bertha 12			
OTTO, Gottfr.Herm.	49	Bremen	57-0606
Anna 49, Heinr.Ohlm. 7			
OTTO, Henry	28	Wenzwig	58-0545
OTTO, Hermann	18	Dessen	56-0411
Jacob 23			
OTTO, Joseph	22	Satrum	56-0629
OTTO, L.	42	Curhessen	58-0399
Martha 42, Heinrich 17, Valentin 13			
Gertrud 8, Wilhelm 6, Johannes 3			
OTTO, Louise	21	Gemuenden	60-0411
OTTO, Ludwig	30	Kurhessen	56-0512
OTTO, Sophie	20	Friedensdorf	60-0521
OTTO, Wilhelm	26	Grave	57-0606
Wilhelmine 22			
OTTOMAR, P.	34	Fuenfhausen	59-0613
OVEN, v. A. (m)	19	Unterbach	61-0897
OVERMANN, Heinrich	17	Mouischeid	59-0535
OWAHN, Boettger	34	Bocholt	59-0384
OYSTE, v. Sophie	59	Hagen	62-0467
PAAK, Meta	27	Elvechren	59-0990
PABBO, Marie	20	Twitz	59-0535
PABISCH, Franz	40	Cincinati	62-0836
PABST, Anna	21	Kissingen	59-0990
PABST, August	43	New York	60-1196
Elise 36, Heinr. 9, August 7, Louis 5			
(child) 10m			
PABST, Christian	22	Neustadt	56-0632
PABST, Gustav	22	St.Louis	58-0815
PABST, J.J.(m)	25	Ostfriesland	61-0682
PABST, Johann	48	St.Louis	58-0815
Knud. 26, Franz 29			
PABSTE, Eleonor	24	Erfurt	55-1082
PACHINGER, Joseph	40	Boehmen	58-0881
PACKAN, Franz	31	Hodina	61-0779
Anna 25			
PACKBUSCH, August	24	Eisleben	57-0447
PACOTOU, (m)	14	Rangoon	62-0401
PACZKIEWICZ, Hen't	20	Strassburg	58-0306
(baby) 1			
PADESTA, Geobotto	25	Italy	61-0716
PAEGER, Andreas	60	Oberschlaicha	59-0047
Magdalene 38			
PAEHER, Ferdinand	19	Umstadt	59-1017

NAME	AGE	RESIDENCE	YR-LIST
PAETZ, Armand	34	Tuemmelsee	57-1148
PAGEL, August Wm.	19	Bremen	57-0754
PAGELS, Friedrich	19	Werkau	62-1042
PAGENSTECKER, Alb.	21	Osnabrueck	59-1036
PAHL, H.Fr.	38	Lautenthal	59-0535
Johanna 21, Friedricke 8, August 3			
Fritz 1			
PAHNPEHRICH, Cath.	17	Verel	61-0804
PAIKOWSKY, Adam	54	Berent	58-0881
Mariane 40, Augustina 21, Catharine 17			
Adam 9, Joseph 7, Anton 8m			
PALLECZECK, Adalb.	37	Strigonau	61-0779
Catharine 31, Barbara 9, Maria 7, Anna 5			
Catharine by			
PALMLIE, Theodor	23	Emmendingen	57-1416
PALSCHEN, Meta	15	Fehmarn	60-0521
PAMPEL, Emil Ferd.	30	Glogau/Sax.	62-0608
Rosalie 27, Agnes 4, Lina 9m			
PANNING, Herrmann	19	Langwedel	62-0712
PANSEN, Doris	23	Dorum	58-0306
PANSER, August	24	Suelbeck	60-0622
PANSING, Wilhelm	18	Diepholz	57-0365
PANSSEN, Peter	32	Calcar	58-0306
PANTE, (m)	39	Bielefeld	57-0961
PANTLEN, Augusta	26	Oehringen	57-0422
PANZE, Wilhelm	26	Pommern	58-0399
Wilhelmine 26, Carl 9m			
PANZER, Elisabeth	25	Oberfranken	58-0399
PAOLI, de Giovanni	32	Italy	61-0107
PAPE, Adolph	30	Hannover	56-0819
Wilhelmine 26			
PAPE, Anna	23	Elldeich	62-0712
PAPE, Christian	47	Steinhude	56-0411
Dorothea 44, Marie 19, Dorothea 7			
Sophie 10, Caroline 5			
PAPE, Christine	36	Friemen	62-0001
PAPE, Henrich	24	Wheeling	59-0477
PAPE, Joh.	28	Oese	59-0535
PAPE, Johann	26	Ostereistedt	58-0563
PAPE, Lina	17	Cassel	62-0836
PAPE, Mary	22	Hersfeld	57-1148
PAPEN, Anna	23	Ostaheide	62-0836
PAPEN, Christoph	17	Zeven	59-0535
PAPENBAUM, Ernst	41	Berme	57-1113
Caroline 27, Louise 12, Friedrich 5			
Heinrich 11m			
PAPENDIECK, Andr.	39	Mussleben	61-0482
Johanna 32, C.A. 12, Juliane 6			
Wilhelmine 2			
PAPENDIECK, Carl	26	Bremen	62-1112
PAPENDIEK, Georg	33	Milwaukee	59-1036
J. 27, Ernst 5, Eleonarde 1			
PAPENGE, Siben(m)	14	Gestemuende	59-0613
PAPENSIECK, Aug'ta	34	Bremen	58-0563
Hermann 9, Elise 8, Christian 6			
PAPP, Georg	30	Obertief/Bav.	60-0429
PAPPENBERG, Georg	25	Offenbach	57-1407
PAPPER, Friedr.	25	Schwihau	60-0521
PAPPLOE, Julius	30	Pyritz	56-0632
Antonia 21			
PAPST, Albrecht	17	Chemnitz	55-0630
PARADIES, Meta	17	Hagen	57-0776
PARAVAGNA, Antonio	72	Italy	61-0167
PARENSTEDT, E.(m)	50	New York	62-0836
PARKNER, Carl Wm.	22	Bruck	58-0563
PARMIGIANI, Pelgr.	31	Italy	61-0107
PARRHYSIUS, Armand	25	Erfurt	57-0422
PARSONS, B.	32	America	56-1216
(wife) 28, C.(f) 4, W.(f) 9m			
PASCHEN, Sophie	44	Dankersen	57-1067
PASCHMEYER, Sophie	28	Achim	55-0634
PASCHWITZ, Ernst	24	Alsdorf	59-1036
PASHAUER, M. Elis.	17	Blankenbach	57-1416
PASSE, B. Elis.	18	Triemen	56-1117
PASSOW, (m)	38	Mazatlan	62-1169
PATALRA, Vincent	32	Seretz	62-1042
PATHEI, Louise	23	Boehmen	57-1407
PATRONSKA, Cathar.	20	Boehmen	62-0730

NAME	AGE	RESIDENCE	YR-LIST
Marie 31			
PATSCHE, Paul	50	Wambach	60-0334
Cath. 39, Heinr. 25, Daniel 6			
PATT, Wieland	22	Rongellen	59-0477
Bartram 21			
PATZELBERGER, Jos.	40	Beaverdam	59-0951
PATZER, Elisabeth	26	Hesse-Darmst.	60-0371
PAUBA, Adalbert	26	Chlumka	59-0613
PAUCK, Louis	17	Bueckeburg	57-0654
PAUER, Carl	20	New York	62-0467
PAUER, Wilhelm	25	New York	59-0477
PAUL, Adam	26	Hesse-Darmst.	60-0371
PAUL, Christ Heinr	26	Lockhausen	56-0589
PAUL, Christian	51	Schmalkalden	57-0924
Cath. Elis. 48, Ernestine 20			
Geo. Friedr. 18, Cath. Marie 16			
Louise 14, Reinhold 8, Leo 6			
PAUL, Heinr.	22	Kreutzreihe/H	55-1238
PAUL, Heinrich	54	Grossenhain	62-0712
Elisabeth 53, Georg 21, Elisabeth 66			
PAUL, Johann	60	Schottlingen	61-0520
PAUL, Justus	19	Melle	56-0279
PAUL, Maria	24	Veckerhagen	57-0924
PAULA, Joh.	47	Rostock	57-1113
Franzisca 45, Franz 21, Sternaz 14			
Maria 12, Amalie 10, Johann 7, Pauline 1			
PAULI, A. Marie	29	Niederstelter	59-0384
PAULICH, N.(m)	40	Illinois	61-0804
Gertr. 9			
PAULIS, Cathar.	16	Boeddiger	59-0214
PAULOWSKY, Josephn	26	Danzig	62-0758
PAULSACKEL, Gustav	18	New Orleans	59-0048
PAULSEN, Anna	17	Luedingworth	56-0413
PAULSEN, Henry	17	Zeven	57-0961
PAULSEN, Joh.	26	New York	60-0334
PAULUS, Babette	32	Dinkelsbuehl	58-0885
PAULUS, Ernst	22	Spueck	62-1112
PAULUS, Friedrich	19	Tiefenbach/Pr	55-0628
PAULUS, Friedrich	32	Spoeck	62-0730
Ferdinand 27			
PAULUS, Margaretha	19	Neuenkirchen	60-0521
PAULUS, Monika	16	Sicklingen	57-1192
PAUSCH, Otto	30	New York	62-0111
PAUSEN, Jette	19	Burgkundstadt	61-0482
PAUTZ, Charles	28	Werder	57-0654
Henriette 23, Friedrich 2			
PAVENSTEDT, Edward	50	New York	61-0482
PAVLOWSKY, Johann	32	Boehmen	62-0758
PAYCKEN, Julius	16	Bremen	59-1036
PAYSER, Roesch.	19	Immenrode	59-0990
PEABODY, Charles	25	Southampton	59-0384
PEASLER, Edward	23	Berlin	50-1017
PECEL, Benedict	37	Losina	60-1141
Cathrina 37, Johann 14, Joseph 9, Wentz 7			
Frank 3, Albert 9m			
PECH, Carl Theodor	23	Zeutz	60-1117
PECH, Fr'dke Herm.	20	Grossen	60-1117
PECH, Wenzel	23	Borek	61-0779
PECHAUFF, Kunig.	26	Coburg	56-1117
PECHER, Joseph	32	Wahnbeck	62-0306
PECHMANN, I.J.W.	30	Kl. Suentel	55-0932
PECHSTEL, Anna	23	Bodisgruen	55-0413
PECHT, Peter Fr'dr	22	Bothel	56-0411
PECK, Diedr.	26	Kallheim	60-0334
PECK, Heinrich	33	Sdt.Oldendorf	57-0606
Henriette 38, Emilie 7, Hermann 4			
Alwine(twin) 1, Albert(twin) 1			
PECKARECK, Joseph	38	Kluck	57-1026
Anna 42, Maria 14, Catharina 9, Anna 7			
Francisca 5, Joseph 3			
PECKMANN, Wilhelm	23	Bartshausen	62-0608
PEDANET, Marie	16	Selle	62-0111
Adele 15			
PEECK, Heinr.	40	Gruenenplan	62-1112
PEEKOVER, Ellen	20	New York	62-1042
PEHNTE, Gust.	20	Wolfenbuettel	57-1192
PEIDECKER, John	33	NYC.	55-1238
PEIFER, Jost	27	Eisenhausen	56-0723

NAME	AGE	RESIDENCE	YR-LIST
PEIL, Anna	19	Bettendorf	56-0512
PEINE, Theresia	30	Dossel	62-0467
PEIPER, Martin	35	Harwen	55-1082
Louise 24			
PEISSNER, J.	24	Felseck	56-0512
PEISTEL, August	36	Newlewin	57-0776
Pauline 32, Paul 7, Pauline 5, Rudolph 3			
August 1			
PEITHMANN, (f)	73	Bramsch	58-0881
PEITMANN, Peter	33	Amsterdam/Hol	55-0812
PEITZMEIER, Ferd.	37	St.Louis	58-0925
PELARICK, Fred.	28	Leipzig	59-0477
PELLEN, Wilhelmine	22	Seckenburg	57-1407
PELS, Moses	15	Wanes	60-0521
Eduard 13			
PELSTER, Bernh.	32	Steinfurt	59-0384
Bernh. 20			
PELTZER, A.	20	New York	62-1042
PELZ, Georg	28	Schinderling	55-0628
PENAAT, Henry H.F	17	Bunde	57-0422
PENDERET, (f)	31	England	61-0107
PENG, Wilhelm	25	Schlesien	58-0399
PENTZEN, Otto	55	Charlottentha	57-1026
Henriette 54, Johann 27, Wilhelm 22			
Franz 16, Maria 24			
PENZ, Wilhelm	25	Schlesien	58-0399
PENZEL, Caroline	13	Landwuest	55-0630
PEPER, Ernst	22	Eickhorst	62-0401
Carl 15			
PEPER, H.	18	Vichershude	59-1036
PEPPLER, Cath.	23	Birklar	57-0422
PERAZZO, Mattes	35	Italy	61-0107
PERGER, Fritz	46	Muenster	61-0779
PERICH, Catharine	23	Oberreidenbch	62-0467
PERKELWINKEL, Joh.	32	Essnerberg	56-0589
PERKINS, Maurice	25	Tuebingen	61-0804
PERL, Ernst	45	Lauenstein	57-0606
Gertrude 40, Johanna 17, Louise 16			
Dorothea 13, Augusta 10, Ernst 7, Lina 6			
Heinrich 3, Fritz 1			
PERLETH, Sebastian	43	Laubach	61-0478
Catharina 40, Basilius 19, Robertus 14			
Mathilde 4			
PERRY, (f)	32	France	61-0167
PERTH, Adelbert	25	Fremon	57-1026
Maria 32			
PESCHEK, Catharine	26	Boehmen	62-0001
PESCHEL, Joseph	20	Gronau	56-0589
PESCHEL, Mathilde	15	Kossenheim	56-0847
PESCHMANN, Carl	37	Erlingholm	60-0521
PESDIRZ, Joseph	27	Swiebnitz	57-0436
Johann 18			
PESKE, Willem	30	Succow	57-0961
PESTNER, C.	24	Hildburghause	62-0993
PETER, Anna Maria	15	Mahlbach	61-0478
PETER, Chr. Goth.	38	Stadt Roda	57-1148
PETER, Dorothea	20	Zimmern	60-0334
PETER, Heinrich	30	Grueneplan	59-0214
PETER, Jac.	27	Ruppertsburg	59-1036
PETER, Jacob	40	New York	62-1169
PETER, Johann	30	Immigenheim	56-0527
PETER, Johannes	46	Arnsheim	56-0413
Louise 35			
PETER, Johs.	27	Ordenhausen	61-0682
Eva Cath. 21			
PETER, Ludwig	28	Gennern	56-0723
PETER, Marie Elise	18	Walldorf	57-0924
PETER, Paulus	58	Schmalkalden	58-0576
Marie 56			
PETER, Peter	25	Odenhausen	57-0924
Caroline 25, Catharine by			
PETER, Wm.	19	Lengenich	62-0467
PETERI, Friedrich	14	Kasten	57-1280
PETERMANN, Fr.	28	Charleston	57-1192
PETERMANN, Joseph	27	Grossostheim	60-0398
PETERMAUS, Elise	20	Storndorf/Hes	55-0628
PETEROFF, Sophie	28	Muenchberg	60-0521
Caroline 10			
PETERS, Aug.	30	Bremen	57-1148
PETERS, Carl	46	US.	59-0951
Doris 35			
PETERS, Caspar	19	Oesern	61-0167
PETERS, Charles	26	America	56-1216
PETERS, E.L.(m)	50	Cincinati	62-0836
PETERS, Friedrich	57	Heinrichsruhe	61-0930
Wilhelmina 51, Albertina 22, Amalia 17			
Agnes 15, Herrmann 9m			
PETERS, H.(m)	24	Krempeln	61-0897
PETERS, H.F.	19	New York	59-0477
PETERS, Heinrich	49	Elm	62-0401
PETERS, Jacob	58	Ospem	58-0306
Theodore 51, Gertrude 23, Johann 21			
Petronella 20, Michael 19, Gerhard 17			
PETERS, Joh. L.	19	Meiningen	55-1082
PETERS, Johann	18	Bramstedt	57-0776
Carsten 14			
PETERS, Johann	19	Moordorf	57-0447
PETERS, Johann	66	Louisendorf	58-0306
Helene 49, Gerhard 24, Heinrich 22			
Eduard 20, Johann 17			
PETERS, Johann	16	Hannover	62-0758
PETERS, Jos.	30	Daglesgruen	60-0521
PETERS, Louise	33	Washington	62-0836
Dorothy 5, Wm. 4			
PETERS, Louise	33	Washington	62-0836
Dorothy 5, Wm. 4			
PETERS, Marie	22	Hildesheim	60-0521
PETERS, Meta	43	New York	62-1112
PETERS, Michael	35	Bavaria	62-0758
Maria 25, Margaretha 3			
PETERS, Sophie	18	Verden	56-0847
PETERS, Thud.	26	Lienen	60-0334
PETERS, W.H.(m)	34	Norden	62-0401
PETERS, William	34	California	59-0214
PETERSEN, Fried'ke	28	Bassum	55-0634
PETERSEN, Wilh'mne	21	Otterndorf	62-0938
PETIG, Heinrich	36	Altendampf/L.	62-0608
Wilhelmine 25, Heinrich 3m			
PETITCLAIR, Jel.	36	France	61-1132
PETRI, Chr.	38	Gabsheim	60-0521
PETRI, Conrad	25	Berkach/Darm.	60-0429
PETRI, Henry	32	Ottersberg	60-1141
Catharina 27			
PETRI, Louis	34	Usingen/Nass.	62-0342
PETRICH, Ottilie	21	Posen	57-0776
Rosalia 24			
PETRIN, Elise	19	Marburg	56-0589
PETRING, Fr.	37	Buende	59-0990
(m) 10, (f) 9, (m) 6, (m) 2			
PETS, Carl	33	Strelitz	57-0776
Maria 26			
PETSCH, Friedrich	29	Ourfeld	55-0812
PETURA, Jos.	38	Popowetz	57-0961
Catharina 33, John 9			
PETZ, Georg	58	Lachweiler	56-0847
Anna 19			
PETZ, Margarethe	17	Wuestenselbit	55-0628
PETZINGER, Heinr.	14	Langenhain	59-1036
PETZLER, Caroline	24	Ulm	59-0047
PETZNICK, Franz	55	Selchow	56-0819
Ernestine 23, Anna 16, August 13			
PETZWASCH, Marie	18	Mies	58-0881
PEUSSNER, Margaret	21	Gross Fehden	61-0779
PEUSTER, Johannes	45	Wetzlar	62-1112
Conrad 15, Friedr. 5, Elisabeth 13			
Johannette 12			
PEVAL, Franz	33	Boehmen	61-0482
Marie 34, Marie 10m			
PEYSER, Mar.	18	Sondershausen	59-0990
PEZOLT, Ant.Theod.	20	Rosswein/Sax.	60-0622
PFADENFINDER, Ad.	39	Bielefeld	57-1280
Caroline 32, Friederike 5, Wilhelm 7			
PFAFF, Ad.	22	Herotz	59-1036
PFAFF, Carl	20	Waldeck	56-0951
PFAFF, Elisabeth	25	Ettinghausen	61-0779
Maria 14			

NAME	AGE	RESIDENCE	YR-LIST
PFAFF, Johannes	37	Schenkbergsfe	57-0847
A.Catharina 38, Elisabeth 8			
PFAFF, L.H.	21	Michelau	62-0993
PFAFF, Petronilla	28	Oberwintern	61-0770
PFAFFENBERGER, Mrg	19	Bavaria	60-0371
PFAFFENBUCH, David	19	Sipenhausen	56-0629
PFAFFMANN, L.	37	New York	62-1042
Marie 42, Louise 9			
PFAHL, Hyronimus	44	Hildesheim	61-0682
PFAHLER, Margareta	33	Bubenheim	57-0754
PFALZGRAF, Elisab.	26	Schrecksbach	62-0342
Joh.Adam 5, Johanna Cath 23			
PFANKUCH, Ludwig	43	Gottsburen	58-0563
Marie 32, Carl Wilhelm 5, Marie Wmne. 4			
Joh.Frd.Lud. 4m			
PFANNENSCHMIDT, Fr	27	Goslar	57-0606
Christine 37, Auguste 14, Carl 7			
Bertha 4, Minna 1			
PFANNKUCHE, Adam	20	Bremerhaven	56-1117
PFANNKUCHE, Friedr	26	Northeim	58-0925
Christ. 30, Rosalie 22, Mary 21			
PFANNKUCHEN, Fritz	18	Seelbeck	56-0723
PFAROW, Wilhelmine	55	Strassburg	57-0961
PFARRER, Barbara	9	Weckesheim	62-1112
PFARRER, H.	28	New York	62-1112
Johanna 24			
PFARRER, Louise	17	Vielingen	59-0214
PFARRER, Wilhelm	28	Rochester	59-0214
PFAU, Michael	31	Meerkelsheim	59-0477
PFAUNER, Ph. (m)	54	Grefenhausen	62-0111
P. (m) 23			
PFAUTZER, Ad.(m)	20	Coelln	60-0521
PFEFFER, Christian	24	Hemstedt	61-0478
PFEFFER, Georg	16	Bingen	60-1053
PFEFFERKORN, Gottf	24	Fredersdorf	57-1280
Christiana 20			
PFEIFEL, Volkmar	48	Erfurt	55-1082
PFEIFER, Andreas	46	Gotha	62-0758
Pauline 20, August 14, Christian 11			
Julius 9			
PFEIFER, J.F.W.(m)	23	Burgstade	62-0401
PFEIFER, Thomas	37	Freudenicht	60-0521
Margaretha 28, Francisca 11m			
PFEIFER, Wm.	18	Homburg	62-0836
PFEIFER. Conrad	37	Sellnrod	61-0047
Isabelle 35, Heinrich 8, Friedrich 5			
Cathrina 11m			
PFEIFF, Jacob	22	Odenhausen	57-0924
PFEIFF, Louise	29	Chicago	59-1036
PFEIFFER, Adam	19	Ellenberg	59-0214
PFEIFFER, August	22	Shelbyville	57-1192
PFEIFFER, Carl	56	Dorrendorf	56-0411
Friederika 19, Franz 6m			
PFEIFFER, Caroline	18	Ottenburg	55-0932
PFEIFFER, Cath.	20	Kappebudeck	56-1216
PFEIFFER, Charles	18	Muehlhausen	57-1192
PFEIFFER, Dor.	33	Schleitheim	62-1112
PFEIFFER, Doris	59	Wertheinm	59-1036
PFEIFFER, Georg	23	Wolkendorf	57-1026
PFEIFFER, Heinrich	59	Gladenbach	62-0712
Anna 54, Jacob 20, Anna 15			
PFEIFFER, Johann	26	Stadtlin	57-1026
PFEIFFER, Marie	17	Oberstetten	62-0730
PFEIFFER, Peter	25	Altenkirchen	56-1044
PFEIFFER, Peter	23	Richmond	59-0384
PFEIFFER, Theodor	18	Niederbach	57-1113
PFEIFFER, Wilhelm	19	Senna/Pr.	60-0371
PFEIFLE, Georg	22	Gaeltlingen	60-0334
Jacob 31			
PFEIL, Catharine	30	Neuler	57-1067
PFEIL, Friedrich	30	Crumpa	55-0812
Maria Ther. 26, Maria Ther. 2			
PFEIL, Justus	27	Burgminden	58-0545
PFEIL, Nicolaus	56	Ana	56-0819
PFEUFFER, Nich.	47	Hellbeck	60-0998
PFINGST, Georg	15	Hofgeismar	61-1132
PFINGSTEN, Dorethe	27	Pohle	57-0509
PFINGSTEN, Louise	18	Antendorf	59-0384
PFISTE, Joh.	27	Bundorf	56-1216
PFISTER, Anna	32	Au	59-0990
(m) 6			
PFITA, Daniel	32	Buchs	60-0785
PFLOGENER, Regina	23	Urphar	60-0334
PFLUEGER, Fr'drke.	22	Maden	62-0730
PFLUEGER, Wm.	21	Springe	61-0482
PFOERDTNER, Elise	19	Bergheim	60-0521
PFOERTNER, Wm.	26	New York	59-1036
Maria 23			
PFOERTNER-HOELLE,M	28	Berlin	61-0716
PFOTENHAUER, Fr'ke	26	Laasen	60-1032
Carl 4			
PFOTTI, Hermann	18	Hoexter	55-0845
Heinrich 20			
PFRAENGER, Gottl.	26	Emleben/Sax.	55-0538
PFRANGER, Heinrich	45	Hildburghsn.	57-1280
PFROMEN, Margareta	20	Schenklengsfd	60-0521
PFUEL, Heinrich	17	Curhessen	58-0399
PFUHL, Conrad	48	Rittenau/Hess	55-0628
Martha Elis. 47, Anna Gertrud 26			
Elisabeth 15, Christian 2			
PHEIL, Ernst	29	Waldheim	56-1260
PHILIP, Johann	35	New York	57-0422
PHILIPP, F.	30	Pesth/Hungary	62-0993
PHILIPP, Georg	36	Zettmannsdorf	61-0478
PHILIPPS, Elisab.	39	Burggen	57-1067
Peter 13, Heinrich 10, Caspar 7			
PHILLIPOT, Vital	50	France	61-0482
PHINEAS, M.(m)		Goettingen	57-0578
PIATTNER, Catharin	23	Tschappina	59-0477
PICHLER, J.H.	29	Olbersdorf	62-0836
PICK, Ad.	19	Carlsbad	59-0951
PICK, Caroline	25	Boehmen	62-0938
PICKEL, Casp.	42	Wernighausen	56-0723
PICKEL, Georg	19	Walldorf	59-0535
PICKEL, Johann	18	Clibach/Hes.	55-0628
PICKERING, (f)	32	US.	57-1150
PIEBUTE, Johann	41	Nordhausen	55-0845
Elisabeth 39, Catharine 10, Marie 10			
Anna 6, Christian 4, Ludwig by			
PIECHATZEK, Paul	19	Oppeln	57-0422
PIEHL, Johann	46	Gr. Woelwitz	56-1260
Dorothea 36, Friedrich 22, Charlotte 10			
Wilhelm 6, Gottlieb 5, Augusta 4			
Julius 9m			
PIEL, Augusta	30	Uslar	58-0881
Johanne 6, Alwine 1			
PIELEMEIER, Fr.	27	Benkdorf	57-0606
Justine 24			
PIELENG, Carl	18	Calmbach	59-0214
PIELMANN, Franz	22	Osterode	60-0785
PIEPER, August	17	Damme	59-0477
PIEPER, Conrad	33	Wesel	60-0521
Emma 23			
PIEPER, Heinr.	28	Damme	59-0951
PIEPER, Marie	21	Bleiwaesche	56-0723
Josephine 20			
PIEPER, Marie	20	Berlin	59-0613
PIEPERMANN, Wilh.	45	Elze	61-0779
Dorothea 35, Dorothea 14, Caroline 12			
Wilhelm 8, Christine 6, Elise by			
PIEPHO, Ferd.Louis	25	Muenden	57-0422
PIEPKO, Henry	18	Rahden	59-0384
PIETSCH, Franz	30	Steindorf	56-0413
PIETZCH, Joh'a W.	22	Netschka	62-0983
PIKARSKY, v. Jos.	27	Glumen	56-0951
PILZ, Anna	22	Rockenburg	61-0716
PIMPER, Anna	22	Ahrbach	55-0630
PINCUS, J.	40	New York	62-1169
PINDEL, Johann	38	Gemuend/Bav.	61-0770
Catharine 31, Catharine 4, Georg 3			
Therese 6w			
PINGER, Andrea	21	Naples	60-0785
PINKEL, Georg	21	Elsingen	58-0399
PINKERT, Wm.	17	Boston	62-0836
PINTHER, C.F.	23	Teich-Wolfram	62-0993
PIPER, Caroline	30	Wattenhausen	61-0520

NAME	AGE	RESIDENCE	YR-LIST
PIPO, Eleonore	22	Rahde	56-0589
PIPPER, Jette	22	Raden	57-1280
PIPPERT, Ernst	35	Unhausen	60-1141
PIRF, Mr.H.	57	Baltimore	59-0477
Magdalene 28			
PISCATOR, Jacob	30	Lenn	58-0604
PISCHT, Therese	26	Paderborn	56-0411
PISCO, Edw.	20	Bruenn	62-0938
PISER, Marie	58	New York	57-1280
PISSE, Leonhard	40	Muehlbach	57-0447
Barbara 39, Maria 12, Friedr. 9, Marg. 1			
PISTEL, Catharine	21	Steibra/Bav.	60-0429
PITKIN, J.C.	36	New York	62-0836
PITSCH, John	23	Hartford	59-0214
PITSCHER, Josua	31	Lennel	57-1148
PITZER, A.Margaret	26	Hartenrod	59-0412
PITZER, Johannes	47	Wornshausen	60-0533
Anna 52, Johannes 17, Jost 15			
Elisabeth 8, Margaretha 7			
PLACK, Louis	32	Cincinnati	58-0306
(mother) 65			
PLAETTNER, Carl	15	Saxony	62-0758
PLANCKE, Maxmilian	19	Hannover	60-0429
Georg 24			
PLANERT, Franz	31	Leipzig	57-0606
Wilhelmine 27, Ida 4, Bertha 2, Minna 11m			
PLANIZ, v. Julie	17	Mergensheim	62-0938
PLANTHOLD, Jos.	38	Osnabrueck	60-1161
PLANZ, Casper	17	Eudorf/Curh.	60-0622
PLANZ, Friedr.	18	Kirchheim/KHe	62-0342
PLAPPERT, Wm.	46	Ruedenhausen	61-0669
PLARER, Joh.	36	Thonhausen	62-0401
PLASS, Louise	25	Minden	61-0167
PLATE, C.	29	New York	62-1169
Meta 8, Theod. 4			
PLATE, Ernest	18	Weserlingen	57-0422
Augusta 55, Jane 21, Charles 15			
Theodor 9m			
PLATE, Johannes	40	Seburg	57-0422
Wilhelmine 31, Henry 9, Johannes 8			
Mathilde 6m			
PLATHE, Claus	29	New York	60-0785
PLATO, Charlotte	40	Magdeburg	62-0938
PLATON, Friedrich	31	Carlshoff	57-0776
PLATTE, Sophie	16	Aplern	61-0520
PLATZECK, Julie	18	Schwersens	62-0467
PLAUM, Joh.Jacob	25	Hartenrod	59-0412
PLAUT, Amant	18	Neustadt	59-0613
PLAUTZ, Carl	40	Pommern	56-1044
Wilhelmine 42, Augusta 17, Wilhelm 14			
Carl 10, Hermann 7, Albert 5			
Albertine 11m			
PLEUSS, Ott.	23	Bassum	62-0938
Mary 24, Bertha 2, Christine 9m			
PLOCH, Fr.(m)	22	Ernsthausen	60-0334
Pletch (m) 6m			
PLOEGER, John	28	Hemelingen	57-1192
PLOGER, Wilhelm	19	Horsmer	57-0447
PLOTTI, Hermann	18	Hoexter	55-0845
Heinrich 20			
PLOUHAR, Johann	36	Boehmen	58-0881
Catharina 25, Matthias 3			
PLUM, Jos.	36	New York	60-1196
PLUMHOFF, Gottlieb	36	Baltimore	58-0604
Heinr. 9			
PLUMPER, C.(m)	19	Nehum	61-0482
POCHEL, Regina	33	Kothen	57-1026
PODERMANN, Anna	30	Westerwiehe	61-0804
PODIER, J.	40	Paris	62-0938
PODISTA, Geobetto	26	Italy	61-0716
POEHLER, Gottlieb	17	Merbeck	56-0819
POEHLER, Theo.	28	New York	61-0804
Amalie 19			
POEHNE, Fr.(m)	28	Bueten	61-0482
Ernestine 24			
POET, Gottlieb	23	Prussia	57-0847
POETSCH, August	29	Gruenenhof	60-0398
POETT, (f)	40	San Francisco	60-0521
(f) 24, Maria 5, Joseph 2			
POETTER, Wm.	31	Lengwich	62-0730
POETTKER, Fr.	28	Lemke	62-1042
POETZEL, Wilh.	24	Braunschweig	56-1044
POFAHL, Aug.W.	40	Neu Wuhrow	57-1113
Henriette 40, Justine 15, Emilie 12			
Ferdinand 9			
POGGENBURG, Doris	36	Holtum	61-0716
POGGENBURG, Gustav	16	Holtum	56-1011
Maria 21			
POGGENBURG, Heinr.	14	Eichberg	60-0521
POH, Sebastian	20	Philadelphia	59-0477
POHL, Friedr.Ernst	18	Wendorf	59-0214
Wilhelm 16			
POHL, Georg	21	Dresden	62-0712
POHL, Gustav	36	Radstein	56-0589
Benedikt 5			
POHL, H. Fr.	38	Lautenthal	59-0535
Johanna 21, Friederike 8, August 3			
Fritz 1			
POHL, Joseph	32	Schlesien	58-0399
POHL, Margarethe	22	Schlagreuth	59-0214
POHL, Marie	29	Burg	59-0047
POHL, Pauline	26	Zachasberg	60-1032
August 4, Hermann 2			
POHLER, August	18	Hiddesen	56-1044
Augusta 26			
POHLEY, Kunigunde	18	Bischwind/Bav	60-0622
POHLKER, G.H.	41	California	62-1042
POHLMANN, Bernh.	17	Aezberg	59-1036
POHLMANN, Caroline	34	Hilden	61-0897
August 9, Maria 5, Carl 11m			
POHLMANN, Emilie	24	Corbach	56-0629
POHLMANN, Friedr.	28	--orf/Waldeck	55-0538
POHLMANN, J.	21	Frankfurt	62-0993
POHLMANN, J.Friedr	23	Raitenbach	56-0819
POHRUEDER, Fritz	21	Cincinnati	59-0951
Philipp 18, Catharine 44			
POLENDERMANN, Mart	15	Rennbach	57-1280
POLL, Bernhard	25	Herdecke	56-0279
POLLACK, Jacob	18	Koenigswart	61-0716
POLLAK, Minna	24	Kuthen	60-1117
Rosalie 16			
POLLEBOM, Joh.Wilh	29	Greven	59-0214
POLLMANN, M.C.(m)	26	Coelln	61-0716
POLTERMANN, Friedr		Melle	57-0436
POLZIN, August	20	Colberg	62-0758
POLZIN, Bertha	18	Griebau	62-0758
POMMEREHNE, Fritz	32	Braunschweig	55-1082
PONDSACK, Hinrich	25	Leeste	59-0214
PONHOLZER, Maria	26	Osterau	58-0815
PONTALBA, de M.	47	France	62-1112
PONTEIL, Armand	33	France	60-1196
PONTINC, Michael	24	Stockstadt	60-0398
PONY, Hermann	19	Rodenberg	59-0384
POOHRASNITZ, Alois	14	Nickolsburg	58-0925
POOK, Ludwig	30	Kirchohsen	55-0413
Louise 24			
POOL, W.K.(m)	28	Odessa/Russia	62-0166
POOS, Heinrich	34	Petershagen	57-1122
Christiana 35, Wilhelm 20, Heinrich 14			
Hermann 11, Wilhelm 10, Christian 5			
Friedrich 3, August 11m			
POPA, Franz	27	Flatow	57-0704
POPP, A.Margaretha	21	Stambach	56-1117
POPP, Anna Marie	19	Leobschuetz	59-0535
POPP, Barbara	28	Schweinfurt	59-0477
POPP, Georgine	24	Meiningen	61-0478
POPP, Johann	38	Langentheiler	61-0482
POPP, M.(f)	17	Bavaria	57-0555
POPP, Marg.	25	Sillershausen	61-1132
POPPA, Friedrich	27	Dessau	57-0606
POPPE, Anton	29	Zwickau	59-0951
POPPE, Engelbert	25	Bojan	55-0845
Therese 26, Therese 7			
POPPE, Friedrich	46	Wolbrechtshsn	57-0422
Wilhelmina 47			
POPPE, Georg	32	Brooklyn	62-0730

NAME	AGE	RESIDENCE	YR-LIST
POPPE, Heinrich	22	Buehren/Hann.	55-1238
POPPE, Marie	21	Meiningen	58-0815
POPPE, Minna	28	New York	62-0836
Emma 1			
POPPELI, L.	30	Reims	62-0467
POPPEN, Sievert	42	Rorichum	61-0520
Harmke 42, Ettge 19, Anna 17, Herrmann 16			
Antge 9, Hinderk 7, Nantje 5, Geerd 3			
Harmke 2			
POPPINGA, Ulrich	16	Norden	58-0563
POPPINGHAUSEN, Aug	22	Erfurt	57-0961
PORGELS, Anna	48	Wien	59-0535
Maximilian 15, Hermine 13			
PORTH, Emilie	21	Schmagendorf	60-1161
PORTH, Henriette	19	Speier	56-1216
POSENER, Conrad	28	Posen	57-1192
Rosina 22			
POSER, Johanna	49	Berge	62-0993
POSLER, J.(m)	38	Missouri	61-0897
POSSER, Paul	16	Schlicht	55-0413
POST, Jul.	26	Gr.Roeschen	59-0990
POST, v. H.C.	30	New York	62-0938
(wife) 28			
POSTBERG, H.	29	Meienburg	62-0836
Justine 31, Sophie 2, Bertha 6m, Lena 24			
POSTEL, Marie	19	Nordleda	62-1042
POSTEL, v. D. (m)	24	Spickerneufld	62-0836
POTRATSKE, Joseph	49	Lipkordie	57-0850
Pieta 50, Joseph 13, Franz 11			
POTRATZ, August	25	Ossowo	57-0924
POTT, August	29	Oldershausen	61-0482
Willi 4			
POTT, Augusta	34	Hannover	57-0654
POTT, Michael	56	Elberfeld	56-0819
Catharine 1			
POTTBERG, Luwdwig	17	Darmstadt	58-0885
POTTGEN, Friedrich	19	Fruenoehl	55-0812
POTTING, Joh.	26	Barrenhausen	60-0521
POTTWIG, H.	21	Nienburg	59-1036
POUSOLD, L.(m)	20	Corlin	62-0730
PRAEFRIED, Wm.	56	Echzell	59-0951
PRAGER, Marie	20	Mitterweilers	59-0477
PRAGER, Perez	59	Eltmann	57-1148
Jeanette 19			
PRAGER, W.	37	Neudorf	55-0932
PRAGER, Wilhelmina	18	Eisenberg	62-0758
PRALLE, Heinrich	29	Bremen	62-0712
PRALLE, Herm.	21	Oldenburg	57-1150
Friedericke 18			
PRALLE, Wilhelmine	21	Oelhausen	57-1407
PRANGE, Johann	23	Steimke	56-0723
(child) 3			
PRATER, David	23	St.Louis	57-1192
PRATER, Heinrich	49	Leutenberg	61-0930
PRATZ, Joh.	3	Anlishagen	61-0669
PRAUN, John	38	Velberg	60-0521
Cath. 29, Josepha 6, Joseph 4, Edward 2			
Ludwig 8m			
PRAYNER, W.A.	23	Dresden	55-1082
PRECHT, Ed.	30	Germany	60-0785
PRECHT, V.(m)	40	Bremen	62-0730
PRECHTEL, Cathrina	21	Muehlhausen	60-0533
PREDIGER, Justus	30	Oberellenbach	61-0779
PREE, Wilhelm	17	Weilburg	56-0819
Caroline 16, Louise 15			
PREHM, Michael	54	Lischin	58-0881
Anna 56			
PREIS, Carl	21	Weimar	62-0758
PREISER, Marie	26	Rodingen	55-0932
Emilie 16			
PREISING, Emilie	19	Bremen	56-0589
PREISINGER, Cathar	22	Sengnhof	59-0613
PREISS, A.W.	33	Hattorf	60-1196
PREISS, Georg	48	Reisach	60-0533
PREISS, Heinrich	47	Niederofleide	57-0776
Cathrina 47, Johannes 18, Cathrina 16			
Louise 14, Elisabeth 10, Reinhard 7			
Anna 5, Christina 3			

NAME	AGE	RESIDENCE	YR-LIST
PREISS, John	18	Schwartzefeld	60-1141
Adolph 14			
PREISS, Mathias	40	Gebhardsreuth	60-0622
Barbara 31, Barbara 3, Catharina 5			
Margaretha 7, Theresia 4m			
PREISS, William	32	Wuertemberg	56-1011
Anna 27			
PREISSLER, Anton	18	Wollstein	57-0776
PRELLE, Friedrich	49	Mahlum	58-0881
Elisabeth 50, Carl 17, Ludwig 14			
Wilhelmine 11, Caroline 9			
PRELLER, Carl	23	Reichenbach	55-0932
PRENNINGER, August	37	Indiana	61-0482
PRENZEL, Philip	18	Cassel	60-1161
PRESS, Heinrich	47	Niederofleide	57-0776
Catrina 47, Johannes 18, Cathrina 16			
Louise 14, Elisabeth 10, Reinhard 7			
Anna 5, Christina 3			
PRESSEL, Marie	23	Steinabuehl	56-1117
Barbara 13			
PRETZ, Conrad	28	Unterschweina	60-1053
PREUSS, Edw.	30	Louisville	57-0422
PREUSS, Edw.	24	New York	59-0477
PREUSS, Francisca	20	Pallenreuth	60-0521
PREUSS, Georg	47	Bavaria	60-0371
PREUSS, Wilhelm	55	Brechen	56-0629
PREUSSER, Andreas	46	Waldmuenchen	56-0847
PREUSSER, Hulda	25	Philadelphia	60-0521
PREUSSER, J Friedr	32	Laucha/Pr.	55-0538
Wilhelmine 27			
PRIAR, Caroline	18	Schellenburg	59-1036
PRIBE, Franz	36	Strakonitz/Bo	55-0538
PRIESING, Henry	27	Hettersen	57-0422
PRIGGE, Albert	42	Hagen/Hann.	62-0342
PRIGGE, Albert	17	Uthlede	62-0836
PRIGGE, Ernst	18	Lotte	62-0836
PRIGGE, Henry	22	New York	62-0730
PRIGGE, J.P.	34	Altenwalde	60-0411
Anna 35, Augusta 9, August 9m			
PRIGGE, Marg.	20	Hambergen	56-1117
PRILL, Carl H.J.	22	Heina	59-0384
PRILLWITZ, Joh.	33	Ostrau	55-1082
Louise 24			
PRINTZ, Anna Cath.	18	Mengsberg/CH.	60-0429
PRINZ, Heinrich	50	Rutersdorf	59-0372
PRINZ, Mathilde	25	Schlesien	58-0399
PROBST, Carol.	26	Dankelsheim	62-0938
PROBST, Lorenz	30	Unterweiser	56-0723
PROEBSTING, Edw.	36	Osage	59-0384
PROEHL, Gustav	18	Wiltenpern	57-1113
PROHMANN, I.J.W.	30	Kl. Suentel	55-0932
PROKOP, Franz	18	Friedland	57-0654
PROMOLIE, Amalie	21	Muenchen	57-0021
PROTT, Henry	23	Bettenhausen	57-0422
PROTZ, Cath.	23	Wuertemberg	57-0606
PROVOST, Marie	30	France	62-0730
PRUCHA, Marie	32	Boehmen	62-1042
Emanuel 4, Marie 8m			
PRUEFER, E.A. (m)	34	Kattenborn	55-0413
PRUSSEN, Heinrich	27	Blomberg/Lipp	57-0847
PRUSSNER, Henriett	21	Pillenbrock	57-0447
PRUTZ, Carl	26	Stettin	62-0836
PSENHEITH, Emilie	21	Bockenem	57-1026
PUCHS, Caroline	23	Saalfeld	55-1082
PUCHSTOR, J.(m)	37	Immenthal	61-0897
Maria 36, Johann 9, Ida 7, Gerhd. 6			
PUCHTA, C.	21	Volkmansgruen	57-0555
PUCHTA, Elisabeth	21	Muenchberg	61-0682
Anna 19			
PUCK, Clamus	54	Huesede	56-1117
Lisette 54, Heinrich 20, A.Marie 23			
Dorethe 18, Friedrich 7, Hermann 6			
PUCKHABER, Marie	50	Beckel	62-0938
Herm. 12			
PUCONICK, Catharin	29	Bromberg	56-0951
Sophie 57			
PUELS, C.(m)	13	Burgkundstadt	62-0836
PUELS, John	42	Williamsburg	62-1042

NAME	AGE	RESIDENCE	YR-LIST
Barbara 46			
PUELS, Mich.	24	New York	62-0836
PUERS, Eugen	27	Duesseldorf	62-1112
PUFF, Johann	24	Schellenwald	57-0847
Catharina 24, Rosalia 9m, Rosalia 17			
PUFF, Marg.	27	Rodach	57-0555
PUFOGEL, Luer	14	Baden	59-1036
PUGGENBURG, Doris	36	Holtum	61-0716
PUGGENSIEK, Ernst	34	Kappeln	59-1036
PUHAN, Max	21	Thorn	62-1112
PUHL, Conrad	20	Hesse-Cassel	56-0512
PUHL, F.	29	Gr.Drahnow	62-0836
Elwine 28, Emilie 2			
PUHL, Johann	24	Merscheid	59-0214
PULKRAWEK, Anton	24	Popowetz	57-0961
Anna 19			
PULKRAWEK, F.	32	Mentour	57-0961
Anna 22, Franz 5, John 3			
PULLACK, Georg	28	Turlendorf	60-0521
PULS, Simon	30	Lippe	58-0545
Louise 28			
PUNDMANN, Fr. Wm.	34	Westercappeln	57-1192
PUPKE, Anna	19	Orte	57-1026
PUPP, Caroline	19	Burgkundstadt	61-0482
PUPPE, Gottlieb	16	Bergwitz	59-0047
PUREN, Alex	20	Riga	61-0716
PUTCHEN, Marg.	18	Leefus	60-0334
PUTZ, Johann	33	Regen	56-0847
Joh.Dorothea 33			
PUTZ, Wm.	54	Obermaubach	57-1416
PUTZER, Jos.	45	Fuenfkirchen	57-0578
PUVOGEL, Johann	26	Baden	55-0845
Anna 17, Elisabeth 14			
PYCHLAU, Oscar	17	Riga	56-1117
PYLL, Friedr.	25	Cleve	61-0167
QUAASDORF, Carl Ed	22	Alt Schonefld	62-0983
QUADE, Johanna	21	Soldin	60-0533
QUAGLIA, Eliza	24	Fuchstadt	57-0422
QUANDER, Franz	24	Jarischau	56-1044
QUARD, Peter	37	Ziethen	56-0629
QUARSCH, Anna	29	Nuernberg	58-0604
QUEDENFELD, Louis	57	Sondershausen	57-1192
QUENSTAEDT, Carl	22	Breslau	61-0779
QUENTEL, August	40	Ndr.Grenzebch	60-0411
QUENTMEIER, Louise	52	Lippe Detmold	57-1280
Caroline 19			
QUEROCHER, Marie	19	Holzkirchen	60-1032
Ursula 24, Johann 3			
QUEST, Louis	30	Davenport	57-1192
QUIBEL, J.	47	Herdelsbach	56-0512
Christina 19			
QUICK, Lorenz		Winterberg	56-1117
(f) 17			
QUIROLA, Stephan	20	Italy	62-1042
QUITTING, Adolph	30	Dieseldorf	59-0412
RAAB, A.Maria	43	Untereisenhm.	62-0100
RAAB, Cath.E.	20	Oberstellen	62-1112
RAAB, Diedr.	17	Wetzlar	59-1036
RAAB, Elis.	29	New York	62-0467
Carl 2			
RAAB, Elisabeth	34	Ansbach/Bav.	55-0628
RAATZ, Elisabeth	22	Batzheim	59-0477
RABA, Georg	40	New York	60-0371
Charlotte 46			
RABE, Adelheid	15	Brake	58-0925
RABE, Christian	26	Freienhagen	57-0924
RABE, Georg	32	Tittau	57-1113
Luise 34, Adamine 12, Luis 10, Johanna 5			
Ernst 3, Joseph 1			
RABE, Ludwig	31	Blasheim	57-0436
Anna Marie 24			
RABE, Susanne	48	Suhs	56-1260
Andreas 7			
RABEL, Charles	28	Neurode	57-0961
RABENAN, Heinr.	25	Garbenteich	59-1036
RABENKAMP, Lina	25	Bonfort	60-0785
RABENSTEIN, C.	24	Ostheim	62-0938
RABER, Anna	19	France	62-1112

NAME	AGE	RESIDENCE	YR-LIST
RABITSCH, Rosal.	32	Bassum	57-0654
RACEK, Matthias	44	Borek	61-0779
Maria 37, Johann 15, Matthias 13			
Wenzel 9, Franz 8, Marie 6, Anna 3			
RACHELBRANDT, Carl	21	Gandersheim	57-0606
RACKEMEIER, Heinr.	35	Lerbeck	57-1067
Marie 26, Heinrich 2			
RACKER, Bernhard	29	Neuenhausen	56-1117
RADECKER, Wilhelm	29	Lingen	55-1082
RADELHEIMER, Leop.	18	Laupheim	59-0477
RADEMACHER, Eduard	19	Bielefeld	57-0447
RADEMACHER, Elise	18	Bremervoerde	58-0925
RADEMACHER, Ern'ne	20	Blegow/Prus.	61-0770
H.Johanna 18			
RADEMACHER, J.H.	50	St.Georgiwold	55-0413
Louise 24			
RADENBECK, Friedr.	58	Bierde	55-0812
Soph. Marie 52, Heinrich 26, Lisette 21			
Wilhelmine 16, Louise 12, Sophie 11			
Friedr.Wilh. 8			
RADENHAEUSER, Joh.	22	Faehr	62-1112
RADERT, Fr.	28	Cammer	57-1067
RADGE, Carl	26	Hinterpommern	58-0399
RADLER, Caspar	32	Ob.Schwarzach	62-0983
RADTKE, Marie	15	Prellwitz	56-0819
Wilhelmine 11			
RAEDHIN, Anna M.	26	Druckendorf	57-1113
RAEDLEIN, Barb.	34	Gr. Granstedt	56-0723
RAEPPLE, Christ.	17	Illingen	57-0850
RAESS, Marie	57	Niederstetten	57-1067
RAETHEL, Ann Marg.	34	Schlossgattnd	57-1148
RAETMEYER, C.	20	Varenholz	58-0306
RAEUBER, Eduard	19	Seehausen	60-0533
RAEUBER, Geo. Casp	21	Machtlos	61-0779
RAEUNING, Heinrich	60	Nidda/Hess.	61-0770
Phillipp 23, Heinrich 18			
RAFF, Andreas	22	Gr. Grenbach	60-0785
RAFF, Louise	32	Holzhausen	56-0512
Charles 5			
RAGALE, Franz	36	Schneidemuehl	57-0924
RAGGOW, August	30	Colberg	56-0723
Bertha 12			
RAGMANN, G.(m)	18	Wiesbaden	61-0716
RAGOT, Julie	20	Bavaria	59-0214
RAGOT, Nicolas	49	Italy	62-0166
RAHDE, Heinrich	32	Klauhorst	57-1067
RAHDE, Louise	34	Giessen	57-1067
Friedrich 1			
RAHDEN, L.(m)	19	Eggeln	62-0730
RAHE, Franz Hinr.	26	Oesede	62-0983
RAHEN, Heinrich	20	Versmold	56-1044
Wilhelmine 20			
RAHL, Dorothea	33	Kuehndorf/Pr.	60-0622
RAHM, Georg	25	Heil. Moschen	55-0628
RAHM, Johann	36	Friedrichsrod	56-0847
Heinrich 20			
RAHM, Verona	22	Schaffhausen	62-0938
RAHNE, Charlotte	19	Herford	60-0429
RAHNEFELD, Dorothy	48	Ehringdorf	56-0847
RAHNEFELD, Gottl.	44	Pirka	56-0847
RAIDEL, Barb.	23	Schwarzenberg	56-1216
RAIMUND, Peter	40	Bojan	55-0845
Catharine 40, Anna 12, Anton 9, Therese 5			
Moritz 5, Wendolin 2			
RAITTEL, Georg	26	Mengenreuth	60-0521
RALAND, Wilhelm	22	Adenstedt	55-1082
RALH, Dorothea	33	Kuehndorf/Pr.	60-0622
RALHUT, Dor.	37	St. Louis	62-0938
RALL, Edw.	16	Neukirch	62-1112
RALLIGECK, Elisab.	16	Barrau	57-0961
RALVERING, Johann	24	Amsterdam	59-0951
RAMHOLD, Philipp	28	Braunfels	57-1407
Louise 30			
RAMIEN, Cornel.	30	Stuckhausen	60-0521
RAMIG, Carl Fried.	19	Friedorf	56-0629
RAMISCH, Joh.	31	Citow	57-1113
Rosalie 28, Joseph 5, Anna 3, Wenzel 6m			
RAMISCH, Magdalena	37	Rosenhain	59-0384

NAME	AGE	RESIDENCE	YR-LIST
Matthilde 17, Maria 14, Bertha 12, R.B. 8 Emma 6m			
RAMISCH, Wenzel	24	Cittow	57-0850
Catharina 33, Rosalie 4			
RAMME, Christ.	18	Fakelstedt	57-0422
RAMMELKAMP, August	45	Malangas	60-0334
RAMMELKAMP, Elise	35	Halle	60-0334
Bernh. 25			
RAMMELT, Carl	24	Wiehe	59-0535
RAMMER, Anton	40	Bodendorf	59-0535
Anna 42, Marie 21, Michael 20, Georg 17 Barbara 13, Juliane 7, Elisabeth 11 Johann 5, Ignatz 9m			
RAMMERS, Georg	24	Altershausen	59-0535
RAMMES, Johann	30	Bavaria	60-0371
RAMPENTHAL, Friedr	25	Gross Furra	56-1011
RAMSAUER, Anton	26	Baiern	55-0634
RAMSEY, Rob.	40	Boston	59-1036
RAMSP, Marcus	37	Hattstadt	62-1042
RAMSPERGER, Leonor	32	New York	62-1112
Herm. 6, Emilie 4			
RANALLACKE, Cath.	21	Freiburg	61-0482
RANISH, Joh.	30	Bohemia	60-1161
RANKE, A.J.(m)	28	New York	62-0401
Henriette 30			
RANKE, Heinr.	19	Iverlohn	60-0334
RANSCH, Maria	17	Lengsfeld	56-0512
RANZ, Jacob	18	Unterbalzheim	60-0334
RANZEHOFF, Emil	18	Bechelsheim	58-0815
RANZIGER, Therese	38	Reifberg/Bav.	62-0608
RAPHAEL, S.	42	Witzenhausen	56-1216
RAPP, Carl	26	Leopoldshofen	62-0730
RAPP, D.	60	Rottweil	60-0334
Sophie 48			
RAPP, Ernst Heinr.	44	Luedingworth	56-0413
Pletch (m) 6m			
RAPP, Jacob	25	Leustetten	59-0990
RAPP, Joh.	57	Buffalo	59-0990
RAPP, Wilhelmine	21	Furien	56-0512
RAPPEL, Barb.	24	Helmstedt	59-1036
RAPPIN, Carl	16	Goettingen	56-0512
RAPPL, Wendelin	29	Isgier/Bav.	60-0429
Margaretha 24, Sebastian 1, Catharina 22			
RAPPOLD, W.(m)	17	Birkenweisbch	62-0836
RAPPOLT, Herm.	24	Nidda	59-0214
RAPS, Georg	32	Tenkensee	60-0521
RASBACH, Valentin	15	Mecklenburg	57-0606
RASCH, Emilie	18	Reutlingen	62-0467
RASCHE, Carl	30	Damme	58-0306
(wife) 27, (child) 3			
RASCHE, Heinrich	18	Hille	56-0411
RASCHEN, A.Marie	16	Berlin	59-0613
RASENBUSCH, Dina	10	Borken	62-0938
Ephraim 9			
RASENSTEIN, Fanny	22	Beverungen	59-0214
RASMUSSEN, Emma	7	Luetjenburg	57-0422
RASSHEN, J.H.	29	Bremen	59-0951
Rebecca 29, Rebecca 1			
RASSI, Gustav	38	Tessin	61-0167
RASSKUPFF, Jas.	19	Cabenz	60-0998
RASTELLER, Ludwig	36	New York	60-0521
RATAICZAK, Joseph	25	Romanshof/Pr.	55-1238
Louise 24			
RATH, Carl	16	Holzhausen	56-0723
RATH, Christian	18	Sansteth	56-1011
RATH, Wm.	23	New York	62-0467
RATHGEBER, Franz	29	Gotha	62-0166
RATHGEN, John	22	Scharmbeck	57-0654
RATHJEN, Bruno	25	New York	61-0897
RATHMANN, Chr.	25	New York	57-0422
John 19			
RATHSBURG, Christa	42	Burkau	57-0654
RATJEN, Augusta	23	Bremen	56-0951
RATMER, Hirschel	17	Benthen	56-1216
RATTHERT, Christ.	19	Todtenhausen	59-0372
RATZER, Friedr.	43	Muenchen	58-0306
Franziska 44			
RAU, Anna M.	22	Mardorf	62-0879
RAU, Friedr. W.	33	Obereffelder	62-1112
RAU, Friedrich	36	Neustadt	56-1117
RAU, Georg	52	Kirchhein	57-0776
Elisabeth 47, Johannes 25, Ludwig 13 Sophie 7			
RAU, Jac.	22	Waldstetten	60-1196
RAU, Jettchen	19	Hungen	57-1122
RAU, Johann	40	Eichelsachsen	62-0712
RAU, Ludwig	39	Bayreuth/Bav.	61-0770
RAU, Peter	28	Heringen	61-0482
RAUBER, Christ.	30	Unterwegfurth	57-0654
Christine 24, Catharine 5			
RAUBER, Wilhelm	19	Seehausen	55-0932
RAUCH, A.	41	Rottbach	62-0993
M. 33, R. 11, J. 9, J. 7, A. 5, A. 2			
RAUCH, Conrad	32	Hamberg	57-1067
Elisabeth 31, Conrad 9m			
RAUCH, Franz	45	Leipzig	55-0630
Theresia 30, Titus 7, Helena 3			
RAUCH, Georg	33	Heimaden	58-0563
Margaretha 28, Michael 4, Margarethe 2			
RAUCH, Joseph	33	Volkmarsen/He	62-0608
Aloisia 34, Ignatz 9, Albert 7 Margareta 5, Kunigunde 3, August 6m			
RAUCH, Sebastian	22	Altenstieg	61-0482
RAUCH, Thomas	39	Heroldsberg	61-0779
RAUCHFUSS, G.C.	18	Boitzsch	62-1112
RAUER, Toss	30	Riebens	57-0654
RAULF, C.	56	Dorste	62-0993
A. 53, C. 23, C. 13, A. 9			
RAUPACH, Johann	24	Gr.Waltersdrf	56-0847
RAUSCH, August	28	Kreuzbach	57-1067
RAUSCH, Catharina	17	Grebenau	56-0632
RAUSCH, Catharine	22	Mannsbach	57-1067
Valentin 10m			
RAUSCH, H.(m)	23	Grebenau	61-0669
RAUSCH, Joh.Heinr.	39	Olda/Sax.	61-0770
Martha 35, Louise 14, Lisette 10, Selma 9 Friedrich 7, Richard 2, Emilie 9			
RAUSCH, Johann	27	Nail	58-0881
Cunigunde 29, Lina 1			
RAUSCH, Mich.	61	Seligenstadt	60-0998
Elizabeth 51, Maria 19, Francisca 14 Jos. 9, Gustav 8, John 6			
RAUSCH, Wm.	26	New York	57-0654
RAUSCHENBERGER, JG	46	Soldin	60-0533
Amalie 37, Johann 16, Wilhelm 4 Joh. Franz 2, Ferdinand 3m, Marie 59			
RAUSCHER, G.(m)	18	Guttenberg	62-0730
RAUSCHKE, Johann	34	Grunau	58-0576
RAUSECK, John	36	Podelhota	56-1011
Josepha 38, Maria 10, Antonia 8 Francis 4, Joseph 2			
RAUTENBERG, Bernh.	26	Osnabrueck	62-0879
RAUTENHAUS, Marg.	23	Frieda	60-0334
RAUTMANN, Heinrich	31	Dingelstedt	56-0629
Dorothea 29, Dorothea 6m			
RAUTMANN, Julius	56	Langenstein	56-0629
Julius 20, Dorothea 17			
RAVELL, D.(m)	40	France	62-0730
REBELL, Anton	20	Bramsche	59-0477
REBELLO, Miguel	24	Paris	60-0785
REBHAN, Barbara	53	Unterling	62-0467
REBMANN, Franziska	23	Weisengich	55-0413
Louise 24			
RECCIUS, Emily	44	Peitz	57-1148
Otto 14, Emily 11, Franciska 7			
RECHT, Sophie	30	Kasalup	61-0716
Caroline 8, Moritz 6, Josepha 4, Max 9m			
RECHTEBACH, Gustav	20	Meiningen	57-0924
RECHTEN, H.(m)	50	Lilienthal	62-0730
RECHTERN, Henry	20	Achim	57-1148
RECK, Fr.	17	Windsheim	55-0932
RECKENBACH, Ad.	24	Pitzburg	59-1036
RECKER, Wilhelm	27	Suedhorst/Han	55-0538
RECKERS, Joh.H.	56	Wuellen	56-1117
A.Marg. 53, Christine 21, Hermann 24			
RECKNAGEL, A.	19	Cassel	55-0932

NAME	AGE	RESIDENCE	YR-LIST
RECKNAGEL, Friedr.	22	Serba	60-1161
RECKS, Carl	22	Polle	55-0932
REDEKER, Friedrich	36	Hohnhorst	55-0630
REDEMANN, Gerhard	36	Waarendorf/Pr	55-1238
REDER, Elisabeth	53	Stockheim	57-0754
Marie 18			
REDER, Joseph	40	Hendungen	61-0478
REDONLY, Francois	26	Bavaria	59-0214
REDWITZ, Joh.Georg	59	Nordhalben	56-1117
REDWITZ, Wolfgang	23	Alsengundstdt	60-0998
REEFERS, Jan. F.	23	Ochtelbur	55-0413
REEMANN, Ernst	28	Bramberg/Pr.	60-0052
REES, E.(f)	16	Kurhessen	57-0555
Cath.(f) 18			
REES, Heinrich	42	Bicken	62-0467
Catharine 42, Lisette 19, Emma 11			
Heinrich 6, Theodor 3, C.Albert 9m			
REESE, Anna	18	Lemvoerde	59-1017
REESE, C.	30	New York	62-0938
REESE, Christian	45	Friedrichshsn	55-0628
Anna Elisab. 45, Christoph 14			
Anna Gertrud 12, Friedrich 7, Julius 6			
Anna Cath. 4, August 10m			
REESE, Christoph	22	Grabbe	56-0589
REFF, A.(m)	73	US.	60-0521
REFFELT, Hermann	18	Bramsche	61-0047
REFFELT, Marie	60	Bramsche	61-0669
Joh. 60			
REGEL, Daniel	19	Pla	55-0812
Anna Cathar. 21			
REGEL, Ferdinand	44	Prosekel	56-0819
Henriette 52, Henriete 18			
REGENER, Friedrich	48	Magdeburg	57-0447
REGENSBURG, Wilh.	27	New York	59-0048
Christine 28, Wilhelmine 6, Wilhelm 4			
REGENTHAL, Wilh'ne	19	Amelsen	60-0533
REGER, Henry	24	Germany	59-0613
REGISTER, v. Max	19	Ingolstadt	61-0716
REGNER, Friedrich	26	Sommerville/O	55-1238
Hendrika 22, Emilie 2			
REGROUT, (m)	48	St.Malo	60-0785
REHACKE, Fr.	37	Kostamlat	56-0629
Catharina 26, Joseph 7, Anton 3			
REHBAUM, Albert	37	Frankenhausen	60-0533
Amalie 40, Guenther 20, Hermann 18			
Henriette 14, Carl 8, Laura 6, Richard 6m			
REHBOCK, Diedrich	16	Steinhude	56-0411
Jacob 23			
REHBOCK, Louise	25	Osterappeln	56-0411
REHFELD, Friedrich	41	Anger	56-1044
Friedrike 38, Dorothea 21, Friedrich 20			
Carl 13, Friedrike 10, Wilhelmine 8			
Wilhem 5			
REHL, Marg.	22	Ellingrode	57-0447
Maria 28			
REHLEIN, Ursula	28	Ebonsfeld/Bav	60-0429
REHLING, Diedrich	21	Ilbese	57-1067
Wilhelm 19			
REHM, Charles	19	Kirchhain	57-0422
REHN, Cath.	17	Gundhelm	62-1042
REHN, Christ.	50	Unterbalzheim	60-0334
Eva 50, Susanna 18, Maria 15, Jacob 11			
REHNERT, Charles	31	Berlin	57-0422
REHORST, Adolph	21	Osnabrueck	61-0779
REHORST, Sophie	19	Rahden	57-1280
REHS, Elisabeth	14	Halsdorf	58-0399
REHSE, Gerhard	19	Neundorf	56-1117
REHWEIN, G.E.(m)	25	Altenburg	61-0482
REIBSAM, Amadeus	28	Spal	56-0279
Maria 29			
REICH, Gertrude	18	Grosteinheim	62-0836
REICH, Heinr.Wm.	33	Elsenberg	61-0779
REICH, Jacob	28	Schellen	62-0983
REICH, Libertha	14	Altenburg	62-0758
REICH, Wilhelm	31	Muenchen	58-0815
REICHARD, Heinrich	26	Hessen	60-0371
REICHARD, J.G.(m)	18	Eschbach	61-0897
REICHARDT, Caspar	50	Pennsylvania	61-1132
REICHBOLD, Daniel	55	Stamheim	57-1067
Vollbrecht 28			
REICHE, Aug.	22	Gruenenplan	62-0166
Adolph 19			
REICHE, Gottlieb	58	Offenbach	62-1169
REICHE, Ludw.	55	Gruenenklau	58-0925
REICHE, Wm.	33	Gruenenplan	62-0401
REICHEL, Caroline	16	Bavaria	56-1044
REICHEL, Christ	30	Heringen	61-0482
REICHEL, Friedrich	22	Hetzles	58-0563
Kunigunde 26			
REICHEL, Friedrich	26	Schlotheim	61-0930
REICHEL, Fritz	12	Althuetten	56-1117
REICHEL, Henriette	52	Munchberg	60-0785
Joseph 2			
REICHEL, Herm.	28	Owen	60-0785
REICHEL, Joh.Jac.	24	Wustenselbitz	62-0879
REICHEL, Johann	18	Brand	56-0527
REICHEL, Johann	30	Diepholz	57-0365
REICHELT, Carl	26	Wittgenau	56-1044
REICHENBACH, Aug.	25	Engern	57-1407
REICHENBACH, B.G.	25	Koerner	62-0993
REICHENBACH, Doro.	27	Steinau	57-1113
Ernst 13, Marie 4			
REICHENBERGER, Joh	31	Burgtreswitz	60-0622
REICHENECKER, Frdr	18	Wuerttemberg	60-0411
REICHENMECKER, B.	22	Romelbach	62-0730
Friederike 15			
REICHENSTEIN, A.	27	Colzendorf	56-0847
REICHENSTEIN, L.	18	Zetel	62-0879
REICHERT, Anna	21	Meinbressen	55-0932
REICHERT, Anna M.	54	Illenschwang	61-0716
REICHERT, Baltasar	34	Bavaria	60-1161
Susan 27, Caspar 8			
REICHERT, Friedr.	34	Himbach	59-0384
REICHERT, J.Carl	18	Prussia	62-0758
REICHHOLDT, Peter	25	Stammheim	56-0527
Cath. 26			
REICHMANN, Georg	15	Alsfeld	55-0634
REICHMANN, Isak	35	Pockenheim	55-0812
REICHMANN, Max	35	Wien	59-0477
REICHOLD, Heinrich	30	Stammheim	56-1260
REICHWEIN, C.Frdke	44	Milau/Saxony	57-0924
August 14, Friedrich 12, Marie 10			
Hermann 8, Gustav 5			
REID, Gregor	30	Waldshut	62-1112
REIDELBACH, Maria	31	Fulda	60-0622
REIDENBACH, J.G.	26	Augusta/GA	62-1112
Eugenia 24			
REIERING, Gerhard	32	Cincinati	59-0214
REIF, M.	48	Meiningen	62-0993
REIFERT, David	28	Altenburg	58-0545
REIFF, Louise	26	Bavaria	62-1169
REIHMEYER, Charles	45	New York	62-0001
REIKER, Th.	45	Freren	55-1082
Louise 24			
REIL, Georg	29	Cassel	62-0306
REILING, Johann	23	Halle	57-0606
REILING, Wilhelm	16	Berson	57-1192
REIM, Carl	26	Oberkirchheim	62-1112
REIM, Mathias	36	Wolpertswende	59-0951
Rosalie 27, Marie 4			
REIMANN, Carl	18	Neudorf	56-0589
REIMANN, G.(m)	44	Baltimore	61-0804
Lina 19			
REIMANN, Georg	17	Melsungen	61-0478
REIMER, Carl	34	Colberg	62-0758
Albertina 36, Albertina by			
REIMER, Christina	26	Stadtamhoff	57-0654
REIMER, Christlieb	52	Zitzenrode	58-0576
REIMER, Dor.	37	Rumeln	61-0482
Louis 13, Adele 8, Adolph 6			
REIMER, Dorothea	35	New York	62-0111
REIMERS, Heinrich	18	Syke	58-0399
REIMERS, J.(m)	28	New York	61-0804
REIMERS, Lena	33	New York	61-1132
REIMERT, (m)	40	New York	62-0836
REIMERT, Wilh'mine	24	Borgholzhsn.	56-0411

NAME	AGE	RESIDENCE	YR-LIST
REIN, Cath.	28	Oberkirchheim	62-1042
REINAL, Johs.	16	Niederreith	55-0413
REINBACH, Cathrina	22	Odenhausen	57-1113
REINBOLD, August	30	Schwarzenberg	57-1280
Catharina 25			
REINBOLD, Joh.	21	Backenheim	59-1036
REINCHEN, Christne	16	Hagen	62-0983
REINE, Marie	58	Giershagen	56-0951
REINECK, Johann	33	Grodmada	56-0411
Susanna 27			
REINECKE, C.(m)	25	Billinghausen	61-0804
REINECKE, Philipp	35	Muenster	59-0384
Maria 33			
REINECKE, Therese	23	Warburg	59-0214
REINECKEN, Felix	34	Waldshut	62-1112
REINEKING, Friedr.	23	Erder	56-1260
REINERS, J.H.	27	San Francisco	59-1036
REINERS, Johann	6	New York	62-1112
Hinrich 4			
REINEWALD, Wilhelm	29	Osnabrueck	56-1117
Louise 24			
REINHARD, C.H.	35	Breslau	56-0550
REINHARD, Heinr.	30	Boston	61-0897
REINHARD, Heinrich	29	Rotha	57-0776
REINHARD, J.Voltma	35	Wilberrode	59-0412
REINHARD, Joseph	38	Bischofsheim	62-0879
REINHARD, Lorenz	36	Hehfert	57-1067
REINHARDT, Christ.	50	Chemnitz	55-0845
Clara 13			
REINHARDT, Christ.	53	Underkiffach	59-1036
REINHARDT, F.A.(m)	55	Knautheim/Sax	62-0342
REINHARDT, Florntn	55	Hela	56-1044
REINHARDT, Georg	30	Geisnidda	56-0723
REINHARDT, J.Georg	25	Meiningen	61-0770
REINHARDT, Joh.	33	Dresden	59-1036
REINHARDT, Mathias	15	Sindelfingen	60-0622
REINHARDT, Peter	22	Baltimore	62-0342
REINHAUER, Wm.Carl	27	Cassel/K.Hess	62-0342
REINHOLD, Caroline	26	Goettingen	58-0545
REINHOLD, Christne	20	Bersdorf	60-0411
REINHOLD, Chrstine	19	Niederlosnitz	55-0538
REINHOLD, Gustav	28	Ronneburg/Alt	55-0538
REINHOLD, J.L.	48	Bottendorf	61-0682
REINHOLD, Juliane	58	Liegnitz/Sil.	60-0622
Maria 20, Pauline 17, Julius 14			
REINHOLD, M.(m)	27		61-1132
REINHOLZ, Franz	54	Boehmen	62-0758
Franziska 44, Anna 20, Marie 13			
REINING, Charles	48	New York	61-0897
REINING, Georg P.	20	Obermunsbach	60-1196
REINKE, Joach.	41	Louisenthal	57-0654
Jane 41, William 18, Charles 16			
Friedrich 14, Augusta 5			
REINKEN, Wm.	32	Dreye	62-0730
REINKENOBBE, Elis.	25	Engelshausen	56-0589
REINKING, Carl	21	Neinberg	56-0550
Louise 46			
REINKING, Henry	31	Estorf	59-0384
Louise 23			
REINKING, Wm.	14	Bremen	62-1042
REINLAENDER, Chr.	57	Buffalo	55-0932
REINLER, Wm.	23	Wille	60-0521
REINMANN, Marie	13	Stetten	57-1280
REINMUELLER, Ph.	20	Hanau	62-0730
REINMUTH, O.F.	26	Glaschau	62-0938
REINOLD, Catharine	55	Beckum	62-0730
Catharine 15			
REINOLD, Sophie	22	Beckum	61-0482
REINS, Carl	19	Withen	61-0520
REINS, Wilhelm	21	Wrexen/Wald.	60-0622
REINSCHLE, Johann	21	New York	62-0342
REINSDORF, Chr'tne	6	Otterndorf	62-0712
REINSFELD, Conrad	28	Schehenmuehl	56-0632
REINSTEIN, Babette	18	Kaiserlindach	60-0521
REIPERT, Carl	15	Seligenstadt	60-0334
REIPSCHLAEGER, A.	45	St.Louis	62-1042
REIPSCHLAEGER, Fr.	17	Brinkum	57-0578
REIS, Georg	14	Heringen	60-0521

NAME	AGE	RESIDENCE	YR-LIST
REIS, Jette	31	Niederweden	62-0836
Beta 21			
REISACKER, K.(m)	22	New Haven/CT	61-0897
REISCHAUER, W.(m)	21	Bueckeburg	55-0634
REISING, Johann	55	Somborn	60-0398
Joh.Georg 18, Balthasar 16, Johannes 14			
REISING, Sophia	26	Oberoden	57-1148
REISRING, Louise	20	Leteln	57-1067
REISS, Albert	30	Baden	60-0371
REISS, Conrad	35	Rhuenta	58-0576
REISS, Valentin	19	Eisenheim	61-0520
REISSE, Ad.(m)	29	St.Louis	62-0836
Caroline 17			
REISSENUSTER, Crln	22	Coberg	60-0998
REISSMANN, Chrstne	57	Greiz	60-0785
REISSNER, J.A.	31	Zeistwitz	55-0413
Louise 24			
REITER, Babette	20	Hainsfahrt	60-0521
REITER, Caroline	31	Hildesin	56-0629
REITER, Christian	20	Wetzlar	57-0704
REITER, Heinrich	28	Giershagen	56-0951
Maria 6			
REITLER, Peppi	33	Perrischau	57-1192
Rosine 5, Moritz 3			
REITZ, Adam	17	Einhartshsn.	57-0924
REITZ, Anna	17	Kleeberg	62-1042
REITZ, Cath.	19	Hochelheim	55-0413
REITZ, Fritz	12	Wolpshagen	57-1122
REITZ, G.	28	Essleben	62-0993
REITZ, Jac.	30	Ndr.Dienzbach	59-0951
REITZ, Phil.	18	Okarben	57-0578
REITZ, Wilhelmine	56	Melsum	57-1122
REITZE, Anna Cath.	22	Hadamar	57-0754
REIZ, Peter	29	Velding	61-1132
REMENCLAR, Gretch.	21	Molsum	58-0399
REMER, Wm.	22	Lippstadt	62-0467
REMMER, M.E.	24	Steeg	59-0477
REMMERSHAUSEN, C.	28	Herrenbreitun	57-1067
REMMERT, Heinrich	28	Berghausen	56-1044
Wilhelmine 28, Elisabeth 58, Mathias 18			
Wilhelm 5, Heinrich 3, Georg 9m			
REMMERT, Herm.	21	Bocke	62-0232
Ed. 46			
REMMING, Herm.	18	Lengerich	60-0785
REMMLA, H.	18	Minden	58-0399
REMNING, Herm.	18	Lengerich	60-0785
REMOHAUSEN, Marie	56	Rastadt	57-1067
REMPE, Ferdinand	15	Minden	60-0533
REMPP, Andreas	32	Ipplingen	62-0879
REMWEDE, Margareta	34	Obergimpel	60-1141
Magdalene 8			
RENAUD, (f)	52	France	61-0897
Charles 10			
RENDER, Heinr.	20	Ellhofen	60-0785
RENGER, Catharine	33	Ohrenberg	60-1032
RENNEBAUM, Heinr.	33	Sieber	57-0924
Augusta 29, Adolph 4, Johanna 2, (baby) 1			
RENNEBOHM, F.W.	57	Hohe	59-1036
Hanna 47, Hannchen 21, Friedr. 18			
Wilhelmine 15, Caroline 13, August 11			
Focke 9, Heinrich 4, Wi. 1			
RENNER, Friedr.	17	Landau	62-1169
RENNER, James	18	Niederaulheim	57-0422
RENSCH, Maria	17	Lengsfeld	56-0512
RENSSMANN, Wilhelm	16	Zeulenrode	55-0932
RENTER, Eva	31	Langenhain	59-1036
RENTZHAUSEN, Aug.	21	Hamburg	56-1216
RENZ, Fidus	30	Hayngen	58-0576
Anna 24			
RENZ, Pastor	28	Fort Wayne	61-0804
Ad.(m) 9, Herm. 8			
RENZ, Sebastian	59	Cincinnati	57-1192
RENZEL, Eleonore	18	Buedingen	58-0881
REPPEL, Mart. Joh.	32	Ditzelbach	61-0520
REPS, Johannes	22	Dillstedt	55-0630
REPSCHLAEGER, Fr.	21	Prussia	57-0555
REPSCHLAEGER, J.C.	33	Prussia	57-0555
Karoline 33			

NAME	AGE	RESIDENCE	YR-LIST
REQUEBERT, B.	21	France	61-0167
RESAG, Fr.(m)	32	Bremen	62-0608
RESCH, Joseph	48	Breitenbrunn	55-0538
Theresia 40, Magdalena 22, Michael 19			
Theresia 21, Marie 18, Josepha 12			
Anna 11, Albert 9, Joseph 8, Ludwig 4			
Georg 2, Michael 1			
RESCH, Philippine	24	Birkenfeld	58-0545
RESS, Johann	34	Jessendorf	62-0100
RESSEL, Caroline	18	Friedland	62-0879
RESSEL, Florian	40	Schoenewald	62-0879
Marianne 42, Joseph 18, Franz 16			
Caroline 14, Florian 12, Therese 10			
Anton 6, Maria 50			
RESSEL, Rudolph	26	Braunsberg	60-1141
RESSENBERG, Wm.	26	Hoexter	60-0521
RESSLER, Lorenz	24	Germany	61-0167
Eva 21			
REST, Bernh.	51	Volkmarsen	62-0306
REST, Franciska	26	Bremen	56-1216
Joseph 9m			
REST, Friedrich	32	Volkmarsen/He	62-0608
RETBERG, Wilhelm	29	Helprechtshsn	59-0384
RETHFELD, Carl	22	Wuest	58-0881
RETHMANN, Joh. Hch	49	Hagen	57-0422
RETTBERG, Const.	20	Nordheim	57-1148
RETTIG, Georg	21	Solingen	61-0482
RETZELER, Dav.	22	Laupheim	62-0730
RETZER, Friedr.	43	Muenchen	58-0306
Franziska 44			
REU, Catharina	22	Wiesenbach	56-0632
REUDIGS, Heinrich	15	Brinkum	58-0881
REUDSEL, Minna	21	Seigelhorst	58-0306
REUHE, Theresia	18	Helsenbergen	60-0622
REUKAUF, John	18	Rodach	56-1011
REUL, Wilhelm	29	Nainhain	57-1122
Friederika 29, Anton 6m			
REUL, Zachar.	20	Bischoffsheim	59-0613
REULING, G.	27	Assenheim	59-0990
REUM, Fried.AUg.	28	Neuenhoff	59-0412
REUMANN, Georg	28	Moeckers	61-0478
REUSCHENBERG, D.G.	15	Bederkesa	58-0563
REUSS, Christine	25	Oxhausen	59-0535
REUSS, Valentin	28	Biblis	62-0342
REUSWIG, Ernst	20	Mehrholz	59-0990
REUTER, Elisabeth	33	Crumbach	62-1169
Christine 11, Andreas 9, Nicolaus 7			
Anna 5			
REUTER, Georg	21	Wunstorf	57-0606
REUTER, Georg III	26	Zellhausen/HD	60-0429
REUTER, H.Chr.	33	Bremervoerde	57-0365
Margarethe 27			
REUTER, Joh.	22	Brandoberndor	59-0412
REUTER, Johann	32	Prussia	61-0682
Margaretha 32, Nicolaus 4, Johann 2			
REUTER, Johannes	29	Fauerbach	59-0384
Catharine 23			
REUTKEMEIER, Herm.	30	Hohenhausen	61-0478
REUTLEIN, J.	27	Saxe-Coburg	56-0512
REUTLINGER, J.G.	34	Trendel/Bav.	60-0622
REUTSCHKA, Marg.	29	P---itz/Boeh.	55-0538
REUTSCHLER, Chr'ne	18	Gutenberg	58-0545
REVERS, Joseph	50	Ramsdorf	62-0983
Margarethe 33			
REVET, Chr.	24	Louisiana	62-1169
REXHAUSEN, Gust.	33	Salzwedel	62-1112
REXROTH, Georg	29	Darmstadt	60-0371
REYNERS, C.L. (m)	49	US.	62-0730
REYTER, Caroline	31	Hildesin	56-0629
RHEIN, August	41	Schlucht/Han.	56-0819
RHEIN, Barbara	28	Germany	59-1036
RHEIN, Eduard	16	Wuerzburg	56-0847
RHEIN, Gust.	19	Minden	59-0535
RHEIN, Johannes	36	Gennern	56-0723
Johanna 69			
RHEINFELD, Elise	22	Wularsheim	57-1416
RHEINLAENDER, Chr.	30	Goettingen	56-1117
RHODE, Wilhelm	55	Ziethen	56-0629
Albert 18, Ferdinand 13			
RHODES, Thomas E.	24	England	59-0613
RHONS, Philipp	21	Goettingen	59-0613
RIBONI, Angelo	40	Colattza	60-1141
Dorothea 27, Eliza 4			
RICHARD, Anton	39	Preussen	57-0606
RICHARD, C.	30	New York	59-0951
RICHARD, Carl	18	Strut	62-0306
RICHARD, Julia	21	Oldenburg	57-0422
RICHBER, Elisabeth	21	Oberglim	55-0630
RICHERS, W.	32	Sulingen	59-1017
RICHTBERG, Heinr.	38	Hessen	61-0682
Margaretha 34, Maria 13, Elisabetha 11			
Catharina 8			
RICHTER, Anna Cath	19	Dresden	62-0983
RICHTER, Anton	16	Wobel/Lippe	57-0847
Emilie 19			
RICHTER, Anton	65	Curhessen	57-0847
Maria 58			
RICHTER, Catharina	28	Bavaria	60-0371
Wolfgang 23			
RICHTER, Christine	21	Goswitz	57-0754
RICHTER, Christine	26	Stein	61-0669
RICHTER, Ferdinand	24	Hoschheim	56-1117
RICHTER, Friedr.	31	Perre Hause	59-0214
RICHTER, Friedr.L.	23	Schreiberhsn.	62-0993
RICHTER, Friedr.Wm	57	Stolberg	57-0422
Henrietta 51, Lewis 24, William 22			
Henrietta 20, Augusta 17, Friedrich 8			
RICHTER, Friedrike	20	Egeln	62-0730
RICHTER, Georg	22	Muehlhausen	60-1196
RICHTER, Gustav	25	Hildburghause	59-0214
RICHTER, Heinrich	43	Noerten	56-1216
RICHTER, Hermann	22	Lengerich	59-1036
RICHTER, J.H.(m)	27	Holtewik	62-0232
RICHTER, Johannes	25	Gersfeld	57-1067
RICHTER, Joseph	23	Carlsruhe	59-0214
RICHTER, Lina Mary	21	Hattingen	56-0413
RICHTER, Louise	9	Blomberg	56-0512
RICHTER, Marie	25	Leisnig	55-0932
RICHTER, Rudolph	24	Gera	61-0779
Rosamunde 24			
RICHTER, Wilhelm	24	Rheinland	60-0371
RICHTER, Wilhelm	22	Rothau	59-0047
RICK, Jacob	13	Tissa	60-0785
RICKEL, Fritz	21	Bufenshausen	57-1407
August 24			
RICKEL, Joh.Jos.	23	Bayern	56-1044
RICKELL, Adolph	43	Badbergen	61-0047
RICKERTSON, Theod.	20	New Bedford	60-0785
RICKLESS, J.G.L.	26	Jever	58-0881
RICKMANN, Louise	22	Holzhausen	58-0925
RIDDER, Heinrich	29	Wadersloh	59-1036
RIDDER, Hermann	22	Wormeln	60-0533
RIDELLE, M.B.	30	New York	62-0938
Mrs. 23			
RIEBE, Charles	28	Hamburg	57-0961
RIEBE, Eduard	26	Pyritz	56-0632
RIEBELING, Fr'drke	21	Minden	58-0399
RIEBELING, Gg.Hch.	27	Mengsberg/CH.	60-0429
RIECHMANN, C.F.	56	Suedhemmers	62-0938
Christiane 50, H.C. 20			
RIECHUS, Diedrich	14	Dedendorf	60-0533
RIECKE, Friedr.Car	14	Dedesdorf	59-0613
RIED, Christ.	23	Germany	56-1216
RIED, Crescenz	29	Stettin	57-0422
RIEDEL, Balth.	17	Fauerbach	59-0384
Catharina 18			
RIEDEL, Fr.Will.	22	Darmstadt	57-1148
RIEDEL, M.H.(m)	17	Dresden	61-0478
RIEDEL, Paul	28	Darmstadt	57-1407
Pauline 27			
RIEDEL, Walburg	30	Hohenweiler	59-0613
Elise 35			
RIEDEMANN, Eberh.	19	Barensdorf/KH	60-0622
RIEDEMANN, Heinr.	19	Dissen	59-0535
Justus 14			
RIEFENBERG, Friedr	30	Kuebingen	60-0521

NAME	AGE	RESIDENCE	YR-LIST
RIEFFENSTAHL, Jul.	29	Rochester	57-1148
RIEG, Barbara	23	Huettlingen	57-1067
RIEGEL, Georg	27	New York	61-0804
RIEGELER, Franz'ka	20	Eneus	61-0047
RIEGEMANN, Marie	41	Lechtingen	57-1407
RIEGER, Chr.(m)	34	Tauberzell/Bd	60-0622
RIEGER, D.	28	Schillingfirs	62-0993
C. 20			
RIEGER, Friedrich	24	New York	61-0047
RIEGER, Minna	24	Hohenhaslach	62-1112
RIEGGER, Eufrosina	20	Thornheim	62-0938
Anton 14			
RIEHL, August	55	Kirtorf	55-0630
Heinrich 23, Margaretha 47, Dorothea 21			
Catharine 17, Friedrika 11, Catharina 7			
Johannes 15, Justus 8			
RIEHL, Elisa	47	Homburg	62-0467
RIEHL, Joh.	16	Mardorf	60-0334
RIEKE, Friedrich	37	Barsenhausen	57-0447
Conradine 32, Henriette 9, August 7			
Friedrich 4, Wilhelmine 10m			
RIEKE, Ida	21	Wolffenbuttel	56-0723
RIEL, Fried.	28	New York	59-0477
RIEM, Minna	21	Stoeckheim	56-0951
RIEMANN, Conrad	47	Rotenburg/Hes	55-0628
Anna Maria 53, Maria 20, Conrad 16			
RIEMANN, Georg	22	Hetzerode	57-0776
RIEMANN, W.(m)	19	Bremen	60-1161
RIEMER, Therese	31	Baiern	57-1280
RIEMSCHNEIDER, Ad.	24	Curhessen	55-0634
RIENKS, T.J.	45	Gasthuisen	62-0467
Johann 28			
RIEP, Carl	19	Wetzlar	60-0334
RIEPE, Anna M.	19	New York	61-0804
RIEPER, Jacob	20	Altona	60-0533
RIEPP, Benedicta	35	Eichstaedt	58-0306
RIES, Babetta	17	Germany	61-0167
RIESE, Ludwig	24	Solsche	56-0411
RIESE, Mathias	60	Altforst	56-0847
Anna 22			
RIESENBACH, P.J.	35	St.Antoni	60-1196
RIESER, Augusta	41	Johanngeorgen	62-0342
RIESER, Carl	32	New York	62-0730
Pauline 29, Caroline 11m			
RIESS, Catharina	24	Lambach	58-0563
RIESS, L.	24	Italy	62-1042
RIESSER, Ludwig	42	Georgenstadt	61-0167
RIESTER, Georg	57	Untereichen	59-1036
RIETZ, Amalie	44	Pirkan	58-0925
RIFAUT, Mrs.V.	42	France	62-1112
Miss V. 30			
RIFFKEN, Tete (f)	22	Logum	55-0413
RIFLING, Heinrich	38	Selbershausen	61-0770
Christiane 32, Georg 8, Paul 6			
Maria Anna 3, Bernhardt 6m			
RIGGER, Sebastian	30	Sorgau	57-1192
RIHM, Anna E.	55	Kirtorf	55-0630
Christian 26, Philipp 23, Johannes 12			
RIKO, Johann	40	Glaskowo	57-0704
Caroline 43, Amalie Fried 17, Ernst 8			
Fried. 6			
RILLING, Elisab.	18	Gomaringen	62-0730
RINAL, Martin	23	Kreuzsabar	57-0447
Elisabeth 28			
RING, John	30	Southampton	59-0384
RINGEL, Theresa	16	Markelsdorf	56-1204
RINGELING, G.	46	New York	62-1112
Mrs.H. 33, Eugen 8, Olga 4			
RINKE, Christoph	51	Rosenthal	61-0930
Christine 52, Andreas 27, Johannes 26			
Franz 24, Georg 22, Margarethe 20			
Carl 18, Christoph 15, Joseph 10			
Rosine 24, Carl 11m			
RINNEMANN, Johann	16	Soehlbach	56-0723
RINTELN, Elise	32	New York	60-0785
Maria 6m, Adam 9, Wm. 8			
RINTINY, Vocke	25	Auricholdendf	57-1280
RIPKE, Malwine	25	Germany	59-0951

NAME	AGE	RESIDENCE	YR-LIST
RIPKENS, R. (m)	23	Borigmoor	55-0413
RIPP, Adam	28	Betzenroth/He	61-0770
Catharine 26, Heinrich 1			
RIPPE, Ernst	9	Anemolter	56-0819
RIPPE, Friedrich	17	Bremen	61-0770
RIPPE, Herm.	19	Werder	57-1150
RIPPE, Joh.	26	Braunschweig	59-0384
RIPPE, Rathje	18	Thedinghausen	62-0730
RIPPERT, Catharine	18	Watzenborn/He	62-0608
RIPS, Louise	21	Hoya	59-0214
Henriette 1			
RISSE, Carl	43	Iserlohn	57-0436
RISSE, Gertrude	36	Lichtenau	58-0815
RISSER, Juliette	23	Paris	62-0938
RISSMANN, Caroline	22	Grave	57-0606
RISSMEIER, H.(m)	23	Hildesheim	61-0897
RIST, Joh.	55	Pondhudson	57-1192
Dor. 40, Caine 58			
RIST, Theodor	22	Curhessen	58-0399
RITTE, Augustina	27	Altendorf	57-0754
RITTE, Georg	18	Cassel	59-0951
RITTER, Andreas	48	Maue	56-0589
Catharine 24			
RITTER, August	24	Linsburg	59-0535
Christine 25, August 9m			
RITTER, Babette	18	Schwarzenbach	60-0521
RITTER, Caroline	19	Tueschau	60-0521
RITTER, David	15	Nolhfelden	60-0411
RITTER, Fr.	18	Fulda	62-0938
RITTER, Friedrich	18	Erfurt	61-0930
RITTER, Heinrich	21	Doehlen	56-0411
RITTER, J.Casimir	18	Boos	61-0682
Appolonia 59, Eva 24			
RITTER, Johann	25	Volkenreuth	62-0879
RITTER, Margaretha	56	Doesdorf/Hann	61-0770
RITTERS, Ludvica	48	Gruenberg	61-0897
RITTMANN, Math.	59	Nemde	62-0938
RITTMEISTER, Elise	17	Wendorff	60-0521
RITZ, Cath. Elis.	23	Dunkelrod	56-0819
RITZ, Georg	28	Pfordt	59-0214
RITZ, Jacob	40	Dielheim	59-0412
RITZ, Marie	16	Friedewald	56-1260
Franz 14			
RITZE, Ehrhard	33	Baden	62-0467
Magdalena 29			
RITZLAFF, Carl	24	Hinterpommern	58-0399
RIVA, Pietro	32	Milan	62-0608
ROBEN, Gesche	28	Oldenburg	59-0535
ROBER, Amalia	28	Badenruber	56-0512
Ludwig 28			
ROBERTS, A.	43	England	62-0938
ROBERTS, Mary Ann	27	England	57-0578
ROBING, Anna	19	Ernsthausen	57-1280
ROBINSON, Edw.	60	New York	62-1112
Therese 54, Marie 26			
ROBL, Margarethe	48	Franknschleif	56-0847
ROBUS, Christoph	35	Rotterode	57-0606
Anna Cath. 34, Bernhard 7, Ernestine 9m			
ROCHEL, Marie	24	Dresden	56-0847
ROCHELS, Minna	20	Bremen	56-0819
ROCHS, Dorothea	26	Zell	62-1042
ROCK, Christian	55	Elberfeld	61-0716
Elisabeth 16, Caroline 14, Friedrich 9			
ROCK, Christine	20	Leteln	57-1067
ROCK, Heinrich C.	43	Elberfeld	59-0047
ROCKHEBUB, Charlot	21	Coeln	59-0613
ROCKSTROH, Carl	45	New York	62-0879
RODA, Fr.(m)	33	Angerstein	62-0836
RODE, Dor.	11	Hannover	57-0654
RODE, Elisabeth	17	Braunschweig	59-0384
RODEFELD, Wilh'mne	42	Minden	58-0399
Louise 18, Christian 11, Heinrich 5			
RODELBERGER, Leonh	33	Kaltensonthm.	61-0770
Michael 30, Eva 33, Marie 1			
RODEMANN, Anton	24	Lippe	57-0555
RODEN, Diedr.	32	Westenholz	57-0847
RODENBECK, Friedr.	58	Bierde	55-0812
Sophia Marie 52, Heinrich 26, Lisette 21			

NAME	AGE	RESIDENCE	YR-LIST
Wilhelmine 16, Louise 12, Sophie 11			
Friedr.Wilh. 8			
RODENBERG, Heinr.	47	Messlingen	57-1122
Sophie 40, Wilhelmine 17, Christine 13			
Christian 10, Louise 9			
RODENBURG, Joh.	36	New York	59-0951
Meta 24, Heinrich 5, Meta 3, Johann 3m			
RODENHAEFER, J.F.	29	Wilmington	61-1132
Christine 27			
RODENHASS, Carl	22	Ostfriesland	60-0785
RODER, A.(m)	28	Bavaria	60-1161
RODER, Gottlieb	21	Strelitz	57-0754
RODER, Wilh.	9	Buchholz	60-0398
RODEWIG, Henry	46	Klingruegen	57-1026
Betty 51, Friedrich 19			
RODGERS, A.(m)	30	London	62-0401
RODIEK, Wilhelm	25	Hude	57-1113
RODOWE, Gustavus	25	Hindersen	57-0422
RODT, Martin H.	39	Dorum	60-1141
ROEBER, Fr'dr.Carl	18	Giessen	61-0779
ROECHINGER, Rosine	17	Diermens	56-0411
ROECKE, Christian	27	Hemmersen	57-0961
ROECKER, John	27	New York	62-0730
ROEDEL, Margaretha	36	Hohensberg/Bv	62-0608
ROEDER, Adam	44	Russdorf	57-0447
Cath. 40, Epalisa 12, Barbara 9			
ROEDER, Caroline	29	Dheinfeld	59-0412
ROEDER, Catharine	49	Borgholz/Hess	62-0608
Catharine 18			
ROEDER, Elias	55	Kochstedt	56-0847
Catharine 22			
ROEDER, Heinr.	19	Langenslo/Hes	62-0608
Daniel 16			
ROEDER, Heinrich	54	Speckswinkel	62-0100
Anna C. 52, Heinrich 15, Johann 12			
Anna E. 8			
ROEDER, Johann	18	Hesselried/He	61-0770
ROEDER, Maria	18	Buchholz	60-0398
ROEDER, Mich.Jos.	23	Lohr	57-0606
ROEDER, Nannette	26	Sanmunster	58-0563
ROEDER, Robert	20	Weissenfeld	60-0411
ROEDIGE, Otto	41	Papenburg	59-0384
ROEDIGER, August	20	Eisenach	55-0634
ROEGGE, Geo. Heinr	22	Heithofen	56-0951
ROEHL, L.(m)	45	Neuenburg	57-0555
Charlotte 14, August 13, Fr.(m) 11			
J.O.(m) 8			
ROEHMER, Johann	28	Felsberg	58-0576
Elise 27			
ROEHRIG, F.W. (m)	46	Goettingen/Ha	60-0622
ROEHRIG, Philip	38	Udenhausen	59-0214
ROEHRING, Mathias	19	Koblenz/Main	56-0632
ROEHRKASTEN, Maria	18	Schuttlingen	56-0819
ROEHRS, Anna	29	New York	59-1036
Jann 11m			
ROEHRS, Heinrich	29	New York	62-0730
Marie 24			
ROEHRS, Henrk.(m)	19	Hastede	60-0429
ROEHRS, Herm.	29	New York	60-0334
ROEHRS, Joh.	36	New York	57-0961
ROEHRS, Margaretha	25	Langwedel	60-0334
ROELCH, Barbara	29	Gehaus	57-0918
ROELFS, Hermann	16	Lehe	58-0576
ROELKER, Maria	17	Osnabrueck	62-1042
ROEMER, August	18	Raalkirchen	62-1169
ROEMER, Helene	20	Allertshausen	59-0951
Elisabeth 17			
ROEMER, Johannes	35	Climbach	55-0630
ROEMER, Lorchen	17	Gruenberg	62-0836
ROEMER, Peter	55	Schweinbraten	55-0538
Anna 53, Dorethe 21			
ROEMER, Therese	18	Wiederau	62-0836
ROEMERMANN, Heinr.	47	Dorste	56-0629
ROENBECK, Friedr.	21	Neu Strelitz	56-1216
Anna 19			
ROENICK, Max	20	Altenburg	59-0047
ROENKER, Elisabeth	17	Flatterlothsn	58-0815
ROENNER, Berth.	18	Grueneberg	59-0951

NAME	AGE	RESIDENCE	YR-LIST
ROEPER, Christ.	71	Erstleben	59-0951
ROEPKE, Carl	36	Stettin	57-0606
ROEPKE, W.(m)	45	New York	61-1132
ROERING, Franz	25	Arnsberg	56-0279
ROES, Franz	31	Stockstadt	61-0482
ROES, Georg	43	Halsdorf/Han.	60-0622
Elisabeth 41, Conrad 15, Catharine 12			
Friedrich 7, Elisabeth 6, Conrad 4			
Martha 6m			
ROES, Gesine	18	Hagen	62-1112
ROESCH, Catharina	20	Wittorf	57-1113
ROESCH, Ludw.	23	Eggenstein	62-0401
ROESE, Adolph	21	Hameln	56-1216
ROESE, Caroline	23	Schlen	60-0533
ROESE, Elisabeth	25	Frankenberg	57-0776
ROESE, Elise	23	Wolffsangen	61-0478
ROESE, Friedrich	44	Sehlen	57-0776
Juliane 39			
ROESEL, Albert	34	Munchenbernsd	60-0785
Emilie 24, Moritz 2			
ROESEL, Erdmann	17	Munchenbernsd	60-0785
ROESENER, Anton	27	Cammer	57-1067
ROESER, Catharine	22	Wolfskaute	57-0754
ROESER, Elisabeth	22	Halsdorf	58-0399
ROESEUVE, Heinr.	28	Bueckeburg	55-0634
Eleonor 27, Carl Friedr. 20, Sophie 20			
ROESKE, Fr.(m)	32	Leipe	60-1196
ROESKE, Friedrich	31	Nalenzka/Pol.	56-1260
Caroline 28, August 9m			
ROESLEIN, Wm.	17	Rietberg	62-0836
ROESS, Anna	29	Oberaula	59-0535
Elisabeth 6, Abel 4, Martha 1			
ROESSER, Friedrich	30	Fuchstadt	57-0422
ROESSLER, Barbara	26	Pfaffenreuth	62-0467
Joh.Carl 7, Justine 15			
ROESSNER, Fr.	23	Kattenborn	55-0413
ROESTER, Heinrich	30	Alsfeld	57-0447
Elisabeth 40			
ROESTER, Ludwig	31	Ellingrode	57-0447
ROETH, Catharine	26	Mainz	62-0938
ROETTIG, Joh.Aug.	20	Muehlhausen	57-1148
ROETZ, Gerhard	19	Crapendorf	55-0932
ROEVER, Chr.	16	Kuhstedt	57-1148
ROEVER, Diedrich	23	Steinhude	56-0411
ROEVER, Johann	54	Miess	59-0613
Anna 34			
ROEVESAAT, Joh.Hch	32	Kleinloog	58-0563
ROFF, Andreas	22	Gr. Grenbach	60-0785
ROFKAR, Anna	20	Tarmstedt	57-1148
Elise 19			
ROGGE, Georg	24	Rodderse	56-1117
ROGGE, Joh. Fr.	19	Hannover	60-0411
ROGGENBAUDE, Math.	15	Breitenstein	60-0521
ROGGENBORG, Heinr.	15	Oeldinghausen	59-0477
ROGGENDORF, Joach.	28	Zernin	57-0776
ROGNER, Marie	17	Schellert	60-0521
ROHACKE, Fr.	37	Kostamlat	56-0629
Catharina 26, Joseph 7, Anton 3			
ROHDE, Carl	31	Bisses	60-0533
Otto 16			
ROHDE, Catharina	20	Uder	57-0422
ROHDE, Friedrich	16	Hille	56-0411
ROHDE, Johann	30	Neuenhain	57-1067
ROHDE, Louise	24	Hannover	56-1044
ROHDFELD, Marie	19	Hille	56-0411
ROHE, Franz	20	Endeln	59-0951
Anna 20			
ROHE, Rudolph	34	Bramsche	59-0477
ROHKRAEMER, Bernh.	25	New York	60-0521
Rosamund 18			
ROHL, Georg	26	Herstein	60-0334
ROHLAND, Friedrich	24	Zeitz	56-0819
ROHLEDER, Henriett	42	Oldenburg	57-0422
ROHLEDER, Herman	48	Boehmen	61-0478
Ottilie 25			
ROHLER, Heinrich	24	Wuertt.	55-0634
ROHLMEYER, Joh. D.	14	Sebbenhausen	60-0533
ROHMBERGER, C.	38	US.	62-1042

NAME	AGE	RESIDENCE	YR-LIST
ROHR, August	21	Stadtloesch	56-0847
ROHR, Fritz	26	Wunstorf	57-0447
ROHR, Moritz	26	Berlin	61-0107
ROHRBACH, Anna Eva	17	Hessen	56-1044
ROHRBACH, Elisab.	21	Iba	60-1161
ROHRBACH, Magnus	25	Hessen	60-0371
Johannes 55, Maria 52			
ROHRIG, Dorothea	22	Hannover	57-0606
ROHRLACK, Gustavus	34	Krjritz	57-0422
Armand 30, Albertine 25, Anna 2			
ROHRSEN, Johann	52	Hohnhorst	55-0630
Engel 42, Heinrich 15, Christine 19			
Maria 17, Sophie 12, Hans 9, Maria 6			
Engel 3, Conrad 6m, Maria 70, Dorothea 34			
ROIHAHN, Carl	29	Sivershausen	57-1280
Sophia 25			
ROLAND, John	36	Elspe	57-0422
ROLAND, Max	17	Linsheim	59-0048
ROLCKMANN, H.W.	25	Hanover	57-0654
ROLF, Gottl.Diedr.	27	Bielefeld	57-0704
ROLFE, Armand	23	New York	57-0654
ROLFFE, William	53	Windsor	57-0654
ROLFING, Ludwig	19	Friedewalde	56-0411
ROLH, J.M.(m)	25	Lidolsheim	61-0897
Rosine 50			
ROLL, Anton	24	Attendorn	57-0606
ROLL, Conrad	24	Weigersbach	60-1141
ROLL, Jacob	20	Unterriexinge	61-0770
ROLLE, Ernst	37	Reichenau	57-0654
Ernestine 13, Emily 9			
ROLLERI, Salteno	24	Italy	62-0166
ROLLHAUS, Catty	42	New York	57-1150
ROLLINGER, Anton	28	St.Leon	61-0482
ROLLKA, Kurt Henry	26	Sachsen	58-0545
ROLTSAR, Joh.	30	Hussum	56-0512
ROMAHN, L.	24	Danzig	62-0993
ROMANN, Anton	21	Lingen	62-0879
ROMANN, Za.	41	Koblina	56-1044
ROMEIS, Andreas	29	Brukenau/Bav.	55-0628
ROMER, Samuel	34	Erlau/Hungary	56-0819
ROMLINGER, Frankli		Elbingen	59-0613
ROMMEL, Geo.Friedr	22	Sachs.-Mein.	58-0545
Sophie 24			
ROMMEL, Gottlieb	20	Canstadt	61-0167
ROMSYKE, Herm.	48	Lotuss	62-0232
Ed. 46			
RONNER, Heinr.	30	New York	60-0785
RONSTEDT, Joh.Conr	19	Feddewarden	56-0819
ROOS, Rosina	8	Tharnashardt	59-1036
ROPENBERG, Moses	37	Koestrich	62-0879
Betty 28			
ROPPELT, Anna	22	Greuth	56-0847
RORAPPER, Johann	25	Wilsenbeck	60-0785
RORENE, Pietro	36	Genova	62-1042
Cath. 24, Annette 22, Marie 20			
ROSCH, Anna	32	Jarhausen	62-0730
ROSCHILD, Moritz	17	Schoenbrunn	59-1017
ROSE, Anton	32	Rosebeck	55-0812
Friederika 34, Elisabeth 17, Johann 3			
Maria 58, Maria 10w			
ROSE, August	26	Braunschweig	56-0819
Ernestine 51			
ROSE, Helene	21	Oberneuland	57-1148
ROSE, J.	38	Germany	56-0550
ROSE, Joseph	20	Gerbecke	56-0512
Heinrich 25, Elisabeth 28			
ROSE, Theodor	20	Hannover	57-1148
ROSEBROCK, Joh.F.	18	Dressen	59-0535
ROSEL, Matth.	18	Kristum	55-0413
ROSEMEYER, Bertha	25	Warburg	59-0384
ROSENAU, Capt.	33	Vegesack	62-0111
ROSENBAUER, Joh.	19	Schran	60-0334
ROSENBAUM, Hanchen	23	Peckelsheim	60-0533
ROSENBAUM, Hen.(f)	20	Fordon	57-0578
ROSENBAUM, Julchen	19	Niederstein	55-0630
Caroline 21			
ROSENBAUM, Levi	16	Niederstein	55-0630
ROSENBAUM, Lina	9	Kalamazoo/MI	62-1169
ROSENBAUM, Sam.	30	Pyrmont	57-1148
ROSENBAUM, Valent.	32	Blankenburg	60-0785
ROSENBERG, Bettch	18	Lohr	60-0785
ROSENBERG, Carolne	18	Fritzlar	60-0521
ROSENBERG, Fr'dke.	49	Wagenfeld	57-0776
ROSENBERG, Johanna	19	Fordon	57-0578
ROSENBERG, Levi	30	Oberaula	56-0629
Betty 25, Carl 9			
ROSENBERG, Minna	27	Bremen	55-0634
ROSENBERG, Samuel	26	Buende	55-0932
ROSENBERG, Samuel	15	Cochau	59-1017
ROSENBERGER, Cath.	24	Schoenborn/Bv	55-1238
Louise 24			
ROSENBERGER, Marie	21	Wiesenberg	60-1032
ROSENBLATT, Carol.	17	Hausen	59-1036
ROSENBLATT, Jetche	14	Geisa/Weimar	62-0608
ROSENBLATT, Manus	18	Mannsbach	60-1161
ROSENBROCK, H.H.	18	Dressel	57-0847
ROSENFELD, Hirsch	19	Waldmanshofen	60-0521
ROSENFELD, Johann	19	Brakel	60-0533
ROSENGARTEN, Jos.	18	Schiffelbach	62-0712
ROSENKRANZ, Carl	37	Schwalbach	55-1082
Louise 24			
ROSENKRANZ, Friedr	42	Schwedt	57-0961
Henrietta 42, Friedrich 14, Mary 12			
Richard 9, Conrad 5, George 11m			
ROSENMEYER, (m)	22	Warburg	58-0306
ROSENSTEIN, Simon	27	Beverungen	59-0214
ROSENSTENGEL, F'ke	48	Vollmerdingen	57-0021
Anna Marie 55, Friedrich 21, Heinrich 15			
ROSENSTIEL, Fr'dke	28	Jaegersburg	61-0482
Emilie 23			
ROSENSTOCK, Jonas	22	Volkmarsen	56-1044
ROSENTHAL, A.(m)	23	Chicago	62-0111
ROSENTHAL, Abraham	37	Hannover	57-0654
ROSENTHAL, Fr.(m)	33	Prussia	57-0555
Augusta 30, August 8, Emilie 1			
ROSENTHAL, Friedr.	24	Pulvermuehle	57-0422
ROSENTHAL, H.	25	Berlin	58-0604
ROSENTHAL, Heinr.	30	Zehlendorf	57-0447
Henrike 29, Franz 1			
ROSENTHAL, Helene	26	Olpe	56-0589
ROSENTHAL, Hermann	27	Osterholz	57-0924
Minna 34			
ROSENTHAL, J.D.	35	Rieda	62-0730
Marie 33, Joh.H. 6, Carl 4			
ROSENTHAL, J.G.(m)	49	Neuenburg	57-0555
P.(f) 33, C.A.(m) 3m, Justine 19			
F.W.(m) 17, Henriette 15			
ROSENTHAL, L.	56	Gruenenplan	62-0938
ROSENTHAL, L.	50	Gruenenplan	62-1112
ROSENTHAL, M. Cath	22	Olpe	58-0306
ROSENTHAL, Salomon	24	Bruchhausen	57-0924
ROSENTRETER, W.	32	New York	61-0804
(f) 25			
ROSER, Joh.Aug.	20	Brueckenau/Bv	62-0608
Hildegard 24, Therese 22			
ROSER, Johann	48	Brueckenau	60-0533
Margaretha 42, Theresa 20, Johann A. 18			
ROSICKY, Johann	35	Boehmen	62-0001
Joseta 34, Wilhelmine 21, Marie 9			
ROSIE, Louise	48	Stuttgart	56-0512
Wilhelmine 23, Louise 20, Auguste 15			
Emily 7, Emma 7, Carl 7, Henry 7			
ROSIGSMANN, Gerhd.	26	Halle	59-1036
ROSINSKY, A.(m)	29	Gera	61-0804
Christine 22			
ROSINSKY, Johanna	20	St.Louis	57-1192
ROSMUNDE, Chris.de	18	Goeppingen	59-0613
ROSS, Anna	18	Ellingrode	57-0447
ROSS, Bertha	18	Unterlind	59-0951
ROSS, Joh.	22	Bremen	59-1036
ROSSBACH, Adam	27	Vilmar	59-1036
ROSSE, Margarethe	56	Nordheim	56-0847
Diedr. 3			
ROSSI, Giovanni	32	Italy	61-0107
ROSSING, J.F.	35	Nemde	62-0938
(baby) 3m			

NAME	AGE	RESIDENCE	YR-LIST
ROSSLOSSKY, Marie	32	Nabfell	57-1407
Anna 18			
ROSSMAESSLER, Otto	22	Leipzig	59-0384
ROSSMANN, Anna	22	Gehrde	62-0467
ROSSMANN, D.(m)	34	Badbergen	62-0467
ROSSMANN, G.C.	32	New York	57-1148
ROSSNER, Conrad	22	Graefenberg	60-0429
Anna 33, Friedrich 7			
ROSSNER, Peter	40	Coburg	57-0776
ROST, Friedrich	22	Reisdorf	60-1053
ROST, Louis	24	Jever	57-1148
ROSZHIRT, Mathaeus	21	Bayern	57-1280
Margaretha 27			
ROTBERG, Marg.Elis	47	Meckelsdorf	56-0819
Joh.Ernst 15, Heinrich 9, Johann Georg 20			
ROTBINGER, Carl	36	Hachstuhl	55-0812
Theresa 26			
ROTE, M.	20	Hameln	56-0550
ROTENBERGER, Joh'a	34	New York	56-0819
ROTENHAUSLER, Clem	18	Artisburg	60-0785
ROTERS, Anna Cath.	25	Gaupel	62-0232
ROTERS, Maria C.	27	Legden/Pr.	60-0622
ROTH, Anna Marg.	15	Maibach	62-0401
ROTH, August	14	Stolzenau	60-0533
ROTH, Carl (Dr.)	33	Giessen	60-0429
ROTH, Christine	30	Elenhausen	57-1122
ROTH, Elise	22	Meiningen	55-0634
ROTH, Heinrich	32	Sulzburg/Bav.	55-0538
ROTH, Johann	25	Rentweinsdorf	60-1053
Margaretha 32, Barbara by			
ROTH, Margaretha	22	Alsfeld/Hess.	62-0608
ROTH, Nicolaus	28	Brokenau/Bav.	55-0628
ROTH, U.	26	Neudorf	62-0993
ROTHAUER, Johann	42	Ahorn	55-0932
ROTHBALLER, J.Bapt	22	Leuchtenberg	60-0429
ROTHBART, David	16	Offenbach	59-0048
ROTHE, Carl	20	Wollfede	57-1122
ROTHE, Gerhard	15	Fond du Lac	59-1036
ROTHE, Heinrich A.	27	Bremen	59-0477
ROTHEN, Conrad	59	Ndr.Ofleiden	62-0712
ROTHERMUND, R.F.	23	Alfeld	61-0897
ROTHERT, Herrmann	22	Hemke/Hann.	61-0770
ROTHKOPF, Marie	19	Boehmen	62-0758
ROTHLINGSHUEFER, A	29	Kaubenheim	61-0482
ROTHMANN, H.W.	30	Nemde	62-0938
ROTHMUELLER, Marg.	23	Minden	55-0413
ROTHMUND, Maria J.	30	Wintersulgen	60-0622
ROTHSCHILD, Abram	22	New York	59-0048
ROTHSCHILD, Aron	20	Frankfurt	62-0938
ROTHSCHILD, Bertha	18	Schluchtern	58-0604
Joseph 17			
ROTHSCHILD, Isaac	19	Langenschwarz	60-0411
ROTHSCHILD, J.	27	Borken	62-0938
Rosa 23			
ROTHSCHILD, Johana	23	Zierenberg	57-1192
ROTHSCHILD, Levi	29	Waltersbruch	62-0232
ROTHSCHILD, Moritz	20	Hofgeismar	55-0634
ROTHSCHILD, Simon	17	Schluechtern	60-0785
ROTT, Heinrich	28	Menslage	56-1216
ROTTENBERR, Lueder	16	Hagen	57-0776
ROTTENHOEFER, Geo.	22	Volkach	60-0785
ROTTER, Margaretha	53	Reisch	61-0770
ROTTHAS, Doroth.	24	Bremen	56-1216
ROTTMANN, Georg	20	Mallinghausen	58-0925
ROTTWINKEL, Herm.	36	Cincinnati	60-0785
ROTZIEN, Joh.Mich.	42	Prussia	62-0758
Wilhelmine 33, Friedrich 12, Johann 10			
Rudolph 8, Eduard 5, Paul 2, Ernst by			
ROUSSEL, Emma	32	France	62-1042
A. 40, E. 16			
ROUSSI, Gabrielle	44	France	62-0938
ROVIGNO, Carlo	26	Italy	61-0716
ROVS, Georg	27	Nassau	58-0399
RUAPP, John	30	Dollingen	59-0477
RUBB, Jacob	36	Altenkirchen	57-0704
RUBBERT, E.(f)	24	Waldcappeln	57-0555
RUBE, Wm.	21	Nidda	62-0836
RUBENKAMP, Alb'tin	21	Hannover	61-0716
RUBENSTOK, Dorotea	25	Vahrenholz	56-1260
RUBERT, Peter	23	Zugenreite	57-1280
RUCHLER, Theodora	17	Artisburg	60-0785
RUCHTI, Georg	28	Diestershofen	56-1117
RUCK, Dorothea	30	Meiningen	57-0924
RUCK, Joh. Wilh.	17	Feuchtwangen	55-0628
RUDDERFORTH, H.	45	England	56-0550
Jeanette 34			
RUDELS, Friedr.	22	Aizendorf	60-1196
RUDLOFF, Fr. (m)	59	Werneck	62-0730
Elise 52			
RUDOLF, Adam	17	Hertingshsn.	55-0630
RUDOLF, Heinrich	28	Ruppertenroth	55-0630
RUDOLPH, Anna	19	Wittgenau	56-1044
RUDOLPH, August	32	New York	61-1132
Anna 9			
RUDOLPH, Catharine	42	Verna/Hessen	57-0924
RUDOLPH, Friedr.	25	Hardisleben	61-0482
RUDOLPH, Gottfr.	42	Ellhofen	60-0785
Christine 37, Friederike 22			
RUDOLPH, Johann	24	Cassel	60-0785
RUDOLPH, Johann	30	Krautheim	60-1161
RUDOLPH, Johannes	16	Verna	57-0924
RUDOLPH, Martin	26	Heimershausen	62-0306
RUDOLPH, Philipp	58	Boxberg	60-1032
Franziska 48, Anna 5, Philipp 13			
Joseph 18, Marie 17, Nanette 24			
(baby)(died) 1			
RUDOLPH, Theresa	21	Tiefengruben	62-0712
RUDRAFF, Anton	23	Biberich/Nass	61-0770
RUEBBECKE, Carl	29	Bruchhoff	60-0334
RUEBER, Johann	33	Bavaria	61-0482
Elisabeth 34, Jacob 5			
RUEBSAME, Elise	55	Hoefele	62-1169
RUEBSAMM, Joh.	17	Weilburg	60-0334
RUECKDESCHEL, Mary	32	Kornbach	56-0951
RUECKER, Jacob	43	Selters	59-0384
Cath. 53			
RUECKER, Jacob	24	Remscheid	62-1169
Mrs. 22			
RUECKERT, Ferdin.	30	Berlin	56-1044
Emilie 29, Marie by			
RUECKERT, Georg	22	Work	60-0334
RUECKERT, Gottfr.	60	Eupen/Pruss.	59-0047
Gertrud 52, Alexander 16, Bertha 14			
Marie 9, Carl 7			
RUECKERT, Justine	24	Holsheim	56-1216
RUEDEBUSCH, Anna	38	Sandhotten	60-0521
RUEDEBUSCH, Anna	23	Grossenkneten	60-0521
Herm. 58, Bernh. 28, Anna 23, Maria 20			
RUEDEBUSCH, August	15	Hockenberge	60-0521
RUEDEBUSCH, Heinr.	25	Huntlosen	60-0521
Marie 18			
RUEDEN, Bernhard	19	Bernstrupp	60-0334
RUEDIGER, Jean	19	Cassel	60-0411
RUEDIGER, Johanna	21	Remptendorf	59-0613
RUEDIGER, Marie	29	Stuttgart	59-0477
RUEDIGER, Theodor	19	Halberstadt	56-0589
RUEF, J.H.(m)	25	Freiburg	61-0482
RUEFER, Johannes	29	Curhessen	55-0634
RUEFFER, Jacob	38	Wallersdorf	62-0608
Catharine 28, Catharine 24, Adam 8			
Anna Maria 6, Juliane 5, Conrad 10m			
RUEGER, Emil	26	New York	62-1042
RUEGER, John	23	Brooklyn	62-0232
RUEGER, Paul	40	Pfaffendorf	56-0819
RUEGER, Theodor	25	New York	62-0467
RUEHL, Catharina	27	Egersheim	55-0812
RUEHL, Elisa	47	Homburg	62-0467
RUEHL, Elisabeth	53	Reiskirchen	55-1082
Louise 24			
RUEHL, Emilie	24	Dorndorf	57-0447
RUEHL, Friederike	21	Egersheim	55-0812
RUEHL, Justus	21	Pflungstadt	57-1067
RUEHLING, Anna	13	Neumarschen	56-0411
RUEHR, Magdalena	28	Mistelgau	61-0520
RUEKRUEGEL, Johann	41	Pittersdorf	61-0520
Margaretha 31, Johann 9			

NAME	AGE	RESIDENCE	YR-LIST
RUELBERG, Carl	26	Grossalmerode	60-0429
RUELBERG, Marie	23	Gr. Almerode	60-1032
Pauline 2, (child) 5m			
RUELLE, Heinrich	20	Brakel	60-0533
RUELLER, Joseph	29	Heck	62-0983
RUEMPEL, Heinr.	18	Oppenroede	60-0521
RUEPKE, Hermann	20	Dissen	61-0478
RUEPP, S.	28	Arau	59-0477
Amalie 22			
RUEPPEL, Ph.	20	Odensachsen	62-0467
RUERGNER, Otto	24	Zensburg	59-1036
Oscar 26			
RUERUP, Hinrich	20	Volmerdingsen	57-0021
RUESS, Heinr.	28	Ulm	60-0521
RUESTER, Minca	52	Untereichen	60-0334
RUETE, Th.W.(m)	19	Scharmbeck	61-0804
RUETER, Heinrich	17	Hille	56-0411
RUETH, Regina	24	Baden	62-0758
RUETHER, Wilhelm	38	New Bedford	59-0372
RUETTGEROTE, Frdke	24	Braunschweig	59-0372
RUETZ, Jacob	31	St.Gallen/Sw.	60-0371
RUGE, Meta	20	Hagen	62-0232
RUH, Barbara	33	Philadelphia	62-1042
Chr. 11m			
RUHE, Carolina	21	Minden	55-0634
RUHE, Rab.(m)	18	Ruckers	56-0819
RUHEMA, Isaak	17	Samotschin	57-0704
Abraham 15			
RUHL, August	21	Cassel	60-0398
RUHL, Caroline	17	Ruckers	62-0306
RUHL, Ferdinand	21	Herbstein/Hes	62-0342
RUHL, J.J. (m)	20	Lehra	61-0897
RUHL, Johann	27	Merkenfritz	58-0576
Gertrud 28, Heinrich by			
RUHLAND, Mary	23	Eglshof	59-1036
RUHM, J.(m)	29	Tiegendorf	62-0306
RUHMA, Eduard	28	Dolitsch	55-0845
Caroline 29, Moritz 25, Georg by			
RUHR, Joseph	16	Damme	59-0477
RULAND, Amalia	25	Germany	61-0804
RULAND, Benedict	19	Strut	62-0306
RULFS, G.	28	Wilmington	59-1036
Cath. 21			
RUMLER, Fed.	24	Wersberg	60-1141
RUMMEL, Henriette	23	Hesse-Darmst.	60-0371
RUMMEL, Luwdig	25	Cornweiler	60-0398
Johann 24			
RUMMELER, Ferdinan	27	Dornbern	57-0654
RUMP, Anna	30	Illinois	62-0938
RUMPFF, Louise	17	Biedenkopf	60-0521
RUMPFF, William	25	Dubuque/Iowa	57-0961
Adele 21			
RUNDDORF, Carolina	40	Peitz	57-1148
August 21, Emil 18, Julius 15, Theodor 11			
Ida 2			
RUNGE, Gustav	37	Philadelphia	59-0951
RUNGE, Joh.Gottfr.	24	Gammlo	60-1196
RUNGE, Lucia	24	Bremen	61-0897
RUNGE, Wilhelm	25	Radewald	57-1067
RUNKEL, D.	35	Marburg	59-1036
Mary 35, Philippine 5, Heinrich 3			
RUNNE, Heinrich	24	Hannover	56-0847
RUOFF, Maria	27	Nuernberg/Bav	55-0628
RUOFF, Sebastian		Tettwangen	57-1280
RUPEL, Johannes	32	Kirchheim	57-0704
Anna Cath. 29, Justus 9m			
RUPP, Adam	32	Spreisach	57-0021
RUPP, Rosine	20	Eggenstein	62-0401
RUPP, Wilhelm	26	Bavaria	62-1169
RUPPE, Barbara	29	Meiningen	57-1148
RUPPEL, Conrad	34	Alsfeld	57-0606
RUPPEL, Georg	30	Burklar	56-0589
RUPPERT, E.	20	Marburg	59-0990
RUPPERT, Georg W.	19	Niedermittlau	56-1117
RUPPERT, Joh.	20	Weidenhausen	60-0398
RUPPERT, Leonore	32	Washington	62-0836
RUPPKE, Chr.	36	Bromberg	55-1082
Louise 24			
RUPPLE, Jac.	36	Schaffhausen	62-0938
Benjamin 17			
RUPPRECHT, Aug.	22	Mirgassen	59-0990
RUPPRECHT, Joh.	24	Rockenbach	60-0521
RUPPRECHT, Marg.H.	20	Noerdlingen	57-0422
RUPPRECHT, Wilhelm	21	Emden	58-0925
RUPRECHT, Elisab.	34	Graefenberg	59-0535
RUPRECHT, Pauline	23	Schoelen	57-1280
RUREDE, Fritz	15	Suhlingen	56-1044
RUSCH, Carl	21	Soltau	57-0578
RUSCHERN, Amalia	28	Pirna	56-0279
RUSCHKUEHL, Fr.(m)	27	Baltimore	62-0467
RUSCHLANGE, Aug.	25	Cloppenburg	59-1036
RUSENATH, Hanna	22	Ubbedissen	55-1082
RUSJINS, Otto	29	Antwerp	62-0401
RUSS, Elisabeth	18	Ellenroth/Hes	62-0342
Anna Cath. 15			
RUSS, Jacob	22	Koenigswald	60-1032
RUST, Christoph	55	Wernerode/Han	55-1238
Sophia 51, Sophia 14, Dorothea 7			
RUST, Francis	34	Nesselroeden	57-0422
Sophia 33, Sophia 6, John 3, Hermine 11m			
RUST, Friedr.	17	Huetthagen	60-0334
RUST, Joh.C.	45	US.	59-0951
Helene 39, Sophie 12, Marie 10, Helene 4			
Catharina 2			
RUST, Margar.	20	Altershausen	59-0535
RUST, Wilhelm	32	New Orleans	59-0048
Caroline 26, Frank 8, Louise 6m			
RUSTE, Heinrich	19	Osterholz	61-0682
RUSZE, Heinrich	19	Osterholz	61-0682
RUTCH, Joh. Georg	26	Lobenfeld	59-0372
RUTENHUSEN, Wlmne.	15	Bremen	62-0401
Johanna 7			
RUTER, Heinrich	28	Giershagen	56-0951
Ferdinand 16			
RUTER, Louis	30	Petershagen	57-1122
Ida 6, Louise 10			
RUTERS, Heinr.	59	Coesfeld	59-1036
Stina 18, Hedwig 17, Jos. 14			
RUTMANN, Albertine	26	Ettenheim	62-0712
RUTROEDE, Heinrich	16	Oberbrake	58-0925
RUTTINGER, Carl	26	Wachenheim	62-0306
RUTTMANN, Joh.	29	Lauersbach/Bd	60-0622
RUWE, Joh.	42	Louisville	59-1036
Wilhelm 31			
RUX, Carl	44	Wischnewki/Po	56-1260
Wilhelmine 40, Louise 17, August 13			
Carl 7, Johann 3			
RYBA, Johann	35	Tabor/Boehmen	62-0608
Anna 32, Marie 8, Johann 4, Joseph 10m			
RYTER, Christian	20	Wetzlar	57-0704
SAAL, Joh.	39	Brooklyn	56-1216
Edw.H. 37			
SAALFELD, J.(m)	38	Hannover	62-0836
SAALFRANK, Joh.G.	24	Kurhessen	56-1044
SAAM, Helena	27	Mattenbach	60-0398
SAAM, Sybilla	30	Niederlindach	56-1117
SAAZ, Fr.	40	Huxoll	57-1148
SABEUSCH, August	24	Polen	57-1122
SACHLEBEN, Georg	35	Schoeningen	55-0628
SACHS, Chr. Fr.	37	New York	62-0730
Catharine 37, Peter 5, Kanny (m) 9m			
SACHS, Frz.	21	Hannover	62-0836
SACHS, Helene	56	Breslau	56-0589
Friederike 15			
SACHS, Johann	20	Wolferode	56-1117
SACHSE, Eckert	14	Singlis	62-0836
SACHSE, Friedr.Wm.	24	Sondershausen	56-0411
SACHTLER, Christof	35	Werndorf	57-0654
Charlotte 45, Ferdinand 17, Louise 16			
Charles 13, Friedrich 9, Caroline 4			
Franz 11m			
SACK, Christiana	21	Giessen	61-0779
SACK, Fr. (m)	29	Holzhausen	56-1117
SACK, Johann	34	Mukendorf	57-1280
SACOWITZ, Johann	36	Zempelburg	56-1260
Caroline 33, Johann 9m, Augusta 9			

NAME	AGE	RESIDENCE	YR-LIST
SADDER, John	64	Illinois	59-0384
SADLO, Mathias	23	Minetz	56-0411
SADTLER, Benjamin	34	Easton	58-0925
SADTLER, Philipp B	88	Baltimore	58-0925
SAEGER, Georg	31	Langenberg	57-1067
Elisabeth 32, Michael 13, Georg 8			
Johann 5, Michael 9m			
SAEGER, S.C.(m)	27	Prussia	57-0555
Louise 22, Augusta 1			
SAENGER, Christian	26	Hesse-Darmst.	60-0371
Elisabeth 26, Eva 2			
SAENGER, Elise	25	Roth	60-0533
Elise 6m			
SAENGER, Herm.	26	Sirakus	56-0527
SAENGER, Johanna	17	Danzig	62-0758
SAERKE, Ernst	19	Blomberg	59-0613
SAEUMENICHT, Fr'dr	20	Bremen	57-0961
SAGEBIEL, W.(m)	43	Hannover	57-0606
SAGEHORN, Heinr.	34	Vichershude	59-1036
SAGEHORN, Hermann	42	Wuldorff	55-0634
SAHLBERG, Tettjen	32	Vilmar	59-1036
SAHLFELD, Julius	18	Hannover	59-0048
SAHR, Margaretha	24	Faile	59-0372
SAILER, Marie	52	Wirthen	59-0990
(f) 28, (m) 3, (baby) by			
SAIVALL, Martin	24	Posen	58-0399
Ernestine 18			
SALES, Franz P.	48	Wien	61-0107
SALGE, Carl	24	Windheim	58-0545
SALGE, Friedrich	55	Windheim	57-0924
SALINGER, Jos.	38	Tropplawitz	57-0654
SALINGER, Philip	23	Wiensdorf/Pr.	60-0429
Henriette 17			
SALLER, Heinrich	40	Illinois	60-0429
Engel M. Dor 36, Engel M. Dor 16			
Joh. Heinr. 11m			
SALM, Rosina	18	Bavaria	57-0847
SALOMO, Ch.	68	Strebeck	55-1082
Louise 24			
SALOMON, Isidor	18	Berlin	59-1017
SALOMON, Johann	32	Emskirchen	62-0306
Barbara 23, Anna 4, Margareta 9m			
Dorothea 59, Joh.W. 27, Catharina 31			
Eduard 6m			
SALOMON, Minna	16	Berlin	59-1017
Helena 14, Emma 11			
SALZBRUNNER, Gottf	37	Ziegelheim	61-0482
SALZER, Johannes	66	Wetzlar	60-0521
SALZHORN, Friedr.	17	Wengesdorf	57-1122
SALZKORN, Christ.	39	Gross Furra	56-1011
Ernestine 37, Hermann 14, Bertha 9			
SALZMANN, Anna	24	Volkerode	56-0847
SALZMANN, Franz	65	Muenzburg	57-1026
SALZMANN, Georg	15	Kerstenhausen	62-0712
Christine 52			
SAMBS, Peter	22	Sulzbach	55-0932
SAMIN, Conrad	46	Gollbach	57-1113
SAMMET, Paul	18	Salzbach	60-0334
SAMOISKA, M.	40	Krakau	59-0477
SAMS, Leopold	26	Ischel	55-0932
SAMSEN, H.	38	Sande	62-1042
SAMSON, Hannchen	20	Rhade	57-1026
SAMSON, Julius	39	Germany	62-0166
SAMTER, Mich.	25	Grossdorf	57-0654
SAMUEL, Janette	21	Lobsens	59-0613
SAMUEL, Julia	26	Shoellisen/Bo	56-0819
Minna 24, Rosa 16			
SAMUEL, Pauline	18	Stettin	56-0723
SANDEMANN, Aug.	26	Skedtz	60-0998
SANDER, Adelheid	28	Mittes Bueren	56-1260
SANDER, Adolph	19	Lumfoerde	60-0785
Emma 21			
SANDER, Albert H.	19	Stuttgart	60-1053
SANDER, Augusta	53	Kaudewitz	56-0951
Marg. 14			
SANDER, Bertha	26	Krotoschin/P	55-1238
Louise 24			
SANDER, Carl H.	24	Posen	56-1044
SANDER, Ch.Hch.	25	Dephorn	57-0847
Maria 21			
SANDER, Christian	35	Oldendorf/Han	55-1238
Carolina 31, Christian 5, Louise 44			
Charlotte 59			
SANDER, Franz	37	Altwalmod	56-1260
SANDER, Franz	50	Bremen	62-0879
SANDER, Friedr.Lud	45	Sulzenbruck	55-0812
Ernestine 51, Heinrich 19, Amalia 16			
Gustav 14, Friedrich 10			
SANDER, Friedrike	14	Wagenfeld	57-0776
SANDER, Gottlieb	42	Kaudewitz	56-0951
SANDER, Heinrich	15	Oberndorf/Han	55-0628
SANDER, Herm.	23	Menzen	62-1042
SANDER, Louis	23	Oberzell	59-0477
SANDER, Louise	25	Jertjen	56-0629
SANDER, Michael	32	Ostheim	56-0951
SANDER, Sophie	18	Rohren	59-0412
SANDER, William	34	Obernkirchen	57-0654
Augusta 34, Louisa 11, Amalia 9, Gust. 7			
Adolphus 5, Charles 19, Augusta 4			
Minna 3, Mary 3m			
SANDERMANN, Conrad	22	Felsen	59-0477
SANDERMANN, Friedr	29	Lauterbach	57-1192
Elisabeth 21			
SANDERMANN, Hch.Cl	17	Reischendorf	57-1148
SANDERS, Armand	22	Aurich	57-0422
SANDERS, Diedrich	58	Grambke	59-0613
Catharine 56			
SANDERSFELD, B.	48	Berne	62-0467
Anna 47, Mathilda 21, Anna 14			
Fr.August 20, Claus G. 16, Johann D. 9			
Bernhard 8, Johann Chr. 3			
SANDHOLZER, Gebh.	49	Newton	60-1196
SANDKUHLE, Margar.	22	Herbergen/Han	60-0622
SANDROCK, Christ.	54	Altendorf	57-1407
Catharina 19, Lora (died) 5			
Heinr.(died) 10			
SANDROCK, Heinrich	22	Vacha	57-1113
SANN, Joh.	40	Wetterfeld	61-0669
SANNING, Sophie	24	Westercappeln	62-0836
SANNWALD, Marie	25	Nagold	61-0897
SANTERS, Josephus	30	Texas	60-0785
SANTROOW, v. (f)	20	New York	62-0938
SAPP, Johann	28	Lahr	57-1026
SARG, Joseph	30	Braeunlingen	61-0779
Robert 12			
SARN, Magdalene	26	Obergimpern	60-0052
SARON, G.	34	Paris	62-1042
M.(m)			
SARRANTE, B.(m)	29	France	61-0482
SARSFELDT, Bernh.	21	Braunfels	57-1148
SARSTADT, Carl	30	Magdeburg	59-0384
SARSTEDT, Adolph	21	Newton Cor.MA	55-1238
SASS, Ernst	25	Prussia	57-0555
SASSE, Johann	21	Werseke	62-0730
Friedrich 9			
SASSIEN, Carl Hch.	24	Hillau	56-0550
SASTRUP, Peter	17	Stade	61-0682
SATERLING, Marie	22	Bollerschaft	57-1122
SATRAND, Joseph	34	Ziniwes	56-0629
Anna 50, Mar. 27, Anton 4, Franz 2			
Joseph 6m, Joseph 17			
SATTES, Jacob	13	Philadelphia	56-1216
Cathar. 7, Kunigunde 34			
SATTLER, Jac.Peter	53	Greifenstein	61-0930
Peter 27, Philippine 57, Magdalena 19			
Carl 8			
SATTLER, Jos.	25	Daglesgruen	60-0521
SAUER, Agnes	19	Laufach	60-1053
SAUER, Anna	21	Obernzenn	58-0576
SAUER, Anna Elisb.	19	Lohme	57-0754
SAUER, August	26	Sablath	60-0533
SAUER, Barbara	19	Ladenburg/Bad	60-0622
SAUER, Catharine	15	Baiern	57-0606
SAUER, Dor.	59	Wurzburg	60-0785
Sus. 60			
SAUER, Elise		Luestringen	62-1042

NAME	AGE	RESIDENCE	YR-LIST
SAUER, Ernst	39	Constadt	55-0812
Christine 34, Natalia 8, Ernst 6			
Rudolf 11w			
SAUER, Fried.Wilh.	26	Alzey	59-0214
Magd. 27, Anna E. 9m			
SAUER, Joh.	27	Herbstadt	61-0669
SAUER, Johannes	16	Prussia	61-0682
SAUER, Marg.	22	Eyershausen	61-0669
SAUER, Marie	22	Ekerode	57-1416
SAUER, Martin	27	Petzingen	60-1141
SAUER, Wenzel	32	Nebylan	61-0779
Maria 26, Wenzel by, Martin 6			
Adalbert 13			
SAUER, Wilhelm	20	Pessendorf	57-1026
SAUERBERG, Wilhmne	45	Meiningen	56-0723
Barbara 33			
SAUERLAND, Ludwig	34	Niederlisting	57-1280
Marie 54			
SAUERMANN, (m)	25	Baiern	59-0535
SAUERMANN, Thomas	22	Baiern	58-0399
SAUGER, Christina	50	Seburg	57-0422
SAUKE, Ernst	19	Blomberg	59-0613
SAUKOP, Wenzel	40	Schisty	57-1026
Josephine 33, Franziska 9, Joseph 7			
Maria 6			
SAUL, Justus	19	Melle	56-0279
SAUST, Anna	27	Magdeburg	59-0477
Therese 2			
SAUTEN, v. (f)	55	Bremen	61-0897
SAUTER, Agnes	48	Hechingen	57-1192
Sophia 26, Theresia 17			
SAUTER, Babette	25	Neuhof	56-0632
SAUTMANN, Friedr.	18	Aldorf	59-0412
SAUTMANN, Ludwig	15	Ruessen	59-0412
SAUTTER, Eduard	27	Oberstaedt	60-0411
Paul 20, Adelheid 22			
SAVERNIER, Philipp	22	Bamberg	57-1416
SAWALL, Martin	24	Posen	58-0399
Ernestine			
SCALA, Matthias	24	Strizorin	61-0779
Anna 22, Joseph by, Catharina 10			
SCHAAB, Christian	30	Schkoe	57-1280
Carl 25			
SCHAAF, Eva	59	Seeheim	62-0401
Carl 28			
SCHAAF, Georg	34	Engelrode	61-0669
Cath. 9, Joh. 7, Andr. 4			
SCHAAF, John	15	Clembach	60-1141
SCHAAF, John G.	25	New York	62-0166
SCHAAL, Eva	45	Ruesselsheim	60-0622
SCHABACKER, Johann	24	Weissenborn	57-0961
SCHABEN, Hermann	36	USA.	56-0550
SCHABERT, Agnes	17	Haepelburg	59-0951
SCHABIN, Heinrich	17	Koelln	56-0819
SCHACH, Anna Barb.	17	Kohlhammer	55-1082
SCHACH, Gottlieb	50	Leonberg	56-1260
Barbara 50, Heinrich 9, Friederike 6			
SCHACHT, Friedr.	34	Philadelphia	57-1407
SCHACHT, Johannes	20	Curhessen	58-0399
SCHACHTSCHNABEL, J	17	Petersrode	57-0422
SCHACK, Christian	37	Celle	56-1011
SCHACK, Louisa	35	Clausthal	56-1011
SCHACK, Robert	25	Lippene	56-0819
SCHACKE, Adolph	43	Hesse-Cassel	62-0712
Therese 33, Sylvester 17, Wilhelm 10			
Joseph 8, Maria 9m, Sylvester 60			
Theodor 17			
SCHAD, August	19	Schwarza	57-0847
SCHAD, Augusta	27	Herbstein	62-0232
SCHAD, Johann	28	Bueckenau	61-0520
SCHAD, Ludwig	18	Schwarza	60-0411
Catharina 19			
SCHAD, Sibylle	23	Walsdorf/Bav.	61-0770
SCHAD, Wilhelm	17	Steinbach	62-0879
SCHADE, Anna Barb.	17	Kohlhammer	55-1082
SCHADE, August	15	Bramoge	59-1017
Johanne 17			
SCHADE, CH.	44	Essen	59-0613
SCHADE, Cath.	24	Herzfeld	55-0932
SCHADE, Elise	20	Gomberg	58-0545
SCHADE, Gertr.	19	Weinberg	55-1082
SCHADE, Gotth.	38	Soehland	60-0334
SCHADE, Wilhelm	34	Weiderothe/KH	60-0429
Christine 35, Jacob 10, Elisabeth 7			
Catharina 4, Peter 11m			
SCHADEWEL, Rosine	32	Gruenau	57-1148
SCHADT, Maria	23	Rupertsburg	57-0924
SCHADT, Wilhelm	27	Ella/Nass.	60-0371
Maria 28, Georg 2, Joseph 1			
SCHAECKEL, Wwe.		Lemvoerde	59-1017
Caroline 19			
SCHAEDEL, A. Marie	21	Grossenhausen	56-1117
SCHAEDEL, Aug.	21	Hildburghsn.	57-0961
SCHAEDEL, Fritz	37	Meiningen	62-0758
SCHAEFE, (m)	28	New York	62-1169
SCHAEFER, Adam	57	Oberlauringen	57-0422
Dorothy 49, Eva 21, Catharina 19			
Lorenz 8			
SCHAEFER, An Marie	32	Curhessen	55-0634
SCHAEFER, Aug.	30	New York	59-1036
SCHAEFER, August	23	Ritterode	55-1082
SCHAEFER, August	29	New York	61-0716
SCHAEFER, Carl	20	Osterode	62-1112
SCHAEFER, Carl Chr	35	Ohio	62-1169
Wilh. 20			
SCHAEFER, Caroline	21	Alsfeld	59-0412
SCHAEFER, Caspar	22	Friedewalde/H	55-0628
SCHAEFER, Caspar	22	Hessen	60-0371
SCHAEFER, Caspar	37	Dankmarshsn.	61-0779
SCHAEFER, Casper	22	Rademuehle	60-1032
SCHAEFER, Cathrina	20	Biesendorf	58-0604
SCHAEFER, Cathrina	19	Adorf/Darm.	62-0342
SCHAEFER, Christ.	27	Vahrenholz	56-1260
SCHAEFER, Chrstine	18	Petersdorf	56-0819
SCHAEFER, Conrad	27	Netzhausen	55-1082
Louise 24			
SCHAEFER, Conrad	24	Kirchlotheim	57-0847
SCHAEFER, Elisa	30	Voccawind	56-1011
Eva 26			
SCHAEFER, Elisab.	56	Richelsdorf	61-0520
Maria Elisab 18			
SCHAEFER, Elisab.	48	Niederweiler	59-1036
SCHAEFER, Fr'drika	38	Niederlosnitz	55-0538
SCHAEFER, Fr.	17	Hainchen	59-0990
W. 15			
SCHAEFER, Freidr.	40	Magdeburg	60-0398
Wilhelmine 42, Henriette 17, Wilhelmine 7			
SCHAEFER, Friedr.H	35	Obernkirchen	55-0812
SCHAEFER, Fritz	40	Baltimore	60-0785
SCHAEFER, Georg	39	Obersuhl	55-0413
Louise 24			
SCHAEFER, Georg	26	Hannover	56-0951
SCHAEFER, Georg	15	Grossenmoor	56-1117
SCHAEFER, Georg	54	Breitenbrunn	57-0961
SCHAEFER, Gottlieb	24	Petersdorff	55-0845
Anna 18, Caroline 20, Heinrich by			
SCHAEFER, Gottlieb	45	Schlesien	56-1044
SCHAEFER, H.C.(m)	39	New York	62-0401
SCHAEFER, Heinr.	19	Aithe	59-0412
SCHAEFER, Jac.	15	Hitzerode	61-0669
SCHAEFER, Jacob	20	Vollmarshsn.	57-0924
SCHAEFER, Jacob	42	Schmie	62-0879
Louise 32, Heinrich 1			
SCHAEFER, Jo.Eleon	56	Petersdorf	56-0819
SCHAEFER, Johann	17	Borkenheim	60-0533
SCHAEFER, Johann	23	Wahnfeld	59-0214
SCHAEFER, Johann	16	Langenstein	59-0951
SCHAEFER, Johannes	28	Weissenhasel	55-1238
SCHAEFER, Johannes	48	Wolf	56-0629
Catharina 34, Catharina 8, Heinrich 9m			
SCHAEFER, Johannes	16	Brunhautshsn.	61-0482
SCHAEFER, John	35	Nolhfelden	60-0411
Caroline 37, Johannes 7, Ernst 5, Mary 2			
Jacob 2m			
SCHAEFER, Leopold	15	Marienborn/He	55-1238
SCHAEFER, Ludwig	26	Giessen/Hess.	60-0371

NAME	AGE	RESIDENCE	YR-LIST
SCHAEFER, Ludwig	22	Ehrbach	57-0447
SCHAEFER, M.(f)	20	Bischhausen	57-0555
A.(f) 16			
SCHAEFER, Magdalen	24	Merfeld/Hess.	61-0770
SCHAEFER, Marie	19	Husede	56-0951
SCHAEFER, Martin	19	Cassel	59-0477
SCHAEFER, Mich.	35	New York	61-0482
SCHAEFER, Peter	22	Obertiefenbch	57-0422
SCHAEFER, Philip	27	Sachsen	58-0399
SCHAEFER, Philipp	30	Leuchtern	57-0606
SCHAEFER, Reinhard	20	Eitershagen	56-0723
SCHAEFER, Sabine	28	Schluechtern	61-0482
SCHAEFER, Sophie	18	Heidelberg	56-0847
SCHAEFER, Susanne	25	Duerkheim	62-0730
SCHAEFER, Wilhelm	21	Gondershausen	60-0371
Catharina 20			
SCHAEFERMEIER, Hch	40	Prussia	58-0885
SCHAEFERS, Wilhelm	18	Kirchhaslach	59-0412
SCHAEFFER, Carl	28	Minden	61-0930
SCHAEFFER, Georg	61	Bischofsheim	59-0477
SCHAEFFER, Heinr.	22	Steinberg	55-0413
SCHAEFFER, Heinr.	16	Wenjes	55-0413
SCHAEFFER, Heinr.	25	Niederwetter	57-0447
SCHAEFFER, Heinr.	24	Niederwetter	57-0447
SCHAEFFER, Heinr.	28	Bremen	57-1026
Veronica 25			
SCHAEFFER, Helene	25	Hauswalz	57-0447
SCHAEFFER, Joh.	36	Wilshausen	56-0629
Cathar. 32, Philipp 7, Georg 4			
SCHAEFFER, Johann	57	Landau	58-0576
SCHAEFFER, Marg.	25	Pluten	57-0447
SCHAEFFER, Marie	19	Landau	58-0576
SCHAEFFER, Wilhmne	23	Carzig	57-0776
SCHAEFFLER, Gottfr	29	Gr. Doberitz	61-0930
SCHAEFFLER, Wilh.	18	US.	59-0951
SCHAEFLER, Carl	31	Herrieden/Bav	55-0628
SCHAENFLE, Carl	19	Hebsack	57-1067
SCHAERER, Eva	21	Gr.Lautenbach	56-1117
SCHAERHAGEN, Herm.	29	Kl.Mimmelage	59-0613
SCHAETZKE, August	19	Breslau	58-0881
SCHAETZLE, Simon	33	Bavaria	61-0482
Magdalena 28, (boy) 1			
SCHAEUMANN, Rose	21	Neubridsteler	60-0521
Moritz 14, Therese 23			
SCHAFER, C.(m)	25	Kozmin	62-0306
SCHAFER, Friedrich	17	Untergeis	56-0819
SCHAFER, Joh.Georg	30	Flensburg	57-1416
Martha Elis. 28, Heinrich 6			
SCHAFER, John	29	Niederwetz	57-0654
Catharine 28			
SCHAFER, Valentin	20	Fraurombach	57-0654
SCHAFER, Wilhelm	17	Rehe	59-0477
Louis 16, August 13, Wilhelmine 41			
SCHAFERCORD, Luise	26	Wimbeck	61-0478
SCHAFFER, Dorethe	38	Carlshaven	57-1122
SCHAFFER, Marg.	27	Niederstoll	57-0654
SCHAFFNER, Anna	28	Schellenwald	57-0847
SCHAFFNER, Joseph	26	Freiburg	57-0606
SCHAFFNER, Samuel	30	Schinznach	60-1053
SCHAFHAENTLE, Jos.	26	Baden	57-0606
SCHAFMACKER, Carol	23	Kirchheim	56-0411
Christine 20			
SCHAFRANECK, Carl	32	Leipzig	59-0047
Henriette 35, Anna 10, Marie 8, Antonie 6			
Eugen 1			
SCHAKE, Susanne	22	Viermuenden/H	55-0628
SCHALBURG, Jesse	21	Bremen	60-0334
SCHALEK, Matthias	42	Boehmen	62-0001
Marie 32, Thomas 9, Marie 7			
SCHALK, G.(m)	30	Porterville	62-0836
SCHALK, John	60	New York	62-0938
SCHALK, Marg.	27	Rodenburg	55-0932
SCHALLER, August	22	Bremen	62-0608
SCHALLER, Christ.	24	Waldeck	58-0399
SCHALLER, Jos.	33	Waltershof	61-0482
Eleonore 32, Johann 12, (boy) 9m			
SCHAMBACH, Johann	22	Rudelswalde	62-0467
SCHAMBERGER, G.A.	24	Knetzgau	59-0477

NAME	AGE	RESIDENCE	YR-LIST
SCHAMEL, Anna	18	Mistelgau	61-0520
SCHAMHART, Moritz	34	Farrenholz	50-1017
SCHANK, Friedrich	19	Philippsthal	60-1032
SCHANKE, Johanna	20	Lugnitz	57-1026
SCHANNBERG, Mary	15	Kurhessen	56-0512
SCHANSEN, Cathrina	22	Misselwarden	55-1048
SCHANTZ, Albert	50	Messingen	60-1161
Agnes 39, Baltus 16, Anna 14, Joh.J. 10			
Margr. 2, Martin 6m			
SCHANZ, C.(m)	28	Nehren	62-0730
SCHANZ, Mich.	48	Wittingen	62-0111
SCHANZE, Catharine	13	Wabern	62-0712
SCHANZE, Herm.	26	Grossenenglis	56-0723
Elizabeth 33			
SCHAPER, Christine	35	US.	59-0951
SCHAPER, Helena	23	Pyrmont	55-1048
Carl 16			
SCHAPER, Max	25	Berlin	61-0167
SCHAPER, Sophie	21	Braunschweig	57-0606
SCHAPPE, Aug.	30	Gruenenplan	62-1112
SCHAPPER, Christne	56	Stemmen	59-0535
Johanna 13			
SCHARF, (m)		Wenzigerode	57-1280
SCHARF, J.A.	23	Hemmstadt	62-0836
Caroline 14			
SCHARFE, Dorette	22	Wuerzburg	60-1032
SCHARFENBERG, Wm.	42	Darmstadt	60-1161
Marie 33, Carl 9, Joseph 20			
SCHARK, G.A.(m)	61	US.	57-0578
SCHARNKE, Ernst	44	Magdeburg	57-0654
SCHARPF, Rosine	27	Rosswelden/Wt	62-0608
Anna Marie 22, Margaretha 18			
SCHASTNY, Joh.Wenz	54	Zulistau/Bav.	57-0924
Maria 45, Eva 12, Catharina 7			
SCHATTE, Heinrich	18	Holtensen	57-0924
SCHATZ, Friedrich	24	Schoeneberg	57-0704
SCHATZ, Joseph	29	Bavaria	60-1161
SCHAUB, Ed.Jul.	51	Witzenhausen	57-0961
SCHAUB, Ludw.	32	Blasbach	60-0521
Jeanette 29, Louise 3, Joh. 6m			
SCHAUDER, Fr'z Ant	42	Hartheim	57-1026
SCHAUDI, Marg.Bar.	21	Ipsheim/Bav.	60-0429
SCHAUER, Gottlieb	28	Preussen	58-0399
Auguste 28, Marie 7			
SCHAUER, Louise	59	Preussen	58-0399
SCHAUER, Wilhelm	35	Wischnewki/Po	56-1260
Caroline 28, August 6, Wilhelm 6			
Johann 3, Augusta 3m			
SCHAUERMANN, Cath.	20	Oberlais	62-0712
SCHAULADE, Emil	54	Danzig	60-0998
Anna 26			
SCHAUM, Carl	23	Gleiberg	57-0924
Elisa 24			
SCHAUM, Cath.	24	Kirchgrun	60-1161
SCHAUM, Matthias	17	Nitzingen/Wrt	62-0608
SCHAUMACHER, Gust.	44	Duesseldorf	59-1036
SCHAUMBUR, Conrad	26	Heimershausen	57-0776
SCHAUMBURG, Anna M	22	Neukirchen	58-0563
SCHAUMBURG, Martin	32	Halse	57-0422
William 24			
SCHAUMBURGER, Jac.	30	Eppenrat	59-0477
SCHAUMER, Joseph	29	Bayern	56-1011
SCHAUSEIL, M.Luise	21	Eisenach	62-0467
SCHAUSS, Adelheid	29	Rothenburg	57-1280
SCHAUSS, H.(m)	17	Wagenfeld	59-0951
SCHEBE, Rosine	69	Cassel	56-0951
Sophia 28			
SCHECK, Monica	19	Neustaedten	60-0334
SCHEDEL, Barbara	28	Neureit	59-0372
SCHEEL, A.(m)	15	Heelsen	62-0836
SCHEELE, Diedr.Hch	22	Verden	57-0606
SCHEELE, Heinrich	26	Borssel	59-0535
SCHEELE, Johann	21	Hastedt	62-0879
Hermann 18			
SCHEEREN, Heinr.	16	Tuttlingen	60-0334
SCHEERER, Alvers	39	Langenselbald	61-0047
SCHEERER, Cathrina	39	Steinberg	62-0712
Marie 14			

NAME	AGE	RESIDENCE	YR-LIST
SCHEERER, Elisab.	18	Kurhessen	56-1044
SCHEERER, Gottfr.	22	Koenigsberg	60-0521
SCHEFER, Margarete	34	Kirtorf	55-0630
SCHEFFER, Emil	42	Louisville	62-1112
Wilhelm 15, Emil 9, August 7			
SCHEFFER, H.G.(m)	40	Boston	61-0897
SCHEFFER, Heinrich	23	Foekelsberg	59-0214
SCHEFFER, Joseph	18	Muenster	60-0785
SCHEFFLER, Christ.	26	Friedingen	60-0411
SCHEFFLER, Wlhmne.	22	Wetzlar	57-0704
SCHEHE, Lorenz	39	Trauensen	56-0512
Mary 40, Barbara 12, Jacob 7			
SCHEHLE, H.H.	21	Bothel	56-0411
SCHEIB, Dorothea	32	Bechtheim/Nas	61-0770
SCHEIBELE, Cathar.	27	Wuerttemberg	60-0371
SCHEIBELHUT, Jos.	30	Grossenlueder	56-0589
SCHEIBENBERGEN, J.	38	Dayton	62-0836
SCHEIBER, Carl	29	Unterwieden	57-1067
SCHEIBLE, Johann	17	Ehnasensweilr	62-0342
SCHEICH, Christian	19	Noertingen	59-0214
SCHEID, Catharina	25	Lindelbach/Bd	57-0847
SCHEID, Peter	59	Pennsylvania	61-1132
SCHEIDE, Wilh'mine	18	Hedem	57-0447
SCHEIDEMANTEL, H.	40	Schluechtern	61-0482
SCHEIDLER, Wilhelm	18	Schonau	60-0398
SCHEIDT, Adele	16	Kunsdorf	59-0951
SCHEIFE, Carl	32	Meseritz	56-0819
Carol.Wilh. 23, Ernest Louis 8m			
SCHEIFEL, Math.	23	Uberkingen	55-0413
SCHEIFERS, Wm.	58	Bredenborn	59-1036
SCHEIFLER, Charlot	24	Bleicherode	62-0938
SCHEIN, Louise	16	Kiselbach	58-0545
SCHEIT, Georg	40	Bergsteten/Bv	55-0628
Magdalena 50, Johann 17, Georg 15			
Joseph 14, Adam 12, Michael 10			
SCHEITER, Anna M.	18	Eisenach	61-0107
SCHEITLIN, Emil	15	St.Gallen	59-0951
SCHEKELS, Sophie	23	Cammer	57-1067
SCHELDT, Chr.	50	Driesdorf	55-0413
Louise 24			
SCHELE, Gustav	14	Bielefeld	57-0447
SCHELER, Johann	53	Schmelz	60-1161
Marg. 61, Barbara 16			
SCHELF, Johann	30	Quillenreit	57-1280
SCHELHASE, George	22	Reichensachse	56-1011
SCHELLENBERG, Carl	27	Baiern	57-0606
SCHELLENSCHMIDT, G	33	Saldin	59-0477
Marie 32, Carl Ed. 2, Fried.W. 6m			
SCHELLENTZAGER, L.	19	Eisenach	62-0938
SCHELLER, J.Caspar	34	Sulzdorf	58-0881
SCHELLHASS, E.F.	36	Utica	59-0214
A.E. 25, Herm. 1			
SCHELLHORN, Gottf.	33	Gerra	59-0535
SCHELLPFEFFER, Fr.	25	SChoenwalde	57-0422
SCHELLWIRTH, C.H.	16	Stuttgart	57-1067
Albert 14			
SCHELTEN, B.(m)	23	Leer	62-0730
SCHELZKY, Christ.	33	Nachterstadt	56-0951
SCHEMMEL, Carl	23	Grunau	57-0924
SCHEMPP, Barbara	18	Waldstetten	60-1196
SCHEMRICH, Sophie	17	Schwarza	60-0411
SCHENCK, Catharina	20	Adorf/Darm.	62-0342
SCHENDEL, Martin	25	Wischel	56-0632
SCHENK, Eva	62	Koenigwart	59-0951
SCHENK, Joseph	34	Kocherbach/He	60-0622
SCHENK, Magd.M.	33	Perouse	62-0879
SCHENK, Michael	17	Neubronn	56-0413
SCHENK, Simon	23	Landsberg	59-0613
SCHENKE, (m)	18	Neunkirchen	59-1036
Anna 60			
SCHENKEL, Carl	58	Dortmund	59-0990
(f) 51, (f) 19			
SCHENKER, Johanna	35	Mehla	61-0520
Carl Frdr. 10, Wilhelmine 4			
Christian Fr 2			
SCHENT, Heinr.	25	Kirchzandern	60-0785
SCHEPAL, Maria	44	Schondorf	57-1026
SCHEPER, Maria	18	Loxstedt	61-0520
SCHEPP, Anton	34	Pohlgoens	55-0413
SCHERB, Jacob	18	Ruederich	60-0411
SCHERB, Martin	28	Moellerich	57-0754
SCHERER, Cathar.	24	Silverbach	56-0512
SCHERER, Catharine	39	Steinberg	62-0712
Marie 14			
SCHERER, Heinrich	19	Wolter	62-0467
SCHERER, Paul	32	Tennessee	61-0482
SCHERER, Peter	47	Ellweiler	59-0384
Cath. 32, Cath. 14, Caroline 9, Jacob 7			
Peter 5, Louise 3			
SCHERF, Louise	20	Germany	61-0482
SCHERLING, Friedr.	40	Laucha/Pr.	55-0538
Wilhelmine 40, Antonia 9, Anna 8			
Rudolph 6, Friedrich 3			
SCHERLING, Heinr.	28	Alsfeld	62-0730
SCHERLOCH, Felix	21	Kleinpardorf	60-0521
SCHERMEISTER, Emly	19	Genstaedt/Pr.	61-0770
SCHERTEL, Friedr.	24	Bayreuth	59-0535
SCHERTEL, Marie	23	Bueckeburg	59-0535
SCHERTLEIN, Philip	25	Wertheim	62-0712
SCHERZEN, Wm.	40	Savannah	60-0785
SCHESCKE, Gertrude	19	Nentershausen	55-1238
SCHESINGER, Israel	21	Curhessen	55-0634
SCHETTER, Johann	26	Altheim	56-0819
SCHEU, Phe.(f)	22	Egershausen	61-0669
SCHEUCH, Josephine	22	Lassa	57-0447
SCHEUCH, M.	20	Marburg	57-1150
SCHEUER, Jette	19	Herdenberg	60-0521
SCHEUERMANN, Crlne	48	Rudingen	61-0482
SCHEUERMANN, P,	16	Speierdorf	62-0993
SCHEURING, Joseph	25	Neubrunn	61-0770
Margaretha 27, Anna 1			
SCHEUVE, Hans Hch.	15	Kreuz Riehe	60-0429
SCHEWE, Joh.Phil.	36	Beckedorf	56-0589
Caecilie 19			
SCHEY, Aron	24	Gorznow	57-1148
SCHIAU, Sophie	21	Bielhorst	59-0214
SCHICK, Franz	23	Sinzheim	59-0384
SCHICK, Georg Frdr	18	Wuestenroth	60-1053
Joh. David 16			
SCHICK, Johanna	24	Enzweihingen	56-0512
SCHICK, M.Ida	33	Laupheim	59-0477
SCHICK, Maria	22	Wuertemberg	57-0606
SCHICK, Richard	15	Amoneburg	56-0413
Caroline 15			
SCHICK, Wilhelm	21	Amoeneburg/KH	62-0342
SCHICKART, M.(m)	22	Roehrach	61-0897
SCHIEBECK, Joseph	30	Boric	57-1026
Anna 27, Catharina 5, Elisabeth 2			
Carl 6m			
SCHIEFELBEIN, Ferd	27	Swinemuende	60-0521
SCHIEFELBEIN, Lou.	27	Graudenz	57-0776
SCHIEFERDECKER, M.	30	Heinstadt	60-1141
SCHIEHMANN, S.	22	Krofbach	59-0477
SCHIELER, Elisab.	22	Kurhessen	56-1044
SCHIELHABE, Wenzel	58	Lippmitz/Boeh	62-0712
Veronica 57			
SCHIEMANN, Henr'tt	20	Gumbinnen	58-0881
Minna 6			
SCHIER, H.(m)	24	Prussia	57-0555
SCHIER, Heinrich	54	Clausthal	59-0990
SCHIERHEITZ, Bernh	48	Damme	59-0951
Marg. 37			
SCHIERHOLZ, Aug'ta	24	Detmold	61-0482
Marie 22			
SCHIERR, Lisette	17	Fuerth	60-1032
SCHIESS, Louis	20	Duesseldorf	56-1011
SCHIESSEL, Andrew	40	Barrau	57-0961
Catharina 27, Mary 62			
SCHIETE, M.(m)	17	Eisenach	62-0730
SCHIFF, Gustavus	23	Heidenoldendf	57-0422
SCHIFF, Jette	19	Langenschweiz	61-0770
SCHIFF, Rieke	23	Ortenberg	60-0533
SCHIFFMANN, Julius	18	Kerkow	56-0819
SCHIFFMANN, L.(m)	29	Missouri	61-0897
SCHIFFNER, Charlot	26	Jueterbogk/Pr	60-0371
Louise 1			

NAME	AGE	RESIDENCE	YR-LIST
SCHIFFNER, Ernst	34	Zickau	56-0951
Franziska 44			
SCHIKA, Jacob	43	Wubitz	55-0845
Rosalie 41, Marie 10, Barbara 17			
Franziska 11, Ignatz 9, Josepha 3			
SCHILBE, Elisab.	19	Lischeid	55-0630
SCHILD, Elisabeth	16	Coelbe	62-0879
SCHILD, Peter	15	Muenster	59-0384
SCHILD, Simon	17	Hesdorf	58-0815
SCHILDEROTH, Cath.	26	Langenheim/He	62-0608
George 2, Elise 8m			
SCHILDKNECHT, Joh.	27	Neustadt	59-0535
SCHILDRACHTER, Dor	34	Homburg	60-0785
SCHILL, Johann	57	Curhessen	58-0399
A.M. 48, Johannes 17, Johannes 12			
SCHILLER, Franz'ka	29	Muhlhausen/Bd	61-0770
SCHILLER, Michael	69	Wuerzburg	60-1032
SCHILLHANEK, Matth	49	Nebylan	61-0779
Catharina 49, Joseph 20, Barbara 19			
Matthias 15, Franz 7, Philomena 3			
SCHILLING, Alex'dr	16	Weissungen/Sx	62-0342
SCHILLING, August	29	Parkersburg	59-0477
SCHILLING, Carl	22	Lerbeck	57-1067
SCHILLING, Elisa	28	Scharmbeck	57-1067
Hinrich 6			
SCHILLING, Elise	24	Curhessen	55-0634
SCHILLING, F.	15	Scharmbecksto	56-0512
SCHILLING, Frd'ke.	28	Schneid	55-0845
SCHILLING, Friedr.	17	--ck/Meckl.St	55-0538
SCHILLING, Geo.	19	Hannover	62-0730
SCHILLING, Gustav	25	Seesen/Hann.	55-1238
SCHILLING, Heinr.	49	Neidlingen	59-0214
Magdalena 16			
SCHILLING, Jac.	29	Grottstedt	61-0669
Eva 23, Chrste(died) 3m			
SCHILLING, Johann	50	Suhl	55-0630
Helena 44, Conrad 14, Louise 10, Hedwig 6			
Robert 4			
SCHILLING, Johann	43	Friedrichsdrf	56-0819
Christine 46, Ferdinand 23, Ernestine 17			
Augusta 12, Wilhelm 9, Robert 6			
SCHILLING, Louise	20	Minden	60-0785
SCHILLING, W.	34	Katzenellenbo	59-0990
SCHILLING, Wlh'mne	30	Heinchen	60-1032
Marie 48, Johanna 4			
SCHILLINGER, Anna	25	Ueberlingen	61-0779
SCHILLINGER, G.(m)	52	Baltimore	62-0836
SCHILTINGER, J.(m)	23	Germany	62-0467
SCHIMCK, Adelbert	59	Boehmen	62-0730
Anna 47, Johann 20, Anna 23			
SCHIMKE, Ernst	23	Altforst	56-0847
SCHIMMEL, G.(m)	22	Neisse	62-0730
SCHIMMEL, Mar.Elis	26	Pohl Goens	59-0384
SCHIMPFKY, Ernst H	21	Frankenberg	61-0770
SCHINBROD, Friedr.	36	Germany	57-0578
SCHINCH, A.	58	Glauchau	57-0850
Wilhelmine 38, Ida 19, Louis 15			
Gustav 14, Marie 11			
SCHINDER, Ernst	28	St.Louis	62-1042
SCHINDHEIM, Friedr	29	Meiningen	55-0634
Sabine 44, Margaretha 17, Catharine 14			
Carl 11, Marie 10, August 9			
SCHINDLER, Wenzel	30	Boehmen	62-1112
Veronica 35, Wenzel 6, Rosalie 5, Josef 3			
Franz 6m			
SCHINELZ, Babette	21	Gunzenhausen	55-0812
SCHINEWEG, L.(m)	16	Essenerberge	62-0730
SCHINGERRE, Cathar	23	Wuertemberg	59-0412
SCHINKE, G.	55	Woltersdorf	59-0990
(wife) 39, (f) 22, (f) 16			
SCHINKE, Gabriel	25	Woltersdorf	59-0990
SCHINKE, Wentzel	52	Bablerwitz/Bo	59-0047
Gabriel 18			
SCHINKE, Wenzel	32	Woltersdorf	59-0990
(f) 34, (m) 8, (m) 2			
SCHINKER, Carl	31	Preussen	55-0634
Dorothea 28, Carl 1			
SCHINNABECK, M.	26	Wuertemberg	59-0214

NAME	AGE	RESIDENCE	YR-LIST
SCHIRER, Anton	52	Deutsch Boehm	57-1280
Therese 50, Franz 28, Wenzel 26			
Andreas 20, Theresia 7			
SCHIRER, Eduard	18	Boehmen	61-0478
SCHIRER, Joseph	77	Deutsch Boehm	57-1280
Franziska 17			
SCHIRMER, C.(m)	27	Martinlamitz	61-0804
SCHIRMER, Charlott	32	New York	61-1132
Emma 6, Carl 4, Willy 3, Fritz 11m			
SCHIRMER, Louise	26	Bremen	58-0885
SCHIRMER, Ludwig	27	Kosciellius	56-0629
SCHIRMER, Marie	16	Bremen	59-0951
SCHIRNECK, Gustav	37	Meiningen	55-0634
SCHITTENHELM, Jac.	16	Duerrenmettst	60-0334
SCHITTHELM, Elisab	13	Gerolsheim	60-1032
SCHITTLER, Heinr.	29	Niederurnen	62-0401
Marg.Reb. 25, Heinr. 2, Cath. 3			
Anna Nath. 1m			
SCHLABERG, Regina	39	San Francisco	59-0613
Carl 9, Franz 8, Therese 18			
SCHLABITZ, Emil	20	Varl	62-0879
SCHLABOHM, Otto	20	Althemsberg	56-1117
SCHLAECHTER, Franz	30	Paderborn	56-0411
SCHLAEGER, Gustav	17	Frankenhausen	60-0533
SCHLAEGER, Wilhelm	28	New York	59-0048
SCHLAFFER, Anna M.	22	Moosbach	58-0563
SCHLAGENHASS, Fr.	34	Oberreuth	57-0754
Margaretha 42			
SCHLANZ, Georg	28	Kieslegg	59-1036
SCHLAPPMANN, Herm.	22	Westercappeln	55-0932
SCHLATTER, Maria	17	Rothenburg	60-0398
SCHLECHT, Magdalen	18	Breitenstein	60-0521
SCHLECHTWEG, Casp.	21	Sachsen	58-0399
SCHLECK, Carl	28	Bockenheim	62-1112
SCHLEELEIN, S.V.	30	Reusch	61-0804
SCHLEGEL, Carl	51	Mellzen/Sax.	55-0538
Christiane 28, Pauline 8, Caroline 1			
Heinrich 6m			
SCHLEGEL, Jacob	52	Buchau	60-0521
Josephta 50			
SCHLEGEL, Joh.Geo.	58	Remstedt	57-0422
Christiane 52, Charles 26			
SCHLEGEL, Xaver	19	Buchau	60-0334
SCHLEGER, Sophie	17	Minden	57-1280
SCHLEHMANN, August	14	Stolzenau	55-0634
SCHLEI, Heinr.	40	Quincy	62-1112
Francisca 42, Augusta 14			
SCHLEICH, Jacob	24	Haitz	59-0372
SCHLEICH, Louise	24	Haitz	59-0372
SCHLEICH, Wilhelm	24	Kertorf	60-0334
Jacob 22			
SCHLEICHER, Friedr	27	Kreisdorf	60-1032
SCHLEICHER, J.F.	40	Coburg	61-0897
Friedricke 30, (dau.) 6m			
SCHLEIDELER, Minna	21	Borgholz	60-0334
SCHLEIDEN, Dr.Hon.	40	Washington	62-1169
SCHLEIER, Nicolaus	24	Walkenfeld/Bv	55-1238
Louise 24			
SCHLEIERMACHER, A.	19	Waldeck	58-0399
SCHLEIF, Christian	66	West Prussia	58-0399
Euphrosine 46, Louise 29, Euphrosine 18			
Justine 15, Mina 13, Carl 10, Caroline 6			
Emilie 11m			
SCHLEITER, H.B.	28	Rosenthal	58-0885
SCHLEMILCH, Joh.	34	Oberimbach/Bv	60-0429
SCHLEMM, Carl	26	Sooden	56-1117
Am. 15			
SCHLEMMERMANN, Ann	16	Duering/Han.	56-0819
SCHLENCK, Carl	18	Berwicke	57-1416
SCHLENCK, Elisab.	30	Louisville	58-0885
Anna 11m			
SCHLENK, B.(m)	22	Rida	59-0951
SCHLENKER, (f)	40	Berlin	59-0951
SCHLENSKER, Heinr.	35	Hille	57-1280
Elisabeth 21			
SCHLENSKER, Louise	23	Hille	56-0411
SCHLENZKER, Carl	56	Preuss.Minden	58-0399
Elise 57			

NAME	AGE	RESIDENCE	YR-LIST
SCHLERMANN, Carl	62	Gerswalde	62-0879
SCHLESELMILCH, Joh	15	Zeil	56-0951
SCHLESINGER, Benno	16	Geleshausen	58-0885
SCHLESINGER, Esth.	19	Kirchenberg	50-1017
SCHLESINGER, Lady	36	New York	59-0613
SCHLEUDERMANN, Cat	17	Oldendorf	60-0521
SCHLEUME, Hanchen	22	Lobsens	59-0613
SCHLEURING, Kunig.	22	Masbach	61-0482
SCHLICHTING, Mar.W	24	Ansbach	58-0925
SCHLIEPHACKE, Sim.	26	Magdeburg	60-0521
SCHLIERENBECK, F.	15	Lehrte	59-1036
SCHLIERF, Franz	25	Katzenmuehlen	57-1026
SCHLIESSER, Ulrich		Wain	59-0477
SCHLINGE, Wilhelm	33	Skantersheim	59-0047
SCHLINGHAIDE, Crlt	52	Minden	59-1036
SCHLINGHEYDE, Aug.	20	Bielefeld/Pr.	55-0628
SCHLIRZ, Christine	40	Schlotten	57-0924
Elisa 10			
SCHLITT, Anna Cath	20	Schwabenroth	62-0342
SCHLITTER, Caspar	20	Niederurnen	62-0232
SCHLITTSHOEFER, Ad	30	Breslau/Pr.	55-0628
SCHLITZ, Heinrich	18	Trieberg	61-0682
Franz 15			
SCHLOBACH, Friedr.	33	Oberweimar	56-0589
Caroline 19			
SCHLOBOHM, Heinr.	23	Dorum	57-1067
SCHLOCKEBIER, Hel.	23	Niederzwehren	62-0712
SCHLOEDER, Anna	29	Kilburg	62-0111
SCHLOEMER, Meta	30	Bremen	55-0544
SCHLOEMER, Therese	24	Bleiwaesche	56-0723
Heinrich 3			
SCHLOENDORF, L.A.H	30	New York	59-1036
Mary 4			
SCHLOENDORF, Louis	34	New York	58-0604
SCHLOENINGER, Pepi	24	Laupheim	60-0521
Sophie 18			
SCHLOESLER, Conrad	40	New York	62-0232
SCHLOETTER, Franz	32	Brenken	57-1280
Marie 27			
SCHLOSS, Jacob	27	Weitersbach	62-0608
Margaretha 24			
SCHLOSS, Max	16	Kueps	59-0214
SCHLOSSER, Gertrud	43	Brella	57-1122
Jacob 16, Nicolaus 13, Marie 9, Peter 10			
SCHLOSSER, Heinr.	16	Homberg/Hesse	57-0924
SCHLOSSER, Joh.Pet	22	Hubingen/Nas.	56-0819
SCHLOSSHAGEN, Ant.	48	Volkmarsen/He	62-0608
Catharine 46, Louise 14, Emilie 10			
Marie 9, Gertrud 6			
SCHLOSSHAHN, Elise	52	Carlshafen	60-1053
Georg P. 21, Joh. Carl 17			
SCHLOSSHAHN, Heinr	25	Carlshafen	60-1053
SCHLOTT, Christine	13	Seckbach/Curh	60-0622
Anna Maria 8			
SCHLOTTERBACH, Wm.	23	Mittelstadt	62-0730
Barbara 19			
SCHLOTTERBECK, Mrt	20	Betzingen	62-0712
SCHLOTTHEIM, v.E.	44	Minden	62-1042
Johanna 27, Hans 1			
SCHLOTTMANN, Plne.	20	Altona	59-0372
SCHLUCK, Johann	20	Klosterboeren	56-0512
SCHLUCKEBIER, Joh.	56	Diesen	56-0411
Anna 57, Gertrud 17, Jacob 15			
SCHLUE, Friedrich	30	Hildesheim	57-0447
Franzisca 27			
SCHLUEK, Georg	24	Hirschfeld	57-0704
SCHLUERB, Th.	23	Schotten	62-1169
SCHLUETER, Carl	18	Wildemann	56-1117
SCHLUETER, Christ.	20	Schoettlingen	55-0628
SCHLUETER, Dietr.	23	Schwey	56-1117
SCHLUETER, Friedr.	34	Grasdorf	56-1011
SCHLUETER, Friedr.	18	Minden	58-0399
SCHLUETER, Heinr.	35	Hille	56-0411
Caroline 35, Friedrich 17, Louise 17			
Heinrich 6			
SCHLUETER, Heinr.	18	Oese	56-1117
SCHLUETER, Heinr.	18	Minden	58-0399
SCHLUETER, Wilh.	17	Oese	59-0535

NAME	AGE	RESIDENCE	YR-LIST
SCHLUMANN, Ernst	26	Kalkhorst	57-0654
Ferd. 31, Caroline 27			
SCHLUMANN, Joseph	24	Manster	60-0521
Theresia 19			
SCHLUMP, Johanna	28	Neubamberg	60-0334
SCHLUMP, Michael	24	Schelldorf	57-1113
Marie 23, Johann 1			
SCHLUMPBERGER, O.	24	Hausen	61-0482
SCHLUND, Elise	24	Rogen	56-0512
SCHLUND, Heinr.	27	Wertheim	60-0334
SCHLUPP, Fr.	28	Duesseldorf	62-0401
(wife) 24			
SCHLUT, Mathias	19	Schwarzennach	57-1122
SCHLUTER, Henry	21	Thedinghausen	57-0654
SCHLUTTER, Carl A.	15	Luebbecke	60-1117
SCHMAENK, Julius	32	Warendorf	58-0885
SCHMAKOWSKY, Wilh.	50	Strahlen	57-1113
SCHMAL, Johannes	56	Danzhausen	56-0723
SCHMAL, Jos.	33	Hammelberg	62-0401
SCHMALFUSS, August	32	Baltimore	62-0879
SCHMALFUSS, Lydia	13	Zenterode	59-1036
SCHMALT, Diedrich	17	Bramsche	59-0477
SCHMALT, Joseph	23	Cloppenburg	58-0306
SCHMALZ, Philipp	47	Neugrub	58-0576
Barbara 44, Conrad 12			
SCHMANDER, Jac.Got	22	Leonberg	62-1169
SCHMANT, (m)	25	Warburg	58-0306
SCHMARR, Peter	17	Grebenau	62-0401
SCHMAUE, Joseph	37	Goentzkau	55-0932
SCHMAUTZ, Jean	31	Nantes	60-0334
Jeane 60, Marie 22, Daniel 19			
SCHMECK, Robert	38	Lignitz	56-0847
SCHMED, Richard	31	Lewin	60-0785
SCHMEDEKE, Wm.	18	Drakenburg	60-1141
SCHMEER, H.(m)	32	Meiningen	60-1161
Anna 27			
SCHMEIKAL, Magdal.	19	Littitz	58-0881
SCHMEIKERT, Friedr	15	Hall	60-0334
SCHMEISSER, F.W.	28	Frankenhausen	59-0535
Henriette 29			
SCHMEISSER, Georg	30	Hambach	57-0447
SCHMEISSER, Maria	19	Zaisenhausen	59-0412
SCHMEISSING, M.	16	Sand	57-0555
SCHMELZ, Georg	36	Illertissen	60-0521
SCHMELZ, Heinrich	14	Elbersdorf	56-0819
SCHMELZ, Hyronimus	22	Triemen	56-1117
SCHMELZKOPF, Ed.	30	Braunschweig	62-0712
SCHMELZPFENNIG, J.	21	Freden	59-0951
SCHMERSAHE, K.G.C.	35	New York	61-0897
Heinr. 9			
SCHMERZ, Henry	30	Baltimore	57-0961
SCHMID, Friedrich	33	Peine	56-0819
SCHMID, Lisette	52	Minden	57-0924
SCHMIDER, Franz	51	Eigen	57-1026
Josepha 53, Rosalia 21, Franz 19			
Gregory 15, Josepha 14, Anna Maria 12			
Anna 10, Johann 3			
SCHMIDT, (f)	28	Bremen	62-1169
SCHMIDT, A.M.	24	Laupheim	59-0477
SCHMIDT, Adam	36	Assel	56-0413
Christine E. 43			
SCHMIDT, Adelheid	15	Sonneberg	57-1192
SCHMIDT, Adolph	19	Schwambeck	59-0214
SCHMIDT, Agnes	18	Neuhaus	59-0477
SCHMIDT, Amalie	50	Nieherin	60-1196
SCHMIDT, Anagela	25	Bernsburg/Hes	60-0371
SCHMIDT, Andreas	19	Schwoelln	58-0881
SCHMIDT, Anna	18	Seligenstadt	60-0521
SCHMIDT, Anna	26	Graebenau	57-1113
Heinrich 24			
SCHMIDT, Anna	39	New York	62-1042
Frd. 9			
SCHMIDT, Antonia	18	Orte	57-1280
SCHMIDT, August	21	Cassel	56-1260
SCHMIDT, August	26	Arnswalde	57-1067
SCHMIDT, August	24	Hauwe	58-0881
SCHMIDT, August	30	Nauheim	61-0482
Philippine 20, Christ 3			

NAME	AGE	RESIDENCE	YR-LIST
SCHMIDT, August	22	Plauen/Saxony	57-0924
SCHMIDT, Balthasar	27	Salzungen	61-0478
SCHMIDT, Barbara	19	Fischbach	60-0521
SCHMIDT, C.	30	Hischeidt	62-0993
SCHMIDT, C.(m)	31	Schleitz	57-0555
SCHMIDT, C.C.	20	Elpersheim	59-0990
SCHMIDT, C.G.	24	Schuetzingen	59-1036
SCHMIDT, C.H.	42	Siegen	56-0512
Anna 42, Emil 21, Clara 15, Louisa 14			
Joseph 7			
SCHMIDT, Carl	25	Eisenach/Sax	60-0052
SCHMIDT, Carl	23	Ense	57-0754
SCHMIDT, Carl	36	Koslowo	61-0779
Henriette 35, Marie 12, Caroline 2			
SCHMIDT, Carl	16	Schildesche	61-0897
SCHMIDT, Carl	18	Dielingen	57-1407
SCHMIDT, Carl	30	Greste	61-0716
Louise 58, Adolph 24, August 21			
SCHMIDT, Cath.	26	Weidenthal	59-0384
SCHMIDT, Cath.	17	Unterstoppel	59-0990
SCHMIDT, Cath.	63	Oberngais	62-1169
SCHMIDT, Cathar.	31	Oberhone	61-0478
SCHMIDT, Catharina	22	Homberg	60-0622
SCHMIDT, Catharina	32	Burghausen	59-0477
Johanna 36			
SCHMIDT, Catharine	26	Stadtsteinach	60-1032
Barbara 6, Catharine 3, (baby) 4m			
SCHMIDT, Catharine	22	Holzhausen	61-0478
SCHMIDT, Catharine	18	Ostheim	59-0412
SCHMIDT, Catharine	45	Berlin	59-0951
Catharine 10, Emma 8			
SCHMIDT, Cathrina	24	Hamberg	57-1067
SCHMIDT, Ch.	14	Neunkirchen	59-1036
Elise 15			
SCHMIDT, Charlotte	21	Stuttgart	59-0477
SCHMIDT, Chr.	15	Gr. Buseck	62-0467
SCHMIDT, Chr.	23	Merlen	62-1112
SCHMIDT, Christ.	24	Buschahn	55-0845
SCHMIDT, Christina	35	Darmstadt	57-0606
Susanne 7, Heinrich 6, Wilhelm 4			
SCHMIDT, Christine	25	Honolulu	60-0785
SCHMIDT, Christoph	25	Kieselbach	57-1026
Cath.Elisab. 24, Johannes 4, Maria 6m			
SCHMIDT, Conrad	25	Hersfeld/Curh	60-0622
SCHMIDT, Conrad	26	New York	59-0214
(wife) 23			
SCHMIDT, Cornelius	24	Herbstein/Hes	62-0342
SCHMIDT, Diedrich	30	Memingen	57-0509
SCHMIDT, Dora	17	Halsdorf	58-0399
Elisabeth 14			
SCHMIDT, Dorothea	30	Goppingen	60-0334
Johanna 4			
SCHMIDT, Eduard	16	Zittau	58-0881
SCHMIDT, Edw.	27	Luetjenburg	57-0422
John 27			
SCHMIDT, Edward	22	Neustadt	60-0411
SCHMIDT, Elisab.	36	Elm	62-1042
SCHMIDT, Elisabeth	26	Sprenglingen	60-0371
SCHMIDT, Elisabeth	19	Kl.Kladenbach	60-0371
SCHMIDT, Elisabeth	55	Kerstenhausen	62-0712
Carl 10			
SCHMIDT, Elise	22	Ruettershause	55-0812
SCHMIDT, Emilie	35	New York	62-0730
Charles 8			
SCHMIDT, Ernest	16	Salzgitter	59-1036
SCHMIDT, Ernestine	20	Kemel	56-0723
SCHMIDT, Ernst	21	Neustadt/Sax.	55-0538
SCHMIDT, Ernst	20	Koenigshofen	57-0606
SCHMIDT, Fr.	16	Salzingen	55-0932
SCHMIDT, Fr.(m)	16	Meiches	55-0413
SCHMIDT, Franz	45	Danzig	62-0758
Barbara 24, Anna 4, Franz by, Johann 30			
SCHMIDT, Franz	15	Naumburg	59-0048
SCHMIDT, Fried.	25	Dingelstedt	56-0629
Christine 26, Dorothea 4, Christine 4m			
SCHMIDT, Friedr.Wm	28	Berlin	58-0885
SCHMIDT, Friedrich	16	Saxony	56-0847
SCHMIDT, Friedrich	24	Jecha/Schwrzb	56-0819

NAME	AGE	RESIDENCE	YR-LIST
SCHMIDT, Friedrich	57	Saalfeld	58-0576
SCHMIDT, Friedrich	36	Bilzingsleben	62-0608
Marie 37, Wilhelmine 10, Lina 3, Emma 9m			
Elisabeth 27, Wilhelmine 23, Andreas 24			
SCHMIDT, Friedrich	16	Sachsen	58-0399
SCHMIDT, Friedrich	45	Main	62-0879
Eva Rosa 42			
SCHMIDT, Friedrike	20	Trinkentafen	60-0334
SCHMIDT, Friedrike	25	Muenden	57-0606
SCHMIDT, G.M. (m)	27	Obereckelshm.	61-0804
SCHMIDT, G.W.	40	Bremsnitz	56-0589
Gertrude 21			
SCHMIDT, Genoveva	27	Hamstaedt	59-1036
SCHMIDT, Geo.Otto	25	Poppenlauer	57-0422
SCHMIDT, Georg	19	Schworlitz	60-0785
SCHMIDT, Georg	27	Friedburg	60-0998
SCHMIDT, Georg	35	Zettmannsdorf	61-0478
SCHMIDT, Georg E.	22	Hildburghause	62-0879
SCHMIDT, Georg Wm.	43	Pfersdorf	56-0951
SCHMIDT, George	18	Laimbach	61-0478
SCHMIDT, Gerd H.	41	Bovenden	61-0482
Heinrich 55, Emilie 55			
SCHMIDT, Gerhard	57	Louisville	59-0214
SCHMIDT, Gottfried	55	Prellwitz	56-0819
Caroline 35, August 25, Charlotte 20			
Ernestine 18, Friederike 14, Emilie 10			
SCHMIDT, Gottfried	53	Berlin	59-0613
Ida 27			
SCHMIDT, Gottlieb	20	Schmalkalden	56-1117
H.Gottlieb 10			
SCHMIDT, H.J. (f)	26	Herbstein	55-0413
SCHMIDT, Heinr.	20	Besse	59-0214
SCHMIDT, Heinr.	27	Vilmar	59-1036
SCHMIDT, Heinrich	34	Lembach/Hess.	55-0538
Elisabeth 33, Marie 9, Elisabeth 6			
SCHMIDT, Heinrich	18	Angeroth	56-0951
SCHMIDT, Heinrich	24	Gotha	56-0279
SCHMIDT, Heinrich	22	Nieder Dieten	60-0371
SCHMIDT, Heinrich	16	Nesse	56-1260
SCHMIDT, Heinrich	39	Guetersdorf	57-0704
SCHMIDT, Heinrich	26	Schmirga	58-0576
SCHMIDT, Henry	34	San Francisco	61-0804
SCHMIDT, Herm	22	Pabris	60-0521
SCHMIDT, Herm.	18	Bauerbach	59-0535
SCHMIDT, Hermann	17	Preussen	56-1044
SCHMIDT, Hermann	41	Colberg	62-0758
Wilhelmine 36, Franz 13			
SCHMIDT, Hermann	17	Hannover	58-0399
SCHMIDT, Hinrich	50	Halsdorf	58-0399
Gertrude 28, Elise 6, Dora 3, Conrad 9m			
SCHMIDT, J.	25	Hofstatten	56-0512
SCHMIDT, J.	36	Hessenthal	62-0993
SCHMIDT, J.(m)	28	Wuerzburg	61-0804
SCHMIDT, Jac.	21	Mandort	60-0521
SCHMIDT, Jacob	36	Hochheim/Nass	60-0371
SCHMIDT, Jacob	26	Ekershorn	57-1416
August 9, Friedr. 7			
SCHMIDT, Jacob	40	Rottheim	58-0399
SCHMIDT, Joh.	44	Oettingen	57-1150
Therese 17, Marie 11			
SCHMIDT, Joh. Geo.	28	Wendelstein	58-0563
SCHMIDT, Joh.Carl	17	Bukarast/Bav.	59-0047
SCHMIDT, Joh.Engl.	31	Stinzhausen	58-0604
SCHMIDT, Joh.Fr.	29	Meilheim	61-0482
SCHMIDT, Joh.W.	25	Ditzum	57-0578
Marie 27			
SCHMIDT, Joh.Wilh.	49	Stockhausen	57-0422
Anna 42, Catharina 9, Dorothy 5			
Margaret 3, Margaret 15, Henry 23			
SCHMIDT, Johann	28	Ansbach/Bav.	55-0628
SCHMIDT, Johann	43	Obersain	55-0630
Maria 15, Amalie 30, Margaretha 13			
Catharine 5, August 8, Peter 2			
SCHMIDT, Johann	40	Rurfeld	60-0998
SCHMIDT, Johann	16	Leonberg	56-1260
SCHMIDT, Johann	52	Schoenwald	56-1260
Justine 15, Elisabeth 23			
SCHMIDT, Johann	26	Kirchein	57-0776

NAME	AGE	RESIDENCE	YR-LIST
Catarina 20			
SCHMIDT, Johann	19	Wulsburg	61-0682
SCHMIDT, Johann	38	Wuerzburg/Aus	62-0608
Barbara 38, Anna 8			
SCHMIDT, Johann	22	Mannheim	62-0712
SCHMIDT, Johann	23	Darlar	59-0214
SCHMIDT, Johann	27	Bischoffsthro	59-0214
SCHMIDT, Johann	22	Steinfeld	62-0879
SCHMIDT, Johann B.	25	New Orleans	58-0881
SCHMIDT, Johann W.	36	Beilstein	55-0630
Elisabetha 32, Heinrich 7, Henriette 3			
Friederike 9m			
SCHMIDT, Johannes	24	Wurtemberg	56-0512
SCHMIDT, Johannes	30	Aufenthal	57-1113
SCHMIDT, John	46	New York	59-1036
SCHMIDT, Johs.	22	Rhoden	55-0413
SCHMIDT, Joseph	48	Wuestewalters	57-1407
SCHMIDT, Joseph	24	Deus	57-1407
SCHMIDT, Joseph	18	Neuffen	59-0613
SCHMIDT, Jost	35	Castel	61-0478
Margaretha 23, Johanna 3			
SCHMIDT, Justus	31	Heiligenstadt	60-0398
SCHMIDT, Kort K.	22	Ihrhove	57-0422
SCHMIDT, Kunigude	24	Coburg	57-0654
SCHMIDT, Leo	27	Breitensee	61-0669
SCHMIDT, Leopold	25	Gohau	56-1044
SCHMIDT, Liberata	32	Stadel	60-0334
SCHMIDT, Louis	44	Jehnhausen	59-0477
Louise 42, Eleonore 19, Robert 17			
Wilhelmine 13, Caroline 9, Arnold 8			
Berta 6			
SCHMIDT, Louise	19	Kurhessen	56-1044
SCHMIDT, Louise	41	Bremka	59-0477
SCHMIDT, Ludwig	20	Wuerttemberg	60-0411
Katharine 17			
SCHMIDT, Ludwig	19	Neuenstadt	60-0398
SCHMIDT, M.(m)	50	Boston	60-0521
SCHMIDT, Marg.	62	Marburg	60-0521
SCHMIDT, Marg.	24	Helmstedt	59-0384
SCHMIDT, Margar.	55	Bieber	57-1113
SCHMIDT, Margareta	25	Bieber	57-0924
SCHMIDT, Margareta	25	New York	59-0214
SCHMIDT, Margarete	17	Arginstein	56-0589
SCHMIDT, Maria	20	Gannenheim	55-0845
SCHMIDT, Marie	25	Cassel	56-0951
SCHMIDT, Marie	25	Hessen	56-0847
SCHMIDT, Marie	18	Obergeis	56-0819
Anna Cathar. 20			
SCHMIDT, Marie	39	Magstadt	59-0613
Christine 16			
SCHMIDT, Martin	59	Muennerstadt	58-0881
Margarethe 59			
SCHMIDT, Math.(f)	21	Tedinghausen	60-0521
SCHMIDT, Mich.	29	Unterleinach	61-0669
SCHMIDT, Michael	26	Bavaria	60-0411
SCHMIDT, Oscar	19	Frankfurt a/O	61-0478
SCHMIDT, Ottilia	25	Halle	59-1036
SCHMIDT, Paul	23	Meiningen	62-0758
SCHMIDT, Pauline	25	Strehlen	61-0804
SCHMIDT, Peter	36	Falkenburg	57-0776
SCHMIDT, Peter	39	Louisville	62-0467
SCHMIDT, Ph.(m)	24	Terndorf	62-0467
Louise 16			
SCHMIDT, Philipp	45	Giessen	57-0606
SCHMIDT, Philipp	40	Kirchhausen	57-1407
SCHMIDT, Rosalie	21	Gampertshsn.	61-0682
SCHMIDT, Selma	22	Jena	60-0334
SCHMIDT, Simon	23	Jettingen	57-0654
SCHMIDT, Sophie	26	Grebenau/Hess	62-0608
SCHMIDT, Th.(m)	24	Philipsthal	57-0422
SCHMIDT, Theod.	16	Skanday/Sax.	55-0538
SCHMIDT, Thomas	23	Landsberg	59-0613
SCHMIDT, Veronica	28	Vilkirch	60-0622
SCHMIDT, Veronica	42	Boehmen	62-1042
Anna 14			
SCHMIDT, W.(m)	30	Neuenburg	57-0555
C.(f) 23, Fr.(m) 6m, Emilie 6, C.(m) 4			
A.(m) 20			

NAME	AGE	RESIDENCE	YR-LIST
SCHMIDT, Wilh.	24	Remscheid	62-1169
SCHMIDT, Wilhelm	37	Daber	56-0819
Charlt.Fr'ke 34, Mary Therese 11			
Anna Amanda 9			
SCHMIDT, Wilhelm	51	Niengraben	61-0520
Catharina 50, Christine 17, Christoph 10			
Maria 7			
SCHMIDT, Wilhelm	20	Rothausen	56-1216
SCHMIDT, Wilhelm	20	Eichelsachsen	59-0214
SCHMIDT, Wm.	17	Uchte	62-0467
SCHMIDT, Wm.	21	Leipzig	61-1132
SCHMIDTKING, Ernst	14	Obermehler	57-0924
SCHMIDTMANN, Theod	24	Hedemuenden	62-0608
Dorothea 24			
SCHMIDTMEYER, Aug.	18	Ludershof	57-0422
SCHMIDTMEYER, Xav.	27	Milwaukee	57-0654
SCHMIDTNER, Cath.	15	Erlangen	60-0785
SCHMIDTS, Mathias	28	Ober-Oels/Pr.	55-1238
SCHMIDTS, Peter	21	Illmen/Pruss.	55-1238
SCHMIEDEKAMP, Fr.	31	Kaldorf	57-0606
SCHMIEDEL, Joh.	30	Buchholz	55-0932
Aug. Tekla 7, C. H. M. 2			
SCHMIEDING, Carl	30	Lindorf	59-0384
SCHMIESING, Bernh.	25	Varenholz	58-0306
SCHMIT, Jacob	37	Wallau	57-1122
Marie 54			
SCHMITS, Carl	23	Elberfeld	55-0634
SCHMITT, Andreas	42	Wisconsin	59-0214
SCHMITT, August	62	Baltimore	62-0342
SCHMITT, Casp.	24	Waldgirmis	59-0214
SCHMITT, Josephina	18	Brueckenau	60-0533
SCHMITT, Ursula	26	Unterdurrbach	60-1053
Johannes 9, Valentin 9, Julius 7			
SCHMITTER, (f)	40	Germany	57-0578
SCHMITTER, Ed.	48	Eschwege	62-1042
SCHMITZ, Bernhard	23	Gescher	61-0482
SCHMITZ, Franz	50	Wuellen	56-1117
Joseph 20, Angela 44, H. (f) 12			
Theodor 8			
SCHMITZ, J.William	30	Siegburg	59-0384
SCHMOCK, Johanna	22	Uslar	57-0578
SCHMOEL, F.(m)	22	Bueckeburg	57-0555
SCHMOER, Christ.	26	Pohle	59-0384
SCHMOLE, Margareta	28	Guntzenhausen	56-0819
SCHMOLL, Johanna L	40	Nordheim	62-1112
SCHMOOR, Gustav	26	New York	60-0785
SCHMUDTZE, August	26	Bremen	57-0654
SCHMUGGE, Marie	58	Schloppe	61-0930
SCHMUTZER, Christ.	56	Leimbach	57-1148
Mary 56, Charles 27, William 20			
Theresia 18, Andr. 11			
SCHMUTZLER, Friedr	26	Lippersdorf	56-0589
Dor. 56			
SCHNAB, Mathias	38	Germany	61-0167
Robert 14, Michael 9, Sabine 2, Ch. (f) 1			
Georg 12			
SCHNABEL, Ernst	35	Schoenwalden	57-0754
Joh.Chrstne. 35, Friedr. Wm. 13			
Henriette 11, Augusta 4, Ernestine 2			
SCHNABEL, Mar.Cath	27	Lich	59-0214
Anna 9m, Friedr. 36			
SCHNACKENBERG, Ann	34	Verden	56-0819
SCHNACKENBERG, C.	37	Verden	56-0819
SCHNACKENBERG, Con	16	Zeven	59-0535
SCHNACKENBERG, Joh	19	Nordsohl	57-0422
SCHNACKENBERG, Mrg	26	Fischerhude	57-0606
SCHNACKENBURG, Hch	18	St.Juergens	59-0951
SCHNADE, Marie	24	Prosekel	56-0819
SCHNADIG, Kaufm.	26	Heddernheim	57-1113
SCHNAK, Christian	34	Strelitz	57-0776
Dorothea 34			
SCHNAPP, Catharine	18	Horle	57-0924
SCHNAPP, Margareta	22	Horb/Bav.	60-0429
SCHNARR, Maria	18	Giebenau	60-0521
SCHNARRE, Bertha	22	Minden	59-0384
SCHNASSE, August	52	Lage	55-1048
Florentine 44, Auguste 21, Eleonore 19			
Friedrich 15			

NAME	AGE	RESIDENCE	YR-LIST
SCHNAT, Friedr.	16	Hesslingen/Wt	60-0429
SCHNATZ, Eliza	19	Bottendorf	60-1141
SCINAUDER, Babette	33	New York	62-0836
SCHNAUS, V.	18	Hauswurz	62-0993
SCHNAUT, Carolina	18	Heeslingen/He	55-0628
SCHNECK, Johanna	17	Neustadt	59-0951
SCHNECKENBERGER, M	26	New York	59-0214
SCHNEDECKE, Fig.H.	40	Charleston	60-0429
SCHNEDLAGE, Rudolf	36	Quackenbrueck	60-1032
SCHNEEBERGER, M.B.	23	Wuertemberg	57-0606
SCHNEEGRAS, Daniel	46	New York	62-0758
SCHNEEMANN, Anna	22	Finne	61-1132
SCHNEEWEISS, Heinr	24	Hannover	55-0628
SCHNEGELBERGER, Ma	17	Braunswend	59-0412
SCHNEIBEL, Ephata	21	Neustadt	60-0521
SCHNEIDER, Adam	14	Geroda	60-0533
SCHNEIDER, Adam	23	Somborn	60-0398
SCHNEIDER, Andr.	38	Astheim	62-0401
Heinrich 15			
SCHNEIDER, Anna M.	59	Worms	62-1042
SCHNEIDER, Aug.	26	Erfurt	62-1042
SCHNEIDER, August	33	Petershagen	59-0477
Maria 46			
SCHNEIDER, August	30	Breslau	60-0398
SCHNEIDER, C.(m)	40	San Francisco	62-0836
SCHNEIDER, Carl	30	Grauengruen	55-0812
SCHNEIDER, Carl	20	Cannstadt	61-0167
SCHNEIDER, Carl Wm	30	Wiessenthal	57-1067
SCHNEIDER, Charles	21	Stuttgart	57-1148
SCHNEIDER, Conrad	15	Herstein	60-0334
Agatha 24			
SCHNEIDER, Conrad	31	Lohne	57-0776
SCHNEIDER, D.(m)	37	Herbstein	62-0232
Helene 25			
SCHNEIDER, Daniel	18	Untershausen	62-0712
Margaretha 17			
SCHNEIDER, Doris	30	Memphis	62-1042
SCHNEIDER, Elisab.	17	Langenstein	61-0482
SCHNEIDER, Elisab.	22	Curhessen	58-0399
SCHNEIDER, Emilie	15	Battenhausen	57-0924
SCHNEIDER, Eva	26	Schmachteberg	56-0951
SCHNEIDER, Ewald	14	Boston	57-1192
SCHNEIDER, Felix	38	Lauterbach	56-0723
SCHNEIDER, Fr'dke.	18	Vroch	57-1067
SCHNEIDER, Fr'dke.	39	Muehberg	61-0482
Emma 5			
SCHNEIDER, Fr'zka.	29	New York	62-0111
Theodor 7			
SCHNEIDER, Fr.	20	Wisseck	56-0951
Ludw. 2			
SCHNEIDER, Franz	34	Hohenmelz/Pr.	55-0538
Wilhelmine 34, Reinhold 12, Magnus 11			
Alvine 9, Anna 7, Ernst 2, Selma 1			
SCHNEIDER, Franz	26	Herbstein/Hes	62-0342
SCHNEIDER, Georg	31	Grebenau/Darm	62-0342
David 36, Catharina 30, Johannes 8			
SCHNEIDER, Georg	24	Langenhain	59-1036
Anna 28			
SCHNEIDER, George	39	Chicago	61-1132
SCHNEIDER, Heinr.	54	Oberzwehren	56-0527
Elise 26			
SCHNEIDER, Heinr.	18	Bernsburg/Hes	60-0371
SCHNEIDER, Heinr.	30	Wohra	57-0754
SCHNEIDER, Heinr.	21	Ndr.Schelt/Na	61-0770
SCHNEIDER, Henriet	24	Rhode Island	61-1132
Johanna 22, Ernestine 4			
SCHNEIDER, Herm.	20	Cappelwindeck	60-1196
SCHNEIDER, Herm.	18	Ahlsfeld	61-0478
SCHNEIDER, Hermann	16	Meiningen	62-0758
SCHNEIDER, J.	35	Schwarzenborn	62-0993
SCHNEIDER, J.B.(m)	34	Cincinati	61-1132
SCHNEIDER, J.E.W.	14	Marburg	62-0467
SCHNEIDER, J.H.(m)	20	Marzhausen	61-0897
SCHNEIDER, Jacob	14	Nahbollenbach	61-0930
SCHNEIDER, Jacob	28	Bruchsal	62-0712
SCHNEIDER, Joh.	23	Muenster	62-0401
Anna Mar. 24, (dau.) 1m			
SCHNEIDER, Joh.	28	Lancaster	62-0401

NAME	AGE	RESIDENCE	YR-LIST
SCHNEIDER, Johann	21	Fauerbach	56-0723
SCHNEIDER, Johann	24	Speckswinkel	57-0754
SCHNEIDER, Johann	30	Wiera	57-0021
SCHNEIDER, John	39	New York	61-0716
SCHNEIDER, Joseph	25	Grefenhausen	62-0111
SCHNEIDER, Josepha	34	Kilzberg	61-0478
SCHNEIDER, Leopold	22	Bohemia	56-0847
SCHNEIDER, Louis	25	Wilikurmess	55-0845
SCHNEIDER, Louise	42	New York	62-0608
Franz 15, Louise 9			
SCHNEIDER, Louise	18	Hilgershausen	60-0398
Anna 16			
SCHNEIDER, Ludwig	25	Goettingen	57-0436
SCHNEIDER, M.	27	Sonnenberg	62-0993
SCHNEIDER, Mar.	30	Baiern	57-0606
SCHNEIDER, Marg.	23	Altrip	59-0990
SCHNEIDER, Marg.	26	Calen	59-0951
SCHNEIDER, Margar.	25	Aschfeld	56-0819
Emilie 21			
SCHNEIDER, Margart	50	Maehren	61-0478
Christian 19			
SCHNEIDER, Maria	23	Sachs.-Altenb	59-0372
SCHNEIDER, Marie	30	Heidelberg	60-0521
Catharine 28			
SCHNEIDER, Mathias	33	Bavaria	62-0712
Anna Maria 25			
SCHNEIDER, Nicol.A	21	Winkel	59-0477
SCHNEIDER, Pauline	19	Reutlingen	57-1192
SCHNEIDER, Peter	17	Minden	59-1036
Christina 21			
SCHNEIDER, Philipp	18	Hessen	58-0399
SCHNEIDER, Siebert	22	Wohra	57-0754
SCHNEIDER, Sophie	15	Alsfeld	57-1067
SCHNEIDER, Valent.	28	Schenklengsfd	61-0520
SCHNEIDER, Vincent	62	Puftzinn	58-0815
Theresia 57, Maria 19			
SCHNEIDER, W.	18	Berghausen	59-0990
SCHNEIDER, Wilhelm	27	Eicha	60-0334
SCHNEIDER, Wilhmne	26	Giessen	61-0897
SCHNEIDER, Wm.	27	Bovenden	61-0482
SCHNEIDERHANZE, H.	28	Sachsen	60-0398
SCHNEIDEWIND, Crln	28	Besingfeld	61-0478
SCHNEIDEWIND, Mich	23	Kreisdorf/Bav	60-0371
SCHNEIER, Caspar	36	Baiern	58-0399
Johann 9, Eva 39, Barbara 7			
SCHNEITERLOHNER, R	25	France	62-0166
Emma 1			
SCHNELL, Cath.	19	Almerode	55-0413
SCHNELL, Charlotte	28	Darmstadt	60-0411
SCHNELL, Edward	15	Lehe	61-0716
SCHNELLE, A. Marg.	20	Coburg	61-0478
SCHNELLE, Theodor	17	Goslar	57-1067
SCHNETE, B.(m)	22	Coesfeld	62-0836
SCHNETE, Joh.	26	Barwinkel	59-1036
SCHNEWALD, F.W.(m)	29	St.Louis	60-0785
SCHNEWLIN, H.	28	Stein	56-0589
SCHNIELZ, Babette	21	Gunzenhausen	55-0812
SCHNING, G.	22	Eckertshausen	56-1216
SCHNITTER, Barb.	26	Gerterode	61-0669
SCHNITTGER, Anne	54	Buenden	56-1011
Anne 18			
SCHNITTGER, Heinr.	28	Vlotho	56-0723
SCHNITTGER, Heinr.	25	Wittlade	57-1122
SCHNITZLER, Gottf.	34	Kaufbeuren	60-0411
SCHNOPP, Ad.	17	Leipzig	60-1196
SCHNUDJE, Hermann	18	Brueggen	59-0613
SCHNUECKE, Gustav	22	Westrup	59-0613
Carl 32			
SCHNUES, Barbara	62	Knetzkau	59-0047
Margaretha 32, Barbara 27, Franziska 23			
Margaretha 6, Walpurga 3			
SCHNUGEN, Frederic	56	Hildburghause	57-0654
SCHNUNBERG, Henry	20	Osnabrueck	57-0654
Catharine 25			
SCHNUPP, John Chr.	17	Eisenach	57-0509
SCHNURR, Heinrich	48	Graebenau	57-1113
Maria 40, Heinrich 12, Margar. 9, Maria 7			
Nicolaus 4, Hartmann 2			

NAME	AGE	RESIDENCE	YR-LIST
SCHNUTENHAUS, R.	26	Chursangwitz	62-0938
SCHOBER, Sophie	20	Bremervoerde	61-0804
SCHOBERT, Anna	24	Weissenstadt	56-0411
SCHOBERT, Margaret	17	Schoenlind	56-0951
SCHOCK, Caroline	17	Steinbach/Wrt	60-0622
SCHOCK, Johann	30	Grabenau	56-1260
Marcianne 28, Wilhelm 6, Johann 4			
Caroline 9m			
SCHOEBEL, Johann	20	Seifersdorf	56-0951
Josephine 29			
SCHOEDDE, August	34	Hersfeld/Hess	62-0608
SCHOEDER, Carolina	28	Bismark	60-1161
SCHOEFFEL, Margret	23	Schmelz	60-1161
SCHOELERMANN, Just	19	Dorum	60-0785
SCHOELGENS, Schol.	35	Aachen	62-1042
SCHOELZEL, Johann	49	-----tsch/Pr.	55-0538
SCHOEMANN, Mary	25	Neuerburg	60-1141
SCHOEMBERG, V.Wolf	23	Moritzburg	60-0411
SCHOEN, Hermann	20	Wieblingen/Bd	60-0622
SCHOEN, Johann	38	Roemerstadt/A	61-0770
SCHOEN, Leopold	24	Leiwitz/Pr.	55-0538
Paulina 26, Oscar 3, Marie 9m			
SCHOENAST, Emanuel	36	Bieberwied	60-0533
SCHOENBACH, Herman	17	Eisenberg	61-0520
SCHOENBERG, Selig	16	Podgosch	56-1044
SCHOENBOAN, Mart.	30	Neermoor	55-0413
Louise 24			
SCHOENE, Ana Marta	24	Grossensee	57-1067
George 9m			
SCHOENE, Johannes	30	Buttlau	57-1067
SCHOENEBERG, Chr.	36	Schoeneberg	57-0704
Carlne.Luise 36, Friedr.Wm. 9, Augusta 7			
Emilie 4, Carl Ludwig 6m			
SCHOENEMANN, (m)	26	Vechta	58-0306
SCHOENENBERG, (f)	30	New York	62-0836
SCHOENER, Joseph	30	New York	62-1042
Louise 6			
SCHOENEWALD, Franz	18	Coeln	55-0628
SCHOENEWALD, Gust.	24	Frankenberg	57-0924
SCHOENEWALD, Heinr	20	Frankenberg	57-0924
Justus 17			
SCHOENEWOLF, Georg	26	Wollstaedt	57-0776
Anna 25, Maria 23			
SCHOENFELD, Gustav	29	Bremerhaven	61-0047
SCHOENFELD, J.Chr.	28	Milwaukee	61-0779
SCHOENFELD, Jacob	16	Obernkirchen	60-0785
SCHOENFELDER, J.A.	39	Koenigshain	62-0836
SCHOENFELDT, Simon	35	Landorff	59-0951
Bettchen 22, Jettchen 9, Hannchen 8			
Meyer 7, Herrmann 6, Emil 4, Sophie 6m			
SCHOENHARDT, Peter	26	New York	61-0167
Nanette 19			
SCHOENIAN, Heinr.	29	Braunschweig	59-0372
Maria 31, Heinrich 5, Friedrich 2			
SCHOENING, Barbara	17	Verweisoch	60-1032
SCHOENING, Henriet	27	Hofgeismar	60-1032
SCHOENING, J.F.(m)	15	Hordinghausen	56-0951
SCHOENING, J.Gottl	28	Lintorf	56-0951
SCHOENNING, Fritz	26	Brake	60-1141
Louise 26			
SCHOENTAG, Martin	18	Bodenhausen	57-1407
SCHOENTHALER, Wm.	28	Auerbach	59-0412
SCHOEPERT, Joseph	23	Kurz	56-0723
SCHOEPFER, Joseph	16	New York	58-0885
SCHOEPFLE, Sophia	17	New York	60-1053
SCHOEPPACH, Johann	45	Voilsdorf	61-0478
SCHOEPPACH, M.Barb	42	Voilsdorf	61-0478
Eleonore 20, Amalie 14, Carl 9, Emma 11m			
SCHOEPS, Barbara	27	Weidnitz	62-0836
SCHOER, Caspar	24	Haselbrunn	62-0467
SCHOESEL, J.A.(m)	15	Heinersreuth	61-1132
Cath. 28, Joh. 13, Elis. 17, Andr. 9			
Joseph 6, Christine 4, J.A.(m) 2			
Cath. 1m			
SCHOESTER, Jac.	40	Alsace	62-0467
SCHOETTELMEIER, H.	34	Richmond	57-1150
SCHOEWERTING, Aug.	18	Osnabrueck	59-0477
SCHOFF, Kappel	19	Schluechtern	60-0521

NAME	AGE	RESIDENCE	YR-LIST
SCHOKEMUELLER, Fr.	22	Ob.Baurschaft	57-0021
SCHOLAND, Johann	18	Bleiwaesche	56-0723
SCHOLL, George	26	Rottendorf	60-1141
Martha 18			
SCHOLL, Isabelle	20	Fuchsberg	57-0754
SCHOLL, Johann	23	Zollenberg	57-0436
SCHOLL, Julius	25	Carlsruhe	59-0048
SCHOLL, Laura	20	Hanau	62-0730
SCHOLLE, Anton	20	Brakel	60-0521
Marie 23			
SCHOLLER, Louis	20	Berlin	50-1017
SCHOLZ, Aug.	44	Detroit	59-0951
SCHOLZ, Gottfried	46	Raussen	56-0629
Johanne 36, Rudolph 7			
SCHOLZ, Julius	37	Savannah	58-0925
SCHOLZE, Ernst	35	Rosenthal	57-0654
SCHOMAKERS, Helene	21	Darme	62-0993
SCHOMBART, Edward	32	Cincinnati	59-1017
SCHOMBER, Philipp	68	Kesselsbach	62-0712
SCHOMBURG, C.	19	Bremen	62-1042
SCHOMBURG, P.(m)	27	Oldendorf	57-0555
SCHON, Anton	23	Wuerzburg	59-0951
SCHONEBURG, G.Ad.	26	New York	59-0384
SCHONEWALD, Felix	18	Prussia	57-0847
SCHONFELD, F. Wm.	23	Bremen	55-0634
SCHONFELD, Fr.(m)	24	Bueckeburg	57-0654
SCHONHEER, Fred'ke	19	Carlsruhe	56-0847
SCHOO, Joseph	24	Schuettorf	58-0563
SCHOON, Christiane	58	Treinsche	58-0604
SCHOON, Emily Paul	28	Zeutz	60-1117
SCHOOTE, Becka	21	Hagen	60-0785
SCHOPPE, Heinrich	26	Einbeck	55-0630
SCHORCH, Fr.	35	Gutmannshsn.	55-0932
SCHORMANN, Elise	22	Ulrichstein	60-0334
SCHORN, Joh.	24	obermerzbach	59-0477
SCHORN, Joseph	40	New York	60-0521
SCHORNBECK, Heinr.	31	Huelsede	55-0845
Sophie 55, Friedrich 21			
SCHORR, Elisabeth	25	Neuses	59-0047
SCHORR, Friedr.	22	Altershausen	58-0815
Joh.Conrad 23			
SCHORTT, Wm.	26	Bremerhaven	62-0401
SCHOSTALL, Joseph	32	Saar	57-1150
SCHOTER, Maria	25	Hofheim	59-0477
SCHOTT, Anna Marg.	18	Spanik/Bav.	55-0628
SCHOTT, Carl	29	Sommerhausen	58-0563
Barbara 28, Kunigunde 2m			
SCHOTT, Johann	28	Schletzerod	56-1117
SCHOTT, Marg.	48	Schletzerod	56-1117
Catharina 21			
SCHOTT, Margaretha	23	Sparreck	60-0521
SCHOTTE, Christian	37	Muehlhausen	57-1192
Dor. 29, Johanna 3			
SCHOTTERHEIM, H.F.	27	Elbing/Pr.	55-0544
Minna 29, Clara 6, Hugo 11m			
SCHOTTLAENDER, Ad.	29	Copenhagen	57-1148
SCHOVERLING, W.(m)	25	New York	60-0785
SCHRADER, Doris	42	Braunschweig	59-1036
SCHRADER, Heinrich	47	Nienburg	55-0634
Sophie 47, Louise 20, Caroline 17			
Heinrich 19, Dorette 14, Minette 11			
Hinrich 9, Conrad 15			
SCHRADER, Johann	31	Weissenfels	61-0930
SCHRADER, Josefina	55	Holzhausen	56-0413
SCHRADER, Lucie	22	Ankum	57-0924
SCHRADER, Ludwig	20	Latzen	56-0819
Julie 25			
SCHRADER, Wilh'mne	25	Voldagsen/Br.	62-0608
SCHRADER, Wilhelm	21	Grossberkel	56-0819
SCHRAEDER, Cathar.	27	Evansville	62-0730
Gustav 3			
SCHRAGE, Heinrich	26	Elbese	55-0932
SCHRAML, W.	27	Baiern	57-0606
SCHRAMM, Andreas	36	Herreth/Bav.	57-0924
SCHRAMM, Friedrich	28	Siegen	59-0372
SCHRAMM, Georg	32	Herbartswind	57-1113
SCHRAMM, Joachim	38	Raudnitz	56-0629
Maria 31, Amalia 17, Jacob 14, Wilhelm 10			

NAME	AGE	RESIDENCE	YR-LIST
Jacob 35, L. 33, Carl 5, Lucie 4			
Ludwig 3, Zel. 9m, David 57, Marie 58			
SCHRAMM, Wm.	29	Tremar	61-0716
SCHRAMMEK, Stephan	31	Drachkan	61-0779
Barbara 29, Martin 6, Johann by			
SCHRAN, H.C.(m)	41	Cleveland	60-0785
SCHRANCK, Carl Fr.	20	Geppingen	56-0411
SCHRANZ, Robert	18	Minden	57-0606
SCHRARTING, Kunig.	28	Bremerhaven	57-1280
SCHRAUB, Conrad	21	Curhessen	55-0634
SCHRECK, Elise	27	Biebern/Hesse	60-0622
SCHRECK, Johann	26	Wasserloos	57-1026
SCHREIBER, Adam	25	Baiern	59-0412
SCHREIBER, Carolne	35	Braunschweig	59-0372
SCHREIBER, Fr'zka.	16	Oettingen	58-0815
SCHREIBER, Friedr.	28	Kuefenbach	57-1407
Elise 26, Carl by			
SCHREIBER, Heinr.	22	Rehna	59-0048
SCHREIBER, Joh.C.	36	Hessen	62-0306
Augustina 32, Justine 8			
SCHREIBER, Joh.Geo	32	Ibra	57-0654
Elise 26, A.Gela 8m			
SCHREIBER, Louis	21	New York	56-1216
SCHREIBER, M.	29	Sulzthal	62-0836
Marg. 31, Fanny 7, Franz 4, Carl 3m			
SCHREIDT, Charles	20	Weindorf	57-0654
SCHREIER, Andr.	24	Eicha	60-0334
SCHREIFLER, Ludwig	17	Hahlsdorf	57-0754
SCHREINER, (f)	40	France	57-1150
(child) 3			
SCHREINER, Georg	28	Buechenau	57-0447
SCHREINER, Johann	19	Wohra	57-0754
SCHREINER, Joseph	25	Bavaria	60-0371
SCHREINER, Lorenz	27	Wickersdorf	62-0467
SCHREISSGUT, Julie	44	Lahr	62-0730
SCHREPELTS, Anna M	22	Enniglohe	56-0723
SCHREPFER, H.(m)	18	Coburg	60-0785
SCHRETTER, Anasts.	32	Lermos	60-0533
SCHREVE, Ludwig	32	Blankenhagen	58-0576
SCHRIEFER, Johann	36	Schlussdorf	62-0608
SCHRIESENER, Mrs.	46	England	62-1112
Charles 1			
SCHRIEVER, John D.	33	Neuenwalde	62-0467
SCHRIMPER, Louise	28	Vehlage	59-0951
SCHRIMPF, Joseph	43	Staufendorf/B	55-0628
SCHRIMPF, Wilhelm	49	Houston	56-1216
SCHROD, Chr.Friedr	45	Oberoppurg	58-0881
Sophie 39, Hermann 16, Wilhelm 13			
Alfred 7, Robert 1, Friederike 25			
SCHRODER, August	25	Muenden	56-0819
Wilhelmine 20			
SCHRODER, Ed.G.	20	New York	62-0730
SCHRODER, Friedr.	16	Wellingen	57-1122
SCHRODI, Caspar	25	Pfromstetten	60-0429
Johanna 21, Franz 9m			
SCHROEDER, A.Cath.	27	Bremen	59-0477
SCHROEDER, Anna	16	Bockeln	55-1082
SCHROEDER, Anna	20	Dedendorf	60-0533
SCHROEDER, Anna M.	28	Neudeishausen	57-1113
SCHROEDER, Armand	26	Klosterweil	57-1148
SCHROEDER, August	16	Lamstedt	60-0334
SCHROEDER, August	18	Diepholz	57-0422
SCHROEDER, August	19	Aerzen	57-0447
SCHROEDER, Augusta	25	Toellenbeck	56-1260
Heinrich 2			
SCHROEDER, Beate	24	Tarnowo	56-1117
SCHROEDER, Betty	22	Germany	56-1216
SCHROEDER, Carl	44	Lommatsch	57-0578
Louise 42, Marie 8			
SCHROEDER, Carl	23	Newmark	57-0776
SCHROEDER, Carl	26	Quakenbrueck	58-0925
SCHROEDER, Carl	34	New York	59-1036
Sophia 28, Carl 8, Sophia 6			
SCHROEDER, Carl	32	Detroit	62-1042
SCHROEDER, Caspar	36	Wipperode	56-1011
SCHROEDER, Cath.	22	Wardenburg	57-1113
SCHROEDER, Chr'tne	31	Schleiz	61-1132
SCHROEDER, Claas	25	Glimstedt	59-0951
SCHROEDER, Concord	54	Diepholz	59-0951
Rosalie 24			
SCHROEDER, Diedr.	23	Schweringen	56-0723
SCHROEDER, Ditmar	24	Fuerstenberg	57-0754
SCHROEDER, Elisab.	20	Ostercappeln	56-1204
SCHROEDER, Elisab.	16	Dedendorf	57-0961
SCHROEDER, Elise	20	Loxstedt	61-0520
SCHROEDER, Elise	30	Haldorf	59-0951
SCHROEDER, Emilie	42	Boston	59-0990
SCHROEDER, Engel	20	Bekedorf	55-0630
SCHROEDER, Ernest	26	Lieme	57-0422
SCHROEDER, FRiedr.	23	Dueste	59-0477
SCHROEDER, Fr.	36	Hedem	57-0447
Louise 34, Lisette 7, Wilhelmine 5			
Wilhelm 2, Carl by			
SCHROEDER, Fritz	21	Cincinnati	59-0951
Philipp 18, Catharine 44			
SCHROEDER, Georg	25	Obermaehler	57-0509
Dorette 21, Berthe 9m			
SCHROEDER, Gottl.	25	Carzig	57-0776
SCHROEDER, H.(m)	28	San Francisco	61-0804
Sophie 29, Catharine 3, Margaretha 18			
SCHROEDER, H.(m)	39	Rietburg	62-0232
Anna M. 35			
SCHROEDER, Heinr.	22	Sulingen/Hann	55-0538
SCHROEDER, Heinr.	16	Berlin	56-0723
SCHROEDER, Heinr.	25	Husselfeld	57-1026
SCHROEDER, Heinr.	25	Bothen	58-0399
SCHROEDER, Henry	36	Todenmann	59-0384
Sophie 30, Sophie 60, Henry 9, Sophie 7			
William 3			
SCHROEDER, Herm.	33	San Francisco	60-1196
Adeline 17			
SCHROEDER, J.D.	47	Louisville	62-0938
SCHROEDER, Johann	40	Kreutzriehe/H	55-1238
SCHROEDER, Johann	42	Columbia	62-0467
SCHROEDER, Johanna	17	Bremen	60-0334
SCHROEDER, Klaarke	56	Weener	57-0422
SCHROEDER, Lisette	22	Wiedenbruch	59-0384
SCHROEDER, Louise	28	Kurhessen	56-1044
SCHROEDER, Ludwika	24	Vechta	62-0730
SCHROEDER, Magd.	19	Sommerda	57-0422
SCHROEDER, Marg.	18	Thedinghausen	62-0730
SCHROEDER, Maria	15	Suling	59-0412
SCHROEDER, Mary	21	Oberissigheim	60-1141
SCHROEDER, Maurice	21	Sommerda	57-0422
SCHROEDER, Nicolas	35	New York	62-1169
SCHROEDER, Robert	22	Gottsbuehren	57-0021
SCHROEDER, Wilhelm	31	Koenigsberg	57-0776
Emilie 10, Wilhelmine 30			
SCHROEDER, Wilhelm	17	EIchselsachse	59-0214
SCHROENECK, J.A.	36	Eschelbronn	62-0836
SCHROETER, Johanna	25	Lugnitz	57-1026
SCHROETER, Jul.Frd	16	Lenzensalza	59-0477
SCHROETER, Otto	20	Erfurt	57-1148
SCHRON, Christiane	58	Treinsche	58-0604
SCHROPELTS, Anna M	22	Enniglohe	56-0723
SCHROTH, Franz	39	Berlin	62-0342
SCHRUK, Ignaz	38	US.	61-0167
SCHRUMPF, Christ.	56	Meiningen	55-0634
Matthias 15, Gottlieb 12			
SCHUBARSKY, Maria	18	Boehmen	61-0716
SCHUBART, Sophie	28	New York	58-0815
SCHUBER, Barb.	36	New York	61-0897
Lucia 7, Georg 4			
SCHUBERT, Balthasa	23	Dornbach	60-0398
SCHUBERT, Carl Gtl	53	Schlettau/S.	60-0429
Chr.Concord. 53, Louisa Agnes 18			
Emily Bertha 11, Adolph Louis 9			
SCHUBERT, Christ.	34	Naida	60-0411
SCHUBERT, E.W.K.	25	Camenz	61-0167
SCHUBERT, Georg	15	Schwirzbitz	56-1044
SCHUBERT, Georg	36	Mistenfeld/Bv	62-0608
SCHUBERT, Joh.Geo.	49	Oertheim	59-0412
SCHUBERT, Johanna	22	New York	59-0214
August 9			
SCHUBERT, Ph.	25	Wertheim	60-0334
SCHUBERT, Wilhelm	19	Kleefeld	62-0758

NAME	AGE	RESIDENCE	YR-LIST
SCHUBMANN, Franz	26	Borholz/Pr.	60-0371
SCHUCHARDT, Carol.	19	Cassel	55-0634
SCHUCK, Anna	19	Leobschuetz	59-0535
SCHUCKMANN, Mary	45	Charleston	57-1148
SCHUECHEL, August	18	Salmuenster	59-0535
SCHUECHNER, Friedr	29	Epperstedt	62-0712
SCHUECKING, Const.	29	Coeln	62-0730
SCHUELE, Jacob	34	Wuertemberg	57-0606
SCHUELE, Johanna	36	Stilingen/Bad	60-0622
SCHUELER, Carl	17	Hammersleben	62-0608
SCHUELER, John	59	Osterode	60-1141
SCHUELLER, Georg	29	Masbach	61-0482
Majas 24, Barb. 6, Georg 3, Majas 7			
SCHUENEBURG, L.(m)	20	Hassenhausen	61-0482
SCHUENEMANN, Fried	16	Laluenfoerde	59-0214
SCHUENEMANN, Georg	19	Hastede	60-1141
Metta 18, Adelheid 15			
SCHUENEMANN, J.	18	Bremen	62-0938
SCHUEPERT, Johann	38	Hafenloar	59-0372
SCHUEPPNER, Johann	21	Goennern	59-0412
SCHUERER, Joh.	45	Lanz	59-1017
Elisabeth 29, Maria 15, Theresia 11			
Elisabeth 9			
SCHUERHARDT, Elise	15	Marburg	60-0334
SCHUERMANN, A.M.	26	Nesse	61-0682
SCHUERMANN, August	45	Hille	58-0545
SCHUERMANN, Casp.	30	Altenhueffen	59-1036
SCHUERMANN, F.W.	27	Detmold	57-0365
Mathilde 27			
SCHUESSEL, Elise	21	Gelsa	57-1067
SCHUESSLER, Anna	39	Welrodekilza	55-0538
SCHUESSLER, C.Th.	18	Lohr	62-0938
SCHUESSLER, Cath.	17	Zell	57-0021
SCHUESSLER, Rasmus	29	Wien	58-0604
SCHUETH, F.(m)	23	Veringhausen	62-0879
SCHUETH, Minna	27	Bosberghausen	62-0879
SCHUETTE, Augusta	16	Ninburg	60-0521
SCHUETTE, Elise	52	Havanna	58-0885
SCHUETTE, H.J.	28	Hildesheim	62-1112
SCHUETTE, Heinr.Wm	40	Otterndorf	57-1150
Rebecca 35, Carl 9, (baby) by			
SCHUETTE, Heinrich	19	Dohnsen	58-0563
SCHUETTE, Henriett	20	Epe	56-1117
SCHUETTE, J Friedr	36	Hattendorf	56-0589
Friedericke 18			
SCHUETTE, Johann	31	New York	57-1148
Carolina 27, Charles 5, Sophia 4m			
SCHUETTFURT, Heinr	18	Buende	60-0334
SCHUETZ, Anna	24	Hinterbalzhsn	60-0521
Elisabeth 4, Joseph 2, Anna 1			
SCHUETZ, August	27	Grabowke	56-0819
SCHUETZ, Charles	41	Wisconsin	59-0214
SCHUETZ, Chr.	28	Darmstadt	57-0606
SCHUETZ, Eduard	24	Schirnrod	60-0622
SCHUETZ, Ferd.	36	Nordhausen	60-0521
SCHUETZ, Franz	29	Hinterhalzhm.	60-0521
SCHUETZ, H.(m)	23	Kurhessen	57-0555
SCHUETZ, Heinrich	30	Minden/Wald.	55-0538
Catharine 25			
SCHUETZ, J. Jacob	18	Frankfurt a/M	61-0682
SCHUETZ, Joh.	27	Hutschdorf	62-0983
Margar. 23, Barbara 6m			
SCHUETZ, Joseph	40	Grenzdorf	56-0847
Louise 18			
SCHUETZE, Carl	19	Wernigerode	59-0214
SCHUETZE, Henriett	21	Oels	57-0754
SCHUETZE, J.Friedr	32	Osterau	57-1026
Caroline 34, Theodor 6m, Joh. Friedr. 3			
SCHUFFERT, Christ.	43	Iserlohn	55-0634
Maria 56, Friedrich 18, Carl 10, Gustav 9			
SCHUHMACHER, Georg	30	Vechta	56-0819
SCHUHMACHER, Heinr	17	Monrial/Pr.	60-0622
SCHUHMACHER, Joh.	32	Weiler/Prus.	55-1238
Louise 24			
SCHUHMACHER, Wilh.	40	Holzminden	59-0535
Emilie 38, Anna 9, Bertha 8, Hugo 6			
Maximilian 6, Dora 9m			
SCHUHMACHER, Wm.E.	24	Hagen	56-0411
SCHUK, John	47	Obermarken	61-0107
SCHUKAI, Carl	33	Conitz	56-1260
SCHUL, Catharina	43	Storndorf/Hes	55-0628
Hartmann 15, Elise 20, Elisabeth 6			
SCHULDER, Carl	27	Milwaukee	62-0111
Marie 20			
SCHULE, Friedrich	53	Krehlingen/Ha	55-1238
Heinrich 31, Friedrich 22			
SCHULENBERG, Herm.	27	Grosswerden	59-0477
SCHULER, Barbara	39	Magstadt	59-0613
Cath. 4			
SCHULER, Gertrud	40	Rosenthal	56-0723
SCHULHERR, J.L.	59	Pahres	61-0804
Caroline 55, Caroline 31, Babette 25			
SCHULHOF, E.	20	Henny-hausen	56-0512
SCHULHOFF, Herm.	25	Horinghausen	59-0477
SCHULL, Christian	24	Buttendorf	57-1280
SCHULLER, Joh.	20	Frommern	59-0384
SCHULLWORTH, Ad.	27	Stuttgart	61-0897
SCHULMANN, Bernhd.	36	St. Louis	57-0654
(wife) 28			
SCHULMANN, Fanny	21	Moenchsrot/Bv	55-0628
Heinrich 13			
SCHULMANN, Marg.	59	Washington	62-1042
SCHULMEIER, Peter	34	Giessen	57-0606
SCHULTANS, Hannche	22	Nentivishause	59-0214
SCHULTE, Carl	17	Bridenei	57-1280
SCHULTE, Carl	39	Hauda	62-0730
SCHULTE, Gerhard	23	Weener	57-0578
Edzard 28			
SCHULTE, Marcus	23	Illienworth	62-0608
SCHULTE, Marie E.	57	Brockhausen	56-0951
SCHULTE, Mary	24	Mettingen	57-1192
SCHULTE, Wilhelm	19	Eidinghausen	56-0411
SCHULTEN, Albert	50	Hilten	61-0478
Gertchen 31, Swen 11, Jean 8, Bert 6			
Heinrich 9m			
SCHULTHEISS, P.(m)	29	Buchenrod	62-0467
SCHULTHEISS, Wmne.	16	Neustadt	61-0482
SCHULTISS, Therese	26	Genna	61-1132
SCHULTZ, Berthold	20	Herzfeld/K-He	62-0342
SCHULTZ, Cath.	58	Reichelstein	60-0785
SCHULTZ, Friedr.	28	Nessentin	56-0951
Louise 50			
SCHULTZ, Jacob	28	Dramstadt	57-1122
SCHULTZ, Johann	26	Neuberg	57-1122
SCHULTZ, Wilhelm	34	Preussen	58-0399
Caroline 29, Ferdinand 5, Louise 11m			
SCHULTZE, A.(m)	20	Braunschweig	61-0804
SCHULTZE, Anton	30	Wesphalen	61-0682
SCHULTZE, Elisab.	15	Braunschweig	59-0384
SCHULTZE, Henry	23	Cassel	59-0384
SCHULTZE, Herm.	20	Berlin	62-0401
SCHULTZE, J.H.(m)	20	Scharmbeck	57-0080
SCHULTZE, Wilhelm	53	Peterburg	59-0951
SCHULTZE, Wilhmne.	23	Bertholtzhsn.	59-0951
SCHULZ, (m)	43	Neuenburg	57-0555
P.(m) 10, A.(f) 8, E.(f) 5			
SCHULZ, Antonia	26	Stettin	57-1150
SCHULZ, Aug.	20	Gr.Kotten	57-1148
SCHULZ, Carl	27	Riebau	55-0932
Dorothea 25, Friederike 3m, Ludwig 20			
Friederike 18			
SCHULZ, Carl	44	Crossen	61-0047
SCHULZ, Christian	25	Jankendorf	56-0819
SCHULZ, Christian	39	Parchim	57-0436
Wilhelmine 26, Frieda 3			
SCHULZ, D.A.	30	San Francisco	62-1169
SCHULZ, Dorothee	25	Wahrburg	61-0478
SCHULZ, Edw.	30	Braunschweig	57-0422
SCHULZ, Eliza E.	21	Melle	57-0961
SCHULZ, Emilie	36	Stettin	57-1026
Carl 9, Emilie 7			
SCHULZ, Fr.	33	New York	57-1148
Adelheid 27			
SCHULZ, Fr.	25	Hadamar	59-0990
SCHULZ, Franz	18	Frankenstein	55-0628
SCHULZ, Friedrich	19	Riebau	55-0932

NAME	AGE	RESIDENCE	YR-LIST
SCHULZ, Friedrich	39	Riebau	55-0932
Elisabeth 27, Carl 9m, Friedrich 3m			
Wilhelm 6, Heinrich 3			
SCHULZ, Friedrich	40	Schloppe	61-0779
Caroline 40, Joh. August 10			
Herm. Gustav 8, Augusta 6, Wilhelm 4			
Louise by			
SCHULZ, Friedrich	15	Nedelstedt	57-1280
SCHULZ, G.	27	Schmolz	56-0512
SCHULZ, Georg	45	Sachs.-Mein.	55-0630
Christoph 10, Martha 17			
SCHULZ, Heinrich	22	Oppenhausen	56-0413
Peter 19			
SCHULZ, Hermann	30	Schloppe	61-0779
Rosine 30, Marie by			
SCHULZ, J.C.	45	Bremerhaven	58-0925
SCHULZ, Jacob	40	Neudoerfel	56-0951
SCHULZ, Joh.Friedr	50	Riebau	55-0932
Maria 47, Friedr. 9m, Maria 23			
Dorothea 21, Catharina 15, Wilhelmina 12			
Friedrich W. 9, Alwina 2			
SCHULZ, Justus	33	Port au Princ	61-1132
SCHULZ, Marie	21	Amt Stuckhsn.	57-1280
SCHULZ, Nick	29	Bremmerfeld	60-1196
SCHULZ, Richard	27	Elberfeld	57-1148
SCHULZ, Theodor	14	Melle	55-0634
SCHULZ, Therese	29	Pinnow	62-0401
SCHULZ, Wilhelm	32	Carzig	57-0776
Justine 33, Wilhelm 7, Emilie 5, Julius 2			
SCHULZ, Wilhelm	25	Ribau	57-0447
Dorothea 17			
SCHULZ, Wilhelm	43	Posen	58-0399
Wilhelmine 30, Juliane 10, Henriette 7			
August 5, Johann 2			
SCHULZ, Wilhelmine	19	Paschenberg	57-0422
SCHULZ, Wm.	29	Jankendorff	59-1036
SCHULZE, Anna	18	Hetzerode	57-0776
Michael 45			
SCHULZE, Carl	36	Dabrowa	62-0306
Christiane 26, Wilhelm 9m			
SCHULZE, Christian	20	Dornheim	55-0630
SCHULZE, Friedrich	39	Succow	57-0961
SCHULZE, Gustav	29	Schleiz	57-1026
SCHULZE, Henry	27	Groshart	58-0545
SCHULZE, Johanna	37	Kamenz	60-0334
Emil 10, Herm. 9, Otto 6			
SCHULZE, Louis	17	Braunschweig	59-0477
SCHULZE, Pauline	31	Sachsenberg	60-0521
SCHULZEN, Cath.	24	Neustadt	62-1042
SCHUMACHER, Barbra	22	Unteraltenhm.	60-1053
SCHUMACHER, Barbra	27	Zender	57-1192
SCHUMACHER, Cath.	17	Luedingworth	56-0413
SCHUMACHER, Elisab	10	Essen	60-0521
SCHUMACHER, Fr.(m)	44	Schweringen	56-0723
Wilhelm 9m			
SCHUMACHER, Friedr	20	Wuerttemberg	55-0634
SCHUMACHER, G.	18	Bremen	59-0990
SCHUMACHER, Heinr.	18	Preuss.Minden	60-0371
SCHUMACHER, Herm.	14	Hassendorf	60-0521
SCHUMACHER, Julius	18	Herschen	62-0306
SCHUMACHER, K.Barb	18	Alfalter	56-0632
SCHUMANN, Aug.	45	Crimmitschau	62-0938
Herm. 16			
SCHUMANN, Carl	30	Motten	62-0712
Barbara 40, (dau.)(died) bob			
SCHUMANN, Cathar.	15	Otterndorf	56-0413
SCHUMANN, Christne	29	Lobenstein	56-0723
SCHUMANN, Fr.(m)	42	Culmbach	62-0730
SCHUMANN, Friedrke	22	Muenden	57-1192
SCHUMANN, Gottlieb	55	Carbusen	59-0214
SCHUMANN, Heinrich	28	Meiningen	55-0634
Friedrich 24, Elise 23			
SCHUMANN, Louise	30	St.Louis	59-1036
SCHUMANN, Margaret	47	Kreisdorf/Bav	60-0371
Margaretha 10			
SCHUMANN, Salomon	30	Hellingen	57-0924
SCHUMANN, Sophie	27	Lobenstein	57-0924
SCHUMER, Joh Conr.	18	Beckedorf	56-0589

NAME	AGE	RESIDENCE	YR-LIST
SCHUMER, Nicl.	30	Luxemburg	61-0482
SCHUMM, Barbara	39	Hellingen/Pr.	60-0622
Elisabeth 11			
SCHUNCK, H.(m)	28	Baltimore	62-0467
SCHUNICHT, Amalie	50	Nieherin	60-1196
SCHUPER, Ferdinand	37	Halberstadt	55-0812
SCHUPP, Ba.(m)	27	Langewiesen	62-0111
SCHUPPE, August	30	Gruenenplan	62-0938
SCHUSTER, Carl	34	Altenschonbch	60-1117
SCHUSTER, Friedr.		Detmold	56-1044
SCHUSTER, Heinrich	23	Hampfeld	58-0815
Philip			
SCHUSTER, Joh.	28	Baiern	57-0606
SCHUSTER, Louise	24	Bavaria	62-1169
SCHUSTERN, Elisab.	56	Luenten	60-0334
SCHUTER, Gertrud	40	Rosenthal	56-0723
SCHUTHE, Martin	48	Sarbske	58-0881
Wilhelmine 32, Alwine 13, Louise 12			
Carl 9, Ferdinand 6, Augusta 4			
Caroline 3m, Justine 30			
SCHUTZ, Friedrich	19	Riebau	55-0932
SCHUTZ, Friedrich	39	Riebau	55-0932
Elisabeth 27, Carl 9m, Friedrich 3m			
Wilhelm 6, Heinrich 3			
SCHUTZ, Joh.Friedr	50	Riebau	55-0932
Maria 47, Friedr. 9m, Maria 23			
Dorothea 21, Catharina 15, Wilhelmine 12			
Friedr. Wm. 9			
SCHWAAB, Louise	17	Schmikartshsn	55-0932
SCHWAB, Christiana	38	Meckniel	57-0776
Sophie 14, Wilhelm 6, Lizelle 6			
Caroline 3			
SCHWAB, Christoph	24	Plieningen	62-0879
Friedr.Wilh. 1			
SCHWAB, Friedrich	29	Eicha	60-0533
SCHWAB, Jacob	17	Ruempa	60-0785
SCHWAB, Johann	49	Recksbach	57-0776
Anna 47, Justina 7, Philipp 5			
SCHWAB, Sim.	27	Ingolstadt	61-0669
SCHWAB, Simon	7	Kleinsteinach	55-0845
SCHWABACH, Doroth.	17	Hofheim	57-0606
SCHWABBE, Bernh.	30	Haidersetten	60-0334
SCHWABE, Emanuel	55	Roedelheim	59-1036
SCHWABE, H.	22	Germany	56-0550
SCHWABEN, Joseph	30	Muenchen	56-0279
SCHWACHHEIM, Fr.	40	Madison	59-0477
SCHWAERZ, Simon	21	Kaldorf	57-0606
Christine 19			
SCHWAGER, August	37	Wallerstein	60-0622
SCHWAHN, Wilhelm	19	Schrecksbach	62-0342
SCHWALEN, Anna	19	Wittlinghsn.	55-1082
Louise 24			
SCHWALENBERG, Hch.	23	Grosslapfert	56-0411
SCHWALM, Anna	58	Goertzheim	59-0535
Catharina 18			
SCHWAN, Marg.	19	Geldern	56-1117
SCHWAN, Philipp	37	Gussen	57-1122
SCHWANDNER, Johann	30	Bruck	56-1117
SCHWANEMANN, Peter	21	Ihenworth	58-0563
SCHWANER, Friedr.	58	Frankenberg	57-0924
Cath.Elisab. 58, Conrad 30			
Joh.Wilhelm 24, A.Catharina 21			
SCHWANER, Marie	17	Frankenberg	57-0924
Helfer 14			
SCHWANEWEDEL, Joha	18	Dorum	60-1141
SCHWANN, Johann	30	Lauterbach/He	61-0770
SCHWANN, Theodor	16	Walsdorf	57-0578
SCHWANTNER, Martin	27	Neukestran	57-1067
Marie 24, Mathias 2			
SCHWANZ, Catharine	27	Sachsen	58-0399
SCHWARKE, Christ.	17	Hahnenkamp	57-1407
SCHWARNEBECK, Auga	20	Berlin	60-1141
SCHWARSMANN, Gesch	23	Moender	57-1148
SCHWARTING, A.H.B.	22	Abbehausergro	59-0477
SCHWARTING, Jacob	24	Uelerland	56-1260
SCHWARTING, Reb.	18	Aschwarden	59-0990
SCHWARTZ, Cathrina	29	Heiningen	59-0535
SCHWARTZ, Georg	36	Felsberg	56-0632

NAME	AGE	RESIDENCE	YR-LIST
SCHWARTZ, H.	27	Russia	62-0938
SCHWARTZ, John	36	New York	62-0730
SCHWARTZ, Ludw.	44	Braunschweig	59-0990
(m) 19			
SCHWARTZE, Anna	19	Dresten	55-1048
SCHWARTZKOPF, Joh.	20	Blowic	59-1036
SCHWARZ, (m)	25	Prussia	58-0306
SCHWARZ, Andreas	25	Muenchen	58-0815
SCHWARZ, August	40	America	60-0785
SCHWARZ, August	35	St.Louis	58-0604
Sophie 26			
SCHWARZ, Bertha	19	Coethen	61-0804
SCHWARZ, Catharine	20	Sterbfritz	61-0520
SCHWARZ, Clara	18	Prag	60-1196
SCHWARZ, Elise	32	Eisrode	56-0723
SCHWARZ, Franz	24	Fulda	55-0845
SCHWARZ, Friedr.	18	Bremervoerde	55-0634
SCHWARZ, G.A.	38	Philadelphia	62-0938
Mrs.A. 30			
SCHWARZ, Hermann	28	Brosen	56-0411
Augustus 20			
SCHWARZ, Jac.	16	Roedenau	61-0669
El. 24			
SCHWARZ, Jacob	17	Schoenwald	56-0951
SCHWARZ, Louise	24	Hanbrunn	58-0815
SCHWARZ, Mathilde	24	Rinteln	58-0563
SCHWARZ, Sophie	22	Wemsheim	56-0411
SCHWARZ, Theodor	39	Louisville	57-1192
Anna 21, Theodor 3, Georg 2			
SCHWARZKOPF, Cath.	28	Staffelhofe	58-0815
SCHWARZKOPF, Citty	20	Boehmen	61-0478
SCHWARZKOPF, Crlne	18	Schneittach	56-1216
SCHWARZMANN, John	35	Reuth	57-1026
Margaretha 32			
SCHWARZROCK, Paul	42	Grieben	56-0723
Elisabeth 22			
SCHWECKER, An Chr.	26	Wollstein	57-0776
SCHWEDT, Sara	18	Sachsen	59-1036
SCHWEERS, Chs.	57	Kirchhatten	60-0521
Anna 48, Friederike 23, Peter 14			
SCHWEERS, Helene	27	Lohne	62-0401
SCHWEGLER, Friedr.	20	Entersbach	61-0520
SCHWEHR, Dorothea	24	Beckedorf	56-0589
Friederike 2			
SCHWEICHARD, Anna	20	Tuebingen	59-0613
SCHWEICHARDT, Marg	33	Heddenheim	57-1192
Christian 6			
SCHWEICKART, Cath.	17	Heidelberg	58-0604
SCHWEICKHER, David	28	Kirchberg	58-0399
SCHWEIG, Johannes	28	Wollhausen	59-0384
SCHWEIGER, Louise	17	Isenburg	60-1032
SCHWEIGER, Peter	20	Schweinkofen	58-0885
SCHWEIGHART, Wlmne	18	Sults	60-1196
SCHWEIKERT, Barbra	19	Wuerttemberg	60-0371
Magdalena 22			
SCHWEIKERT, Joh.S.	49	Emskirchen	62-0306
Margareta 39, Andreas 10			
SCHWEINEFUSS, Clem	37	Oite	59-0412
SCHWEINFURT, Marg.	20	Neuses	62-0730
SCHWEINITZ, Carl F	19	Meiningen	55-1082
SCHWEINITZ, v.G.J.	28	Austria	62-0166
SCHWEINSHAUT, Adam	29	Koenigshofen	62-0712
SCHWEINSHAUT, S.	25	Koenigshofen	62-0836
SCHWEITZER, Christ	28	Unterkepach	59-0477
SCHWEITZER, Christ	28	Unterkepach	59-0477
Susanne 25			
SCHWEITZER, Johs.	15	Apenheim	62-0166
SCHWEITZER, Marie	20	Neukirchen	62-0879
SCHWEITZER, Richd.	18	Neustadt a/O	59-0477
SCHWEIZER, Carolne	22	Mittelstadt	62-0730
SCHWEIZER, Joh.Wm.	22	Harochbach	61-0478
SCHWEIZER, Wilhelm	30	New York	59-0048
SCHWELA, Catharine	23	Boehmen	60-0785
SCHWELERMANN, Eng.	30	Telgte	60-0998
Elise 27			
SCHWENDTKER, Heinr	53	Hille/Prussia	62-0608
Elisabeth 53, Caroline M. 20			
Marie Louise 16, Sophie 9			
SCHWENDY, Ferdin.	28	Prussia	57-0555
SCHWENGE, Marie	18	Paddewig	56-0589
SCHWENK, Anna	40	Fuerstenheide	57-1407
SCHWENK, Heinrich	38	Dagersheim	58-0563
Heinrich 11, Carl Heinr. 8, August 31			
SCHWENK, Julius	34	Kleinerstadt	61-0482
Dorothea 34			
SCHWENKE, Chrstine	21	Mengringhsn.	61-0520
SCHWENKE, Georg	23	Sellfach	57-1122
Christine 48, Emilie 13, Louise 17			
SCHWENKE, Heinrich	37	Minden	57-0776
SCHWENKER, Adolph	25	Germany	59-0951
Lucie 24, (child) bob			
SCHWENKER, Carolne	22	Minden	56-0411
SCHWENKER, Heinr.	17	Hille	56-0411
SCHWENTKER, Carol.	19	Hille	56-0411
SCHWENTKER, Wilh.	34	Willen	55-0932
Chr. 30			
SCHWENZER, Adolph	33	Berlin	61-0682
Friedricke 35			
SCHWER, Hendrika	36	Suedlahn	62-0983
SCHWERDT, E.	17	Salzungen	62-0993
SCHWERDTFEGER, Car	40	Sievershausen	59-0214
SCHWERDTFEGER, Chr	21	New York	59-0951
SCHWERS, Caroline	21	Steinhude	56-0411
Marie 10			
SCHWERTZ, Herm.	38	Runneln	61-0482
SCHWERZEL, Martha	29	Bischoffsrode	60-0398
SCHWESINGER, E.	20	Hildburghause	62-0993
SCHWESSEL, Johanes	18	Bottendorf/He	55-1238
SCHWETJE, Anna	33	Lesum	61-0632
SCHWID, Franz	42	Boehmen	58-0881
Maria 32, Clara 15			
SCHWIED, Marie	14	Bremen	60-0521
SCHWIER, Heinr.	34	Minden	62-1042
SCHWIETERING, Fr´z	27	Ahaus	61-0482
SCHWIMME, Ulrich	28	Frankenhausen	56-0951
SCHWIND, Friedrich	16	Antwerp	57-1192
SCHWING, Conrad	26	Curhessen	55-0634
SCHWINGE, Hermann	20	Paddewich	57-0776
Anna 22			
SCHWINGEL, Johann	18	Heimershausen	57-0776
SCHWINGER, Eduard	18	Sponn	56-1117
SCHWINICH, Ida	20	Haltern/Hann.	55-0544
SCHWITZ, J. Wilh.	30	Siegburg	59-0384
SCHWOHS, E.	25	New York	59-0951
Sophie 20			
SCHWONS, Niclaus	34	US.	55-1048
SCOTT, Alice	34	Southampton	59-0477
SCOTT, Ernst	29	Lemmesch	62-0467
SEBERGER, Cathrina	24	Hambach	57-0447
SEBIG, Friedrich	28	Niederodenbch	59-0384
SEBO, Wilhelm	17	Oberglogau	56-0589
SEBY, Felix	58	Altingen	61-0047
SECHLER, Georg	35	New York	62-0730
Caroline 25, Fr.(m) 5, Georg 3			
SECKER, Conrad	18	Suling	59-0412
SECKER, Doris	16	Brotum	56-1216
SEDLAE, Wenzel	26	Boehmen	62-0001
SEEBACH, Conrad	38	Luderbusch	55-0932
Anna 50, Johannes 18			
SEEBECK, August	16	Loxstedt	56-0819
Augusta 23			
SEEBECK, Cath.	26	Westerbeverts	59-0951
SEEBECK, Christine	26	Loxstedt	60-0521
SEEBECK, Georg	17	Driftsethe	59-0951
SEEBECK, Joh.D.	29	San Francisco	62-1169
Dorothea 26, (suckling) 9m			
SEEBECK, Joh.H.		Brooklyn	57-1150
SEEBER, Friedrike	27	Suhl	57-0924
SEEBOHM, Ad.	19	Minden	55-1082
SEEBOHM, Heinrich	27	Edersfeld/Bav	55-0628
SEEDORF, Diedrich	21	Lessumstotel	57-1026
SEEGELBAUM, Barb.	59	Ofen	62-1042
SEEGER, A.	30	Iber	62-0993
M. 26, A. 1			
SEEGER, Carl	20	Cassel	59-0384
SEEGER, Johann	24	Germany	62-0467

NAME	AGE	RESIDENCE	YR-LIST
SEEGER, Theodor	21	Baltimore	62-0836
SEEGER, Wilhelm	33	Buchholz	57-0447
SEEGER, Wilhelmine	32	Buchholz	57-0447
Wilhelm 7, Carl 9, Otto 1m, Wilhelm 33			
SEEKAMP, Gesche	22	New York	62-1112
SEEKAMP, Henry	28	Achim	57-1192
Soph. 18			
SEEKAMP, Johanna	24	Brake	59-0477
SEEKER, Sophie	18	Brockum	59-0214
SEEL, Joh.Christ.	34	Tiefengruben	62-0712
Friedr.Mart. 13			
SEELE, Caroline	40	New York	56-1216
Anna 7, Albert 11m			
SEELEN, v. Georg	56	Wiebrechtshsn	62-0993
SEELIG, Amalie	20	Pirstein	60-0521
SEELIG, Elisabeth	25	Speckwinkel	57-0754
SEELIG, Johann	30	Erdmannsrode	60-0622
SEELMAYER, Marie	25	Muenchen	60-0521
SEELMEYER, Friedr.	30	Polle/Hann.	55-0538
SEER, Anna	20	Nortwede	57-1122
SEERNERS, Anna M.		Gerdens	56-0629
SEGELER, Fr.(m)	28	Berlin	62-0608
SEGELKE, Joh.	17	Bremen	62-1042
SEGERT, Bernhard	37	St.Louis	59-0951
SEGGEBROCK, Maria	25	Lyhren	61-0520
SEGGERMANN, J.H.	24	Strackholt	56-0629
SEGGERN, v. Heinr.	36	Gruppersburen	58-0925
SEGGERN, v. Henry	46	New York	58-0815
SEGGERN, v.H.F.	47	Delmenhorst	59-0477
Meta 36, Heinrich 9			
SEGGEWISCH, Marg.	70	Stadtlohne/Br	62-0608
SEGITZ, Babette	16	Erlangen	61-0167
SEHR, Catharine	24	Bavaria	62-0758
Clara 18			
SEHRT, John	40	Baltimore	60-0785
SEIBEL, Catharine	18	Roth	61-0520
SEIBEL, Elisabeth	22	Rohde	57-0924
SEIBEL, Elisabeth	54	Atzenau	60-0398
SEIBEL, Johann	21	Grefenhausen	62-0111
SEIBEL, Kilian	21	Leinburg	57-0961
SEIBERT, Caspar	48	New York	59-1036
Elisabeth 43, Elisabeth 21, Carl 19			
Maria 15, Emilie 9			
SEIBERT, Conrad	37	New York	59-1036
Cathar. 38, Catharina 39, Emilie 13			
Louise 9, Herrmann 8, Heinrich 6, Emma 5			
Anna 4, Carl 2, Minna 9m			
SEIBT, August	34	New Jersey	57-0365
SEICHTER, Susanne	23	Salzburg	60-0521
Friedrich 9m			
SEIDEL, August	30	Oberhusdorf	57-1113
Barbara 30, Augusta 7, Bruno 4			
SEIDEL, Carl	57	Schlesien	62-0758
Marie 35			
SEIDEL, Carl Aug.	26	Oberhusdorf	57-1113
SEIDEL, Ernestine	48	Mecklenburg	55-0845
Octavia 10, Arthur 9, Leopold 8, Em. 5			
Traugott 4, Trini 3, Minna 15			
SEIDEL, Florian	19	Algers	56-0951
SEIDEL, Friedrich	37	Sachsen	57-0776
Juliane 39, Ernst 5, Hermann 10m			
SEIDEL, Joh.Charl.	26	Froehlichdorf	57-1148
SEIDELL, Henriette	57	Dresden	57-0606
SEIDEN, John	28	Temeswar	57-0654
SEIDENZAHL, Louise	55	Petershagen	61-0482
SEIDL, John	45	Eggenberg	57-0422
SEIDLER, Andreas	26	Elbersberg	57-0754
SEIDLER, Herm.	21	Oberwaid	59-0535
Amalia 19			
SEIDLER, Margareta	25	Bischoffsgrun	58-0563
SEIFERMANN, Caspar	57	Minden	56-1044
Lisette 20, Marie Cath. 18, Heinrich 18			
Wilhelm 16, Franz Caspar 14, Wilhelm 49			
SEIFERT, Caroline	25	Schmeheim	60-1161
SEIFERT, Christoph	65	Buchwalde	55-0812
Eleonore 60			
SEIFERT, E.C.Alb.	14	Mainz	61-0482
SEIFERT, Eva	30	Siefershausen	57-1407
SEIFERT, H.	17	Esslingen	59-0990
SEIFERT, Johanne	18	Pfaffenries	56-0527
SEIFERT, Johannes	28	Gulozheim/Bav	61-0770
Catharina 22, Heinrich 3m			
SEIFERT, Lorenz	45	Sandberg	56-0279
Phillipp 23			
SEIFERT, Mich.	21	Oberbach	62-1042
SEIFERT, Michael	40	Unterweissenb	56-0951
Heinrich 3			
SEIFERTH, Margaret	14	Grauenmaas/Bv	62-0608
SEIFFERT, Christ.	32	Steinau	62-0712
Eva 25, (dau.) bob			
SEIFFERT, G.(m)	59	Helmsbrecht	62-0730
L.(m) 15			
SEIFFERT, Ida	19	Gotha	55-0634
SEIFORT, Chr.	25	Altenberg	56-0411
Maria 25			
SEIFRIED, Conrad	22	Heimerdingen	62-0306
SEIFRIED, Friedr.	22	Kalmbach	61-0482
SEILER, Conrad	28	New Orleans	58-0885
SEILER, Margareth	31	Germany	59-1036
John 7			
SEILER, Wilhelm	30	Neustadt	60-1053
SEILER, Wm.	19	Bruchsal	62-0730
SEILKOPF, Ernst	56	Lauenhagen	62-0836
Sophie 46, Sophie 18, Fr. (m) 16			
Cath. 14, Marie 8, (dau.) 9m			
SEIM, Ernst	26	Mahlbach	61-0478
SEIM, Johannes	34	Mahlbach	61-0478
Margaretha 37, Catharina 13, Johannes 11			
Peter 8, Wilhelm 7, Elisabeth 6			
Heinrich 4, Conrad 9m			
SEINKE, Anna	25	Germany	59-0951
SEIP, Elisabeth	28	Hochelheim	55-0413
SEIP, Johannes	52	Leihgestern	57-0924
SEIPEL, Chr.	26	Usenborn	55-0413
SEIPEL, Jost Heinr	57	Curhessen	55-0634
Adam 37, Leeschen 23, Christine 3			
SEIS, Anna Cath.	26	Ort	62-0879
SEITER, P.J.(m)	36	New York	61-0897
SEITERLEIN, Maria	22	Rothenburg/Bv	55-0628
SEITERMANN, Phil.	28	Krummbach/Hes	62-0608
SEITNER, Johann	46	Solzbach	55-0932
Elisabeth 48, Johann 17			
SEITS, Franz	15	Gotha	56-0847
SEITZ, Anna	21	Lorsen	60-0785
SEITZ, Barbara	36	New York	61-0779
SEITZ, Casimir	32	New York	62-1169
SEITZ, Christine	22	Markgroningen	60-1032
SEITZ, Friedrich	36	Wendenbostel	58-0881
Wilhelmine 35			
SEITZ, Maria	27	Allendorf	55-0630
SEITZ, Richard	24	Blankenloch	62-1112
SEKE, Anna	21	Sand	57-0555
SELAN, Thomas	46	Bohemia	60-1161
Maria 40, Sosh. 18, Cath. 13, Joh. 10			
Anna 6, Franz 1			
SELIG, Adam	40	Ilm	60-1141
Anna 24, Clinious (m) 2			
SELIG, C.(m)	21	Hersfeld	62-0836
SELIG, Friedrich	28	Niederodenbch	59-0384
SELIG, Georg	49	Hersfeld	56-0629
Gertrude 45, Wilhelmine 14, Henriette 12			
Gust. Adolph 8, Bertha Maria 5			
SELIG, Seligmann	24	Hainhausen	60-0533
SELIG, Valentin	23	Hersfeld	57-0704
SELIGER, Friedr Wm	17	Harpenfeld	56-0951
SELIGMANN, Joseph	19	Hattenbach	56-1011
SELING, Anna C.	22	Malkomes	57-0847
SELL, Anna	26	Hammelburg	58-0815
Therese 3			
SELL, Eduard	21	Niederursel	58-0881
SELL, Ludw.	14	Michelbach	60-0521
SELLE, Gottlieb	43	Neu Schonewld	57-0704
Henriette 47, Bertha 16, Augusta 14			
Wilhelm 12, Henriette 6, Emilie 4			
Friedrich 2			
SELLFLEISCH, Augta	20	Roda	56-0847

NAME	AGE	RESIDENCE	YR-LIST
SELLHAUSEN, Barb.	31	Washington	62-0938
Minna 4			
SELLHAUSEN, F.	36	Washington	62-0938
SELLHEIM, Anna	21	Conradsdorf	60-0521
SELLHEIM, Hermann	22	Schotten	59-0477
Julie 28			
SELLHORST, Theod.	22	Lippenstaupp	60-0334
SELLMANN, Georg	25	Etensfeld	56-0723
SELLMER, Gottfried	44	Romanshof	56-0632
Joh.Caroline 30, Emil.Augusta 12			
Joh. Ludwig 10, J.Gottfried 7			
SELLNER, Martin	36	Salluschen	57-0924
SELTENREICH, G.(m)	33	New York	62-0111
SELZING, Henry	25	Philadelphia	60-0411
Louise 26, Bertha 2, M. El. (f) 5			
SEMINETH, Elis.	28	Alsleben	60-1196
SEMKE, Claus	20	Nordsohl	57-0422
SEMKEN, Heinr.	32	US.	59-0951
SEMLER, Elise	18	Singlis	62-0836
SEMLER, F.L.	26	Stutzhaus	57-1067
SEMLER, Friedrich	24	Itzehoe	61-0682
SEMM, Therese Elis	19	Meiningen	62-0712
SEMMERNER, Heinr.	26	Stade	57-0776
SEMMLER, Carl	43	Darmstadt	57-1407
SEMMLER, Mary	24	Cassel	60-1141
Frank 9m			
SENDEL, Friedr.Aug	20	Eisleben	57-0924
SENDELBECK, Anna	18	Kreussen	59-0990
SENDER, v. Adolf	25	Cincinnati	55-0932
SENF, Ed.	17	Cassel	57-1192
SENFT, Gust.	25	California	62-1042
SENGSTACKEN, Heinr	39	Floegeln	57-1150
Elisabeth 34, (baby)			
SENKSTACKEN, Peter	23	Meckelstedt/H	60-0622
SENNE, Fr.	24	Estorf	62-1042
SENNE, Hans	19	Kreuz Riehl	55-0630
SENNEWALD, Justine	22	Erfurt	57-1067
SENNEWALD, Martin	30	Erfurt	60-0411
Friederike 25, Justine 6, Anna 2			
William 2m			
SENNHOLZ, J.Friedr	32	Vornhagen	56-0589
Agnes 18			
SENNING, Georg		Altenbrunslar	59-0214
SENT, Gustav	37	Dessau	56-0819
SENTH, Georg	19	Ahlsfeld	61-0478
SERHT, Heinrich	23	Lehrbach	55-0630
SESSINGHAUS, Fr´dr	14	Hannover	57-1192
SETTELE, Ludwig	20	Giegelbach	56-0847
SETZER, Catharine	30	Miltenberg/Bv	62-0608
Anton 28			
SETZER, Fr.(m)	28	Spatzenhof	57-0555
G.(f) 23, Chr.(f) 6m, Gottfried 6			
SEUBEL, Elise	22	Germany	61-0167
SEUBERT, Marg.	27	Hetzlars	59-0535
SEUBERT, Margareta	15	Sindeldorf	62-0879
Michael 13			
SEUBERT, Maria	28	Kirchhain	59-1036
SEUFER, Conrad	50	Philadelphia	62-0938
SEUFFERT, Valentin	34	Steinfeld	61-0520
Margaretha 30, Victoria 5			
SEUNBERGER, D.	27	Actenfeld	56-0512
SEUSING, Carl	17	Heinersdorf	56-0629
SEUSS, Johannes	32	Bayern	61-0930
Barbara 38			
SEVENZIG, Elisab.	36	New York	62-1169
Senny 9, Emma 4			
SEVERIN, Christian	40	Anger	56-1044
Elisabeth 33, Christian 13, Heinrich 11			
Wilhelm 9, Carl 7, Maria 6			
SEVERIN, Wilhelm	25	Anger	56-1044
SEVERT, A.(m)	27	New York	61-0482
SEYBEL, Anna E.	25	Oberholzhsn.	60-0533
SEYBOLD, Andr.	14	Laufen/Wuertt	60-0429
Regina 34, Friederike 10			
SEYBOLD, Jacob	18	Tuebingen	60-0411
SEYBOLD, Joh.Mich.	35	Wuertemberg	57-0606
Leonh. 26			
SEYBOLD, Rosina	23	Wuertemberg	57-0606

NAME	AGE	RESIDENCE	YR-LIST
SEYFAHRT, Ferd.	18	Crimmitschau	57-0422
SEYFAHRT, Wilhelm	49	Charleston	57-1026
SEYFANG, Cath.	21	Wuertemberg	59-0535
SEYFANG, Matth.	23	Ohio	59-0535
SEYFERT, Georg	28	Hannover	57-0961
SEYFRIED, Caroline	27	Oberjungbach	56-0589
Joh.Georg 26			
SEYFRIED, Ferd.	21	Driegisau	59-1036
SEYP, Emil	27	Buffalo	58-0885
SEZFRIED, Ferd.	21	Driegisau	59-1036
SHERSEY, Henry	23	England	60-0334
SHORT, Augusta	24	Blearsville	58-0306
SHROEN, Eva E.	21	Solms	56-1117
SHUPEL, Anton	34	Mecerisch	57-1416
Anna 38, Franz 15, Marie 9, Therese 40			
SIBICH, Heinr.	30	Theimendorf	56-0411
Juliane 25			
SICHELSTILL, Andr.	31	Axtheit	57-1280
Margaretha 31, Anna 5, Elisabeth 68			
SICHER, Lorie	20	Berdika	55-0845
SICK, Elise	21	Reidlingen	60-0521
SICK, Friedrich	17	Naugard	57-0654
SICKERT, Albert	19	Kluetzken	56-0629
SIEB, Anna	24	Wunsiedel	60-0411
SIEB, E.	27	Coburg	62-0993
SIEBE, Christian	19	Varl/Pr.	60-0622
SIEBE, Joh.	25	San Francisco	59-0951
Christiane 24			
SIEBEL, Fr´dr. Wm.	25	Solingen	55-0634
Julie 25, Heinr. Wilh. 1			
SIEBELIUS, Franz	20	Ndr.Ingelheim	60-1053
SIEBELS, Mary Cath	24	Wiarden	57-0422
SIEBENEICHER, Jos.	20	Stolz	59-0477
SIEBENHAUS, John	38	Sulzheim	60-0411
SIEBERT, Catharina	15	Ob.Vorschuetz	57-0754
SIEBERT, Conrad	53	Schoenberg/He	55-0628
Catharine 49, Margaretha 22, Hanjost 18			
Anna Maria 15, Elisabeth 13, Anna Cath. 7			
Christine 5			
SIEBERT, Fritz	19	Arolsen	56-0819
SIEBERT, Heinrich	22	Neunrupperhsn	55-0628
SIEBERT, Jonas	41	Eplerode/Hess	55-0538
Agnesia 41			
SIEBERT, Jos.	29	Hadamar	57-1148
SIEBKING, Chr.	16	Hille	56-0411
SIEBOLD, Heinrich	22	Pattenberg/CH	60-0622
SIEBOLT, August	19	Jever	62-0938
SIEBOLT, Vincent	59	Baden	62-0467
SIEBRANDT, Siebran	26	Wayens	57-0422
SIEBS, Christ.	28	Paddingmittel	58-0306
(wife) 26			
SIEDE, Michael	40	Brutzig	57-0704
Anna Maria 38, Regina 9, Maria 6			
Gottfried 3, Christian 9m			
SIEDENTOPF, H.(m)	17	Moordorf	62-0232
SIEDRICH, Johann	84	Flaeurlingen	58-0563
Franz 37, Agnes 38, Marie 12, Johann 10			
Joseph 8, Alois 6, Eduard 4, Franz 3m			
Josephine 45			
SIEFERT, Adolph	15	Adelsheim/Bad	60-0429
SIEFERT, Christ.	57	Eisenach	59-1036
Amalia 60			
SIEFERT, Fr.Jul.	24	Aufenthal	57-1113
SIEG, Johann	35	Petzick	57-0924
Louise 26, August 4, Johanne by			
SIEG, Wilhelm	27	Grunau	57-0924
SIEGEL, Georg	30	Kubert	55-0630
Magdalena 25			
SIEGEL, Minna	22	Hugershausen	60-0521
SIEGENTHALER, Ulr.	52	Minnesota	59-0214
Emil 8, Julius 9			
SIEGER, Christ.	27	Weinheim	56-0512
Georg 5			
SIEGLER, Adam	28	Steinfeld	61-0520
Cathrine 23, Eduard 6m			
SIEGLER, Anton	36	St.Louis	59-0214
SIEGLER, Johann	51	Muenster a/Na	59-0214
Magdalena			

NAME	AGE	RESIDENCE	YR-LIST
SIEGMUND, August	19	Schwarzenburg	58-0399
SIEGMUND, Edward	36	Buchau	57-0654
SIEGMUND, Wm.	27	Probstei	57-0654
SIEGRIST, Peter	32	Friedrichstal	62-0938
Lydia 28, Martha 3, Pauline 6m			
SIEKER, Wilhelm	21	Vahrenholz	56-1260
SIELEMANN, H.	48	Melle	59-0990
(f) 46, (f) 15, (m) 10			
SIELER, Amalie	19	Rauda	62-0879
SIEMENS, H.	28	Norden	55-0932
SIEMENS, W.(m)	40	Silver Creek	62-0232
SIEMON, Conrad	65	Hessen	61-0682
Cathrina 66			
SIEMON, Georg Casp	19	Sachsen	59-0412
SIEMON, Heinrich	22	Borken	57-1067
SIEMON, Hr.	28	Johannisthal	55-0932
Martha 28			
SIEMONS, Ella Marg	28	Norden	57-1148
SIEMONS, H.	22	Halle	57-0961
SIEMS, Gerhard	18	Bederkesa	57-0847
SIEMS, Johann	18	Hannover	62-0758
SIERING, Wilhelm	52	Waldeck	55-0634
Elisabeth 50, Heinrich 30, Daniel 30			
Cathrina 7, Heinrich 6, Cathrina 4			
Heinrich by			
SIEVERMANN, Ant.	44	Hecke	57-0578
SIEVERS, Anna	24	Maulbach	61-0047
SIEVERS, Aug.	24	Stolzenau	62-0938
Louise 34			
SIEVERS, Barb.	44	Washington	62-0938
SIEVERS, Conrad	38	Hannover	58-0576
SIEVERS, Fritz	22	Pyrmont	57-0509
SIEVERS, L.(m)	28	Chicago	62-0730
SIEVERS, Max	26	Paderborn	61-0047
SIEVERT, Friedrich	27	Besingfeld	61-0478
SIEVERT, Heinrich	36	Illershausen	59-0047
Elisabeth 45			
SIEWE, Ant.	30	Sorgau	57-1192
SIEWERMANN, Elise	26	New York	59-0477
Marie 19			
SIEWERT, Christoph	43	Selchow	56-0819
Caroline 31, Emilie 8, August 3, Carl 9m			
SIGEL, B.(m)	24	Washington	62-0836
SIGISMUND, Liebgot	30	Gallitz	57-0776
Elisabeth 37			
SIGMUND, Jacob	18	Mannheim	60-0398
SILBACH, Elisabeth	21	Manheim	60-0521
SILBER, Hannchen	26	Hildesheim	56-0723
SILBER, Jacob	23	Sommerach	59-0477
SILBERBAUER, Barb.	34	Wien	59-0384
Carl 5			
SILBERBERG, Benj.	19	Volkmarsen	62-0306
SILBERER, Anna	39	Manitowoc/Wis	61-0770
SILBERG, Elias	20	Termentingen	61-0107
SILBERG, Mench.	19	Kutna	61-0107
SILBERHORN, Georg	55	Wernsbach	59-1036
Margareth 43, Johanna 9m			
SILBERSCHMIDT, Fan	17	Geisa	59-0477
SILBERSTEIN, Isaac	40	Germany	62-0938
SILBERWEISS, Anton	22	Frankfurt a/M	61-0520
SILLER, Joh.Philip	25	Neuenkirchen	57-0924
SIMECK, Joseph	28	Popowitz	56-1011
Maria 27, Francis 7, Wenzel 5, Stephen 3			
SIMER, Jette	25	Wagenfeld	62-0836
SIMMAU, William J.	22	Giessen	57-0654
SIMMONDE, P.H.	47	St.Thomas	57-1192
SIMON, Adam	20	Melsen/Curh.	60-0622
SIMON, Amalie	26	Hochst	60-0785
SIMON, Benjamin	32	France	60-1196
Emil 11			
SIMON, C.	22	Ruhlkirchen	62-0993
SIMON, Fr.	26	Sondershausen	57-0365
SIMON, Franz	41	Schlitz/Bav.	61-0770
Philippine 35, Wilhelm 15, August 10			
Elise 7, Heinrich 5, Emil 3, Dorothea 1			
SIMON, Johann	49	Hachborn	55-0630
Elisabetha 43, Elisabetha 16, Heinrich 19			
Philipp 14, Elisabetha 8, Balthasar 6			

NAME	AGE	RESIDENCE	YR-LIST
Catharina 4			
SIMON, Johann	21	Zellhausen/HD	60-0429
SIMON, Nomann	33	Osterode	60-1141
SIMONS, Blanke	29	Herford	59-0477
Sophie 4, Fritz 3, Mathilde 11m			
SIMONSMEYER, Heinr	30	Brosen	56-0411
Charlotte 25, Hermann 28			
SINGER, G.(m)	27	Gr.Buseck	62-0467
SINGER, Kunigunde	23	Lahmeisache	59-0214
SINGEWALD, G.	50	Baltimore	57-1148
SINTOPP, Heinrich	24	Rechenbuettel	56-0411
SINZ, Victor	20	Basel	59-0477
SIPKOWITZ, Louise	24	Bergersdorf	58-0604
SIPPACH, Ch. Louis	35	Brundobra	60-1053
Jacobine 28, Lina 2			
SIPPEL, Ludwig	20	Schweina	56-0819
Christine 16			
SIPPEL, Nic.	18	Vockerode	62-1112
SIPPER, Joh. Georg	20	Sachs.-Weimar	55-0634
SIRFLING, Ernst	59	Altenburg	62-0306
SIRT, Martin	28	Regen	56-0847
SITTIG, Cath.Elis.	26	Hannover	57-0606
SITTIG, Friedrich	20	Goettingen/Ha	55-1238
SITTINGER, Julius	32	Chemnitz	55-0630
Maria 26, Dorothea 65, Agnes 36, Selma 2			
Otto 9m			
SIVORES, Andreas	43	Italy	62-0166
SIX, Friedrich	30	Meiningen	55-0634
SKALICKY, Geo.	34	Boehmen	62-1112
Therese 25, Jos. 8, Franz 6, P. 4			
Therese 2			
SLABY, Adelbert	27	Hetcan	57-0961
SLAMA, Rosalie	21	Boehmen	61-0716
SLOTEKNOEL, Heinr.	21	Blomberg/Prus	57-0847
Henriette 36			
SMEFFERS, Jacobine	17	Halden	56-0951
SMIDT, Edward	22	Neustadt	60-0411
SMIDTS, Gottfried	52	Haan	60-0411
Henriette 46, Robert 22, John 18			
Albert 16, Emma 9, Ernst 3, Hulda 2			
SMIDTS, Joh. Wilh.	22	Haan	60-0411
Anna Elise 29, Peter 45, Wilhelmine 44			
Gustav 18, Fr. Charles 10, William 7			
Bertha 4, Leopold 2m			
SMIKALLA, Elias	30	Kl.Grauden	58-0881
SMITH, Henry	50	Cincinnati	57-1148
SMITH, James	57	Boston	59-1036
SMITH, John	24	New York	61-0107
SMITH, S.H.	50	New York	62-1169
SMITH, William	29	Southampton	59-0477
SNEUING, Herm.	18	Dehnekamp	61-0167
SNIEFFERS, Jacobna	17	Halden	56-0951
SNIPP, Elise	23	Hannover	58-0925
SOBESTOM, Adolph	9	Hannover	62-1112
SOCK, Anna	21	Altenburg	61-0482
SOEDING, Caspar	61	Altenhagen	56-1216
SOEGER, Heinrich	23	Hunfeld	56-0589
SOEHL, Joh. H.	16	Beckedorf	56-0589
SOEHLKE, Georg	26	New York	59-0214
SOEHNER, Agnes	18	Walddueren	60-1032
SOEHNHOLZ, Heinr.	59	Foehren/Hann.	60-0371
Wilhelm 10			
SOELLNER, Marie	21	Soell	57-0578
SOERENSEN, Louise	20	Bremervoerde	61-0804
SOERGER, Malwine	24	Reidlingen	60-0521
SOERINSEN, Doris	20	Bremervoerde	60-0622
SOGEMEIER, August	20	Hesselteich	60-0398
SOHL, Joh.Heinrich	28	Erfurt	57-1067
SOHLKE, Louise	37	Strasburg	60-1053
SOHMS, Susanna	40	Hoffenheim	60-0398
Heinrich 12, Philipp 9, Carl 2			
SOHUPER, Ferdinand	37	Halberstadt	55-0812
SOLDAN, Maria	19	Frankenberg	57-0924
SOLL, Heinrich	23	Rendsburg	58-0881
SOLMS, Friedrich	25	Sadbergen	56-1117
SOLSCHECK, Albert	27	Berlin	62-0758
Johanna 33, Ida by			
SOLZER, Cathar.	53	Foehl	56-0413

NAME	AGE	RESIDENCE	YR-LIST
SOMMER, A.Barbara	18	Bann	60-1053
SOMMER, Carl	49	Jaegersdorf	56-0723
SOMMER, Carl	25	Esrode	61-0669
SOMMER, Chr.	23	Okarben	57-0422
SOMMER, Georg	18	Ahorn	55-0932
SOMMER, Herm.	20	Dedesdorf	58-0815
SOMMER, Johannes	36	Weiterode/CH.	60-0429
SOMMER, Maria	19	Doringstadt	57-0847
SOMMER, Maria	21	Veitlahn	62-0166
SOMMER, Nathan	22	Hildesheim	57-1026
SOMMERFELD, Christ	55	Cartzig	57-0704
Louise 54			
SOMMERFELD, Eman.	39	Liebenberg/Pr	62-0342
SOMMERFRUCHTE, C.F	26	St. Louis	61-0482
SOMMERKORN, Emil	13	Breslau	60-1161
SOMMERLOTT, Carl	70	Saalburg	59-0477
SOMMERLUTH, Carl	23	Apelern	57-1280
SOMMERMEYER, Edw.	20	Gardelegen	58-0885
SOMMERUD, H.	23	Horp	56-0512
SONDERMANN, Gust.	26	Witterod/Hess	56-0819
Christiane 29, August 9			
SONNDINGEN, Suzann	18	Landau	56-0847
SONNEMANN, Sigmund	22	Bibergen	57-1192
SONNENBERG, David	39	Fuerstenheide	57-1407
SONNENBERGER, G.	51	Friedersdorf	62-0993
SONNENTHAL, Fanny	22	Sulzbach	57-1148
SONNKALL, E.	36	Rohrbach	56-0354
SONNTAG, Carl	26	Albertshausen	59-0214
SONTAG, Franz W.	24	Attendorn	57-0606
SONTMANN, Friedr.	18	Aldorf	59-0412
SONTMANN, Ludwig	15	Ruessen	59-0412
SOORHOLDT, J.F.(m)	28	Eschum	55-0413
SOOSTEN, v. Cath.	18	Koehten	58-0815
SOOSTEN, v. Diedr.	28	New York	58-0815
SORACCO, Mich.	24	Italy	62-1042
SORENSON, Wilhelm	19	Bremerhaven	58-0885
SORG, Anna	66	Gehra	59-0535
SORG, Marie	27	Feldsteinbach	56-0279
Beata Louise 40			
SORGE, Wilhelmine	26	Bohlscheiben	60-0429
SORGER, Moritz	19	Schwarzbach	60-1032
SORRIES, Friedrich	29	Bremervoerde	57-0447
SOTTING, Martin	29	Bolanden	61-0047
Christine 23			
SOULAGNET, J.M.	30	France	62-1112
SPACULA, Jul.(m)	25	Erfurt	61-0482
SPAETH, Caroline	21	Oltens	58-0604
SPAEZECK, Ad.	33	Lemberg	57-0961
SPAHN, Bernhard	52	Brandoberndor	59-0412
SPAHN, C.(m)	24	Fuerth	61-0897
SPAHN, Georg	31	Goernheim	55-0845
SPALINGER, Jacob	20	Unterriexinge	61-0770
SPALT, Wilhelm	19	Stuttgart	56-0512
SPANGE, Cecelia	22	Brockdorf	57-1026
SPANGENBERG, Doret	21	Northeim	57-0578
Johanne 19			
SPANHAKE, An.Dorth	26	Wunstorf/Hann	57-0754
SPANNAGEL, Wilhelm	16	Minden	57-0924
SPANNER, William	30	Rotenburg	60-0411
Anna Cathar. 31			
SPANSEL, Margareta	17	Streitberg	60-0521
SPARENBERG, Wm.	19	Cappeln	57-1122
SPARER, Magdalena	29	Letza	56-1117
SPARES, Hinrich	16	Bremervoerde	57-1026
SPARK, Friedrich	24	Hall	58-0925
SPARK, Georg	21	Stromberg	56-1044
SPARKUHL, Joh.	18	Havana	59-1036
SPATECK, Ad.	39	Seelau	62-0401
SPEAR, Elias	27	Galesburg/IL	62-1112
SPECHARDT, Juliane	59	Wersau	61-0897
SPECHT, Ant.	18	Damme	57-0961
SPECHT, B.	17	Berlichingen	62-0993
SPECHT, Chr.(m)	26	Winzen	56-0723
SPECHT, Franz	44	Issum	61-0716
Catharine 32, Mathias 12, Peter 7			
William 4, Helene 9, Catharina 2			
Elisabeth 6m			
SPECHT, Heinr.(f)	39	New York	60-0521
Minna 8, Wilhelm 4, Johann 9m			
SPECHT, Heinrich	21	Ober Assber	61-0478
SPECHT, Heinrich	30	Carlsruhe	59-1017
SPECHTMAEBEL, Fr´z		Darmstadt	57-0961
(wife) , (girl)			
SPECKDER, Meta	17	Roennebeck	61-0107
SPECKER, (m)	22	Wien	58-0306
SPECKERT, Am.	29	Wagenschwend	59-0990
(f) 10			
SPECKMANN, Friedr.	16	Schinckel/Han	60-0429
SPECKMANN, Gesine	16	Amt Hagen/Han	62-0608
SPEER, Hermann	23	Guttentag	56-0847
SPEERLI, J.F.	26	Kilchberg	62-0836
SPEICHER, Maria	19	Germany	62-0467
Dumian 12			
SPEIDEL, Kumins	28	Fungingen	57-1416
SPEITLE, Catharine	20	Lauffen	62-1112
SPELINA, Joseph	38	Strizorin	61-0779
Magdalena 25, Joseph by			
SPELLMEYER, Heinr.	15	Blasheim/Pr.	55-0628
Dorothea 17			
SPELLMEYER, Rud.	28	Lotte	62-0467
Cath. 28, Sophia 11m			
SPELMEYER, Elisab.	20	Harlinghausen	56-0589
SPENCE, R.G.	28	England	62-0938
SPENGLER, Arnold	49	Kirchberg	55-0630
Anna 42, Bernhard 18, Georg 7, Anna 2			
SPENGLER, Georg	38	Gerhardsofen	61-0478
Margaretha 35, Kunigunda 9			
SPENGLER, Joh.	19	Auendorf	59-0535
SPENGLER, Juliane	20	Echzell	60-0785
SPENGLER, Wm.	23	Arheilgen	60-0785
SPENNEBERG, Melch.	32	Cincinnati	59-0412
SPENNESBERGER, Jos	29	Mennichen	58-0399
Magdalene 32			
SPERBER, Kunigunda	20	Lossbergsger.	60-1053
Joh.Gerhard 28			
SPERD, Sybilla	36	Kuntzhausen	59-0047
Anna S. 13			
SPERFLAEGE, Heinr.	50	Watbergen	56-0527
SPERLING, Aug.	19	Sheboygan	58-0604
SPERLING, Friedr.	20	Cheboyan	57-0422
SPERLING, Johann	43	Nadelwitz	61-0930
SPERLING, Joseph	57	Boehmen	60-0411
Franziska 55, Maximilian 2, Adolph 9m			
Sophie 29, Therese 16			
SPERLING, Therese	27	Magdeburg	59-0477
Anna 2, Robert 4m			
SPERS, Johann	18	Helfenberg	62-0879
SPERTZEL, Georg	37	Mottgens	58-0881
Gertrud 7			
SPERZEL, Anna	35	Mottgers/Curh	60-0429
Joh.Georg 11, Margaretha 9			
SPETH, Jos. Anton	29	Engenberg/Bav	60-0622
Marie 29, Johan Anton 8			
SPEWACEK, Ant.	35	Belvecky	57-1148
Anna 39, Franz 5, John 3			
SPEWACEK, Fz.	38	Leschau	57-1148
Ludmilla 33, Mary 9, Joseph 8, Anna 6			
SPEYER, Carl	37	Mahle	55-0845
SPICKER, August	33	New York	61-0716
SPICKER, Friedrich	31	Cassel	61-0930
SPICKHARDT, Marie	40	Haila/Hess.	61-0770
Jacob 15			
SPIECHER, Carl	18	Sachsa/Pruss.	57-0924
SPIECIS, Georg	29	New York	58-0815
SPIEGEL, Augusta	36	Helminghausen	59-0613
Sophia 2			
SPIEGEL, Martin	35	Wickels	56-0819
Joseph 32			
SPIEGEL, Moritz	20	Schoenbuch	56-1044
SPIEGEL, Rosine	29	Laibach	61-0478
SPIEKER, Louise	58	Posen	59-0412
Justine 23			
SPIER, Anna Barb.	50	Cassel	55-0634
Andreas 21			
SPIER, D.(m)	23	Wittelsberg	62-0730
SPIER, Ernst	25	Suedthorsten	60-0622

NAME	AGE	RESIDENCE	YR-LIST
Carl 20			
SPIER, Lowy (m)	14	Wittelsberg	60-0334
SPIER, Marcus	19	Willinghausen	62-0712
SPIES, H.	64	Germany	59-1036
A.L. 62, M. 8			
SPIETH, Augusta S.	22	Esslingen/Wrt	60-0622
SPILKER, August	24	Nedelstedt	57-1280
SPILKER, Charles	19	Baltimore	62-0111
SPILLE, Joh.Derric	35	Fiebing	57-0422
SPILLING, Barb.	48	Marburg	59-0384
Dorothea 18, Jacob 15			
SPINDLER, August	27	Saalburg	59-0477
Heinrich 59, Johanna 55, Franzisca 17			
Louise 9			
SPINDLER, Augusta	16	Gampertshause	61-0682
Sophia 27			
SPINDLER, Fr.(m)	23	Dalhausen	61-1132
SPINDLER, Julius	19	Hofgeismar	59-0951
SPINDLER, Otto	42	Cassel	62-0001
SPINDLER, Wm.	35	Saalburg	62-0467
Christine 35, Anna 13, Ida 9, Wm. 3			
Lina 9m			
SPINTER, Daniel	62	Blegow/Pruss.	61-0770
Charlotte 67			
SPIRO, Moritz	15	Bromberg	56-0723
SPITTEL, Fr. A.	32	Molsdorf	56-0589
Joh.Wilh'mne 31			
SPITTLER, Joh.N.	18	Schwarzburk	59-0951
SPITZBARTH, Adolph	38	Marseille	60-0429
SPITZER, J.G.(m)	27	Muenchen	62-0166
SPLAUER, Rieke	18	Burgkundstadt	60-0521
SPLITTGERBER, Erns	30	Buden/Posen	57-0654
Henriette 28, Julianne 5, Wilhelmine 3			
Michel 58			
SPLITZEN, Marie	19	Debstedt	58-0885
SPOCK, Chr.	30	Ostheim/Weim.	62-0608
Ottilie 36			
SPOELBRING, Wm.	22	Osnabrueck	62-0342
SPOERER, Friedrich	54	Ritterhude	56-0413
Louise 30			
SPOERL, Nicl.	27	Naila	62-0730
SPOHLER, Anna	19	Niederort	56-0819
SPOHR, Fr.(m)	45	Hameln	62-0467
Emil 22			
SPOHS, Hermann	21	Aerzen	60-0785
SPOLK, Heinrich	24	Stromberg	56-1044
SPORLEDER, August	24	Holzminden	57-0606
SPORLEDER, Augusta	15	Hannover	59-0384
SPORNHEIMER, Elis.	35	Staudenheim	62-0467
Heinr. 17			
SPORTGEN, Herm.	29	Asperheide	61-0716
Marie 22, Heinr. 2, Catha. 3m			
SPREEN, Carl	48	Grossendorf	59-0951
Engel 48			
SPREEN, Joh.	19	Oppendorf	60-0521
SPREEN, Sophie	19	Gressendorf	59-0535
SPREEN, Wilhelmine	19	Rahden	57-1280
Dorette 16			
SPRENGEMANN, J.	55	Buende	60-0334
Wilhelm 22			
SPRENGER, J.J.	37	Lancaster	62-0730
Catharine 34, Emma 13, Carl 7, Frank 4			
Marschall 2			
SPRENGER, Margaret	24	Oldendorf	60-0521
SPRENGMANN, Wilh.	18	Buenden	56-1011
SPREUER, Joh.	27	Aschenbach	60-0334
SPRINDEL, Julius	22	Ludwigsburg	61-0897
SPRING, Ernst	29	Hohensalza	61-0482
SPRING, Therese	19	Dietelsheim	61-0482
SPRINGER, Heinrich	28	Oldenburg	58-0815
SPRINGER, Therese	22	Michelsdorf	55-0932
SPRINGER, Ursula	25	Langenau	59-0384
SPRINGMEYER, Aug.	18	Dissen	57-0422
Christina 50, Charlotte 9			
SPRUCK, Hagolin	20	Markenzell	62-0712
SPRUNG, Charles	33	Berlin	57-0654
SPRUNG, W.	45	Boehmen	62-1112
Franziska 43, Anton 21, Joseph 19			
Franz 17, Wenzel 12, Petronella 9			
Marie 6, Victoria 4, Alois 9m			
SPUCK, Catharine	59	Roedchen	57-0924
Wilhelm 23, Ludwig 32, Catharine 25			
Heinrich 5, Wilhelm 1, Heinrich 30			
Elisa 28, Ludwig 6, Dorothea 4			
SPUCK, Dorothee	25	Raetchen	56-0527
SPUERING, Heinrich	20	Thedinghausen	57-0606
STAAB, Barbara	26	Cassel/Hessen	55-0628
STAAB, Conrad	24	Hoesbach	60-1053
STAACK, Aug.	16	Bremerhafen	59-1036
STAATS, Bertha	27	Wolfenbuettel	62-0608
Marie 2			
STAATS, H.C.	15	Hahlen	62-0938
STABEL, Ch.(m)	23	Bingen	61-0482
STABEVAN, Julius	24	Laubach	57-1122
STABUS, Conrad	24	Schifenbach	58-0399
STACHELIN, C.	38	US.	62-1042
Mrs. 30, Theresa 10, Jacob 6, Sophie 3			
Martha 23			
STACHNOTH, L.(m)	22	New York	61-0897
Emil 4			
STADE, Friedericke	21	Oberweimar	56-0589
STADEN, v.Rebecca	20	Bremervoerde	61-0804
STADER, Philipp	40	Lenn	58-0604
Christine 40			
STADLER, Dorothea	26	Stuttgart	56-0527
Joseph 17			
STADLER, Heinrich	29	Canada	62-0342
STADTHOFF, Alb.	56	Schuerum	57-0422
Mary 45, Harm 19, Werner 18, Gesche 16			
Bernarda 14, Hoja 11, Hemke 8, Albert 4			
STAEBLER, L.(m)	27	Lauffen	62-0730
STAEHLER, Wm.	25	Wetzlar	59-0477
STAEMPFLE, Johanna	20	Schelhausen	62-1169
STAERKER, J.A.	42	Baltimore	61-0804
STAETZ, Joh.G.	45	Ploching	59-0214
Catharina 43			
STAFFEHL, Charles	36	Westen	57-1192
Charlotte 26			
STAGGENBURG, Berta	30	New York	59-0951
Bertha 5, Henry 3, Henriette 2			
STAHL, Cath.	23	Worms	61-0897
STAHL, Georg	27	Rothenburg/Bv	55-0628
STAHL, Sebastian	30	Wulmeister	55-1082
STAHLHUT, Charlott	26	Meibosen	62-0401
Ferdinand 16			
STAHLHUT, Friedr.	19	Windheim	58-0545
STAHLMANN, Chrstne	19	Bielefeld	60-0429
STAIGER, Marie	30	Endingen	61-0482
STAKENSKY, Alex.	20	Dresden	62-0730
STALLFORTH, Alfred	19	Herford	56-1117
STALLFORTH, Bernh.	20	Bremen	62-0758
STALMANN, Jakobine	32	Cassel	57-1280
Fritz 9m			
STAMM, Heinrich	23	Michelau	56-0413
STAMM, Leonh.	27	Altershausen	59-0535
STAMM, Rika	23	Herlinghausen	61-0779
STAMM, William	23	New York	60-0411
STANG, Georg	35	Bugenau	57-0704
Elisabeth 37, Maria Elisb. 7			
STANG, Georg A.	28	Berlin	60-1053
STANG, Georg A.	18	Tuttlingen	59-0214
STANG, H.(m)	19	Marburg	61-0482
STANG, Marie	22	Heinboldshsn.	55-0538
STANGE, Carl Fr.	57	Detroit	59-0214
STANGE, Heinrich D	16	Lehe	59-0613
STANSELL, H.(m)	41	England	60-0521
STAPP, Philip	46	Goetzenhein	60-0429
Margaretha 19, Elisabeth 15, Friedrich 12			
Philip 10			
STARCK, William	40	Strassburg	57-0961
Willemina 33, Hermina 3, Armand 2			
STARCKE, John H.	24	Mugeln	56-0550
STARK, Carl	31	Jena	58-0925
STARK, Fanny	19	Ermelshofen	62-0467
STARK, Franziska	19	Erfurt/Pr.	60-0622
STARK, G.W.	28	Schwarzenbach	55-0932

NAME	AGE	RESIDENCE	YR-LIST
STARK, Meinholf	23	Hegenstorf	55-0630
STARK, Otto	19	Biebrich	59-0990
STARKE, C.H.(m)	22	Leipzig	57-0080
STARKE, Carl	30	Ansbach	56-0723
STARKE, Carl Juls.	23	Schlettau/S.	60-0429
Fr'dke.Chrst 23, Paulne.Selma 11m			
STARKEBECK, Heinr.	46	Salzuffeln	57-1416
STARKIE, Maria A.	20	England	60-1196
STARY, J.	37	Nemschuetz	62-0993
C. 35, A. 5, W. 3, A. 2m			
STASASTA, Johann	40	Prague	60-0052
Barbara 27, Antonia 27, Franz 3, Anna 6m			
STASCHMANN, Franz	22	Lienen	60-0334
STASNY, Johann	44	Boehmen	62-0758
STASSEN, Babette	17	Bavaria	59-0214
STASSMEIER, Friedr	28	Lippe-Detmold	58-0399
STATTBERG, Gottfr.	49	Burgstadt	56-1216
Doroth. 29, Friedr. 9m			
STATZENBERG, M.	53	Miess	59-0613
STAUBITZ, Andr.	33	Wittelsberg	61-0804
STAUBITZ, R.	19	Niederweimar	57-1192
Elisabeth 23			
STAUCH, August	17	Wildberg	56-1117
STAUCH, Caroline	26	Wien	57-0918
STAUCH, Martin	36	Trautheim/Bad	60-0622
STAUDER, Carl	30	New York	62-0467
Caroline 32, Heinrich 4, Minna 11m			
STAUDTER, Franz'ka	32	Weibersbrunn	60-1053
STAUTE, Louis	16	Altenburg	59-1036
STAUTZ, Elisabeth	19	Eufingen	59-0384
STAUTZ, J.Philipp	47	Eufingen	59-0384
Sophia 47			
STEB, Victoria	23	Deggingen	62-0879
STECH, Johann	35	Grodmada	56-0411
Louise 28, Wilhelmine 11m			
STECHER, Conrad	49	New York	59-0214
Anna Maria 26, Johannes 3			
STECK, Heinrich	18	Sandheim	56-0411
STECKEL, Fried.	26	New York	62-1112
STECKET, Elisabeth	21	Henneberg	57-1122
STECKNER, Franz	23	Luetzen	57-1067
STEDEROTH, Fr'dke.	22	Nentershausen	60-0533
Wilhelmine 20			
STEEB, J.M.	18	Elpersheim	59-0990
STEEECK, P.	37	Brooklyn	62-0836
Anna 37, Georg 2, Anna 6m			
STEEGE, Ferdinand	28	Alt Barkoczyn	61-0779
STEEGMANN, (f)	38	Cassel	61-0897
STEEGRAFE, Ad.	25	Vegesack	62-1169
STEEHRS, H.(m)	40	New York	62-0730
John 9			
STEEMANN, Heinrich	39	New York	58-0925
STEENCKEN, Johann	17	Hannover	58-0545
STEENKEN, A.(m)	24	New York	61-0167
STEFANI, Joseph	29	Italy	59-0613
STEFFEL, Heinrich	52	Sauerhof	56-1044
STEFFEL, Maria	16	Hadacke	61-0779
STEFFEN, Ad.	46	Leichlingen	57-1192
Anna 44, Augustine 18, Mathilde 14			
Hulda 4, Ernst 9m			
STEFFEN, Carl Fr.	27	Philippshof	62-0608
Friedrike 27, Johanna 6m			
STEFFEN, Carst.	16	Gestenseht	56-1117
STEFFEN, Mina	19	Ansbach	58-0925
STEFFEN, Wilhelm	39	Philadelphia	62-0938
STEFFENS, A.H.	36	New York	62-0836
Fr.(f) 30			
STEFFENS, Joh.	38	Zeven	59-0535
STEFFENS, Johann	31	Koblenz/Main	56-0632
STEFFENS, Lisette	21	Bremervoerde	60-0622
STEFFENS, Margreta	52	Otterndorf	62-0712
STEGE, Fr.H.	25	New York	61-0804
STEGEL, Anna	31	Soegel	60-1141
STEGHERR, Xaver	24	Hafenhoven	60-0533
STEGMANN, Caroline	23	Halle	60-0334
Emilie 23			
STEGMUELLER, Herm.	23	Braunschweig	59-0477
STEHLING, Therese	31	Schoenfeld	61-1054

NAME	AGE	RESIDENCE	YR-LIST
STEIDEL, Anton	30	Altenburg	55-0845
STEIDEL, Georg	30	Wien/Aus.	55-0538
STEIFF, Louise	29	Leidorf	59-1036
STEIFF, Philippine	22	Leidorf	59-1036
STEIGER, Carl	17	Gaunerichheim	62-1112
STEIGER, Fr.	31	Spielberg	60-1161
Maria 22			
STEIL, Cath.	24	New York	62-0467
Anna 3, George 9m			
STEIL, Henry			61-1132
STEILER, Georg	20	Driftsethe	59-0951
STEIN, Abraham	70	Neu Pekal A	58-0815
STEIN, Anna Gert'd	21	Curhessen	55-0634
Heinrich 20			
STEIN, Anna Marie	18	Darmstadt	57-0654
STEIN, Bertha	15	Schwanfeld	56-1216
STEIN, Carl	34	Frankfurt	59-0477
Kunigunde 34, Ot. 5			
STEIN, Caroline	27	Schlieben	60-0533
STEIN, Cath. Elis.	24	Eisenach	59-0372
STEIN, Cath.Elise	14	Gerstungen	57-1067
STEIN, Catharina	22	Bernsburg/Hes	60-0371
STEIN, Friedrich	27	Wiederau	59-0535
STEIN, Hirsch	19	Hintersteinau	60-0785
STEIN, Israel	14	Schweinshaupt	60-0622
STEIN, Peter	60	New York	62-1112
Mrs. 58			
STEIN, Rosette	18	Strassburg	58-0306
STEINBACH, A.	37	Evansville	62-0938
STEINBACH, E.	38	New York	62-1042
STEINBACH, M.(m)	52	England	61-1132
STEINBACH, Sara	29	Privosten	59-1036
STEINBECK, Franz H	25	Preussen	56-1044
STEINBERG, Friedr.	18	Rawicz	62-0938
STEINBERG, Helene	18	Wetter	56-0629
STEINBOCHS, Elise	19	Wilmershaim	56-0512
STEINBOCK, August	32	Sachsen	59-0412
STEINBORN, Lewis	52	Oldendorf	57-0422
Louisa 55			
STEINBRENNER, Rosa	19	New York	59-0535
STEINBRING, Johana	16	Berlin	56-0847
Rosina 38			
STEINBRINK, Christ	26	Hohenebra	59-0477
STEINBUEGEL, Georg	18	Relenbach	57-0447
STEINDL, Johann	35	Margarethen	57-0850
Maria 40, Joseph 2, Aloise 3m			
STEINEBACH, Jacob	32	Bremen	56-0819
Heinrich 26			
STEINECKE, Johann	44	Caldorf/Lippe	55-1238
Louise 24			
STEINER, Elise	58	Koenigswart	61-0716
STEINER, Heinrich	15	Ludwigsburg	59-0951
STEINER, Johann	33	Baiern	57-0606
STEINER, Louise	25	Amoesgrund	58-0815
STEINER, Tobias	32	Wuerzburg	59-0372
STEINER, Wm.	24	Koenigswart	61-0716
STEINERNAGEL, Anna	28	Eidorf	57-0447
STEINERT, Anna	26	Neumark/Bav.	55-0628
STEINERT, Franz	28	Duderstadt	57-0606
STEINHAEUSER, Jete	20	Burgkundstadt	61-0482
STEINHAEUSER, Wm.	11	Stuttgart	57-1067
Adolph 27			
STEINHAUER, Georg	25	Erdmannrode	57-1067
STEINHAUER, John	26	Heyna	60-0411
STEINHAUER, Marie	54	Falkenberg	59-0990
STEINHAUER, Sebald	30	Aulendorf	57-0509
STEINHAUS, Joh.	20	Volkershausen	57-1026
STEINHEIM, Mariane	18	Heiligefeld	58-0815
STEINHOF, Christ.	36	Osterbruch	55-0630
Wilhelmine 30, Christine 9m			
STEINHOFF, Chr.	36	Sudheim	62-0401
Helene 37, Heinr. 9, Caroline 8			
Augusta 4, Johanna 2, August 6m			
STEINHOFF, Eden	32	Ackum	60-1141
Mary 27, Bernhard 5, Lisette 4			
STEINKAMP, Christ.	50	Lefer	57-1280
Wilhelmine 47, Louise 18, Friederike 15			
Charlotte 13			

NAME	AGE	RESIDENCE	YR-LIST
STEINKAMP, Gerard	24	Schuettorf	57-0422
STEINKE, Friedrich	36	Wittlohs	56-0629
Margaretha 28, Heinrich 7, Magdalena 6			
Friedrich 3, Dorothea 3m			
STEINKE, Georg	28	Breitenbronn	56-1117
STEINLE, Louise	21	Laufen/Wuertt	60-0429
Catharine 20			
STEINLEIN, Wilh.	22	Frankfurt	59-1036
STEINMETZ, J.C.	20	Grebenstein	62-0836
STEINMETZ, Johann	19	Curhessen	58-0399
STEINMETZ, Joseph	27	Gotha	61-0930
STEINMETZ, Magd.	25	Wachbach	59-0990
STEINMETZ, Maria	22	Eiterhagen	57-0754
STEINMETZ, Marta E	19	Altendorf	57-0754
STEINMETZ, Max	31	Philadelphia	59-1036
STEINMETZ, Wilhelm	32	Altenbruch	61-0682
STEINMEYER, H.(m)	26	Schoettmar	57-0422
STEINMEYER, H.(m)	16	Bremen	61-0682
STEINMEYER, Heinr.	18	Bremen	57-0447
STEINMEYER, Henry	34	St.Louis	57-1148
Mary 30, Christiane 11m			
STEINMEYER, Robert	20	Reutlingen	60-1141
STEINNGER, Jul.	16	Borrauh	56-1044
STEINORG, Ernst Em	35	Osnabrueck	55-0634
STEINRICHTER, Mary	20	Pfaffenburg	56-0847
STEINWARTE, Christ	30	Finhorst	57-1192
Dor. 53, Sophia 21, Louise 23			
STEINWEDEL, Betty	19	Spaden	56-0413
STEINWEG, S.(m)	19	Borgentreich	62-0467
STEIS, Margaretha	25	Chiffdorf	57-1192
STEISE, Clara	30	Albertloh	58-0604
STEITZ, Heinrich	28	Stamheim	57-1067
Elisabeth 26			
STELGES, Trina	20	Nortwede	57-1122
STELL, Anna	23	Sompla	56-0847
STELLERICH, Joh.	24	Hochstadt	59-0384
STELLING, Fr.	27	New York	62-1042
STELLING, Fz.	22	Helmstedt	57-1192
STELLING, Jette	22	Culmberg	62-0730
STELLJES, J.H.	30	New York	62-0836
Adelheid 27, Johann(died) 9m			
STELLJES, Meta	18	Hannover	58-0545
STELTER, Johann	22	Drahnow	58-0576
Wilhelm 24			
STELZ, Joh.	20	Leidhecken	57-1192
STELZ, Johannes	16	Florstadt	57-1192
STELZLE, Franz	25	Meinzingen	60-0334
STELZNER, Carl	37	Chemnitz	55-0845
STEMMER, Franz	29	Ratzenried	62-0938
STEMMERIG, B.	22	Nordwalde	58-0604
STEMMERMANN, Mart.	19	Apelern	56-1260
STEMMERMANN, Math.	18	Koehlen	56-1117
STENDER, Alois	17	Wernigerode	57-0447
STENECK, Martin	31	New York	62-0608
STENGELE, Joseph	23	Worndorf/Bav.	60-0622
STENGELIN, Jos.	26	Siebeldingen	62-0111
STENMANN, Bernhard	27	Albertloh	58-0604
STENNER, Fr.(m)	23	Orenstaedt	62-0401
STENNESBERGER, Jos	29	Mennichen	58-0399
Magdalene 32			
STENSCHEL, Julius	20	Breslau	56-1216
STENZEL, Emil	35	Othmarchau	57-0918
STEPANOWSKY, Mart.	42	Borek	61-0779
Barbara 33, Wenzel 9, Joseph 8			
Adalbert 4, Maria by			
STEPHAN, Anna	43	Amberg	61-0482
STEPHAN, Fr.	23	Lukbach	57-1416
STEPHAN, J.R.		New York	59-0613
STEPHANEK, Fr.	49	Jenositz	57-0961
Catharina 40, Mary 20, Catharina 6			
Antonia 4, Joseph 9, Anton 8			
STEPHEN, Heinrich	38	Cincinnati	62-0608
Anna 21			
STEPHENS, L.(m)	30	England	60-0334
STEPHENS, Maria	19	Luxem/Pr.	55-1238
STERLING, J.C.	20	Watertown	62-0938
STERN, Abraham	15	Prag	57-1192
STERN, Babette	24	Friesenhausen	62-0467

NAME	AGE	RESIDENCE	YR-LIST
STERN, Betti	22	Barhaven	60-0785
STERN, Carl	15	Schoenewald	56-0951
STERN, Eva	60	Landorf	59-0951
STERN, Fanny	40	Feuerbach	60-0785
STERN, Ferdinand	26	Attendorf	59-0951
Meyer 15			
STERN, Haehnlein	15	Teckenbart	60-0785
STERN, Heinrich	26	Sternbach	57-0365
STERN, Helene	29	Ruemmelsheim	60-0785
Charlotte 28			
STERN, Hirsch	19	Hintersteinau	60-0785
STERN, Isack	18	Gemuenden	58-0399
STERN, Jethe	24	Schluchtern	58-0604
STERN, Jette	24	Antenhausen	60-0785
STERN, Johanna	21	Baden	56-0847
STERN, Johannes	18	Oberehen	57-1122
STERN, Koppel	19	Rotenkirchen	60-0785
Betti 22			
STERN, L.Herm.	25	Melle	57-1192
STERN, Lazarus	20	Sommerhausen	58-0306
STERN, Sophie	24	Cochau	59-1017
Lotte 32			
STERN, Wolff.	23	Klatenbach	60-0398
STERNBERG, Johanna	19	Lauberzechbch	62-0730
STERNDORFF, Haje L	36	Norden	57-1067
STERNHEIMER, Benj.	59	Hainstadt	61-0716
Amalie 58, Johanna 22			
STERNKAMP, Joh.T.	27	Ascheberg	59-0214
(wife) 28			
STEU, Jeanette	34	Schwitz	62-0467
STEUBER, Armand	28	Steinbruecken	57-0961
STEUBER, David	17	Bromokirchon	62-0879
Elisabeth 15			
STEUBER, Joh.Peter		Oberklee	57-1067
STEUDTEN, J.G.	53	Wechselburg	55-0932
STEUERER, Conrad	24	Baden	60-1196
Louis 19, Wendelina 54			
STEURER, Ernst	32	Anstbach	60-1032
STEVENS, Ed.	31	England	62-1112
Charles 8			
STEWENER, Carl Aug	17	Melle	56-0819
Carol.Charlt 15			
STEYBE, Jacob	27	Isny	61-0482
STIBIL, Johann	39	Allighang	58-0885
STICH, Barbara	58	Ostereiffel	62-0712
Catharina 22, Anna Maria 32, Maria 4			
STICH, Casp.	35	Flossenberg	60-0521
Marg. 30, Elisabeth 6, (daughter) 6m			
STICH, Franz Leop.	24	Zerbst	60-0398
STICKAU, Friedr.	23	Desdel	60-0521
STIEBITZ, Carl	18	Poppendorf	55-0932
STIEFEL, Hefe	54	Abterode	62-1112
STIEFEL, Sarchen	16	Vockerode	56-0819
STIEGAST, Ph.(m)	20	Lippe-Detmold	57-0555
STIEGLITZ, Andreas	36	Aldersheim/Bv	56-0632
Marie 18			
STIEGLITZ, Marcus	34	New York	57-0918
Sara 28, Henriette 6, Nathan 4, Louis 2			
Franziska 8m			
STIEL, Justus Conr	15	Rauscheberg	62-0342
STIELER, Heinrich	15	Fielingen	57-0924
STIEMANN, Henr.	39	New York	59-1036
STIEMER, Fr.	19	Suhl	56-0512
Christiane 16			
STIER, Bernhard C.	44	Obernmehler	56-0951
STIER, Christine	21	Kleinmehlsa	62-0166
STIER, Georg	33	Obermehler	57-0924
Bertha Frdke 27, Pauline 5, Louis 2			
STIERING, Sophie	14	Sueste	57-1148
STIERING, Wilhelm	21	Asmushausen	56-0629
STIETZ, Louise	52	Hubenrade	61-0682
Elise 21, Elisabeth 19, Maria 10			
STIEVEMANN, B.(m)	35	New York	62-0730
STIFT, Ernst	18	Ringleben	61-0482
STIHLO, Fritz	30	Rattig	57-0776
Friederike 26			
STIKA, Johann	39	Tankow	55-0845
Catharina 39, Maria 17, Joseph 14			

NAME	AGE	RESIDENCE	YR-LIST
Barbara 11, Anna 9, Catharine 7, Franz 3			
Johann 1			
STIKLING, zum Cath	50	Werel	61-0804
Heinr. 18			
STILLEMUNKES, C.	19	Urweiler	62-0111
STILLER, Richard	29	Bertsdorf	55-0932
Johanne 29, Paulus 9m, Robert 3			
STILZING, Ernst	15	Rothenburg	57-0436
STIPP, Fz.	18	Rheine	57-1192
STOBAEUS, Babette	40	Melrichstadt	58-0885
Pauline 16			
STOCK, Anna Marie	21	Grebenau	56-0632
Peter 5			
STOCK, Carl	51	Windheim	60-0533
Sophie 51, Lisette 15			
STOCK, Catharine	21	Cramfeld	58-0306
STOCK, Christine	20	Leteln	57-1067
STOCK, Franz	44	Lanersville	58-0604
(wife) 43			
STOCK, Friedrich	22	Bixfeld/Curh.	60-0622
STOCK, Fritz	25	Detmold	61-0779
STOCK, Henriette	24		59-0613
STOCK, Hermann	36	Hohenhausen	56-0632
Sophie 46			
STOCK, Johanna	58	Fritzlar	57-1192
Wilhelmine 22, Catharina 20, Caroline 16			
Christine 18			
STOCK, Johanne	60	Hameln	60-0785
STOCK, Leonhardt	27	Storndorf/CH.	60-0622
STOCK, Ludwig	22	Storndorf	55-0413
STOCK, Maria Elisb	34	Sorgenzell	62-0306
STOCK, Philipp	25	Lemgo/Lippe	62-0608
STOCK, Theodor	26	St.Louis	58-0815
Sophie 30, Carl 7, (dau.) bob			
STOCK, Wilhelm	20	St.Annen	57-0447
STOCKBRANDT, Ernst	28	Lenstrup	57-0447
STOCKE, Franz	31	Dirnstein	60-0521
STOCKER, Ludwig	18	Wuerttemberg	60-0411
STOCKER, Max	20	Linz	60-0521
STOCKHAUSEN, R.		Deutz	59-0613
STOCKMANN, Fr'drke	19	Uslar/Hann.	62-0608
STOCKMANN, Fr.	21	Ostenholz	58-0563
STOEBENER, Carolne	18	Moenchshof	56-0847
STOEBER, Johann	15	Lindhorst	61-0520
STOECKICH, Erdmann	27	Kraftsdorf	62-0879
STOECKING, Anna	20	Magdeburg/Pr.	55-0538
STOECKLER, Carl	23	Rothenburg	57-0436
STOECKMANN, Chr.	41	Benhorn	58-0563
Marie 36, Friedrich 13, Christoph 6			
Dietrich 5			
STOECKMANN, Heinr.	26	Heinhorst	60-0533
STOEHR, August	15	Glashuetten	57-0436
STOEHR, Christoph	35	Obergeis	56-0819
Anna Maria 27, Elisa 7, Heinrich 6			
Nicolaus 4, Anna Barb. 11m			
STOEHR, Franz	34	Goessweinstn.	59-0990
STOEHR, Georg	28	Luetzelsachse	62-1169
STOEKKER, Monika	56	Moehlingen	57-0436
Martha 30, Gottlieb 28, Catharina 22			
Joseph 20			
STOELZING, Georg T	20	Rothenburg	57-0436
Wilhelmine 28			
STOEPS, Alwine	26	Munchenbernsd	60-0785
STOER, August	24	Boston	60-0411
STOERDE, Herm.	32	Berlin	62-0730
STOERMER, Marg.	21	Poppenhausen	59-0384
STOERNER, George	26	Londerstadt	60-1141
STOERR, Paul	30	Leutkirch/Wrt	60-0622
STOEVE, A.D.(m)	25	Berge	62-0401
STOEVE, Herm.	32	Berlin	62-0730
STOEWAKS, Chr.	36	New York	62-0730
Marie 20			
STOFFELS, Gertrude	24	Apendorn	58-0306
Johann 20, Elisabeth 17, Maria 15			
Mathilde 12, Johann 7			
STOFFELS, Heinrich	55	Appendoorm	58-0306
Mrs. 53, Franz 25			
STOFFT, Elisabeth	22	Coelln	59-0048
STOFLE, W.	39	Berlin	56-1216
STOH, Wilhelmine	22	Arolsen	62-0730
STOHMANN, Meta	19	Leeste	62-0836
STOLD, Carl	18	Carlshafen	59-0214
STOLDT, Gust.	21	Detroit	56-1216
STOLL, Carl	23	Baden	62-0467
Anne 51			
STOLL, F.	27	Arnswalde	57-1192
STOLL, Franz	24	Ellweiler	59-0384
Caroline 3			
STOLL, Georg	22	Lauterbach	58-0545
STOLL, Johann	42	Geroldshausen	61-0478
STOLL, Otto	28	Marienwerder	57-0654
STOLLBERG, August		Eisleben	57-0021
STOLLMYER, Engel	52	Cappeln	57-1122
Anna 16			
STOLTER, Fr.(m)	36	Prokesch	60-1161
Anna 59, Caroline 20			
STOLZ, Friedrich	43	Posen	57-0776
STOLZ, Gottf.Fr.	16	Auendorf	59-0535
STOLZ, John	55	Vienna	56-1011
Julia 23			
STOLZE, Eduard	34	Ringleben	60-0533
STOLZING, Maria	26	Rothenburg	60-0398
STOMDICK, Wm.	42	St.Louis	59-0477
Marie 46			
STORCK, Augusta	16	Bielefeld	62-0879
Julius 14			
STORCK, Marie	16	Wallenrod	62-0879
Catharine 19			
STORR, Eva	43	Echingen	62-0232
STORR, Wilh.	31	Ehningen	56-1216
STORZ, Christian	24	Osnabrueck	60-1032
Conrad 23			
STOTZ, Fr. H.	24	Weimar	55-0932
Frieda 18			
STOTZ, Gottl.	37	Duerrewangen	59-0384
STOTZER, Liborius	29	Oberlauringen	57-0422
Cunigunde 35, Anna 15			
STOULT, Sophie	45	New York	62-0938
Henry 8			
STOVE, R.	27	Remscheid	62-1169
STOY, Ferd.	25	Dornberg	62-1042
STRABAL, Joh.	40	Lossina	57-1113
Magdalena 37, Martin 11, Joseph 8			
Marie 4, Wenzel 9m			
STRACK, Albert	26	Arolsen	57-1192
(f) 25			
STRACK, Dor.	23	Arolsen	57-1192
STRACK, Fanny	23	Michelsen	56-0847
STRADSMANN, August	16	Roedinghausen	60-0334
STRADTMANN, Joh.H.	31	Henderson	62-0879
Catharine 32			
STRAEHLE, J.G.	18	Aldingen	62-0993
STRAHM, Michael	24	Krassingen	60-0998
Margueritt 24			
STRANG, Johanna	28	Oberstedt	61-0478
Friedricke 3, Louise 6m			
STRANG, Mar.Magd.	20	Oberstedt	61-0478
STRASS, Caroline	19	Schoenlind	60-0785
STRASS, Moritz	18	Schoenlind	56-0951
STRASSBURGER,	24	New York	59-0951
STRASSER, Aloys	45	Augsburg	57-1280
Amalia 52			
STRASSMANN, H.(m)	40	Dedesdorf	62-0232
STRATE, Gerh.	24	Oelde	58-0306
STRATER, Heinrich	24	Boston	58-0815
Jose. 22			
STRATHAUS, Chr.	36	Langenberg	60-0521
STRATHEMANN, Wilh.	24	Roedinghausen	56-1011
Friedrich 17			
STRATHO, Max	30	Paderborn	61-0047
STRATMANN, Adelh.	25	Gilhausen	57-1148
STRATMEYER, Johann	57	Sullingen	61-0482
STRAUBE, Just.	21	Stotterheim	57-0961
STRAUBEL, Albert	15	Saalfeld	60-0398
STRAUCH, Carl	20	Herstelle	56-0589
Anne 18			

NAME	AGE	RESIDENCE	YR-LIST
STRAUCH, Johannes	44	Trauenheim/He	62-0608
STRAUCH, Louis	21	Oelde	58-0306
STRAUCH, Maria	49	Herstelle/Pr.	55-1238
Louise 24			
STRAUL, Michael	59	Reinrod	59-1036
Elise 35, (baby) 9m			
STRAUS, Mateus	45	Bolsingen	57-1280
Maria 45, Michel 12, Maria 9			
STRAUSS, A.(m)	21	Obersemen	62-0836
Ester 55, Betty 26			
STRAUSS, Abraham	44	Riedesheim	61-0047
STRAUSS, Abraham	53	Runkel	57-1026
Hirsch 18, Ester 19			
STRAUSS, Elka	25	Storndorf	62-0879
STRAUSS, Friedrike		Bederkese/Han	60-0622
Margareth 21			
STRAUSS, Helena	25	Hanau	60-0398
STRAUSS, Johanna	38	Louisville	62-1112
STRAUSS, Leopold	19	Pilsen	59-0214
STRAUSS, Moses	19	Eckertrode	60-0398
STRAUSS, Oscar	34	Breslau	59-0384
STRAUSS, Philippin	28	Berchholtheim	60-0785
STRAUSS, Salma	23	Storndorf	62-0879
STRAUSS, Samuel	18	Naples	60-0785
STRAUSS, Sophie	18	Assmannshsn.	56-1044
Elisabeth 15			
STRAUSS, Wilh'mine	24	Festenberg	56-1117
STRAUSZ, Aaron	19	Ndr.Wellstedt	57-1280
STRECKFUSS, Heinr.	26	Bremen	59-0951
STREEP, Conrad	26	Magdeburg	58-0576
Catharine 21			
STREHL, Gustavus	34	Frankfurt	57-0422
A.Mary 27			
STREICHER, Zachar.	27	Wuertt.	55-0634
Adam 25, Agatha 17			
STREIT, Carl Fried	23	Basel	50-1017
STREIT, Casper	29	Poppenlauer	57-0422
STREIT, Charles Au	51	Reichenau	57-0654
Mary 50, Christiane 20			
STREIT, Elise	34	Eisenach	57-0509
Heinrich 7, Sawine 4			
STREIT, Gregor	23	Steisslingen	56-0629
Anna 22, Crecenz 1, (baby) bob			
STREMEL, Carl	23	Biedenkopf	60-1196
STRENGER, Jos.	26	Stedefreund	60-0334
Friederike 18			
STRETKER, Charie	24	Muenster	59-0214
STRICHER, Caroline	21	Salzungen	56-0847
STRICK, Dor.	26	Magdeburg	62-0836
Johanna 7, Julius 5, Adelheid 11m			
STRICK, Rudolph	24	Nashville	56-0819
STRICKER, Julius	31	Berlin	60-0371
Augusta 26, Julius 6, Otto 5, Bertha 1			
STRICKER, Louise	23	Schwebheim	59-0384
STRICKER, Margaret	24	Rauchensteig	56-0589
STRIEGEL, Friedr.	33	Niedermisburg	61-0047
Barbara 32			
STRIEGLER, C.Georg	50	New York	60-0533
STRIENING, Georg	21	Niederurf	57-0850
STRITERSKY, Joseph	33	Boehmen	62-0001
STRITETZKY, F.	35	Jaroschoff	62-0993
C. 30, Fr. 8, C. 8, A. 11m			
STROBECK, August	24	Halberstadt/P	55-0538
Robert 9m, Robert 9m			
STROBEL, Catharine	24	Leesten/Bav.	55-0628
STROBEL, Fr.Herm.	28	Naumburg	59-0214
STROBEL, Magdalene	30	Zell	57-0850
Paul 39, Carl 4, Franz 1			
STROBER, John	39	Modbarith	60-1141
STROCHLEIN, Georg	35	Calcutta	61-0520
STROELE, J.G.	37	Germania P.	62-0467
Catharine 29, Friedrich 6, Catharine 2			
Rosa 11m			
STROELL, Bened.	30	Goetzlei	59-1036
STROELTING, Wilh.	24	Elbingen	56-0723
STROH, Catharine	32	Okarben	57-1148
Catharine 9, Christine 8, Margaretha 4			
Christine 52			
STROH, Peter	41	Okarben	57-0422
STROHMANN, Cathar.	18	Altersberg	56-1117
STROHMER, Andr.	25	Baltimore	57-1148
STROHMEYER, (f)	46	Braunschweig	57-0578
Fr. 45			
STROHMEYER, August	23	Oehlshausen	57-1407
Minna 24, Fritz 5			
STROHMEYER, August	26	Schoeningen	61-0482
STROMBERG, Wlhmne.	42	Baltimore	62-1112
STROMBERGER, John	26	Sulzburg/Bav.	55-0538
STRONG, W.	36	New York	62-1042
Isabelle 13, Victoria 11			
STROTHEIDE, Fr. R.	35	Waldstetten	60-1196
STROTHOFF, Emma	18	Hagen	61-0804
STRUBREITER, Jos.	39	Jachen	55-0932
Franciska 30, Josephia 5, Joseph 2			
STRUCK, Cathrina	52	New York	60-0429
STRUCKMANN, F.(m)	24	Rocke	57-0555
STRUEBICH, Ulrich	29	Seesen	57-1148
Johanne 27, Dorothea 58, Auguste 5			
Philippine 4, Aug. 11m			
STRUEGGER, Gerhard	27	Hannover	58-0399
STRUENING, J.(m)	32	Washington	62-0836
STRUEVER, M.E.	20	Meiningen	58-0399
STRUEWING, G.(m)	39	Cincinati	62-0836
G.(m) 59			
STRUPEL, Anton	34	Mecherisch	57-1416
Anna 38, Franz 15, Marie 9, Therese 40			
STRUSS, Diedr.	59	Schweringen	61-0482
STRUSS, Johann H.	20	Thedinghausen	57-1113
Johann H. 20			
STRUSS, Wilken	14	Dedendorf	57-0961
STRUTZ, Gottlieb	24	Fakelstedt	57-0422
STUAN, Friedrich	22	Steinhausen	56-0629
STUBENHOFER, Seb.	23	Walheim	56-1117
STUBIG, J.C.(m)	25	Nauheim	61-0482
STUCK, H.(m)	19	Bischhausen	57-0555
STUCKARDT, B.(m)	40	Soemmerda	62-0836
STUCKARDT, Marcus	35	Oberfeld	61-0779
Elisabetha 29			
STUCKEN, Christina	27	Wittenberg	57-1280
STUCKENSCHMIDT, H.	19	Buehren	59-0535
STUCKERT, Anna B.	22	Reinheim	62-0467
STUEBEL, Moses	16	Wustensachsen	57-0961
STUEBER, Ana Maria	24	Neumark	58-0881
STUEBER, Johann	28	Altheim	62-0758
STUEBER, Jos.	28	Neumarkt	62-0467
STUEBING, Conrad	43	Breitenborn	60-0398
Elisabeth 39, Elisabeth 18, Heinrich 14			
Catharine 8, Johannes 6, Margaretha 3			
STUECKAN, Wilhelm	24	Daestel	57-1280
STUECKE, Ernst	25	oldenburg	59-0477
STUECKEL, A. Marie	23	Grossenhausen	56-1117
STUECKLER, Johann	30	Baiern	57-0606
STUEHLER, Anna	16	Hofheim	62-0730
STUEHMER, Frz.	24	Rodenkirchen	62-0938
STUEMM, Caroline	20	Carlsruhe	60-0785
STUERENBERG, Bernh	16	Rathinghausen	59-0951
Marie 18			
STUERKE, C.	42	New York	62-0938
Joh. 9			
STUETZER, August	18	Bernhausen/Sx	62-0342
STUETZER, Ursula	15	Nuernberg	56-0847
STUHLFELDER, Josef	31	Jedling/Bav.	61-0770
STUHLMANN, Fr.(m)	23	Baltimore	62-0467
STUHR, Carl	55	Frankenhausen	59-0951
STUMP, Joh. Martin	19	Wuerttemberg	60-0371
STUMPENHAUSEN, E.	27	Wietzen	61-0482
STUMPF, Anton	30	Olpe	57-0606
STUMPF, Christine	22	Obringen	60-1161
STUMPF, Georg Ph.	44	Eschelbronn	62-0306
Rolette 38			
STUMPF, Johann	24	Erlangen	57-0447
STUMPF, Johannes	45	Hagen	57-0776
STUMPF, Laurette	30	Berne	59-0613
STUMPF, Margarete	21	Meiningen	56-0527
STUPEL, Therese	40	Prachalz	57-1416
STURLA, GeorgAngel	40	Italy	62-0166

NAME	AGE	RESIDENCE	YR-LIST
STURM, Ferdinand	24	Colberg	62-0758
Jacob 62, Catharine 52, Minna 31			
Wilhelm 15, Albertina 10			
STURM, Jacob	17	Fuerth	61-0167
STURM, M.(m)	25	Fuerth	62-0836
STURM, Marie	22	Sparreck	60-0521
STURM, Max	28	Muenchen	59-0384
STURM, Mich.	30	Leimgruben	60-0521
STUTENROTH, Elise	28	Neubunslar	57-1192
STUTTE, Lisette	24	US.	59-0951
STUTZMANN, Ph.Jac.	23	Philadelphia	59-0535
STUVE, Heinrich	15	Schweringen	56-0723
SUCHLAND, Emma	22	Eisenach	62-0758
Ernestine 20			
SUCK, Fritz	36	Bremen	57-1148
Mathilde 38, Friedericke 22, Charles 16			
SUCK, Helene	59	Bremen	60-0521
Frdke. 25, Helene 15			
SUCKE, Christine	19	Pickelsheim	59-1036
SUCKE, J.Friedr.	57	Obtsbessingen	59-0477
SUCKER, Johanna	21	Friedemuss	56-0411
SUD, Joh.Baut.	20	Basel	50-1017
SUDDENDORF, Heinr.	28	Wuellen	56-1117
SUDEN, H.	26	California	62-1042
SUDHOFF, Lisette	26	Beckum	62-0467
SUDTELGTE, Bernh.	59	Telgte	60-0521
SUECK, Aug.	38	Boehmen	62-0467
Franziska 35, Marie 6			
SUEMENLINZ, Erstne	46	Stadthagen	61-0682
SUENDERMANN, Beta	23	Achim	56-1044
SUEPFLE, Wilh'mine	17	Neckartheidin	60-0411
SUEPKE, J.H.	16	Riemsloh	58-0604
SUERT, Joh. Heinr.	28	Stockum	56-0411
SUESS, Ad.(m)	38	San Francisco	61-1132
SUESS, Reinhold	25	Sachsen	55-0634
Volkmar 26, Susanne 25			
SUETZLER, Barbara	24	Wiesenthal	60-0785
SUFFERTE, Johanna	44	Erfurt	55-1082
SUHR, Christian	22	Steinbahn	61-0478
SUHR, Elise	25	Schwey	61-0482
SUHRE, Marie	14	Halle	59-1036
SULGER, Philipp	24	Wetzlar	57-0704
Augusta 27, Hermann 4, Alfred 9			
SULKOWSKY, (m)	40	Austria	61-0107
SUMMER, Friedrich	23	Westeritz	60-0334
SUMMERMEYER, Aug.	31	Brosen	60-0998
SUMMLER, Aug.	45	Oberwesel	59-0951
SUMPFELD, Heinrich	16	Rotenburg	55-0932
SUNDHEIM, Emilie	24	Hann. Muenden	55-1082
SUNNING, Martha	18	Hannover	62-1112
SUPPES, Carl Fr.	26	Landenhausen	62-0608
SUSSDORF, Georg	18	Philippsthal	60-0622
SUSSKIND, Johanne		Steinstrass	56-0550
SUSSKIND, Marx	18	Steinstrass	56-0819
SUSTMANN, Wilh'mne	17	Wabern	62-0712
SUTORIUS, Jacob	22	Grosshebach	61-0520
SUTTER, Adolphus	33	Lippe	57-0422
Charlotte 27, Sophia 4, Lewis 2			
SUTTER, Adolphus	33	Lippe	57-0422
Charlotte 27, Sophia 4, Lewis 2			
SUTZE, Ferd.	17	Wetzlar	56-0629
SWIDITZKY, Fr.Edw.	20	Doebern	57-0754
SWOBODA, John	34	Cittow	57-0850
Catharina 34, Anna 6			
SYCORA, Anton	41	Boehmen	62-1042
Anna 35, Franz 22, Johs. 14, Joseph 8			
Anton 9m			
SYDOW, Caroline	30	Rambezin	61-0930
TAATGE, Heinrich	21	Lindhorst/Lip	55-0628
TABBE, Heinr.	59	New York	62-0836
TABYANO, Frantz	22	Seichnitz	57-1407
Marie 33, Anna 31			
TACHT, Elisabeth	20	Hoesbach/Bav.	60-0429
TACKING, Friedr.	36	Philadelphia	57-1150
TADDICKEN, Caecile	15	Ellerbeck	61-0482
TADENBERG, Loiuse	24	Wiarden	61-0482
TADGE, Joh.	22	Lindhorst	55-0932
TAEBEL, Adolph	22	Bergen/Hann.	62-0608
TAEHN, Franz	28	New York	62-1169
TAEL, Betty	50	Bremen	59-1036
TAFFT, Christine	63	Pommern	58-0399
TAGLIABNE, Julia	31	Haia	61-0716
TAGSOLD, Georg	16	Harenberg	57-0447
TAKE, Catharine	54	Berleburg	60-1032
Georgine 20			
TAKE, Georgine	20	Melzungen	60-1032
TALAMINE, J.	10	New York	59-0477
Magdalene 7			
TALKERT, Sarah	32	Paris	62-0111
Marie 10			
TALLERT, Theresia	33	Kaschau	60-0521
Rosalie 4			
TALLMANN, Johann	22	New York	60-1161
TALOR, Marg.	40	San Francisco	62-1042
Clara 8, Fritz 1			
TAMLYN, H.	35	New York	62-1042
Ellen 30, George 1, Mary 4			
TAMM, Augusta	26	Bischleben	61-0482
TAND, Marie	34	Marienkulm	56-0847
TANGER, Theod.	21	Dresden	56-1216
TANGMANN, Josephin	17	Oldenburg	59-0214
TANNER, Peter Fr.	54	Helmbrechtls	62-0879
TANZ, Johanna	51	Naumburg	61-0047
Lina 21, Friederike 24			
TANZLER, August	33	Sachsen	55-0634
Bruno 11			
TANZREITEN, Ther.	26	Wien	59-0951
TAP, Dorothe	61	Stockstadt	59-0214
Mariane 31, Reinhard 3			
TAPHORN, Ant.	18	Damme	57-0961
TAPP, Fed.	32	Friedeberg	60-1141
Wilhelmina 32, Hermann 4, Robert 9m			
TAPPE, Louise	19	Hextor	57-1407
TAPPERT, Dorothea	18	Wolbrechthaus	60-0398
TAPPHEIMER, Johann	28	Ruggell	60-0533
Elise 28, Johann 2, Agatha 2m			
TARRENHAGEN, Rosal	19	Goettingen	59-0613
TASCHE, Ferdinand	18	Volkmarsen/He	62-0608
TAUBERT, Anna	40	Frankenau	60-0429
Hermann 18, Ernestine 16, Bernhard 14			
Emilie 11, Bertha 5			
TAUBERT, Heinrich	45	Ruppersdorf	58-0881
Johanna 37, Alexander 16, Gustav 14			
Alwin 11, Anton 2, Amalie 9			
TAUBERT, Joh.Heinr	42	Troebnitz	56-0589
Diena 21			
TAUSCHECK, Ferdin.	34	Boehmen	62-0758
Barbara 28, Maria 4, Barbara by			
TAUSCHER, Christ.	35	Niederlosnitz	55-0538
Johanne 32, Ernst 9, Louis 8, Moritz 7			
Hermann 5, Lina 3, Marie 2			
TAUVERT, Ernst	27	Gera	58-0306
TAYLOR, Marg.	30	St.Louis	59-0951
TEASTERSTONE, Art.	32	England	60-0334
(wife) 32, John 12			
TEBBEN, Gerhard	18	Wachtum	60-0533
TECHTEMEYER, Conrd	19	Horsten/CH.	60-0429
TEDDEN, Fr.(m)		Lehe	61-0716
TEDELER, Julie	36	Bernstein	57-1122
TEER, Traugott	24	Eiseborn	60-0785
TEGELER, Carl	21	Loewen	57-1280
TEGMEIER, Johann	55	Rilpen/Hess.	55-1238
Marie 19, Sophie 7			
TEIBEL, Louis	16	Marienburg	62-0938
TEIBUTE, Johann	41	Nordhausen	55-0845
Elisabeth 39, Catharine 10, Marie 10			
Christian 4, Anna 6, Ludwig by			
TEICHERT, Barb.	28	Bayern	56-1044
TEICHMANN, Minna	19	Hofgeismar	56-0279
TEIGLER, Jos.	32	Coesfeld	61-0482
Elisabeth 27			
TEINAUER, Christof	41	Neudorf	58-0399
TEIS, M.E.(f)	23	Hosbag	57-0555
TEKAMP, Gertrude	39	Ramsdorf	62-0983
TEKAMP, Hinr.Herm.		Nichtern/Nass	62-0983
Marianne 6, Sophie 3, Hendrich 1			

NAME	AGE	RESIDENCE	YR-LIST
TEKAMP, Rheinhard	39	Wenderswick	62-0983
TELLE, Emil	21	Dresden	59-0613
TELLINGHAUS, Joha.	45	New York	61-0482
Anna 21			
TELLINGHAUSEN, E.R	39	Hannover	62-0467
Trientje 29, Gretje 3, Jantzen 1m			
TELNIES, Chr.	37	Barleben	57-1067
TELOBUSCH, Joh.	19	Hohlen	59-0951
TEM, Margaretha	18	Reichelsheim	59-0047
TEMME, Heinrich	28	Berlebeck/Lip	62-0608
TEMMING, Carol.	28	Magdeburg	62-0938
R. 27			
TEMPEL, Anton	29	Chicago	59-0214
TENKHOFF, Carl	27	Muenster	61-0804
TENNIE, August	25	Lugde	56-1117
TENSKE, Michael	42	Wassarken	55-0812
TEOBALD, F.A.	25	New York	59-0384
TEPE, Clemens	39	Damme	59-0951
Lisette 35, Agnes 8, Alex. 4			
Elisabeth 11m			
TEPPE, Gerh.Hinr.	39	Engter	57-0924
Anna Marie 40, Louise 10, Joh.Heinrich by			
TEPPEL, Anton	33	Posen	60-0785
TERA, Johannes	63	Luebeck	59-0951
Emma 10			
TEREK, August	22	Borgloh	60-0785
TERFLOTH, G.	28	US.	59-0951
(wife) 20			
TERNES, Georg	29	America	56-1216
Julia 28, (dau.) 4, (dau.) 11m			
TESCAR, Th.	33	Skau	59-0477
Marie 21, Wenzel 11m			
TESCH, Emanuel Fr.	26	Zeni	56-1117
TESCHNER, F.	23	Hildburghause	62-0993
TESKE, Ernst David	44	Cartzig	57-0704
Doro. Sophie 43, M.Louise Aug 15			
Matilda Flor 13			
TESMER, Emil	17	Heilbronn	62-0879
TESTERINDE, L.Ch.	43	Sheboygan	61-0897
TETJE, Augusta	25	Helsingen	57-1192
Lucie 23			
TETTAU, v. Hans	18	Magdeburg	62-0712
TETTENS, Caroline	20	Boehmen	61-0897
TEUBNER, Ferdinand	19	Breslau	56-0279
TEUSCHER, Carl	38	Buchheim	55-0812
TEUSS, Heinrich	33	Uenzen	58-0881
Meta 36, Anna 9, Dietrich 8, Heinrich 5			
Johann 5m			
TEUTBORN, Pauline	26	Frankenhausen	59-0384
TEUTSCHMANN, Elise	21	Althausen	58-0545
TEVES, Joseph	19	Beverungen	56-1204
TEWS, Friedrich	25	Berlin	56-1044
TEXTOR, C.F.	27	Bremen	57-1192
TEXTOR, F.	19	Marburg	59-0990
THALER, Johann	28	Untersteinhof	62-0712
THALKS, Gerhard	29	Thiernau	59-1036
Folkert 17			
THAMANN, Heinrich	34	Cincinnati	58-0306
(wife) 22, (child) 7, (child) 3			
THAMER, Caspar	56	Berfa	57-1067
THANLE, H.(m)	19	New York	62-0232
THANUR, Heinr Carl	17	Curhessen	55-0634
THEBUS, August	17	Hubenrod	58-0881
THECKS, D.	12	England	62-0938
THEDICK, Bernhard	25	Alfhausen	56-1117
THEES, H.D.	25	Brunsbrock	59-0535
THEIL, Jos.	31	Canth/Silesia	60-0429
THEILMANN, Adolph	35	Schoenau/Aus.	55-1238
THEIMER, Franz	52	Maehren	62-0712
Caroline 52, Juliane 23, Joseph 19			
Benjamin 17, Josepha 9, Johann 7			
THEIN, Johann	22	Heesberg/Sax.	55-0628
THEIS, Anna Marg.	18	Ruedinghausen	58-0925
Anna Maria 20			
THEIS, Catharina	22	Geismar	57-0850
THEIS, Catharine	20	Flensungen	62-0467
THEIS, Heinr.	24	Berkelbach	56-0951
Elise 30			

NAME	AGE	RESIDENCE	YR-LIST
THEISSEN, Marie	43	New York	59-1036
THEIST, Anna	25	Triemen	56-1117
THEMANN, Anna	27	Coeln	60-1141
THEOBALD, Julia	24	France	61-1132
THEUERER, Charles	50	New York	60-0785
THEUERER, Georg	52	Marktbibart	58-0563
Margarethe 33, Andreas 8, Magdalena 4			
Johann 9m			
THEUERKAUF, A.	37	Cincinnati	57-1192
Sophia 32, Anna 3, Catharina 11m			
THEUNE, Roderich	22	Benstedt	56-0589
THEURING, Wm.Edw.	28	Merseburg	59-0412
THIAS, Franz	45	St.Louis	62-1042
THIBARTH, John	31	Friedrichstal	62-0467
THIEL, Christiane	59	Melsungen	59-1036
Christiane 21			
THIEL, Hermann	26	Illinois	58-0881
Mathilde 23, Hugo 1			
THIEL, Louis	55	Louisville	59-1036
Rosine 41			
THIELBAR, Derric	27	New York	57-0422
THIELE, Arm.Lewis	38	Michigan	57-0654
THIELE, August	26	Hannover	57-0555
THIELE, Carl	37	Aurich	57-0578
THIELE, Carl	34	Grossmachno	59-0047
Henriette 23, Emilie 4, Carl bob			
THIELE, Caroline	14	Uslar/Hann.	60-0622
THIELE, Charles	15	Horn	57-0422
THIELE, Friedrich	28	Bierde	55-0812
Lisette 24, Friedrich 3m			
THIELE, Heinrich	31	Stroella	58-0576
Sophie 42, Anna 12			
THIELE, Louise	17	Mariensee	57-1192
THIELE, Otto	35	Sacramento	59-1036
THIELE, S.	33	Philadelphia	57-1150
Julius 4			
THIELE, Will.	19	Nienburg	57-1148
THIELEKE, Heinrich	26	Dessau	61-0682
Louise 22, Louise 1			
THIEMANN, C.(m)	30	New York	60-0785
THIEMANN, Carl	58	Rahden	57-1280
Marie 56, Dorrette 23, Marie 21			
THIEMANN, Maria	29	Koenigsberg	60-0785
Marg. 9, Max 7			
THIEMANN, Mary	40	Damme	57-0961
THIENNER, Guenther	18	Uderfleben	60-1032
THIERAUCH, Georg	19	Horningstof	60-0334
THIERFELDER, Emily	30	Crimmitschau	57-0606
Adolph Rich. 3, Wilh.Pauline 5			
THIERGAERTNER, A.M	28	Mkt.Brandenba	59-0477
THIERMANN, Carl	18	Lohe	57-1122
THIERMANN, H.(m)	26	Louisville	62-0467
Heinrich 14			
THIERMANN, J.Herm.	31	New York	59-0048
THIERMANN, Wilhelm	38	Bremerhaven	57-0776
THIERMANN, Wm.		Lehe	62-0467
Helene			
THIES, Wilh.	38	Steimbke	57-0850
Marie 38, Johann 12, Friedrich 16			
August 8, Louise 7, Wilhelm 5m			
THIESING, Chrstine	21	Nichtern	62-0983
THIESS, Henry	30	Westendorf	57-0422
THIESS, M. (m)	30	Bruessel	61-0897
THIESS, Ulrich	19	Schiffdorf	56-1117
THIRA, Joseph	32	Budweis/Boehm	62-0608
Barbara 24, Catharina 2, Maria 7m			
THIRA, Matthias	25	Budweis/Boehm	62-0608
Anna 21, Anna 6m			
THISE, Gustav	18	Heidelberg	60-0371
THOBE, J.D.	27	Addrap	62-0938
THODE, E.G.(m)	45	New York	62-0467
Wilhelm 9			
THOELE, Hermann	42	Bremuh/Han.	61-0770
THOENE, Franz	19	Westphalen	57-0606
THOERICHT, Ambrosa	50	Kochlige	57-0021
Marianne 42, Philipp 22			
THOGODE, Wm.	18	Beverstedt	60-0521
THOGODT, Rebecca	25	Bevenstedt	59-1036

NAME	AGE	RESIDENCE	YR-LIST
THOLEN, F.J.	35	Holthausen	55-0413
Louise 24			
THOM, Carl	35	Kassbaum	61-0478
THOMA, Otto	24	Gottmadingen	56-0589
THOMANN, Georg	27	Unterweiler	62-0712
THOMAS, Andreas	28	Albertshausen	61-0779
Margaretha 25, Wilhelm 6			
THOMAS, Aug.	15	Nienburg	59-1036
THOMAS, Augustus	30	Fakelstedt	57-0422
THOMAS, Charles	20	Arnstadt	57-0422
THOMAS, Chr.	19	Schwiegershsn	59-0535
THOMAS, Franz	35	Muenster/Hann	60-0622
THOMAS, Friedrich	56	New York	57-0961
THOMAS, J.G.	54	Teich-Wolfram	62-0993
E.F. 58, H.A. 9			
THOMAS, Josef	39	Boehmen	62-1112
Francisca 32, Cara 12			
THOMAS, Suzanne	21	Memmingen	56-0527
THOMAS, Wm.	17	Leidingstadt	62-0467
THOMEL, Carl	23	Wittenberg	62-0983
THON, Friedrich	32	Petershagen	57-1122
THON, Heinrich	21	Martinfeld	57-0447
THON, Philipp	30	Martinfeld	57-0447
THONE, Cath.	32	Mainz	59-0613
THOR, Thomas	44	Boehmen	61-0930
Anna 33, Franz 7, Joseph 2, Franziska 14			
Maria 9			
THORBECK, E.	38	Proyts	57-1192
THORBERG, Otto	51	Meppen	55-0845
THORMANN, Joh.	16	Totensteins	59-0384
THORMANN, Lisette	15	Schwichtler	59-1036
THORMANN, Val.	32	Ketsch	56-1216
THORNER, G.Moritz	31	Osnabrueck	56-0951
THORSPRECKEN, Fr.	18	Bremen	56-1044
THORWART, Heinrich	20	Giessen	62-0232
THRONHOEFER, Maria	28	Bayern	62-0712
THUDIUM, Georg	56	Lochingen	61-0669
Rosine 26, Cath. 24, Chr.(f) 20			
Chr.(m) 16			
THUEMMLER, John	58	Muelsen	57-0422
Caroline 57			
THUERNA, Elise	16	Muenden	58-0399
THUERNAU, Engel M.	18	Beckedorf	56-0589
THUERNAU, Joh.	16	Luedersfeld	59-0951
THUM, Theresia	26	Gissigheim/Bd	60-0622
THUMANN, Friedrich	16	Rotenburg	55-0634
THUMSEN, Christ.	33	Chicago	59-0477
THUMSER, Anna Cath	19	Schwingen	58-0306
THUN, v. Catharina	20	Lehe	60-1161
THUR, Christlieb	59	Kolpin	57-0422
Caroline 56			
THURICH, Marie	11	Leipzig	57-1026
THUSS, Anna W.	28	Berg	56-0723
THYWISSER, Georg	32	Aachen	57-0918
TIBALDI, Calli	42	Italy	61-0716
TIDEMANN, Ernst	21	Bremen	59-0477
TIEBLER, Ferd.	16	Schorndorff	55-0845
TIEDAU, Chr.	52	Hemmendorf	57-0422
Minna 45, Charsine 18, Augustus 9			
TIEDEKE, Johannes	17	Boehmen	61-0478
Henriette 26			
TIEDEMANN, Carl	30	St.Louis	59-0613
TIEDEMANN, Cathar.	16	Alfestaedt	61-0478
TIEDEMANN, Herm.	33	Ebersdorf	61-0167
TIEGLER, Justus	23	Bauchenbach	57-1122
TIEHL, Hermann	16	Maulbach	61-0478
TIEKEN, Elisabeth	18	Koehten	58-0815
TIELEKE, Friedrich	49	Dorum	57-0422
Helen 40, Doris 18, Augustus 6			
Friederike 8			
TIELMANN, Elise	33	Stadtbergen	57-0776
Elisabeth 15, Franz 11, Druetgen 6			
Wilhelm 4, Louise 2			
TIEMANN, Harm F.	33	Fiebing	57-0422
TIEMANN, J.Henry	21	New York	62-0758
TIEMANN, Johann	19	Oerel	60-1161
TIEMEYER, Heinrich	23	Vehrte	61-0482
TIENKEN, Dr.	18	Frellstorf	62-0938

NAME	AGE	RESIDENCE	YR-LIST
TIENKEN, Heinrich	25	New York	58-0815
TIENKEN, Sophie	29	New York	62-0730
TIEROFF, G.H.(m)	17	Bayern	56-1044
Catharina 20			
TIETJEN, Anna	24	Flossenburg	60-0521
TIETJEN, Chr.	18	Hemilingen	62-0938
TIETJEN, Doris	21	Wellen	56-0819
Sophie 26			
TIETJEN, Friedrich	32	Hagen	58-0925
TIETJEN, Heinr.	40	Kingston	62-0232
TIETJEN, Henry	24	New York	62-1112
TIETJEN, Herm.	18	Wardenburg	57-1113
TIETJEN, Joh.	34	Charleston	61-0804
TIETJEN, Joh.	33	Bevenstedt	59-1036
TIETJEN, Julie	30	New York	62-0467
TIETJEN, Minna	20	Dorum	60-0521
Wm. 9			
TIETJEN, Reb.Ma.	19	Wahldorf	59-0477
TIETJENS, Cath.	18	Meinershagen	59-1036
TIETYEN, Martin	18	Neuhausen/Han	60-0622
TIETZ, August	34	Carzig	57-0776
Augusta 29			
TIETZEN, J.	16	Ohlenstedt	56-0512
TIGGEMEYER, Fr.	20	Westerwehe	56-1216
TILGE, Friedrich	17	Philadelphia	59-0951
TILIA, Steph.	24	Schmilowo	56-1216
TILKING, Friedr.	24	Langfoerden	59-0951
TILL, Anna	22	Tholmar	57-1280
TILLACK, Jacob	32	Harwen	55-1082
Louise 24			
TILLIG, Emilie	30	Indianapolis	62-1112
Fanny 4, Maria 2, Theod. 6m			
TILLIGAN, Johann	23	Ziniwes	56-0629
Michel 17			
TILLMANN, Joseph	36	New York	59-0477
TILLMANN, Therese	39	Bucher	56-0512
Theodor 11, John 8, Wilhelm 3			
TILTHUTH, Caroline	28	Minden	56-0951
TIMKE, Wilhelm	31	Amelith	59-0214
TIMKEN, Hermann	28	Lilienthal	58-0881
TIMM, Carl	39	Neukirch/Han.	60-0622
TIMM, Carl	38	Neuenburg	57-0555
Caroline 23, Emilie 2, Bertha 9m			
TIMME, A.	34	St.Louis	59-0951
TIMME, C.	31	Arnsee	62-0993
L. 39, F. 39, F. 13, L. 11, E. 3, F. 1			
TIMME, Herm.	33	Schmerten	60-0334
Heinr. 23			
TIMMERMANN, Johann	25	Sudweihe	62-0730
TIMMERMANN, Matild	21	Diepenau	59-0951
Friedrich 15			
TIMMLER, Caroline	26	Obergleis	56-0589
TIMNER, Demuth	40	Wellingen	57-1122
Cathrine 11, Caspar 9, Nella 8			
Heinrich 10			
TINEMANN, Caline	24	Elderich	56-0629
Emilie 18			
TINN, Johs.	24	Hundshausen	55-0413
TINNSCHMIDT, Danl.	19	Schvezstedt	55-0845
TIPPE, Anna	54	Anemolter	56-0819
Henriette 48			
TIPPEL, Catharine	20	Hatzbach	58-0399
Catharine 30, Johannes 5			
TIPPEL, Justus	39	New York	62-1042
Elise 30, (daughter) 9m			
TISCHBEIN, Julie	44	Bettenhausen	62-0938
Fickchen 23			
TISCHBEIN, Moses	16	Bettenhausen	60-0785
TISCHER, Gottlieb	41	Oels	57-0754
Susanne 41, Ernst 15, Auguste 6			
Christiane 11m			
TISCHLER, Georg	45	Mainecke	57-1407
TISSMANN, Joh.G.	24	Mobendorf	60-0398
TITIEN, Adelheid	18		57-1280
TITIEN, Margarethe	29	Osterholt	59-0613
TITJEN, Henry	24	New York	62-0938
TITJEN, Herrm.	45	San Francisco	59-1036
TITLER, Heinrich	25	Bremervoerde	56-1260

NAME	AGE	RESIDENCE	YR-LIST
TITZ, Christine	22	Tepnitz	57-0578
TOBIAS, Heinrich	24	Bielokar/Pr.	60-0052
TOCKSTEIN, Joseph	51	Strakonitz/Bo	55-0538
Maria 27, Anna 17, Adolph 11, Alois 2			
Anna 6m			
TOD, Heinrich	33	Wiefels	61-0482
Elise 30, Sophie 9, Marie 7, Elise 6			
Tonij 4, Heinrich 1			
TODT, J.G.	29	Uelzen	58-0399
TODT, Moritz	22	Bremen	62-0983
TODTBRANDT, Aug.	25	Lippe-Detmold	57-0447
Conradine 30, Herm. 5			
TODTS, Johanna	30	Dassel/Hann.	62-0608
TOEL, Caroline	50	Bremerhafen	56-0629
Auguste 26			
TOEL, E.G.	25	Bremen	59-1036
TOELCKE, Lina	17	Lage	55-1048
TOELKEN, Adelheid	24	Bremen	62-0349
Meta 22			
TOENCH, Heinrich	34	Oberhilsen	57-0924
TOENJES, Armand	31	Ruttel	57-1148
TOENJES, Friedr.	17	Reinhardshsn.	61-0478
TOENJES, J.	22	Bederkese	58-0925
TOENJES, Marg.	28	Ruttel	57-1148
TOENNIES, J.Lueken	26	Backband/Hann	62-0342
Helene 28, Gesine 3, Johanna 11m			
TOENNIS, Herm.	40	Cincinnati	62-0836
TOENSCH, Anna Elis	34	Verna/Hessen	57-0924
TOEPELMANN, August	19	Bremen	59-0372
TOEPFER, Marie	24	Eisenach	60-0334
Carl 3			
TOEPPE, Heinrich	34	Volkhassen	56-0411
TOGADE, Claus	19	Wollings	56-1117
TOLLE, H.	23	Oldenburg	59-0990
TOLLER, Johannes	26	Strigowitz	57-1113
TOLLER, Wenzel	43	Nebellau	57-1113
Catharina 43, Anna 12, Franz 9, Barbara 9			
TOLLKOPF, Joseph	27	Mantau	58-0881
Magdalena 23, Franz 2			
TOLLMEIER, Fr.	52	Varnholz	57-0606
Friedricke 54, Simon Heinr. 18			
Wilhelmine 19			
TOMASZESKA, Fr'zka	21	Budzin/Pr.	62-0342
TONJES, Johanna	17	Ritterhude	57-0606
TONNE, Wilhelmine	24	Landesbergen	61-0779
Heinrich 3			
TONNER, Carsten	24	Tarmstedt	57-1148
C.Joh. 25			
TONNJES, Lur	15	Gnarenburg	59-0535
TONTRUP, Eleonore	16	Eichstedt	62-0730
TONWOLLE, Louise	18	Frankfurt a/M	61-0682
TOPEL, Carl Heinr.	18	Sarbske	58-0881
TOPINKA, Wenzel	32	Boehmen	61-0930
Marie 31, Franziska 11m, (male)			
TOPP, Heinrich	17	Westphalia	60-0371
TORCK, Lueder	16	Kasbrock	61-0478
TORKE, Berend	22	Hannover	57-0847
TORNOW, Carl	24	Berlinchen	62-0879
TORNOW, Lewis	23	Neuhoefen	56-1011
TOSER, Herm.	32	Milwaukee	61-0804
TRABACCO, Filippo	29	Italy	61-0716
TRABANT, Elisabeth	45	Schluechtern	56-1216
Helena 15			
TRABERT, Franciska	22	Freissbach	57-1067
TRABKE, Robert	18	Potzkau	56-1044
TRABUSINNER, Josef	35	Wien/Aus.	55-0538
Marie 28			
TRACHTE, August	26	Somerset/Lipp	62-0608
Heinrich 19			
TRAEGER, August	19	Cassel	57-0754
TRAEGER, Friedr.CG	38	Calbe	57-0924
Henriette 35, Emilie 8, Friedrich 3			
TRAEUMER, Carl	29	Meiningen	62-0758
TRAICHHAUS, Frdke.	23	Tecklenburg	57-1026
TRAINER, Franz	39	Volkbach	56-1260
TRAMM, Simon	14	Hohnheim	60-0785
TRAPP, Anna B.	29	Erlbach	62-0306
TRAPP, Bernhard	29	Laubach	61-0478

NAME	AGE	RESIDENCE	YR-LIST
Abelonia 27, Carl 3, Theresia 9m			
TRAPP, Gotthilf	20	Hagelbeck	56-0629
TRAPP, Joh.	35	Seeligfeld	56-0629
Caroline 33, Caroline 9, Hermann 5			
Ottilie 3, Emilie 6m			
TRAPP, Julius	34	Bluemenhagen	58-0881
Maria 31, Bertha 3			
TRAPPER, Friedrich	23	Lopphoff/Bav.	62-0608
TRAPPER, Joh.	26	Azurdorff	60-0521
Kunigunde 7			
TRATT, Christian	17	Raasen	57-0924
Georg 19			
TRAUB, Moses	23	Strassburg	59-0047
Emilie 34			
TRAUERMANN, Helene	22	Sonderhausen	60-0521
TRAUERNICHT, Th.	22	St.Louis	61-0107
TRAUM, Heinrich	44	Hesse-Darm.	62-0712
Marie 37, Catharina 13, Heinrich 9			
Catharina 58			
TRAUT, Matthaeus	27	Herbstein/Dar	62-0342
TRAUT, Matthaeus	27	Herbstein/Hes	62-0342
TRAUTMANN, Th.(m)	48	Wisconsin	62-0712
TRAUTNER, Carl	17	Cahla	56-0589
TRAUTWEIN, Rosa	24	Worms	61-0482
TRAUTWETTER, Emil	36	Berlin	59-0214
TREBING, Conrad	19	Breitenborn	60-0398
TREIBIG, J.Friedr.	29	Meiningen	61-0478
TRELS, Eilert Gerd	51	Oldenbrock	55-0812
TRENDELMANN, Chr.	18	Cammer	57-1067
TRENZEL, Lothar	19	Melborn	56-0354
TREPLIN, Herm.	35	Braunschweig	56-1117
TRES, F.	28	Malsdorf	62-0993
TRESINE, de L.	21	Jersey	62-0938
(wife) 18			
TRESSENBERG, Aug.	31	New York	59-0214
TRESSET, Wilhelm	18	Sondershausen	57-0365
Johanna 23			
TRETBOR, Gustav	25	Ferning/Boehm	56-1260
TRETTIN, Friedrich	59	Drosedo	57-0704
Ferdinand 39, Alb.Caroline 40			
Henriette 37, Hermann 11, Bertha 9			
Wilhelm 7, Friedrich 5, Albert 4			
Eduard 8m			
TRETZINGER, Heinr.		Dittelsheim	57-1026
TREUSS, Lina	40	New York	59-1036
G. 7, Friedr. 5, Ralph 4			
TREVELYAN, (m)	30	Havana	62-0836
TREWERT, Henry	19	Assmissen	57-0422
TRIEBEL, Dan.	24	Suhl	56-1117
Friederika 35, Emma 10, Robert 3			
TRIEBEL, Ludw.	43	Schweinshaupt	60-0622
TRIEBERT, Henry	46	Baltimore	57-1148
TRIEFEL, H.F.	25	Windorf	59-0535
TRIEGLOFF, A.W.	22		57-1192
TRIEKE, Carl	40	Friedland	57-0447
Friedrike 38			
TRIER, Isaac	59	Frankfurt	62-0467
TRIER, Ludwig	14	Burgel	59-0384
TRIESCHMANN, Cath.	31	Nausis	62-0730
Daniel 8, Barbara 5			
TRIESELER, Friedr.	21	Sehlde	59-0535
TRIESSER, Georg	24	Cincinati	59-0384
Marg. 34, Maria 4, Ida 4m			
TRIMKE, Wilhelm	25	Oelagsen	56-0847
Carl 5			
TRINHERMS, J.Fr'dr	28	Brochhausen	56-0589
Heinrich 3			
TRIPPE, Elisabeth	32	Medebach	62-0730
TRITJEN, Johann	20	Buelstedt	60-0334
TRITTIN, Paul Rob.	15	Frankfurt	62-0983
TROECHLE, L.(m)	29	New York	62-0467
TROEMEL, Wilh.H.	20	Leipzig	59-1036
TROLL, Anna	21	Ob.Vorschuetz	57-0754
TROMBE, Domingo	28	France	61-0167
TROMMEL, Friedrich	55	Dillenburg	62-0712
Catharine 46, Friedrich 22, Helene 20			
Christian 18, August 16, Otto 14			
Julius 12, Emil 10, Louis 5, Robert 11m			

NAME	AGE	RESIDENCE	YR-LIST
TROMMERSHEISER, Fr	20	Tiefenbach/Pr	55-0628
Louise 56			
TROSS, Stephen	50	Williamsburg	61-0804
TROST, Anna	59	Homberg	61-0779
Heinrich 19			
TROST, Heinrich	23	Lippstadt	57-1407
TROST, Maria	27	Steinbach	56-1260
TROSTE, Elis(died)	18	Lichting	57-1407
TROTTMANN, Marie	31	Baiern	58-0399
TRSEGER, Gottlieb	28	Weikenreuth	55-0630
TRUBE, Joh. Carl	26	Wotzerode	56-0819
TRUBER, Cath.	29	Bavenhausen	62-0730
C.G.(m) 3			
TRUBER, Ernst H.	18	Eschwege	62-1042
TRUCKENBRODT, J.N.	23	Obersiemen	61-0897
TRUMPF, Gustav	24	Braunschweig	56-1117
TRUNK, Carl H.	30	Eisenach	59-0951
Franziska 30, Alma 2			
TRUTSCHEL, Julius	22	Leidewitz	59-0048
TUBBESING, Mathild		Soest	59-0613
TUBUTE, Johann	41	Nordhausen	55-0845
Elisabeth 39, Catharine 10, Marie 10			
Anna 6, Christian 4, Ludwig by			
TUCK, Clemens	54	Huesede	56-1117
Lisette 54, Heinrich 20, A.Marie 23			
Dorothee 18, Friedrich 7, Hermann 6			
TUCKERMANN, Carl	27	Mecklenburg	55-0845
TUEGEL, Caroline	16	Suedhemmern	62-0401
TUERK, Adam	57	Sachs.Weimar	58-0399
TUERK, Georg	57	Sachs.-Weimar	58-0399
TUERNAU, Johann	15	Bremen	61-0716
TULEGA, Anna	19	Littwitz	60-0785
Anton 9			
TULINEN, Jos.	18	Hecke	59-1036
TULIS, Joseph	31	Podolitz	55-0845
TUMME, Caroline	34	Duesseldorf	60-0785
TUNACK, August	33	Geslluse	57-0776
Charlotte 28, August 3, Friedrich 2			
Wilhelm 8			
TUNITSCHI, Johann	21	Kokschin/Boeh	59-0047
Wenzel 19, Marie 20			
TURICH, F.W.	26	Goettnitz	56-0723
TURNAU, Fr. (m)	28	Lauenhagen	62-0836
Engel 21			
TURNER, James	48	Missouri	62-1169
TUSCH, Margaretha	20	Bavaria	60-0371
TUSCHHOFF, Carl	32	Rhoden/Wald.	57-0924
TUSSHOELLER, Max J	27	Siegburg	59-0384
TUTMANN, Dorette	22	Seehausen	60-1032
TWART, Friedericka	49	Posen	59-0412
Wilhelmine 15, Friedrich 6, Carl 4			
TWEITMANN, J.H.(m)	16	Burgdam	62-0401
TYARKS, Elisabeth	53	Tettens	61-0482
TYARKS, Emma	20	Tettens	61-0482
Amatie 13, Herman 15			
TYARKS, G.B.(m)	19	Schartens	61-0482
TYARKS, Gerhard	16	Wattens	57-0961
TYARKS, Jan J.	56	Persene	56-0629
Alfke 53			
TYLKING, Wilh'mine	20	Sulbach	61-0482
UBBE, Janna	28	Campen	55-1082
UBERE, Wilh.	20	Neudorf	55-0932
UBHOFF, Henry	30	Heinsbach	59-0384
Carl 25			
UCHELPOL, Wilhme.	15	Hilter	62-0467
UCHTMANN, Sophie	16	Hartenbostel	58-0925
UCKERMANN, Christ.	33	Schoetmar	60-1141
UDERICH, Catharina	24	Ellingerode	56-1117
UERF, Marie	19	Melbach	59-0047
UFFHAUS, Wilhelm	29	Gotha	55-0634
Louise 26, Ida by			
UHARD, Pierro	39	Italy	62-0166
UHDE, Charlotte	45	Marburg	57-0436
Hermann 10, Mathilde 4, Caroline 2			
UHDEN, Carl	22	Buchholz	62-0401
UHL, Joh.	18	Liets	57-0447
UHL, Louis	28	Nidda	59-0214
UHLAND, Wm.	30	Bruchdorf	62-0401
UHLEN, Clemens	42	Louisville	60-0785
Christine 45			
UHLENBRINK, Adelh.	19	Wessum	59-0951
UHLENBROCK, Anton	27	Muenster/Pr.	62-0608
UHLENHACKE, Heinr.	30	Glandorff	56-1117
UHLIEN, Gustav	22	New York	60-0785
UHLIG, Carol.Hedw.	16	Hohenstein	62-0983
UHLING, Bernhard	38	Wessum	57-1148
Armand 24, Henry 16			
UHLING, Eva	25	Erzberg	60-1141
UHLMANN, August	51	Plauen	60-0398
UHLMANN, Carl	36	Plauen	57-1280
UHLY, Bertha	26	Fischbach/Bav	62-0608
UHRBROCK, H.(m)	15	Hoya	61-0804
ULBRECHT, Julius	31	Obergraefenhe	59-0535
Therese 27			
ULBRECHT, Wilhelm	39	Frohberg	59-0535
Ed. 24			
ULERMOEHLEN, C.W.	44	Washington	60-0785
August 50			
ULIBER, Ignatius	54	Fritzlar	57-0654
Elisabeth 53			
ULIN, Mrs.	24	Baltimore	59-0477
ULLMANN, Adam	36	Thonberg	61-0779
Christiane 15			
ULLMANN, Jette	25	Eschenau	59-1036
Isidor 14			
ULLMER, C.	20	Ingersheim	62-0993
ULLRICH, Conrad	31	Halbensachsen	57-0850
ULMER, Marie	23	Waltershofen	59-0613
ULOTH, Geo.	33	Bessel	56-0512
M. 30, Heinrich 3, John 9m			
ULRICH, Adolph	20	Neustadt	59-0613
ULRICH, Adolph	18	Boberthausen	59-0951
ULRICH, Arm.	29	Ohio	57-1148
ULRICH, August	25	Osterode	56-0819
ULRICH, Bruno	24	Wilsenbeck	60-0785
ULRICH, Charles	29	Dettersdorf	57-0961
ULRICH, Christine	55	Chemnitz	56-0847
Anna 33			
ULRICH, Edward	21	Bremerhaven	59-0214
ULRICH, Ernestine	17	Senna/Pr.	60-0371
Maria 19, Bertha 13, Louis 21			
ULRICH, Fr.(m)	25	Dauersdorf	56-0723
ULRICH, Friedrike	24	Marienwerder	57-0704
Adeline 17, Ernestine 21			
ULRICH, Georg	62	Koenigswald	60-1032
Heinrich 19			
ULRICH, Heinrich	31	Berlin	61-0779
ULRICH, J.(m)	20	Boehmen	61-0897
Wm. 18			
ULRICH, Jacob	23	Haltensleben	59-0372
ULRICH, Johann	18	Meckmuehle	57-0606
ULRICH, Julius	36	Genthin	55-0812
Mathilde 24			
ULRICH, Wilhelm	28	Harpke	58-0815
ULSEMER, Otto	20	Wuerzburg	61-0482
ULTMANN, Bertha	22	Stachheim	60-0521
ULTSCH, August	18	Weismein	58-0399
UMBACH, Martha	22	Marburg	59-0990
UMBACH, Wm.	19	Newark	62-0467
UMERLE, Chr.	42	Stuttgart	56-0512
Amalie 19, Emily 14, Pauline 1, Gust. 15			
UNBEWUST, Christ.	18	Fernbreitenba	56-0279
Wilhelmine 23			
UNGAR, Josepha	40	New York	62-0938
Baldwin 9			
UNGAR, Pauline	19	Mainz	62-1169
UNGER, Barbara	19	Weschnitz	62-0712
UNGER, Bertha	23	Oberlungwith	60-0533
UNGER, Caspar	20	Liebenstein	62-0712
UNGER, Catharine	32	Rothenburg/Bv	55-0628
UNGER, Elisabeth	20	Neuffen	59-0613
UNGER, Johannes	27	Sueps	59-0613
UNGER, Matthias	24	Westheim	58-0576
Susanne 23, Sabine by			
UNGERICH, Heinr.	41	Kreuznach	60-1196
UNKART, Bruno	19	Schierschnitz	58-0563

NAME	AGE	RESIDENCE	YR-LIST
UNKART, C.G.	48	Coburg	56-0354
UNOLD, Jak.	46	Balzheim	59-1036
Cathar. 38, Cathar. 17, Gottlieb 14			
Georg 12, Johann 11, Caspar 7, Cathar. 40			
UNSCHICK, Ph.	21	Muenster	59-0384
UNSCHULD, Christne	25	Carlsruhe	56-1011
UNTERBECK, Chrl.An	19	Loebejuin/Pr.	60-0429
UNTERLAENDER, Abr.	29	Fuerth	56-1260
UNVERZAGT, G.(m)	17	Elsoff	62-0467
UPHOF, Friedr.	14	Hille	56-0411
UPHOFF, Caroline	28	Minden	58-0399
UPHOFF, Chr.	26	Hille	55-0411
UPHOFF, Hermann	37	Warendorf	58-0885
UPHOFF, Louise	21	Hille	55-0411
UPHOFF, Marie	20	Minden	58-0399
UPHOFF, Weit B.	54	Ochtelburg/Ha	55-0544
Faulke 44, Bernhard 17, Annchen 15			
Foke 12, Johann 9, Bartelt 6			
UPMANN, Carl Fr'dr	35	Westphalia	60-0371
URBACH, Fr.(m)	23	Steinau	62-0730
URBAHN, Matth.	31	Welwaren	59-0384
Anna 30, Vincenz 6, Anna 4, Ferd. 9			
Therese 6m, Anna 23			
URBAN, Balthasar	54	Laimbach	61-0478
Heinrich 28, Anna Liese 26, Catharina 18			
Casper 14			
URBAN, J.	31	Schmolau	62-0993
J. 9			
URBAN, Joseph	36	Welwaren	59-0384
URINS, Louise	20	New York	62-0938
URRM, Sophie	15	Strausburg	60-0785
URSENBACH, J.	67	Schwitz	62-0467
Sophie 64, Henry 32, Zelima 23			
URSTADT, Heinr.	17	Kurhessen	56-1044
URTUF, Cath.	17	Braunschweig	59-0384
UTAFSY, Carl	34	Ungarn	62-0938
UTESTADT, Georg	28	Walldorf	57-0924
Emilie 27, Georg Heinr. by			
UTRECHT, Friedrich	17	Deissel	57-1192
UTRINCK, Johann	22	Atzeg	56-0279
UTTERSTEDT, Nicol.	19	Walldorf	56-0629
UTZ, Magdalena	32	Bavaria	60-0371
VACE, Rebecca	22	Cluspach	56-0512
VADENFINDER, Adolf	39	Bielefeld	57-1280
Caroline 32, Friederike 5, Wilhelm 7			
VAETH, Jacob	35	Weibersbrunn	60-1053
VAETH, Joseph	24	Markheidenfld	60-1053
VAGEDES, Bernhard	25	Soegel	60-1141
Anna 26			
VAGEL, Ontars	43	Wesenthal	60-0998
Elizabeth 33, Albert 10, Caroline 8			
Wilhelm 4, Carl 2			
VAGEN, Johann	23	Koehlen	56-1117
VAGT, Magdalena	22	Bremen	57-0654
VAHL, H.H.	24	Niederbecken	59-0951
VAHRENHORST, Chrlt	20	Mehnen	57-1192
VALENTIN, Franz	43	Bohemia	60-1161
VALLERI, M.J.(m)	34	Havre	62-0401
VALLERS, C.D.	30	Neuenhuntorf	59-0477
VALLMUELLER, Lina	19	Baden	60-1196
VANAU, Maria	21	Breitenbach	55-0630
VARELT, Elisabeth	26	Schoenhof	57-1148
VARNHOLZ, Armand	27	Guetersloh	57-0961
VARRELMANN, Ferd.	17	Bassum	56-0629
VARRELMANN, Heinr.	23	Hannover	58-0881
VASS, Chr.	38	New York	59-0951
VASSNACK, Emil	18	Remscheid	57-1148
VASSOLD, Georg	28	Neuenkirchen	58-0563
VATER, Benno	24	Dresden	61-0682
VATER, Herm.	28	Marchuetz	62-0836
Henriette 33, Solmar 5			
VATER, Johann	32	Curhessen	57-0847
VAUCLAIR, Francois	38	France	61-1132
VAUPEL, Sophie	23	Loehlbach	60-0411
VEERHUSEN, Falkert	38	Aerdorf	57-1192
Margaretha 28			
VEGILAU, Jul.Fr'dr	29	Redenthin	57-0704
Wilhelmine 32, Franz Leo. 9m			

NAME	AGE	RESIDENCE	YR-LIST
VEHN, Marg.	28	Bayern	56-1044
VEHN, ter Gerard	39	Emden	57-0422
Mary 33			
VEIGEL, Johann	27	Hessingheim	60-0334
VEIT, Carl Fr.	19	Heilbronn	62-0730
VEITSCH, Caroline	19	Kingel/Wurt.	60-0052
VELDE, v.d. Cath.	35	Gehrde	62-0836
VENEIS, Victoria	34	Strehbergmuhl	60-0622
Magdalena 15, Anna 5			
VENN, Carl	15	Driburg	60-0334
VENSEL, Michel	27	Schmitzdorf	55-0630
Anna 26, A.Maria 9m			
VENT, Traugott	27	Ehringsdorf	56-0723
Ann 26			
VERCH, Emilie	30	Posen	55-0812
Adeline 9, Robert 8, Oscar 3			
VERDIER, A.	32	France	62-1112
VERNALEKEN, Max	35	Curhessen	58-0399
Franziska 42, Eduard 13, Theodor 5			
Clara 3, Ida 9m			
VERNALIKEN, August	27	Volkmarsen/He	62-0608
VERRA, Paph.	35	Napoli	62-1042
VERSPOHL, Elisab.	25	Borchhorst	59-0412
VERZY, de Fredrik	30	Baltimore	59-0048
VESPER, Sophia	17	Friedrichshsn	55-0628
VESPERMANN, Minna	21	Sieben	56-1260
VEST, Lorenz	39	Bavaria	62-0758
Marie 39, Caroline 13			
VESTE, Nicoline	16	Schuettueber	58-0815
VETTE, Sophia	25	New York	58-0399
VETTER, Casper	33	Roda	56-0847
VETTER, Christian	19	Coburg	56-0847
VETTER, Ed.	21	Wulfsthal	59-0990
VETTER, Nic.	57	Salmsdorf	61-0167
VETTER, Richard	23	Pfiffelbach	61-0804
Linna 22, Minna 11m			
VETTERLEIN, Ferd.	16	New York	62-1112
VEY, Eva	23	Oberschwabach	57-1067
VEY, H.P.(m)	48	Baltimore	62-0730
VEY, Rudolph	23	Herlheim	57-1067
VEZZA, Paph.	35	Napoli	62-1042
VIAND, Mrs.	47	Paris	59-0477
VICEDENN, Georg	14	Burgweisach	59-1036
VIDEN, Helene	28	Crefeld	59-0613
VIEHACKER, Joseph	23	Wending/Bav.	61-0770
VIEHBROCK, Johanna	21	Hambergen/Han	60-0622
VIEHMANN, Ant.	20	Hornsheim	60-0334
VIEHMANN, Ed.(m)	18	Babenhausen	62-0836
VIELLEIBER, Marie	25	Oberstweiler	55-0812
VIERLA, Wenzel	40	Boehmen	58-0399
Marie 30, Joseph 9			
VIESON, Josef	23	Vechta	58-0306
VIETOR, O.	25	Varel	58-0604
VIEWEG, John B.	30	Lieme	57-0422
Julia 17, A. 40, Jane 26			
VIG, Therese	23	Freiburg	57-0606
VIGELIUS, Wilhelm	23	Limburg	56-0279
VILAIN, Antonia	30	Berlin	56-0632
VILETS, W.	36	Belgia	62-0938
VILLINGER, Anton	21	Freiburg	62-0993
VINER, Jos.	48	New York	62-1042
VINKE, Heinr.	16	Hille	56-0411
VINZIA, Luigo	33	Italy	61-0716
VION, M.(m)	35	Havana	61-0167
VISSEN, Ulrike	41	Williamsburg	58-0604
Ernst Ludwig 14			
VITTING, Aug.Herm.	24	Neustadt/Pr.	62-0608
VLOTH, Geo.	33	Bessel	56-0512
M. 30, Heinrich 3, John 9m			
VOBET, Gottlieb	14	Merchingen	59-0477
VOCKE, Georg	20	Minden	58-0576
VOCKE, Heinr. Wm.	17	Meinden	56-0629
VOEGE, Died.	27	Margelse	55-0413
VOEGELDING, Joh.He	35	Leer	59-0412
VOEGELE, Louise	21	Renningen	59-0214
VOEGTLI, Maria	16	Himmelried	62-0166
VOEHL, Catharina	24	Frankenberg	57-0924
Heinr.Andr. 15			

NAME	AGE	RESIDENCE	YR-LIST
VOEHRINGER, Wilh.	30	Leiningen	60-1032
Caroline 28, Carl 4			
VOEL, Heinrich	32	Hommelshain	59-0412
Lina 20, (daughter) bob			
VOELKE, Georg T.	48	Gebhardsreuth	60-0622
Barbara 36, Anna 14, Andres 8, Joseph 2			
VOELKEL, Heinrich	32	Hommelshain	59-0412
Lina 20, (daughter) bob			
VOELKENING, Friedr	35	Lauenhagen	59-0214
VOELKER, Christ.	43	Schwarzbach	60-0785
Cath. 36, Joseph 6, Cath. 3, Anna 55			
Caspar 26			
VOELKER, Elisabeth	24	Oberweimar	57-1192
VOELKER, Heinrich	19	Offelten	56-0589
Joseph 9m			
VOELKER, Herm.	32	Luenten	60-0334
VOELKER, Marie	20	Falkenberg	59-0990
VOELKERS, Caroline	16	Winzlar	56-1011
VOELKERT, Minna	23	Kieselbach	60-0334
Wilhelm 9m			
VOELLER, Friedrich	50	Henfstedt	61-0478
Euphrosine 51			
VOELMELE, Wilhelm	27	Hannover/Han.	55-1238
VOELPEL, Philip	67	Mehrenburg	57-1026
VOELTER, Ernst	25	Eschdorf	56-0819
VOELZ, Wilhelm	30	Griebnitz	58-0576
Caroline 30, Hermann 5, August 2			
VOERKEL, Mary Elen	49	Lindenau	57-1067
Valentin 22			
VOETZ, Wilhelm	30	Griebnitz	58-0576
Caroline 30, Hermann 5, August 2			
VOGEL, Abraham	27	Elberfeld	62-0232
VOGEL, Amalie	20	Lauterbach	60-1053
VOGEL, B.C.	30	Muehlhausen	58-0881
VOGEL, Babette	17	Redwitz	55-0630
VOGEL, Babette	20	Hermweiler/Pr	62-0608
VOGEL, Carl	20	Elberfeld	56-0847
VOGEL, Christ	34	Walheim	60-0334
VOGEL, Elisabeth	25	Graefenberg	59-0535
VOGEL, Fr.	35	New York	62-0938
VOGEL, Franz	27	Hofbieber	59-0951
Mary 28			
VOGEL, G.(m)	42	Thalheim	62-0730
VOGEL, Gustav	24	Sdt.Lengsfeld	62-0342
VOGEL, Heinrich	22	Curhessen	55-0634
Maria 18			
VOGEL, Heinrich	23	Rautenberg	61-0779
VOGEL, J.G.(m)	24	Graefenberg	61-0682
VOGEL, Joh.	25	Orenroth	60-0334
VOGEL, Johann Fr.	25	Thurnau	56-1117
VOGEL, Johann G.	40	Muenchaurach	59-0047
Elisabeth 39			
VOGEL, Johanne	26	Othlingen	60-0785
VOGEL, Johannes	41	Jever	57-1113
VOGEL, Johannes	28	Arnsfeld	62-0938
VOGEL, Mars	19	Kannstadt	62-1112
VOGEL, Michael	14	Suhl	55-0630
VOGEL, Michael	36	Frankenheim	56-1216
VOGEL, Pankratz	54	Redwitz/Bav.	60-0429
Magdalena 40, Barbara 14, Adam 10, Carl 3			
VOGEL, Rosa	18	Rilsen	60-1117
VOGEL, Rosine	16	Schwabitz	62-0836
VOGEL, S.M.(m)	58	Leitkirch	61-0804
VOGEL, Wilhelm	15	Tuebingen	55-0845
VOGELDORF, Dor.	32	Posen	57-1192
VOGELE, Pauline	24	Sinsheim	60-1053
VOGELEI, Lenore	52	Tanne	57-0850
VOGELLER, Maria	18	Havelkamp	59-0412
VOGELPOHL, August	19	Aithe	59-0412
VOGELSANG, Anna	19	Bremen	58-0881
Wilhelmine 44			
VOGELSANG, H.(m)	35	Boehmen	61-0897
VOGELSANG, Heinr.	16	Lixnen	58-0815
VOGELSANG, Jacob	47	Lixnen	58-0815
VOGELSANG, Jul.	24	Bremen	57-1148
VOGELSANG, Margar.	21	Bremen	57-0080
VOGELSANG, Maria	27	Bremen	59-0951
VOGES, Christian	24	Langenheim	57-0847

NAME	AGE	RESIDENCE	YR-LIST
VOGLER, Friedrich	21	Baltimore	56-1216
VOGLER, Wilhelm	24	Zigchin	59-0214
VOGT, An Cath.Marg	25	Schmetschen	58-0563
VOGT, Anton	31	Dornolzhausen	55-0413
VOGT, C.A.	20	Biedenkopf	62-0993
VOGT, Clara	20	Melle	57-0447
VOGT, Engel	16	Espelkamp	59-0951
VOGT, Friedrich	28	Kreisbueren	59-0372
VOGT, Friedrich	39	Delmenhorst	59-0477
VOGT, Herm.	24	Lohausen	62-0166
VOGT, Jacob	17	Lick	59-0048
VOGT, Peter	68	Germany	61-0167
VOGT, Theresia	19	Hinfeld	57-0704
VOGTS, Claus	18	Glinstedt	59-0951
VOIGT, Anton	48	Schlesien	58-0399
VOIGT, Carl Gottl.	32	Rochlitz	62-0879
VOIGT, Diedrich	40	Brinkum	57-0578
VOIGT, Ed.(m)	24	Merseburg	56-0723
VOIGT, Elisabeth	29	New York	57-1148
VOIGT, Friederike	20	Colberg	56-0723
VOIGT, H.A.	30	Birkenride	62-0993
J. 30, A. 4			
VOIGT, Theodor	19	Leipzig	59-0047
VOILIN, August	27	Niagara Falls	62-0467
VOLGER, Christian	44	Columbia	58-0885
VOLK, (m)	29	France	58-0306
VOLK, Babette	17	Kroedlingen	62-0730
VOLK, Magdalena	26	Daimbach	57-1407
VOLK, Paul	23	Ahorn	55-0932
VOLKAMER, J.M.	30	New York	62-1042
VOLKE, Andreas	30	Bischhausen	55-0812
Elisabeth 24, Dor. Carol. 4w			
VOLKELT, Herrmann	20	Camburg	60-0411
VOLKENAND, Conrad	15	Wittershausen	55-0538
VOLKENING, Fr.	38	Lauenhagen	62-0836
Sophie 32, Fr.W. 8, Heinr. 9m			
VOLKENING, Helene	31	New York	59-0951
VOLKER, Helene	19	Essen	60-0411
VOLKMANN, Charles	24	Gross Furra	56-1011
Amelia 24, Emily 6m			
VOLKMANN, J.M.	42	Wuerzburg	62-0730
VOLKMANN, Johann	23	Heuchelheim	62-0467
VOLKMANN, Martin	25	Untersleben	60-1141
VOLKMANN, Oscar	20	Wittenberg	61-0478
Richard 18			
VOLKMAR, Georg	26	Stankowo/Aust	60-0622
Josepha 21			
VOLKMAR, Georg	18	Kirchhasel	57-0704
VOLKOMMER, Jos.	42	Brooklyn	56-1216
Ros. 16			
VOLKWEIN, Jacob	27	Westhoyel	58-0604
VOLL, John	23	Nachtillhsn.	57-0422
VOLLERS, Ludw.	21	Spon	57-1416
VOLLERS, Minna	17	Spaden	62-0758
VOLLMAHN, Fritz	32	Hoya	57-0924
Elisabeth 34, Fritz by, Helene 18			
VOLLMANN, Fr'drke.	41	Wolenmshausen	57-1067
VOLLMANN, Gottlieb	37	Grosswender	57-1067
VOLLMANN, J.Sophie	43	Drexten	57-0924
Emilie 17			
VOLLMANN, Joseph	27	Tetschen	57-0704
VOLLMAR, Mar.Ther.	21	Leiboltz	57-1067
VOLLMER, Friedrike	25	Hohenstein	57-0021
VOLLMER, Jacob	56	Calw/Wuert.	61-0770
VOLLMER, Jacob	57	Stuttgart	62-0758
VOLLMEYER, (m)	31	Philadelphia	62-1112
VOLLMUELLER, Lina	19	Baden	60-1196
VOLLRATH, A.	27	Frankenhausen	56-0512
VOLLRATH, Angelika	27	Sporntheim	59-0951
VOLMER, Heinr.	19	Lauenhagen	62-0836
VOLMERDING, Marie	24	Bremen	60-0334
VOLTERS, Harmke	50	Neermoor	55-0413
VOLZ, Anna Cath.	20	Bernsburg/Hes	60-0371
Catharina 17			
VOLZ, Anna Maria	28	Winterbach	56-0819
VOLZ, Wilhelm	30	Wasserloos	60-0334
Marie 24			
VONDRAN, C.E.(m)	26	Eckartsberga	61-0482

NAME	AGE	RESIDENCE	YR-LIST
VONENTER, Boseth.	18	Bayern	57-0654
VORHAUER, Anna	21	Breitenbach	56-0411
VORNHOLZ, Friedr.	25	Thedinghausen	62-0879
VORS, Johannes	24	Buffalo	59-0384
Johanna 38			
VORSHEIM, Hermann	26	Muenster	60-0533
VORSPOHL, Theodor	23	Borghorst	59-0951
VORSTE, Heinrich	28	Prussia	57-1122
VORSTEHN, Bernhard	20	Delmenhorst	59-0477
VORWERK, Diedrich	17	Emstick	60-0533
VOSEBRING, Herm.G.	22	Quakenbrueck	57-0704
VOSHAGE, August	23	Vahlbruch	56-0819
VOSS, Andr.	43	New York	61-0804
Anna 33			
VOSS, Augustus	26	Rojanowo	57-0422
VOSS, Fr.Ad.St.	34	Westercappeln	57-1192
Cath.M.St. 32			
VOSS, Henriette	23	Neuenburg	57-0555
VOSS, Mary	24	Neuhaus	57-0654
VOSS, Minna	18	Gordelheim	57-0776
VOSS, Wilhelm	26	Wobel/Lippe	57-0847
Sophie 24			
VOSS, Wm.	11	Laer	59-1036
VOSSBRING, R.(m)	19	Cincinnati	62-0730
VOSSBRINK, Cath.A.	13	Gehrde	62-0836
VOSSKAMP, H.	35	Strohe	62-0730
Charlotte 2			
VOSSMANN, Friedr.	25	Ahrten	58-0399
VOULATUIN, Frances	30	France	62-0467
Anne 3, Louise 6m			
VREEMANN, Rosa	19	Oppenheim	60-0785
VRIES, de F.G.	48	Winkel	62-0938
Gertrude 43, Claus 19, Gerd 17			
Heinrich 11, Hermann 6, Gertrude 59			
Gertrude 13, Elise 8, Mathilde 5m			
Henriette 3			
VRJZL, Chr. B.	30	Neermoor	55-0413
Louise 24			
WAAS, Heinrich	25	Echzell	58-0881
WACHA, Franz	30	Boehmen	61-0716
Anna 29, Maria 4, Johann 8m			
WACHENFELD, J.Jac.	41	Nolhfelden	60-0411
Catharine 43, Henry 19, Charles 15			
Anna Cath. 13, Louise 9, Anna Mary 7			
WACHENFELL, Jacob	19	Oberzwehren	56-0527
WACHER, Barbara	17	Solmsdorf	59-0477
WACHMANN, Louise	16	Hille	56-0411
WACHT, Emily	25	Berlin	57-0654
Hedwig 5			
WACHTER, Margareta	30	Weizendorf	57-0754
WACKER, Eugen	30	Stuttgart	62-0938
WACKER, Johanna	22	Bruchsal	62-0836
WACKERNAGEL, Nicl.	22	Zeitz	57-1113
WAECHTER, Elise	40	Bielefeld	56-1044
Heinrich 6, Augusta 4			
WAECHTER, Fritz	21	Hanau	59-0951
Caroline 51			
WAECHTER, Nicolaus	48	Tyrol	59-0048
WAECHTERSHAUSEN, J	20	Offenbach	60-1141
WAECKER, Xaver	30	Altheim/Baden	56-0819
WAEFERLING, Ludwig	43	Badenwerder	60-1196
WAETGEN, Heinrich	15	Offenwarden	60-0411
Anna Hedwig 14			
WAGAESTER, Cathar.	50	Niederhone/He	61-0770
Elisabeth 13, Friedrich 11			
WAGEMANN, Friedr.H	26	Preussen	56-1044
Franziska 24			
WAGENER, Anton	28	Donauwoerth	55-0932
WAGENER, Anton	18	Koblenz/Main	56-0632
WAGENER, Charlotte	22	Dillstedt	61-0478
WAGENER, Christian	23	Salzungen	61-0478
WAGENER, Gottlieb	25	Preussen	58-0399
WAGENER, H.(m)	56	Geilshausen	61-0669
Marie 50, Elise 18, Joh. 12			
WAGENER, Ludwig	25	Bieber	57-0924
Catharine 28			
WAGENFUHR, A.(m)	24	Ilsenburg	61-0897
WAGENHAUSER, Bernh	67	Kl.Steinach	62-0306
Barbara 66, Bernhard 30			
WAGENKNECHT, Aug.	23	Taura	58-0576
WAGENLAENDER, Mar.	17	Groningen	59-0477
Barbara 14			
WAGENSEIL, Joseph	19	Isny	56-0629
WAGESTER, Georg	19	Niederhohn	56-0723
WAGNER, Amalie	21	Marksteft	62-0730
WAGNER, Anna	18	Bettendorf	56-0512
WAGNER, Anna	26	Watzenbach	56-0723
WAGNER, Bernh.	53	Grampach	58-0815
WAGNER, Bernhard	13	Sickershausen	62-0730
WAGNER, Bertha	30	Prenzlau	57-0422
Hugh 5, Richard 3, Magdalena 2, Arnold 6m			
WAGNER, C.(m)	20	Nuernberg	61-0804
WAGNER, Carl	13	Biedenkopf	57-1067
WAGNER, Caspar	46	Rauschenburg	57-1280
Dorette 56, Catharina 12, Conrad 9			
WAGNER, Casten	24	Lusen/Pruss.	55-1238
WAGNER, Catharina	40	Offenbach/Hes	62-0342
WAGNER, Ch.	24	Sickershausen	62-0730
WAGNER, Ch. Gottf.	38	Sachsen	60-0411
Joh. Christ. 41, Aug. Louise 11			
WAGNER, Christian	34	Heiligenstadt	60-1032
Elise 30			
WAGNER, Conrad	34	Feuersbach	60-1161
Cath. 26, Conrad 4			
WAGNER, Dietrich	30	Grebenstein	60-1053
WAGNER, E.(f)	52	Sand	57-0555
WAGNER, Elisabeth	19	Niederaula	57-0704
WAGNER, Elisabeth	23	Bieden/Hessen	62-0608
WAGNER, Emil	18	Hundshausen	55-0413
WAGNER, Emilie	19	Meiningen	62-0758
WAGNER, Ernst	38	Gissen	62-0758
WAGNER, Fr.(m)	23	Fordon	59-0951
WAGNER, Friedrich	36	Niederhausen	57-1407
Elise 35, Georg 10, Wilhelm 8, Marie 6			
Elisabeth 5			
WAGNER, Georg	31	Adelsdorf	55-0845
WAGNER, Georg	18	Hettenstein	59-0047
WAGNER, Georg F.	16	Gieboldehsn.	55-0413
WAGNER, Gustav	23	Dittendorf	59-0951
WAGNER, H.	25	New York	59-0613
WAGNER, Heinrich	19	Hessen	59-0372
WAGNER, J.L.	19	Kl. Bathwar	58-0604
WAGNER, Joh.	22	Hessen	60-1161
WAGNER, Joh.	21	Boehmen	62-1042
WAGNER, Joh. Georg	58	Dillstadt/Pr.	62-0608
Anna Marg. 58, Amalie Rosam 27, Louise 22			
Herrmann 19, Jette 15, Johannes 13			
WAGNER, Johann	38	Weiler/Pruss.	55-1238
Cathrina 29, Catharina 7, Margaretha 6			
Anna 5, Nicolaus 4, Mathias 1			
WAGNER, Johann	15	Riedesheim	61-0047
WAGNER, Johann	24	Bamberg/Bav.	62-0342
WAGNER, John	51	Hausen	59-1036
Friedr. 19			
WAGNER, Jos.	50	Griesbach	55-0413
Louise 24			
WAGNER, Joseph	28	Schwabelweiss	61-0520
Therese 23			
WAGNER, L.	33	Bronnau	59-0990
(baby) by			
WAGNER, Margreta	19	Kettenkamp	60-1032
WAGNER, Maria	38	Offenbach	58-0881
Hermann 15, Johann 13, Louis 9, Marie 5			
WAGNER, Maria	30	Altorf	61-0520
Margaretha 7			
WAGNER, Marianne	20	Schwirbitz	56-1044
WAGNER, Michael	22	Jarotschin	56-0847
WAGNER, Minna	25	Nidda	59-0214
WAGNER, Peter	58	Ohio	56-1216
WAGNER, Theresia	24	Knittelbach	57-1026
WAGNER, Wilhelm	29	Hochweisel/He	62-0608
Barbeta 25, Wilhelm 4, Friedrich 10m			
WAGNER, William	42	Stolberg	57-0422
Emma 18			
WAGNER, Wm.	34	Hessen	62-0730
Eva 30, Julia 6, Wm. 4, Conrad 26			

NAME	AGE	RESIDENCE	YR-LIST
Catharine 24			
WAHL, Catharina	23	Vaterrode	56-0847
WAHL, Herm.	36	Braunschweig	60-0785
WAHL, Maria	16	Wenjes	55-0413
WAHLEN, Franz	21	Altona	60-0533
WAHLER, Christoph	42	Salzungen	61-0478
Margaretha 25, Christiane 20, Maria 18			
Friederike 16, Christian 14			
Heinr.(died) 8m, August 3, Christel 2			
WAHLER, Waldemar	27	Roetchenbroda	57-1192
WAHLERS, Friedr.	25	Stelligt	59-0535
WAHLSING, Fr.	49	Rosenhagen	57-1067
Christine 40, Christine 17, Wilhelmine 16			
Louise 12, Friedrich 9, Hanne 8			
Lausanne 6, Sophie 3			
WAHN, Heinrich	17	Oberaula	56-1044
WAHRTMANN, Hm.	17	Gehrde	59-0535
WAIBEL, v. (f)	32	France	62-0938
Amalie 4, Liene 24			
WAID, Johann	18	Gissigheim/Bd	60-0622
WAINER, Mary	19	Blaubeuren	57-1192
WAJHANN, Georg	41	New York	60-0334
WALBEN, Jacob	28	Barrau	57-0961
Theresa 31, Joseph 10m			
WALBRUNN, D.(m)	25	Missouri	61-0897
WALCH, Anna	22	Kalte Nordhm.	57-1280
WALCHER, Adam	37	Unterbalzheim	60-0334
Susanne 37, Johann 14, Anna 9, Barbara 8			
Magdalena 7, Anna 5, Catharina 6m			
WALD, Anna Maria	20	Bischwind/Bav	60-0622
WALD, Heinrich	17	Philippsthal	60-0622
WALD, Margar.	28	Cassel	59-0535
WALDA, Heinrich	18	Quetzen	55-0812
Friedrich 18			
WALDECK, J.	26	Lengfeld	56-0512
Betty 26, Caroline 20			
WALDHAUER, Johann	33	Priesingen	57-1026
WALDHEIM, Hedwig R	22	Willazhufen	61-0107
WALDINGER, Wilhmne	36	Barmen	57-0961
Charles 15, August 9, Laura 4			
WALDMANN, Fr.	33	Seesen	57-1148
Friedricke 21, August 6m			
WALDMANN, Heinz	27	Muehlhofen	62-1112
WALDMANN, Hermann	21	Gerstungen	58-0576
WALDOERFER, Joh.Ge	30	Madison	59-0613
WALHOFF, Joh.	26	Garbenteich	59-1036
WALKA, Maria	24	Wien	59-0214
WALKENHORST, Jos.	29	Mawitz	56-0527
WALKER, Christian	26	Lockhausen	56-0589
Johanne 27			
WALKER, Jos.	25	Unterbalzheim	59-1036
WALKER, Pauline	15	Wuertemberg	57-0436
WALL, Matthias	28	Roetenbach	57-0447
Catharine 24			
WALLACH, Marianne	44	Schwarzenborn	55-0628
Fromine 20, Johanne 18, Jacob 17			
Roeschen 15, Betty 12, Regina 7			
WALLAN, D.H.(m)	35	New York	60-0785
Jahn (f) 27			
WALLANCH, Peter	19	Schwarzenborn	60-0785
Dina 45			
WALLBRACH, Jul.	56	Wetzlar	61-0669
WALLBRECHT, A.(m)	26	Liebenau	60-1196
WALLEISEN, Georg	23	Sandheim	56-0411
WALLENHAUPT, Joh.	21	Wickersrode	57-0924
WALLENSTEIN, Kaeth	25	Hohenlohe	60-0785
WALLENSTEIN, M.	30	Laubach	62-1112
Jettchen 59, Salomon 30, Fanny 35			
WALLERS, Joh.	19	Verden	58-0306
WALLERSTEIN, Betty	27	Hanau	62-0938
WALLERSTEIN, F.	23	Bischoffsheim	62-0938
WALLESER, Justin	26	Baden	59-0477
WALLING, Heinr.	15	Moordorf	62-0232
WALLIS, (f)	42	Canada	56-1216
WALLIS, F.	42	Chicago	62-1112
Sidonie 24			
WALLMANN, Christ.	33	Linden	56-1216
WALLMANN, Julius	27	New York	56-1216

NAME	AGE	RESIDENCE	YR-LIST
WALLNER, Cath.	57	Rothbuegel	59-0384
Cath. 28, Joseph 5, Carl 3			
WALPER, Johannes	17	Gilfershausen	60-0429
WALSER, J.	31	Wangen	62-1042
WALTE, Joseph	20	Bohemia	55-0634
WALTE, Susanna	22	Schwarza	57-0847
WALTE, Susanne	27	Schonweissbch	57-0447
Catharine 24			
WALTEMAT, Charlott	27	Bremen	57-1192
WALTER, Adolph	24	Fritzlar	57-0654
Louise 23			
WALTER, Andreas	25	Schirnsdorf	60-0533
WALTER, Andreas	25	Jagstheim	60-1032
WALTER, August	34	Prussia	58-0885
WALTER, Augustina	18	Hessen	62-0306
WALTER, Chr.	39	Mengerskirchn	59-1036
Cath. 30, Maria 24			
WALTER, Chr.Carl	42	Muenchen	58-0925
Maria 38			
WALTER, Elisabetha	18	Steinbach	60-1053
WALTER, Elise	21	Hitzerode	61-0669
WALTER, Ernst	19	Asch	57-0447
WALTER, Fanny	21	Muehlhausen	60-0521
WALTER, H.	58	Raiding	59-1036
Caroline 50, Friedrich 28, Heinrich 11m			
WALTER, H.(m)	50	Leipzig	60-0785
Peter 22			
WALTER, Heinr.Fr'd	23	Crimmitschau	57-0924
Dorothea 33, Marie 11, Wilhelmine 8			
WALTER, Heinrich	26	Heppenheim	62-1112
Anna M. 25			
WALTER, J.	16	Steiner	56-0512
WALTER, Jacob	36	Buchau	59-0384
Aloys 14			
WALTER, John	33	Fustel	60-1141
WALTER, Jos.	18	Ried	62-1112
WALTER, Joseph	52	Bobenhausen	55-0845
Catharina 18, Carl 18, Catharina 16			
Marie 12, Friedrich 3, Heinrich by			
WALTER, Joseph	26	Heppdiel	60-1032
WALTER, Theresa	26	Muenster	61-0047
Ferdinand 5, Johanna 11m			
WALTER, Wilhelm	19	Dornhagen	57-0754
WALTERMANN, Bernh.	29	Beelen/Pr.	62-0608
WALTERS, Heimann	61	Jersey	61-0897
Helene 45, Dorette 15			
WALTHER, Anna	28	Windischbach	61-0520
Andreas 48, Anna Maria 36, Franz 12			
Julius Albin 3			
WALTHER, C.L.(m)	22	Thalheim	62-0401
WALTHER, Carl	25	Glashuetten	55-0932
Malis 23, Conrad 4			
WALTHER, Cath.	61	Calen	59-0951
WALTHER, Conrad	36	Weiss	60-0334
WALTHER, Friedrike	42	Jena	62-1169
Hermine 23, Clara 13, Carl 9, Louis 8			
Edmund 2			
WALTHER, G.	30	Philadelphia	62-1112
WALTHER, Georg	55	Kruspis	55-1082
Anna Cath. 50, Anna 21, Elisabeth 14			
Friedrich 10, Johann 8, Elisabeth by			
WALTHER, Heinrich	28	Basdorf	57-1407
WALTHER, Leopold	25	Arnstadt	60-0398
Amalie 22			
WALTHER, Louise	36	Muehlen	60-1053
WALTHER, Mar. El.	23	Reichensachsn	61-0478
WALTHER, Martin	16	Darmstadt	57-1407
Bernhard 18			
WALTHER, Mich.	22	Nanndorf	59-0477
WALTHER, Reinhardt	55	Muentzenberg	62-0712
WALTJEN, Heinr.	58	Bremen	61-0897
WALTJEN, Heinrich	20	Bremen	56-0723
WALTROOP, Joh.	16	Leeste	59-0477
WALTRUP, Johann	34	Aldenhausen	57-0447
WALZ, Carl	31	Weilersteisin	59-1017
WALZ, Christ.	28	Marinkuhlen	60-0334
WALZ, Georg	22	Waldmichelbac	59-0412
WALZ, Gottfr.	26	Ebhausen	62-0166

NAME	AGE	RESIDENCE	YR-LIST
Barbara 26			
WALZ, Heinrich	19	Frieberg/Hess	60-0371
WALZ, J.G.(m)	17	Wannweil	61-0482
WALZ, Louis	22	Schlessingen	58-0815
WAMBACH, Adam	40	Albshausen	57-0754
Maria 36, Elise 9, Anna 4			
WAMBOLD, Hanna	21	Cronheim	60-0521
WAND, Joh. Georg	39	Obermehler	57-0924
Friederike 33, August 11, Bertha 9			
WANDER, Wilhelm	40	Welrodekilza	55-0538
WANDMACHER, W.	30	New York	62-0836
Meta 22, Henriette 20, Anna 3m			
WANDREI, Wilhelm	26	Kimnolewohan	57-1113
Louise 22			
WANDVAHL, Caroline	13	Eichhorst	56-0411
WANEK, Martin	34	Boehmen	61-0930
Anna 25, Petronilla 5m			
WANEMEYER, C.	30	Uptloh	62-0938
WANETZ, John	52	Boehmen	62-0938
Catharine 54, Johann 21, Franz 16			
Carl 12, Marie 19			
WANFRIED, Ernst	23	Greussen	60-0533
WANGEMANN, Sophie	23	Seckenburg	57-1407
WANITZ, Aug.	19	Rueckleben	55-0932
WANKEL, Theresa	53	Fulda	59-1036
Wm. 21			
WANKELMANN, Fr.	38	Mehnen	57-1192
Meta 33, John 8			
WANKELMANN, Wilh.	17	Mehnen	57-1192
Charlotte 17			
WANN, Hironimus	26	Neisse	55-0845
Louise 15			
WAPPNER, Christian	25	Heiligenstadt	62-0342
WARDENSCHLAG, Jul.	34	Strassburg	59-0951
Babett(died) 6			
WARDMANN, Julius	19	Kirchzandern	60-0785
WARHARNICH, Matias	36	Boehmen	56-0411
WARK, Chr.	23	Braunschweig	55-0932
WARKMEISTER, Eliza	52	Rodenburg	60-1141
Mary 21			
WARLIK, Marie	30	Holkonitz	57-1416
WARMUND, Carl	20	Wiesbaden	59-0535
WARMUTH, Ann	24	Euerdorf	61-0669
WARNECKE, Johann	30	Selchow	56-0819
WARNECKE, Minna	20	Bremervoerde	61-0804
WARNECKE, Wilh'mne	26	Teiterberg	58-0815
WARNECKE, Wilh.	25	Teiterberg	58-0815
WARNER, Joseph	38	Buffalo	62-0730
Kathie 35			
WARNER, Maria	16	Bisenz	62-0730
Louis 9, Leopold 8			
WARTERS, W.	24	Canada	59-1036
James 9m			
WASENER, Johanna	28	Nagolsheim	61-0779
WASMUTH, Catharina	22	Roda	57-1280
WASMUTH, Johann	23	Rohde	57-0924
WASSERHAUSER, Elis	24	New York	59-0951
Louise 3, Anna 3m			
WASSERMANN, Jette	49	Mkt.Deggingen	61-0804
Jette 21, Regina 18, Haga 16, Helene 4			
WASSININ, Friedr.	32	Palmer	58-0885
WASSMANN, Ludwig	37	Eimbeck	62-0983
Minna 32			
WASSMUTH, Marie	19	Pickelsheim	59-1036
Pauline 21			
WASSNUSS, Balduin	38	Nordhausen	60-0429
Emma 33, Balduin 6, Erich 4, Oscar 2			
WASSUNG, Philipp	4	Mainz	59-0613
WATERMANN, G.(m)	30	New York	62-0467
WATERMANN, Sophie	30	Rehren	57-0847
August 14			
WATERMEYER, F.W.	21	Bremen	59-0384
WATSACK, Carl	17	Graefenau	60-0521
WATSON, J.	24	England	62-1112
WATSON, Wm.	27	England	62-0938
WAX, Nicolaus	32	New Orleans	62-1169
WEBE, Maria	55	BUchholz	60-0398
Elisabeth 25			

NAME	AGE	RESIDENCE	YR-LIST
WEBER, Ad.	27	Alt Wildungen	62-0730
WEBER, Andreas	30	Dembach	57-1407
Wilhelmine 28, Friederike by			
WEBER, Anna	35	Wetzikan	58-0925
WEBER, Anna	28	Speyer	59-0384
WEBER, Anna	25	Furth	62-1112
WEBER, Barb.	23	Herford	59-0384
WEBER, Carl	12	Neckartenzlin	62-0730
WEBER, Carl Fr.	39	Dresden	56-0629
Henriette 32, M. Louise 15, Pauline 7			
WEBER, Carl Jul.	52	Suhl/Pr.	55-0628
Herrmann 21			
WEBER, Catharina	68	Holzhausen	56-1117
WEBER, Catharine	25	Schwarzenborn	57-0754
WEBER, Catharine	21	Schleid	57-0447
WEBER, Catharine	24	Fischbach	62-0001
WEBER, Christoph	22	Hempelstadt	56-0632
WEBER, Conrad	33	Alsfeld	56-0847
WEBER, Conrad	27	Bodungen	57-1192
WEBER, Dietrich	26	Sandstaedt	57-0850
WEBER, E. (Dr.)	31	Vernau	59-0951
Sophie 23			
WEBER, Elisabeth	16	Schweringen	56-0723
WEBER, Elisabeth	55	Kurhessen	56-1044
Catharina 26, Elisabeth 10			
WEBER, Elisabeth	25	Rauschenberg	62-0938
WEBER, Elise	25	Germany	59-0951
WEBER, Fr. (m)	18	Schweringen	56-0723
WEBER, Fr.(m)	26	Halberstadt	62-0608
WEBER, Friedr.	9m	Wernau	59-0951
WEBER, Friedrich	21	Meyenburg/Han	60-0622
WEBER, Friedrich	26	Schwarzennach	57-1122
WEBER, Friedrich	26	Wendbostel	59-0535
WEBER, H.(m)	32	Schweningen	61-0897
WEBER, Heinr.	21	Stangenruth	56-0527
WEBER, Heinr.	24	Schillingstdt	59-1036
WEBER, Heinrich	23	Bremen	60-1032
WEBER, Herm.	25	Obersontheim	62-0836
WEBER, J.	34	Grombach	62-0993
M. 36, A. 10, E. 4, G. 1			
WEBER, Jacob	26	Graefenberg	59-0535
WEBER, Joh. Elise	56	Leipzig	58-0885
WEBER, Joh.Friedr.	55	Buer	56-1044
Elisabeth 40, Joh.Friedr. 8			
WEBER, Johann	18	Langenstein	62-0608
Catharine 22			
WEBER, Johanna	23	Ratebor	55-0812
WEBER, Johanna	44	Oberheidl	57-0850
WEBER, Johanna	30	Michelstadt	59-0477
Carolina 23, Mathilda 19			
WEBER, Johannes	22	Hessen	57-0447
WEBER, Johannes	22	Bamberg	62-0712
WEBER, John G.	20	Hamburg	60-1053
WEBER, Louise	18	Gittelde	56-0723
WEBER, Louise	32	Seesen	56-0527
WEBER, Louise	20	Detmold	60-0334
Louis 14			
WEBER, Marie L.	17	Brockhausen	56-0951
WEBER, Marie Lenor	18	Brockhausen	56-0951
WEBER, Math.H.	57	Lingen	56-1117
A.(f) 50			
WEBER, Michael	33	Kabelsdorf	61-0478
WEBER, Michael	39	Reifberg/Bav.	62-0608
WEBER, Rosine	18	Kupferzelle	62-1169
WEBER, Sophie	58	Fischbach	62-0467
Theodore 21			
WEBER, Theodora	43	Arnstadt/Thur	55-0628
Fritz 17			
WEBER, Valentin	44	Obersuhl	56-0723
Fromine 20			
WEBER, Wilhelm	16	Schweringen	60-0533
WEBER, Wilhelm	38	Holzhausen	56-1117
Sophie 38, Sophie 9, Wilhelm 6			
WEBER, Wm.	28	Arheilgen	60-0785
Johann 23			
WEBER, v. Albert	28	Jena	57-1148
WEBERICH, Mary Ann	49	Hammelburg	61-0779
WEBES, Johanna	23	Ratebor	55-0812

NAME	AGE	RESIDENCE	YR-LIST
WECERKA, Franz	34	Boehmen	61-0482
Rosalie 30			
WECH, Anton	37	Lischin	58-0881
Barbara 38, Catharina 7, Johann 3			
Maria 6m			
WECHTKAMP, Maria	91	Hiller	59-1036
WECKELER, Kilian	23	Zell	56-1260
WECKER, Heinrich	25	Stemmen	56-1260
WECKERT, Heinr.	17	Sachsenhausen	59-0535
WECKESSER, Georg C	27	Moeckemuehl	57-0924
WECKMANN, Johannes	16	Ostheim/Hess.	62-0608
WEDDING, Johann	56	Luenten	60-0334
Wilhelm 21, Grethe 19, Heinr. 6			
Gerhard 5			
WEDDING, Marie	38	Altstaedte	60-0334
Heinr. 35, Bernhard 5, Margaretha 4			
Margaretha 7			
WEDDINGFELD, Luise	17	Bremen	62-0938
WEDEKAMP, Heinrich	20	Bielefeld	57-0447
WEDEKIND, Fritz	26	Bremerhaven	61-0716
WEDEKING, Christof	34	Beckeloh	61-0520
Sophie 27, Dorothea 5, Wilhelm 2m			
WEDEL, Friedrich	58	Irenbusch	56-1011
Carolina 58, Albertine 26, Charles 25			
William 22, Wilhelmine 18			
WEDELSTADT, v.Carl	29	Grabow	61-0930
WEDEMEYER, Christ.	18	Hannover	55-0634
WEDEMEYER, E.	41		62-0993
E. 36, A. 16, W. 10, E. 7, C. 4, W. 11m			
WEDEMEYER, Friedr.	18	Drangstedt	56-1117
WEDEMEYER, Gottfr.	21	Probsthagen	60-0785
WEDEMEYER, H.(m)	29	New York	62-0111
WEDEMEYER, Philipp	26	Sillium	58-0925
WEDHAWERM, Eliese	24	Maar	56-0527
WEECKE, Fr. (m)	29	New York	56-0951
M. 36			
WEECKE, Louise C.	29	Engershausen	56-0951
Heinrich 3			
WEESEMANN, Louise	47	Morsenberg/L.	62-0608
Hermann 19, Florentine 16, Fritz 13			
WEFEL, Cath.	19	Haltern	62-0401
WEFERS, Luedger	27	Emdessen	61-0107
WEGENER, Ch.	66	Cheersdorf	59-1036
WEGENER, Fr.	44	Trebbin	57-1148
Amalie 25, Wilhelmine 14, August 9			
Armand 4			
WEGENER, Friedr.	25	Werblitz	59-0384
WEGENER, Friedrich	34	Berlin	56-0819
Christiane 33			
WEGENER, Friedrike	16	New York	62-0467
WEGENER, Fritz	25	Langwedel	62-0712
WEGENER, Gottlieb	55	Prussia	57-0555
Elisabeth 47, Gotthelf 24, Chr.(m) 20			
Gottlieb 7, Christine 17, Elisabeth 1			
Ernst 9			
WEGENER, Mathilde	22	Kleinpardorf	60-0521
WEGJAHR, Charlotte	22	Emsdetten	62-0938
WEGMANN, August	17	Lengerich	62-0467
WEGMANN, Cath.L.	27	Lengerich	57-0422
Wilhelmina 22			
WEGNER, Wilhelm	28	Neu Wuhrow	60-0371
WEHBERG, Elise	36	Ankum	59-1036
WEHMANN, Carl	26	Wingassen	60-1053
WEHMANN, H.(m)	16	Burgdam	62-0401
WEHMEYER, Fr.(m)	58	Lippe	57-0555
L.(f) 48, L.(f) 26, L.(f) 9			
WEHNER, Anna	24	Salzungen	55-0413
WEHNER, Friedr.	37	Elster	59-0951
WEHNER, J.A.	39	Dornbach	62-0993
C. 28, P. 3			
WEHNING, Herrmann	26	Emstaedt	61-0930
WEHR, Christine	23	Heuthen	57-0606
WEHR, Joseph	21	Heuthen	57-0606
WEHR, Michael	13	Heuthen	57-0436
Wilhelm 11			
WEHRENBERG, Diedr.	30	Schweringen	60-0533
WEHRICH, Friedrike	28	Chemnitz	56-0847
Jacob 29			

NAME	AGE	RESIDENCE	YR-LIST
WEHRKAMP, Wm.	19	Citter	59-1036
WEHRLI, Anna	9	Kuettingen	59-0951
WEHRMANN, Friedr.	24	Ostermunsel/H	61-0770
WEHRMANN, Joh.G.	23	Rheinland	60-0371
WEIBEL, Jos.	38	Elmira	62-0232
WEIBER, Ignatius	54	Fritzlar	57-0654
Elisabeth 53			
WEIBLINGER, Johana	21	Oberhinkhofen	62-0467
WEICHERT, Barbara	28	Romelshausen	57-0776
Philipp 22			
WEICHSELBAUM, C.	36	Fuerth	61-0716
WEICHSELBAUM, Carl	30	New York	57-1148
WEICHSELBAUM, Crln	16	Bitzfeld	57-1148
WEICHSELBAUM, Theo	21	Frankfurt/M.	56-0413
WEICKER, Georg	37	Baltimore	62-1042
Joh. 9			
WEICKERT, Carl	20	Reichstadt	58-0563
WEIDEMANN, Carolne	20	Lihrn	55-0630
WEIDEMANN, Henry	47	Lyhren	59-0384
Wilhelmine 50, Wilhelmine 15, Johann 12			
Christ. 8, Engel Marie 6, Hanne 36			
Sophie 5			
WEIDEMANN, J.(m)	18	Singlis	62-0836
WEIDEMANN, Nanny	20	New York	59-0951
WEIDENFELD, Leopld	15	Langendorfles	62-0712
Wilhelmine 18			
WEIDENHAMMER, Amal	39	Grossenstein	60-1053
WEIDENHOEFER, A.	30	Vegesack	62-0993
WEIDINGER, Adele	19	Reudnitz	62-0730
WEIDINGER, Barbara	27	Hilpoltstein	56-0632
WEIDINGER, Johann	30	Brueckenau	60-0533
WEIDLICH, G.H.	20	Aurich	62-0993
WEIDLING, Christ.	30	Preussen	57-0606
Friederike 21			
WEIDMANN, Caroline	17	Adelsheim	59-1036
Christoph 19			
WEIDUNGER, Carolne	23	Elsingen	58-0399
WEIERMANN, Rosa	58	Burgkundstadt	62-0730
Lena 20			
WEIERT, Joh.	15	Soell	57-0578
WEIFEBORN, Margar.	18	Frankfurt a/M	57-1407
WEIGAND, Cath.	21	Bavaria	60-1161
Marg. 21			
WEIGAND, J.C.	37	Gulchstein	59-0384
WEIGAND, Mathias	58	Bernbach	57-0436
Georg 56			
WEIGAND, Rosine	28	Laibach	61-0478
Caecilie 30			
WEIGAND, Traugott	20	Schwarzenburg	58-0399
WEIGEL, Eduard	32	Roswaag	60-0411
Mary 46, Johanna 16, Conrad 14			
WEIGLE, Dorothea	20	Leutenbach	61-0520
WEIGLE, Friederike	24	Backnang	61-0716
WEIGOLD, L.Ph.	19	Auerbeck	59-0613
WEIH, Mary	14	Steinbach	60-0411
WEIHL, Carl	25	Homberg	59-0990
WEIHMANN, Johann	28	Brandt	56-0527
WEIHNAU, Carl	30	Witzenhausen	56-0847
WEIL, Babette	30	Wostraczien	62-1112
WEIL, Carl	19	Hesse-Darmst.	58-0399
WEIL, Carl	18	Herzens/Boehm	59-0047
WEIL, Ernst	40	Muenster	59-0384
Elisabeth 17, Cath. 15			
WEIL, H.J.	22	Espa	59-0384
WEIL, H.S.(m)	33	Germany	62-0467
WEIL, Jacob	19	Fuerth	56-1044
WEIL, Julius	21	Horeenz	59-0477
WEIL, Samuel	36	Illinois	62-0758
Anna 20			
WEIL, Sara	27	Adelsheim	56-1216
WEILAND, Peter	30	Mischede	60-0334
WEILER, Ed. (m)	29	Hersberg	57-0447
Johanna 34			
WEILER, Margar.	23	Langenau	59-0384
WEILER, Otto	28	Herzberg/Pr.	55-1238
Louise 24			
WEILERS, Minna	28	Berlin	62-0730
WEILKOPF, Ernest	32	Roloven	57-0654

NAME	AGE	RESIDENCE	YR-LIST
WEILRING, Gerh.	33	Lasser	59-0951
WEIMANN, Amalie	20	Holtensen	57-0924
WEIMANN, Friedrich	30	Rehburg	56-1044
WEIMANN, Leonhard	36	Bonzenweiler	56-0632
WEIMAR, Jacob	22	Alsfeld/Hesse	62-0608
WEIMAR, Martin	26	Rod	57-0509
WEINBERG, Clara	25	Zirden	56-0951
WEINBERG, Elise	25	Wildeshausen	60-0785
WEINBERG, Mariane	18		56-0629
WEINBERGER, Balth.	27	Brueckenau	62-0879
WEINBERGER, Heinr.	22	Lauterbach	62-0879
WEINBERGER, Johann	29	Hesse-Darmst.	56-1044
WEINDORF, Jac.	38	New York	62-1112
WEINEK, Elisabeth	25	Oberzwehren	56-0527
WEINEMANN, Bramke	21	Feuchtingen	57-0961
WEINGAERTNER, Chr.	49	Weigertheim	60-0334
Helene 20, Wilhelmine 15, Friedr. 13			
WEINGUTH, Ferd.	48	Lehpehne	56-0951
Marie 35			
WEINHARDT, Paul	23	Rottenburg	57-0021
Pauline 21			
WEINKAUF, John	17	Bavaria	57-0847
WEINMANN, Fanny	20	Gunzenhausen	59-0951
WEINMANN, Minna	33	Fuerth	59-0951
Ernst 3, Georg 2			
WEINMANN, Reinhold	19	Roemhild	62-0879
WEINMANN, Sara	34	Feuchtlingen	57-0961
WEINSCHENK, Louise	24	Muehlberg	61-0482
WEINSTEIN, Marcus	27	Warsten	57-1148
WEINSTEIN, Matilda	18	Fritzlar	57-0961
WEINSTEIN, Matilda	18	Hessen	57-0961
WEINSTOCK, Carolne	20	Cassel/Hessen	62-0608
WEINSTOCK, Rosa	24	Kackhausen	59-0477
WEIPERT, Henry	14	Wernges	57-0654
WEIPPERT, Michael	29	Maasbach/Bav.	62-0608
Bernhardine 26, Reinhard 5, Jacobine 2			
WEIRATHER, Franz	29	Elbingenalp	55-0413
WEIRAUCH, Minna	16	Gottmannshaus	60-0521
Johann 59			
WEIS, Bertha	17	Giesen	55-1048
Hermann 15			
WEIS, Rosina	21	Pahres	56-0629
WEISBAECKER, Herm.	26	Heidhausen	55-0812
Christine 32, Christine 5, Wilhelm 4			
Louise 11w			
WEISBECHER, Martin	15	Obernau	61-0779
WEISBROD, Andr.	28	New York	62-0836
WEISE, J.G.(m)	26	Munningen	61-0482
WEISE, Minna	20	Berlin	57-1148
Fr. 16			
WEISE, Oscar	18	Lobschuetz	56-0589
WEISEL, Catharina	29	Robertshausen	56-0589
WEISENBORN, Carl	24	Braunhausen	56-1011
George 20			
WEISENBORN, Wilh.	31	Langensalza	62-0306
WEISER, Paul	27	Oppeln	57-0422
Francizka 23			
WEISER, Wilhelm	24	Schmillinghsn	57-1113
WEISHAAR, Emerich	20	Luderbusch	55-0932
WEISHAUPT, Cath.	20	Augsburg	57-1280
WEISHAUPT, Conrad	29	Granchenwies	57-1192
Wendelin 15, Josepha 47, Marianne 23			
Lucie 8			
WEISHAUPT, Werner	18	Altendorf	57-0754
WEISMANN, A.(m)	38	St.Louis	61-0804
Nanette 28			
WEISS, A.(m)	30	New York	60-0785
WEISS, Adolph	19	Unterhadau	59-0613
WEISS, Anton	59	Danzig	62-0758
Catharine 50, Franz 24, Joseph 21			
Marianne 18, Josephine 16, Jacob 13			
WEISS, Augusta	32	Marburg	59-1036
WEISS, Carl	24	Moeskirch/Bad	61-0770
WEISS, Christ.	29	Unterkessach	59-0214
WEISS, Christ.	44	Boistedt	59-0613
Clara 47			
WEISS, Christian	26	Nitzingen/Wrt	62-0608
WEISS, Christian	27	New York	59-0048
WEISS, Ester	26	Jarotschin	56-0847
WEISS, Eva	24	Kaichen	59-0047
Catharine 2			
WEISS, Fanny	25	Choldau	60-0785
Albert 16, Josephine 14			
WEISS, Fr.	38	Boston	62-1042
Marie 32, Laura 7, Marie 6			
WEISS, J.G.E.	39	Langgrun	62-0467
Gottlieba 42, Wilhelmine 14, Herm. 9			
Beata 7, Edw. 5, Heinr. 2			
WEISS, Jacob	24	Roda	56-0847
WEISS, Joh.B.	24	Goldlauter	58-0563
Fr.Wm. 22			
WEISS, Johann	34	Ob.Ottersbach	60-0334
Catharina 28, Philipp 3			
WEISS, Johann	20	Reichenberg	57-1026
WEISS, Johann	24	Mainz	57-1407
WEISS, John	17	Obertiefenbch	57-0422
WEISS, Jos.	24	St.Leon	61-0482
WEISS, Julia	17	Posen	62-0166
WEISS, Kunigunde	20	Gotha	56-0847
WEISS, M.	41	Unterschleich	59-0990
(f) 41, (f) 16, (baby) by			
WEISS, Marianne	24	Grasbronn	59-0412
WEISS, Martin	26	Troestan	60-1032
WEISS, Mathilde	20	Littwitz	60-0785
Joseph 9m			
WEISS, Michel	19	Bernadutt	59-1017
WEISS, Moritz	17	Neustadt	61-0804
Cath. 15			
WEISS, Otto	24	Breslau	56-0819
WEISS, Regina	37	Laudenbach	60-0334
WEISSBACKER, Theo.	28	Paderborn	57-0021
Bernhardine 26			
WEISSBECKER, Heinr	30	Salmmatter	60-0785
WEISSBROKER, Jacob	58	Ichtershausen	55-0538
Louise 49, August 27, Henrietta 18			
Emilie 21, Caroline 21			
WEISSE, Aug.	32	Altenburg	59-0990
(f) 31, (f) 5, (f) 3, (son) by			
WEISSENAU, Ottilie	28	Goldbach	59-0384
WEISSENBERGER, Lse	33	New York	59-0613
Albert 10			
WEISSENBORN, David	30	Bischoffsrode	60-0398
Elisabeth 30, Marie 2, Carl 6m			
WEISSENSEE, Clemen	19	Fulda	57-0754
WEISSENSTEIN, Emma	20	Bockenheim	60-0785
WEISSERT, Eisele	20	Illingen	59-0477
WEISSERT, Jacob	32	New York	59-0477
WEISSERT, Jacob	32	Illingen	59-0477
Eisele 20			
WEISSHAAR, Elisab.	34	Creuzburg	61-0804
WEISSHAUPT, Anna D	19	Altendorf	56-0629
WEISSKOPF, Anton	24	Metternich	57-1416
WEISSLOHM, Doris	23	Achim	60-0785
WEISSTANNER, Theo.	18	Rheinwald	59-0477
WEIT, Christian	52	Wetterburg	57-1280
WEITEFELD, Elisab.	49	Volkmarsen	56-0847
Marie 8			
WEITENHAUSEN, Lina	20	Gruenberg	61-0897
Louise 9m			
WEITKOPF, Gottlieb	30	Bremen	58-0576
WEITLICH, Carl A.W	17	Marburg	62-0879
WEITZE, Ad.	15	Prussia	61-0669
WEITZEL, Elisabeth	15	Storndorf	62-0879
WEITZEL, Gertrude	18	Boddiger	59-0214
WEITZEL, Johann	20	Wangerod/Hes.	55-1238
Sybilla 15			
WEIZE, Wilhelm	40	Fuerstenau	61-0716
WEIZEL, Skolastica	21	Lindersfeld	56-0632
WEIZEL, Theodor	22	Linderfeld	56-0632
WEIZLER, Carl	17	Bergen	59-1017
WEKING, E.F.	32	Friedwald	62-0836
WELBROCK, Rebecca	21	Bremen	57-1026
WELCH, Heinrich	25	Hundelshausen	60-0429
WELCKER, Franz	27	Herzogenaurac	56-1117
WELCKER, Heinrich	22	Bieden/Hess.	62-0608
WELDELE, Leopold	21	Steinbach	59-0384

NAME	AGE	RESIDENCE	YR-LIST
WELHOWER, Johann	24	Falkenburg	57-0447
WELING, Sophie	51	Rainsen	56-0629
WELJEN, Heinr.	19	San Francisco	59-0951
WELLENSCHLAEGER, W	40	Frankfurt a/M	62-0467
WELLER, Conrad	26	Obergeis	56-0819
WELLER, Joseph	26	Brochterbeck	60-0533
Heinrich 24			
WELLER, Louise	30	Hoboken/NJ	62-1112
Emilie 6m			
WELLHAUSEN, H.(m)	32	Holtensen	61-0482
WELLICH, Ludwig	18	Unterkessach	59-0214
WELLING, S.	18	Devonshire	59-0384
WELLINGHAUS, Fried	30	New York	59-0613
WELLINGHOFF, Heinr	19	St.Louis	56-1216
WELLJE, Dietrich	30	Schweinsbruck	57-0850
WELLMANN, C.F.	24	Herford	59-0535
WELLMANN, Carl	19	Oppendorf	56-0413
Therese 6			
WELLMANN, Diedr.	26	Hannover	57-0847
WELLMANN, Fr´drke.	24	Uhra	59-0535
Charlotte 20			
WELLMANN, Helene	24	Meienburg	62-0836
WELLMANN, Johann	21	Heiligenlohe	56-0847
WELLNER, Conrad	32	St.Louis	62-0467
WELS, Ulrika	20	Repzin	61-0478
WELSING, Herm.	32	West Point	61-0482
WELTER, Jean	46	Holland	62-1112
WELTERING, Georg B	32	New Orleans	58-0815
WELTY, Bonifacia	38	Aachen	62-0111
WEMBERGER, Casp.	24	Grosswerden	59-0477
WEMPE, Herrmann	25	Garthe	59-0951
WENDEBURG, Louise	22	Beverstedt	60-1141
WENDEBURG, Marie	20	Stintstedt	62-0232
WENDEHUT, Christne	51	Borna	60-0785
WENDEL, John	41	New York	60-0785
WENDEL, Lena	22	Neuenlandermo	55-1082
WENDEL, Ludwig	32	Rauch	59-0613
WENDELKEN, Lina	18	Cassebruch	56-0589
WENDLER, Elisabeth	51	Weisdorf	56-0632
Margarethe 17, Barbara 16			
WENDLER, Marg. Dor	22	Moenchberg/Bv	55-0628
WENDMAN, Andreas	27	Hahnbach	58-0925
WENDORF, Emilie	32	Greifswald	59-0951
WENDT, Bernhardine	22	Osnabrueck	56-0413
WENDT, Ernst	21	New York	57-1150
WENDT, H.J.	22	Thedinghausen	59-0477
WENDTE, Annette	16	Verden	57-1148
Louise 18			
WENER, Bernhard	27	Muhlberg	60-1117
WENER, Mariane	32	Schweinfurt/B	60-0371
WENGER, Joseph	26	Koblenz	57-1280
WENGEROTT, Ludwig	20	Gemund	57-1416
WENISCH, Johann	47	Teufstetten	58-0563
Catharina 28, Wm.Friedrich 15			
Louise Marg. 13, Marie 1			
WENKE, Catharine	19	Lotheim	56-0413
WENKE, Georg	22	Osnabrueck	60-1032
WENKE, Heinrich	30	Leiste	61-0716
WENKE, Marie	30	Regen	56-0847
WENKE, Marie	21	Bremen	59-0951
WENKMEISTER, M.	23	Dresden	62-1112
WENKO, Ludwig	23	Meschede	57-1067
Josephine 50, Sophie 26, Cathrine 16			
Theresia 13, Josephia 10			
WENNECKE, Martin	16	Deus	57-1407
Catharine 19			
WENNELKAMP, Arnold	22	Warburg	59-0384
WENNING, Joh.Heinr	38	Muenster	57-1148
WENS, Heinrich	58	Stolzenau	59-0047
Sophie 37, Caroline 10, Dorothea 4			
Fritz 1			
WENSEN, Edw.	31	Rodelstadt	59-0214
WENT, Marg.	18	Hannover	57-1148
WENTE, Christian	16	Ostendorf	57-0847
WENTE, Christoph	47	Antendorf	59-0384
Louise 40, Christoph 18, Louise 15			
WENTE, Friedrich	25	Borstel	59-0613
Clarchen 9			

NAME	AGE	RESIDENCE	YR-LIST
WENTE, Sophie	22	Hattendorf	56-0589
Heinrich 3			
WENTELKEN, Martin	28	US.	55-0845
Anna Maria 28, Joh. Marie by			
WENTHE, Friedr.	15	Hoya	59-1017
Dorothea 17			
WENTJEN, Claus	38	New York	61-0897
WENTZEL, Camillus	32	Duesseldorf	62-1112
WENTZEL, Carl	18	Manslau	57-0754
WENTZEL, H.	19	Alfeld	59-1036
WENTZEL, Henry	33	Leidhecken	57-1192
WENZ, Henry	34	Roth	57-1192
WENZEL, Carolina	43	Boehmen	61-0930
Anna 9			
WENZEL, Elisabeth	18	Curhessen	58-0399
WENZEL, Hyronimus	39	Tiefenort	57-1026
Anna Marg. 39, Anna Marie 9, Heinrich 5			
Carl 6m			
WENZEL, Marg.	20	Rodenkirchen	56-1117
WENZEL, Mary	21	Frankenberg	56-0692
WENZING, Charles	19	Stein	57-1192
WERBACH, Michael	32	Unt.Aeltershm	59-0047
Andreas 48, Anna B. 45, Anna M. 19			
Anna Marie 16, Andreas 11, Dorothea 7			
Michael 4, Leonhard 1			
WERDEHOF, Theresia	57	Hegenstorf	55-0630
WERFT, Emma	18	Burgstadt	62-0836
WERKMEISTER, Ch´ne	28	Bernburg	62-0712
WERKMEISTER, J.	15	Scharmbecksto	56-0512
WERMELSKIRCH, Geo.	28	Zwickau	62-1169
WERMERSKIRCH, H.	27	New York	59-0384
WERMERSKIRCHEN, C.	48	Grossvernich	62-1042
Pauline 19, Melchior 17, Robert 15			
Alois 9			
WERNER, Adam	31	Fritzlar	60-0411
WERNER, Albrecht	21	Hastedt	57-1192
WERNER, August	28	Cincinnati	61-0804
WERNER, Bernh.	18	Garthe	59-0951
WERNER, Carl	28	Remptendorf	58-0925
WERNER, Carl	52	Prag	58-0576
WERNER, Carl	34	Waldeck	62-0306
WERNER, Catharina	22	Zimmersrode	56-0847
WERNER, Ernst	39	St.Louis	57-1150
WERNER, Franziska	30	Wittenberg	62-0758
Victor 8, Johann 5			
WERNER, Friedr.	18	Mannheim/Bad.	62-0342
WERNER, Heinrich	50	Buchenau	56-0723
Magdalena 50			
WERNER, Johann	17	Albtshausen	56-0723
WERNER, Johannes	36	Schreifel	55-0812
Marie 56, Johann Peter 4			
WERNER, Johannes	48	Buchenau	56-0723
Johanna 48			
WERNER, Justus	37	Bohrenfurth	55-1082
WERNER, Louis	23	Germany	62-0467
WERNER, Marie	30	New York	59-0048
Ernst 11m			
WERNER, Minna	16	Bitterfeld	62-0983
Marie 14			
WERNER, Pauline	20	Laupheim	59-0477
WERNER, Valentin	22	Germany	61-0167
WERNETH, P. (m)	41	Forchheim	61-0897
WERNIGK, Emily	28	Heiligenstadt	57-1192
WERNING, Herm.	38	New York	58-0306
WERNSDORFER, H.J.	41	Prolsdorf	59-0477
WERSABE, Friedrich	37	New York	62-0758
Catharine 31			
WERSDORFER, Ph.	36	Schnei	62-0467
M.(m) 9			
WERSEBIE, Georg	43	Meyenburg/Han	60-0622
WERTEMEYER, Maria	26	Hille	56-0411
WERTHEIM, M.(m)	16	Erdmannsrod	62-0730
WERTHEIM, Selig	27	Eilenfeld	60-0785
WERTHEIMER, Nathan	14	Ailringen	61-0716
Malca 18			
WESCHE, Charles	29	Osterwieck	57-0654
WESELY, Johann	29	Boehmen	62-0758
WESEMANN, Carl	34	Hannover	56-0512

NAME	AGE	RESIDENCE	YR-LIST
Josephine 33			
WESEMANN, Wilhelm	30	Bremervoerde	57-1407
WESERMAKER, W.	23	Lingen	58-0399
WESFITZKY, Joseph	36	Kotzly	56-0411
Franzisca 36			
WESP, Philipp	32	Frankfurt/M.	55-1238
WESS, Benedict	25	Steinbach	61-0520
Maria Elis. 24, Susanna 9m			
WESSEL, Anna	23	Geestemuende	59-1036
WESSEL, Chr.	17	Hille	55-0411
WESSEL, Ebern	23	Barmen	61-0682
WESSEL, J.G.D.(m)	21	Grosskoehren	61-0482
WESSEL, Lisette	19	Solste	56-1117
WESSEL, Wilhelmine	22	Bremen	59-0214
WESSELHOEFT, J.Gu.	25	Hamburg	55-1238
Mary Ottilie 23			
WESSIG, Berta	9	Braunschweig	55-1048
WESSLING, Diedr.	45	Cincinnati	62-0938
Marie 52			
WESSLING, Heinr.W.	28	Badbergen	62-0879
WEST, Fr. Ferd.	22	Dresden	56-1117
WESTENDORFF, Ferd.	22	Bramsche	58-0306
WESTENDORFF, Franz	20	Bramsche	58-0306
WESTENMANN, Friedr	20	Suedfelde	57-1122
WESTERBURG, Hannch	20	Westerburg	61-0482
WESTERHOFF, Anton	19	Schalten	60-0334
WESTERHOFF, Clara	24	Oyte	59-0535
WESTERHOFF, Engel	20	Cloppenburg	58-0306
WESTERHOFF, Joh.	24	Louisendorf	58-0306
WESTERKAMP, Christ	21	Osnabrueck	57-1192
WESTERMANN, Fr'dke	22	Meyenburg/Han	60-0622
WESTERMANN, Franz	19	Neuenkirchen	60-0785
WESTERMANN, Gottl.	38	Stelligt	59-0535
Marie 36, Friedrich 8, Dietrich 6			
Doris 1			
WESTERMANN, Metazo		Misselwarden	55-1048
WESTERWELLER, Joh.	63	Bobenhausen	55-0845
WESTFELD, Marie	20	Sabbenhausen	56-0723
WESTH, Charlotte	27	Luebbecke	60-0334
WESTHOFF, Bertha	32	Ellerfeld	56-0413
Catharina 18			
WESTINER, Michael	32	Bavaria	62-0758
WESTMEIER, Caspar	18	Wolfenrod/CH.	60-0429
WESTMEYER, Cathar.	18	Wafferode	58-0399
WESTPHAL, Albert	19	Bockeln	55-1082
WESTPHAL, Diedrich	39	New York	57-1150
Lucie 34, Gesine 13, Emilie 14, John 9			
Diedrich 8, Emilie 6, Georg 1			
WESTPHAL, Ferd.	39	Freiburg/Pr.	55-1238
WESTPHAL, Heinrich	30	Hannover	57-0847
WESTPHAL, Henry	58	New York	62-0712
WESTRUP, Elise	29	Greven	59-0214
WESTRUP, Margareta	38	Osnabrueck	56-1260
Heinrich 6			
WETEMANN, Wilhelm	39	Landesbergen	56-0819
Sophie 40, Heinrich 12, Friederich 9			
Caroline 8			
WETH, Johann L.	29	Steinbach	58-0576
Anna 23			
WETKAMP, Joh.	24	Schmitten	60-0521
WETTER, Chr.(m)	47	Rodach	57-0555
B.(f) 41, C.(m) 9, G.(m) 7, Gottfried 5			
WETTER, Ferd.	31	Schwanei	57-0422
WETTER, Hermann	38	Wisconsin	59-0214
WETTER, Wilhelm	26	Berleburg	57-0509
WETTERAU, Gebhard	21	Richelsdorf/P	55-1238
Catharine E. 24			
WETTERHOLM, Ernst	22	Deutz	60-0398
WETTERICH, Friedr.	19	Gerabronn	57-0422
WETTIG, Christ.	26	Weisenau	55-0845
Martha 24, August 2			
WETTIG, John	40	Seitendorf	57-0654
Mary 35, Joseph 18, Ferdinand 16			
WETTLAEUFER, Heinr	58	Kurhessen	56-1044
Friedrich 23, Anne Marie 23			
WETTNAGEL, Elisab.	18	Lanz	62-0712
WETTSTEIN, Jacob	52	Louisville	57-1150
WETZEL, Aug.	19	Cassel	57-1148

NAME	AGE	RESIDENCE	YR-LIST
WETZEL, Dor.H.(f)	25	Lobenstein	56-1117
WETZEL, Emilie	20	Suhl	56-1117
WETZEL, Heinr.	42	Kruspis	55-1082
Louise 24			
WETZEL, Jacob	31	Buchheim	59-0535
WETZEL, Joseph	68	Baden	62-0730
Joseph 36			
WETZEL, Joseph	32	Boehmen	62-0758
WETZEL, Mary Elis.	24	Kleinwelzbach	56-0819
WETZEL, Matth.	61	Sorgau	57-1192
Victoria 38			
WETZEL, Paul	28	Alpshausen	57-0754
WETZELL, Catharine	25	Darmstadt	57-1148
Elisabeth 23			
WETZER, H.J.	38	Saalburg	59-0477
Christiana 38, Pauline 13, Bertha 9			
Herman 8, Amalie 6, Louise 3, Henry 9m			
WETZIG, C.	22	Collm	58-0885
WETZLAR, Lob	17	Bavaria	57-0847
WETZLER, Carl Fr.	24	Rheingoennhm.	62-1169
WEULE, August	27	Thiede	55-0630
WEWER, Antonius	28	Duesseldorf	62-1112
WEY, Wilhelm	35	Wernhausen/Sx	62-0342
WEYL, Chr.	34	Emerikenheim	59-0951
Albert 7, Bernh. 4, Ferdin. 2			
WEYMANN, Kunig.	59	Saxe-Coburg	56-0512
WEYN, Christine	39	Ndr.Ofleiden	62-0712
WEZEL, Marie Elis.	24	Kleinwelzbach	56-0819
WHICKER, Alfred A.	17	England	60-0334
WIBEBER, Bona	34	Wangen	62-1042
Barbara 24, Maria 1, Luzian 6m			
WICHARD, Jos.	59	Holtrop	61-0482
Minna 9			
WICHEL, Fr.	35	New York	61-0107
WICHELMANN, Friedr	20	St.Louis	59-0214
WICHELN, John	21	Martum	57-0654
WICHELN, Z.(m)	17	Narlum	60-0521
WICHER, Sophie	18	Stendach	57-1280
WICHERT, Ch.	35	Walkermuehl	59-0951
WICHERT, Heinrich	28	New York	61-0482
WICHLER, Valentin	27	Rosdorf	57-0447
WICHMANN, Carl	36	Cathrinhagen	57-0847
Sophie 32, Carl 8, Hinrich 3, Ludwig 10m			
WICHMANN, Heinrich	33	Hupede	60-0334
Friedr. 22			
WICHMANN, John	33	Baltimore	60-0785
WICHMANN, M.	34	San Francisco	61-0482
Emma 20			
WICK, D.	14	Marburg	59-1036
WICK, Jacob	19	Marburg	60-0334
WICK, Margaretha	21	Billenhausen	60-0622
WICKENHOEFER, J.J.	17	Roeddenau	57-0754
WICKENS, Johannes	21	Strausburg	60-0785
WICKER, Hermine	28	Braunschweig	56-0413
WICKGESSER, Joh.	29	Lischeid	55-0630
WICKGRUBEN, Franz	35	Reuhearmming	56-0951
Gertrude 23			
WIDEMANN, Helene	17	Hersburg	57-1407
WIDMANN, David	28	Doefingen	58-0576
WIDMANN, Lorenz	26	Albersbach	55-1082
WIDMER, C.G.(m)	27	Zuerich	61-0482
WIDMEYER, Matthias	29	Petersdorf	56-1260
WIDSACK, Louis F.	50	Rudnick	57-0422
Charlotte 33, Theresa 12			
WIEBAND, Apollonia	46	Bieber	60-1053
WIEBER, Peter	27	Niederklein	60-0429
Wilh. Jos. 21			
WIEBKE, Christine	17	Ilserheide	57-1067
WIECHERS, Friedr.	33	Walsrode	58-0563
WIECHERS, Sophie	14	Neubruchhause	62-1112
WIECHMANN, Anna M.	14	Holsen	56-0723
WIECHMANN, Carolne	32	Mannheim	57-1192
WIECHMANN, E.G.(m)	19	New York	62-0730
WIED, Heinr.	18	Gr.Klotzenbur	60-0398
WIEDECK, John	58	Petershagen	57-1122
WIEDEKAEMPER, F.	48	St.Louis	59-1036
Marie 25			
WIEDEMANN, Johann	29	Tapfheim/Bav.	55-1238

NAME	AGE	RESIDENCE	YR-LIST
Ignaz 42, Elisabeth 36, Ludwig 8			
Theresia 5, Elisabeth 9m			
WIEDEMANN, Nepomuc	24	Washington	57-1192
WIEDEMEYER, Wilh.	32	New York	57-0422
WIEDERHOLD, Theod.	18	Gr.Weschungen	56-1011
WIEDERHOLT, Johana	22	Wernigerode	57-0422
WIEDEY, Charles	40	Baltimore	57-1148
Wilhelmine 30, Henry 8, Sophia 6			
Charles 11m			
WIEDIGER, Charlot	58	Ohio	61-0520
WIEDING, v.Derric	56	Mengelbostel	57-0422
WIEDMANN, Maria	5	Wuerttemberg	60-0371
Joseph 11m			
WIEGAND, Alma	23	Blankenheim	59-0372
WIEGAND, Annette		Damar	57-1067
WIEGAND, Augusta	23	Marburg	55-1082
WIEGAND, Elisabeth	23	Langenstein	57-0754
WIEGAND, Elise	18	Philipsthal	57-0924
WIEGAND, Heinrich	53	Birishof	57-1067
Elisabeth 47, Barbara 17, Peter 18			
WIEGAND, Johann	43	Isny	61-0482
Marie 42, Pauline 13, Robert 9, Fanny 8			
WIEGAND, Johann M.	32	Hellmershsn.	57-1067
WIEGAND, Jost	50	Eifahr	61-0478
Elisabeth 20, Elisa 18, Jacob 16			
Louise 1			
WIEGAND, Leontine	25	Fulda	61-0682
Natalia 20			
WIEGAND, Philipp	39	Laubach	61-0478
Blondine 49, Conrad 9			
WIEGAND, Wilhelm	53	Apelern	57-0847
Christine 55			
WIEGANDT, Geo.	19	Bavaria	60-1161
WIEGANT, Engh	23	Herstein	60-0334
Anna 21			
WIEGANT, Martin	20	Rheinsachsen	60-1032
WIEGANT, Peter	27	Muehlhausen	59-0412
WIEGEL, Carl	38	Fuerstenberg	56-0951
Agatha 24			
WIEGERS, H.	24	Mariensee	57-1192
Louise 24			
WIEGLEB, Henriette	35	Greisen	62-0712
WIEGMANN, Geo.Lud.	24	Dipenau	59-0412
Soph.Maria 26, Wilhelmine 2			
WIEGMANN, Heinr.	21	Margelse	55-0413
WIEGNER, Gottlieb	31	Athens	60-0521
WIEHE, Henry	40	New York	62-0836
WIEHLKER, Anna	41	New York	57-1150
WIEKARD, Christ.	24	Hatten	60-0521
WIEKER, Anna Mart.	17	Wiekdorf	56-0411
WIELAGE, Gerh.	24	Barwinkel	59-1036
WIELAGE, John	34	Baltimore	62-1042
WIELAGE, Th.(m)	15	Gr.Drehle	62-0836
Marie 13			
WIELAND, Apollonia	46	Bieber	60-1053
WIELAND, Caroline	21	Lemmersbach	60-1032
WIELAND, Gustav	21	Wuerttemberg	57-0776
WIEMANN, Cath.	23	Versmold	59-0990
WIEMANN, Hermann	25	Detmold	56-0819
WIEMELER, Hermann	31	Greven	59-0214
WIEMER, P.F.A.	28	Neustadt	59-0477
WIENAND, Clementin	22	Alsberg	56-0819
WIENER, Johann	22	Grossbardorf	61-0716
Maria 21, Franz 9			
WIENKE, Heinrich	60	Varrel	60-1161
Cathr. 52, Marg. 21, Heinr. 19			
Elisabeth 17, Cathr. 15, Marie 13			
WIEPOLT, H.A.(m)	35	Legden	62-0232
WIESE, Catharine	40	New York	61-0897
WIESE, Christian	33	Wehden	56-0413
Catharina 36			
WIESE, Eduard	16	Darmstadt	60-0785
WIESECKE, Wilhelm	25	Laase	60-1032
WIESECKEL, Joh.	34	Williamsburg	60-0785
Marg. 58, Joh. 9			
WIESELDEPPE, H´ch	30	Lippe-Detmold	55-1238
WIESEN, Friedr.	15	Bremervoerde	61-0482
WIESENGER, Heinr.	22	Bremervoerde	55-0634

NAME	AGE	RESIDENCE	YR-LIST
WIESNER, Adolph	18	Bremervoerde	57-1026
WIESNER, Friedrich	14	Bremervoerde	57-1026
WIESSLER, Agathe	32	Heuweiler	58-0881
WIESSMER, Johanne	54	Milwaukee	60-0521
WIETERHAHN, L.	28	Pittsburg	62-1042
WIETHOFF, Wilhelm	18	Merkelwede	62-0836
WIETIG, Friederike	23	Oebisfelde	57-0606
WIETING, Justus H.	49	Heaness/Hesse	57-0847
Anna M.E. 48, Anna 19, Justus 17			
Andreas 15, Anna M. 14, Anna Martha 9			
Hinrich 7, Sebastian 4			
WIEWEL, Clemens	36	New York	62-0879
Gertrude 21			
WIGAND, David	25	Schwarzborn	56-1260
WIGAND, Heinrich	18	Philippsthal	60-0622
Wilhelm 24			
WIGAND, Magnus	19	Dammersbach	62-0712
WIGANDT, Heinrich	27	Wasenberg	56-0589
WIGEMANN, A.Barb.	18	Lauffen	56-1117
WIGERT, Anna	26	Greven	59-0214
WIGGER, Carl	27	Albertloh	58-0604
WIKLES, Margarete	30	Lelitz	57-1280
WILBERG, Julius	23	Potsdam/Prus.	55-1238
WILBINGER, Marie	26	Ridlingen	60-0521
WILCKE, Heinrich	56	Bodenwerder	57-0606
Elisabeth 28			
WILCKE, W.	57	Holzminden	57-0606
Wilhelm 30, Friedericke 27			
WILCKENS, Daniel	19	Bremen	56-1117
WILCKENS, Heinrich		Schoenmoor	58-0881
Meta 20			
WILCKENS, John	30	Holtdorf	57-0654
WILD, Albert	28	Bremen	55-0932
WILD, Anna	20	Wildeshausen	62-0879
WILD, Johann	39	Sterrengen	62-0306
WILD, Theodor	22	Schonberg/Bav	56-0819
WILD, Valentin	16	Liebenstein	62-0712
WILDE, Edmundus	26	Warendorf	58-0885
WILDEBRANDT, Rud.	16	N.Brandenburg	61-0897
Augusta 19			
WILDENBERGER, G.	23	Brenhausen	57-1416
WILDGRUBE, Leopold	21	Dessau	56-0411
WILDHAGE, Anton	50	Hattendorf	56-0589
Wm. 18			
WILDT, Tekla	21	Barknau	56-1044
WILFERS, Joh.Nicol	17	Helmbrechtls	62-0879
WILHELM, A.	28	Curhessen	58-0399
A.K. 28, Christine 9m			
WILHELM, Andr.	26	Wernshausen	57-0447
WILHELM, Cath.	20	Rossbrunn	61-0482
WILHELM, Heinr.	46	New York	60-1161
Cath. 36, Elisab. 3			
WILHELM, John	39	Bergholz	57-0654
Friedericke 44, Gustavus 15, Mary 14			
William 12, Albertina 8, Ferdinand 6			
Albert 4			
WILHELM, R.(m)	28	Haffenoyl	59-0951
WILHELM, Robert	25	Lindau	55-0845
WILHELM, Werner	36	New York	59-0990
WILHELMI, Georg	17	Zwoenitz	56-1216
WILHELMS, Adelheit	33	New York	58-0815
WILING, Wilhelm	48	Steinhude	56-0411
WILKE, Christian	30	Assel	56-0413
Ulrika 19			
WILKE, Elis.	35	Koenigsberg	60-0785
WILKE, Emil	14	Denstadt	57-1407
WILKEN, Lane	33	New York	57-1192
WILKEN, Ludw.G.	19	Etzel	58-0925
WILKENING, Carolne	19	Hemmeringen	57-1192
WILKENING, Louise	18	Kohlenfeld	61-0520
WILKENING, Wilhmne	15	Winzlar	56-1011
WILKENNING, Herm.	46	New York	59-0477
WILKENS, Carl	17	Hesse-Cassel	62-0712
WILKENS, Claus	40	Philadelphia	62-0467
WILKENS, Conrad	16	Marsum	57-1150
WILKENS, Diedr.	27	New York	62-0712
Gesine 25, Anna 5			
WILKENS, Joh.	26	Varrel	60-1161

NAME	AGE	RESIDENCE	YR-LIST
WILKER, Marie	21	Osnabrueck	62-0467
WILKER, Marie	18	Osnabrueck	59-1036
WILKING, Catharina	21	Landstuhl	61-0682
WILKING, Diedrich	15	Dexendorf	56-0723
WILKINSON, W.C.	33	Kappeln	59-1036
WILKOMM, Friedrich	22	Wircassen	60-1053
WILL, Andreas	44	Hesse-Darm.	62-0712
Margaretha 42, Jacob 11, Elisabeth 9			
Margaretha 6			
WILL, Friedr.	29	Neu Luboza	56-0629
Louise 22, Augusta 2			
WILL, Georgina	30	Neudietendorf	57-1148
WILL, Heinr.	40	Sudersfeld	60-0785
Catharine 44, Christ. 15, John 12			
William 9, Marie 7, Heinrich 4			
Christ. 73			
WILL, Heinrich	26	Waffendorf	56-0632
WILL, Johannes	15	Breitenbach	57-0776
Johann 13			
WILL, Ludw.	21	Eggenstein	62-0401
WILL, Ludwig	19	Goldlauter	57-1280
WILL, Marg.	23	Baltimore	62-0232
WILL, Margaretha	19	Wolfgrube/Hes	60-0371
WILL, Marie E.	37	Alsfeld	57-0606
WILL, Peter	24	Prussia	62-0758
WILL, Salome	19	Bavaria	60-0371
WILLAKER, Andreas	24	Wassbuhl	62-0001
WILLE, Cath.	18	Luedersfeld	59-0951
WILLE, Cath.Sophie	21	Lindhorst	56-0589
WILLE, Friedrich	20	Herstelle	62-0730
WILLE, Johannes	23	Osterrode/CH.	60-0622
WILLEMSEN, Wm.Hch.	31	Oldersum	61-0779
Sophie 28, Heinrich 7, Jacob 5, Marcka 2			
Trina by, Harm 23			
WILLENBERG, Carol.	32	Lohne	62-0401
Johanna 5, Marianne 3			
WILLER, Anna	36	Bosel	60-0785
WILLERKE, Johanna	25	Mehle	61-0669
WILLERS, Hermann	34	Bremen	62-0879
WILLERSIN, Friedr.	25	Gueglingen/Wt	60-0429
WILLGRUBS, Georg	26	Westmergrave	59-0951
Mencke 29			
WILLIAM, John	61	Hosbach	60-0411
Cath. Mary 60, Henry 6			
WILLIAMS, William	50	England	60-0334
(wife) 49, Margaret 17, John 19			
Elisabeth 22, Ellen 8, Robert 12			
WILLICH, Louis	17	Unterkepach	59-0477
Sophie 21			
WILLIMANNS, Arnold	2	Heidelberg	56-0629
Pauline 25			
WILLING, Andreas	26	Herrnhof	56-1117
WILLING, Wilhelm	7	Wetzlar	57-0704
WILLINGER, B.(m)	27	Cincinnati	62-0467
WILLMANN, Cathrina	35	Braunlingen	58-0881
WILLMANN, Dorothea	20	Westenholz	57-0847
WILLMASER, Doroth.	19	Marburg	57-0436
Franz 18			
WILLMER, Charlotte	34	Nienburg	59-0477
(baby) 9m			
WILLNER, Christian	20	Hahnenkamp	57-1407
WILLOUGHBY, W.	58	New York	62-1042
Mrs. 54, Willy 10			
WILMERS, Heinrich	32	Wessum	59-0951
WILMERTH, L.E.	23	New York	62-0938
WILMING, Gerhard	21	Hestrup	57-1148
WILMS, Ernst C.H.	30	Zelle	61-0682
WILMS, Eta	30	Wayens	57-0422
Henry 4			
WILSON, Anna	16	England	61-0167
WIMMEL, Edw.	23	Minden	57-0847
WIMMEL, Heinrich	22	Glauberg	61-0520
WIMMER, Andreas	37	Edersfeld	56-0819
Eva Maria 35, Mary Barbara 9, Georg 7			
WINANDS, Martin	43	Cincinnati	62-0467
WINCKELMANN, Heinr	50	Wense	58-0563
Catharina 44, Wilhelm 19, Jacob 15			
Catharina 20, Friedrich 9			

NAME	AGE	RESIDENCE	YR-LIST
WINCKELS, Beta	10	New York	59-1036
WINDECK, Carl	20	Coeln	61-0482
WINDECK, Gertrude	58	Coeln	61-0482
WINDEL, Hedwig	59	Sudheim	62-0401
WINDHEIM, H.	29	New York	59-1036
WINDHEIM, Otto	22	Chicago	59-0214
WINDHORST, Chr.He.	24	Rade	59-0412
WINDHORST, Friedr.	18	Rahden/Pr.	60-0622
WINDHUSEN, Johann	21	New York	61-0779
WINDISCH, J.G.	23	Egglofstein	61-0482
Johann 32			
WINDLER, Heinrich	30	Calmitz	60-0411
WINDOLPH, Christ.	24	Geisleben	57-0447
Therese 26			
WINDOLPH, Joh.Paul	16	Geisleden	61-0167
WINDUS, Wilhelm	42	Sooden	56-1117
Elise 44			
WINGBERMUEHL, Mary	24	Bernstrupp	60-0334
WINIGER, Seb.	38	Bavaria	62-1169
WINKEL, Martha	21	Heimarshausen	59-0535
WINKEL, William	19	Hannover	60-0411
WINKELHOFF, J.	27	Liebenburg	59-0477
WINKELMANN, A.(m)	27	New York	62-0467
WINKELMANN, Anna	18	Ponte	62-0730
WINKELMANN, Carlne	58	Nienburg	58-0881
WINKELMANN, Diedr.	29	Lesen	56-0819
WINKELMANN, Elis.	18	Hohenaverberg	57-0924
WINKELMANN, Gertr.	20	Riesberg	61-0804
WINKELMANN, Henry	23	Wense	57-0422
WINKELMANN, Herm.	28	Nettenauberge	59-0384
WINKELMANN, Sophie	53	Verden	56-0847
Elise 14			
WINKLER, Ambrosius	26	Grossenstein	60-1053
WINKLER, Barb.	18	Steinheim	61-0669
WINKLER, Carl	40	Altenburg	62-0758
WINKLER, Catharine	24	Rothain	57-1407
WINKLER, Charlotte	31	Franklin	57-0961
WINKLER, Friedr.	30	Niederopen	60-0521
WINKLER, Joh'a Chr	17	Schmollin	57-1026
WINKLER, Joseph	46	Schlesien	56-1044
Joseph 19, Carl 14, Albert 6, Anna 17			
Martha 9, Hedwig 46			
WINKLER, Kunigunde	29	Eilersbach/Bv	55-0628
WINKLER, Marie	20	Halderwang	60-0533
WINKLER, Rudolph	28	Eldagsen	62-0712
WINKLER, The. (f)	18	Leobschuetz	57-0422
WINKLER, Wilhelm	24	Altona	56-0951
Dorothea 39			
WINKR, Salome	26	Lunwoda	57-1416
WINNAMANN, Anton	45	California	62-0166
Elisabeth 23			
WINNEKE, Anton	36	Eneus	61-0047
WINSESOCH, J.Soph.	24	Schlettwein	62-0306
WINTER, Anna	26	Leipzig	61-0682
Hulda 5			
WINTER, Carl	33	Bunzlau	62-1169
Amalie 31			
WINTER, Carl Fr'dr	46	Gnadenfels	56-1044
Johanna 47, Magdalena 14, Hermine 12			
WINTER, Caroline	24	Hameln	62-1112
WINTER, Caspar	25	Rotenburg/Hes	55-0628
WINTER, Charles	19	Rhanne	57-0961
WINTER, Ferdinand	28	Endorf/Pruss.	56-0632
WINTER, Friedrich	7	Luetjenburg	57-0422
WINTER, Georg	24	Quentel	60-0411
WINTER, Hermann	24	Langerliebe	56-0589
WINTER, J.	35	Perleberg	62-0993
WINTER, Johann	34	Bronn/Bav.	61-0770
WINTER, Johann	31	Wasseraltinge	62-0730
WINTER, Jos. Anton	26	Oberlinzkirch	61-0770
WINTER, Justine	26	Holzminden	57-0606
WINTER, Lina	23	Saalfeld	62-0467
WINTER, Lydia	18	Stuttgart	62-0938
WINTER, Peter	39	Elvingen	62-0730
WINTER, Simon	36	Mossbach/Bav.	60-0622
WINTERBERGEN, Ma.	25	Winterberg	56-1117
Sa.(m) 17			
WINTERCORN, Caspar	28	Kinbach	61-0770

NAME	AGE	RESIDENCE	YR-LIST
WINTERHALTER, Jos.	30	Freiburg	57-0606
WINTERKORN, Michl.	23	Lulzfeld/Bav.	62-0608
Marie 23			
WINTERS, Adelheid	20	Vegesack	58-0545
WINTERS, Wilhelm	30	Westen	56-0847
Margaretha 24			
WINTERSTEIN, Josef	20	Nidda	57-1407
WINTSCH, Felix	52	Zuerich	61-0930
Anna 35			
WINTSCH, Heinr.	25	Zuerich	62-0836
WINZEMANN, Anna	47	Laufen	59-0384
Pauline 15, Carl 9			
WINZER, Anna	26	Leipzig	61-0682
Hulda 5			
WIRCHES, James	38	SImman	57-0654
William 34			
WIRGERS, Jacob	31	Aurich	57-0578
Hindertje 34, Jacob 10m			
WIRMELER, Hermann	31	Greven	59-0214
WIRSCHING, Dorth.	50	Veilsdorf	55-0413
Louise 24			
WIRTH, Adam	24	Unterstamheim	59-0477
WIRTH, Anna	27	Flotz	59-1017
WIRTH, Charles	26	Giessen	57-1148
WIRTH, Friedh.	32	Philadelphia	62-1112
Louise 5			
WIRTH, Friedr.Andr	52	Prussia	62-0758
Eleonore 50, Christiane 28, Friedrika 26			
Augusta 17, Aurelia 14, Theodor 11			
Rudolph 5, Hermann 4			
WIRTH, Mary	20	Holzhausen	56-0512
WIRTH, Robert	16	Bamberg	62-1112
WIRTHS, Caspar	14	Remscheid	56-1044
WIRTZ, Susanna	50	Maehren	61-0478
Catharina 28, Anna Maria 26, Johann 24			
WISCH, Heinrich	17	Curhessen	55-0634
Jacob 16			
WISCHEK, Franz	34	Chemnitz	60-1141
Cathrina 34			
WISCHER, Jacob	42	New Orleans	61-0107
WISCHKER, Justus	19	Langendein	57-1122
Elisabeth 15			
WISCHMEYER, Ed.	16	Minden	56-1216
WISCHMEYER, Matias	36	Osede	56-0819
WISEMANN, Cathrina	22	Rauschenbach	57-0754
WISKE, Marie	20	Londorf	57-0606
WISLISCHEL, Mathis	45	Heiligenkreuz	57-0924
Anna 31, Josepha 10, Martin 8, Anna 6			
Matthias by			
WISMUTH, Jos.	33	Leiderode	62-0938
WISSER, James	34	Blauchurz	57-0654
WISSER, Rud.	24	Lemberg	62-0938
WISSING, Bernh.	37	Hacksbergen	59-0951
Henriette 24, Johanna 9m			
WISSMANN, Joh.	29	Waldstetten	60-1196
WISSNER, Conrad	29	Climbach	55-0630
Maria 32			
WISTERFELD, Elise	24	Muenden	56-0411
WITKOP, Justine	30	Aplern	61-0482
Friedrich 19, Caroline 16			
WITMANN, H.(m)	20	Eberbach	62-0836
Anna 16			
WITT, August	30	Bromberg	56-1044
Ernestine 29, Augusta 3			
WITTAUER, Magd.	20	Windischnlaib	60-0521
WITTCHEN, Cathrine		Geestemuende	59-1036
WITTCHER, Otto	17	New York	60-0334
WITTE, C.H.R.	16	Osnabrueck	62-1112
WITTE, Charles	37	Falkenburg	57-0654
Louise 30, Friedrich 8, Wilhelmine 7			
Emily 5, Julius 3			
WITTE, Herm.	40	Westphalia	62-0467
Therese 15, Ferdinand 9, Elisabeth 8			
ELisabeth 28			
ITTE, Joh. Gerh.	19	Bersenbrueck	57-0704
ITTE, Male (f)	35	Bremen	61-0897
ITTE, Meta	17	Bremen	61-0779
ITTE, Sophie	38	Isny	61-0482

NAME	AGE	RESIDENCE	YR-LIST
WITTE, Wilhelmine	29	Anemolter/Han	60-0622
Fritz 4			
WITTEKIND, Mayer	40	Kissingen	57-1148
Regina 30, Siegmund 4, Babette 1			
WITTELMANN, Georg	38	Thomsenreuth	55-0845
Friederike 24			
WITTEN, Herm.	19	Ritterhude	57-0606
WITTENBERG, Heinr.	25	Kroge/Hann.	57-0847
WITTFELD, Diana	52	Reda	57-1416
WITTHOEFT, Fr.	25	Seehausen	55-0932
WITTIG, Ch.(f)	25	Darmstadt	60-0785
WITTIG, Christian	26	Weisenau	55-0845
Martha 24, August 2			
WITTIG, Mi.	58	Coburg	60-0785
Marg. 53, Edward 16			
WITTIG, Moritz	26	Maasen	56-0279
WITTINGFELD, Carol	17	Trattheim	60-0398
WITTJEN, Caroline	26	Bremerhaven	59-1036
WITTKAMP, Louis	38	Hameln	56-1260
Dorothea 38, Leopoldine 10, Louis 5			
Juliane 7, Andreas 9m			
WITTKE, Christine	25	Carzig	57-0776
WITTKUGEL, Wilhelm	18	Obernkirchen	56-1117
WITTLE, Marie	24	Muellgarte	55-0845
WITTLER, Bernhard	38	Greven	57-1192
Loudewina 46, John 9, Henry 7, Mary 5			
Josephine 11m			
WITTLER, Elisabeth	58	Damme	57-0961
WITTLER, Gottl.Ddr	24	Bielefeld	57-0704
Fd'ke.Amalia 21			
WITTMANN, Joh.	25	Sigl	55-0413
WITTMANN, Johann	31	Auerbach	60-0533
Margaretha 29, Conrad 2			
WITTMANN, Peter	29	Reutershofen	61-0478
Rosalie 23			
WITTMER, Bernhard	30	Savannah	58-0925
WITTMER, Ed.	26	Wohlau	56-0951
WITTNIG, Joseph	25	Nordwalde	60-0785
WITTPEN, Carst.	19	Sellstedt	56-1117
WITTPEN, H.P.	17	Loxstedt	61-0520
WITTPENN, Meta	15	Wistedt	56-1117
WITTROCK, Anna	24	Cloppenburg	58-0925
WITTROCK, Herm.	37	Brinkam	58-0815
WITTSACK, Augustus	10	Rudnick	57-0422
William 8, Charles 5, Adolphus 6m			
WITTSTEIN, Emilie	30	Bremerhaven	59-0477
Gustav 6, Adolph 11m			
WITTSTEIN, Marie	16	Nienburg	60-0785
WITTUP, Bernhard	25	Brochterbeck	60-0533
WITZ, Leopold	19	Kottenplan	58-0885
WITZEL, Johannes	26	Hesse-Cassel	56-0512
WIX, Heinrich	28	New York	62-0232
WOBSER, Albert	20	Labes	61-0930
Caroline 49			
WOCHER, August	17	Buende	59-0477
WODRICH, Wilhelmne	19	Jarmen/Pr,	60-0429
WOECKENER, Johanna	47	Rehda	58-0563
Carl 16, Wilhelmina 13, August 11			
Aug.Chr. 8, Johanna 1			
WOEGTMANN, Dina	23	Ankum	59-1036
WOEHLER, Carl	24	Armsen	57-1067
Augusta 25			
WOEHLKE, Minna	19	Bruchhausen	57-0924
WOEHLKEN, Friedr.	49	Mattfeld	57-0850
Margaretha 46, Heinrich 14, Johann 9			
Friedrich 7, Maria 4, Christian 11m			
WOEHRDEN, Georg	26	New York	59-0384
WOEHRER, Joseph	44	Alkosen/Aust.	55-1238
Louise 24			
WOELCKE, Marie	22	Wallenbruecke	57-1113
Ilsab. 22			
WOELFL, Johann	24	Muehlbach	61-0478
WOELFLE, J.C.	19	Oefingen	62-0938
Anna 19			
WOELK, John	23	Gross Warzula	56-1011
Henry 20			
WOELL, Adam	20	Albshausen	57-0754
WOELLENWEBER, (f)	30	Louisendorf	58-0306

NAME	AGE	RESIDENCE	YR-LIST
(baby) 1			
WOELLENWEBER, (f)	38	Philadelphia	62-0938
WOELLENWEBER, Nic.	56	Louisendorf	58-0306
(wife) 47, Agnes 23, Susanne 19			
Elisabeth 17, Henriette 15, Nicolaus 13			
Wilhelm 7, Philipp 7, Jacob 6			
Friedr. Wm. 3			
WOELTJEN, Diedr.	18	Darvesden	59-1036
WOERLEIN, Barbara	22	Offenbach	56-0819
WOERNER, Conrad	28	Zell	56-0723
WOERNER, Gottf. F.	15	Heiningen	59-0535
WOERNER, Johannes	30	Baltimore	62-0401
WOERNER, W.F.	23	Asperg	62-0993
WOERTH, Friedr.	47	Bonn	59-0048
WOERZ, Anton	20	Laupheim	59-0477
WOERZ, J.	26	Cambright	59-0477
WOERZ, Joseph	35	Bieberwied	60-0533
WOESENER, Carl	27	Braunfels	57-0704
Caroline 27, Joseph 9, Marie 6, Johann 2			
WOFF, Robert	20	Mussdorf	62-0100
WOGE, Jacob	39	Oldenburg	58-0576
Eleonore 35			
WOHL, Valentin	14	Rossbach	61-0897
WOHLA, Franz	30	Hrachotusk	57-1067
Elisabeth 27			
WOHLERS, Johann	15	Selingen/Hann	57-0847
WOHLERS, Johann	21	Cassel	57-1407
Bernhard 24			
WOHLERS, Julie	32	Bremervoerde	59-0990
WOHLFAHRT, Eva	46	New York	60-0622
WOHLFAHRT, Herm.	25	Hanau/Hess.	60-0052
WOHLGEMUTH, Benno	17	Wien	62-0232
WOHLGEMUTH, Fr.(m)	31	Freudenstadt	61-0482
Fridaline 31			
WOHLGEMUTH, Phil.	29	Hessen	56-1044
Anna Cath. 27, Sebastian 3, Christina E 1			
WOHLLEBEN, Joh.	34	Kabelsdorf	61-0478
WOHLRAAB, Sophie	26	Langendorfles	62-0712
WOHLRABE, Carl	55	Roldisleben	62-0730
Friedericke 55, Ernestine 19			
Wilhelmine 16			
WOHLRABE, Carl W.	27	Erfurt	60-1032
WOHLTMANN, Gesine	20	Hofen	59-0990
WOHNEMANN, Daniel	28	Borkummohr	57-1280
Margarethe 29			
WOLBERS, M.C.	26	Hesselte	62-0993
WOLBMANN, F.	42	Boehmen	62-0467
Franziska 30, Carl 6, Anna 11m			
WOLBORN, Philipp	37	Bodensee	57-0422
Magdalena 33, Mathilde 8, Philipp 4			
WOLBRECHT, Hedwig	26	Rinteln	58-0399
WOLD, Barb.	27	Unt.Aschenbch	59-0990
WOLDE, George	23	Bremen	62-0401
WOLF, Andreas	57	Friedberg	57-1280
WOLF, Anna	30	Froschenreuth	60-0533
WOLF, Anton	26	Jettelhofen	57-0754
WOLF, Carl	28	Okershausen	59-0372
WOLF, Carl	25	Detmold	59-0384
WOLF, Carl Julius	19	Thierschneck	58-0881
WOLF, Christian	34	Gotha	56-0413
Carolina 52			
WOLF, E.S.(m)	13	Eschelbronn	62-0836
WOLF, Ernestine	28	Kattenborn	55-0413
WOLF, Gottfried	37	Leibel	57-1280
Christiane 29, Carl 6m			
WOLF, H.	50	Posen	56-0550
WOLF, Johann	45	Hofheim/Nass.	55-0628
Elisabeth 38, Thomas 7, Peter 5			
Elisabeth 9m			
WOLF, Laurence	32	Darmstadt	57-0422
WOLF, Lisette	30	Priesen	57-0704
Louis 4, Jette 2			
WOLF, P. (m)	45	Elbingenalp	55-0413
WOLF, Philippine	27	Wetzlar	59-0384
WOLF, Robert	28	Coeln	62-0712
Jeanette 28, Max 5, Carl 3			
WOLF, Robert	20	Mussdorf	62-0100
WOLF, Wilhelm	26	Lilbenhausen	57-0447

NAME	AGE	RESIDENCE	YR-LIST
Sophie 24			
WOLFAHRT, Michael	30	Koenigshofen	60-1161
Marianna 26, Johann 2, Susan 6m			
WOLFER, Christine		Elbingen	59-0613
WOLFERS, Otto	20	Elberfeld	57-0924
WOLFF, Ad. (m)	25	Hersfeld	62-0730
WOLFF, Amalie	45	Milwaukee	62-0938
WOLFF, Andreas	30	Stefling	57-1067
WOLFF, Anna	24	Traustadt	57-1067
WOLFF, Anton	58	Ditzelbach	61-0520
Anton 25, Conrad 13, Johanette 16			
WOLFF, Benj.	41	France	62-0938
Sara 31, Line 6, Ernestine 3, Emil 1			
WOLFF, Bertha	26	Mannheim	59-1036
(baby) 2m			
WOLFF, Cath.	17	Sulzheim	61-1132
WOLFF, Charles	22	Schoenfeld	57-0961
WOLFF, Christiana	27	Deiz	57-0961
WOLFF, Christine	21	Eppingen	59-1036
WOLFF, Emma	21	Perleberg	59-0477
WOLFF, Ernestine	19	Weinsberg	60-0334
WOLFF, Franzisca	22	Weiderstadt	56-0951
WOLFF, Gottfried	33	Burg	59-0047
WOLFF, Gottlieb	30	Dresden	56-1044
Amalie Frdke 25			
WOLFF, Heinrich	54	Buchenau	57-1067
Gertrude 53, Jacob 16, Ludwig 12			
WOLFF, Heinrich	31	Westerharre	58-0881
Anna 31, Marie 4			
WOLFF, Heinrich	55	Huelshagen	59-0214
WOLFF, J.	36	Ernstale	56-0512
WOLFF, Joseph	40	Kestran/Boehm	57-1067
WOLFF, Julius	29	Witters	56-0819
WOLFF, Justus	24	Darmstadt	56-1216
WOLFF, Madame	24	Moscow	59-0477
(child) 9m, (servant) 20			
WOLFF, Marcus	30	Bremen	62-0467
WOLFF, Michael	22	Greupenheim	62-0467
WOLFF, S.	25	Texas	59-0951
WOLFF, Wilhlem	28	Grosskalber	58-0399
Margaretha 21			
WOLFRAM, Joh. Jac.	39	Leesten/Bav.	55-0628
Margaretha 36, Michael 14, Johann 7			
Simon 5, Simon John 4, Anna Cath. 11m			
WOLFRAMM, Friedr.	34	Parisa	56-1216
Carol. 29, Liberta 24			
WOLFSHEIMER, Janet	26	Reichenberg	56-0629
WOLFSOHN, David	15	Lobsens	57-1148
WOLKA, Johann	33	Crzeianka	60-0334
WOLKEN, Henry	20	Wrisse	57-0422
WOLLAND, Dor.	25	Bielefeld	57-0961
WOLLENHAUPT, Burch	22	Hannover	56-1011
WOLLENSCHAL, Soph.	35	Helmstedt	57-0850
WOLLENSTUNFT, B.E.	26	US.	58-0306
WOLLIN, Noa	20	Prussia	57-0555
WOLLMANN, Jos.	36	Pablowitz	59-0990
(f) 26, (m) 4			
WOLLMAR, Heinrich	14	Friedrichshsn	55-0628
WOLLNER, Marie	23	Donau	62-0467
Anna 22			
WOLPERT, Jacob	27	Wannweil	61-0482
Christiane 24			
WOLSCHENDORF, C.	32	Schleitz	57-0555
WOLTEMATH, J.H.	71	Coppenbruegge	62-0938
Louise 61, Carl 42, Louise 15			
Dorothea 12, Augusta 9, Johann 7, Carl 5			
Rosa 34			
WOLTER, A.Cathrine	22	Nentershausen	56-0279
WOLTER, Friedrich	57	Vitzig	57-0704
Rudolph 26, Otto 20, Caroline 31			
Ottilie 21, Augusta 11m			
WOLTER, Joh.	19	Berlin	50-1017
WOLTERS, Doris	18	Harpenfeld	56-0951
WOLTERS, Friedrich	35	Hassel	58-0925
WOLTERS, Heinrich	25	Westenholz	57-0847
Marie 19, Joh. 6m			
WOLTERS, Heinrich	25	Westenholz	57-0847
WOLTHMANN, Meta	21	Sandstedt	56-1011

NAME	AGE	RESIDENCE	YR-LIST
WOLTJEN, Ch.	23	Philadelphia	60-0785
Lizzie 20			
WOLTMANN, August	22	Bremen	60-1032
WOLZBACHER, Thekla	24	Winterbach	56-0819
WOMELSDORF, J.Pet.	28	Hamburg	60-1053
WONDRA, Matthias	35	Prym	55-0845
WOOD, Georg	45	Toledo	60-0334
WOORTKOETTEN, B.	23	Nordwalde	60-0785
WORACECK, Caroline	52	Schwisau	62-0836
WORCH, Cath.	22	Homberg	62-0401
WORM, Fr.(m)	40	Neuenburg	57-0555
Chr.(f) 48, C.L.(m) 18, A.J.(f) 16			
J.F.(m) 14, Henr.(f) 10, Wilhelmine 3			
WORRM, Sophie	26	Carzig	57-0776
WORSTENDICK, Mar.W	15	Berghausen	56-1044
Catharine Fr 10			
WORSTMANN, Jette	19	Reichmansdorf	60-0521
WORTMANN, Heinrich	25	Luedingworth	56-0413
WOSSEDALCK, Heron.	39	Mericua	57-1113
Anna 39, Joseph 15, Franciska 13			
Peter 11, Karolina 9, Franz 5, Paul 6m			
WOTTUBA, Martin	41	Mokz	55-0845
Anna 43, Josepha 14, Maria 11, Franz 6			
Rosalie by			
WRAZECK, Matthias	38	Pento Zahosie	56-1011
WRBATA, Wenzel	32	Boehmen	62-0758
WREDE, Joh.Heinr.	48	Westenholz	58-0563
Joha.Louise 45, Dorothea 22, Heinrich 20			
Christoph 9			
WREDE, Sophia	28	Wollingst	56-0512
WREDE, Wilhelm	41	Bremen	61-0770
WREDEN, Meta	24	Wollings	56-1117
WRTISCH, Thomas	38	Boehmen	58-0881
Marie 43, Marie 11, Franz 5, Magdalena 28			
WUBBENA, SImon	25	Tergast	60-0398
Nelke 54, Meint 17			
WUEHRMANN, Fr.	21	Dorum	58-0563
WUELBERN, Christ.	17	Alfstedt	56-1117
WUENSCHEMEIER, Lud	21	Feuchtwangen	57-0606
WUERFEL, Amalie	30	Colleda	55-0630
WUERFEL, Caroline	23	Landshuth/Pru	55-1238
WUERGER, Wilhelm	28	Hoffen	57-1280
WUERTEMBERGER, Arm	14	Walldorf	59-0477
WUERTEMBERGER, Geo	43	Brandau	59-0477
Marie 40, Georg 15, Maria 11, Joseph 9			
Friedrich 8			
WUERTEMBERGER, Ka.	26	Oberramstadt	59-0477
WUERTH, Gebhard	33	Wuerttemberg	55-0634
Johann 19			
WUEST, August	30	Eschhausen	61-0478
WUEST, Jacob	35	Aarau/Switz.	60-0371
WUEST, Louise	20	Laufen/Wuertt	60-0429
WUEST, Oscar	18	Noerdlingen	56-1260
WUESTEFELD, Mich.	16	Blankenau	59-0214
WUESTENBERG, Aug.	28	Philadelphia	59-0214
WUESTENHOFER, Mich	23	Hausen	60-1053
WUESTHOFF, Frdke	36	Solingen	59-0412
WUESTHOFF, Heinr.	15	Rade	59-0412
WUHE, Wilhelm	13	Hannover	55-1082
Louise 24			
WULF, Fr. (m)	48	Friedrichstal	62-0730
Christiane 48, Christiane 18			
Wilhelmine 16, Friedrich 13, Edward 9			
William 7, Juliane 5, Friederike 2			
WULF, J.	16	Scharmbecksto	56-0512
WULF, Wilhelm	36	Obediesen	57-1280
WULFECKER, Xaver	25	Grossthalheim	60-0521
WULFF, Edward	22	Carlsruhe	60-1141
WULFF, H.A.	40	Neustadt	59-0477
WULFF, Sophie	19	Vilsen	56-1044
WULFING, Charles	25	St.Louis	57-1192
Hermine 18, Christiane 45			
WULFKUHLE, Ch.	60	Kohlstedt	60-0998
Bengst 24, Claud 25, H.(m) 35, Frake 24			
WULZE, Friedrich	40	Ahrenfeld	57-0422
Louisa 28, Sophia 7, Louisa 16, Minna 3			
Carolina 9m			
WUNDER, Carl	30	Wagenfeld	57-0924

NAME	AGE	RESIDENCE	YR-LIST
WUNDER, Gust Juls.	23	Altenburg	60-0429
WUNDERLICH, Amalie	20	Redwitz	56-0527
Anna Margar. 15			
WUNDERLICH, Chr'ne	26	Landwuest	55-0630
WUNDERLICH, Edw.	29	Milwaukee	57-1192
Helene 27			
WUNDERLICH, Emilie	18	Reichstadt	56-0411
WUNDERLICH, Jacob	22	Preussen	55-0634
WUNDERLICH, Johann	16	Kubert	55-0630
Adam 22			
WUNDERLICH, Magd.	16	Redwitz	56-0527
WUNDERLICH, Valen.	32	Sophienthal	57-0606
Catharina 28			
WUNDERLICH, W.	28	Asch	62-0993
WUNSCHEL, Georg	27	Wordorf	56-0589
Margarethe 24			
WUPPERFURTH, John	27	Leichlingen	57-1192
WURFEL, Carl	55	Schweidnitz	56-0512
Johanne 55, Anna 24			
WURMBACH, Ernst	18	Mussen	57-1280
Caroline 21			
WURST, Christian	19	Calw	56-0951
Anna 27			
WURST, Joseph	36	Michelsdorf	55-0932
Barbara 34, Joseph 7, Amalie 12, Rosa 9			
Barbara 34, Joseph 7, Amalie 12, Rosa 9			
Emilie 2			
WURST, Vinc.	25	Dittersbach	55-0932
WURSTENER, Caspar	25	Schneidheim	56-1011
WURSTER, Christ.	46	Grafenburg	62-0111
Christ. 16			
WURSTER, Joh.	20	Freudenstadt	59-1036
WURTMANN, An Marie	32	Elsfleth	57-1026
WURZEL, August	39	Zicher	57-1407
Anna 38, Johanna 10, Marie 8			
Wilhelmine 7			
WURZEL, Cath.	22	Seligenstadt	60-0334
WURZER, Johann	32	Hochdorf	56-1117
WURZMANN, Fd.	13	Eltmann	57-1148
WUST, Joseph	42	Lauterbach	60-1053
WYLZINSKY, v. Ign.	30	Kroeben	57-0578
WYMANN, Th.(m)	53	Boston	61-0482
XANTUS, J.(m)	40	Washington	62-0730
YAMY, Fried.	34	New York	62-1112
YERKEL, Joh.Eleon.	57	Dresden	57-1026
YNDERS, Mar. Cath.	19	Abhenruh	61-0478
YORK, Werner	18	Lemgo	59-1036
YOUNG, Johannes	23	Baltimore	62-0401
Carl 26			
YOUNG, de Peter	44	Philadelphia	59-0048
Sarah 58			
YSSLEBER, Georg	34	Friedlos	56-0819
Marie 35			
YUNG, Anna	19	Habelschwerdt	59-0477
YUNG, Elise	28	Coeln	59-0477
YUNG, G.S.	34		59-0477
Dora 28, Georg 5, Theodor 3			
YUNG, Joh. Jac.	32	Rhein Baiern	55-0634
ZABEL, Conrad	44	Wernswig	55-0845
ZACHARIAS, Georg	55	Bischoffsrode	60-0398
Eva 45, Christoph 21, Rebecca 18			
Orthega 16, Sophia 12, Maria 8			
ZACHER, Andreas	42	Stannig	58-0881
ZACHER, Stephan	32	Philadelphia	59-0214
ZACHO, Nicolaus	22	Leer	56-0847
ZAHN, Carl Aug.	15	Trepnitz	57-0578
ZAHN, Maria	25	Bueckeburg	62-1042
Fr. 3			
ZAHN, Sophia	25	Nassau	60-1141
ZAHRT, Catharine	42	Mahlbach	61-0478
ZAJIK, Franz	24	Boehmen	62-0758
ZALENKA, Joseph	42	Nischwalitz	55-0845
Catharine 34, Franz 10, Joseph 6			
Johann 4, Barbara 14			
ZAN, Woytech	21	Pieseck	57-1113
ZANDER, G.A.(m)	34	Muenden	61-0804
ZANDER, Heinrich	26	Kolleda	57-0447
ZANG, Eve	19	Olenberg	60-0998

NAME	AGE	RESIDENCE	YR-LIST
ZANG, Gottfried	32	Stockstadt	62-0879
Barbara 29			
ZANKE, Rud.	30	Naumburg	61-0167
ZAPF, Edward	21	Rode	60-0411
ZARNITZ, Carl	26	Baltimore	59-1036
Francisca 23			
ZAURS, Chr.	53	Philadelphia	61-0167
ZAZECK, Joseph	26	Mischowitz	56-0411
Therese 26, Josephine 3, Marie 11m			
ZECH, Anna L.	36	Noerdlingen	62-0836
ZECH, Hugo	19	Hannover	62-0758
ZECHBAUER, Friedr.	20	Wolkershausen	58-0399
ZEEB, Veit	54	Wannweil	61-0482
Elisabeth 45, Johannes 22, Veit 17			
Jacob 15, Barbara 13, Christine 9			
Maria 7, Gottl. F. 6, Albert 9m			
ZEH, Johann	20	Seckbach/Curh	60-0622
ZEH, Simon	42	Dettelbach	61-0779
ZEHFUCHS, Gustav	31	Darmstadt	58-0885
ZEHL, Hanne	19	Meiningen	56-1260
ZEHN, Gottlieb	41	Wartenburg	56-0951
Wilhelm 23			
ZEHNDER, J.C.	22	Menzingen	56-0951
ZEIDLER, Adolph	16	Bremervoerde	58-0563
ZEIDLER, Johann	28	Duerstein	56-1117
ZEIDTE, Christiane	19	Bayreuth/Bav.	61-0770
ZEIER, Jos.	51	Bruechenau	60-1196
ZEIGER, Wm.	27	New York	60-0785
ZEILER, Anton	31	Hardt	58-0881
Heinr. Ludw. 21, Philippine 24			
ZEILER, Bartel	32	Etzenricht	62-1169
ZEILNER, Catharine	25	Biermann	56-0847
Johanna 21			
ZEIMER, Rosa	19	Schwihau	60-0521
Lotte 19			
ZEIMER, Rosa	27	Malinetz	62-0836
ZEIP, Wilhelm	40	Bremen	62-0879
Beta 33, Diedrich 10, Christian 8			
Johanna 6			
ZEIS, Adam	27	Fuerth	60-1032
ZEISEL, Joh.	29	Doberschuetz	60-0521
ZEISS, Heinrich	27	Lobenstein	57-0606
Wilhelmine 27, Emilie 9m			
ZEISS, J.Aug.Louis	28	Lobenstein	57-1067
Sophie 20, Tekla 13			
ZEISS, Stephan	21	Gesen	58-0399
ZEITLER, H.	31	Rauschensteig	62-0993
ZEITLER, Susanne	53	Bayern	56-1044
Anna 16			
ZEITNER, Elisabeth	35	Grafenholz	56-1044
ZEITZ, Andreas	26	Hainrode	57-1407
Johanna 32			
ZEITZ, Andreas	28	Unt.Aschenbch	59-0990
ZEITZ, Heinrich	14	Goettingen	55-0634
ZELL, Herm.	29	Wallage	60-0998
ZELL, J.W.	40	America	56-1216
Lucy 22, Helen 13			
ZELLE, Friedrich	32	Staden	59-0412
Emilie 27, (boy) bob			
ZELLER, Amalia	25	Casdorf	59-1036
ZELLER, Clementine	24	Huettlingen	57-1067
Marianne 30, Marianne 3, Clemens 9m			
ZELLER, Friedr.	37	Boehmen	61-0897
ZELLER, Johanna	20	Riedern	61-0669
ZELLER, Ludwig	28	Adelsbach	60-0334
Susanna 40			
ZELLINGHAUS, W.	45	New York	58-0604
ZELLMANN, Christ.	24	Allendorf	57-1407
ZELLMANN, Joh.Gotl	28	Romannsdorf	57-0704
ZELLNER, Christian	59	Jankendorf	56-0819
Johann 17			
ZELLNER, Gustav	15	Romannshof	58-0576
ZEMANN, Franz	42	Boehmen	61-0897
Magdalena 41, Leopold 8, Catharine 6			
Marie 4, Franz 9m			
ZEMANN, Johann	17	Boehmen	57-1407
Fritz 13, Caspar 7, Molika 4			
Catharina 45			

NAME	AGE	RESIDENCE	YR-LIST
ZEMLICKA, Joseph	36	Tabor/Boehmen	62-0608
Anna 33, Joseph 9, Marie 7, Franz 4			
Johann 6m			
ZEMLICKA, Matthias	56	Tabor/Boehm.	62-0608
Catharina 55, Elisabeth 24, Catharine 22			
Barbara 18, Albert 16			
ZEMLICKA, Matthias	33	Tabor/Boehmen	62-0608
Theresa 28			
ZENNER, Franz	41	Poldwitz	60-0785
Emilie 32, Fenna 8, Henrietta 5, Franz 6			
ZENTGRAFF, Joh.	15	Weimar	55-0413
ZEPF, Leopold	34	Duerkheim	62-1169
ZERB, Georg	48	Litzenlinde	55-0812
Christine 48, Louise 12, Maria 9			
Friedrich 7			
ZERBER, Gottfried	27	Rombezin	61-0930
ZESEMSKY, John	52	Pentozahosie	56-1011
ZESEWITZ, Joh.Wilh		Halle	57-0606
Joh.Fr.(f) 21			
ZESSLER, H.W.(m)	17	Luehne	57-0080
ZETZMANN, Elise	27	Steinfeld	57-1026
ZETZMANN, M.(died)	22	Grottstedt	61-0669
ZEUCHNER, Wilhelm	39	Preussen	55-0634
ZEYER, Max	19	Bruecknau	61-0047
ZICKGRAF, Johannes	31	Rheingoennhm.	62-1169
ZIEBER, Christine	30	Liegnitz	60-0533
ZIEGEL, Franz	33	Assamstadt	62-0306
Catharine 42, Charlotte 4			
ZIEGELBACH, Ferd.	15	Cassel	59-0951
ZIEGEMEYER, Louis	23	Hameln	56-1260
ZIEGENMAYER, A.F.L	28	Buddenstedt	62-0467
Marie 34			
ZIEGER, Joh.Rosina	51	Choren/Sax.	60-0622
Anna Maria 18, Carl Gottlob 16			
ZIEGFELD, Julius B	24	Amerika	58-0815
Mirls 23			
ZIEGLER, Carl	45	Bielen	59-0214
ZIEGLER, Carl	30	Baltimore	62-1112
Catharine 27, Carl 11m			
ZIEGLER, Carl Math	24	Gr.Wenkheim	58-0881
Adelheid 22, Franz 2			
ZIEGLER, Christian	37	Kirchheim	62-0306
ZIEGLER, David	20	Kurhessen	56-1044
ZIEGLER, Franz	28	Halsheim/Bav.	55-1238
Louise 24			
ZIEGLER, Georg W.	19	Harburg	60-1196
ZIEGLER, J.Ad.	23	Seusswark	61-0482
ZIEGLER, Johann	31	Schwarzenborn	56-0527
ZIEGLER, Michael	34	Theinfeld	57-0422
Gertrude 34, Michael 1			
ZIEGLER, Susanna	19	Birk/Bav.	61-0770
Catharine 26			
ZIEGLER, Wilhelm	46	Duesseldorf	59-0372
ZIEHN, Conrad	40	Unteruzer/Sax	62-0342
ZIEHN, Eduard	30	Gotha	58-0399
J.M. 28, F.W. 6, A.B. 5, C.W. 9m			
ZIELBERG, Joh. H.	21	Carlshafen	60-1053
ZIENER, Friedr.	33	Meiningen	62-1112
ZIERENBERG, Carl	25	Lewuthal	57-0654
ZIERHORST, Wm.	38	Wesel	59-1036
ZIESCHE, Johann	45	Chemnitz	59-0214
Carl Aug. 18			
ZIETLOW, Mathilde	29	Bovenden	56-0279
Anna 9			
ZIETZ, Ernst	20	Mainz	58-0925
ZIGELER, Susanna	19	Birk/Bav.	61-0770
Catharine 26			
ZIGLER, Christian	37	Kirchheim	62-0306
ZILCH, Adam	19	Koerle	57-0754
ZILCH, Georg	18	Ibach	56-0819
Madeleine 22			
ZILICH, Johannes	28	Borken/Hessen	57-0924
ZILIOR, Eva	22	Breitenstein	57-1067
ZILLER, Wilhelm	37	Winkheim	58-0576
ZIMMER, Ernst	24	Oberstruse	62-0758
ZIMMER, Georg	48	Lehnerts	56-0589
ZIMMER, Johann	56	Kochstedt	56-0847
Sophie 26			

NAME	AGE	RESIDENCE	YR-LIST
ZIMMER, Lucas	27	US.	61-0167
ZIMMERER, Joseph	30	St.Louis	56-0723
ZIMMERLEIN, J.	38	Gestungshause	56-0512
Eva 37, Johann 6, Niclaus 3, Stephen			
ZIMMERLING, Fr.(m)	25	Laerkerick	62-0401
ZIMMERMANN, Aug.	17	Zielbach	61-0669
ZIMMERMANN, B.(m)	21	Otterswanz	60-0334
ZIMMERMANN, Barb.	48	Trasadingen	62-1112
Elisabeth 22, Magd. 17, Barb. 18			
ZIMMERMANN, Caroln	28	Elberfeld	55-0634
ZIMMERMANN, Christ	18	Friedberg	57-1192
ZIMMERMANN, Conrad	36	Grave	57-0606
Louise 27, Friedrich 4, Conrad 1			
ZIMMERMANN, Dan.	27	Bischberg	59-0214
ZIMMERMANN, Doroth	45	Culmbach	58-0563
Elisabetha 21, Sophia 20			
ZIMMERMANN, Edward	26	Philadelphia	59-0477
ZIMMERMANN, Elisab	26	Seligenstadt	62-0730
ZIMMERMANN, F.	18	Frankenhausen	56-0512
ZIMMERMANN, Fr.Hch	43	Wrisse	57-0422
ZIMMERMANN, Georg	44	Birchhofen	56-0723
Margaretha 28			
ZIMMERMANN, Gott.	31	Gernitz	56-0527
Heinrich 3			
ZIMMERMANN, Gottf.	37	Grosstrenten	57-0924
A.Christine 32, Wilhelm 6, Henriette 4			
Wilhelmine by			
ZIMMERMANN, H.	30	Hohneggelsen	56-0512
Wm. 25			
ZIMMERMANN, H.(m)	45	New York	61-0804
Barbara 17			
ZIMMERMANN, H.A.	31	Coeslin	56-0723
ZIMMERMANN, Joh.	25	Stelcowes	57-1148
ZIMMERMANN, Joh.	32	Hoffenheim	60-0398
Maria 24, Catharine 9m			
ZIMMERMANN, Louise	33	Wahlhausen	57-1407
ZIMMERMANN, Sophie	21	Braunschweig	56-0413
ZIMMERMANN, W.(m)	12	Althuetten	56-1117
Rosalie 50			
ZIMMERMANN, Wenzel	18	Althuetten	56-1117
ZIMMERMANN, Wilh.	23	Gaisberg	59-0214
ZIMMERMANN, Wm.	22	Werdorf	60-0521
ZIMMERMANN, Wmne.	14	Marburg	60-0785
ZIMMERMANN, Wmne.	20	Rinteln	57-1407
ZINK, Adam	33	Ellenbach	57-1280
ZINK, Caspar	67	Eisenach	57-0509
Balthasar 40			
ZINK, Ferdinand	31	Colberg	56-0723
Anna 52			
ZINK, Marg.	24	Hundefeld	62-0836
ZINK, Martha	32	Feldkirchen	59-1036
ZINK, Willibald	37	Engelsbach/SG	55-1238
Louise 24			
ZINKEL, Andr.	29	Coburg	60-1161
ZINKHAN, Mary	23	Neuengronau	61-0804
ZINN, Carl	19	Philippsthal	60-0622
ZINN, Valentin	24	Speckwinkel	57-0754
ZINN, Wilhelm	17	Schlitz	62-0879
ZINSER, Julius	28	Neustadt	57-0754
ZINSSER, Carl	28	Roenrod	60-0334
ZIOCK, Heinrich	55	Hettingen	58-0815
Elisabeth 52, Mathilde 22, August 16			
Emilie 12			
ZIPFEL, Friederike	22	Rutha	56-0589
ZIPFEL, Margaretha	17	Reichheim	59-0214
ZIPFER, Louise	19	Carlsruhe	56-1011
ZIPPENFELD, Emilie	20	Attendorn	57-0606
ZIPPERLEIN, Chr.	32	Unterkessach	62-0836
ZIRBEL, Carl	24	Minden	57-0924
ZIRKELBACH, Heinr.	20	Stockheim	55-0812
ZIRKELBACH, Nic.	55	Stockheim	56-0951
Philip			
ZIRKELBOCK, Joh'na	15	Schauch	56-0512
ZISCHNER, Georg	27	Greislbach	57-0847
Walburga 31			
ZITTLER, Eduard	25	Osnabrueck	55-0634
ZITZLAFF, Johann	57	Petzick	57-0924
Michel 24, Caroline 22, Wilhelmine 77			

NAME	AGE	RESIDENCE	YR-LIST
ZITZMANN, Ludwig	21	Steinheide	60-1141
ZITZNER, Anna M.	51	Moschendorf	59-0990
(f) 19, (f) 13, (f) 11, (f) 10			
ZOBELEIN, Anna	36	Roettenbach	61-0520
ZOCH, August	31	Marienwald	61-0770
Joh.Wilh'mne 31, Henrit.Luise 6			
August Wilh. 4, Ludwig Herm. 2			
ZOCHIEGNER, Friedr	37	Brunneburg	55-0634
Friederike 32, Pauline 27, Richard 7			
Anna 5, Maria by, (son) by			
ZOCKENDORF, Cath.	23	Ollen	58-0815
ZOCKENDORF, Marie	17	Sudwalde	58-0815
ZOECKLER, Johann	51	Wheeling/WVa.	57-1148
Mary 41			
ZOECKLER, R.(m)	20	Rueckborn	62-0836
ZOELLNER, Charles	18	Hellefeld	57-0422
ZOELLNER, Elisab.	59	Holzdorf/Hess	62-0608
ZOELLNER, H.A.(f)	22	Liverpool	61-0482
Wilhelm 2			
ZOELZIN, Anna	28	Herzhausen	57-0850
ZOERB, Johs.	45	Hochelheim	55-0413
Louise 24			
ZOHME, Hen.	21	Gradenstedt	59-1036
ZOLL, Caspar	29	Euersdorf	60-0533
ZOLLMANN, Theod.	27	Limburg	59-1036
ZONG, Nico.	18	Caffmannsreut	59-0951
ZORF, Conrad	23	Pohlgoens	55-0413
ZSCHOMMLER, Ehrgot	47	Moesheim	58-0576
Amalie 20, Laura 15, Aurelia 13, Lea 10			
Lorenz 7, Robert 5			
ZUBE, Friedrich	36	Trockenhuette	61-0779
Susanne 34, Wilhelmine 24, Wilhelmine 9			
August 7, Mathilde 2, Ferdinand by			
ZUCH, Julius	36	Arnswalde	57-1067
Henriette 31, Rudolph 5, Bertha 2			
ZUCKER, Peter	59	Hausen	59-1036
ZUFALL, Elisabeth	17	Rittenau/Hess	55-0628
ZUIRE, Friedr.	28	Muehlhausen	60-1196
ZUMBILL, Marie	43	Wolperstwende	59-0951
ZUMLOH, Th.(m)	33	Warendorf	62-0836
ZUMPFT, Aug.	25	Sayn	62-0938
ZUMPFT, Marie	28	Homberg	62-0730
ZURGRAF, Jean	25	Wuergis/Nass.	62-0608
ZURHOELLE, Johanna	32	Lippstadt	57-0704
ZURMANN, Anna Marg	18	Wilhelmsdorf	62-0306
ZURNETTENSTADT, M.	15	Gehrde	59-0951
ZURWELLER, Heinr.	23	Bissendorf	61-0482
Ludwig 16			
ZUWALSKY, Georg	24	Budzin/Pruss.	62-0342
Magdalena 22			
ZWICK, Eduard	26	Worndorf/Bav.	60-0622
ZWICK, Herm.	27	Gruenberg	61-0897
ZWICKER, Christine	33	Landwuest	55-0630
ZWINGE, Casp.Harms	36	Warendorf	58-0885
ZWISLER, Wilhelmne	58	Reutlingen	60-0334
Constantia 22			
ZYKA, Jacob	48	Budweis/Boehm	62-0608
Marie 47, Wenzel 10, Martin 7			
Catharine 10m